EVERYTHING
FOR SALE

ALSO BY ROBERT KUTTNER

The End of Laissez-Faire:
National Purpose and the Global Economy After the Cold War
(1991)

The Life of the Party:
Democratic Prospects in 1988 and Beyond
(1987)

The Economic Illusion:
False Choices Between Prosperity and Social Justice
(1984)

Revolt of the Haves:
Tax Rebellions and Hard Times
(1980)

EVERYTHING FOR SALE

The Virtues and Limits of Markets

ROBERT KUTTNER

A Century Foundation Book

THE UNIVERSITY OF CHICAGO PRESS

The University of Chicago Press, Chicago 60637
Copyright © 1996 by Robert Kuttner
Preface copyright © 1999 by Robert Kuttner
Foreword copyright © 1996 by the Twentieth Century Fund, Inc.

Library of Congress Cataloging-in-Publication Data
Kuttner, Robert.
    Everything for sale : the virtues and limits of markets / Robert Kuttner.
        p.   cm.
    "A Century Foundation book."
    Includes bibliographical references and index.
    ISBN 0-226-46555-1 (pbk. : alk. paper)
    1. United States—Economic policy—1993– 2. Industrial policy—United States.
3. Environmental policy—United States. 4. Full employment policies—United
States. 5. Capitalism—United States. 6. United States—Commercial policy. 7. Free
enterprise—United States.   I. Title.
HC106.82.K87   1999
338.973—dc21   98-48861
                                                                                    CIP

⊗ The paper used in this publication meets the minimum requirements
of the American National Standard for Information Sciences—Permanence of Paper
for Printed Library Materials, ANSI Z39.48-1992.

For Gabriel and Jessica

Ah, purity
And the purists,
Talking,
Talking of hearts that are pure
And an art that is pure
And an earth that is not at the moment but should be
Some day
Pure.

Talking, talking,
Talking in what would appear to be total ignorance
Of the following simple, pure fact about purity: purity
Is as rare in its purest state
As the absolute vacuum
Of which the physicist speaks in his classroom when somebody
Knowing too much suggests that all falling bodies
Do not fall equally fast.
"But they would," the physicist says, "they would if you took
All the air away."

        All the air away?
Who would take all the air away? Is there anyone,
Anyone present, anyone living,
Who would make such an issue of purity that he'd take
All the air away?
I must meet him.
I must shake his pure white hand and say to him, "Blast!
If you take all the air away, you'll fall equally fast."

Reed Whittemore, 1956

Contents

Foreword

Given the demise of centrally planned economies and the relative prosperity of the United States, one might expect Americans to be preaching to the world about the superiority of their system: mixed capitalism. Instead, the political flavor of the moment asserts the necessity to abandon what we have in favor of a purer, more rough-and-ready version of a market economy. The billboards on the road to this promised economic Utopia offer now familiar policy prescriptions for what ails America: privatization, deregulation, downsizing, shrinking entitlements, and lower taxes. The intellectual underpinning of this thrust is a nearly religious adherence to the belief that virtually all public-sector activity, including financial support for the poor, protection of labor-union rights, and even macroeconomic policies, does more harm than good. Adherents view the simplified models of laissez-faire economists as revealed wisdom about what sort of world their proposals will produce.

Faith in idealized market structures also has spawned a political jihad intent upon stripping away the community and governmental safeguards against market abuses and imperfections—safeguards that are central to the modern American system constructed during the Great Depression and after World War II. In addition, an overtly and proudly selfish ideology finances and propels the drive to cut taxes on the wealthy, punch holes in the social safety net, and "unchain" business from the shackles of regulation and litigation. The conservative catechism castigates those who would "reward need" by supporting public programs for the poor and, at its most radical, even rejects Adam Smith's conviction that the state must provide the bedrock of the educational and physical infrastructure of an industrialized society.

The extreme version of the current fundamentalist conservative economics seems to imply that there is no such thing as a market failure—that in every circumstance the market will produce better results than alternatives. This view is not universal; in fact, the majority of scholars recognize that it carries an important point to the level of absurdity. The ravages of an unpoliced marketplace are well known. At a minimum, modern commerce and economic growth depend on clear rules of the game, enforceable contracts, independent courts, community infrastructure, and public investment, especially in education.

Despite the divisions of academic opinion, in the political arena, many Democrats and moderate Republicans are stumbling all over each other to prove their conversion to the one true faith of laissez-faire economics. And the media often appear mesmerized by the tactics and apparent certainty of slick, well-financed conservative idea merchants and politicians. Yet even in the teeth of this prevailing wind, a number of economists, politicians, and journalists are offering compelling critiques of a set of originally reasonable ideas carried to their most illogical extreme. Prominent among them is the author of this book.

Robert Kuttner has written a number of influential books about the American economy, including *The End of Laissez-Faire: National Purpose and the Global Economy After the Cold War*; he is a widely syndicated newspaper columnist and founding coeditor of *The American Prospect* magazine. In this work, Kuttner proves that it is possible to acknowledge and even embrace the many virtues of the marketplace without insisting either that it is without flaws or that it will fulfill every human need. In so doing, he addresses one of the most pressing needs in public discourse today. In recent years, debate on this subject has been unbalanced, driven by the zealotry of political partisans and purists. In the pages that follow, Kuttner provides an insightful and thoroughly documented antidote to the fevered advocacy of these true believers. Indeed, his common-sense approach to the real-world issues of health care, communications, transportation, and legal affairs actually provides the reader with a sense of relief. It seems, after all, that we are not crazy; real human beings in the real economy must cope with all sorts of daily experiences in markets that just do not always get things right. If there is to be reformation in the way we think about economic issues, Robert Kuttner is certain to be one of its most important intellectual leaders.

The Twentieth Century Fund owes its existence to the conviction by one very successful businessman, Edward Filene, that markets alone would not produce a stable and growing democratic nation. He was convinced that an active and informed public sector was necessary to build a just and growing nation. The Fund has supported a number of works that respond to our founder's charge. In the years after the Great Depression, the Fund addressed these issues in a number of volumes, including Evans Clark's *Financing the Consumer, Labor and Government* and *Debts and Recovery, 1929–1937* by Albert G. Hart. Later, that early interest continued with such publications as Jan Tinbergen's *Shaping the World Economy* and Hyman Minsky's *Stabilizing an Unstable Economy*. More recently, the Fund published Edward Wolff's *Top Heavy: A Study of the Increasing Inequality of Wealth in America* and set up a task force to explore market speculation and corporate governance, with a background paper, "Who's Minding the Store?" by Robert J. Shiller. In addition, we are currently supporting an examination of the future of capitalism that was begun by Leonard Silk and is being completed by his son Mark Silk, as well as a look by Barry Bluestone and Bennett Harrison at how inequality and flawed public policy undermine economic growth and a study by James Galbraith of the inequality crisis.

Markets and capitalism are central to our society. But, as Robert Kuttner makes clear, a little modesty on the part of the most strident champions of the market would go a long way (after all, even the pope is infallible only on special occasions); it might well move public discourse on economic policy beyond simplistic answers and mechanical solutions to complex, real-world circumstances. On behalf of the Trustees of the Twentieth Century Fund, I thank Kuttner for his timely and significant contribution to the debate about economic policy.

Richard C. Leone, President
The Twentieth Century Fund

Preface

When I wrote the first edition of *Everything for Sale,* which appeared in early 1997, my purpose was to challenge the dominant idea that nearly all of economic life is best organized as a pure market. In fact, some realms of the economy work very efficiently as markets—ordinary manufacturing, retail sales, and personal services, among others. In these realms, supply and demand operate roughly as advertised, to give consumers bountiful choices at reasonable prices. Competition serves to discipline producers and reward innovators. Prices function as roughly accurate signals of what buyers desire and what things cost to make. But elsewhere, in much of the economy, market forces tend to price things wrong or to produce unchecked opportunism and instability.

In realms such as health care and pollution and education, the prices and quantities yielded by private purchasing power give society either too little (education and research) or too much (pollution); or the attempt to maximize profits leads to perverse incentives (health care). In other realms, such as airline travel and electric power, unregulated market forces generate monopolies, frustrating the goal of efficient consumer choice. Still other realms, such as banking and securities markets, require careful government regulation because the individual seldom knows enough to protect himself and speculative impulses can wreak broader economic damage.

Moreover, many of the things we hold dear, such as the right to vote or the liberty of one's person, are not appropriate to market mechanisms at all. They are not properly commodities, but in a market society they are all too vulnerable to commodification. Today commercialism is relentlessly encroaching on realms where it doesn't belong, as public office is all but auctioned off and shadow markets in healthy infants and body parts are all but quoted on the stock exchange. Taken together, something like half the economy cannot and should not be a textbook market. Even the well-intentioned effort to make things more marketlike can backfire, as this book will suggest in detail.

My purpose was neither to lionize nor to damn the market, but to invite the reader to explore with me where in society market principles were suitable, where they were misleading, and where they were dangerous, and how market forces are best constrained and turned to public purposes. My subtext was a plea to appreciate the complexity of human society and to resist the utopian fashion of the age to turn nearly every human association into a market transaction.

Since I wrote this book, one market in particular has gone haywire and not for the first time—the international financial market. I did not treat this market in great detail in this book, since it was the subject of my previous book, *The End of Laissez-Faire* (Knopf, 1991) which the reader is welcome to consult.

In the 1980s and the 1990s, enthusiasts of the free market commended its benefits to developing economies and to formerly communist countries, most particularly with regard to financial flows. The claims seemed irrefutable. Command economies were wildly inefficient because they priced things wrong. Commissars could not possibly second-guess the decentralized, self-correcting mechanism of the market. That's why Russian factories produced unwanted products of low quality, while Russian consumers faced empty shelves. What the formerly communist countries needed, therefore, was the bracing discipline of supply and demand. Get the commissars out of the way, and a free market would simply emerge. By the same token, third-world countries, with shallow markets and often corrupt or dirigiste connections between government and industry, needed much the same medicine.

Laissez-faire enthusiasts especially commended the link between these fledgling market economies and the global marketplace. By embracing the market remedy and opening themselves to global capital flows, emerging economies would not only "get prices right" domestically, they would win the confidence of foreign investors and gain access to global markets.

This hope has proven dangerously naive. One of the forms of market failure is the propensity of markets to overshoot—to become euphoric on the upside and overly gloomy on the downside. Financial markets are particularly vulnerable to such giddy, roller-coaster swings. Within one country, it is possible for governments to stabilize and temper these boom-and-bust propensities, through central banks, financial regulation, and reservoirs of countercyclical purchasing power such as social insurance and defense spending. But few such effective stabilizers exist globally. While a large economy such as the United States, with very deep domestic financial markets and well-honed institutions, can survive financial panics, small emergent markets turn out to be all too vulnerable to fads beyond their control once they fully open their borders as recommended by the marketizers.

In the case of East Asia, foreign capital seeking supernormal returns abruptly swamped these newly liberalized capital markets. When overbuilding ensued and returns began sagging, the capital rushed out just as fast as it had rushed in, devastating their currencies and economies. By late 1998, the Asian financial panic had spread to Russia and to much of Latin America and was threatening recession in the U.S. and Europe. To some extent, the emergent market economies needed institutional reforms, but what caused the collapse of 1997–98 was not a sudden day of reckoning for institutional practices that had served East Asia well for two decades. Rather, it was the imported instability of global financial speculation.

Moreover, a closer look at these economies suggests that different countries had different challenges. Russia had never built a functioning civil society, which is the precondition of efficient capitalism. Japan suffered from what Keynes would have called a "liquidity trap." The more the government tried to ignite a demand-led recovery, the more anxious consumers stashed away savings. Its banks and other financial institutions had been designed for a much more managed economy. Cutting them loose to face the discipline of market forces risked setting off a deeper recession. In East Asia, different nations faced a variety of overdue structural reforms. Generalized austerity only makes things worse—and so does imported financial speculation. What these countries need is not more exposure; they need some respite.

But in nearly every case the IMF's remedy of austerity only constricted growth, diminished the confidence of the international investor community, and created an impossible policy trap in which politicians had to resort to politically unbearable and economically self-defeating belt-tightening in order to restore confidence on the part of traders who had likely been out of the market for a long time. Imagine if the U.S. had been counseled to raise interest rates and cut spending during the Great Depression as a signal to foreign investors.

So once again, financial markets turn out to be the most precarious ones of all. A money market is the market on which the rest of capitalism depends. Seemingly, it is the most purely marketlike, since the supply and demand discipline imposed by investors and traders yields minute adjustments in the value of a variety of financial instruments. Yet notwithstanding this exquisite market discipline, financial markets can turn dangerously irrational.

Systemically, the effect of free capital mobility is not just periodic crises but a chronic deflationary bias for the system as a whole, as nations seek to win the confidence of international investors. In a downturn, this can take the form of competitive devaluations, as in Europe in the 1930s and Asia in the late 1990s.

In an inflationary period, it can take the form of high real interest rates, as in Europe and America in the 1980s. The common effect is needless instability, creditor hegemony, slow growth, and pressure on nations to jettison high wages and decent social benefits.

Presumably, the world learned this lesson once. Coming out of the Great Depression and World War II, the architects of the postwar recovery acted to constrain private global capital flows. In principle, the original 1944 Bretton Woods regime remedied both the speculation and the deflation, and created some room for national stabilization policies. Fixed exchange rates and limits on capital flows effectively banished speculators from the temple. Occasional adjustments in parities were the province of central banks and treasuries; their common goal was stability, not profiteering from chaos. IMF and World Bank credits helped shaky nations recover by resuming expansion, not by exporting deflation.

Today's Bank and Fund, however, are a far cry from the original Bretton Woods institutions, which were anchored by a more powerful U.S. dollar and a more activist U.S. government. After the relative weakening of the dollar and the collapse of fixed exchange rates in the early 1970s, Bretton Woods mutated into its antithesis—a system devoted to resurrecting the reign of speculative capital and to enforcing austerity.

Now, with the Asia collapse and the imminent ruin of Russia, even bearers of conventional wisdom are having second thoughts. Longtime champions of free trade, such as Columbia University economist Jagdish Bhagwati and Paul Krugman of MIT, now find financial flows to be different from product flows; financial markets are not self-regulating after all. Advocates of exposure to global markets as a strategy for "getting prices right," such as Harvard's Jeffrey Sachs, are noticing that financial markets often get prices disastrously wrong on both the upside and the downside. The mainstream has noticed that China and India, which resisted the formula, are riding out the storm. Almost everyone is faulting the IMF's zeal for austerity.

What is startling is that the same policymakers who commend laissez-faire as policy often find that the viability of the system requires them to violate it. For although global capital flows are more or less free and currency values are more or less set by market forces, governments and central bankers do recognize, if only through periodic *ad hoc* interventions, that the stakes are simply too high to let speculative capital and currency swings determine the fate of the real economy.

Five times in the past two decades, the U.S. and the other great powers have intervened in very significant ways to counteract the impulses—and the damage—of speculative forces in capital markets. These included the concerted intervention in late June 1998 to prevent the yen from crashing and taking the Asian economy with it, the Mexican rescues of 1983 and 1995, the Louvre Accord of 1988 to stabilize the dollar against the yen, and the Plaza Accord of 1985 which produced a period of coordinated reductions in interest rates.

Note that three of these occurred under the Reagan Administration, which elsewhere was fiercely committed to free markets. Note also that the recent coordinated moves to shore up the yen were undertaken out of fear that a weakening yen would trigger a chain of devaluation throughout Asia and very serious recession—more market irrationality. The Western powers have pressed the Chinese to continue pegging the Hong Kong dollar to the U.S. dollar and to continue defending the Chinese yuan—two more violations of the idea that currency values should be set by market forces. But while Western governments are willing to engage in *ad hoc* interventions to contain crises, at this writing they remain uneasy about returning to a more regulated economy generally. Thus despite some encouraging early harbingers of revision, the conventional economic wisdom still reigns.

I take small comfort in the observation that it evidently requires a crisis to generate second thoughts about the perfection of markets. It would be preferable to rely on the power of logic and persuasion. That is the aspiration of this book.

Robert Kuttner
November 1998

Acknowledgments

I acknowledge, with deep appreciation, the heterodox members of the economics profession, some of whom may feel they are in slightly awkward company. Some are close friends and colleagues, others are casual acquaintances who have generously provided materials and explained concepts. All give me hope that a more complex and institutional view of economy and society is not a lost cause. Thanks to: Robert Heilbroner, Barry Bluestone, Bennett Harrison, Maryellen R. Kelley, Paul Romer, George Akerlof, Richard Freeman, Richard Nelson, Lawrence Katz, Lawrence Mishel, Dean Baker, Rebecca Blank, James Galbraith, Robert Eisner, Robert Frank, Richard Thaler, and especially Albert Hirschman.

Among business historians, legal scholars, social scientists, journalists, and other near-economists, I appreciate counsel from Tom McCraw, Richard Vietor, Robert Lane, Louis Lowenstein, Jon Hanson, Joseph Bower, Shoshana Zuboff, William Emmons, Wolfgang Streeck, David Moss, Joel Rogers, Mark Granovetter, Paul Dempsey, Will Hutton, James Fallows, Neil Talbot, Richard Valelly, Nancy Kete, Viviana Zelizer, and Amitai Etzioni.

I extend special thanks to the Twentieth Century Fund, its president, Richard C. Leone, and associates Greg Anrig and David Smith; to my editor at Knopf, Ash Green; to Jennifer Bernstein and to John Brockman. I am also grateful to my colleagues at *The American Prospect*, especially to Paul Starr, Robert Reich, and Jon Cohn, partners in the enterprise of rebuilding a public philosophy which can sustain a mixed economy. Thanks, too, to my editors at the Washington Post Writers Group, Alan Shearer and Anna Karavangelos; to David Greenway and Marjorie Pritchard of the Boston *Globe*; to Steve Shepard and

Bruce Nussbaum at *Business Week*, in whose columns many of my explorations on markets and their limits first appeared; and to Elisabeth Sifton.

Close readers of all or major parts of the manuscript included: Richard Leone, Greg Anrig, David Smith, Robert Heilbroner, Barry Bluestone, Deborah Stone, Jim Morone, Ben Harrison, Joseph Quinn, Richard Vietor, Arnold Relman, Marcia Angell, Tom McCraw, Jon Hanson, and William Emmons. They saved me from a variety of errors; any errors that remain are entirely mine.

Research assistance, at various stages of this project, was provided by Andy Fairbanks, Beate Sissenich, David Casagrande and Jennifer Goren.

Thanks also, for a variety of kindnesses, to Sid Wolfe, Suzanne Goldberg, Jim Carroll, Shannon Woolley, and Reuven and Orli Avi-Yonah.

Finally, and most profoundly, thanks to my beloved Sharland. Love is not for sale.

EVERYTHING
FOR SALE

INTRODUCTION

The ideal of a free, self-regulating market is newly triumphant. The historical lessons of market excess, from the Gilded Age to the Great Depression, have all but dropped from the collective memory. Government stands impeached and impoverished, along with democratic politics itself. Unfettered markets are deemed both the essence of human liberty, and the most expedient route to prosperity.

In the United States, the alternative to laissez-faire has never been socialism. Rather, the interventionist party, from Hamilton and Lincoln, through the Progressive era, Franklin Roosevelt and Lyndon Johnson, sponsored what came to be known as a "mixed economy." The idea was that market forces could do many things well—but not everything. Government intervened to promote development, to temper the market's distributive extremes, to counteract its unfortunate tendency to boom-and-bust, to remedy its myopic failure to invest too little in public goods, and to invest too much in processes that harmed the human and natural environment.

Since the constitutional founding, however, the libertarian strain in American life has often overwhelmed the impulse toward collective betterment. Today, after two decades of assault by the marketizers, even the normal defenders of the mixed economy are defensive and uncertain. The last two Democratic presidents have been ambivalent advocates for the mixed economy. Mostly, they offered a more temperate call for the reining in of government and the liberation of the entrepreneur. The current vogue for deregulation began under Jimmy Carter. The insistence on budget balance was embraced by Bill Clinton, whose pledge to "reinvent government" soon became a shared commitment merely to reduce government. And much of the economics profession, after an era of embracing the mixed economy, has reverted to a new fundamentalism cherishing the virtues of markets.

America, in short, is in one of its cyclical romances with a utopian view of laissez-faire. Free markets are famous for overshooting. Real-estate bubbles, tulip manias, and stock-market euphorias invariably lead to crowd psychologies and painful mornings-after. The same, evidentially, is true of ideological fashions.

So this is a good moment for a sober sorting out. How does the market, whose first principle is one-dollar/one-vote, properly coexist with a political democracy whose basic rule is "one person/one vote"? When does the market run riot? What are the proper boundaries of market principles? What should not be for sale?

ii

Even in a capitalist economy, the marketplace is only one of several means by which society makes decisions, determines worth, allocates resources, maintains a social fabric, and conducts human relations. Actual capitalist nations display a wide variation in the blend of market and nonmarket. A basically capitalist system is clearly superior to a command economy. But the nations where markets have the freest rein do not invariably enjoy the most reliable prosperity, let alone the most attractive society.

In this age of the resurgent market, we are promised that technology, ingenuity, and freedom from the dead hand of government will revive economic efficiency and material progress. Yet, despite the triumph of market principles, market society is no Utopia. Compared with the golden era of the postwar boom and the mixed economy, this is a time of broad economic unease. As society becomes more marketized, it is producing stagnation of living standards for most people, and a fraying of the social fabric that society's best-off are all too able to evade. One thing market society does well is to allow its biggest winners to buy their way out of its pathologies.

Even as the market enjoys new prestige, ordinary people are uneasy with many of the results. With greater marketization comes not just opportunity but opportunism; a society that prizes risk also reaps insecurity. Taken to an extreme, markets devalue and diminish extra-market values and norms—on which viable capitalism depends.

The promise of growth has also run into questions of sustainability. Even mainstream economists wonder about the effect on the natural environment if the third world were to enjoy even half the living standards and the claim on natural systems of the United States and Europe. The standard economic calculus does not know how to measure the costs of depletion of natural systems, since these are not accurately captured in current prices. And in market logic, by definition, what is not reflected in the price system does not exist.

All of this should cast serious doubt on the presumption, so fashionable of late, that the natural form of capitalism is laissez-faire. Beyond a certain point, excessive marketization may not be efficient *even for economic life*. In this book, I seek to explore where that point lies; to search for criteria to understand better where the market is best left alone and where it needs help; to reclaim a defensible middle ground; and to suggest the policy implications that follow, in several realms.

iii

The mixed economy of a generation ago was constructed on the ruins of depression and war. It produced a quarter-century of unprecedented growth and prosperity. It allowed a blend of dynamism and stability, of market and political community. When economic growth faltered after 1973, a new, radically classical economics gradually gained influence in the academy and in politics. Resurgent business groups, once cowed by the New Deal–Great Society era, became unabashed crusaders for laissez-faire. The increasing marketization of global commerce undermined the institutional capacity of nation-states to manage a mixed economy, and discredited center-left parties.

The period of "stagflation" discredited economic management and conferred new prestige on laissez-faire. If further confirmation were needed, the erosion and collapse of communism impeached not just state socialism, but European social democracy and American neo-Keynesianism as well. The political counterrevolution that culminated in the 1980 election of Ronald Reagan enjoyed a rendezvous with an intellectual reversion that had been sweeping the economics profession for at least a decade. Each drew strength from the other.

In scholarly economics, theorists such as Milton Friedman, who had been marginal, became central. The concrete study of economic history and economic institutions became archaic. The smartest rising economists used ever more complex mathematics, based on the premise of a "general equilibrium"—a concept that presumed a smoothly self-correcting market and implicitly urged that markets become purer and that more realms of society become markets. Newly self-confident conservative economic theorists colonized other academic disciplines. Market concepts became widespread in law, political science, and economic history. As experts on public policy, these economists became the intellectual champions of privatization, deregulation, and liberation of the global marketplace. It all boiled down to one very simple core precept: market is better.

This book begins with the working hypothesis that a capitalist system is a superior form of economic organization, but even in a market economy there are realms of human life where markets are imperfect, inappropriate, or unattainable. Many forms of human motivation cannot be reduced to the market model of man.

There is at the core of the celebration of markets a relentless tautology. If we begin, by assumption, with the premise that nearly everything can be understood as a market and that markets optimize outcomes, then everything else leads back to the same conclusion—marketize! If, in the event, a particular market doesn't optimize, there is only one possible inference: it must be insufficiently marketlike. This epistemological sleight of hand is an astonishing blend that blurs the descriptive with the normative. It is a no-fail system for guaranteeing that theory trumps evidence. Should some human activity not, in fact, behave like an efficient market, it must be the result of some interference that should be removed or a stubborn human refusal to appreciate markets. It cannot possibly be that the theory fails to specify accurately how human behavior works. The thrust of free-market economics for a quarter-century has been a search to narrow the set of special cases where market solutions cannot be found for market failures. Today, the only difference between the utopian version and the mainstream version is degree.

In interpreting political economy, parsimony—Occam's celebrated razor— is the most overrated tool in the scholarly medicine cabinet. The beauty of the market model is its elegant simplicity. A perfect market can be modeled; the analyst can perform neat simulations, using very sophisticated mathematics. But the more complex the departures from a perfect market, the less relevant is the cherished analytic apparatus or the Platonic ideal of a pure market.

Academic champions of the market concede, often with irritation, that real-world institutions are messy; that labor markets are not like product markets, whose merchandise "clears" based on adjustments of price; that actual bundles of capital equipment are "lumpy," and not prone to smooth, frictionless equilibration as in the algebra. But as the economist ventures into the institutional thicket, she strays from the norms of her profession. She had better be tenured first. Thus, in part because of the attractiveness of its own core model, academic economics has lately become a purer version of itself—almost a lobby for the idea that the real economy should strive to emulate the model. The Cambridge economist John Eatwell once remarked, facetiously, "If the world is not like the model, so much the worse for the world."

As my subtitle implies, I am a believer in a balance between market, state, and civil society. I arrive at this belief primarily from a reading of economic and political history, which suggests that pure laissez-faire is socially and even economically unsustainable. Although defenders of a mixed economy often argue their case on equity grounds, there is significant evidence that, quite apart from questions of distributive justice, the very stability of the system requires departures from laissez-faire. My previous books have all treated, in different ways, the intersection of economics, politics, policy, and ideology. They have all dealt with the boundaries between state, market, and society. In these earlier works, I challenged one of the central claims of the marketizers—that equality necessarily comes at the expense of efficiency. I also examined the corrosive influence of international laissez-faire on the project of operating a mixed economy at home. And I explored the practical political difficulty of center-left parties serving their natural constituency in an era of limited budgets and resurgent laissez-faire.

In this book, I hope to go deeper into the dynamics of the market itself, searching for first principles. Where, really, do markets perform roughly as advertised? Where is the market model a reasonable approximation of human motivation, and where is it misleading? By what criteria are we to know when the market has overstepped its proper bounds? How do different kinds of markets fail to optimize outcomes? What patterns of failure recur? How are we to know when we are in a realm where markets produce rough efficiency and rough justice, versus one where markets produce avoidable calamities? When is the best response to market failure to contrive procedures or outcomes that are more "marketlike"? When does that approach only make things worse? Where is the proper boundary between market and nonmarket?

In the search for principles on which to reinvent a mixed economy, one must begin by according great respect to the market. For markets do many things very well. The reader will find herein a brief tour of the market's virtues before proceeding to a summary of its limits. It is evident that command economies are not viable; that prices are indeed potent signals of what it costs to produce a good or a service and what consumers will pay; that when prices unreasonably depart from market discipline they yield too many of the wrong goods or too few of the right ones, and insulate producers from the bracing tonic of competition—leading to stagnation. The trouble is that markets do not reliably yield such results; on the contrary, markets sometimes produce perverse outcomes for fairly prolonged periods.

The quest for a viable mixed economy necessarily leads back to government and politics, for the democratic state remains the prime counterweight to the market. Marketization, of late, has swamped the polity. The dynamics are cumulative. Government has less popular legitimacy, and fewer resources with which to treat escalating problems. The less government is able to achieve, the more it seems a bad bargain. American liberals and European social democrats often seem unable to offer more than a milder version of the conservative program—deregulation, privatization, globalization, fiscal discipline, but at a less zealous extreme. Few have been willing to challenge the premise that nearly everything should revert to a market.

To rebuild an alternative philosophy of political economy, one must first shake the hegemony of the laissez-faire market. I hope to accomplish this with evidence, not tautology. The last intellectual refuge of the marketizer is the claim that, even if markets sometimes fail, political interferences are likely only to compound those failures. Here, also, we must get down to cases. Governments seek to override markets for a variety of purposes—to stabilize, to promote growth, to limit detrimental side effects, to temper inequalities, to cultivate civic virtues. But governments also operate in a political crucible, and require political consent and fiscal resources. In the search for strategies to temper and tame the market, we need to seek ones that are within the competence of the state, that restore vitality to the enterprise of politics, and nourish rather than overload civil society.

iv

The book is divided into three broad sections and a conclusion. Chapters 1 and 2 give markets their due, examine their intellectual premises, and then explore where the market and its zealots overreach. Chapters 3, 4, and 5 look concretely at realms of society that necessarily depart from pure market principles: the market for human labor, the market for health and life, and the purest market (but also the most hazardous when left to its own devices): the market for money. I then turn to how society collectively compensates for the market's limitations. Chapter 6 deals with the sources of technical innovation and economic growth, and the necessary departures from laissez-faire that promote prosperity and development. Chapters 7 and 8 consider regulation of the market in several economic and social realms. The final chapter brings us back to the uneasy coexistence of markets and politics, and looks toward a new synthesis.

I have excluded several intriguing areas where market principles dwell uneasily with nonmarket ones, such as education, the arts, the economics of public spaces, religion, charity, and sport. The list is almost endless. By being selective, I've sought to take representative examples of the commingling of market and extra-market, with sufficient detail and breadth to draw useful generalizations, without overwhelming the reader (or writer).

Before we get ahead of our story, let me close this introduction with some important disclaimers:

First, I will not be treating, except in passing, the market's moral limitations. Nor will I be addressing at length the market economy's most widely conceded handicap—its "macroeconomic" failure to equilibrate supply and demand at the level of the economy as a whole. Nor is this mainly a book on markets and inequality. I address these topics briefly in the context of labor markets.

Each is surely a limitation of the market, but each already has an ample literature.

Rather, I will be addressing the market's limitations in realms where most economists believe it ordinarily succeeds—the realm that academicians call "*micro*economics." How do actual markets work in actual domains of daily economic life? How do markets deliver the goods, in realms from daily bread to health care to technical innovation itself? What are the practical choices when markets don't deliver, can't deliver, and shouldn't deliver? How do market principles necessarily coexist with nonmarket principles? How good are other systems of allocation and deliberation at accomplishing what the market does badly? How does market failure compare with "polity failure"? And what are the implications for public policy?

Second, this is not a book of economic theory or one primarily for the professional economist. Economists enamored of pure markets begin with the theory, and hang models on assumptions that cannot themselves be challenged. The characteristic grammatical usage is an unusual subjunctive—the verb form "must be." For example, if wages for manual workers are declining, it *must be* that their economic value is declining. If a corporate raider walks away from a deal with half a billion dollars, it *must be* that he added that much value to the economy. If Japan can produce better autos than Detroit, there *must be* some inherent locational logic, else the market would not dictate that result. If commercial advertising leads consumers to buy shoddy or harmful products, they must be "maximizing their utility"—because we know by assumption that consumers always maximize their utility. How do we know that? Because to do anything else would be irrational. And how do we know that individuals always behave rationally? Because that is the premise from which we begin. The truly interesting institutional questions—the disjunctures between what free-market assumptions would predict and the actual outcomes—are dismissed by the tautological and deductive form of reasoning. The fact that the real world is already far from a perfect market is ignored for the sake of theoretic convenience. The dissenter cannot challenge the theory; he can only describe the real world.

A third, related disclaimer: despite sore temptation, this book is not, for the most part, a work of economist-bashing. Of late, the economic model has sometimes seemed a caricature of itself. As economics has become more fundamentalist, the most extreme version of the market model has carried the greatest political, intellectual, and professional weight. At the same time, a large number of professional economists pursues institutional particulars and evidence, as opposed to deductive logic and algebraic manipulation. Their work, often at risk to their professional standing, deserves immense respect. It is cited throughout this book, and I have programmed my word-processor to resist facile phrases like "Economists claim . . ." As more than one American president has complained, economists disagree among themselves, even on matters that ought to be readily quantifiable. My quarrel is with a utopian—really, a dystopian—view of markets, not with economists as a breed.

This book explores how actual markets work in practice, and then distills some tentative principles from the patterns in the practical cases and applies those principles to policy questions. It is written mainly for the lay reader. It is intended as a guide for those intimidated by claims that are often overstated, oversimplified, or just plain wrong.

Fourth, this book is not an exercise in nostalgia. The postwar boom was indeed a uniquely successful period for capitalism—and for a social democratic or mixed economy. Because of a combination of historical accident, political struggle, intellectual innovation, and institutional setting, a viable mixed economy became possible at the level of the nation-state. But it is all too obvious that we can't turn the clock back to the economic system of the postwar boom. The political and institutional forces have changed irrevocably. We have gone from a set of primarily national economies, heavily based on mass-production industries, to a globalized marketplace of infinite variety and rapid change. The mixed economy of the next century will necessarily rely on a different set of public institutions, strategies, and political coalitions.

Finally, this book is intended as a careful sorting out, not a manifesto. In reviewing a broad literature on markets, one finds that the recent paeans to markets are drearily predictable. The author goes through the motions of empirical inquiry, but the conclusion is always the same: You see, markets really are better. This book is not intended as a mirror image. My purpose was not to accumulate ammunition for a preordained punch line—Aha, markets really are worse!

On the contrary, in exploring different real-world markets, I come away with increased respect for the power of markets and the complexity of the story—yet with renewed conviction that the good society requires a mixed economy. The great paradox of our age is that a more complex economy, using such principles as regulated competition and freer trade, indeed maximizes the benefits of market incentives, yet requires competent regulators to set efficient ground rules. This, in turn, demands more adaptive government and more responsive politics and policy. So the grail of an absolutely pure market, disembodied from political interference or from historic time, is not just a fantasy but a dangerous and self-defeating one.

1 / THE RESURGENT MARKET

THE MARKET'S MAGIC

Markets accomplish much superbly. They offer consumers broad choices; they promote and reward innovation. They bring investors together with entrepreneurs. Markets force producers to search for greater efficiency and ruthlessly purge the economy of failures. Market systems are far better than command systems at determining rough economic worth. As economists since Adam Smith have observed, the great paradox of the market is that the individual pursuit of self-interest aggregates to an efficient general good.

At the very core of the market system is the price mechanism. Prices indicate what millions of individual goods and services are "worth" to willing sellers and willing buyers. Prices thereby function to apportion economic resources efficiently: they signal sellers what to produce; consumers how to buy; capitalists where to invest.

When economists speak of the market's efficiency, they generally have in mind the efficiency of *allocation*. Prices steer resources to the uses that maximize output in the form of products and services, relative to the available input of capital and human labor. Prices do so via the discipline of supply and demand. So far so good.

The genius of market pricing is its malleability. Prices can rise or fall instantly and change continually, as they adjust to shifting tastes and costs. Markets, therefore, can claim to embody and express freedom of choice, as well as efficient allocation of scarce resources. Markets epitomize decentralized, atomized decision-making. This concept of ongoing and reasoned refinement of preferences, prices, and quantities is central to the picture of satisfied economic man dwelling in an efficient marketplace.

For economies to operate efficiently, drastic change or abrupt disjuncture is the exception rather than the rule. Occasionally, entire enterprises fail, employees are fired, or something wholly new is invented. But in their ordinary functioning, markets mostly invite *marginal* shifts. Change is constant, subtle, and ineluctable. A retailer or wholesaler continually adjusts prices. Buyers and sellers of shares of stock, through an ongoing auction, shift prices minutely in accord with preferences and predictions, usually by eighths of a point. Consumers, likewise, are said to adjust their preferences at the margin. This week's basket of household purchases is pretty much like last week's; the consumer adjusts only the last few dollars of discretionary income, simultaneously expressing her freedom to choose and helping to make the economy run efficiently.

The process of marginal adjustment comports with the economist's notion of efficient allocation based on price, as well as the social imperative of reconciling stability with change. (It also beautifully lends itself to the mathematics of the differential calculus. That, in turn, causes much of professional economic discourse to be conducted in an idiom of stylized algebra, which tends to omit or disdain historical, social, or political factors that cannot easily be modeled.)

Markets do a lot better than command economies at generating roughly accurate prices in many realms much of the time. Communism failed partly because it trampled civil society and political democracy, partly because it destroyed the price system. In a market economy, if there is unmet demand for a good or a service, an entrepreneur will likely emerge to supply it at the right price. If there is oversupply, or inefficient production, goods will pile up, the price will fall, and relatively inefficient suppliers will shape up or exit the field.

This dynamic also produces pressure for refinement and improvement, for sellers are under merciless competitive pressure to do tasks more efficiently; to find out exactly what the customer wants and to meet her tastes; to invent new products that will fire the consumer's imagination and open his wallet. As tastes change, and new producers overtake old ones, the price system will shift resources accordingly. Capital will appropriately shift out of typewriters and into computers, out of iron and into plastics. Miraculously, the economy as a whole, cued by the price system, will produce the right quantity of what people want, given their purchasing power. A market economy, unlike a command economy, will never produce millions of unfashionable size-ten shoes to fill a production quota set by commissars.

The adjustment of price, according to shifting demand and supply, allows merchandise to move and markets to clear inventory. In economic parlance, a market is said to "clear" when supply and demand has caused the last buyer to purchase the last available product for a price acceptable to the seller, at whatever moment the goods become perishable or sale becomes moot. In a market that cleared perfectly, there would be no empty airline seats, no unsold concert tickets, no rotten fruit, for the price would keep declining until it fetched a buyer. Evidently, even free markets do not clear perfectly. But for the most part they offer a reasonable approximation. That is why there may be a shortage of purchasing power in a capitalist economy, but seldom a shortage of products. When Russia shifted from communist to capitalist, citizens long accustomed to pockets full of rubles, long lines, and empty shelves suddenly found themselves confronting shops loaded with goods that they couldn't afford to buy.

A favorite economists' example of "market clearing" is the fish market. If there is a high demand for lobster, and not many lobsters, the fishmonger raises his price. If there is a surfeit of haddock, and not many willing buyers, the price of haddock comes down; if demand stays chronically low, eventually fishermen shift resources to catching other varieties. The discipline is relentless. Merchants do not behave this way because they studied economics; price adjustment is intuitive. Those with poor intuition fall by the wayside. A product is "worth" what the market deems, not what the vendor imagines. If the market is working properly, the last adjustment in price will clear the store of the last piece of seafood. The market rewards those who grasp the logic and punishes those who miss it. If the seller stubbornly fails to lower his price, at the end of the day he is rewarded with a pile of rotten fish. Roughly the same mechanism operates in the case of toys, Toyotas, financial services, and hairdressers. The interplay of demand and supply explains Adam Smith's famous paradox of why water, necessary for life, is cheap, while diamonds, a nonessential bauble, are expensive. If you look only at demand, the reverse should be true. But water is plentiful and diamonds are rare (and kept even rarer by the diamond cartel—but that's another story).

The price mechanism accomplishes another stunning feat. Modifications in price not only accommodate shifting tastes and variations in supply, but most of the time they also somehow prevent competition from becoming mutually ruinous, and thus allow the seller to earn a "normal" profit. This homeostasis, in turn, is reinforced by the infinite refinements in capital markets that allow producers to finance their enterprises at roughly appropriate capital costs. Thus, the self-correcting equilibrium maintained in countless small markets aggregates to a self-correcting economy as a whole.

SUPER MARKETS

Consider the local supermarket. As an illustration of what markets do well, the institution is aptly named. It is a market *par excellence*. The distribution and retailing of food is mostly unregulated, and fiercely competitive. There are usually several supermarkets in town, which means you can shop around. Supermarkets compensate by creating little oases of market power, putting some products on sale in order to attract customers and to dispose of temporary oversupply. The sale items and prices are not identical at different stores or at different points in time, so the market is competitive but not ruinously so. The shopper is pretty well informed—but not perfectly informed; it takes time and diligence to go from one supermarket to another to get the lowest possible price on milk, *and* bananas, *and* roasting chicken. Most shoppers tend to stay with one supermarket, look hard for bargains, but do the week's shopping at one place and overpay for some items. A minority of shoppers, with more time on their hands, will go to two or three stores and buy only bargains everywhere.

Somehow, at the end of the day, the average consumer's lack of infinite time to go shopping, and less-than-perfect information about the relative prices of a thousand products in several local stores, exactly allows the supermarket to earn a normal profit. If this were not the case, supermarkets would shut down, investors in supermarkets would shift their capital to some other enterprise—and then food prices would rise to some level that would coax entrepreneurs back in. Somehow, too, even though profits relative to sales are razor-thin in the supermarket business—1 or 2 percent is typical—there is enough profit to allow supermarkets to invest in capital improvements such as optical scanners. These, in turn, make the business even more efficient over time.

Supermarkets, too, provide the retail outlet for farmers and producers of processed foods, and thus connect the consumer market to the agricultural one. And somehow, though farmers perennially complain about the prices they receive, the retail prices are generally adequate for farmers to stay in business and make a normal profit over time, too. The less efficient farmers fail; the most efficient ones keep becoming more efficient.

The supermarket also furnishes a portion of the local market for labor. Here again, the price mechanism seems to be just about self-regulating. Though cashiers and meat-cutters are not the most glamorous of jobs, the supermarket manages to pay just enough to attract people who are just competent enough to perform the jobs acceptably. If it paid too little, it would fail to attract skilled help, and the customers would be dissatisfied. If a particular supermarket paid too much, it would eat into its profit margin and be overtaken by some competitor.

Finally, the supermarket is part of the market for capital. Most supermarkets are owned by large corporate chains, whose shares are publicly traded on stock exchanges. If supermarket profits are below par over time, the price of the shares will fall. That also operates as a powerful signal—on where investors should put their capital; on what lines of business conglomerates should enter and exit; and on how executives must supervise their managers and managers their employees.

Though there may be occasional missteps, and though some supermarkets go bankrupt, the interplay of supply and demand in all of these submarkets contributes to a dynamic equilibrium. It results in prices that are "right" most of the time. The supermarket does all this with almost no price regulation, even though its products are highly perishable, it must decide how to stock and display thousands of different food items in response to shifting consumer tastes, and price competition in the supermarket business is fierce. The price mechanism substitutes for elaborate systems of control that would be hopelessly cumbersome to administer. No wonder the champions of the market are almost religious in their enthusiasm. Though supermarkets are closer to an economics textbook than many markets in our society, they are emblematic of industries serving consumers.

Before we wax too rapturous, however, please note two anomalies.

For one thing, even supermarkets are not perfectly efficient. Retail grocers operate on thin profit margins, but the wholesale part of the food-distribution chain is famous for enormous markups. A farmer is likely to get only ten cents out of a box of cornflakes that retails for $3.99. National conglomerates like Procter & Gamble or RJR Nabisco collectively spend billions on advertising and packaging to promote brand loyalty. These expenditures manipulate tastes, but beyond a point add little to the consumer's welfare. Food manufacturers proliferate brands far beyond any rational need to give the consumer choices. At my local supermarket, I counted more than 150 brands of breakfast cereal. This proliferation occurs not because shoppers demand so many choices. Rather, companies like Kellogg's and Post keep complicating consumer choices to grab shelf space and brand loyalty from each other. In the process, they add to their own overhead costs, those of the supermarket, and ultimately those of the economy. The fact that these overhead costs are roughly comparable among different food wholesalers and different supermarkets doesn't mean that consumers "want" 150 brands of cereal; it only means that the price mechanism is not competent to squeeze out this particular inefficiency.

Second, though they are subject to intense price discipline, even supermarkets are far from perfectly free markets. Their hygiene is regulated by government inspectors, as is almost all of the food they sell. Government regulations mandate the format and content of nutritional labeling. They require clear, consistent unit-pricing, to rule out a variety of temptations of deceptive marketing. Moreover, many occupations in the food industry, such as meat-cutter and checkout clerk, are substantially unionized; so the labor market is not a pure free market either. Much of the food produced in the United States is grown by farmers who benefit from a variety of interferences with a laissez-faire market, contrived by government to prevent ruinous fluctuations in prices. The government also subsidizes education and technical innovation in agriculture. Economists debate whether this interference with agricultural markets is a net gain or loss to efficiency.

Still, as a roughly efficient free marketplace, the supermarket is close enough—and evidently good enough. It is interesting that a modicum of regulation is entirely compatible with the basic discipline of supply and demand, and probably enhances its efficiency by making for better-informed consumers and less opportunistic sellers, and by placing off-limits the market's most self-cannibalizing tendencies. Real (inflation-adjusted) prices of food keep declining over time. Consumer choice keeps increasing.

HEROIC ASSUMPTIONS

The supermarket is a good place to begin, because it conforms almost perfectly to the stylized textbook definition of a free market. The theory of markets posits several interrelated assumptions.

Three have to do with competition. In a stylized free market, consumers are said to possess "perfect information." This is almost never literally true, but is often close enough to be a reasonable approximation. Second, there is said to be "perfect competition"—many suppliers and freedom to shop around. Barriers to entry are necessarily low—anybody must be free to open a supermarket. This, in turn, means that producers are not monopolists, and don't have the market power to dictate prices. (Supermarkets do engage in opportunistic price hikes, but prices that are wildly out of line with competitors do not stick for very long, because word spreads and shoppers are driven away.) Prices are thus set by the interplay of supply and demand. Though there may be other forms of regulation, such as food inspection and labeling, there is little direct price regulation from third parties such as government. Third, free markets must have "mobility of factors": capital and labor, as well as consumers, are free to go elsewhere if they don't like their compensation.

A second set of assumptions is behavioral. Firms, by definition, have the single-minded goal of maximizing profits; consumers pursue the goal of rationally maximizing their well-being ("utility") by pursuing the most satisfying products at the best available price. Preferences are said to be set "exogenously"—they reflect the consumer's own tastes. (I address the behavioral assumptions of the market model in chapter 2.) A perfect market also presumes the absence of significant "externalities"—social costs or benefits, such as pollution or public health, not fully captured in the price of the immediate market transaction. There are other, more technical assumptions, but this is the basic list.

What describes supermarkets pretty well describes the production and sale of most consumer goods. It describes the setting of prices for many, but not all, raw materials used by producers. A relatively free market also characterizes many, if not most, services bought by consumers and producers alike. If you don't like your barber, there is likely to be another one down the block. There is no shortage of restaurants, hotels, tax preparers, photocopiers, dry cleaners from which to choose. Likewise, if your business is dissatisfied with the computer-repair service, management consultant, ad agency, office-cleaning company, office space itself, there are many more to choose from, all competing on the basis of quality and price, all—remarkably—earning a roughly normal profit. In all of these realms, the market mechanism mostly works.

This brief description of how the marketplace operates in one industry allows us to appreciate why most economists are so enraptured with markets. Students of economics often hear their teachers compare markets to self-regulating systems in nature. Listening to an economist rhapsodize on how marvelously markets continuously adjust, how they deliver a humble cornflake from stalk to table through several chains of production and distribution without help from a commissar, is a bit like hearing a physicist marveling at the equipoise of the physical universe, or a doctor explaining the wonder of the self-regulating systems of the human body.

When a particular market does not work like a supermarket or a textbook one, the question is what to do about it. Free-market economists, almost intuitively, think market failure is limited to a fairly narrow set of special cases, and that the solution to market failure is more market. But is it? And when is it? And by what criteria do we know? That dilemma is the broad subject of this book.

WHEN THE MARKET FAILS

Consider a market profoundly different from the market for retail groceries—the market for health care. This is no small, special case, since it consumes 15 percent of the entire economy, roughly as much as food does. We shall come back to health care in greater detail in chapter 4, but for now it is worthwhile to review its broad structural characteristics. Health care is anything but a textbook free market, yet market forces and profit motives in the health industry are rife.

On the supply side, the health industry violates several conditions of a free market. Unlike the supermarket business, there is not "free entry." You cannot simply open a hospital, or hang out your shingle as a doctor. This gives health-care providers a degree of market power that compromises the competitive model—and raises prices. On the demand side, consumers lack the special knowledge to shop for a doctor the way they buy a car, and lack a perfectly free choice of health-insurer. Since society has decided that nobody shall perish for lack of medical care, we partly de-link effective demand from private purchasing power, which is also inflationary.

Health care also offers substantial "positive externalities"—diffused benefits not calculated in the instant transaction. The value to society of mass vaccinations far exceeds the profits that can be captured by the doctor or drug company. If vaccinations and other public-health measures were left to private supply-and-demand, society would seriously underinvest. The health system also depends heavily on extra-market norms. Physicians and nurses are guided by ethical constraints and professional values that limit the opportunism that their specialized knowledge and power might otherwise invite.

The fact that health care is a far cry from a perfect market sets up a chain of perverse incentives. In ordinary markets, sellers maximize profits by minimizing costs. But in health care, the profit maximizer's object is to maximize insurance reimbursement. The more complex the procedure and the more inflated the cost base, the more money can be billed to the insurance company. In recent years, private and government insurers have tried to crack down—by intensively reviewing what doctors and hospitals do, publishing book-length schedules of permissible procedures and reimbursements. Providers have fought back, by further complicating their own billing. All this inflates the cost of the whole system.

Worse, the insurance industry's efforts to reduce inflation (in a highly imperfect market) have created a second-order set of inefficiencies. Increasingly, consumers lack the ability to shop around for doctors or insurance plans. Often, they are locked in either because they get health insurance through their jobs, or because a "pre-existing condition" makes them unattractive to other insurers. They then become easy prey for insurance plans that seek to save costs by denying them care that they need, and to which they are ostensibly entitled.

Increasingly, too, insurance companies seek to minimize costs simply by refusing to insure people likely to become sick. This process of risk selection and segmentation, known as medical underwriting, is itself very expensive. So is the endless point-counterpoint of complex preapprovals and reviews of treatments. And so is the proliferation of paperwork. The providers and the insurers are each behaving "rationally" as profit maximizers, but their behavior does not yield a general good; the result is irrational for the system as a whole.

Thus, health care violates all the premises of an efficient free market—perfect competition, perfect information, mobility of factors, and so on. Yet, unless we want people dying from preventable diseases for lack of private purchasing power, the cure does not lie in liberation of the health "market." We'll return to this subject in greater detail in chapter 4.

SECOND-BEST MARKETS

Here is the nub of the issue. Are most markets like supermarkets—or like health markets? And when a market exhibits resistance to market forms of discipline, what is the remedy? The conundrum of the market for health care is a signal example of a concept that will recur throughout this book: The General Theory of the Second Best. The theory, propounded by the economists Richard Lipsey and Kelvin Lancaster in 1956, and largely ignored today, holds that, when a particular market departs significantly from a pure market and yields an outcome that is not "optimal" in market terms, attempts to make it more marketlike in some, but not all, respects will have indeterminate results for economic efficiency—and sometimes perverse ones.

The Second Best theorem suggests that when there are multiple "distortions" in the price and supply disciplines of a given market, the removal of one distortion in the attempt to create a purer market will not necessarily improve the overall outcome. A second-best market typically has second-best forms of accountability—professional norms, government supervision, regulation, and subsidy—to which market forces have adapted. For example, if the health-care system is already a far cry from a free market on both the demand side and the supply side, removing one regulation, and thereby making the health system more superficially marketlike, may simply increase opportunism and inefficiency. In many economic realms, the "second-best" outcome of some price distortion offset by regulation and extra-market norms may be the best outcome practically available. The hapless attempt to get incrementally closer to the "first-best" state of a pure free market—in an arena like health care, where price signals are necessarily distorted—may lead to third-best outcomes.

Another good second-best illustration is the banking industry. Until the early 1970s, banking in the United States was very highly regulated. Regulations governed both the price and the quantity of banking services. A bank, though privately owned, was viewed almost as a public utility. The departures from a pure-market model were multiple:

As in the case of hospitals, entrepreneurs could not open banks at will. Aspiring bankers had to apply for government charters. If the government found that an area was already "overbanked," the charter would be denied, no matter how worthy the applicant. Several Depression-era laws kept commercial banks out of the investment-banking and insurance businesses. And banks were limited to one state, and in several jurisdictions state law limited local bank branching as well.

Banks were also limited in the interest they could charge borrowers, through state usury laws, and in the interest they could pay depositors, through the Federal Reserve's Regulation Q. No interest at all could be paid on checking accounts. Banks were further required to maintain stipulated ratios of loans to total capital. They enjoyed access to emergency borrowings from the Federal Reserve System, as well as government deposit insurance. In return, they were required to undergo periodic examinations by federal and sometimes state bank examiners. A similar, parallel regime regulated savings-and-loan associations, which were almost always nonprofit mutual associations. There were also strict limits on the bank's ability to go into nonbanking lines of business.

Banks were thus strictly regulated on both the asset side of their ledgers (loans) and on the liability side (deposits). They were regulated with respect to price (interest charged and paid) and with respect to quantity (their loan-to-capital ratio). They benefited from strict limits on both the kind and degree of competition they encountered in their environment.

This extensive regulation was a legacy of the Great Depression. In the 1920s, commercial banks had been free to underwrite securities, often with depositors' money. They had also been party to a variety of speculative schemes, which contributed to the crash. In the Great Depression, several thousand banks went broke. Millions of Americans lost their life savings. Beyond the personal tragedy, it is a fact of economics that bank deposits function as part of the nation's money supply. When banks collapse, credit is drawn out of the economy. A financial collapse therefore cascades onto the real economy, starving otherwise viable businesses for credit. In the 1930s, failing banks not only consumed the savings of depositors; they called loans on businesses, demanded payment of mortgages.

In the aftermath of the crash, Congress and the Roosevelt administration resolved that banking was not just another business. Bankers had a unique fiduciary duty, since they were handling other people's money. Beyond that, they were part of the nation's monetary system, and the risk of catastrophic failure was simply too great to indulge. The regulatory regime of the 1930s was not a single grand design; in some ways it had inconsistent elements. (Many economic historians now believe that investment-banking abuses were not a serious culprit in the Great Crash, and that separating commercial banking from investment banking was more an effort to punish perceived scapegoats than a sound regulatory decision.) But it was founded on the broader (accurate) conviction that banks could not be pure creatures of the marketplace. They should not make speculative investments; to help them resist temptation, they were barred from whole industries that were inherently risky. Nor should they compete for depositors' accounts on the basis of interest; to prevent that temptation, all banks were required to pay identical interest rates.

In a pure market, competition disciplines the players; competition is based largely on price; failures simply exit the field. As a realm of the second best, the banking regime that lasted between the 1930s and the 1970s presumed that broad bank failure could not be tolerated; so it strictly limited price competition, and substituted other means of accountability, many of them regulatory.

This regulatory regime, however, did not relieve bankers of several other forms of market discipline. Market and nonmarket disciplines coexisted, as they characteristically do in second-best arenas. In any given community, a prospective consumer and a prospective business customer had several banks from which to choose. If a bank was sloppily managed and depositors had to wait in long lines, the customer could easily go across the street. If loan officers were careless in evaluating applications for credit, a bank would have more than its share of bad loans. The examiners would be on its case; it would have to set aside reserves to cover loan losses. The bank's profits would decline, its stock price would drop, its salaries would be depressed, and in the extreme case it would be forcibly merged with another bank and people would lose their jobs.

Thus, though this was emphatically a second best, rather more heavily regulated than, say, supermarkets, the banking system was an effective hybrid of market and nonmarket forms of discipline. The environment remained highly capitalist, though not laissez-faire. Despite very significant regulation, banks were definitely profit maximizers. Bankers had every incentive to operate efficiently. Indeed, the system bred a generation of bankers who were prudently conservative, in their dress, their manner, their career patterns—and in their aversion to speculation. Banking was emphatically not entrepreneurial. It could almost be reduced to a set of checklists and formulas. A well-worn joke in the savings-and-loan business had it that S&L executives followed the "3-6-3" rule. Take in deposits at 3 percent, make mortgage loans at 6 percent, and be on the golf course by 3:00 p.m. There was plenty of room for high-flying entrepreneurship elsewhere in the economy, just not with insured depositors' money.

None of this seemed to harm either the larger economy, where credit was plentiful, or the banking business. During the period 1945 to 1973, there were only 105 bank failures, costing the deposit-insurance agencies less than a billion dollars. And during the same period, the economy as a whole grew by nearly 4 percent per year. For the decade after 1984 there were more than 100 bank failures every year.

Economists and historians can debate whether the high performance of the U.S. economy during the postwar period operated because of, or in spite of, the mixed form of capitalism and the extensive regulation characteristic of that era. There is no way to resolve that debate precisely. But circumstantially, it certainly seems that the mixed economy was doing something right.

The banking business gradually became more marketized in the early 1970s. The proximate cause was inflation, which led to financial and political pressures to lift the caps on interest rates. Partial deregulation then led to more intense price competition and pressure for more deregulation. By the 1980s, Congress, guided by an administration enamored with laissez-faire, had forgotten most of the lessons of the Great Depression and the special fiduciary role of banks, and was treating banking like just another business. In the savings-and-loan debacle, Congress gave thrift institutions extensive free-market liberties on the asset side of the ledger (loans), but retained deposit insurance on the liability side. This was an invitation for S&Ls to speculate with government-guaranteed money.

The full story of this evolution is explained in chapter 5. For now, let us treat it as an instructive case of the perils of ignoring the Theory of the Second Best. Banking, by its very nature, could never be totally deregulated. So the kind of pure-market price disciplines that govern, say, supermarkets were simply not attainable. But the free-market ideologues (abetted by opportunists in the banking industry and willing legislators and regulators) mistakenly assumed that partial deregulation was a big step forward. That mistake cost taxpayers $160 billion in the ensuing bailout.

It also cost the economy an incalculable amount of economic growth. For, during the subsequent period of shakeout, lenders suddenly became excessively risk-averse. In the late 1980s, when the regulatory climate suddenly changed, banks came under pressure to "clean up" their balance sheets. Bank regulators suddenly sharpened their pencils and began downgrading performing loans whose collateral was depressed in a recession. This abrupt tightening of credit standards pushed thousands of viable businesses into needless bankruptcy, and deepened the recession.

Looked at as an illustration of the Theory of the Second Best, the banking and S&L scandals suggest what happens when a necessarily mixed sector of the economy tries to substitute excessive marketization. Except for a very few fringe romantics in the economics profession, nobody thinks banking can be a pure free market. Almost nobody thinks we can do without a central bank, the Federal Reserve. Commercial banking is part of the nation's monetary system. Bankers use other people's money, and most small depositors lack the financial sophistication to calibrate precisely yield against risk when they decide which bank gets their savings deposits. A banking collapse would bring in its wake a financial collapse and a depression in the nonfinancial economy.

So banking, like health care, is necessarily a second-best realm. In the effort to bring things closer to the first best of a pure market, banking deregulation removed nonmarket forms of discipline, creating a net deterioration. In the market model of politics (Public Choice theory—see chapter 9), regulation invariably makes things worse, because the regulatory arena is politicized. What Public Choice leaves out is that the process of deregulation is every bit as politicized, every bit as laden with self-serving behavior, as the process of regulation. The history of banking deregulation is replete with cases of influence peddling, special pleading, and corruption of both the legislative and bank-supervisory processes. Indeed, the prior regime of regulation, where rules were clear and norms of supervision were well entrenched and hard to breach, was probably far less vulnerable to political corruption and opportunistic behavior on the part of politicians than the regime of rolling deregulation that followed it.

The saga of banking regulation raises the question of contending conceptions of efficiency. The intellectual and ideological champions of deregulation, in banking and elsewhere, invariably claimed that removal of regulatory strictures would increase the efficiency of the banking system and, by extension, of the economy. Let market forces loose—and they would perform their usual miracles of steering resources to their optimal uses, relying on price signals. Those most eager for credit would pay a higher price, and the credit would be theirs. Investors with a taste for higher risk and possible reward would be freer to gamble. In the case of banking, this meant allowing bankers to compete for deposits on the basis of price, by bidding up interest rates on deposits; and to seek out more aggressively loans that would pay the highest returns and thus would prove themselves the most worthy uses of credit.

The market, again by definition, had to be right. If loans to ski resorts, fast-food chains, and the Bolivian government paid a slightly higher return than loans to a local small business or housing complex, then they had to be the more deserving use of the capital. This calculus, of course, ignored the fact that lenders are neither clairvoyant nor immune to corruption. High-interest loans to shaky third-world regimes became a fad in the late 1970s and the 1980s. Bankers and regulators talked themselves into the belief that sovereign states could not go bankrupt. Foreign governments, relying on the old saw that if you go deep enough in debt to a banker you acquire a partner, managed to keep borrowing new money in order to pay interest on old loans. At the peak of the third-world debt crisis in the early 1980s, the outstanding, uncollectible third-world debt to money-center banks equaled more than twice the banks' capital. Regulators for the most part allowed money-center banks to carry these nonperforming loans on their balance sheets at book value. If the regulators had chosen to crack down, or to let pure-market forces sort out the wreckage, America's largest banks were technically insolvent. Eventually, over a decade, the third-world debts were gradually written off, at about sixty cents on the dollar. The putative gain to allocative efficiency achieved by the deregulation of banking was overwhelmed by loan losses.

THE THREE EFFICIENCIES

As the reader may have noticed, so far we have been dealing mainly with one form of efficiency, the form that economists call "allocative efficiency": markets, using price signals, steer resources to uses that maximize outputs relative to inputs; the price system responds to consumer choices, takes advantage of specialization, and hence optimizes performance for a given level of resources.

As noted, this brand of efficiency imagines a snapshot of consumer preferences at a given point in time. It does not consider the issues that concerned John Maynard Keynes—whether the economy as a whole has lower rates of growth and higher unemployment than it might achieve. Nor does allocative efficiency deal with the question of technical advance, which is the source of improved economic performance over time. Technical progress is the issue that concerned the other great dissenting economic theorist of the early twentieth century, Joseph Schumpeter.

A review of both economic history and economic theory suggests that there are three very different concepts of efficiency in economic life. We might call them Smithian, Keynesian, and Schumpeterian. For the most part, the study of markets is dominated by issues of allocation—the efficiency of Adam Smith. Keynesian efficiency, by contrast, addresses the potential output that is lost when the economy is stuck in recession, performing well below its full-employment potential. Increasing allocative efficiency in such circumstances doesn't help. It may even hurt—to the extent that intensified competition in a depressed economy may throw more people out of work, reduce overall purchasing power, and deepen the shortfall of aggregate demand. The economy of the 1990s has offered the paradox of escalating gains to productivity via Smithian efficiency, coexisting with declining purchasing power and declining job security for most ordinary people. Resources are allocated in a more marketlike manner, but overall performance is nonetheless mediocre and living standards are mostly stagnant.

By contrast, World War II is history's great example of an event that grossly violated allocative efficiency yet stimulated broad improvements in living standards. During the war, the United States had wage and price controls, rationing, coerced savings, monopolistic military contracts, and a variety of other affronts to free-market pricing. There was massive state intervention throughout the economy. During the peak of the war effort, nearly 50 percent of production was in response to government procurement contracts, most of which entailed monopoly pricing.

All of this violated ordinary supply and demand; it was profoundly inefficient in an allocative sense. Yet in a Keynesian sense the war was stunningly efficient. In 1941, the economy had still not fully recovered from the Great Depression. Unemployment remained at over 11 percent, and growth from June 1940 to June 1941 was less than 2 percent. But by June 1942, the economy was at full employment. Industry, which had resisted making investments because demand was slack, suddenly poured billions of dollars into war-production plants. Industry was recapitalized, at state-of-the-art technology. A generation of skilled workers was trained to operate it. Although nearly half of what was produced during the war was literally manufactured only to be blown up, the stimulus of war production rekindled economic growth. GNP increased by about 50 percent in just four years, a rate that has never been equaled before or since. By war's end, civilian purchasing power was one-third higher than it had been before Pearl Harbor. Although private-savings rates rose, much of the money that paid for the war was borrowed, through war bonds. But despite a record debt/GDP ratio of 119.8 percent at the war's end—more than double the "dangerous" ratio of the mid-1990s—this high debt was perfectly compatible with the two decades of record growth that followed.

Standard free-market economics simply does not know how to treat these two very different kinds of efficiency in the same analytical frame. As James Tobin, the Yale economics Nobelist, once quipped, "It takes a lot of Harberger triangles to fill up an Okun gap." Tobin was referring to Professor Arnold Harberger's little triangular diagram depicting the economic loss that results from monopoly prices. When monopolists use their market power to sell fewer units of product at a higher price, consumers pay more to obtain less. By extension, any departure from a free-market price results in an allocative loss that can be graphed as a triangle. The "Okun gap" is named for Arthur Okun, the Keynesian chairman of President Johnson's Council of Economic Advisers. Okun was fond of calculating the difference between the actual GNP and the economy's potential output were it at full employment.

The point of Tobin's quip is that little allocative efficiencies do not compensate for big, Keynesian inefficiencies of insufficient purchasing power, low growth, and high unemployment. At the same time, Tobin's deliberately and splendidly mixed metaphor—triangles and gaps—underscores that standard analysis lacks a common metric for assessing in the same conversation the interaction of these two conceptions of efficiency. If a Keynesian intervention reduces allocative efficiency by distorting market prices, but appropriately stimulates demand, standard market economics is literally unable to calculate *a priori* whether the trade-off is worth the candle.

The postwar boom was also built on what I am terming "Schumpeterian" efficiencies. Joseph Schumpeter was the great prophet of technical progress as the engine of growth, and the defender of imperfect competition as the necessary agent of technical progress. Large, oligopolistic firms often turn out to have the deepest pockets. They keep on innovating, to defend their privileged market position and to fend off encroachment. Innovation within a structure of stable oligopoly may be more reliable than innovation in a context of fierce and mutually ruinous price competition. Casual readers (or nonreaders) of Schumpeter may remember him as the prophet of "creative destruction," a phrase that he indeed coined to describe the onrushing turbulence of capitalism. But the usual cartoon of Schumpeter gets his meaning backward. Schumpeter's concern was how a market system could endure *despite* its many propensities toward ruinous competition. He was no advocate of creative destruction.

The modern economy offers many examples of Schumpeterian efficiency. The old regulated Bell telephone monopoly generated excess profits, many of which were plowed back into Bell Labs. A regulated rate structure also created pricing incentives for investing in ever more advanced switching technology, since profits grew with the rate base, and the rate base grew with the base of installed capital.

The German economy is famous for cartels and semi-cartels that resist price competition and emphasize technical progress. The Japanese economy, likewise, blends price competition and nonprice competition. South Korea is perhaps the most noteworthy case of Schumpeterian development that thrived by departing from "correct" pricing. The South Korean government made capital available at negative interest rates to favored industries and not only tolerated but often organized cartels.

James Kurth, a political economist at Swarthmore, has coined the useful phrase "Military Schumpeterianism." This is an ingenious twist on the oft-repeated observation that the postwar boom was built on "Military Keynesianism," by which commentators meant the reliable stimulus of defense spending; this substituted for a more explicit and aggressive Keynesianism of large deficit spending for civilian purposes, socialized savings, public-works investment, and so on. Kurth's point is that, though large and persistent military outlays may have indeed had macroeconomic benefits, defense contracts also had immense benefits for technical innovation, industrial stabilization, and market leadership—the efficiency of Schumpeter.

A series of long-term military contracts to a prime vendor produced assaults against allocative efficiency—the hundred-dollar hammers, thousand-dollar toilet seats, cost-plus windfalls regularly exposed in congressional investigations—yet also produced stunning technical advances and market leadership. Who thinks that Boeing would be the world's leader in aircraft sales absent World War II and the Cold War? As with Tobin's quip about triangles and gaps, standard economics has difficulty weighing the allocative loss of the hundred-dollar hammer against the dynamic gain of jet technology.

The list of technical gains generated by spinoffs from the warfare state is legion. Indeed, the reduction in defense outlays has caused a significant cut in funding for basic research, much of which was provided under the defense umbrella. Recent research by Maryellen R. Kelley of Carnegie-Mellon University suggests that the network of military prime contractors and subcontractors also provides immense benefits in technical diffusion of best-practice manufacturing (which was necessary to meet difficult specifications and fine tolerances), analogous to similar benefits of Japanese keiretsu and German bank-industry-labor interlocks. The common element here is long-term association and forms of competitive discipline that offer shelter from pure price competition.

As a matter of technical economics, there is a Schumpeter/Smith disjuncture that parallels the Keynes/Smith disjuncture. An economy that is performing according to the precepts of allocative efficiency is likely to have both avoidable unemployment and collective underinvestment in technological advance. A perfectly competitive market will spend too little on innovation both because profits will be too low, and because of well-known "externality" dilemmas.

An externality, please recall, is a cost or benefit to the economy as a whole that is not captured by a party to an immediate transaction. A negative externality is a cost, such as pollution, that is imposed on others. A positive externality, such as the broad gain from a new invention or from training an employee, is a benefit to society whose economic return is not fully realized by the innovator. Because investments in innovation are risky and because they often benefit competitors, market forces tend to underinvest in innovation. Indeed, the more "perfect" the competition, the less money is left over to invest in innovations that have broadly diffused benefits but that may not pay off to the investor for decades, if ever. The greater the rate of creative destruction, the less available are the monopoly "rents" that are the innovator's reward and necessary shelter. (In economic terminology, a "rent" is a super-normal profit that would be competed away in a perfect market.)

The more the economy relies on casinolike capital markets, the less the availability of patient capital. But when is oligopoly relatively "efficient," and when is competition mutually ruinous? From a purely Smithian perspective, the question is nonsensical *ex hypothesis*. Oligopoly is never efficient, because more competition is always better. However, as Douglass North, the first economic historian to win the Nobel Prize in economics, observed in his 1993 Nobel Lecture, "It is adaptive rather than allocative efficiency which is the key to long run growth." This is, of course, the efficiency of technical progress—of Schumpeter. We shall return to markets and innovation in chapter 6.

Another problem with allocative efficiency: the market's allocation of resources is only "efficient" based on a given distribution of income—one that reflects not only the verdicts of prior efficient markets, but also historical accidents. "Property is not theft," wrote R. H. Tawney, rebutting the anarchist

Proudhon, "but a good deal of theft becomes property." Remarkably, the set of goods purchased by the existing income distribution is deemed simultaneously "efficient"—and substantially arbitrary.

In principle, we could have a wide range of possible income distributions and start the economic game again, and the usual supply-and-demand discipline would efficiently resume. Though this happens occasionally (as in the case of land reforms, or social revolutions), for the most part the allocative efficiency of the market presumes the actual income distribution bequeathed to us by recent history. By market criteria, therefore, it is allocatively efficient for a millionaire to spend an extra fifty dollars on a fine after-dinner cigar, and for a pauper to starve in the streets for lack of money to eat. The price system doesn't care about that: its job is simply to match willing buyers with available sellers, and to be a buyer you need money.

Conventional economics usually replies that it is still more efficient to let market-determined supply and demand determine prices and prizes; if we don't like the social consequences, we can always redistribute income after the fact. Fine—but who are "we"? This rather airy conclusion innocently overlooks how wealth buys, among other things, power—and how power resists income redistribution.

The usual construct of purely allocative efficiency also begs the question of "Efficiency for what?" Market pricing is an arguably efficient means, not an end. The goals, values, habits, and institutions of a good society may include an essentially market economy, but must be set by extra-market processes and forces. In their enthusiasm for the market mechanism, many theorists insist market values are an end, not a means, and that whatever society results from market forces is by definition the best available, as well as one that has delivered just rewards.

Milton Friedman and his disciples have made valiant but ultimately unconvincing efforts to infer extra-market values from the functioning of the market mechanism. If markets thrive on well-informed consumers, then a market society requires free expression. If markets express voluntary exchange and free choice, then they are the natural handmaiden of liberal democracy. This sounds plausible in the abstract, until we remember that Nazism, fascism, Latin American military dictatorships, East Asian autocracies, and a wide range of other authoritarian regimes coexisted all too well with a basically capitalist form of production and exchange. Liberal democratic values, not to mention social ones, must be found elsewhere. Taken to an extreme, markets tend to destroy them.

AN ACCIDENTAL EQUILIBRIUM

Structurally, the economy of the postwar boom (1948–73) lent itself to non-Smithian kinds of efficiency—and to steady growth. The market economies of that era were national, were sheltered from pure marketization, and were hence more amenable to stabilization and management. The global economic rules of that era—fixed exchange rates, capital controls, managed trade—allowed entrepreneurship to flourish but limited its global dimension. Most of these were a legacy of economic controls instituted during the Depression and the war.

In the aftermath of World War II, a mixed economy was attainable at the level of the nation-state, because the nation-state controlled its borders. That made it possible for nations to have national fiscal, monetary, regulatory, social, sectoral, and developmental policies. These included macroeconomic management; social contracts between industry and labor predicated on noninflationary full employment; economic-development strategies that used subsidy, preferential procurement, and technology forcing via regulation; tight supervision and regulation of financial institutions; and the use of banks as engines of national development. The United States, as the dominant economy and keeper of the peace, helped stimulate global recovery by exporting capital, by serving as the residual market for other nations' product exports, and by serving as architect and guarantor of the Bretton Woods/GATT framework. The basic postwar system of global finance and trade dates to the Bretton Woods Agreement of June 1944, which established the International Monetary Fund and the World Bank. By 1947, the system included the General Agreement on Tariffs and Trade. This triad of institutions, under U.S. sponsorship, sought to reconcile increasingly free trade, stable but adjustable exchange rates, and high rates of economic growth. Until 1973, the secret weapon of the Bretton Woods system was the strength of the U.S. economy as a market and provider of capital, and the role of the U.S. dollar as reserve currency.

In addition, large, stable mass-production firms in basic industry and collective bargaining with labor unions created an industrial context that stabilized wages. The result was a virtuous circle, at the national level, of rising productivity, which translated into rising real wages, which enabled mass consumption of the economic product. This, in turn, created increasing opportunities for investment, which kept the productivity increases coming.

By contrast, in the new economy, nothing stays put very long. Nations have lost their macroeconomic leverage, because capital and product markets are now global. As the first Mitterrand government of 1981–83 learned to its chagrin, if a medium-sized nation runs a macroeconomic policy more expansive than that of

its neighbors, the stimulus will only leak out into imports, producing price inflation and debasement of the national currency. Labor has lost the power to bargain for high wages, because labor markets are increasingly worldwide, too.
Wage workers in poor nations lack the purchasing power to buy what they make,
which means that global supply outruns global demand. Governments today are
hesitant to regulate, since capital is free to move to areas of lower regulation.
The emerging consensus on liberal commerce also deprives governments of
Schumpeterian tools of technical development. And despite the best efforts of
the GATT and its successor, the World Trade Organization, there is no common
standard protecting intellectual property, nor a common understanding of what
constitutes commercial predation. Today's globalized, hyper-marketized economy is more like the world that Adam Smith projected, and the world that his
followers have commended, than the world of either Schumpeter or Keynes.

A COUNTERREVOLUTION

As the institutions of a mixed economy came under assault two decades ago, so
did its intellectual underpinnings. Several factors converged. Private business,
weakened by the Great Depression and the enlarged role of the state in World
War II and the Cold War, gradually recovered both its prestige and political influence. Center-left political coalitions, the intellectual and political constituencies for a mixed economy, began fragmenting. The less economic security the
state was able to deliver, the less enthusiasm its partisans could muster. In the
United States and Britain, radically conservative champions of laissez-faire attained political power, which they used to unleash market forces and further
weaken countervailing institutions. It is particularly instructive to examine the
role of the economics profession.

It is striking that so many professional economists, half a century after the
Great Depression, commenced a second romance with the ideal of a laissez-faire
economy. One can locate three major elements to the counterrevolution. First,
despite Keynes and the mixed economy, the core of the basic economic model
remained radically classical, thanks to the alliance of advanced mathematics and
highly abstract assumptions about human behavior. Notwithstanding Keynes,
that laissez-faire behavioral core was never challenged and awaited only the
right circumstances for its resurgence. Second, the stagnation of the postwar
mixed economy in the 1970s gave prestige to the conservative critics of
Keynesian (macroeconomic) intervention and discredited the Keynesians. Third,
as laissez-faire regained currency in the profession, even liberal economists,
classical at heart, began doubting the wisdom of regulatory (microeconomic)
interventions.

Beginning in the early 1950s, Milton Friedman and the school of economics that later came to be known as "monetarism" put forward the argument that government intervention cannot, in the long run, improve the functioning of markets and will likely worsen outcomes. Friedman opposed all forms of intervention, on libertarian as well as efficiency grounds, but the immediate target of his initial critique was fiscal and monetary intervention. Friedman's dissent was particularly unfashionable at the time, since it challenged the one province where the interventionists seemed to have won the debate—the macroeconomic realm of the economy as a whole.

Though most economists in the United States and Britain continued to have a classical view of human motivation and the market system of pricing, the postwar mainstream had appended John Maynard Keynes's insight that, when the pricing system aggregated to the economy as a whole, supply did not reliably equilibrate with demand. Entire economies could get stuck for long periods in suboptimal equilibria, yielding sluggish growth and protracted unemployment. Keynes liked to observe that the longest such disequilibrium was the Middle Ages.

Activist fiscal and monetary policy was therefore necessary to maintain the level of total purchasing power ("aggregate demand"), so that the economy could operate at its full potential. Contrary to the older, classical view, supply did not generate its own demand. Nor did savings spontaneously generate investment and growth. Entrepreneurs would invest and produce at the available frontiers only when they saw customers armed with effective demand for the products. Given the unreliability of private demand, government demand had to make up the difference. The Keynesian view not only justified state intervention; it impeached the claim of a self-correcting market, and by implication indicted the entire classical model. By the 1950s, Keynesian macroeconomics was well entrenched in the profession, even though it papered over a plain contradiction with the premise of classical microeconomic theory that the price system mostly worked. As late as 1980, Peter Drucker, a conservative, could still write, "Economics today is still very largely 'the House That Keynes Built.' "

The House of Keynes, however, was fragile. Rather than a consistent architecture, it was a 1930s-modern wing awkwardly tacked on to a nineteenth-century classical mansion. Moreover, mainstream economics had embraced only an adulterated form of Keynes, as interpreted by his more moderate disciples. Whereas Keynes himself had a more profound critique of the entire classical schema, the dominant group, who came to be known as "neo-Keynesians," left classical economics essentially intact, buttressing it with the need for government stabilization of total demand. Though Paul Samuelson grandly dubbed this amalgam the "neo-classical synthesis," the theory's classical core remained a plain contradiction that invited a counterrevolution.

In toppling Keynes, Friedman argued that pumping up economic activity, whether through government borrowing or via manipulation of the money supply, was at best a temporary fix. Over time, it would yield only inflation. The long-term constraints on real output would remain unchanged, but the resulting inflation would create distortions and uncertainties that actually retarded growth. As inflationary expectations became embedded in the economy, these would warp price signals, misallocate resources, deter investment, and produce real costs to economic efficiency. Therefore, Keynesian pump-priming, and even old-fashioned central-bank manipulation of interest rates, would both backfire. Friedman not only insisted that government fiscal and monetary intervention could never improve outcomes. Even if, for the sake of argument, it could do so in theory, such intervention was likely to be corrupted in practice by politics. So the actual intervention would invariably be worse than the best intervention available. Better, on both counts, to leave the free market alone.

In the fiscal realm, Friedman proposed a balanced budget. In monetary policy, he proposed a "strict monetary rule." The Federal Reserve should put the money supply on automatic pilot, because, like a novice sailor attempting to compensate for shifts in wave and wind, monetary authorities would be prone to oversteer. By renouncing hapless efforts to manipulate interest rates or the stock of money, central banks would allow markets to determine the most efficient interest rate available, stripped of any "inflation premium" generated by the market's lack of confidence in mistakes politicians might make. Where Keynesians saw the Great Depression as proof that pure markets led to speculative excesses, shortfalls of total demand, and stagnation, Friedman viewed the Depression as a casualty of wrongheaded central-bank policies.

Just as there was a natural interest rate, determined by the supply of savings' interacting with the demand for capital, Friedman slightly later propounded the idea of a Natural Rate of Unemployment. Again, the private economy was capable of generating so many jobs at market wages. Attempts to raise wages beyond a "market-clearing" level via unions or minimum-wage laws, or to push unemployment levels below their natural rate through macroeconomic stimulus, would not only yield inflation but, over time, would even lead to higher unemployment. The common message: the market economy is doing the best it can.

Events seemed to vindicate Friedman's prophecy. In the 1960s, the Keynesians thought they had mastered the art of economic "fine-tuning." By the mid-1970s, growth abruptly faltered and inflation soared. Within the economics fraternity, the end of the boom seemed an object lesson in the hubris of macroeconomic intervention. To add to the disgrace of the neo-Keynesians, unemployment and inflation, which in theory move inversely (as a "trade-off"), rose in unison through much of the decade. This era of "stagflation" unfortunately coincided with left-of-center administrations in the United States, Britain, and West Germany. By 1980, each had left office, humiliated. Again, Friedman's view of tampering with the natural market forces seemed vindicated. And most neo-Keynesians lost the courage of their earlier convictions.

There is, of course, a more institutional analysis of the demise of postwar boom and the sources of 1970s stagflation: the OPEC price shocks introduced an external, structural source of inflation, which became embedded in the price system. This occurred just as the Bretton Woods system of stable currencies anchored by the U.S. dollar was collapsing. Central banks practicing orthodox monetary policy then responded to stagflation by raising interest rates, and putting all the major Western economies on a path of slower growth and higher unemployment. So reduced growth and rising prices collided for reasons that had little to do with Keynesian intervention or with the mixed economy. Eventually inflation was squeezed out, but at terrible cost. In the meantime, the more conservative interpretation, followed by a backlash of conservative policies, won the day.

In the 1950s, Milton Friedman was dismissed as a curiosity. By the 1980s, Friedman and several of his followers had won the Nobel Prize. Ideas such as the Natural Rate of Unemployment had become as much a part of the economic mainstream as supply and demand. (We return to it in chapter 3.) Indeed, so complete was the neutering of Keynes that by the early 1990s it was self-described "neo-Keynesians" who fretted about excessive deficits and worried that unemployment rates below 6 percent were unsustainable. In the intervening forty years, Friedman and his protégés had popularized the free-market gospel through Friedman's own best-selling books and his television series, "Free to Choose." A burgeoning Chicago School had become a generalized theory of the superiority of free markets. "Fundamentally, there are only two ways of co-ordinating the economic activities of millions," Friedman wrote. "One is central direction involving the use of coercion—the technique of the army and the modern totalitarian state. The other is the voluntary co-operation of individuals—the technique of the marketplace."

Among the other doctrines to grow out of the Chicago view was the school that came to be known as Law and Economics. The basic idea is that the law, as a system of rules, commands, and controls, tends to contradict and countermand the natural logic of markets. Rather, according to Law and Economics scholars, jurists and legal scholars should endeavor to make the law facilitative of markets.

A very influential early document was a journal article by Ronald Coase, later to win a Nobel Prize, called "The Problem of Social Cost." The doctrine, dubbed the Coase Theorem by a fellow Chicagoan, like the market ideal itself was breathtakingly audacious, simple, and strikingly analogous to Friedman's view of fiscal and monetary policy: Courts and regulations, like central banks, are basically incapable of improving on economic outcomes that free individuals would otherwise negotiate. If we assume that such negotiations are voluntary, readily attained, and themselves costless—a preposterous assumption, as Coase himself later acknowledged—individuals will naturally bargain their way to reasonable outcomes, no matter what rules courts and regulators set down. Therefore, regulation serves no useful function. The Coase Theorem became the most cited paper in the economics journals, and the Law and Economics movement became a powerful intellectual lobby against regulation.

The new, radically fundamentalist economic model colonized other social sciences as well. In political science, the new school of Public Choice theory held that political democracy should be understood as just another market. If, as specified by the theory, rational individuals sought to maximize their well-being, it logically followed that elected officials had one goal only—getting re-elected. It also followed that interest groups pursued politics only to win benefits at the expense of other interest groups. By analogy to economic theory, this was described as "free riding" or "rent-seeking." Whereas markets by definition optimized, polities by definition diverted resources and worsened outcomes. These theorists defined out of existence a richer model of political democracy in which elected officials, at least some of the time, could pursue a general public interest. That view was dismissed as "sentimental." A pioneer of Public Choice theory, James Buchanan, also won a Nobel Prize.

For young economists, the convenience of this brand of theorizing was that one size fit all cases. Apprentice economists, and fellow travelers in other disciplines, were spared the time-consuming process of reading history or studying the details of complex institutions. They had only to devise the models, collect the statistics, and crunch the numbers. There was little mystery to the conclusion, since it was ordained by the assumption—the market works. You didn't really need to know much about anything, and you could know everything about everything. Some of the most prestigious economists today are astonishingly expert in everything from trade to labor markets to income distribution to financial markets to macroeconomic policy—and by age thirty-five. It suggests either remarkably protean intellects—or dubious shortcuts. In a kind of Darwinian process, economists expert in advanced mathematics and innocent of the details of commercial life drove out those with a more complex curiosity. Today, an Adam Smith would not likely get tenure. His work would be dismissed as journalism or sociology.

THE LIBERAL COLLAPSE

In understanding the dominance of the market ideal today, one must appreciate that the intellectual counterrevolution of the 1970s reflected not only the growing influence of conservative economists like Milton Friedman but also the second thoughts of many liberals. Two very influential books of that era express the trend. Both were written by Brookings Institution economists who considered themselves liberal Democrats, and who served Democratic presidents as chairs of the Council of Economic Advisers. Both books were originally given as Godkin Lectures at Harvard: Arthur Okun's *Equality and Efficiency: The Big Tradeoff*, the 1974 Godkin Lectures, and Charles Schultze's *The Public Use of Private Interest*, the lectures for 1976.

In *Equality and Efficiency*, Okun begins by noting the inherent conflict between the realm of citizenship rights and the realm of private purchasing power. The market slops into realms where it doesn't belong, where money is not supposed to buy influence. The market creates vast gulfs of wealth and income that undermine civil society itself. Although these two principles necessarily coexist in a capitalist democracy, says Okun, we must recognize that the economy usually pays a price in lowered economic efficiency when it opts for greater equality, because such efforts come at the expense of the market mechanism.

I have challenged Okun's "trade-off" premise in my 1984 book, *The Economic Illusion*, which pointed to a wide and substantially indeterminate range of policy interventions, some of which improved both equality and efficiency, and others of which depressed both. My purpose here is not to rehash that debate. Rather, I want to pause for a moment to locate Okun and Schultze as two bellwethers in the evolution of liberal postwar economic thought away from the ideal of a mixed economy, back toward a more fundamentalist, laissez-faire one.

Okun spends the first part of his book as a good liberal, decrying both the vast inequalities of our market economy and the tendency of markets to trespass where they don't belong: "Some of our most cherished rights are auctioned off to the highest bidder. These transgressions may be as important a source of cynicism, radicalism, and alienation as the vast disparities in living standards between rich and poor." In the end, however, Okun's formula is to use taxes and transfer payments to take care of society's losers, but otherwise to let market forces rip. To do less, he insists, would be to sacrifice economic performance. Politics, alas, is outside Okun's field of competence. The trouble with his remedy, as recent history has shown, is that, the more powerfully entrenched the market model becomes, the less appetite have its custodians for redistributing its prizes. Marketization also changes the distribution of political power. As an economist might say, political choices are partly endogenous to the structure of the economy.

Schultze, writing two years after Okun, goes much further. In *The Public Use of Private Interest*, Schultze discerns "a growing body of objective evidence that government is not performing its tasks efficiently." The basic problem, for

Schultze, is a failure of public policy to appreciate the market and to use markets to achieve public ends.

Government doesn't prioritize well, failing to sort out "the frivolous from the important." Government intrudes clumsily: "We have a propensity to intervene in resource-allocation decisions in order to achieve equity and income-distribution goals that might better be handled by some form of tax or monetary-transfer arrangements." And government has only one way of intervening: "removing a set of decisions from the decentralized and incentive-oriented private market and transferring them to the command and control techniques of government bureaucracy."

Schultze's book is suffused with a reverence for markets, a disdain for government, and a dismissal of the idea that public-mindedness can or should be cultivated. "Harnessing the 'base' motive of material self-interest to promote the common good is perhaps *the* most important social invention mankind has yet achieved. . . . If I want drivers to economize on gasoline usages, advertising appeals to patriotism, warnings about the energy crisis, and 'don't be fuelish' slogans are no match for higher prices at the gas pumps. In most cases the prerequisite for social gain is the identification, not of villains and heroes but of the defects in the price system that drive ordinary citizens into doing things contrary to the common good."

Taken as a whole, Schultze's book views "polity failure" as ubiquitous, and market failure as a relatively narrow series of special cases. He calls on public policy to remedy these cases by structuring incentives rather than decreeing "command-and-control" solutions. Thus, if markets generate socially unacceptable income distributions, the remedy is taxes and transfer payments, ideally in the form of vouchers (which are more marketlike). If industry takes a free ride on the natural environment and pollutes, the solution is not to command lower pollution levels, but to create tax incentives and shadow markets that will change the price signals to which industry responds. Somehow, a hopelessly corrupted polity is expected to find its way to this superior remedy, though Schultze doesn't indicate how. In a more technical and also highly influential book published during the same period and co-authored by environmental economist Allen Kneese, *Pollution, Prices, and Public Policy*, Schultze lays out a scheme for incentive pricing as a substitute for "command-and-control" environmental regulation. In the intervening years, "command and control" has passed into the policy discourse as an all-purpose disparagement of the regulatory impulse. The idea that regulation, where absolutely unavoidable, should be "marketlike" has become conventional wisdom.

During the same period, Alfred Kahn, the Cornell economist and later chairman of the Civil Aeronautics Board, was having grave misgivings about economic regulation. In the 1970s, both the left and the right criticized the schema of price and supply regulation then typical of trucking, airlines, railroads, gas pipelines, and telephones. Free-market economists saw this regulatory regime as a gratuitous interference with the price system. Liberal reformers criticized regulatory agencies as captives of regulated industries. Political scientists, who a generation earlier had celebrated "pluralism," found it degenerating into narrow interest politics practiced at the expense of the larger collectivity. If competent public-interest regulation was possible in theory, it was increasingly improbable in political practice. These officials, all self-described liberals, served as expert advisers to Democratic presidents, while dismantling much of the case for a mixed economy. In the emblematic case of airline regulation, what began under President Carter as "regulatory reform" quickly evolved into a drive for complete deregulation.

Yet another liberal economist emblematic of the era, Alain Enthoven, argued against European-style systems of national health insurance, and spent more than two decades searching for a way to structure the profit motive to deliver health care efficiently. In a 1980 book titled (with unintended irony) *Health Plan*, Enthoven approvingly quotes Schultze's disparagement of command and control, and declares: "Regulation depends on coercion, on forcing people to behave in ways they consider opposed to their own best interests. The decentralized competitive market, on the other hand, leaves maximum freedom to individual providers and consumers consistent with achievement of society's purposes."

The mixed economy was in retreat on each major front. Keynesian macroeconomics was seemingly discredited by events. The microeconomics of a partly regulated economy were under growing assault, with relative liberals in the profession and in government leading the charge. And the nineteenth-century behavioral assumptions about economic man were regaining ground, at the expense of more psychological and social brands of analysis.

Thus, by the time Ronald Reagan took office in January 1981, much of the Reagan crusade was pushing on an open door. As the Reagan deficits mooted the use of fiscal policy, liberal as well as conservative macroeconomics saw only one fiscal imperative—budget balance. Liberals as well as conservative economists fretted that unemployment below a Friedman-style Natural Rate of roughly 6 percent—ten million souls—would trigger inflation. Liberals as well as conservatives became cheerleaders for deregulation. Organized business, once tamed and traumatized by the Roosevelt era, awoke from its slumber and began pumping hundreds of millions of dollars into think tanks whose intellectuals would validate and celebrate laissez-faire.

Steven Kelman, in a charming and insightful book titled *What Price Incentives?*, tells of the chasm between economists and noneconomists (mostly lawyers) working on regulatory issues under Carter. The lawyers, Kelman recounts, tended to attribute the uniform antiregulatory bias among the economists to a failure to hire "a broad enough spectrum of economists" and to "beg the economists, if they can't support the [regulatory] proposals, to at least give them the 'best economic arguments' in favor of them." But, Kelman reported, "The economists' answer is typically something like, 'There are no good economic arguments for your proposal.' "

Thus the hegemony of free-market economics and its conception of the efficiency of allocation. The Reagan revolution and its progeny, the Gingrich "Contract with America," did not spring full-blown from a political crusade. The ground was seeded for better than a decade by a counterrevolution in economic thinking. We next turn to the free-market view of human behavior, another area where theory diverges heroically from evidence.

2 / THE IMPERIAL MARKET

MARKETS, BEHAVIOR, AND SOCIETY

As good a neoclassical economist as Arthur Okun could write that "the market needs a place, and the market needs to be kept in its place." Human society plainly needs norms of behavior other than the short-term, instrumental, and purely egoistic norms of the market. But lately, enthusiasts of markets have claimed that most of human activity can and should be understood as nothing but a series of markets, and that outcomes would be improved if constraints on market behavior were removed.

In the past quarter-century, a good deal of economic theory has become less the study of "the allocation of scarce resources," and more the simple celebration of markets. A more complex model of human behavior, reflecting twentieth-century insights about psychology, has reverted to a simplified nineteenth-century conception of rationality. A more complex view of society has given way to the claim that most issues boil down to material incentives, and most social problems are best resolved by constructing or enhancing markets. And, indeed, fewer people today enjoy protections against the uglier face of the market, or social income as a right of citizenship. More aspects of human life are on the auction block. Champions of market society insist that all of this makes us better off.

The picture of an optimal, self-cleansing market system is based on several premises, which together make up the laissez-faire model. As we have seen, some involve the dynamics of price, supply, and innovation. Others purport to describe the logic of social structures. Still others are claims about human behavior and motivation. All need to be qualified as descriptions of reality.

In the laissez-faire model, people behave rationally. Their motivation can be best understood as self-interested, even when it seems to be altruistic. Social structures, norms, and institutional legacies are largely irrelevant except as unfortunate intrusions on the market mechanism. Individual, selfish decisions simply aggregate to a general good, through the price system. Standard theory holds, via the Fundamental Theorems of Welfare Economics, first, that a freely competitive economy yields a single, optimal set of prices that can be understood as a "general equilibrium"; and, second, that this one best set of prices is attained via the free expression of preferences. Implicitly, departures from this one best price-set have costs to economic welfare.

Thus the behavioral assumptions of a rational individual freely expressing and maximizing preferences connect to the efficiency assumptions of the collective outcome. It is noteworthy that modern general-equilibrium theory, foreshadowed a century ago by radically classical economists such as W. Stanley Jevons and Léon Walras, is the work of yet another Nobel Prize winner, Kenneth Arrow, whose declared political preferences are ostensibly left-of-center. His general-equilibrium theory, however, has become the capstone of a brand of political economy that becomes a generalized argument against state intervention. A great many other economists find their preferences as citizens at odds with their professional training.

The alleged optimality of markets depends on the veracity of each of these several interconnected assumptions. However, if people do not behave "rationally" in the terms specified by the economic model, if preferences are unstable, if some markets do not "clear" on the basis of accurate price signals, if income and hence buying power do not closely reflect merit, if some costs and benefits are not captured by the market's price, then the myriad small markets in society do not aggregate to an efficient "general equilibrium." Rather, there is a great deal of indeterminacy in society and hence the possibility that extra-market motivations and measures could yield a superior use of available resources. The pro-market remedy to society's imperfections is training people and institutions to behave more like the specification of economic man. But if much of human life cannot be reduced to a market, the benefits will not materialize.

In the real world, there are many possible configurations of prices consistent with high rates of economic growth. Actual prices reflect not just the calculating, rational individual of the market model, but a messy blend of discernment, habit, misinformation, and nonmarket motivation. Some extra-market motivations, as I will suggest below, not only are socially desirable but actually improve economic outcomes. So the core theorems postulating a single general equilibrium and a unique "correct" optimum are at odds with the dynamics of both actual price-setting and human motivation.

I have been speaking here of an "economic model." There are of course dissenters within the economics profession. In the spectrum of views, however, one is a dissenter precisely in proportion to how imperfectly one believes that the standard economic model describes the world, and how narrowly or broadly the market model can be extended from explicitly economic phenomena to interpret aspects of life that do not seem to be markets. Thus, the purists insist that politics, family life, law, and even explicitly antimarket phenomena like charity can be understood as variants on markets. The dissenters challenge this extrapolation, and also question whether markets optimize outcomes even in narrowly economic realms. But they challenge it at risk to their standing in the profession.

Because of the logical consistency, interdependence, and mathematic elegance of the several aspects of the market model, a dissenter who calls into question one fundamental aspect of the model threatens the entire edifice. Free-market enthusiasts tend to fiercely defend their model as a whole, because of its logical interconnections. "When you dig deep down," Charles Schultze once observed to me, "economists are scared to death of being sociologists. The one great thing we have going for us is the premise that individuals act rationally in trying to satisfy their preferences." This helps explain why the profession tends to marginalize, even ostracize, those who posit that motivation is more complex and that noneconomic factors matter.

I focus here on the purists since it is necessary to grasp what the pure-market model claims before one can measure the claims against the messy, institutional real world. This chapter examines the new fundamentalism in the market conception of society and human nature. It suggests some of the limits and defects of this model—as description and prescription. Consider first the behavioral claims.

RATIONALITY

Those who believe society can best be understood as a series of markets begin by positing a rational, calculating individual whose goal is to maximize "utility." This premise says everything and nothing, since it is true by definition in all cases. But it is a key aspect of the market model, since it is the behavioral part of the logical argument that whatever the market decides must be optimal. In this syllogism, people rationally express their true preferences in their pattern of expenditure, the occupations they pursue, how they divide work and leisure time, choose mates, and so on. It then logically follows that markets accurately serve free choices and aggregate to general welfare. In twentieth-century conservative economics, this inference has come to be known as "revealed preference."

People, by definition, get what they want. If they wanted something else, they would select it. If they wanted something not on the menu (and if it were cost-effective), some entrepreneur would figure out how to provide it.

The doctrine of revealed preference permits a more radically classical economics. Every exchange is presumed "free" and every choice voluntary. One can then deny that some choices are invidiously precluded by prior circumstances, dubious inequalities of status or power, or by markets themselves; that tastes are both somewhat unstable and subject to manipulation; and that extra-market remedies are sometimes the most direct route to outcomes that people really want but cannot find via market institutions. Polls show, for example, that most Americans would like universal health insurance with free choice of doctor. Other nations offer that alternative, via state regulation, at lower aggregate cost than our own system. But the free market does not place it on the available menu.

The picture of a rational individual deliberately and mindfully maximizing utility and adjusting preferences at the margin confers legitimacy on the outcome and facilitates (spurious) mathematical precision. Conversely, if we remove the assumptions of rational utility-maximization and marginal adjustment, the whole affair is much more indeterminate, difficult to model, and subject to political intermediation.

It is perfectly possible to have a broadly efficient capitalist economy while jettisoning the heroic behavioral assumptions. Even if individual preferences were somewhat arbitrary, unstable, and manipulable, entrepreneurs would remain subject to competitive discipline to offer the best product at the most attractive price. Products would still efficiently get to the shelves, and consumers would still broadly hold producers accountable. But the market-determined income distribution would no longer be sacrosanct. There would be a great variety of possible relationships between prices of different goods—all of them tolerably efficient. One would have to acknowledge that regulation might improve outcomes, precisely by "distorting" market-determined prices.

Moreover, some "tastes" are less a reflection of revealed preference than of misinformation, prejudice, and ignorance of broader possibility. Society educates its young partly to train them for useful occupations but also to cultivate a higher general level of knowledge, judgment, discernment, active citizenship, and an appreciation of learning itself. The philosopher Bertrand de Jouvenel, ridiculing the doctrine of revealed preference, observed that, if books were printed in a language he could not read, "possibly I would turn to comic strips; this would triumphantly reinforce the proof that 'people prefer' comic strips. Revealed preferences in fact reveal *ignorance*, the lack of intellectual and aesthetic formation."

A fine example of the instability and malleability of "revealed preference" (and the overreach of the model) is the turning of public opinion against smoking. In 1995, 25 percent of adult Americans smoked, down from a peak of 42.4 percent in 1965. Beginning in 1971, television advertising of tobacco was prohibited, surgeon general's warnings were required, scientific evidence accumulated about links between smoking, cancer, and cardiovascular disease. The percentage of adult smokers gradually declined. In Massachusetts, a 1992 referendum increased the cigarette tax by twenty-five cents and used the proceeds to place print and broadcast ads warning of the hazards of smoking. Between 1992 and 1996, smoking in Massachusetts declined by 18 percent, or triple the rate of decline of the rest of the nation.

The model of revealed preference can neither comprehend this process nor shed useful light on what occurred. By definition, people are maximizing their utility—both when they smoke and after they quit. The theory is agnostic on whether it is better for them to smoke or not. Since smoking is one of the best-documented health hazards, people presumably would be better off if they maximized their utility by quitting instead of smoking. But this inference makes the theorists extremely uncomfortable, since choices manipulated by private efforts are by definition legitimate, whereas those influenced by public education are presumptively suspect as paternalistic or coercive. By specifying "perfect information" as one of its assumptions, the model implicitly is friendly to disclosure requirements that improve the quality of actual, as opposed to hypothetical, consumer information. But, as skeptics of the capacity of government and politics to do anything right, many conservative economists have been wary of disclosure laws, lest they give aid and comfort to the interventionists. Indeed, conservative economists have been oddly hostile to the idea that government-mandated information might be a more objective counterweight to "information" provided by purveyors of products—which information is by definition one-sided, opportunistic, and often misleading.

In an argument that borders on self-parody, some theorists even contend that by choosing to smoke people are not only maximizing their utility but helping the economy. The argument goes like this: Smokers die prematurely. They thus make less of a claim on Social Security funds and on health care. These statistics can be empirically challenged, since smokers are generally likely to die of protracted diseases that are costly to treat—lung cancer, heart disease, emphysema—even if they die younger. Such studies do not empirically examine the literal lifetime outlays on smokers and nonsmokers by the health-care system; they merely extrapolate from the fact that smokers tend to die younger. But suppose the statistics were true. The claim that people are improving their own welfare and society's—by pursuing an avoidable habit that increases their risk of a gruesome, premature death—defies common sense.

Why would intelligent people make such an argument? Because the whole free-market schema hinges on the claim that revealed preferences must aggregate to a general optimum. The investment in the market model is so powerful that its defenders resort to Swiftian logic. Indeed, two Chicago School economists once logically demonstrated that people who commit suicide must be maximizing their utility.

The *locus classicus* of the revealed-preference argument is an article by Gary Becker and his colleague George Stigler, both later Nobel Prize winners from the Chicago School, titled "De Gustibus Non Est Disputandum." Because the consumer is ultimately sovereign, Stigler and Becker insist that "it is neither necessary nor useful to attribute to advertising the function of changing tastes." The benign role of advertising, in their view, is to help consumers to "differentiate products." In comparing "tastes," Stigler and Becker also contrast "good" and "bad" addictions—for example, the habit of listening to classical music versus the habit of using heroin.

The Becker-Stigler article is mainly a series of syllogisms. ("The stock of music capital might fall and the price of music appreciation rise at older ages because the incentive to invest in future capital would decline as the number of remaining years declined, whereas the investment required simply to maintain the capital stock would increase as the stock increased.") The piece sheds no useful insight on the actual dynamics of either the cultivation of musical taste or heroin addiction, or on the formation of preferences generally. On that issue, free-market economics is agnostic. Indeed, the authors conclude, in a moment of uncharacteristic humility, "we would welcome explanations of why some people become addicted to alcohol and others to Mozart, whether the explanation was a development of our approach or a contribution from some other behavioral discipline." Small chance that the explanation would be adduced from theirs.

By positing that there is ultimately no accounting for tastes, Stigler and Becker leave open the possibility that *Homo republicanus* will override *Homo economicus*. Suppose people, good utility-maximizers, choose in their capacity as citizens to create a universal health-care system, or to mandate cigarette warnings, or even to limit "commercial speech." Can the Chicago economist gainsay their free choice? As Albert Hirschman wrote, trumping Stigler, "De Valoribus Est Disputandum."

"ANOMALIES"

Skeptics have long challenged the utilitarian behavioral construct on its own terms. People, surely, experienced emotional as well as rational influences. Utility maximization was plainly a tautology. Nobody had the time to calculate, much less to optimize, every decision. As the "marginalists" were taking over economics, Thorstein Veblen wrote nearly a century ago, "If, in fact, all the conventional relations and principles of pecuniary intercourse were subject to such a perpetual rationalized, calculating revision, so that each article of usage, appreciation, or procedure must approve itself de novo on hedonistic grounds of sensuous expediency . . . it is not conceivable that the institutional fabric would last overnight."

This debate was something of a draw, because tautologies cannot be refuted. Lately, however, a new generation of critics has brought empirical evidence as well as logic. A bright spot in recent academic work on preferences is an uncharacteristically experimental genre at the boundary of economics and psychology. This work tends to make Chicago-style economists very uneasy, because it demonstrates that preferences, far from being rational and consistent, are context-dependent, unstable, and often reflect noneconomic motivations.

Almost forty years ago, Herbert Simon proposed a heterodox theory of Bounded Rationality. People behaved "rationally"—but under serious constraints. "The capacity of the human mind for formulating and solving complex problems is very small compared with the size of the problems whose solution is required for objectively rational behavior in the real world. . . ." Cornell economist Richard Thaler, another dissenter, teases the Chicagoans for excluding from their model human folly. In a debate with Robert Barro, one of the most solemn advocates of the theory that people consistently behave according to "rational expectations," Thaler explained that the difference between his own model and Barro's is that "He assumes the agents in his model are as smart as he is, while I portray people as being as dumb as I am." Thaler wrote later that "Barro agreed with this assessment."

The school of experimental economics reflects nearly two decades of motivational surveys and experiments, pioneered by psychologists Daniel Kahneman and Amos Tversky. These experiments demonstrate inconsistencies and asymmetries of preferences that standard economic theory would expect to be stable and symmetrical. A good example is what Thaler calls "endowment effects": Most people demand more money to give something up than they would pay to acquire it. In the market model, rational economic man prices the same commodity identically, as buyer or as seller. But evidently this does not describe real people.

Experiments show that people will charge more to sell bottles of wine they already have than they would pay to acquire the very same wine, though free-market theory would posit a single, "market-clearing" price. Likewise lottery tickets, pens, inherited stock, and myriad other commodities. Even more remarkably, this "endowment effect" does not apply only to long-held articles that might plausibly have extra sentimental value. It seems to be instantaneous.

Kahneman and Tversky performed an experiment in which they asked people what they would do if they arrived at a theatre to buy a ten-dollar ticket for a play and found they had lost a ten-dollar bill en route. Eighty-eight percent said they would buy the ticket anyway. But when the study proposed that they had purchased the ticket in advance but lost the ticket (rather than the money) on the way to the theatre, only 54 percent said they would spend ten dollars to replace the ticket. Money is of course fungible. The two situations are economically identical, and rational economic man would behave identically in both cases. But real people don't.

Thaler conducted an experiment with Cornell students in which he gave half the class, at random, a Cornell coffee mug that retails for $6.00. The other half received no mug. Students were then invited to sell or keep their mugs. Economic theory predicts that the class would be randomly divided into those who liked mugs more than their monetary value, and those who preferred the money. In theory, a market-clearing price would be established by supply and demand. Roughly half the mugs would trade; and when the market cleared the mugs would be owned by those subjects who subjectively valued them most. But that predicted result did not materialize. The market mostly failed to clear. The median mug-owner demanded no less than $5.25 to part with the mug, whereas the median prospective buyer was willing to pay no more than $2.75. In four experiments conducted by Professor Thaler, only 12.5 percent of the mugs traded, rather than the 50 percent predicted by theory. Thaler comments that people, rather than being the rational calculators specified by the market model, have a "status quo bias," and an "aversion to loss."

A closely related flaw in the standard model is the oft-noted perception that real people simultaneously have more than one "preference schedule." We resolve to eat the salad, but gorge ourselves on the steak. Obsessive behaviors and addictions at one extreme, and "irrational" love of family and country at the other, challenge the one-dimensional model of motivation. People pay a great deal of money to go to "fat farms" to lose weight that they could easily avoid by eating less in the first place. They simultaneously indulge habits they know are bad for them, and play tricks on themselves to frustrate their own habitual and impulsive behaviors. Many smokers deliberately buy cigarettes by the pack, which is more costly, rather than by the carton, in the hope that they will thereby smoke less. Polls even show that a majority of smokers support higher tobacco taxes. Is economic man maximizing his utility when he overeats, or when he pays to undergo a costly weight-loss program? When he overpays for the cigarette, or when he smokes? The Chicago answer is that, by definition, he is maximizing on both occasions, but this is not a very useful conception of human behavior.

A much more convincing explanation is that economic behavior is a struggle between "multiple selves with competing preferences," as Thaler puts it, or between "preferences and meta-preferences," in the words of Albert Hirschman, or what philosopher Harry G. Frankfurt called first- and second-order desires. Long before these modern critiques, Walt Whitman had it right in "Song of Myself":

> Do I contradict myself?
> Very well then I contradict myself,
> (I am large, I contain multitudes.)

The economist Amartya Sen, in a classic essay titled "Rational Fools," suggests that people are motivated by both second-order preferences and transient impulses. Human beings are self-evaluating. We have the self that is, and the self that we'd like to be. As Mark Lutz and Kenneth Lux, two heterodox economists, have observed, "I like to watch TV" is an evaluative statement, but less evaluative than the statement "I wish I didn't like TV so much." We have battles over self-discipline. We sometimes pursue behaviors that express this dilemma, as when Ulysses "lashed himself to the mast" to resist the call of the Sirens, and as millions of Americans do when they "irrationally" put no-interest deposits into blocked Christmas accounts.

Hirschman points to a whole class of "non-instrumental" activities, pursued not to yield a deliberate outcome, but "for their own sake." He writes, "From their earliest origins, men and women appear to have allocated time to undertakings whose success is simply unpredictable: the pursuit of truth, beauty, justice, liberty, community, friendship, love, salvation, and so on. . . . [A]n important component of the activities thus undertaken is best described not as labor or as work, but as *striving*—a term that precisely intimates the lack of a reliable relation between effort and result. A measure of cost-benefit calculus is impossible under the circumstances."

Margaret Jane Radin observes, in her book *Contested Commodities*, that while market economists assert that virtually everything ought to be for sale, given a willing buyer and a willing seller, in reality entire realms, such as "infants and children, human reproduction, sperm, eggs, embryos, blood, human organs, human sexuality, human pain" are arenas where the drive to commodify a domain is "contested" by widespread social values. The goal of "universal commodification," she notes, is held by free-market economists, but by few others.

As the philosopher Mark Sagoff suggests, this distinction not only applies to different levels of the consuming self. Each of us also plays the dual roles of consumer and citizen. Consumers have wants. Citizens have values. Many values are extra-material, and contradict wants. "Social regulation reflects public values we choose collectively, and these may conflict with wants and interests we pursue individually." As consumer, Sagoff writes, I pursue narrow self-interest, and momentarily "put aside the community-regarding values I take seriously as a citizen. . . . I love my car; I hate the bus. Yet I vote for candidates who promise to tax gasoline to pay for public transportation." Voting itself is a nonrational act, since the chance that one vote will affect an outcome is minuscule. The political scientists Sidney Verba and Nelson Polsby tell the story of the time when, on sabbatical in Europe, they drove several hundred miles to cast absentee ballots they knew would cancel each other out. The act of voting is a declaration of faith in the civic process, as well as a declaration of preference.

"Anomalies"—the concept is Thaler's—may be far too modest a term to capture the import of multilayered individual preferences. These findings are far more damaging to the standard market model than it may first appear. For one cannot project a general optimum based on the response of the price system to preferences that are random, unstable, or extra-economic to begin with. If that is true, then general-equilibrium theory is elegant mathematics built on sand.

Moreover, economic decisions are often based on misinformation *ex ante*, and yield disappointment *ex post*. Seemingly, the solution for this is simply a better-informed consumer. But as products and decisions proliferate, that prospect is a receding mirage: there are not enough hours in the day. As essayist Steven Waldman writes, "[S]pend the optimal amount of time on each decision and pretty soon you run out of life."

Indeed, choice itself, one of the most prized trophies of the market system, can become self-negating when taken to an extreme. The market model requires the informed consumer to hold the producer accountable. But an overwhelmed consumer cannot competently play that role. "The more choice available," Waldman writes, "the more information a consumer must have to make a sensible selection. When overload occurs, many simply abandon the posture of rational Super-Consumer." Paradoxically, an excess amount of choice makes the consumer putty in the hands of a sophisticated marketer. Free-market theorists acknowledge this problem as "search costs," but tend to trivialize its significance.

CIVILITY AND MORALITY

For two centuries, critics, left and right, have observed that a functioning society requires more than a series of markets; that civic life requires people to be more than self-interested maximizers of their own utility. As the political scientist Robert Lane notes, "Only a modest element of our daily consciousness is focused directly on market-related things. A much larger portion is occupied by work (which is quite different from a labor market), family, friendship, uncommercialized leisure, education, worship, musing. . . ." Many of these activities have market aspects, but to see them merely as markets misses their essence.

Market values, ripped out of a broader context of socially shared norms, declare that opportunism, cutting corners, taking advantage are not only legitimate but virtuous, since squeezing out the maximum possible price that the market will bear maximizes efficiency. There is a doctrine in free-market economics called "perfect discrimination." The idea is that it maximizes the efficiency of the overall economy when every seller extracts the maximum price that every buyer is willing to pay. The seller, supposedly, is doing a disservice to the efficient allocation of resources if he charges a penny less than the consumer will pay, and he should price the same product differently based on the preference schedules of different consumers. But imagine an economy that has reverted to the North African souk or the slimiest used-car lot—with no price tags. You ask, "How much is that?" and the answer comes back: "How much will you pay for it?" In principle, every price should be negotiable, all the time. But life is too short. When, in the 1860s, modern retailers began offering fixed prices for the convenience of shoppers, it was taken as a signal of fair dealing, trustworthiness, modernism, and convenience for the consumer. Lately, however, more and more product markets are pursuing perfect discrimination. Hotels, rent-a-car franchises, hospital beds, airlines—all have a multiplicity of prices for the same product. An incalculable amount of time is spent either haggling or investigating, or throwing up one's hands and being gouged. It is hard to imagine this as progress.

Many verdicts are necessarily beyond the province of the market. No matter how wealthy you are, you cannot practice medicine unless you have completed an arduous course of study and certification. You cannot literally purchase a seat in Congress unless you can persuade a majority to elect you. But a rich man can endow a medical school, and perhaps induce the school to accept his son. And as money invades politics, seats in Congress are figuratively for sale, if not literally. These encroachments are signs not of the market's virtue but of its tendency to invade realms where it doesn't belong.

Mark Sagoff writes, "No matter how much people are willing to pay, three will never be the square root of six. Similarly, segregation is a national curse, and if we are willing to pay for it, that does not make it better but only makes it worse. Similarly, the case for or against abortion rights must stand on the merits; it cannot be priced at the margin. . . . [W]e do not decide to execute murderers by asking how much bleeding hearts are willing to pay to see a person pardoned and how much hard hearts are willing to pay to see him hanged." As a society and as individuals, we may succeed or fail to make defensible decisions on these and kindred issues of fact and value. But the failures, as Sagoff writes, "are not market failures. There are no relevant markets to have failed."

Another troubling aspect of the imperialism of the market is its agnosticism on questions of public and private morality that plainly matter. The market model shrugs: one taste is as good as another, and there's no disputing taste. This may be true when the consumer is debating whether to order chocolate or vanilla, but not when society is debating whether to abolish slavery. Some "preferences" are antisocial, self-defeating, even sadistic. The satisfaction of a preference, as Sagoff suggests, is an instrumental good, not an intrinsic good. We need to look for the sources of the good society elsewhere. To add insult to injury, the market model insists that its impoverished conception of liberty is the very essence of democracy—free individual choice! Who could ask for more?

Some Law and Economics School scholars, almost pathetically, have sought to resolve issues that irrevocably involve questions of public value by treating them as economic externalities. A paper by Guido Calabresi and A. Douglas Melamed tries to dispatch the issue of slavery by branding it economically inefficient (evidently the gravest indictment the market model can bring). Beyond the plainly unpleasant effects on the slaves, Calabresi and Melamed propose that *observers* of slavery suffer from "uncompensated third party effects"—they feel bad, knowing that fellow humans are enslaved. This "externality" is then counted as a cost. But of course there is no way of quantifying this cost. Smart people on the other side of the debate could invent infinite counterarguments. What if a majority of people in fact gained pleasure, as apparently most white South Africans did, knowing that the subordinate status of blacks enhanced their own material well-being and feeling of superiority? If whites are richer and smarter, does their utility count for more? Would that make slavery or apartheid "cost-effective," and hence legitimate? As everyone but the market ideologues knows, some values must be beyond price. The irony of Calabresi's argument, far-fetched as it is, is that, if indeed people of the oppressor race feel shame or guilt knowing that their fellows are enslaved, these feelings precisely reflect extra-market values.

There are values and norms necessary for a viable society of which markets are not just agnostic but corrosive. The purely utilitarian framework sidesteps ancient issues of justice, virtue, charity, ethics, public-mindedness in favor of what Robert Heilbroner termed "a blanket moral exemption" to whatever results "passed the profit-and-loss test of the marketplace. . . ." Heilbroner adds: "It is part of the nature of capitalism that the circuit of capital has no intrinsic moral dimension, no vision of art or idea aside from the commodity form in which it is embodied. In this setting, ideas thrive, but morality languishes."

This relentless process of "commodification" and commercialization has troubled a succession of conservatives for more than two centuries. Well before Marx saw a "cash nexus" trampling other institutions, conservatives such as Burke, Carlyle, and other traditionalists made a similar critique from the opposite end of the spectrum. Modern conservatives, more sanguine about markets, trip over this dilemma. In mid-1995, Robert Dole, almost simultaneously, was lauding free markets, sponsoring legislation to deregulate telecommunications—and launching a crusade against Hollywood's role in disseminating violence and pornography. "You have sold your souls," he told Time-Warner. "But must you now debase our nation and threaten our children for the sake of corporate profits?" It must have been jarring for Dole's allies to hear him rail against Hollywood's amoral pursuit of profit, making movies and recordings that the consuming public was all too willing to pay for. Even celebrants of the market are sometimes troubled by how it chooses to maximize its earnings—and must look beyond market values to justify their concern.

Connecticut Senator Joe Lieberman, a moderate Democrat, spoke at a 1995 forum sponsored by the pro-market American Enterprise Institute, on "Sex and Hollywood." At one point, Lieberman asked: "Why would the television industry in its pursuit of profit give the public so much of what the public says it doesn't want? It not only defies common sense, but it seems to defy our basic understanding of the way markets work." Lieberman then answered his own question by observing that TV is not a typical market: "[I]t is beamed into our homes free of charge. . . . [p]roducers can make money from a small portion of the market even while offending the majority."

True enough, but note Lieberman's presumption, so characteristic of our age, that markets by definition must be serving consumer welfare. He needs to reach for an idiosyncratic explanation for why TV should be a special case. It comes as a revelation to him that market forces could be corrosive of values that we collectively hold dear as citizens.

When the rock star Jerry Garcia died, *The Wall Street Journal*, the very temple of market worship, ran a snide op-ed article dismissing Garcia as a "drugged-up knockoff of a social experiment that went sour." In a letter to the editor, a reader taunted the *Journal* that, if millions of fans bought his records and attended his concerts, then obviously Garcia had to be a great musician: "The market proved it. That is, if you believe in markets."

Another conservative market enthusiast, Newt Gingrich, with no sense of contradiction, gave a speech praising a program that essentially bribes elementary-school children to read by paying them a dollar a book—"It's called incentives," Gingrich sneered, in case his liberal adversaries were ignorant of the concept—and then closed by calling on his audience to put aside their self-interests for the good of the country. Either material incentives and rational self-interest are a core principle of the conservative creed, or there are greater goods that transcend calculating egoism. One cannot have it both ways.

What makes the market model so compelling—and misleading—is that it treats each transaction as a unique event. Market apostles such as Friedman insist that all exchanges are voluntary unless blocked or distorted by government.

But an individual brings to a market transaction a set of prior rights, values, behavioral norms, and constraints on purchasing power that reflect market and extra-market factors. The system of private property itself, and the general freedom to engage in commerce, are anchored in a constantly changing system of law.

These realities were noted and analyzed in great detail by the great turn-of-the-century European sociologists, Durkheim, Weber, Tönnies, and Simmel, all of whom called for a common social science that recognized the place of non-market as well as market influences. But the discipline of economics went its own way and sought to rip the market out of its social context. If, a century later, there is at last a unified social science, it is, ironically, the one reflecting the behavioral model of free-market economics.

In one of the most important and original works of this century, the historian and social critic Karl Polanyi saw the onrushing market system as the source of the twentieth century's cataclysms. The extreme nationalism and escape into illiberal forms of politics and government, Polanyi argued, were responses to the instability and insecurity wrought by laissez-faire taken to an extreme. Whereas a Friedman sees the market as the quintessence of liberty, Polanyi, a liberal rather than radical critic, saw political democracy as dependent on actions to temper the reach of the market and pace of marketization, and the market as "embedded" in society.

The heedless rush to remarketize everything is proceeding today, oblivious to those historical lessons. A key social question not solved optimally by markets is the appropriate pace of change. Extra-market institutions are needed to reconcile the creative destruction characteristic of pure markets with the stability and predictability of daily life craved by human beings.

The fact that left and right have both criticized the instability of markets, and from seemingly opposite quarters, tends to obfuscate the critique. But if we accept that human beings thrive on a blend of market and nonmarket sources of identity, motivation, and satisfaction, then it becomes clear that the nonmarket aspects of society can be either "conservative" (tradition, religion, custom, ethnicity, community) or "liberal/social-democratic" (a series of extra-market rights and entitlements guaranteed by the state and brokered by politics).

"A well integrated social order capable of sustaining a well performing economy," writes the German-American political scientist Wolfgang Streeck, "may be inherited by tradition, or constructed through politics, or both." Gøsta Esping-Andersen, a Danish sociologist, notes that Scandinavian social democracy was able to thrive because a tradition of strong monarchy, respected central government, and deference to authority was turned to more democratic purposes in the twentieth century under the auspices of labor movements and social-democratic parties. A mixed economy was thus anchored by both traditional (conservative) and modern (political/labor) institutions.

Arthur Okun once observed that "Everyone but an economist knows without asking why money shouldn't buy some things." It is all too easy, however, using the economic method, to reduce forms of intercourse whose essence is extra-market to commercial transactions. James Tobin wrote, "Any good second year graduate student in economics could write a short examination paper proving that voluntary transactions in votes would increase the welfare of the sellers as well as the buyers." Technically, one can even demonstrate that the marginal productivity of some members of society is too low to allow them to purchase the cost of living. Should they perish?

OFF-LIMITS

The political philosopher Michael Walzer, in his lovely book, *Spheres of Justice*, points to the necessity and long-standing tradition of "blocked exchanges": some things are not, and should not be, for sale. We recognize the general view that certain transactions are off-limits to the market whenever we use expressions like "He prostituted himself"—prostitution being perhaps the best-known case of cheapening something precious by monetizing it.

Historically, some things have been placed *ultra commercium* by religion or tradition. The Catholic church once sold both "indulgences" (entree into heaven) and priestly titles. Later, the Catholic church condemned the sin of simony—the sale of ecclesiastical office. The Protestant Reformation was partly a protest against the materialism of Catholicism. In political life, bribery and nepotism have been widely recognized as contrary to proper civic norms—but both have intermittently flourished. Nepotism, after all, was once the essence of dynastic continuity. Lately in America, as the law has cracked down on explicit forms of political corruption, market forces have turned to the creative use of campaign finance as a legal surrogate for explicitly illegal bribes.

In the precapitalist economy, many potential transactions were placed off-limits, and other forms of exchange were permissible that are barred today. There were royal monopolies on many products, and many forms of commerce required a charter from the crown. Skilled trades required licenses from either the state or state-sanctioned guilds; the number of tradesmen was strictly restricted by the guilds, and open price competition was severely limited. Conversely, the state may have had a monopoly on the coin of the realm, but private banks effectively printed money when they circulated bills. Other forms of exchange illegal today were permissible then, such as slavery, indentured servitude, and the ability to purchase release from military conscription by hiring a stand-in.

Interestingly enough, the doctrine of "solidarity," associated since the 1840s with the trade-union movement, influenced the Catholic social teachings of the twentieth century and the Christian Democratic movement. A German Jesuit economist, Heinrich Pesch, S.J., proposed a doctrine of "solidarism," invoking earlier teachings of Thomas Aquinas, which views the economy not as a set of individual transactions, but as an organic whole. Aquinas prefigured modern social Catholic teachings, which locate the individual within a collectivity. Solidarism rejected socialism, and allowed a major place for the market economy, but insisted that the self-interest of the individual must be tempered by a concern for the entire community. This "neo-corporate" conception of society became a central idea of the Christian Democratic movement, which sought a middle ground between socialism and laissez-faire anchored in Catholic social teaching. The church, of course, is the longest-running counterweight to the dogmas of a pure market. Trade unions are perhaps the second oldest.

In the modern era, the nation-state has limited the market's reach via regulation. Even if market forces so desire, it is impermissible to emit certain pollutants into the air, to hire workers below a certain age or wage, to buy votes explicitly, to trade stocks on the basis of insider knowledge. We take other aspects of life away from market criteria when we stipulate that nobody shall die for want of medical care. We set these limits to protect a market society from the market's own baser instincts. Such norms are not self-evident or implicit from market logic. They evolve, in response to changing conditions, values, and political choices.

We also set limits on markets to enhance human freedom. The loss of liberty that results from a sudden, unmerited termination of one's job, capricious eviction from one's home, inability to pay the doctor, absence of decent schools for one's children, is every bit as real and often more serious than the loss of the liberty to pollute or to choose among a hundred brands of breakfast cereal. Contrary to the market theorists, the pure free market is not a seamless web, nor is the mixed economy a slippery slope to socialism.

In his classic essay, "Two Concepts of Liberty," Sir Isaiah Berlin proposed that negative freedom—the freedom to be left alone—is a limited and impoverished conception of liberty. "Men are largely interdependent, and no man's activity is so completely private as never to impact the lives of others in any way." Berlin defined positive freedom as the individual's wish to be his own master: "I am not Robinson Crusoe. Nor am I disembodied Reason. . . . [M]y ideas about myself, in particular my sense of my own moral and social identity, are intelligible only in terms of the social network of which I am an element. . . . My individual self is not something which I can detach from my relationship with others, or from those attributes of myself which consist in their attitude towards me." Sir Isaiah concluded that "The liberty of the strong, whether their strength is physical or economic, must be restrained." Restraint on the liberty of the strong is a principle of political democracy central to the Federalist Papers, but it challenges a central precept of market economics.

Society's conception of what should be properly for sale and what limits should be placed on commerce has changed over time—in both directions. In the period from the 1790s to the 1930s—Polanyi's "Great Transformation"—the boundaries shifted relentlessly in favor of market exchange. In the premodern era, there were reciprocal obligations between vassal and serf. Neither land nor labor was for sale, as in modern markets. By the 1830s, land and agricultural products were both treated as pure commodities, and English laborers had to take their chances on the labor market. But in the period between the Great Depression and the 1970s, the market was dramatically constrained by regulatory and income-transfer policies, as well as policies empowering trade unions and limiting the global mobility of capital. In the past two decades, policy, fashion, and the balance of political power have enlarged the market's reach once again.

The sociologist Viviana Zelizer explores the economically paradoxical ways in which society has valued children over time. Economists such as Gary Becker argue, deductively, that parents treat children literally as commodities. Zelizer's far richer and more empirical work suggests something much more complex. In the eighteenth and early nineteenth centuries, when market values were less pervasive, children were nonetheless valued substantially in terms of their contribution to the household economy. But in the twentieth century, with bans on child labor and a rising middle class, the economically "worthless" child was increasingly treated as a "priceless" object. The very concept of childhood is socially constructed, and its material aspect is only one factor among many. Contrary to both Marx and to Chicago economists, there are huge aspects of socioeconomic life that are culturally conditioned, and cannot be usefully comprehended as merely material calculations at one remove.

BOUNDARY VIOLATIONS

As the market vogue has gained force, realms that used to be tempered by extra-market norms and institutions are being marketized with accelerating force. Ordinary people of all philosophical stripes often decry "commercialism," but think they have little power or reason to reverse its march, whereas market advocates insist that the untrammeled encroachment of the market is necessary for economic efficiency.

In this debate, as in others, there is no single, optimal path. When society decides that the interstate-highway system should be free of billboards, or that national parks should have only limited forms of commerce, or that a small fragment of the broadcast spectrum should be commercial-free, or that automated telemarketing machines are prohibited, or that there is a distinction between "advertising" and "news," society is providing islands of respite from marketization. As long as commerce has plenty of other avenues, these constraints hardly impair meaningful consumer choice or economic efficiency.

Increasingly, such barriers are the exception. Rather, the market is overtaking areas that once operated on the basis of other principles. The Olympics, the province of amateur sport, have become one giant infomercial. As schools struggle for funding, they become easy prey for entrepreneurs such as Chris Whittle, whose Channel One bribes school officials with TV monitors in exchange for an ability to deliver a captive young audience to advertisers with the implicit endorsement of the school. Educators have widely criticized the Whittle "news" offering as a thin gruel. Studies have found no improvement in the current-events comprehension of students exposed to its content. Other corporations bombard schools with slick "curricular" materials intended to get the corporate message across to impressionable minds. After the *Exxon Valdez* spill, Exxon distributed a pseudo-documentary to schools, emphasizing the heroics of the cleanup, and minimizing the company's role in the accident that caused the disaster. This is another boundary violation—the encroachment of commercial motive into an institution whose purpose is education.

In the mass media, the pressure of advertising keeps breaching the boundaries between commercial messages and "programming" or "news." The coexistence of a free press and its commercial sponsors has never been smooth. From its inception, the press has been underwritten by advertisers. But norms gradually developed, reflecting free expression and professionalism, which differentiated journalism from advertising and insulated journalists from explicit advertiser pressure. These norms have also been reinforced by public policy. The 1912 Newspaper Publicity Act prohibits advertising disguised as news stories, and the FTC in 1967 ruled that paid ads had to carry the word "advertising" at the top of the page. The FCC has limited the number of commercial minutes per hour, and has required disclosures of covert promotions. But the market keeps finding ways to breach these rules.

Although print publishing is somewhat better defended against these assaults, broadcasting has been heavily commercialized almost from its inception. The essential economic logic of commercial book publishing is that a reader pays the cost of the book by choosing to buy it. The essential principle of commercial broadcasting is that the product is "free" to the viewer, but the program is crafted to find an audience to deliver to a sponsor. Noncommercial norms in broadcasting have never been as strong as in the print media, and the boundary between program content and commercials grows ever blurrier.

With broad-spectrum cable TV, whole shows and even entire channels are a hybrid between a product pitch and entertainment. Pseudo-documentaries that are thinly disguised commercials bombard travelers in airport waiting rooms and on planes, and patients in doctors' offices. Two decades ago, network rules and FCC standards kept brand names out of TV programs. Today, product placements are a major new form of advertising. A whole new kind of show is now developed entirely for the potential of product spinoffs. "My Little Pony," "The Care Bears," and "GI Joe" are among the children's TV shows developed explicitly in order to sell tie-in products. Board games, once an innocent children's pastime, are also increasingly developed to promote brand-name products.

What is wrong with all of this? In the case of education, commercialization is antithetical to the pedagogic mission in several respects. Self-serving curricular materials have no place in a school trying to foster critical thinking. Chris Whittle's Channel One reinforces just what schools are trying to wean children away from—short attention spans, shallow factoids, instant analysis. A political democracy also requires that news programs have reasonably serious content, but advertiser dominance debases journalism into entertainment. It leads to a subtle self-censorship, as well as a dumbing down of content.

By market logic, if the show attracts an audience, it must reflect "revealed preference." This mode of disseminating culture panders to a lowest common denominator rather than aspiring to civic and artistic education, or uplift. And because of its onrushing need to invade other realms, the market does not know how to restrain itself. Sources of restraint must originate elsewhere.

The relentless encroachment of the market and its values turns the shallow picture of economic man into a self-fulfilling prophecy. Beyond selling individual products, commercial culture is selling a set of commercial values. The collective message of all the advertising is that material consumption will lead to happiness. Consumption is doubtless pleasurable, and nobody minds a high material standard of living. But at their present extremes, commercial values crowd out other values. Economist Juliet Schor, in her influential book, *The Overworked American*, points to a vicious circle in which the pursuit of material satisfactions promised by advertising leads Americans to work more hours than they really want, in order to have the money to buy the products that never quite yield their promised fulfillments. Over time, people internalize two contradictory conclusions—a cumulative cynicism combined with an unquenchable hunger that perhaps the next product will somehow yield the elusive satisfaction.

The pattern has secondary costs, to the quantity and quality of leisure time. Schor quotes a museum curator sheepishly explaining why his museum had to be combined with a shopping mall: "The fact is that the shopping is the chief cultural activity in the United States." If shopping is the principal leisure activity, watching TV has to be a close second. And of course the relentless message of television is to go out and shop some more. Schor observes, "Many potentially satisfying leisure skills are off limits because they take too much time: participating in a community theatre; seriously taking up a sport or a musical instrument, getting involved with a church or community organization."

By projecting entertainment values, market society also cheapens the civic enterprise. Candidates adapt themselves to the environment of commercialism and market themselves as products. TV viewers come to think of themselves more as consumers than as citizens. Instead of reasoned debate, politics consists of brief sound bites, often vicious ones. Just like restless consumers, voters retain little brand loyalty to parties or officials, and acquire growing cynicism about the entire civic enterprise. As politics becomes more driven by money, officials of both parties go where the money is—to wealthy individuals and businesses. This alliance stunts the impulse to temper the reach of the market.

Commercial pressures also encroach on sacred symbols, both religious and secular. The commercialization of Christmas is an old story that keeps setting new records. More recently, under pressure from retailing lobbies, secular holidays have been debased into mainly three-day shopping weekends. Fewer and fewer people remember the origin or purpose of "Presidents' Day," "Veterans Day," "Memorial Day," or even the Fourth of July—one of the few holidays still held on its original date.

The trend toward commercialism is so ubiquitous that it is difficult to realize there are other roads, which preserve a legitimate nonmarket sphere while still allowing the market plenty of room to provide society's material goods. In the 1920s, there was a huge struggle over whether radio would be commercial. In Britain and other fundamentally capitalist nations, noncommercial broadcasting won the initial round and commercial broadcasting was prohibited. Commercial competitors to the BBC were allowed in the 1970s, but not before an ethic of high quality and public service had taken root.

In the United States., where quality radio news had almost disappeared by the 1970s, the advent of National Public Radio demonstrated that there was a large potential audience for literate, well-informed public-affairs programming. Although government still contributes 18 percent of NPR's budget at this writing, public radio today is close to self-supporting. This service is a "product" for which market forces evidently could not divine an audience, but the audience materialized via other avenues.

By offering listeners a high-quality noncommercial service, public radio induces behavior that is absurd in terms of the market model of human nature. Why would listeners fork over twenty-five or fifty dollars to support public broadcasting when the rational behavior would be to "free-ride"? The answer, of course, is that the very existence of noncommercial radio, besides providing programs that respect the listener's intelligence, fosters an ethic of noncommercialism and behavior to match. From a market point of view, this behavior is irrational if not incomprehensible. It misses the point to say that NPR listeners are indulging their "taste" for charity. What they are doing is expressing a preference as citizens that such programming endure and be disseminated. Note, however, that quasi-commercials are encroaching on public radio, and that market language slips into this oasis of noncommercialism. It is painful to hear my local public radio station refer to its annual on-air fund-raising drive as "telemarketing." It is hip and modern to speak the language of the market, and fuddy-duddy to speak of community.

FELLOW FEELING

One of my children's favorite songs was a classic by the late Malvina Reynolds, called "Magic Penny":

> Love is something if you give it away
> give it away, give it away
> Love is something if you give it away
> You end up having more.

> It's just like a magic penny
> Hold it tight and you won't have any
> Lend it, spend it and you'll have so many
> They'll roll all over the floor.

This conception of love, of course, is the antithesis of the market model, whose essence is scarcity. In market exchange, it is absurd to think you can get more of a commodity by giving it away, except perhaps as a premium or a loss-leader. That's why Reynolds's penny is "magic": in the market you don't get more of something by giving it away. One might strain (as Gary Becker has) and analogize love to an investment, but that somehow fails to capture the idea. Indeed, a number of smart economists have argued precisely that we need to maximize our reliance on the market because altruism and love are themselves scarce commodities. Sir Dennis Robertson, in a well-known essay titled "What Does the Economist Economize," concluded by deciding that the market system efficiently economized love, which was too scarce a commodity to be a reliable basis for human intercourse. By harnessing self-interest, markets reserved altruism, empathy, and fellow feeling for special occasions. In rather the same spirit, Charles Schultze wrote, "however vital they may be to a civilized society, compassion, brotherly love, and patriotism are in too short supply to serve as substitutes [for marketlike incentives]."

The market model of human nature has great difficulty comprehending that altruism is worth *cultivating*; that it is something more than just another arbitrary, self-interested "preference." In a classic Monty Python routine, a man named Mr. Ford is soliciting a charitable donation from a wealthy banker who doesn't grasp the concept of charity:

> BANKER: I'm awfully sorry, I don't understand. Can you explain exactly what you want?
> FORD: Well, I want you to give me a pound, and then I go away and give it to the orphans.
> BANKER: Yes . . . ?
> FORD: Well, that's it.
> BANKER: . . . I don't follow this at all. I mean, I don't wish to seem stupid but it looks to me as though I'm down a pound on the whole deal!

One utilitarian economist, trying to explain the fact that religious commitment cannot be explained by the market model's usual anticipated lifetime "stream of benefits," introduced a new factor—"afterlife consumption." People invest time and money in spiritual pursuits in proportion to their expected utility *post mortem*. Anything to save the model! This cosmic overreach also reveals a more earthly weakness in the method—the fact that people cannot reliably know before the fact whether an act of consumption will actually yield the anticipated satisfactions.

Millions of Americans, of course, work in charitable and volunteer activities. To understand this as a special case of utility maximization misses the point utterly, for the logic is outside the logic of markets.

That most people expect respite from purely instrumental and opportunistic calculations in daily life is demonstrated by the empirical work of experimental economics. Surveys show that most people ordinarily behave in ways that contradict their own self-interest, because of norms of fellow feeling and decency, and because of the "extra-rational" wish that others would do the same for us. Whenever we return a wallet, assist a stranger, pick up anonymous trash, leave a tip at a restaurant far from home that we will never visit again, we are "casting bread upon the waters" in the hope that others will do likewise. We have a mental picture of a more virtuous, civic self that we sometimes act on. Observing altruism in others reinforces community-minded behavior in ourselves. Despite the best effort of the Chicago economists, these expressions of fellow feeling cannot usefully be understood as a contract, or as a special form of selfishness.

Society would be a more Hobbesian place—"nasty, brutish, and short"—if this were not the case.

Experiments also find that more than three out of four people surveyed think it unfair for a profitable company to fire current employees because unemployment is high and the company can find replacements at a lower wage. This pattern, of course, is currently endemic in our feverishly marketized economy. In surveys, 79 percent of respondents considered it unfair for a grocery store to increase the price of a product already in stock because the owner has gotten word that the wholesale price has gone up. A majority of respondents also thought it unfair for restaurants to impose a five-dollar surcharge for Saturday-night reservations. Ninety-one percent of respondents thought it was wrong for a landlord to raise the rent when he learned that a tenant had gotten a raise. Seventy-four percent thought it unfair for a store, a week before Christmas, to sell a popular, hard-to-get doll by auction.

An economist might reply that these majorities simply misunderstand basic principles of economics. Why don't people just learn to behave more like the market model! (This is a bit like the politician who longs for a better class of voters.) The more subtle and plausible explanation is that these respondents are articulating the plain fact that they have complex sets of extra-market values coexisting along with those posited by economic theory. And if the revealed preference of these respondents prizes fair play, loyalty, and commitment along with calculating maximization of utility, then it is economic theory that is a mistaken description of motivation and behavior, and not the behavior that is found wanting by the truth of theory. It also might appear according to the economic model that the public always wants a free lunch and that the respondents are sentimentally identifying with the party who has the lesser bargaining power—the tenant, employee, or customer, rather than the landlord, merchant, or boss. But if we look a little deeper, a better explanation is that most people are saying they value a society in which the stronger does not always take full advantage of the weaker.

By market lights, people hold these views out of ignorance. They are letting sentimental notions about fairness produce economic harm, since a society that departs from market principles is reducing its potential economic output. That argument—the efficiency claim—is the highest ground of the case for the market, and the bulk of this book is devoted to demonstrating that it is exaggerated or mistaken. Often, departing from market norms either is indeterminate for purely material well-being, or improves material outcomes.

Yet another set of experiments contradicts the hypothesis that people value "fairness" only when they are on the weak side of the transaction. People ordinarily leave tips in restaurants they will never see again. A survey asked the question: "If the service is satisfactory, how much of a tip do you think people leave after ordering a meal costing $10 in a restaurant they visit frequently?" The mean response was $1.28. The same question was posed, shifting the venue to "a restaurant on a trip to another city that they do not expect to visit again." The mean response was $1.27. In the tipping example, there is no risk of retaliation. The respondents are simply acting out generalized norms of generosity, empathy, and self-respect. They would be ashamed to think of themselves as the sort of people who would stiff a waiter. The authors of the study commented: "In traditional economic theory, compliance with contracts depends on enforcement. It is a mild embarrassment to the standard model that experiments often produce fair behavior even in the absence of enforcement."

One of the best-documented findings from a long series of game-theory experiments is that most people, surprisingly, will contribute a share of windfall winnings to the public good, even though economic theory would predict that each rational individual would "free-ride" and hope that somebody else will worry about the general welfare. The major exception occurs when the experiment is conducted among economics students, who have evidently been conditioned by their training to prize egoist behavior. In one famous experiment, only 20 percent of economics students chose to contribute to the general well-being, compared with a majority of other students. The author titled his article "Economists Free Ride: Does Anyone Else?" Experiments have also placed "lost" wallets where subjects are likely to "find" them. These experiments find that large numbers of people will take the time and trouble to track down the owner and mail the wallet, cash intact, with no expectation of reward. Why? Evidently, such behavior makes us feel virtuous, and we like the idea of living in a society where empathic, generous acts are widespread. People who display such values are not being merely sentimental; they are also participating in the maintenance of a society with a defensible balance between selfish and generous behaviors—which has economic as well as social benefits. Classroom instruction that teaches the rationality of pure egoism warps this necessary balance.

There are two related dangers wrought by the cult of the absolutization of markets. The first is that market *institutions* drive out extra-market institutions. Faced with an onslaught of competitive pressure, nonmarket institutions, like charity hospitals or public television or "amateur" sport, begin looking and behaving more like profit-making ones. The second danger is that market *norms* drive out nonmarket norms. Market theory advises us to behave more like textbook economic man. Experiments show that this counsel has an effect on the behavior of young economists, and perhaps on others. When everything is for sale, the person who volunteers time, who helps a stranger, who agrees to work for a modest wage out of commitment to the public good, who desists from littering even when no one is looking, who forgoes an opportunity to free-ride, begins to feel like a sucker.

Civility and public-mindedness can be cultivated—or undermined. When market enthusiasts argue that all prices should be "unbundled" for the sake of greater accuracy, or that public services should charge fees to reflect their true costs, or that only the very poor should be the beneficiaries of income transfers, they are pursuing market logic at the expense of extra-market logic—but not necessarily creating a more efficient economy or society. For example, there is no good market reason for free public libraries. Many of the people who use them could afford to pay a small fee to check out books. In principle, if there were demand for this service, an entrepreneur would provide it. But the existence of the free public library creates a subculture that cherishes learning and signals that learning has extra-monetary value. Whereas some readers get to enjoy an unnecessary "subsidy," others could not afford to purchase or even rent books at market rates, and would read less. The free library also creates an oasis of noncommercialism, where all social classes rub elbows. A conventional economist might well concede that literacy is an "externality," and defend free libraries on that basis. But this defense is too narrow, since it misses the cultural and normative essence of the institution. "Unbundling" the subsidy, introducing a means test, or inventing some other device to make free libraries more market-like, would destroy their essence.

At this writing, the Republican majority in Congress has been ridiculing and seeking to abolish President Clinton's volunteer program, the AmeriCorps. At first blush, this seems a tempest in a teapot; the program is small and seems to be allowing young people to spend a year doing good works for a very low salary, while they earn a stipend to be put away toward college tuition. But the hard right has good reason to attack this program, for it is an explicit and deliberate attempt to nurture nonmarket values. People who spend a year doing community service may well come away with a lifelong set of ideals that hold nonmarket values at least as dear as market ones. Even worse, this program represents *governmental* nurturing of service values. The ultra-market right has no problem when some traditional institution, like the church, incubates a service ethic, but by definition the government is held to have no business playing such a role.

This recalls Streeck's point: both traditional institutions and deliberate political creations can serve as counterweights to the market. Some hybrids such as trade unions play this role, anchored in the private sector but given legal recognition by legislation in a collective-bargaining system brokered by the state. A conservative economist looks at a trade union and sees nothing but a monopoly that seeks to push wages above a market-clearing price. But unions are also part of the rich American social fabric once celebrated by Tocqueville. They sponsor

Little League teams, community-service projects, and civic education, as well as serving as agencies of employee "voice" within the workplace. In both roles, they nourish solidarity values as a counterweight to market values.

Today, new policy and ethical dilemmas arise almost daily about the limits of marketization. How should society regulate commerce in body parts? The same conservatives promoting the expansion of market principles supported legislation prohibiting the sale and clinical use of fetal tissue. Should wealthy people, or celebrities such as the late Yankee great Mickey Mantle, be allowed to "jump the queue" for scarce transplants? Should surgical procedures and artificial genetic forms be considered a form of intellectual property and awarded patents? Should college professors become joint venturers with entrepreneurs? Should state functions such as criminal justice be partly privatized, or kept in a separate realm deemed inappropriate for commerce? Should there be any limits on the commercialization of sport? Should policy try to preserve the boundaries between broadcast programming and broadcast advertising, or is it reasonable for free individuals to watch endless infomercials if they so choose?

ALTRUISM AND EFFICIENCY

We cannot infer the Golden Rule or Kant's Categorical Imperative from standard free-market theory. But though we might have extra-market reasons for wanting compassion and civic virtue to be widespread norms, we should also welcome these values on more narrowly economic grounds. A limitation on the reach of the market is necessary to limit the market's self-cannibalizing tendencies within its own realm. A set of extra-market or premarket values—such as honor, trust, loyalty, decency, fairness—makes markets work better, even though market pressures keep undermining those values.

Market theory conceives of economic relationships as purely instrumental. All transactions are at arm's length, and there is no room for sentimentality. The theory construes long-term commitments as implicit contracts, since the contract epitomizes the economic concept of a free, voluntary exchange by calculating, rational individuals. Where opportunism is convenient and worth its nominal cost, the theory commends opportunism. In Law and Economics School theory, there is even a doctrine of "efficient breach": If it is cost-effective for one party to a contract to break it, that party should ignore the contract and pay the price.

However, society pays a heavier price if norms of commitment and trust are casually breached. It saves incalculable time and money if we can assume that most people are trustworthy most of the time; that every transaction does not require endless haggling. Were these norms not widespread, the costs of monitoring would skyrocket and contracts would have to become ever more elaborate to cover every contingency. Many of us have had the experience of having a lawyer propose a document far more extensive than necessary, given what we know intuitively about our business partner. Many contracts are oral or informal, thanks to generalized norms of trust. Were the norms of calculated opportunism commended by many economists ever to become universal, we would become a society imprisoned in our own contracts. Deborah A. DeMott, a law professor at Duke, warns that Law-and-Economics theory, by reducing all relations to short-term calculation, can "witlessly provide the mechanics to undermine the normative core of many relationships." Her illustration is the fiduciary relationship, a legal concept of special confidence and trust. She writes that "the norms imposed by fiduciary obligation operate to discourage the calculated pursuit of self interest that underlies the account of efficient breach." To reduce such special relations to nothing more than ordinary, breachable contracts is to destroy their special nature.

In some spheres, altruism is plainly more efficient than market exchange. Richard Titmuss's classic, *The Gift Relationship*, meticulously compared the British and American systems of blood banks.

American blood banks began as voluntary, nonprofit institutions and were eventually coordinated under the Red Cross. However, by the 1960s, when Titmuss wrote, for-profit blood donation had made substantial inroads. Titmuss found that, contrary to the mythology, just 9 percent of all blood donors "approximated to the concept of the voluntary community donor who sees his donation as a free gift to strangers in society." The sort of people who professionally sell their blood, of course, are exactly the people whose blood the system shouldn't want—alcoholics, junkies, and other desperate people likely to carry communicable diseases (and this was before AIDS). Professional donors, who sold their blood or plasma as often as they could, accounted for nearly a third of all blood products by the late 1960s, and contribute a higher share today. Paid donors have often concealed addictions or histories of disease.

In England, by contrast, sale of blood was prohibited. The British National Health Service ran the voluntary National Blood Transfusion Service, with a conscious goal of encouraging a clean supply of blood and promoting an ethic of voluntary donations. Between 1948, when the program was established, and 1967, the supply of blood rose by 222 percent, from nine annual donations per thousand of population to twenty-nine per thousand. Between 1956 and 1967, the blood supply increased by 77 percent in England and Wales, and 8 percent in the United States.

In England, free-market economists recommended that if British donors were paid for blood supplies would increase and "a movement towards more efficiency in the blood market is a movement towards more efficiency in the economy as a whole." In America, the FTC actually ruled that a nonprofit

Community Blood Bank in Kansas City, which was organized by local hospitals after a scandal-ridden local commercial blood bank closed, was an impermissible monopoly—a conspiracy to restrain commerce.

Professor Titmuss concluded that, quite apart from "moral and social" issues, three economic conclusions emerge:

> The first is that a private market in blood entails much greater risks to the recipient of disease, chronic disability, and death.
>
> Second, a private market in blood is potentially more dangerous to the health of donors.
>
> Third, a private market in blood produces, in the long run, greater shortages of blood.

Titmuss found the price of blood significantly higher in the United States, the supply less reliable; and because of the system's fragmentation and divergent quality, there was far more waste. He noted the paradox that "the more commercialized a blood distribution system becomes (and hence more wasteful, inefficient, and dangerous) the more will the gross national product be inflated. This, of course, is entirely an artifact of transferring a voluntary service to the paid, commodified sector of society."

Here is a plain *economic* benefit beyond the comprehension of the market model. Titmuss's own survey of why Englishmen and -women donated blood revealed that 26.4 percent of respondents cited a general desire to help (Titmuss termed this altruism—"Knowing I might be saving somebody's life"); 1.4 percent suggested gratitude ("Because I am fortunate in having good health myself"); 9.8 percent suggested reciprocity ("My own life had been saved by transfusions"); 10.2 percent cited a sense of duty or a recollection of the war effort; and 31.2 percent cited either a personal appeal ("A workmate convinced me of the need for more donors") or national appeal ("I heard the appeal on the BBC").

Steven E. Rhoads conceives of fellow feeling and commitment as a kind of positive externality. "One might expect to find economists proposing public policies that will help reinvigorate ethics, good will, and civility," Rhoads writes. "One finds no such proposals."

In a sense, it is the market that free-rides on extra-market values that make our market society a bearable place, by tempering the relentless opportunism that the market model commends. Norms of civility are a public good. Without them, the world would degenerate into a society of relentless mutual suspicion. The late Olof Palme used to warn of the dangers of a "society of sharp elbows." Instead of a relatively pleasurable world of commerce, we would have to be constantly on guard against being ripped off. Bankruptcies would proliferate. Banks would have to charge higher interest rates to compensate for the ubiquity of opportunism. Explicit warranties would have to be negotiated for every transaction. Doctors would resort to "defensive medicine" to a far greater degree than they already do. A handshake would become worthless. Society would be a paradise mainly for lawyers. This is the dystopia that the marketizers commend.

In the next section of the book, we turn to the details of this uneasy coexistence in three concrete realms: the workplace, health care, and the financial system, where the perfect model of the textbook and the ideologue is impossible to attain and imprudent to pursue.

3 / THE MARKET FOR LABOR

HUMANS AS FACTORS OF PRODUCTION

Economists and other students of society have long recognized that labor markets are fundamentally different from markets for products. A job or profession is, in one sense, a commodity bought and sold in a market, just as a wage or salary is a price paid by the employer. But work is also a central source of identity and livelihood, a valued (or resented) affiliation, and sometimes a calling. Its venue is not the unsentimental marketplace of a trading floor or an auction house, but an institution with complex hierarchies, friendships, collegialities, reciprocal loyalties, and an ongoing social existence. Labor is also malleable in a way that physical goods are not: there is an almost infinite range of possible combinations of effort and compensation, commitment and opportunism, and no single optimal path defined by maximum freedom of exchange.

A pure-market transaction, remember, is a single exchange at a moment in time. In the real world, that ideal case materializes in a spot market or an auction market such as a stock exchange where bidders are plentiful, prices actually change from minute to minute, and each transaction is a one-time event that clears the market of the merchandise. Long-term price and supply contracts may occasionally override spot markets, but these are voluntary and based on the perception of mutual advantage, usually because of risk aversion. However, in product markets, long-term supply contracts are a relatively trivial departure from the price mechanism. Market theorists raise no objection, because the process of contracting is just another kind of voluntary exchange.

Labor transactions are a whole other story. Here, spot markets are the exception, and departures from market-clearing prices the norm. A few workers still get their jobs through hiring halls and daily shape-ups. But generally workers expect to be doing the same job tomorrow that they do today, for the same employer and at the same pay. Workers do change jobs, but not continually. Pay is adjusted, but not daily. Wages don't fluctuate like stock prices or prices in the fish market. Layoffs occur, but these are exceptional rather than ubiquitous. Labor's price is broadly set by markets, but in an institutional context that presumes a continuing relationship.

These long-term labor relationships are often compared to voluntary contracts in product markets, but the analogy is slippery. Sometimes there actually are explicit long-term contracts between manager and worker, or with the union on behalf of workers collectively. But major aspects of long-term labor "contracts" are tacit and customary. As long as business holds up, you can presume that you will not be fired if you do your job well, even if someone off the street would take the job at a lower wage. Your past dedication will be repaid during hard times in the future. None of that is written down. The result of these social and institutional aspects of the labor markets is that labor prices (wages) do not adjust smoothly and continuously. The price of labor, as economists invariably put it, is "sticky."

Presumably, labor rarely behaves like a spot market because the workplace is not just a marketplace but a social organization with a certain institutional logic and institutional imperatives. Turning it into a pure spot market would assault its viability as an institution. Even the meanest workplace has norms of fairness. If breached, these can affect morale, and hence productivity and profit. For example, different individuals in the same job category in large organizations do not have the identical "marginal productivity," yet it is customary to pay them roughly the same wage.

Not only do similarly situated workers have different productivities, but the output of any one worker fluctuates moment to moment and week to week, depending on mood, effort, morale, health. There is, however, no practical way for management precisely to adjust pay accordingly, on the model of a product market. Paying workers by the piece was one attempt to reward output with more precision. But piecework has mostly disappeared. Some students of labor markets explain the eclipse of piecework largely in terms of its damage to teamwork, morale, and quality. As labor economists have long noted, the employer is not just buying the worker's time but also her effort. Workers possess not just formal skills but what Michael Polanyi called "tacit knowledge," which can be eagerly applied to the enterprise—or resentfully hoarded.

Evidently, it has proved efficient (though not in Adam Smith's sense) for most companies to honor the social character of work, and to pay employees in ways that often diverge from their precise marginal contribution to the company's output at any given moment. That doesn't mean the firm ignores the employee's output or effort. On the contrary, it only means there are more effective ways to induce performance than treating labor as a pure market commodity. People, unlike things, have a broad range of possible outputs. They have a capacity for learning. They notice how they are being treated, and that affects how they perform. The great political economists have all remarked on this. The most elegant and original recent statement is Albert Hirschman's modern classic, *Exit, Voice, and Loyalty*, which observes that "voice"—having an influence—is an alternative to the rather static choice in the market model of staying or leaving. Voice, in turn, engenders loyalty. In order to work, loyalty must be reciprocal. So voice offers a constructive and engaged alternative to sullen exit.

Labor markets violate perfect market conditions in another key respect. It is often efficient for management to pay good incumbent workers slightly above the going rate, because this implicit bonus lets workers know that they are valued and encourages effort and loyalty to the firm. A worker who perceives that his skills are "worth" eight dollars an hour on the open job market, but who is making ten dollars with the prospect of going to twelve, is likely to value his job and give his all for the company. This custom of paying a slight premium over a market-clearing wage to incumbent workers also reduces job turnover, improves communication, reduces company recruitment and training costs, and makes the firm a happier place. Employers who pay the lowest possible wage that attracts workers invariably complain about how hard it is to get good help.

A whole genre of scholarly labor-market research, known as Efficiency Wage Theory, concludes that the efficiency associated with inducing the highest available worker effort, output, and loyalty requires a substantial departure from the treatment of labor purely as a commodity in an auction market. A related case in point is the custom of seniority. Firms often raise pay with longevity, not because productivity always increases with experience—beyond a certain level, productivity often declines with age—but to reward loyal service, and to send other workers signals that they are valued and that this is a good place to work. Respect for seniority also recognizes that older workers are likely to have more costly family obligations—a social rather than a purely economic consideration. The custom of laying off by seniority, or according long-tenured workers "bumping" rights, is usually demanded by unions, but is often voluntarily offered by nonunion employers, for much the same set of reasons. It would disrupt the workplace as a social institution if younger workers could elbow out older ones.

Kindred labor-market institutions such as academic tenure and the system of apprentices and journeymen common to craft occupations, which plainly violate pure-market pricing principles, are interpreted by labor economists as facilitating the sharing of knowledge. Apprenticeship (formal or tacit) may seem rigid, but it is efficient because it assures high standards and gives journeymen the security to pass on their craft to novices. In academia, if a brilliant young lecturer could take his professor's chair at one-third the pay, it would save the institution money—but scholars would think twice about imparting information to their graduate students. This is one more reason why labor markets are not simple auction markets (and why professors who call for pure markets elsewhere seldom renounce tenure). As Lester Thurow has observed, "If wages really were flexible and allocated in a bidding auction, each worker would try to build his own little monopoly by hoarding specific labor skills and information in an effort to make himself indispensable." But in the real world, Thurow adds, "Employers repress wage competition and build employment security. . . . Lower outside wage bids are not accepted, because if they were, workers already on the job would feel threatened. . . ."

Recruitment patterns are also a blend of social and economic. Standard free-market theory presumes perfect information. Somehow, the right worker will find her way to the right job at the right price. But sociological studies of how workers actually find jobs and how employers actually recruit workers make a mockery of the "search theory" of economics. A classic of the genre, the sociologist Mark Granovetter's study "The Strength of Weak Ties," found that a variety of extra-market connections—somebody knows somebody's cousin; a recent recruit's classmate is in the right place at the right time—account for how people actually get jobs. The interesting part of the story occurs after the worker gets the job—more malleability. And when formerly excluded groups—Jews, blacks, Asians, women—break into a previously proscribed labor pool, it has nothing to do with changing marginal productivities but, rather, shifts in political power, law, and, finally, behavior and custom.

As a consequence of all the foregoing departures from spot-market pricing, the market price of labor at any given time is likely to be "wrong," both in the individual firm and in the aggregate economy. Some workers are being paid too much, others too little. Apparently, the logic of the workplace as a social organization demands these anomalies and renders them tolerably efficient. Efficiency Wage Theory says that this brand of pricing is the best available second best, at least for the firm.

However, in macroeconomic terms, this departure from pure-market pricing principles means that labor market, unlike the fish market, doesn't "clear" on the basis of price adjustments. At the end of the day, there is an oversupply of product—namely, people seeking jobs. Some workers are slightly overpaid relative to their marginal product, some are working longer hours than they'd like; others find themselves working involuntarily part-time, or without jobs.

The phenomenon of the involuntarily overworked employee is also a function of imperfections in the labor market itself. Some people on the fast track—say, associates in law firms or junior recruits to investment banks—might prefer to work fifty hours a week—but find themselves working eighty, to demonstrate diligence in competing for a few coveted partner slots. What might have been two forty-hour jobs is one eighty-hour job. In similar, less glamorous cases, such as mandatory overtime in factory jobs, involuntary overwork results from the employer's efforts to game the rules of the fringe-benefit system and minimize turnover. If the employer hires another worker, he is stuck with additional payroll taxes and fringe-benefit costs, as well as training costs. The new worker may also be hard to fire during the next downturn, because of mandated severance costs or lingering remnants of tacit contracts. So it is more "efficient" to require a smaller incumbent work force to work overtime than to take on new employees who desire work. This pattern reflects a blend of opportunisms that may save money for the employer, but it is neither a perfect market nor necessarily efficient for society.

The labor market is imperfect in another key respect. Because of the macroeconomic problem of the economy's tendency to fall into periodic recessions caused by shortfalls of aggregate demand, adjusting (lowering) wages in an effort to clear the labor market is a perverse cure for unemployment. Reduced wages translate into reduced overall purchasing power—and even less demand for workers. In the early 1930s, many people at first thought we could cure the Great Depression by cutting wages. The result was deeper depression. There are other available strategies to maintain full employment, but they lie elsewhere, beyond the realm of more perfect microeconomic pricing. "The pervasiveness and persistence of unemployment," writes Joseph Stiglitz, "is, in my mind, the most telling 'critical experiment' which should lead to the discrediting of the basic competitive equilibrium model which (depending on how you view it) either predicts or assumes full employment."

Readers will likely recognize the dilemma of the imperfect labor market is a variation on the Three Efficiencies of chapter 1. In allocative (Smithian) terms, the price of labor departs significantly from the "correct" market price—the price that precisely equates supply and demand and reflects the worker's marginal contribution to the output of the firm at any given time. But the logic of the firm as a social organization seems to require this divergence. And the departure from a theoretically correct price can produce compensating efficiencies by inducing effort, knowledge sharing, work satisfaction, innovation, and loyalty.

Thus, there is not a single correct or optimal price for labor but a broad range of possible pay scales, reward systems, and strategies to induce and compensate effort. The appropriate market price fluctuates, in part because effort also fluctuates. By the same token, a Keynesian full-employment economy, coupled with education and training outlays, can produce a high growth rate, a socially tolerable income distribution, and rising living standards over time—which more than make up for the fact that some labor is priced "wrong" by Smithian lights.

THE NEW LABOR MARKET

The alert reader will recognize that this entire prologue is slightly archaic. For what is striking about the current era is that labor, suddenly, is in fact becoming rather more like a spot market. The customary extra-market norms in worker-manager relationships, long thought to be institutionally efficient, have been substantially eroded by the resurgence of market forces. During the postwar boom, when the economy was more highly regulated, unions were more powerful, and foreign trade was less important, there was far less institutional turbulence generally, and hence in labor markets. This was the era of mass production and oligopoly. If you went to work for a large, stable company like General Electric or General Motors, AT&T or United Airlines, whether as a wage worker or a salaried manager, the normal expectation was to spend your entire career there, assuming that you did your job reasonably well.

Layoffs occurred, but they were typically cyclical. Most workers furloughed during economic downturns got their jobs back. Today, however downsizing, out-sourcing, leveraged buyouts, relocations, and contingent employment are becoming the norm. Even such redoubts of long-term labor contracts as academic tenure and the civil service are under assault. Few people have anything like the presumptive employment security characteristic of the postwar era. Is this shift necessary? Is it efficient?

A generation ago, labor economists differentiated "primary" and "secondary" labor markets. Jobs in the primary labor market were characterized by career security, regularized contracts, decent pay, fringe benefits, and norms of professionalism. Often they were in occupations that were either regulated and licensed by the state, or self-regulated through professional organizations. Skill was one determinant of what was a primary-labor-market job, but not the only one. Besides the elite professions, occupations in this category also included a good many semiskilled factory jobs in stable basic industries. Despite fairly rudimentary skills that could be acquired in a few weeks, occupations such as automobile assembler could be in effect professionalized thanks to the combination of stable firms in basic industry and strong unions.

In contrast, secondary-labor-market jobs were what used to be called "casual labor." They were marked by high turnover, low wages, an absence of fringe benefits, and minimal or nonexistent reciprocal obligations. Many students of labor in that era thought that, as the economy grew both richer and better bolstered by social insurance, and trade unionism became institutionalized, more and more occupations would gradually be professionalized, and converted from secondary to primary ones. But in the 1990s, the reverse is happening: occupations that were once primary are looking increasingly like casual labor.

It is startling to read standard works on labor economics written as recently as the early 1980s and to compare them with the actual job markets of the 1990s. Arthur Okun, explaining why the price of labor was "sticky" rather than fluid, coined the phrase "invisible handshake." In marked contrast to Adam Smith's invisible hand, labor markets were based on a variety of contracts, formal and tacit, because they depended on myriad reciprocal obligations. As an example, Okun wrote in *Prices and Quantities* (written in 1979–80): "The firm simply cannot tell its senior workers to stay home and draw no pay while it is adding recruits. Such a breach of faith would have major adverse impacts on the subsequent quit rates of established workers and acceptance rates of recruits."

Economist Andrew Weiss, summarizing the Efficiency Wage view, offered this explanation for why firms often pay above a market-clearing wage: "The lower the wage, the more resources the firm would have to spend on supervision to maintain a given level of effort from its workers." The theory also explained firms' reluctance to adjust to reduced demand by cutting pay in terms of the employers' imperfect information: "If all workers were identical, or if all firms were perfectly informed about the productivity of workers . . . a firm would respond to a fall in the value of the worker's output [or reduced demand for it] by cutting the worker's wage. . . . However, if a firm is imperfectly informed about the productivity of its workers, the firm would care about which workers would be induced to quit by a wage cut. The firm would be concerned that the workers that quit would be the ones the firm most wants to retain—workers whose productivity exceeded their wage."

These insights explained another great paradox of labor markets—the fact that firms faced with increased competition or declining demand typically adjusted the *quantity* rather than the *price* of their labor, resorting to layoffs rather than wage cuts. A rational employer, behaving as *Homo economicus*, would presumably extract reductions in his wages. But, typically, firms resorted instead to layoffs, damaging a small fraction of the work force instead of all employees, and giving greatest security to the faithful employees with the longest-term service to the company. Again, the social logic of the workplace trumped the market logic.

But these characterizations, reviewed in the mid-1990s, read like archeological descriptions of a lost continent. Today, employers are breaching virtually all of the conventions so carefully analyzed by the last generation of labor economists—and evidently getting away with it. With heightened competition and successive waves of leveraged buyouts, brutal downsizings have become normal. Relentless layoffs are not merely a temporary response to business cycles, but a way of life. Labor has come to be viewed not as a long-term resource but as an expendable cost center.

Far from cherishing their experienced employees, some Fortune 500 corporations today literally invite their experienced workers to bid to keep their jobs by taking pay cuts. They calculate what pay levels would attract young recruits, and then ask the incumbent employee to match the lower pay. Even unionized companies have gotten around the once sacrosanct doctrine of equal pay for equal work by instituting two-tier pay scales, in which workers with seniority are grandfathered at higher wage scales while new hires perform the same job for less—not just as novices but throughout their careers. Universities have preserved the custom of tenure for an elite few, by enlarging a lower order of lecturers who will never be tenured, and who subsist on short-term contracts, low pay, heavy teaching loads, and multiple jobs.

Large corporations are pursuing strategies of retaining as few core employees as possible, pursuing the maximum possible degree of flexibility in how they take on labor. Consultants offer seminars on how to convert a large portion of the work force from permanent staff to contingent employees. At a 1994 training session sponsored by the Institute for International Research, executives from McDonald's, Manor Care, Connecticut Mutual Life, McDonnell-Douglas, H&R Block, and others offered tips on how to shift from a full-time, permanent work force to a contingent one, without sacrificing quality or productivity.

Temporary and contract employment are now the fastest-growing categories of work. Manpower Temporary Services is now not only the largest U.S. employer but also the largest private-sector trainer. This trend is driven partly by the desire of corporations under new competitive pressure to avoid paying payroll taxes and fringe benefits, but the more fundamental goal seems to be cost-cutting and flexibility. The new information technology facilitates this shift. At the high end of the labor force, business consultants, stock analysts, computer experts, salespeople, etc., can do their jobs as independent contractors, with a laptop, phone, fax, and modem, from any remote location. At the low end, businesses can use temp agencies, independent consultants, or subcontractors to increase or decrease their payroll, day by day.

These strategies allow employers to escape all the implicit contracts and reciprocal obligations that characterized the labor-management regime of a generation ago. If an employee is not permanently attached to the payroll, you don't really owe her anything beyond a day's pay for a day's work. As the labor market becomes more like a spot market, employers are increasingly able to pay their workers precisely in accord with their perceived marginal productivity. Something very much like an auction market sets labor's price. If you sign on with a temp agency as, say, a computer-graphics expert, or a bookkeeper, you will be paid precisely according to the going rate for your skill, which will not change hour to hour but may well change week to week, with the fluctuations of labor supply and customer demand. This system also allows the employer who relies on contract workers and consultants to trade off quality and price on a daily basis, and to pick the man or woman who precisely fills the appropriate niche. Contrary to the old worry about "supervision costs," the work quality evidently speaks well enough for itself. If the contractor or temp wants repeat business, or higher pay, she will do a good job. The more decentralized, customized, and flexible the economy becomes, the more the labor market functions like the spot market once deemed institutionally impossible.

These trends are celebrated by enthusiasts of the new information economy for their decentralization and flexibility. The computer and the Internet are said to portend a virtually frictionless market economy, in which any seller is free to connect with any buyer, worldwide. The transformation in labor relations is cheered by free-market enthusiasts in the economics profession and in the business community, for multiple efficiencies. At long last, the economy's one great holdout, the labor market, is behaving like a true auction market. If unions and the state will just go away, this shift will vastly improve the productivity of work, align contribution with reward, and allow the labor market, finally, to "clear"—solving the problem of inflation-free unemployment.

Some observers take this model to its logical conclusion and propose an economy based on the paradigmatic "virtual corporation"—a highly entrepreneurial firm with a tiny core of owners and nearly everyone else as contract labor. The virtual corporation is customer-driven, with extremely low fixed costs. Its owners must be nimble and efficient, or their firm will be displaced by even more efficient competitors. Better yet, their contractors and temporary employees must also be highly entrepreneurial, since they are being paid precisely according to the value that they can add to the enterprise. Their pay is determined in the marketplace, and it reflects the worth of their human capital.

Thus, as the labor market becomes more of a spot market, its champions, in an inversion of the New Socialist Man proclaimed by Lenin, imagine a New Capitalist man or woman, who internalizes and embodies the values of the marketplace. In this new economy, everyone is a capitalist, whether as an owner of a firm or as a free-lance. This exemplar of the new economy is worth whatever her labor will fetch in the market on a given day. People who have little to offer can expect little back, and have only themselves to blame. If you don't like the insecurity of being a contingent worker at the beck and call of a virtual corporation, then get with the program and become an entrepreneur yourself. As regulations, unions, and customary barriers fall, old and cumbersome corporations will adapt to this model—or be driven out by more flexible and dynamic competitors. The evidence is in large corporations like GE, IBM, Xerox, or GM, which are shedding labor and long-term contractual obligations as fast as they can.

The merger movement also spurs this evolution, in two distinct but reinforcing respects. Incumbent management may feel obligated to honor a tacit social contract with loyal longtime employees; an outside owner new to the enterprise feels no such obligation. And mergers, say, between a Chase Manhattan and a Chemical Bank, create redundancies and opportunities (or pretexts) for streamlining. In the ensuing restructuring, not only will thousands of workers be laid off, but core jobs can be redefined as contingent ones, shrinking the pool of primary employees (and inflexible costs) even further.

An intriguing question is whether this new commodification of labor damages the firm, in all the ways the last generation of labor economists thought it must. How is it that employees who abruptly find themselves with little job security, and with the constant threat of being underbid by younger recruits, nonetheless share information, display loyalty to the firm, and get their work done? A great deal of the business-school literature on human capital contends that corporations are wise to treat their employees as valued assets. Lately, there has been an outpouring of writings congratulating corporations that deliberately try to design work to be intrinsically satisfying, share power, and value the contributions of employees. However, a great many of these experiments last only until the next hostile takeover and the next bout of downsizing, which are of course the result of extreme pressures of the competitive marketplace. Innumerable corporations that once boasted of no-layoff policies, offered "family-friendly" workplaces, and a slew of generous fringe benefits, reverted to ruthless cost-cutting once competitive pressures proved sufficiently intense. The market model would say this shift in strategy "must have" been efficient—otherwise managers would not have pursued it.

Charles Heckscher, a labor sociologist at Rutgers, conducted extensive interviews with middle managers at large corporations. He reported a paradox. The new climate of downsizing and cost-cutting, he found, had middle managers terrified about their own futures. But they had so internalized the values of efficiency, competitiveness, and cost-cutting that their loyalty to the company was not impaired—even though these values prefigured their own eventual dismissal. On the contrary: most had apparently convinced themselves that if they just worked more diligently, the company might achieve its competitive goals and they might be spared the ax. Security may engender commitment and diligence, but so, evidently, does insecurity.

In short, the labor market is indeed behaving more like a product market. But it remains to be seen whether this is efficient for either the economy or the society.

HIGH ROADS, LOW ROADS, AND POWER

In assessing these labor-market trends, there are ultimately two basic ways to think about what is unfolding. Either something about the new information economy truly makes it imperative and efficient and "natural" to treat labor more like a commodity—in which case higher productivity will eventually result and translate into higher material living standards even if coupled with higher anxiety and vast extremes of inequality—or these trends principally reflect shifts in *political power* rather than economic imperatives dictated by new technologies. If the latter is the case, as I will argue, then the new economy really offers a broad set of social choices which we should confront explicitly. And the relative blend of market and extra-market institutions governing labor relations is indeterminate with respect to economic outcomes, at least within a wide range.

In thinking about this, one must carefully differentiate institutional changes that truly are contoured by technology from ones that reflect conscious (or unacknowledged) political and social choices. Many studies of technology and market structure, on both the political left and right, propose that the change from mass-production industries to a knowledge economy brings with it profound changes in macroeconomic forces, labor relations, and the role of the state. Left-of-center political economists Charles Sabel and Michael Piore, for example, optimistically propose that the new production technology, by dispensing with rigid production lines and standard products, allows an economy of "flexible specialization" that both portends a return to craftwork and solves the old Keynesian problem of labor markets failing to clear. If, at last, labor can be priced properly, there should be no involuntary unemployment. And an information economy offers at least the potential of more highly skilled and valued work for all. From the opposite end of the political spectrum, George Gilder, John Naisbitt, and Peter Huber see the new information economy as the quintessence of laissez-faire. Regulation is mooted by ubiquitous competition and relentless change; government cannot possibly keep up; it can only weigh the process down. A frictionless cyber-economy connects buyers to sellers worldwide, and the market decides precisely and efficiently what each good or service (including labor) is worth. The market is finally self-regulating, and the state can finally wither away.

Though recent changes in production and information technologies are indeed epochal, these interpretations seem both too utopian and too deterministic. Despite the new flexibility and turbulence, most workplaces still stay put for many decades. Most people still go to jobs and collect paychecks. Most people do not work as free-lances in cyberspace, or as new-age artisans in small production shops. They work for relatively large organizations with a past, a future, and a physical presence—in a factory, office, shopping mall, hotel, hospital, or university. Studies of actual corporate behavior suggest that firms still retain much latitude to pursue "high-road" or "low-road" strategies with respect to their employees. Some corporations view their employees as long-term assets, even in a turbulent and intensely competitive economy. Others regard workers as expendable. The high-road companies, like the low-road ones, seek flexibility in their labor arrangements, but they pursue flexibility strategies that minimize the damage to their social compact.

For example, Harman International, a five-hundred-million-dollar manufacturer of audio equipment, has a deliberate policy of going to great lengths to avoid layoffs. When demand is temporarily soft, the company resorts to bringing work ordinarily contracted out back inside its plants, and finding maintenance work or sales work for employees ordinarily employed in production. The company calls this strategy "OLE" (pronounced "Olé"), which stands for "Off Line Employment." Harman believes it is good for morale and productivity, but pursues this approach mainly because of the values of its founder and chief executive, Sidney Harman, who is an exponent of worker empowerment. At worst, the evidence is that Harman's human-capital policy does no damage; it may well improve his company's competitive position.

Massachusetts-based Powersoft, a high-end software company, reconciles the apparently contradictory labor-market objectives of flexibility and loyalty by having an in-house team of contingent employees, called Powersoft Temps. Whereas many companies deliberately out-source and rely on contract workers as a strategy to minimize fixed labor costs, Powersoft prizes the loyalty of employees permanently attached to the company yet achieves a good deal of flexibility by having a flying squad that moves around as needed, doing such jobs as entering data, processing customer orders, and mailing out invoices. This device also serves as a recruitment pool, and many of the temps are eventually offered permanent positions. In this case, too, a more humane approach is less reflective of some market imperative than of the personal values of the company's chairman and founder, Mitchell Kertzman.

To shift from high-tech to more traditional industries, Magma Copper, an Arizona-based company long known for labor strife, took the remarkable step in 1992 of negotiating an unheard-of fifteen-year contract with its union, the United Steelworkers of America. The contract grew out of several months of intensive discussion that involved everyone from rank-and-file copper miners to the company's chairman. Among other improvements, the contract provided gain-sharing from productivity improvements. Between 1989 and 1995, productivity at Magma increased by 86 percent. In mid-1995, the company was so pleased with the results that it took out ads in major newspapers praising the union, and began to work closely with the mineworkers' unions in Titaya, Peru, where it had acquired a new source of ore. Note that the union, in this case, is not a docile company union, but a tough and independent adversary, the United Steelworkers of America, who had demonstrated their internal solidarity and ability to damage the company. In this case, a "high-road" approach did not stem from a benign, paternalistic CEO, but grew out of years of strife. These companies are, unfortunately, exceptions in today's turbulent economy, but they suggest that many roads are still possible.

There is little doubt that today's economy is far more marketized than that of the postwar boom, and that this shift has transformed labor markets. However, the chain of cause and effect seems rather more complex and indirect than the simple association of an information economy with laissez-faire proposed by theorists such as Gilder. A more convincing story is that globalization and information technology have eroded the relative power of the two great stewards of the mixed economy—organized labor and the state—and increased the relative power of business to evade tacit contracts with its employees. Once the process of the relentless shaving of labor costs takes hold, the competitive environment becomes more intense, and every employer begins playing the same opportunistic game. The competitive quest for cost-cutting, in turn, increases business's political determination to achieve further deregulation, the better to trim costs—which further undermines the mixed economy, and further undermines the bargaining power of employees.

After all, there was nothing inherent in the old mass-production economy that dictated unionization, wage-and-hour legislation, limits on laissez-faire trade, or the custom of lifetime employment. These certainly did not exist early in the industrial revolution, or even as late as the 1920s. That they existed at mid-century was more the fruit of political struggle than of economic determinism. The factory economy was perhaps somewhat more amenable to unionization, because it agglomerated thousands of workers in the same physical location, which promoted class consciousness and in turn mobilized a political constituency for a mixed economy with constraints on the ability of private capital to treat labor as a commodity. Still, nearly a century elapsed between the rise of the factory system and the maturation of effective industrial unions. And in most of the parliamentary West, it took another half-century, a great depression, and a world war for a shift in relative political power to allow a reasonably balanced social contract between industry and labor.

Prior to 1935, there were plenty of factory workers, but few were members of unions, and little social legislation was on the books. In the United States, the social compact forged in the 1930s and refined in the 1940s and 1950s did not reflect an abrupt change in modes of production; it reflected a new political balance. Likewise, in Europe and Japan, where postwar reconstruction emphasized a quite explicit social-market or social-democratic economy, this was the effect of a profound shift in political power. Throughout the West, the Great Depression and World War II disgraced laissez-faire economics and enhanced the prestige of trade unions and the democratic state. In the former Axis powers and in France, Belgium, the Netherlands, and the Nordic countries, the war obliterated or discredited not just fascism but political conservatism generally. In the more free-market Anglo-Saxon countries, the state enjoyed rare prestige because of its success in winning the war.

Even relatively conservative parties of that era were committed to a welfare state, public investment, economic regulation, and social partnership with trade unions, partly as a bulwark against communism. In Southern Europe, this model drew legitimacy from Catholic social teaching. In Northern Europe, it was more social-democratic; in Japan, it blended the traditional Shinto and Buddhist conceptions of reciprocity and group obligation with an emergent brand of industrial capitalism that retained feudal or tribal undertones. In the United States, the state enjoyed more legitimacy to regulate commerce than usual because of the Cold War. The postwar boom, therefore, pursued the model of a mixed economy in every one of the advanced industrial nations, with variations only in degree. But this was far more the result of geopolitical and domestic political realignments than of industrial evolution. And, for the moment, it substantially demarketized labor.

It is naïve, therefore, to view a particular labor-relations regime either as the natural counterpart of a stage of production, or as a naturally contoured marketplace, even an atypical one with long-term tacit contracts. For more than a century, wage workers have endeavored to win civic and workplace rights to shelter themselves from being treated like a commodity. Their success has waxed and waned, based on their own mobilization, the strength of their political allies, and the impact on domestic politics of external events such as depressions and wars.

As we have seen, the body of modern scholarly work on labor economics (to its credit) concludes that the simple "price-auction" view of labor markets misdescribes reality, and that non–market-clearing outcomes can have offsetting efficiencies. This is true both in the nonunion sector, where tacit contracts can yield productivity gains, and in the union sector, where the contracts are more explicit. But a good deal of this research mistakenly presumes that whatever wage and tenure practices emerged, especially in the majority of enterprises with no union, must have assumed the shape they did because it was efficient. This, after all, is how a market economy is supposed to evolve. Thus, if employers valued long-tenured workers and didn't opportunistically dump those with seniority during periods of high unemployment; or if they paid workers a bit more than a market-clearing wage; or if they offered fringe benefits—all of this must have reflected some social imperative peculiar to labor markets that was efficient to the firm. Managers must have been "optimizing," because market-theory economics insists that market actors always optimize.

These anomalies, the theorists concluded, were seemingly efficient in real-world labor markets, but they had unfortunate macroeconomic consequences such as a propensity to mild inflation or less than full employment. For centrist economists of a generation ago, the remedy was a series of further offsets, in the spirit of the second best: labor compacts or tax incentives to limit wage increases to the rate of productivity growth, or public-sector employment programs to soak up the unemployed. A generation of moderate Keynesians devised ingenious strategies to reconcile necessarily "imperfect" labor markets with high-employment, low-inflation macroeconomies.

But this scholarly conception of labor markets tends to fall seriously short, for it leaves out *power*. It presumes that the arrangements that result are simply the workings of market forces, rather than a political struggle over how market and nonmarket relations are to be structured and for whose benefit. The trouble with this approach is that, when new institutions displace old ones, as they have in the 1980s and 1990s, the theorist is left to throw up his hands and to conclude rather helplessly that something about the economy or the technology of our own era abruptly moots all the earlier insights about efficiency wages and tacit contracts. The new arrangements also must be efficient, or they wouldn't have emerged.

One must be very skeptical of this inference. If workers thrived on security and knowledge-sharing a generation ago, they would likely do so today. If the firm could live with a more social labor market and the economy still generate 4 percent annual real growth back then, it probably could do so now. What has changed is less the contours of technology than the contours of power. Most economists are professionally uncomfortable with issues of power, because that topic is largely assumed away in the neoclassical paradigm, in which all exchanges, by definition, are deemed voluntary. More institutionalist students of labor markets, such as Arthur Ross, John Dunlop, Thomas Schelling, and William Lazonick, do look at labor outcomes (appropriately, in my view) in terms of power and bargaining. But this mode of inquiry puts them at the margins of the market model.

In truth, customs and norms regarding the appropriate treatment of employees ebb and flow over time. Such norms internalize changing power balances, via the power of unions or of the state, or through customary behaviors reflecting extra-market values or embedding earlier political struggles. As market principles become a sacred imperative rather than one contending principle among many, we see the erosion of norms that historically persuaded employers to look for mutual gains from more humane treatment of their workers. I am reminded of that great social-contract theorist, E. B. White. The text is *Charlotte's Web*.

"You mean you *eat* flies?" gasped Wilbur.

"Certainly. Flies, bugs, grasshoppers, choice beetles, moths, butterflies, tasty cockroaches, gnats, midges, daddy longlegs, centipedes, mosquitos, crickets—anything that is careless enough to get caught in my web. I have to live, don't I?"

"Why, yes, of course," said Wilbur.

Charlotte continues:

"I am not entirely happy about my diet of flies and bugs, but it's the way I'm made. A spider has to pick up a living somehow or other."

In today's economy, in contrast to that of the postwar social-contract era, when power relations were more symmetrical, many employers treat employees like expendable cogs. This is advertised as not unlike Charlotte's natural order: "I have to live, don't I? Nothing personal. It's the way I'm made." It is presumed that employers, in a new fiercely competitive environment, must behave unsentimentally and sometimes ruthlessly toward their workers in order to live; and that, if wage employees don't like the result, they should simply become entrepreneurs, too.

Conservative economists, presuming efficient labor markets, also assume away power when they consider discrimination. For Gary Becker, the Nobelist of the Chicago School, racial or gender discrimination must be rational; otherwise it would not be pursued. According to Becker, the white person who practices discrimination that does not make economic sense—for example, refusing to hire a perfectly qualified minority or woman candidate at a competitive wage—is indulging a "taste" for disliking members of certain groups, and paying an appropriate price for it. This delicate language, of course, leaves out the more plausible likelihood that a dominant group enjoys the privileges that come with the systematic subjugation of out-groups. If women cannot become doctors, lawyers, or corporate CEOs, there are more such jobs for men. If blacks are systematically relegated to domestic service and farm labor, that makes the cost of such labor all the cheaper and reserves the better jobs for the dominant group. When women and minorities did gain entry to elite jobs after the 1960s, it did not reflect shifts in tastes or belated acknowledgment of the efficiency of opening doors to all, but shifts in power. In the pure market model, however, groups do not exist, only individuals.

Another failure, characteristic of more orthodox economic analysis, is to conceive of work as a "disutility." That is, people are presumed to view work as a burden and something to be avoided. They work because they have to; their wages compensate them for the unpleasantness (disutility) of work. Alfred Marshall, the father of modern economics, wrote that a person's willingness to work is measured by the wage that is just sufficient "to induce him to undergo a certain fatigue." Because their actual work effort varies, workers must be supervised in order to assure the employer that they are diligently carrying out their jobs. A whole genre of related research uses the rather archaic verb "to shirk." The presumption is that, other things being equal, employees prefer to goof off than to take pride in their work.

It is scarcely worth belaboring the point that work is not just a source of drudgery and inconvenience, but also potentially a craft in which most people would prefer to take pride. Freud had it right when he observed that the two great pursuits of the human experience were love and work. Professor Robert Lane, in his magisterial work on markets and human psychology, *The Market Experience*, points to the multiple developmental functions of work: Work is a source of self-esteem and mastery; an engagement with the social world; a basis for positive or negative self-identity; and the source of ongoing learning. Work gives structure to life; it combats boredom and alienation. Lane, summarizing more than a decade's study of markets and human society, concludes that the signal failure of the market system is its inability either to provide enough work, or to structure enough jobs that allow people to realize their basic human needs for challenge, mastery, the intrinsic satisfaction of being one's own boss, and "cognitive complexity."

Here also, there is a great range of possibility, which is broadly indeterminate in its effect on overall productivity. A great deal of work can be configured to be engaging and satisfying—or to be routine drudgery. The more it is routine, the more the employer can justify treating workers like expendable cogs, and the more workers will live up to their billing as would-be shirkers—and the more the employer will need to follow the economist's imperative to supervise relentlessly.

Conservative market enthusiasts do recognize that work can be joyous as well as burdensome. But in today's ultra-market economy, exhilarating and rewarding work is something mainly associated with entrepreneurship; it is the boss who gets to feel the thrill of creating something, and the wage worker who feels mainly insecurity. Hundreds of books appear yearly celebrating the joys of managing, owning, marketing, and creating value. For owners, the problem is not shirking, but workaholism. Yet there is surprisingly little celebration of the joy of ordinary craft. It is almost as if fulfilling work is too good for the common people. Thus, the emerging class division in postindustrial society widens the gaps not only in material reward but also in work satisfaction. The implicit premise is that, if the ordinary worker can't cut it as an entrepreneur, it's his fault. The boss, faced with a demoralized worker, then invests some of her creative juices in more effective supervision. This is also facilitated by the new information economy. Computers not only allow telephone operators, airline reservationists, supermarket checkout clerks, FedEx deliverymen, and back-office workers in banks and insurance companies to serve customers more efficiently. They also allow a more precise monitoring of workers' output.

Interestingly enough, both the free-market right and the Marxian left in the economics profession use this same concept, of workers' being prone to "shirk"—but infer opposite conclusions. Free-market conservatives pursue this analysis because it conforms to the conception of utility and disutility in their model of human behavior, and because it allows the entrepreneur to be cast as a "principal," and supervisors and employees as his "agents." The Marxians also like this concept because it nicely expresses the class struggle. Bosses treat workers like dirt; so of course workers shirk duties whenever they can. Some left-of-center economists, like William Lazonick, turn the "shirking" view around on the conservatives, by arguing that there are huge productivity gains to be unlocked from the work force if only management would treat workers more generously and learn to reward autonomy and share authority.

If we look back on the twentieth-century history of labor markets and labor relations, and their connection to the evolution of production, it is difficult to escape the conclusion that many paths were, and are, possible; that each system of production can coexist with a wide variety of labor arrangements and a wide range of possible growth rates—but with markedly different consequences for earnings distribution, job security, and work satisfaction. For any stage of technological development, the institutional and regulatory regime can permit most firms to treat most workers as casual labor—or they can create incentives and constraints that promote job security, autonomy, gain-sharing, a learning environment, and long-term affiliations. Public policy can make it easier or more difficult for employers to treat their workers as casual labor.

A globalized economy, with a weakened state and more flexible and decentralized modes of production, is certainly more vulnerable to the commodification of labor. However, with the shift to a service-and-information economy, greater marketization of commerce, and the rise of contingent employment, it is the politics more than the economics that poses the challenge. It is not difficult to imagine a set of policies that would restore a functioning social contract between business and labor, reducing both insecurity and inequality without sacrificing growth (see below). It is more difficult, given the current distribution of political and economic power, to imagine a political mobilization that would challenge the dominance of laissez-faire and carry out opposite policies. We shall return to a policy agenda shortly.

LABOR MARKETS AND INEQUALITY

As labor markets have become increasingly laissez-faire markets, inequality has widened apace. The benign view of this phenomenon holds that skills, at last, are being rewarded appropriately. A more skeptical view holds that income extremes are now far beyond any degree necessary to reward diligence or innovation; that the negative social consequences of inequality far outweigh the gains to allocative efficiency; and that the extreme income inequality associated with pure markets, far from being a source of efficiency, is one more serious blemish of laissez-faire society and one more social calamity wrought by pure markets.

The widening of inequality, beginning in the mid-1970s and accelerating in the 1980s, is one of the best-documented recent economic trends. No matter how you measure it, the income distribution in the United States has become more extreme. During the quarter-century between 1947 and 1973, the economy both grew faster than in our own era, and produced an earnings distribution that gradually became more equal. Median family income, adjusted for inflation, slightly more than doubled. The bottom 20 percent of households, however, realized income gains of 138 percent, while the top 20 percent gained 99 percent. These trends reversed after 1973. In the period between 1979 and 1993, the top 20 percent gained 18 percent, while the bottom 60 percent actually lost real income. And the poorest 20 percent lost the most income of all—an average of 15 percent of an already inadequate wage. Wealth, far more concentrated than income, has now reached its point of greatest concentration since the 1920s. All of the gains to equality of the postwar boom have been wiped out.

This trend has multiple causes, but virtually every one is a variant on a single cause—the increased marketization of society. Laissez-faire markets, in many respects, behave like lotteries. They tend to bestow disproportionate rewards on winners. Lester Thurow, in his book *Generating Inequality*, points to the windfall origin of most large fortunes. In principle, markets are in or near equilibrium, but in practice, they are in constant disequilibrium. A company with temporary, above-average returns can enjoy a big stock run-up and windfall yields for its founders or owners. Some of this is due to skill, diligence, and foresight; some of it simply to luck—the people who decided to invest early in Xerox or IBM rather than Studebaker; the people who had their savings in housing in the 1970s and in the stock market in the 1990s rather than vice versa. Thurow writes: "Large, instant fortunes are created when financial markets capitalize new above-average rates of return," often when a private company sells its first stock offering. And once these lucky fortunes are acquired, they need only normal rates of return to earn incomes that are immense by ordinary standards.

As economists Robert Frank and Philip Cook note in *The Winner-Take-All Society*, as the marketplace becomes the entire world, a superstar in sports or entertainment can command astronomical earnings. The same is true of the leading company in an industry, or a technical innovator—whose market was once a region or a nation but is now the globe. This dynamic creates not only terrible social inequalities, but inefficiencies in the allocation of effort, since millions of people compete for very scarce positions that will yield only a handful of winners. The legions of inner-city youth with hoop dreams of becoming the next Michael Jordan would have been better off pursuing other trades, and might have—if markets sent different signals.

With greater marketization and the erosion of norms of fairness, the earnings of corporate chief executives, successful investors, and media superstars are becoming ever-higher multiples of the earnings of ordinary people. Graef Crystal's work on executive compensation demonstrates not only that CEO salaries and benefits have risen from 35 times that of the average production worker in 1974, to 120 times by 1990, but that there is surprisingly little correlation between how the company is performing and what the boss is paid. Eventually, nonperforming bosses are usually forced out, of course, but the change in norms has meant that at any given time all bosses—the stars and the dogs—command relatively higher pay levels. These exorbitant shares to the executive suite are less the result of markets pursuing efficient solutions than of a shift in power.

At the other end of the earnings spectrum, the routine worker with skills that can be learned in a few hours or days has suffered a relative erosion of bargaining power and hence income. Increasingly, such workers are competing not just with workers in a local labor market or nation, but with the entire world, where there are more than a billion workers unemployed or underemployed, competent to perform routine jobs, and eager to work even for subsistence wages. There have always been surplus workers in poor countries, but until recently the boundaries of the nation-state and the limits of technology prevented the world from functioning as a single, integrated labor market. Today, an American factory worker in Detroit is competing with factory workers in Mexico or Malaysia, who are often working with roughly comparable production technology. A back-office data clerk is competing with clerks in the Philippines who are able to receive data by satellite, enter it according to a sophisticated computer program, and return it to the United States—at a fraction of the U.S. labor cost.

When the increasing polarization of wages first became a subject of public debate, in the early 1980s, right-wing politicians and their intellectual confrères dismissed the entire issue as a red herring promoted by unions and their apologists. Foreign competition was indeed increasing and, yes, domestic wages were declining in a few "rust-belt" industries such as steel and autos. But these were industries where wages had outstripped productivity growth, and the workers were getting just what they deserved. If domestic industries and their workers couldn't meet the competition at prevailing wages, they had either to cut costs or to watch jobs migrate overseas.

Most economists, both mainstream and ultra-conservative, also tended to deny that anything was seriously amiss. The apparent polarization of earnings, these economists contended, was a temporary anomaly.

First, they blamed the slow growth and stagflation of the 1970s. Slower growth meant higher unemployment. Higher unemployment meant that those at the end of the job queue—the poorest, youngest, and least skilled—suffered disproportionately. Restore growth to normal levels and the income-distribution problem would take care of itself.

Second, they blamed a one-time, coincident labor-market event—the entry of both baby boomers and women into the work force. The baby-boom generation, those born between 1946 and 1964, flooded job markets in the 1970s and 1980s. This created a simple supply-and-demand problem: too many workers, not enough jobs. When supply exceeds demand, the price—in this case, wages—falls. Moreover, younger workers were by definition less experienced. So it was only natural that they would command depressed wages relative to older ones. Much of the inequality problem was really a generational one, economists argued. What was true of baby boomers was also true of women. Their sudden entry in job markets increased the total supply of job-seekers; and women, as new entrants, tended to be less experienced than men. There was also lingering discrimination, and women had a tendency to enter and leave the labor force to have children or to follow "primary-earner" husbands to new pastures. On all counts, women's wages tended to be depressed. But this also should be understood as temporary. When the baby boomers were digested into the labor force, and women's participation became normalized, greater equality would return.

The mainstream did acknowledge the role of trade, but minimized it. It was true that, as the economy became more global, increased foreign trade produced some relative losers. But this influence, properly understood, was mostly beneficial. A core principle of laissez-faire economics was comparative advantage. If some other nation could produce at lower cost a good formerly produced in the United States, it made sense for Americans to import that product rather than keep making it, and to find something else for the displaced American workers to do. With hundreds of millions of workers in Latin America and Asia willing to make, say, clothing, at wages of less than a dollar an hour, it was sentimental and irrational to protect apparel jobs in the United States—most of which paid less than the median wage in any case. Economists could demonstrate that the benefit of retaining the job was far less than the cost to American consumers. The preferred policy was to let the job go, and find ways to compensate the losers—pay them transitional benefits, subsidize their retraining. This consensus went from free-market conservatives to moderate Democrats, all of whom called for policies of adjustment as an alternative to protectionism.

Ironically, at the same historical moment when greater marketization was displacing well-paid American jobs, the more zealous enthusiasts of marketization were increasingly disparaging all government programs—even those such as Trade Adjustment Assistance, worker retraining, and other measures intended to facilitate marketization by reducing political resistance and compensating those dislocated. Trade Adjustment Assistance, a program originally devised in the Kennedy years to win union support for freer trade, was cut by 80 percent under President Reagan, and eliminated entirely in the 1995–96 budget cuts. Retraining outlays were also slashed. The political moderates who proposed adjustment as a pro-market alternative to protectionism sought a constructive middle ground, but found themselves isolated as a kind of centrist splinter with little popular or legislative backing.

Moreover, beginning in the Reagan years, tax and income-transfer policy, instead of mitigating the unequal income effects of markets, began cutting in the same direction and intensifying inequality. Transfers to the poor were cut; taxes on labor were raised through successive hikes in payroll taxes, while taxes on upper-bracket incomes and on capital (which is disproportionately owned by the affluent) were cut. Institutions that served to defend wages of relatively low-income workers, such as the minimum wage and the right of unions to organize freely, were weakened.

The confidence among mainstream economists that the inequality of the late 1970s was merely a transient trend turned out to be disproved by events. Baby boomers grew up and were absorbed by the labor force; the cohorts of recent graduates that began entering job markets after about 1985 were far smaller; the percentage of women in the work force plateaued. But the relentless marketization of labor intensified and, not surprisingly, inequality only increased. Moreover, after the recession of 1981–83, economic growth resumed. As defenders of the Reagan administration kept insisting, during the 1983–89 recovery ("the longest peacetime expansion on record"), overall growth rates nearly matched those of the glory days of the postwar boom. And after a recession that coincided unfortunately with the feckless Bush presidency, in the Clinton expansion of 1993–96 growth again resumed smartly, inflation stayed low, unemployment rates dipped below 6 percent and stayed there. But wage and salary inequality continued to widen. Something fundamental had indeed changed.

That something was greater marketization, which acted like a solvent on each of the countervailing extra-market institutions that had previously mitigated the market's tendency to extreme inequality.

MERIT AND REWARD

The rise of marketization, and with it of inequality, has led some commentators to proclaim that inequality is now increasingly based on merit. This is hardly a new idea. Economists as diverse as Adam Smith, Karl Marx, and Alfred Marshall have commented on how wages tend to reflect skills. What has changed lately, however, is the removal of constraints, both positive and negative, that interfered with a more perfect correlation between skill and reward. Supposedly, in the bad old days inequality was based on discrimination and blocked opportunity. Today, however, the sweeping away of old barriers thanks to civil-rights laws and meritocracy, coupled with the liberation of market forces, means that people are now being paid according to their true worth. But pure labor markets, like pure financial markets, tend to overshoot. And it is extremely hard to defend some of the market's verdicts of worth.

Nonetheless, some commentators, such as Mickey Kaus in *The End of Equality*, conclude that it is both futile and economically self-defeating to attempt to override the market's verdicts. Others, such as Charles Murray and the late Richard Herrnstein, and more recently Dinesh D'Souza, find that markets work so efficiently that the declining economic and social condition of minority groups must be the result of their inherent inferiority. But this vein of commentary ignores the randomness of many pay arrangements in a market society, the benefits of discrimination to dominant groups, and the loose connection between the distribution of earnings and the economic performance of society as a whole.

A great many analysts of wage inequality, both liberal and conservative, contend that its main cause is the interplay of globalization and technology. In this view, skills matter more than ever, and routine American workers who were once overpaid relative to their skills are now being compensated according to global norms. Americans of high skills, by contrast, have the entire world as their stage. The widening income-inequality, therefore, is defensible. The remedy, in this view, is education and training. With advanced skills will come advanced wages. Of course, it takes heroic leaps of faith to project a meritocratic model onto the social reality of late-twentieth-century America. Whatever the benefits (and costs) of a purely meritocratic society, the fact remains that some people begin the race with a huge head start, and others with an immense disadvantage.

The education-and-training cure, though benign, is also far too simple a panacea. Very highly skilled workers are more likely to be in short supply, and hence better positioned to defend their earnings, but earnings inequality is in fact increasing, mainly because greater marketization is removing institutions that once promoted wage stability and equality, in multiple ways. A better-trained and -educated work force, though certainly desirable, is only a partial remedy (see "The Skills Debate," page 101). A complete list of the factors increasing inequality must include these:

Globalization. The globalization of markets increases wage inequality in the high-wage countries, in two distinct and reinforcing ways.

First, globalization places labor into worldwide competition. Workers in high-income nations are compensated partly on the basis of their marginal productivity, but also based on local living costs and social norms of fairness. A taxi driver in, say, Boston performs essentially the same job as a taxi driver in Calcutta, with roughly the same productivity—but makes perhaps ten times the wage. Likewise a street sweeper, housemaid, or waiter. However, these service workers in different countries are not in direct competition with each other, except when illegal migration occurs. (You cannot call a taxi driver in Calcutta to take you from Penn Station to La Guardia.) Rather, the taxi drivers' wages are typically some fraction or multiple of their society's median wage; their living standards reflect the productivity of the society as a whole, and social conventions of fairness. If the median family income of a nation is forty thousand dollars, then users of taxis can afford to pay cab drivers ten dollars for an occasional taxi ride, even if some potential immigrant cab drivers might be desperate enough to work for less.

In the factory- and technical-services economy, however, workers are increasingly in direct competition worldwide. Auto assemblers, steelworkers, chip fabricators display comparable skills throughout the world. Broadly comparable production technology is also available worldwide. State-of-the-art steel mills exist in South Korea and Brazil. One of the most potent principles of economics is the "law of one price": in a perfectly free market, the prices of comparable goods will tend to converge. As labor markets have become globalized, the wages of routine workers worldwide have tended to converge—downward. To pursue the example of autos, Ford assembly plants on both sides of the Rio Grande have roughly the same productivity and technology, but Mexican workers are paid about one-seventh the wage of their U.S. counterparts. They receive this wage not because it reflects their productivity—but because there are so many surplus workers in the Mexican labor force. The Marxian notion of a reserve army of the unemployed seemed ludicrous when the advanced nations had low unemployment rates and the mobility of financial and production capital was bounded by regulations, norms, and limits of technology. Today, desperately poor potential workers in the third world are linked to the consumer markets and production systems of the advanced nations, and depressing wages of employed workers in the first world. It is almost as if today's footloose global entrepreneurs were determined to prove Marx right.

Looked at from a Keynesian rather than a Marxian perspective, the problem is a global imbalance of supply and demand. Low-wage workers in poor countries who use advanced production technology and produce for global markets are paid proportionally less than the value of what they add to the world's supply of goods. They literally can't afford to buy what they make. Unlike Henry Ford's famous five-dollar-a-day assembly workers at River Rouge, the Ford production workers in Chihuahua, Mexico, can't afford to purchase the cars they build. Nor can they afford to buy a basket of goods from richer countries proportional to what they themselves add to global supply. Nothing in free-market economics will automatically give them that purchasing power; it takes extra-market forces to raise their wages. This is a globalized variant on Keynes's famous refutation of Say's Law: demand does not necessarily prove adequate to consume supply. And the macroeconomic policy levers that can be used to sustain demand in one country are absent globally. As long as this is the case, the wages of workers in poor countries will tend to drag down wages of workers in rich ones, and this will exacerbate income inequalities in countries that once had functioning social contracts between labor and capital.

Analysts such as Robert Reich have pointed to this dynamic as a particular problem for low-skilled workers, but the same global downward pressure on wages increasingly affects many highly skilled occupations, such as computer programmer—the emblematic job of the information age. India is now a prime source of advanced computer programmers. Global companies like IBM and Digital hire programmers at about two hundred dollars a month in India, and even temporarily bring them to the United States, abusing an exchange program that allows highly skilled workers in temporary short supply to be imported to the United States. As it happens, there are plenty of domestic computer programmers; there just aren't very many that will work for two hundred dollars a month.

As the economy has become more marketized and the ability of wage workers to bargain for a decent share has weakened proportionally, it is mainly owners of capital, and salaried workers with hard-to-find skills, who have reaped the gains. This set of dynamics has widened inequalities, whether one measures wages, annual incomes, individual incomes, or family incomes. Inequality has widened both between high-skilled and low-skilled workers, and within occupations. It has widened between well-educated workers and those with two years of college or less; and it has widened between full-time and part-time workers.

High Unemployment. Throughout the industrialized West, the period since 1973 has been characterized by high unemployment. There is substantial debate about why this has occurred. One factor is the slower rates of economic growth typical of the past two decades, and the slowing of growth is itself a subject of wide debate. A second factor is demographic—more young people of the baby-boom generation, and more women entering labor markets. A third factor is the effect of globalization and marketization on the levers that individual nations once used to maintain full employment. If one nation tries to go it alone with a program of Keynesian economic stimulus, this risks stimulating domestic inflation and a run on the currency. Unregulated global financial markets tend to inject a deflationary bias into the system, by pressing debtor nations to bring their accounts into balance by contracting their economies. Financial markets will punish the nation that grows faster than its neighbors. (Exceptions like Japan and South Korea had highly regulated financial markets.)

It was this laissez-faire bias to slow growth that the Bretton Woods system sought to counteract, by stabilizing exchange rates and making credit plentiful worldwide. After the experience of the Great Depression, the central idea of Bretton Woods was that the system should instead be designed to have a bias toward growth, by putting pressure on creditor nations to expand rather than on debtor nations to contract. The collapse of the Bretton Woods system after 1973 has thus been associated with an era of slower growth and higher unemployment. (The reasons behind the collapse of the Bretton Woods system are treated extensively in my previous book, *The End of Laissez-Faire.*)

Higher unemployment, in turn, tends to reinforce earnings inequality, because it weakens worker bargaining power, especially among less skilled workers. So marketization, in one further respect, has led to more marketization, and greater earnings inequality.

In addition, the intellectual and ideological ascendance of the laissez-faire view has led policymakers to embrace a doctrine that used to be held only by extreme conservatives in the economics profession—the idea of a Natural Rate of Unemployment. The Federal Reserve evidently believes deeply in this effect. Despite the absence of inflationary pressures, the Fed hiked interest rates seven times between 1992 and 1994, dampening the economic recovery, slowing down job creation, and reducing the growth rate from over 4 percent in 1994 to less than 3 percent in 1995.

The idea of a Natural Rate of Unemployment is a more conservative variation on the "Phillips Curve," which describes the supposed trade-off between inflation and unemployment. To review the evidence of recent years is to appreciate how both conceptions are wide of the mark—another example of a brand of economic analysis that presumes mechanistic relationships rather than ones substantially influenced by the institutional context. In the late 1980s, unemployment and inflation were both high and rising. In the early and mid-1990s, both were low and falling. Economist Robert Eisner, a critic of the Natural Rate of

Unemployment, has written, "If there is a natural rate, God apparently treats his children very differently, with [unemployment in] much of Europe in double digits and Japan, despite a severe recession, still at only 3%."

The English economist Joan Robinson challenged the idea of a simple trade-off between inflation and unemployment by calling for new institutions of social bargaining. Low unemployment would need to be inflationary only if labor did not appreciate its long-term interest in price stability and if social conflicts over shares of total product led to wage settlements and price hikes that began an inflationary cycle. The Swedish Keynesians managed to "cheat" the Phillips Curve with two generations of "active labor-market policy" that used macroeconomic stimulus to get unemployment down to about 6 percent, and then relied on public employment and job-training sabbaticals to reduce it to below 2 percent. A key to this strategy was union cooperation in moderating wage pressures despite full employment, and shelter from the full force of low-wage foreign competition. Many other European countries with strong but responsible trade unions enjoyed low unemployment and low inflation for prolonged periods, thanks to mechanisms of social bargaining that allowed gains in output-per-worker to be passed along to employees, but not gains in excess of productivity. This model has been somewhat impeached by the slower growth and higher unemployment rates that began in the 1980s. But if central banks permitted higher growth rates, the social-bargaining approach would be perfectly serviceable, and is in any case not to blame for the joblessness.

The United States has never had the European degree of explicit social bargaining, either ideologically or institutionally. In the late 1970s, when stagflation was the main issue, a number of American economists sought to contrive more marketlike mechanisms that would improve on the inflation-unemployment trade-off by keeping wage gains at or below the rate of productivity growth. One popular but short-lived idea promoted by economists at the Brookings Institution was the Tax-based Incomes Policy (TIP). Firms would be rewarded for wage restraint in their tax treatment. If their pattern of wage growth did not exceed their productivity growth, they would get lower taxes. Another ingenious plan was MIT economist Martin Weitzman's proposal for a Share Economy, in which workers would take a larger fraction of their compensation in the form of profit sharing. This change, Weitzman argued, would bring the long-sought flexible adjustment to labor markets, reduce inflation, and allow firms to remain at fuller employment by spreading available work.

All of these approaches implicitly or explicitly challenge the premise of a Natural Rate of Unemployment consistent with price stability. All represent social inventions in pursuit of a sustainable Second Best, which would improve on the high unemployment rates of a pure free market. Many nations, for prolonged periods, have realized full or near-full employment, coupled with tolerably low inflation. In the 1980s, the nations with relatively high unemployment also had higher inflation. What precludes full employment is not economics but politics.

The record of the Clinton administration suggests how even policymakers who dispute this conception of a Natural Rate of Unemployment are politically constrained to defer to it. Alan Blinder, before he joined the administration, repeatedly criticized the Federal Reserve for keeping real interest rates too high and growth too low. In the 1994 Economic Report of the President, the chapter on macroeconomics, authored by Blinder, declared that long-term interest rates were above historic norms and should be brought down. When he joined the Federal Reserve as deputy chairman, however, Blinder repeatedly insisted that he believed in a Natural Rate of Unemployment—only he thought it might be 6 percent rather than 6.5. Meanwhile, the jobless rate dropped to 5.5 percent, and inflation didn't move. Labor Secretary Robert Reich, after a press conference decrying the fact that productivity growth was increasing but median wages were falling, was dressed down by other members of the Cabinet for signaling a desire for "higher labor costs" and thereby frightening Wall Street.

Far from being a transient phenomenon, high unemployment, with its attendant effects on inequality, has become a long-term feature of a marketized and globalized economy. The forces of financial orthodoxy crusade for balanced budgets, on the premise that fiscal discipline and low inflation will increase savings rates, which in turn will heighten investment and growth. But the record of the U.S. Federal Reserve suggests that, no matter what the state of fiscal discipline, inflation, or savings, the free-market conservatives who currently dominate policymaking have an aversion to full employment.

The Shift from Manufacturing to Services. Coincidentally, while the economy was globalizing it was also shifting from manufacturing to services. Manufacturing, at mid-century, provided nearly a third of all the jobs in the U.S. economy. Manufacturing was heavily unionized. Even jobs that were not unionized were influenced by union pay scales, if only as union-avoidance medicine. Manufacturing jobs also produced relatively "high-value-added" per worker. That is, each production worker in most goods-producing industries worked with a relatively large amount of physical production capital, and generated a lot of product per hour worked. All of these factors made for relatively high wages, as well as a pattern of wages relatively evenly distributed.

The service economy, by contrast, includes a grab bag of very high income jobs and very low ones. It includes brain surgeons and nurses' aides; software engineers and data-entry clerks. It includes technically dynamic sectors, such as telecommunications, and technically static ones, such as babysitting. Other things being equal, the service economy will be a less equal economy, since it combines occupations with more dramatically divergent rates of productivity than the factory economy. As more jobs shift to the service economy, that factor alone tends to widen earnings inequality, because it shifts more people to sectors that seem inherently less inegalitarian. The economist Barry Bluestone has calculated that, in the twenty-five years prior to 1987, the earnings gap between college graduates and high-school dropouts working in goods-producing industries widened by 15 percent, while the comparable gap in the service sector widened by 60 percent.

Moreover, other things are not equal. The service economy, for the most part, is not unionized, except in the public sector. Manufacturing is still heavily unionized. Though factory workers enjoyed relatively high and equal wages, there was nothing inherent in production work that required such an earnings distribution. If more service occupations were unionized, the distribution of earnings would become more equal, but that would not necessarily depress the efficiency of the overall economy or distort labor markets. Whether the economy as a whole sacrificed efficiency and output would depend on how industry reacted to the changed pattern of wages.

Weakened Wage Regulation and Norms. I have suggested that the widening of earnings inequality is less the result of "natural" changes in the distribution of skills or the logic of labor markets than a reflection of shifts in relative power between owners of capital and wage and salary workers. Marketization itself, of course, is a prime cause of that power shift. In this century, two of the principal countervailing forces offsetting the market's tendency to create extreme earnings-inequality have been trade unionism and wage regulation by the state. This context, in turn, engendered labor-market norms that discouraged opportunistic behavior by employers.

In recent years, most notably in the United States and Britain, where conservative policies have had the most dramatic impact, these countervailing forces have been significantly weakened. In the United States, the minimum wage was once equal to roughly 50 percent of the average wage. At this writing it is 34 percent. Even with the modest increase approved in August 1996, it will rise to barely 40 percent. Indeed, the Republican House majority leader, Representative Richard Armey, has been a vigorous advocate of repealing all minimum-wage laws. Coupled with relatively high unemployment (which also erodes labor's bargaining power), this means that wages of workers, especially of those who do not bring to the labor market skills in short supply, tend to lag.

Wage regulation has also been weakened in more subtle ways. The backdoor assault on regulation has cut appropriations to enforce regulations on the books. In the mid-1990s, reports began surfacing of slave-labor camps in Los Angeles textile factories, and of Victorian-style sweatshops in lower Manhattan.

The U.S. Department of Labor has fewer than thirty wage-and-hours inspectors for all of greater Los Angeles, and even fewer for New York.

Non-wage forms of employee compensation, not required by law but long established by custom and by relative bargaining power, are also eroding. Pension benefits, a hallmark of a primary-labor-market job, have been cut significantly since 1980. The proportion of workers covered by some form of company pension plan has declined from 50 percent in 1980, to 44 percent in 1994. The typical form of pension has become the "defined-contribution" rather than "defined-benefit" plan, which means that the worker rather than the company takes the risk of fluctuations in the investments that back the plan. As stock markets have risen, companies have also siphoned tens of billions out of pension plans, on the pretext that they are "overfunded." Even in firms that retain pension plans, the relative contribution from company and from worker has tilted, so that workers are financing retirements out of their own pockets rather than collecting them as a fringe benefit.

Precisely the same dynamic has affected the other main fringe benefit, health insurance. In the cost-cutting era, fewer companies offer health plans at all; there is narrowed choice of plan and of doctor, and more cost-shifting to employees, both by requiring workers to pay a larger fraction of premiums, and by herding them into plans that have higher out-of-pocket costs (see chapter 4).

Deregulation. Beyond explicit labor regulation, more general economic regulation of industry is conducive to earnings equality and stability in several reinforcing respects (see also chapter 7). Traditional regulation of "natural monopolies" such as public utilities limits the entry of new competitors, and guarantees a stable rate of return. That in turn allows stability in employment. Even regulation that regulates price but allows more than one competitor, like the traditional regulation of broadcasting and airlines, tends to depress price competition, which creates a climate favorable to career security and high wages.

Deregulation, of course, reverses this process. With greater price competition in industries such as telecommunications, public utilities, airlines, trucking, hospitals, etc., comes pressure to cut labor costs. Companies that once had strong and docile unions and/or stable pay scales and career ladders, like AT&T, find themselves in relentless price competition with new competitors such as Sprint, which are fiercely nonunion and have lower labor costs. AT&T either cuts its own labor costs or is priced out of the market. Likewise the major trunk airlines, large teaching hospitals, broadcast networks, and so on.

Other aspects of marketization are closely analogous to deregulation in their labor-market effects. For example, companies that were not explicitly regulated, but were in oligopolistic industries (steel, auto, chemicals, defense contracting, etc.), are going through much the same process. Intensified price competition takes the form of intensified pressure to cut wages and benefits. In the public sector, the analogy is privatization. If a contractor can do a job more cheaply than the civil service, the pressure is for the civil service either to lower wages, cut benefits, lay off employees, or contract the job out. In all cases, the resurgence of competition based on labor costs tends to hammer down wages, repeal tacit social compacts, and wreak havoc on assumptions of career ladders and job security.

The Assault on Unions. Management toleration of unions in the United States came in two broad waves, both anchored by rank-and-file activism linked to supportive government policies. The first occurred during the New Deal, when a burst of labor organizing at the grass roots enjoyed a rendezvous with a sympathetic government. Even before Roosevelt took office, the Norris–La Guardia Act of 1932 lifted the threat of unions' being prosecuted as an illegal restraint on commerce. The NRA, then the Wagner Act, guaranteed workers the right to organize, allowing John L. Lewis to proclaim with only slight hyperbole that "President Roosevelt wants you to join the union."

World War II reinforced labor's role as a legitimate social partner. In exchange for social peace and an absence of strikes for the duration of the war, unions were granted influence as wartime advisers on industrial policy, and enjoyed a holiday from antiunion activity by management. The wartime wage and price controls also had the unintended side effect of entrenching pension and health benefits. Companies facing labor shortages could not compete with one another by offering premium wages, but they could and did bid up fringe benefits. By V-J Day, the presence of a union and of fringe benefits in the factory economy had become normal. Labor scholars of that generation made the mistake of presuming that collective bargaining was now a permanent feature of American industrial life.

Business's counteroffensive began almost as soon as GIs demobilized, and bore its first fruit in the 1947 Taft-Hartley Act, passed by the Republican 80th Congress over President Truman's veto. The act outlawed the closed shop, prohibited secondary boycotts, and allowed states to pass "right-to-work" laws that permitted nonunion workers to work side by side with union members. The percentage of unionized workers peaked in the early 1950s.

Far from becoming reconciled to unions, management began resorting to sophisticated union-busting techniques. Though the Wagner Act guaranteed the right to organize freely and to bargain collectively, management could moot that right by firing workers who showed union sympathies. As cases piled up, the redress provided by the NLRB and the courts was typically too little and too late. Companies were given light fines and enjoined to bargain in good faith—years after key leaders were fired and the steam had gone out of the organizing drive.

Research by Harvard labor-law professor Paul Weiler demonstrated that, nation-wide, one worker in twenty who signed a union card was fired in retaliation. This sent a powerful signal to those who might show union sympathies.

In 1978, a legislative effort to toughen the Wagner Act failed to overcome a Senate filibuster, by two votes. When President Reagan took office, one of his first acts was to fire striking air-traffic controllers represented by PATCO, sending private industry a signal that it was now legitimate to replace workers who went on strike. The Wagner Act did not prohibit that practice, but long-standing custom dictated that the strike must be a carefully choreographed and limited form of industrial warfare in which neither side sought to inflict permanent damage on the other. After the PATCO affair, the firing of strikers became increasingly widespread, and the strike went into eclipse.

Greater marketization itself weakened unions in multiple ways. The industry-wide master contract, once the central instrument of labor's determination to "take wages out of competition," was suddenly a relic. As plant closings and relocations became normal, wages came brutally back into competition. Workers in different companies, and even in different plants of the same company, were whipsawed to demonstrate which could produce the biggest savings in labor costs. The winners would get to keep their jobs, at least for the time being. Instead of reflecting union "demands" for better wages and benefit increases, the typical contract negotiation was about management demands for "givebacks." In a nation none too keen on collective remedy to begin with, the failure of unions to deliver benefits, or even to guarantee job security, made them far less attractive to unorganized workers. With management playing hardball, why put your job at risk for a union that would not likely make much of a difference?

In addition, the Lane Kirkland generation of labor leaders, with some notable exceptions, did not emphasize organizing new workers in new industries. They had come of age during the brief era of industrial peace, and enjoyed their self-image as labor statesmen. In the 1950s, the radicals were driven out of most unions, and radicals tended to make the best organizers. The new insurgent movements of the 1960s—the antiwar movement, environmentalism, feminism, and gay rights—had few friends in the mainstream labor movement. People committed to grass-roots activism often found homes elsewhere. Most union resources increasingly went either to tending the existing membership, or to legislative and electoral politics. Organizing was hard, unrewarding work; and with the deck so stacked against labor, even when there was strong sentiment for a union, it was hard to win certification. So established unions grew reluctant to throw good money after bad. All of which meant that, as new industries emerged, the organized fraction of the labor force dwindled.

Globalization and the shift from traditional manufacturing to services and to high technology only intensified the relative decline. By 1995, the unionized fraction of the private-sector labor force had dwindled from a peak of 35 percent to a sixty-year low of 11 percent. As a consequence, one of society's most potent counterweights to the inequalities generated by markets is far less of a presence.

Economists have long debated whether unions and their influence on wages distort economic efficiency. After all, they change the pattern of wages that market forces would otherwise confer, and markets (by definition) are presumed to be efficient. The best, and most empirical, resolution of this debate is found in the 1984 study *What Do Unions Do?* by Richard Freeman and James Medoff, both Harvard economists. Freeman and Medoff meticulously measured wages and productivity in union and nonunion firms. Their findings challenge the oversimplified laissez-faire pictures of unions as monopolists that raised wages beyond justified levels, and hence harmed both productivity and employment.

Unions, Freeman and Medoff found, had two faces. They did use a degree of market power to extract wage increases. But by providing a collective voice for workers, and changing the dynamics of workplace life, they often made contributions to productivity that well justified their presence. Workers know a lot about efficient production, but in the absence of collective representation "are unlikely to reveal their true preferences to an employer, for fear the employer may fire them." If management uses the collective-bargaining process in good faith, they added, "unionism can be a significant plus to enterprise efficiency."

Freeman and Medoff found that this did not apply in all cases. In some unions and some workplaces, wages did outstrip productivity, either because a powerful union won excessive demands, or because the monopoly structure of industry as a whole led to excessive price and wage increases, and "monopoly rents" in which workers shared. Alternatively, the fractious nature of labor relations in particular enterprises precluded the kinds of positive-sum gains produced elsewhere.

These "two faces of unionism" had offsetting effects. They raised wages, but often also raised productivity. Though their wage increases sometimes came at the expense of nonunionized workers, unions nonetheless were on balance a force for greater equality, because they promoted a more egalitarian distribution of earnings and less arbitrary treatment by management, both within and between enterprises and in society generally. The claim that unions increase inequality is wrong; Freeman and Medoff conclude that the increase in inequality induced by monopoly wage effects is dwarfed by three other union effects on wages that reduce inequality: union wage policies favoring lower inequality of wages within establishments; union policies for equal pay for equal work across establishments; and union gains for blue-collar labor which reduce inequality between white-collar and blue-collar workers.

If unions could be good for productivity, why did most managements resist unions? Because managers and owners, for the most part, enjoy the prerogatives of power. They prefer to make their own decisions. As that labor-market sage Mel Brooks put it, "It's good to be the king." Unions also tended to change the distribution of profits and wages, in favor of higher wages and lower profits. However, as Freeman notes, "Most studies of the union profit effect find that unions reduce profits largely in sectors where company market power is extensive and thus are more likely to constitute a redistribution of profits than a major force driving firms out of business." Moreover, "gain-sharing" plans, in which workers and owners share the fruits of improved productivity, may reduce management's share of profits—but raise the overall level of output and of profits.

Reading Freeman and Medoff, and kindred research, one must be impressed yet again with the broad indeterminacy of labor-market outcomes. The purest market does not necessary yield optimal productivity. Social forces can significantly alter the pattern of wages and benefits that owners would otherwise pay their employees, with no easily predictable or mechanistic effect on economic efficiency. That's because there is an almost infinite variety of ways to perform a task and a wide variety of states of employee morale. The pattern of compensation and the style of management chosen by a particular employer constitute only one of many possible paths.

Because of the shifts in the relative power of workers and employers, the particular path chosen by most managers in the present economy is one in which wage reduction is a paramount goal. This clearly reduces worker earnings and increases worker insecurity. It is more marketlike, in the sense that it treats labor more like other commodities. But it is by no means clear that this is the optimal outcome.

The Skills Debate. One of the factors widening income inequality is that some workers, notably those with low levels of education, are being bypassed by the new knowledge economy. Only a generation ago, thanks to plentiful factory jobs, strong unions, and little foreign trade, a worker with modest formal schooling but a strong back and a willingness to work hard could join the blue-collar middle class. It is clear that those days are over. Such jobs still exist, but their numbers and pay scales are dwindling. Very few will be available to the generation now entering the labor force.

There are anecdotal reports from managers of good blue-collar "knowledge" jobs going begging. Reportedly, employers have difficulty filling many of the available positions in the new economy, because too many young people get out of school—even out of high school and junior college—with minimal skills in literacy, "numeracy," and good work habits.

These factors have led to a near consensus that defines a great deal of the earnings-inequality problem as simply a skills problem. In Robert Reich's influential book, *The Work of Nations*, Reich eloquently described the fate of ordinary "routine" workers in a global, knowledge-intensive economy, and pre-scribed education and training as the remedy. Another very influential work, the 1990 Report from the Commission on the Future of the American Workforce, summed up its message in its title: "America's Choice: High Skills or Low Wages!"

A 1995 article by Michael Rothschild, in the Democratic Leadership Council's magazine *The New Democrat*, puts the proposition so extremely it borders on self-parody:

> Thanks to the near-miraculous capabilities of microelectronics, we are vanquishing scarcity. . . . Consequently, the venerable politics of class warfare, which results from an economic reality in which a fixed amount of goodies must be divvied up among too many grasping hands, is dying, along with conventional economic thinking.
>
> The losers this time are those who cannot or will not participate in the knowledge economy. . . . Like illiterate peasants in the Age of Steam, today's unskilled are being left behind by the new economy. . . . Other than the poorest 20 percent of Americans whose illiteracy prevents their participation in the Knowledge Age, everyone senses the promise of the new economy.

Well, not quite everyone. This breathless celebration overlooks the fact that 80 percent of Americans, many of them not only literate but with college degrees and advanced skills, are not sharing in the fruits of the knowledge economy. Two decades of ever-greater marketization have narrowed rather than broadened pros-perity. Note also that Rothschild's formulation makes concern with these trends a minority issue, one aligned with society's losers, and one that a smart political party would disdain, rather than an issue that affects four out of five Americans.

To review the rhetoric of "New Democrats" and their Republican opponents, one would think that the main difference between the two major parties is only in the relative roles of the public and private sectors in making up for this skills gap. Democrats want more public funds for education and training—upgrading of public education, school-to-work transition programs, federally subsidized re-training for displaced workers, and more carrot-and-stick incentives to induce private business to invest more in training. Republicans trust the private sector to do what is best for itself. They point to McDonald's "Hamburger U.," to the train-ing investments by temporary-help firms such as Manpower, and by the software industry. They argue that plenty of money goes into public education and that the need is not for more money but for the injection of better incentives into the edu-cational system. But both parties seem to think that the earnings problem is in large measure a skills problem. Upgrade skills and earnings will follow.

That analysis follows the conventions of free-market economics. If relative wages are falling, it must be because the relative value of workers' human capital has declined; by definition, their pay levels are appropriate because the market says so.

The problem is that the most careful research on this subject suggests that the skills gap is largely a mirage. It is true that there are people at the bottom of the labor market who are effectively not hirable. But this is a very narrow segment of the work force. On the other hand, millions of people who are literate and numerate and offer good work habits still receive dismal wages. Work by the urban anthropologist Katherine Newman on entry-level jobs in Harlem found enormous competition among qualified workers, who could read, write, show up on time, and efficiently serve customers, for a small supply of entry-level jobs. By every indicator, workers are in fact becoming better educated. What has changed is what economists call the "return to skills." Except at the very top, workers are being compensated less generously for the skills they have. The problem, in short, is more on the demand side—the kind of jobs employers are offering and how they compensate employees—rather than on the supply side of the skills that workers bring to labor markets. That deterioration, in turn, reflects mainly a shift in relative bargaining power, not skills.

The most dramatic indicator of what is really at work is the changing relationship of productivity to compensation. Manufacturing productivity (output per hour worked) has increased by about 50 percent since 1973, yet manufacturing compensation has been flat. Overall productivity in the economy lagged during the 1970s, but rebounded during the 1980s and 1990s. Since 1989, overall productivity in the economy has risen at about 1.2 percent a year, yet the median wage has steadily declined. Even in the 1993–95 recovery, when productivity growth exceeded 2 percent a year, median worker compensation barely rose.

Those who dismiss these trends tell a variety of stories. At the heart of them is the new technology. Supposedly, companies are placing new demands on workers, and workers just don't have the skills. But many workplaces display a new blend of advanced technology and stagnant earnings. Routine workers in industries as diverse as retailing, banking, and fabrication of computer chips actually work with very advanced technologies. But they do so in a way that demands little in the way of advanced training or problem-solving skills. Moreover, even workers who do bring higher skills to the labor market have faced stagnant earnings, except at the very top. A more descriptive title for the Report from the Commission on the Future of the American Workforce might have been "America's Choice: High Skills *and* Low Wages!"

It is easy to confuse what is operating here, because it is certainly true that earnings have collapsed most dramatically for those workers with the least education. In the decade between 1979 and 1989, the median real wage of high-school dropouts declined by 18 percent; male high-school graduates by 13 percent; men with one to three years of college by 8.3 percent; even the wages of male college graduates were effectively flat. Only those with two or more years of graduate education enjoyed real increases, averaging 9.7 percent. Women gained relative to men, but only women with college degrees enjoyed net gains over the decade, averaging 12.6 percent.

On the demand side, it is simply not true that industry abruptly raised the hurdle in terms of the skills required to hold a good job. Rather, given the weakness of labor's bargaining power and the flood of displaced blue-collar workers, industry was simply able to draw from a higher-educated pool of applicants for the same old jobs. In the 1980s, as educational levels increased, economists calculated that upward of 20 percent of college graduates were performing jobs that did not require a college degree. By 1990, the typical autoworker had at least a technical degree from a junior college, and many had four-year degrees—though real wages were declining. Though there were spot shortages of unusual specialties, these described only a tiny fraction of the entire labor market.

Economist David Howell, concluding a review of the academic literature on demands for higher skills, reports, first, that industry's demand for worker skills in recent decades did not increase at a rate above the century-long trend. Second, Howell notes, there is a very poor and even worsening match between skills and compensation, which varies widely from industry to industry and even from firm to firm.

In the absence of other changes that would reverse the bargaining asymmetry between labor and industry, it is very unlikely that the human-capital solution would change these patterns in the distribution of earnings. If it takes a graduate degree to realize increases in earnings commensurate with society's average increase in productivity, many workers will not realize such increases, since it is obvious that we cannot send everyone to graduate school. If society did, the earnings premium to graduate education would soon disappear. If we accept Reich's notion that in the new globalized economy it is mainly knowledge workers ("symbolic analysts") who are able to compete worldwide and maintain living standards, even by the most generous definition they are only 10 percent of the jobs in the economy.

Education and training policies do have a place in a strategy to reverse the trend to earnings inequality. Industry's reluctance to invest adequately in training and on-the-job learning is one of the most widely accepted, least controversial cases of externality or market failure. Training is a public good. Nations such as Germany that combine high employment and low inflation have relied on ingenious training programs. Especially for people from disadvantaged backgrounds and for older workers displaced from traditional occupations, school-to-work transition programs, training and retraining schemes, can offer a crucial boost up job ladders. But, given all the other forces generating market-driven inequality, training and education offer at best a partial remedy.

Hypothetically, if we tried to rely on human capital (education and training policies) alone to restore the current earnings of male high-school dropouts to their real 1979 level, University of Chicago economist James Heckman has calculated that it would cost the government $284 billion. To restore the 1979 earnings distribution generally, without redistributing from college graduates to high-school dropouts, would cost more than $2 trillion.

A SOCIAL LABOR MARKET

The most potent proof that something other than technology and skill is driving the increase in earnings inequality can be found by comparing the recent experience of the United States and other advanced nations. The bottom line is that most other countries, though they face similar changes in technology, have not faced the same widening inequality. While the real earnings of manufacturing workers in the United States fell throughout the 1980s, they rose by 1.2 percent a year in Europe and 1.6 percent a year in Japan. Moreover, earnings inequality, already wider in the United States than in most every other industrial country, widened in the 1970s and '80s, though it narrowed or stayed roughly the same elsewhere. In the United States, in 1988, male workers in the bottom 10 percent had earnings equal to just 38 percent of the median. In Japan, the comparable figure was 68 percent; in West Germany, 61 percent.

Though average per-capita income is broadly comparable, Freeman calculates that American men in the bottom tenth earn roughly 45 percent as much as comparable Germans, 54 percent as much as Norwegians, half as much as Italians, etc. It is not the case that Europe paid for its greater equality with lower growth, since European (and Japanese) savings and investment rates, as well as rates of productivity growth, have continued to outstrip those of the United States. Between 1979 and 1990, GDP per worker increased by about 1 percent a year in the United States, compared with 1.5 percent a year in Europe.

What accounts for these differences is simply that Europe and Japan have stronger wage-setting institutions that override the free market's tendency to push earnings to the extremes. Europe has much stronger unions, stronger minimum-wage laws, apprenticeship systems and training programs, and public investment. In addition, Europe has more comprehensive and better-entrenched systems of pensions and universal health insurance, child care, and disability coverage, so that the nonwage portion of worker compensation is also far more egalitarian. All of these mechanisms contribute in the first instance to greater income-equality—and in the second instance to norms of fairness that hold relative equality in high esteem. In addition, another body of research suggests that nations with higher levels of income inequality tend to suffer lower rates of growth, because of the drag on mass purchasing power.

Economist David Card compared earnings trends in the United States and Canada, two nations with broadly comparable economies, and found that, while earnings had become sharply more unequal in the United States during the 1980s, the degree of inequality and poverty in Canada had actually declined slightly. Card, in an article written with Richard Freeman, attributed the change to institutional factors: stronger Canadian unions (anchored by stronger Canadian labor law), more generous social insurance, tougher immigration laws. In Canada, 90 percent of unemployed people collect unemployment compensation, with relatively higher benefit levels and eligibility of up to fifty weeks. In the United States, only about one-third of the unemployed collect such benefits, which expire after twenty-six weeks. Unemployment benefits, of course, not only replace lost earnings. Their existence increases workers' bargaining power. Moreover, though Canada has a lower percentage of college graduates than the United States, many more Canadians attend vocational and training programs.

In the 1980s, it was conventional for conservatives to dismiss Europe as a sinking economic ship, the victim of "Eurosclerosis." Workers were hard to fire; wages were too highly regulated; this made labor markets rigid and inefficient, and caused Europe's higher rates of unemployment. It is true, in an era of slow growth, that the United States has in effect chosen to take its stagnation in the form of lower wages, whereas Europe takes slower growth in the form of higher unemployment. But it does not logically follow that the labor-market regulation is the cause of the slow growth. Economist Rebecca Blank, reviewing the debate about "protection versus flexibility," finds that the simple caricature of European labor markets as being rigid and inefficient and American ones as flexible and dynamic is a series of false dichotomies. As Blank observes, many European social policies, such as greater investment in training, child care, and universal provision of health insurance, in fact enhance labor mobility, whereas the U.S. failure to provide such benefits socially locks American workers into present jobs. "Some social programs may offset the inefficiencies and distortions caused by other political or economic constraints," she notes. Compared with laissez-faire, a package of labor-market regulations, taken as a whole, may yield as good an overall economic performance, with a more equal distribution and greater economic security.

As labor markets become more like spot markets, there are allocative efficiencies to be gained in the matching of workers with jobs, vendors with customers, and pay scales with marginal productivity. But if these allocative gains are not to be vitiated by other losses (in income, security, and aggregate demand), offsetting stabilizers are necessary. The analogy is the old paradox that brakes allow the car to go faster. Consider major mechanisms that might reverse the trend to greater inequality without harming growth.

Full Employment. Tighter labor markets counteract market-driven inequality in several complementary ways. Low unemployment increases the leverage of employees to bargain for a larger share of the profits that now go to owners. Lower overall unemployment also takes some of the sting out of job dislocation, because other opportunities are available. With lower unemployment rates, income distribution further tends to be more equal because there are fewer people without earnings. However, desirability of full employment, widely accepted a half-century ago, has fallen afoul of the doctrine of the Natural Rate of Unemployment—part of the free-market dogma.

Stronger Unions. The central precept of the labor movement used to be "Take wages out of competition." By making comparable employers pay similar workers comparable wages, unionization compelled companies to compete based on innovation and productivity; today's companies increasingly compete by cutting worker pay and benefits. Stronger unions, as political actors, would be a more potent constituency for a mixed economy generally.

Fair Trade. In a global economy without common social standards, underpaid workers in poor countries contribute more to global supply than to global demand. That imbalance drags down pay levels in high-wage countries. Free trade might be made conditional on a floor of common social standards and pay-for-productivity norms.

Wage Subsidy and Social Income. Regulatory measures like the minimum wage, and income transfers such as the Earned Income Tax Credit, can counteract the private market's tendency to pay as little as it can get away with. In-kind benefits, such as universal health insurance, child care, and socially provided pensions, allow labor to become more flexible without sacrificing benefits that traditionally have been provided by employers. Contingent employment would be far more attractive to employees if social benefits were universal rather than perks of permanent, full-time jobs.

Education and Training. Some (but far from all) of the inequality problem can be remedied by improving the skills of the work force. But, given private business's chronic underinvestment in training, the remedy is either social provision of training or a system of mandates to private business. The 1990 Report on the Skills of the American Workforce reported that the United States has "the worst school-to-work transition system of any advanced industrial country" and that "Only eight percent of our front-line workers receive any formal training once on the job, and this is usually limited to orientation for new hires or short courses in team-building or safety."

"Gain-Sharing" Commitments. The approaches of companies such as Powersoft, Magma, and Harman (as discussed earlier in this chapter) suggest that gain-sharing compacts are both available and efficient. But, absent strong unions insisting on such compacts, or government regulations mandating them, most CEOs are primarily loyal to themselves and their shareholders, and prefer to treat employees as expendable. An immense literature of business writing pronounces that a gain-sharing strategy of management yields long-term dividends to the firm. But in today's feverish, financial-market-driven economy, most are more interested in short-term dividends to impress investors and boost the stock price.

Responsible Corporations. A Democratic congressional task force chaired by Senator Jeff Bingaman of New Mexico has proposed creating a new category of corporation that would receive a variety of benefits from the government in exchange for maintaining a more reliable social compact with its employees. The qualifying corporation would receive favorable tax treatment, selective regulatory relief, and certain training and technology subsidies. In return, the corporation would have a greater degree of employee participation, either through unions or work councils; it would resist abrupt downsizing and out-sourcing, and make a good-faith effort to create and maintain high-wage, secure jobs with decent fringe benefits. And it would have a profit-sharing program or other gain-sharing plan. In short, the corporation would treat its employees as stakeholders rather than disposable factors of production.

Specifically, to qualify for this special status, a corporation would have to meet several threshold tests. It would have to contribute at least 3 percent of payroll to a portable, multi-employer pension plan, along the lines of plans offered by the TIAA/CREF teachers' pension fund. It would devote at least 2 percent of payroll to employee training and education that met standards set by industry groups. It would offer a health plan that conformed to a basic model health-care package and pay at least 50 percent of the costs. The qualifying corporation would also be required to have a profit-sharing plan, with bonuses tied to productivity, and/or an employee stock-ownership plan with employee trustees. In addition, it would maintain a compensation plan whereby the ratio of the income of the highest-paid to that of the lowest-paid employee was no more than fifty to one. It would have its own variant of a Community Responsibility Agreement regarding relocations and layoffs. And for companies with more than twenty-five employees, it would either be unionized or have an employee involvement-and-co-determination program. The corporation would also have to be headquartered in a country that banned child labor and prison labor and allowed free collective bargaining; and it would subscribe to a code of conduct regarding its operation in countries without such standards.

The Bingaman plan further includes a Tobin-style tax on the short-term trading of securities. The proceeds of this tax, in turn, would go to finance a social-capital fund, for worker training, school-to-work transition programs, industrial extension, export promotion, and technology research and development.

This sort of legislation, if not carefully drafted, could give many corporations tax breaks for actions they are already taking. Still, it seems reasonable to use either carrots (tax breaks) or sticks (regulations) to revive a more symmetrical relationship between company and worker.

In other advanced industrial nations, such as Germany and Japan, this sort of social compact is the fruit of deliberate state policy, or of a stronger union movement, or both; it reflects a more corporatist or social-market conception of capitalism. In the United States, this more social view of the labor market was temporarily entrenched, as a result of the unusual legitimacy that the state enjoyed during the Depression, World War II, and the early Cold War. But this social conception of the market was partly taken for granted, defied the libertarian streak in the American soul, and never quite became part of the American creed. Today, it needs to be rebuilt, almost from scratch.

Note that this approach flies in the face of key articles of faith deeply held by today's elites: that government should deregulate and let market forces take over; that "free trade" is the highest form of free market and an unambiguous good; that federal spending should be cut; and that full employment would be inflationary and bad for financial markets. The free-market ideology has not only needlessly widened society's inequalities, but also entrenched a dominant way of thinking that precludes remedies.

Three conclusions are clear from this review of labor and markets. First, the main source of rising earnings inequality in the last quarter of this century is greater marketization, in its multiple forms. Second, there is no evidence that a moderately more egalitarian earnings distribution, tempered by extra-market forces, has costs to efficiency or output. Within a fairly wide range, the earnings distribution is broadly indeterminate, and reflects social institutions and distributions of political power. And, third, policy instruments that could return labor markets to a path of economic efficiency coupled with greater income equality are readily available—but all fly in the face of the current vogue for greater marketization.

The labor market is not the only such arena. We now turn to other realms of human society in which the idealized market is impossible to attain, and where the simple pursuit of pure markets reduces efficiency and leaves most people worse off.

4 / MARKETS AND MEDICINE

AN UNHEALTHY MARKET

Nobody really wants a perfect market in health care. Our view of health reflects broadly shared, extra-market values: No hospital should turn away patients in emergencies. No one should want for basic medical care because of limited purchasing power. Children should be vaccinated against preventable diseases. Basic sanitation should be universal. We embrace some of these principles out of a sense of fellow feeling and shared community. As empathic creatures, we may allow market forces to determine whether some people can never afford filet mignon, but not whether some people must die because they can't pay the doctor.

Beyond compassion, social provision of basic public health is enlightened self-interest. Rich and poor alike can contract and spread infectious diseases, perish in epidemics, get sick from tainted meat or impure drugs. It is a nuisance if prudent people must remember to buy bottled water, even for the rich. To put these concepts in the idiom of economics, sanitation is an indivisible public good. Social-health measures offer positive externalities—general benefits that market logic fails to discern and price accurately. Perhaps, too, the insured middle class derives "psychic income" from knowing that even a pauper can see the doctor.

The essence of markets is to produce both winners and losers. But it is unacceptable that losers should lose their health care—for sound, extra-market reasons. We expect health care to be available even when people make the kind of miscalculations that are severely punished by ordinary markets. For example, if a person's insurance company goes out of business, if someone is disqualified from obtaining health coverage because of a lost job, denial of care is too severe a penalty.

Thus the dilemma: Once we express these shared values by creating institutions that substantially divorce life and health from private purchasing power, this huge sector of the economy is something other than a free marketplace disciplined by competition. Paradoxically, however, it remains riddled with people and groups whose main motive is profit. And the most efficient way to make money in the health-care business is to avoid sick people or to limit care— maneuvers plainly at odds with our social objectives.

To discipline opportunistic market behavior in health care, society cannot rely entirely on market incentives, since the market is so structurally imperfect to begin with. Much of the recent history of health policy in the United States has been a hapless effort to bring "market efficiency" and "pro-competitive reform" to a sector that is inherently extra-market. Not surprisingly, most have backfired.

For most of the postwar era, our health system was a rough balance of market forces tempered by extra-market ones. But it had two serious flaws. It left tens of millions of people without coverage. And the tension between market principles and social ones in an essentially private system built in inflationary tendencies. Lately, as insurance companies and corporations have intensified their efforts to rein in costs, the system has tipped; it is becoming a purer market—with unhappy results for all except a few fortunate entrepreneurs.

Among its other flaws, our heavily marketized system fails to perceive that the determinants of long life and good health are not entirely medical. Profit opportunities do not repose in improvements to public health. Yet longevity and healthfulness are substantially social. The normal life span increased markedly during the nineteenth and twentieth centuries, mainly because of better nutrition, improved sanitation, vaccines, and antibiotics that wiped out killer diseases, less exhausting physical work, relief of residential overcrowding, and better knowledge and practice about formerly life-threatening natural conditions such as childbirth. Expensive medical heroics contribute only the last bit of improvement in health.

When investment in heroics comes at the expense of basic public health, it can leave society worse off. Thus, to the extent that markets devalue the social determinants of health, the market misallocates health resources. "A society that spends so much on health care that it cannot or will not spend adequately on other health-enhancing activities may actually be reducing the health of its population," write the health economists Robert Evans and G. L. Stoddart.

That nonmedical factors very significantly influence health and life is confirmed by transnational comparisons. Nations that spend less of their GDP on explicitly medical interventions nonetheless have lower rates of sickness and longer life spans than the United States, if the societies are more broadly egalitarian, offer universal medical coverage, and invest more in basic public health. Two brief examples make the point dramatically. In Japan, longevity increased at an astonishing rate during the postwar era. Average life expectancy rose by seven and a half years in just twenty years—a gain to health equivalent to abolishing premature death from cancer and heart disease combined. Between 1965 and 1989, Japanese life expectancy at birth increased from sixty-eight years for men and seventy-three for women to seventy-six for men and eighty-two for women, primarily because of basic improvements in nutrition, sanitation, and basic public health. This was not a rebound effect from World War II, since mortality figures were even worse in the 1930s. Nor, given that the change is recent, is the explanation genetic. Nor does it reflect increased outlay on medical care. Japan's health outlays have been stable for two decades at 6 to 7 percent of GDP, and reflect a lower-tech approach to care than that of the United States. We shall return to the nonmedical determinants of health shortly.

Even Britain, which has brutally ratcheted down its fifty-year-old National Health Service under seventeen years of Conservative government, now spends less than 6 percent of its GDP on medical care, compared with over 14 percent in the United States and about 9 percent in the average advanced country. Since Britain is a less affluent country to begin with, per-capita health spending in the United States is roughly triple that of Britain. But most of Britain's outlay is social, so nobody does without basic care. And Britain has almost identical morbidity and mortality rates to those of the United States—except that the poorest one-fourth of Britons are substantially healthier than their American counterparts. (It remains to be seen what another decade of widening inequality in Britain would do to these numbers.)

My point is not to deprecate the medical part of the health system. We all appreciate access to good medical care. As the normal life span increases, we will need to spend every medical dollar as astutely as we can. My point, rather, is that market forms of incentive and accountability do not optimize this problem. Health care is inevitably a highly imperfect market. The real question is what kind of imperfect market—with what distribution of benefits and costs, and what strategies of discipline and efficiency.

I will argue in this chapter that health care is perhaps the quintessential case of an economy of the Second Best, a necessary blend of market and nonmarket. But the peculiarly American version of this blend is dysfunctional. It yields what Alain Enthoven termed "a paradox of excess and deprivation." Well-insured people receive care that has become ever more technology-intensive and costly, with the costs driven by the entrepreneurial part of the system. Others, without insurance, get little or no care at all—a public-health catastrophe with both hidden and overt economic costs.

In the 1980s, a second paradox appeared. As private market forces battled the seemingly chronic medical inflation, private regulators such as insurance companies became every bit as intrusive on medical decisions as the most maligned government bureaucrat. The more America tried to rely on the market model to resolve its health-care crisis, the more regulated it became. As another health-policy scholar, William D. White, put it, "How did we move from policies declaring allegiance to competition to what is becoming the most clinically regulated system in the world?" How, indeed?

RIVAL VISIONS OF REFORM

The American health-care system reached a crossroads in the early 1990s. It was clear that the system, one way or another, could not continue inflating at the rates of the 1970s and '80s; and that in many respects the escalating costs, the fragmentation, and the insecurity were products of a common syndrome. It was economically inefficient to have a splintered system made up of thousands of different plans, each with its different reimbursement schedules and treatment protocols. The system wasted more money on paperwork than any other in the world. But was the remedy greater marketization or greater socialization—or a different blend of both?

As costs escalated, the market's response compounded the irrationalities. Insurance plans and corporate sponsors, as private-market actors, sought to restrain their own costs—by avoiding sick people, second-guessing doctors, limiting treatments, and shifting costs to subscribers. This response was rational for the individual firm, but not for society. Consumers became justifiably apprehensive about losing coverage. Doctors were finding the increasing interference by insurers intolerable. Hospitals were nervous about getting paid. Corporations wanted their costs capped. Politically, all of this created a potential alliance between the anxious insured and the uninsured, and between medical consumers and medical professionals. Thus a grand reform coalition seemed possible, with cost containment, universal access, and health-care security as necessary complements.

As the nation teetered on the brink of fundamental reform, the debate was over which version—"single-payer," "play-or-pay," or "managed competition."

"Single-payer" referred to Canadian or Medicare-style universal coverage, in which clinical care could remain decentralized and mostly private, but the coverage and payment mechanism would be social. To restrain inflation, the system as a whole would get a cost cap—an annual budget. Negotiation would determine which sectors would get what share of the overall health budget. Medical professionals and lay advisers would make the often difficult trade-offs—how much for preventive measures, for routine acute care; how much for premature babies; how much for the dying elderly; how much for new costly technologies. At a time when markets were in vogue and governments out, this approach was widely dismissed as too statist and too costly, even though it would likely save money for society as a whole.

"Play-or-pay" meant requiring employers either to offer acceptable coverage to their workers, or to pay a tax that would finance their coverage from a residual insurance pool that would also cover the unemployed. This approach had the virtue of building incrementally on the present system, but the flaw of maintaining the fragmentation. Ironically, it was originally proposed by Richard Nixon in 1972, but rejected at the time by Democrats. In the 1980s, many liberals, led by Senators Kennedy and Rockefeller and the AFL-CIO, reluctantly embraced play-or-pay as the best reform that seemed attainable politically.

The Clinton administration attempted a third strategy, the novel blend called "managed competition," relying heavily on the vogue of markets. For a self-described New Democrat, managed competition offered Clinton both ideological and political appeal. Philosophically, it embraced marketplace competition. Under the Clinton plan, regional planning bodies known as "health alliances" would certify qualified insurance plans, and bargain with providers over costs. Employers would pay 80 percent of the cost of vouchers that could be used by citizens to buy coverage at any qualified plan. Subscribers would be free to switch plans once a year. Very large companies would have the option of sponsoring their own plan (a variant of play-or-pay). Politically, it offered an insider strategy of dealing all the major interest groups in. It seemed to appeal to the big insurance companies, who would get to manage the plans; to doctors and hospitals, who would have the security of getting paid; to employers, who would finally realize cost containment; and to anxious consumers, who would obtain both free choice of plan and security of coverage. This approach, sponsors hoped, would finally bring marketlike discipline to the health-care system in a way that combined security of coverage and restraint of costs. Ideologically, this scheme was pro-market—except that it depended on a great deal of prior and ongoing regulation.

But managed competition failed both as outsider politics and as insider politics. In the end, the public's enthusiasm was numbed by the plan's Byzantine complexity. Clinton rejected the politics of seriously pitting the people against the interests. Despite initial public support for health reform, no energized grassroots constituency for the Clinton plan materialized. The populist drama of patients at risk and doctors nitpicked by insurance overseers collapsed into the perception of back-room dealing. Meanwhile, the industry interest groups, Clinton's presumed insider allies, ultimately concluded that, despite the large elements of market competition, the whole approach involved too much government.

In the aftermath of this failure, universal access has disappeared as a policy goal, and private-market actors have redoubled their own efforts to rein in costs. This form of private regulation provides neither the accountability to consumers nor the universal coverage that the Clinton plan and foreign single-payer plans offer. And it generates its own inefficiencies. Though universal, socially mandated coverage is temporarily off the American political agenda, it still offers the best blend of free choice for consumers and professionals, and the most efficient use of the health dollar. To appreciate why, consider the dynamics of medical markets.

MEDICAL SUPPLY AND DEMAND

Competition is the prime mechanism that renders markets efficient. The sovereign consumer disciplines the opportunistic producer. As I suggested briefly in chapter 1, virtually all of the economist's conditions of perfect market competition are necessarily violated by the medical-care system. On the supply side, there is no free entry. On the demand side, most consumers do not "shop around" for treatments the way they buy cars. Most medical diagnoses and procedures are obscure to the laity, and determined by physicians, not patients. Bills are paid not by consumers, but by insurers. The doctor is on both sides of the transaction; she partly creates her own demand.

Moreover, demand is divorced from private purchasing power, thanks to insurance. Where one's life and health are concerned, money is no object, especially if someone else is paying the bill. A famous law of health economics, coined by Milton Roemer in the 1960s, holds that the demand for hospital beds tends to expand to meet the supply. Tax policy also artificially stimulates demand for medical care, by making health insurance partly tax-deductible, either to the employer or to the individual subscriber.

Also, because many patients are "locked into" their present plans by employer affiliations or pre-existing conditions, many Americans cannot shop around among insurance plans at all, no matter how high their dissatisfaction. Uniquely in health care, the system of payment—the insurance plan or Health Maintenance Organization (HMO)—is bundled with the product—the available doctors. This further frustrates the consumer's power to discipline the producer. Hence, another paradox: the more the health market is subjected to private forms of regulation, the more the consumer's sovereignty is diminished, and the less applicable the market model.

A consumer is also dependent on the system of medical degrees and licensing for assurance of the basic competence of doctors. Libertarian conservatives consider government licensing of professionals a case of state-mandated monopoly and pure excess cost. But imagine a system with no medical licensing. We may think the system of civil law is overburdened by medical tort claims now, but the aftermath of full medical deregulation would bring the courts to a grinding halt.

All of these interferences with market discipline cut in the same direction: they tend to raise prices. Doctors' average earnings have outstripped the consumer price index throughout the postwar era. Pharmaceutical companies have been consistently among the most profitable industries. The new, entrepreneurial health companies have been Wall Street's darlings. And between the late 1960s and early 1990s, health-care costs generally inflated at triple the overall rate of inflation. Managed care has moderated medical inflation somewhat, though, as we shall see, the savings are mostly deceptive.

In addition, the technical dynamism of medical care, the aging of the population, and the inherent labor intensiveness of the healing enterprise add whole other layers of inflationary pressure. The subsidy of both supply and demand signals entrepreneurs to invest heavily in new devices and procedures. Elegant medical technologies command the highest prestige (and pay) in the medical profession. Heroic (and costly) medical feats appeal to the self-image of specialists and capture the imagination of the public. The public thrills to the drama of ever more baroque organ transplants, the rescuing of ever-tinier premature babies, the success of elegant test-tube conceptions, the attachment of severed limbs through microsurgery. These are all technology-intensive, and very expensive.

Though some technological advances do save money—laser techniques for faster and less invasive operations, outpatient scans rather than inpatient exploratory surgeries—they also stimulate demand. And because of a general sentiment that health is a sacred realm beyond base pocketbook considerations, the public tacitly expects that first-class care should be available to everybody. A Harris survey found that 91 percent of respondents agreed that "everybody should have the right to the best possible healthcare—as good as a millionaire gets."

An aging population compounds the problem. Not only are the elderly the likeliest candidates for expensive medical heroics, but as the normal elderly become more aged and frail, even their normal care becomes more costly. Roughly a third of Medicare outlays finance treatment of patients in the last year of life, and half of that amount is spent in the last month. In America, our death-denying culture combines with the medical ethic of prolonging life at any cost to produce exorbitant outlays often devoted to squeezing out a few more days or weeks of an increasingly miserable life. If we gave every patient the benefit of every procedure that might possibly improve health or prolong life, the medical sector would be technically capable of absorbing most of the GDP.

One more subtle factor: As the economist William Baumol has famously noted, service occupations such as doctor and nurse (and schoolteacher, musician, artist, and carpenter) are inherently inflationary, because they are labor-intensive.* For society, the source of increased economic wealth over time is the substitution of capital for labor. This is the very definition of rising productivity. But skilled people in occupations where capital does not replace labor over time still expect their incomes to grow with the rising average wealth of society.

Baumol's favorite example is a string quartet. It performs Mozart in 1997 with exactly the "productivity" of 1797—but expects 1997 wages. A doctor may be working with much more high-tech equipment (itself a source of inflation) in 1997 than in 1957, but a conscientious physician can still perform only so many physicals an hour. Yet the doctor expects his income at least to match the rise in the cost of living. If the doctor who performed three physicals an hour in 1957 is performing the same three physicals an hour today, his measured productivity is unchanged. But if his real income is up, he has contributed to inflation. Doctors can compensate, to some degree, by eliminating house calls, adding nurse-practitioners and physicians' assistants, using time-saving monitoring devices, and reducing the hands-on time spent with each patient. But there are natural limits to this sort of offsetting productivity gain. At the end of the day, it is the doctor who must perform the examination of the patient, or he is no doctor at all. Given all of the above, it is remarkable that the rate of medical inflation has been held to "only" something like triple the rate of general inflation.

THE ACCIDENTAL RISE OF HEALTH INSURANCE

Before World War II, inflationary pressures in medical care were held in check by two forces: the fact that many people could not afford to pay the doctor very much, and the norms of medical professionalism. Until the Great Depression and the war, health insurance was not generally available. Most doctors were only moderately affluent, compared with their earnings growth during and after the post–World War II boom.

Medical doctors had not become seriously self-regulated and licensed by states as a learned profession until a generation or two earlier, in the late nineteenth century. As physicians professionalized, the American Medical Association's canon of ethics recognized that medical doctors held a position of immense power and trust, and recognized the fiduciary aspect of that position

---

* This tendency has come to be known as Baumol's Law.

with ethical constraints on profiteering. Doctors often had sliding fee scales. Needy people got a modicum of medical care from what might be termed "socialism in one practice." Charity hospitals operated by religious orders, as well as public hospitals, served the poor, but the care was catch-as-catch-can.

Uniquely in the United States, the introduction of medical insurance was not the result of an ideological or political shift in favor of an expanded welfare state. Rather, it was the consequence of how private-market forces responded to two historical accidents—the Great Depression and World War II. During the Depression, hospitals, like other industries, were going broke. Health insurance had previously been opposed by the American Medical Association, as an interference with the doctor-patient relationship. Such insurance also had been widely considered actuarially impossible, because of the perils of "adverse selection"—the risk that the people most likely to get sick would be most eager to insure their health. Prior to the Great Depression, "sickness funds" were limited to a few fraternal and ethnic organizations.

In 1929, however, Baylor University Hospital demonstrated that hospital insurance was feasible after all. Baylor contracted to insure the hospitalization of some 1,250 Dallas schoolteachers at a flat rate of fifty cents a month per subscriber. In return, the plan paid for up to twenty-one inpatient days per year. The numbers worked. Other community hospitals soon imitated the Baylor plan. As the Depression deepened, the idea of mass insurance contracts became increasingly attractive to hospitals.

By the mid-1930s, this approach evolved into the Blue Cross system—a loosely coordinated network of hospitalization insurance, authorized by special state legislation, organized by local hospitals, and franchised by the American Hospital Association for the express purpose of making sure that hospitals would get paid. All such plans were nonprofit organizations, charging a flat "community rate" to subscribers and spreading the risk among a broad enough pool of people to be actuarially sound. Doctors' initial opposition to hospitalization insurance was neutralized by provisions guaranteeing that the subscriber could select any doctor and the doctor any treatment.

Physicians remained wary of prepaid insurance for doctor bills. The AMA successfully prevented the 1935 Social Security Act from including health insurance, and as late as 1940 the AMA was opposing even private medical insurance. Gradually, however, the medical establishment relented—on condition that the plans be controlled by physicians. In the 1940s, "Blue Shield" plans for doctor bills proliferated, modeled on Blue Cross, in part to head off commercial medical insurance.

The other big stimulus to health insurance was World War II. The war created labor shortages. Employers, however, were prevented by government wage controls from enticing prospective workers with higher pay. But the War Labor

Board and the Office of Price Administration did permit improved fringe benefits. Many war-production plants began offering health benefits, through either
insurance plans, company clinics, or comprehensive prepaid group systems such
as Henry J. Kaiser's soup-to-nuts Kaiser health plan, the forerunner of the modern HMO. Elsewhere, prepaid group plans, such as the Health Insurance Plan
(HIP) of New York, were organized by liberal social reformers as a kind of private welfare state.

By the war's end, two uniquely American characteristics of the health-care
system were firmly in place. Insurance plans compliantly reimbursed costs
dictated by doctors. And insurance was tied to employment. A generation of
Americans grew accustomed to getting health coverage via their jobs, as if this
odd juxtaposition were the natural order of things. Employer contributions to
group health insurance rose from almost nothing in 1940 to over a hundred billion dollars a year by the mid-1980s.

Once Blue Cross/Blue Shield demonstrated that health insurance was actuarially feasible after all, commercial insurance companies followed. Companies
like Aetna, Prudential, and John Hancock captured half the health-insurance
market. To win the cooperation of doctors and hospitals, the commercial carriers
followed the Blue Cross/Blue Shield practice of deferring to medical professionals. Insurance contracts agreed to pay "reasonable and customary" charges, and
left treatment decisions to doctors.

The health system thus settled into a structure of "fee-for-service" medicine—doctor and hospital billed the patient for each procedure—coupled with
"third-party payment"—most bills were paid by insurers. This legacy, though
substantially wrought by private market forces, created a system with unique inefficiencies and an inflationary bias. These became fully manifest only as the
system matured and as government followed its basic contours in adding insurance for the elderly and the poor in 1965.

By the 1980s, the inefficiencies would be flagrant. But for the first decades
after World War II, the ratio of younger working people to older, sicker ones was
high; corporations were making good profits; and medical inflation gathered
force only slowly. The ratio of health-care costs to GDP rose only from 4.4 percent of GDP in 1950 to 5.9 percent in 1965.

A secondary reason why medical costs inflated slowly at first was that insurance was not available on the open market to most older Americans, at any
price. Except for lucky retirees whose fringe-benefit package extended health
coverage into retirement, health coverage for the aged was not available, because private insurers refused to provide it.

So a great many elderly people simply went without medical care. This
was, in effect, a form of rationing. But it was rationing dictated by market forces.
Nor was this the result of some abstract unseen hand; it was, rather, the work of

conscious policy choices by insurers to deny coverage to elderly subscribers. The poor, likewise, found themselves with no insurance. Society's overall health costs stayed moderate, in part because many people did without.

In 1965, armed with a rare working majority, the Democrats were able to enact both Medicare and Medicaid. It wasn't the comprehensive schema sought by every Democratic president since Roosevelt, but it extended government coverage to the two most vulnerable groups. Though the AMA was implacably opposed to the whole idea, Congress and the Johnson administration offered doctors a costly sweetener—and found sugar coatings for the hospital, insurance, and drug industries as well: The government would do almost nothing to alter the existing structure of the private health-care system. It would simply pay the cost of bringing new subscribers into it—creating new profit opportunities for these powerful industries. Sponsors solemnly promised, contrary to the AMA's warnings, that bureaucrats would never come between patient and doctor. Medicare, like the Blues and commercial insurers, would pay reasonable and customary charges for doctors and hospitals alike. In deference to industry's opposition to government bureaucracy, the Medicare legislation gave private insurance companies the lucrative business of processing claims, a needless and costly layer of middlemen who had to be redundantly monitored by government. Drug companies, similarly, would be reimbursed at going rates. All this created a huge new market for the medical-industrial complex, and increased the inflationary bias.

My colleague Paul Starr terms this characteristically American approach to social reform "passive intervention." Organized business has immense political power in the United States. Occasionally, however, reformers muster enough countervailing power to extend social benefits to new groups of citizens—but not to challenge the structural power of dominant industries. This brand of reform thus comes at a terrible price, since it reflects and inflates existing inefficiencies. In the 1960s, this failure to challenge entrenched provider groups and the structure of their system led the Johnson administration to enact a medical-insurance program with a profound inflationary bias. In the 1990s, the same failure to confront entrenched industry structures led the weaker Clinton administration to a spectacular political failure.

PASSIVE INTERVENTION AND INFLATION

In the three decades after Medicare and Medicaid were enacted, there ensued a series of cops-and-robbers games between the forces of cost containment and the forces of cost escalation. Note that all of this occurred within the context of an imperfect market. Whereas the ordinary entrepreneur in a perfect or nearly perfect market maximizes profits by minimizing costs, the medical entrepreneur in a fee-for-service reimbursement system maximizes profits by inflating costs or increasing volume. A simple blood test may bring reimbursement of a few dollars; a CT scan can be billed at several thousand dollars. Small wonder that the U.S. health-care system uses expensive tests at far above the average rate of advanced nations. With CT scanners, there is at least the presumption that the expensive investment benefits health. But there are countless other examples of sheer waste. The science writer Daniel Greenberg recounts the story of going into the hospital for minor surgery, finding himself with a stuffy nose, and requesting nose drops. Instead, a technician brought in a vaporizing device, billed to Greenberg's insurer at forty dollars a day. The consumer's impulse to argue is stifled by the fact that insurance pays. As we shall see, this set of incentives has recently been thrown into reverse, with the shift to "managed care" and "at-risk" contracts. But before we get to that story, the history of a quarter-century of failures to rein in inflation is worth recounting.

In the late 1960s, the general rate of inflation gathered force, first from the Vietnam War, later from the OPEC oil shocks. Medical inflation, as a special sectoral problem, was not a major driver of these mainly macroeconomic trends, but it became a cause of identified concern, because health-care prices were rising even faster than others.

In 1972, Congress began the first in a series of hapless initiatives in an effort to control medical costs, empowering Medicare to disallow excess costs. Congress also created peer-review bodies, known as Professional Standards Review Organizations (PSROs) to monitor both the quality and the efficiency of medical procedures. (Under the Reagan administration, these were stripped down to Peer-Review Organizations [PROs], privatized, and left with more limited authority.) In 1974, Congress mandated and subsidized a network of state health planning agencies, to constrain redundant medical facilities. This led to the system of requiring health-care entrepreneurs to apply for Certificates of Need, known all too fittingly as CONs, before they could create or expand institutions. This was also repealed as a federal requirement, under Reagan.

At best, these measures restrained medical inflation marginally. Studies found that costs continued to increase, because, as long as profits were to be maximized by maximizing reimbursable costs, entrepreneurs in a fragmented system found avenues around the halfhearted controls. For example, when health-planning agencies began restricting the numbers of new hospital beds, hospitals responded by increasing the capital-intensiveness (and hence the reimbursement rate) of each bed. A hospital bill, once a fairly simple and consolidated bottom line, became an ever more elaborate set of line items. Hospitals began billing literally for every aspirin tablet and every suture. The more the system fragmented, the more the opportunities proliferated to stimulate demand and to find new ways of profiting.

In a second round of cost containment, government sought to reverse these incentives, by promoting prepaid group plans and by changing the system of hospital reimbursement. Group plans, such as California's Kaiser-Permanente or New York's HIP, had long been stepchildren of the medical system, fiercely opposed by the American Medical Association. These plans challenged the prevailing ethic of fee-for-service medicine. Their origins and implicit ideology were almost socialistic; people would pay a fixed monthly fee, then get all the care they needed from doctors affiliated with the plan. Kaiser's roots were in the war-production ethos of the 1940s; HIP's in the social-welfare culture of New York in the 1930s. Both tended to be staffed by socially conscious doctors who embraced a service ethic and took lower pay than their more individualist, entrepreneurial colleagues.

In 1970, as the Nixon administration grappled with rising inflation, a pediatric neurologist named Paul Ellwood proposed transforming the vaguely liberal prepaid group health-care model into a new, safely Republican creature, the Health Maintenance Organization, or HMO. The term, coined by Dr. Ellwood, has passed into the medical jargon. Where the traditional group plan was nonprofit and communitarian in its values, Ellwood's HMO could be nonprofit or for-profit. It could be sponsored by insurance companies, hospitals, or anyone. Ellwood persuaded the Nixon administration to support legislation subsidizing the creation of new HMOs with grants and loans, and requiring large employers who provided health coverage to offer at least one federally approved HMO as an option. This legislation was approved in 1973.

The HMO had two rationales, one political, the other economic. Politically, Democrats and organized labor were pushing a universal national health-insurance plan. HMOs gave the Nixon administration a more "marketlike" Republican alternative that seemingly combined decentralization, consumer choice, and entrepreneurship with the security and cost containment offered by the Democratic single-payer plan. To universalize coverage, Nixon also proposed his companion play-or-pay bill, which, of course, did not become law.

The cost-containment rationale of HMOs was straightforward. Fee-for-service medicine encouraged doctors and hospitals to maximize reimbursable treatment and ignore preventive care. But a prepaid plan must live within a fixed budget, so its financial incentives are reversed. The HMO maximizes its retained earnings or profits by finding the most cost-effective way to treat each patient, by emphasizing low-tech and preventive measures, by relying on physicians' assistants, nurse-practitioners, technicians, and general practitioners rather than on expensive specialists, and by limiting unnecessary surgery and inflated technology. The shift to HMOs, sponsors hoped, would use market incentives to reverse at last the spiral of medical inflation.

At the end of 1995, an estimated fifty-five million Americans were enrolled in HMOs. But, remarkably, the growth of HMOs has had only a marginal effect on the inefficiency of the larger health-care system. Between 1982 and 1990, Blue Cross/Blue Shield premiums on traditional fee-for-service ("indemnity") plans increased by 112 percent. During the same period, HMO premiums increased by 106 percent. The reasons for this unimpressive performance have to do with the broader inefficiencies embedded in the American health-care system of which HMOs are a part, and the fragmentation to which competing HMOs contribute.

Even the ostensible cost-savings of HMOs are partly illusory, because HMOs generally market to healthier populations; sicker people often prefer indemnity plans that allow freer choice of doctor and hospital. Moreover, HMOs tend to "shadow-price" conventional insurance plans, underpricing them by just a shade. As the price of conventional insurance rises, the price of HMO insurance has followed—another example of market power and imperfect competition in the health sector.

Several studies have found that HMO members have fewer and shorter hospital admissions than members of fee-for-service plans. However, it is not clear how much of this savings reflects the selective recruitment of a healthier population by HMOs, how much reflects denial of necessary care, and how much is genuine gain via pursuit of the most appropriate treatment. Nor is it clear that HMOs reduce the rate of increase in medical costs after an initial savings substantially based on risk selection.

The other federal strategy for limiting health-care inflation involved changing the way hospitals got paid. In the early 1980s, Congress revised the Medicare payment system, which by then accounted for about 35 percent of all hospital reimbursements. Instead of compensating hospitals for their actual costs, the Department of Health and Human Services (HHS) adopted an elaborate set of schedules, first developed at Yale University, known as "diagnosis-related groups," or "DRGs."

The DRGs, for 467 separate medical conditions, sought to establish standard reimbursement rates, regardless of length of stay, based on the cost of treating a typical case. Some cases, of course, are more costly to treat than others. But over time, the law of averages would ensure that hospitals received reasonable compensation. They would have a financial incentive not to overtreat any one case, since they would no longer benefit by increasing the intensiveness of treatment. This strategy was further embellished with a Prospective Payment System (PPS), which adjusted reimbursement rates by region.

But even the DRG/PPS system had elaborate special exceptions, waivers, capital-cost reimbursements, subsidies for teaching hospitals, wiggle room for diagnosis inflation, and an exemption for states with their own systems of rate regulation. This system did not significantly restrain Medicare inflation either, though it did reduce the profitability of each Medicare admission. Meanwhile, the Medicaid program for the poor, never as popular or well funded as Medicare, gradually ratcheted down eligibility requirements and reimbursement levels. By the mid-1980s, the typical hospital was losing money on Medicaid, roughly breaking even on Medicare, and shifting its costs to the more generously reimbursed part of the system—that financed by Blue Cross/Blue Shield and the big private insurers. Typically, the identical procedure at a hospital could command any of several different reimbursements, depending on whether the patient was insured by Medicare, Medicaid, Blue Cross, or a commercial insurer, or was paying out of pocket. But despite the game of shift-the-cost, hospitals were running out of payers who would bear full freight.

FROM COST INFLATION TO PRIVATE REGULATION

Three decades of "passive intervention" failed spectacularly. It produced neither universal coverage, security of access, clinical autonomy, nor containment of costs. The effort to shift costs and the countereffort to contain them each became a new source of cost inflation. The market simply proved too much for its half-hearted public regulators. And in the aftermath of the 1994 failure of comprehensive health-care reform, the system reverted to intensified private regulation.

Using "managed care," insurance plans began regulating how hospitals treated patients, rather than just passively paying bills. Given that many metropolitan areas had surpluses of hospital beds, insurers also used their market power to negotiate discounted rates, and to encourage consumers to shift to HMOs, in which cost containment could be even more intensive.

By 1993, traditional indemnity policies covered less than 50 percent of insured Americans, and a majority of health plans were tightly managed—subject to utilization reviews, price discounting, gatekeeping by primary-care physicians, and often prior approval before an insured patient could be admitted to the hospital. Insurance-company reviewers also participated in approving treatment protocols and "discharge planning," setting the number of days a patient could stay in the hospital. As a result of these disciplines, more treatments were performed on an outpatient basis, fewer patients were authorized to see specialists, and hospital stays progressively shortened.

Large employers also took steps to cut their costs. Rather than contracting with insurance companies to underwrite risks, many big corporations became self-insured, retaining an insurance company to manage the plan but not to bear the risk. This move cut administrative costs, but was also motivated to take advantage of a loophole in the Employee Retirement Income Security Act of 1974 (ERISA), which regulates pension and health benefits—but exempts from state or federal regulation the details of health plans of companies that self-insure. Thus, companies that self-insure could arbitrarily change the terms of coverage, and even drop employees who contracted costly illnesses such as AIDS, despite state regulations to the contrary.

Companies also shaved their own expenses by shifting costs to their employees, through reduced coverage, the sharing of premium costs with employees, and the introduction of copay requirements in plans that once paid the entire cost of treatment. During the 1980s, more than 80 percent of collective-bargaining disputes involved proposed cutbacks in health coverage. By the early 1990s, large companies were at last reporting that their own health-insurance costs were rising more slowly. But most of this had come from shifting costs to employees, not from genuine efficiency gains.

Insurance plans, whether sponsored by large corporations, commercial insurers, Blue Cross/Blue Shield, or HMOs, also began organizing networks of approved physicians, who would agree to accept a discounted fee and to follow the plans' treatment guidelines in exchange for patient referrals. And rather than reimbursing hospitals case by case or procedure by procedure—the traditional fee-for-service model—insurance plans and HMOs began negotiating "capitation" contracts that paid flat fees for the treatment of so many insured "lives" and left hospitals and doctors bearing all or part of the financial risk of treatment.

Many insurance plans entered into secret contractual deals with hospitals that seemed to violate the plain language of their contract with the subscriber. For example, the typical health plan contained inpatient mental-health benefits of up to sixty days per spell of illness. But the actual contract between the health plan and the psychiatric hospital might stipulate that the hospital would make sure that the average inpatient stay was only five days, or bear the loss.

Many insurance plans operate on an 80-20 cost-sharing basis: the patient pays 20 percent of charges and the plan pays 80 percent until a major-medical feature kicks in. But contracts between plans and hospitals typically negotiated payment at a discounted rate. So a given operation might be billed at a sticker price of $10,000, of which the subscriber is obligated to bear a copayment of $2,000 (20 percent of $10,000). However, if the insurer has a contract to pay the hospital a discounted rate, say fifty cents on the billed dollar, the insurer would pay only $5,000, not the nominal $10,000 charge. The subscriber, however, gets a copayment bill based on the full (and fictitious), undiscounted rate. So the subscriber, despite a contractual 20-percent copayment rate, actually pays 40 percent ($2,000 out of $5,000). Consumers in several states have filed lawsuits to block this double bookkeeping at patient expense. In June 1995, Blue Cross and Blue Shield of Minnesota settled one such class-action lawsuit, reimbursing subscribers some $3.9 million, and promising to begin charging coinsurance at the real discounted rate rather than the nominal rate. Similar suits are pending in other states.

Far from generating improved efficiencies, employers and insurers were compelling consumers to pay out of pocket or do without. Private-market forces also cost-shifted to government, since their reduced payments to doctors and hospitals had the effect of compelling Medicare, Medicaid, and local public hospitals to make up the loss. Ironically, this result was perceived as a crisis of the public part of the system, which was blamed for being relatively less efficient than the private.

HOSPITAL CHAINS

The shift to consolidation and private regulation can be vividly seen in recent changes in the hospital industry, where investor-owned chains are growing explosively. Historically, one segment of the hospital industry was for-profit, but such hospitals were invariably locally owned. In less than a decade, the vast majority have now become owned by absentee companies, usually the result of merger-and-acquisition binges orchestrated by entrepreneurs.

Hospitals today are experiencing the same kind of cost squeeze, downsizing, and consolidation typical of other industries in the new, hyper-marketized environment. Mergers and joint ventures are proliferating, as hospitals scramble to find ways to remain in the game. Some of these deals border on the bizarre, as when a Catholic charity hospital merges with a fiercely for-profit chain.

In this climate, nonprofit institutions and norms are being squeezed out by for-profit ones. The most aggressive chain is a company called Columbia/HCA, itself the result of three prior mergers. Columbia/HCA, founded only in 1988, now owns 346 hospitals, many of them converted from previous nonprofit status.

The typical acquisition pattern is this: A chain like Columbia/HCA, armed with investor capital and its capacity to borrow in financial markets, comes into a community that has excess hospital beds, and makes a struggling nonprofit hospital an offer it can't refuse. The chain also promises town officials that a tax-exempt institution will be converted to one that generates tax revenues. It often buys off key trustees and other key hospital officials. Once a hospital is "in play," the sale becomes almost a foregone conclusion; the only questions are who will buy it, on what terms, and who will benefit. After a hospital has been acquired, spartan cost economies are instituted—layoffs, increased hours and reduced pay for remaining medical personnel, closing or trimming of facilities deemed unnecessary.

With a reduced cost structure, the for-profit hospital can then offer to contract with insurance plans for so many insured "lives" at a reduced rate, underpricing local competing hospitals. Some hospitals are bought by the big chains only to be closed, in the time-tested way that a monopolist acquires competitors to shut them down and better dictate price. Acquisition of hospitals is often part of a corporate strategy to build a complete network of regional health facilities, ranging from HMOs to walk-in clinics, outpatient-surgery centers, home-care operations, pathology labs, and so on, aimed at further increasing market penetration and power.

In principle, all of this wrings out overutilization and excess capacity, and offers administrative efficiencies. But such rationalization of facilities under private, profit-motivated auspices invites extreme conflicts of interest, as well as pursuit of short-run gain at the expense of long-term efficiency. For example, in the case of Columbia/HCA, representatives of the company sometimes offer board members and executives of nonprofit community hospitals very lucrative deals that border on bribes, in exchange for approving the takeover. Columbia also typically demands letters of confidentiality before it commences negotiations. As a result, the public may never learn all the terms of the deal, or whether the formerly nonprofit hospital sold for a fair price. (Ironically, if these were for-profit hospitals, financial details would have to be disclosed under the securities laws.)

In Tennessee, Columbia/HCA's home state, Nashville Memorial Hospital was bought for somewhere in the range of $60 million to $120 million (the exact figure was never disclosed). The assets were turned over to a newly created foundation. Not coincidentally, the foundation hired as its president the former CEO of the hospital, J. D. Elliot, who had been a key player in orchestrating the deal to deliver the hospital. In Dickson, Tennessee, a local state legislator served as a trustee of Goodlark Hospital before its sale to Columbia, and as president of the foundation afterward. In other contexts, these examples of self-dealing would constitute a flat breach of fiduciary duty and an illegal kickback.

These conversions illustrate how markets fail to price things properly in mixed realms with extra-market goals. In a highly imperfect market (such as the market for a nonprofit hospital), the market price is the "right" price only in the tautological sense that it represents what a willing buyer pays a willing seller at a point in time. This is hardly a free market, since there is only one seller and one buyer, and often collusion rather than arm's-length bargaining between seller and buyer.

Given all the other departures from perfect competition, it is not clear that market principles can properly be applied to the sale of a nonprofit hospital at all. When the property at stake is a community hospital, its present asset value represents many decades of benefactors' making donations for the good of the community. These include charitable contributions, local government subsidies in the form of forgone property taxes, and slightly below-market fees accepted by doctors for the good of the community.

With an acquisition by a for-profit company, what occurs is really the one-time windfall conversion of nonmarket social assets to market ones, and the one-time capture of capitalized forgone profit. In effect, the entrepreneur is arbitraging between two kinds of markets—one of them a social market, in which norms of service limit opportunism, the other a conventional and profit-maximizing market. The entrepreneur pockets the difference, at the expense of the hospital's social objectives. Further, this is hardly an arm's-length transaction, since it often involves a panic sale by a hospital board worried about whether it can stay open at all, coupled with personal inducements offered by the acquiring chain.

As the Tennessee story shows, the conversion of a nonprofit hospital is no free market in another sense—because it is highly politicized, which distorts the market model even further. Columbia/HCA is notorious for spending large sums on lobbying and campaign contributions to win the cooperation of public officials whose approval is needed in these conversions.

In Cleveland, Columbia negotiated a joint venture with four Catholic hospitals operated by the Sisters of Charity of St. Augustine. This is ostensibly a fifty-fifty partnership: the hospitals retain their Catholic identity, but Columbia gets operating control. Catholic hospitals, of course, were set up to serve needy patients. Nuns work for far less than market wages. This kind of joint venture has been very unpopular in the Catholic health-care community, since it represents both a subsidy of for-profit institutions by nonprofit ones, and a plain corruption of the religious mission. John E. Curley, president of the Catholic Health Association, told his 1995 convention, "Simply put, the investor-owned model is not compatible with the Church's mission in health care. . . . Our Church ministry sees health care as an essential human service; investor-owned chains see health care as a commodity to be exchanged for a profit."

For-profit chains like Columbia/HCA claim to increase efficiencies by centralizing administration, cutting waste, buying supplies in bulk at discounted rates, negotiating discounted fees with medical professionals, shifting to less wasteful forms of care, and consolidating duplicative facilities. (By that logic, the most efficient "chain" of all is a universal national system.) But for-profit chains also cut costs by cutting care and by shifting the costs of treating unprofitable cases to other parts of the system. According to *Business Week*, nonprofit hospitals in areas where Columbia/HCA moves in complain that they get stuck with an escalating fraction of charity cases. At Kendall Regional Hospital, near Miami, which Columbia/HCA bought in 1991, uncompensated and charity care declined from $10.1 million to $8.6 million between 1992 and 1994, while the load of nearby Baptist Hospital, a nonprofit, rose from $14.5 million to $19.7 million.

During 1995, fifty-nine sales of nonprofit hospitals to for-profit alone were announced, with more in negotiation. Since charitable institutions are not profit-maximizing creatures to begin with, these sales raise thorny legal, ethical, and economic issues. Should the incumbent trustees benefit financially? Should the acquiring company be obligated to keep the facility open? What public authority should represent the community interest? Under the well-established common-law doctrine, a charitable corporation that has raised funds for one set of purposes is not free to convert its assets to new purposes, nor are executives of charities free to convert assets to personal benefit. But that is precisely what occurs when a for-profit buys out a nonprofit. Some conversions have circumvented this stricture by transferring assets to a nominally nonprofit foundation that is closely controlled by the parent for-profit corporation. At this writing, the attorneys general of several states are investigating whether these conversions violate the rules under which public charities are supposed to operate.

It's not at all clear that these investor-owned networks even create true administrative efficiencies. Their main purpose is to maximize referral strength and market power, to rationalize the reduction of facilities that have become duplicative in the new, leaner environment, to squeeze more out of doctors and nurses, resist costly treatment modalities, avoid the traditional money-losing missions of research, education, and the treatment of uninsured patients, and to negotiate for the maximum number of insured "lives," preferably healthy ones, at the maximum reimbursement or capitation rate. The epidemic of reorganization is also driven substantially by entrepreneurs who see profit opportunities in assets temporarily undervalued by markets, and there are countless instances of hospitals' being sold and then resold, acquisitions followed by spinoffs, and huge windfall profits. All of this is "efficient" only if one believes that everything markets do is efficient by definition. It doesn't necessarily produce the optimal configuration of health facilities, which is a social goal beyond the comprehension of markets.

Another key distinction is also pertinent. Though some hospitals have long been for-profit institutions, the shift to for-profit hospitals that are *shareholder-owned chains* brings an important qualitative shift. Even if a local surgeon is very well paid relative to the local standard of living, and even if the local hospital is a for-profit establishment, these people still have to live in the community and answer to it. That reality tends to temper the goal of pure profit-making with more complex norms, and to place limits on opportunism. Not so with an absentee chain, which simply views a local hospital as another financial asset, to be downsized, reorganized, or closed out, as unsentimentally as a share of stock. To put this point in language intelligible to the economist, one of the very high costs of marketization in health care is the squeezing out of extra-market norms that serve as an economically valuable and socially irreplaceable public good. To paraphrase Captain Yossarian of *Catch-22*, if everyone else is acting like an entrepreneur, the doctor who acts to serve humanity is a damned fool.

This "rationalization" of hospital resources under market auspices is short-sighted and inefficient in yet another sense. It creates an immense cost-squeeze for such justifiably high-cost institutions as specialized ("tertiary-care") hospitals, teaching hospitals, and nonprofit voluntary and public hospitals, which traditionally treat a higher fraction of uninsured patients as part of their community mission. This now becomes more difficult, since there are fewer and fewer payers to bear the cost.

Teaching hospitals, for example, have historically been subsidized indirectly, by charitable contributions, by tax-exempt status, by extra Medicare payments that recognize the higher overhead costs of teaching institutions, and by the willingness of private insurers to reimburse teaching hospitals at higher rates that reflect higher embedded costs. Historically, this system amounted to a tacit cross-subsidy. Free-market economists tend not to like cross-subsidies, since they interfere with the "transparency" that, in a pure market, makes for better-informed and hence more rational decisions by market actors. As the health-care system endeavors to become more marketlike, teaching hospitals are revealed as high-cost providers, and HMOs and insurance plans seek to avoid them or to demand that they lower their rates. However, there is no way for teaching hospitals to lower their rates to levels comparable to nonteaching ones without abandoning the teaching mission—or shifting the cost entirely to students, which is prohibitive.

Education of the next generation of doctors is, of course, another public good—one that the logic of short-term profit maximization cannot recognize. The current system may well produce too many doctors and too many specialists. That is certainly a fair subject for public debate. More rational, extra-market systems in other advanced countries simply recognize the public-good nature of medical education, and finance it directly as a line item in the national budget, setting national goals for specialists and primary-care doctors. This allows a measure of rational planning for the future, and avoids the game of pass-the-cost. This was also the approach offered in the now defunct Clinton Health Security Plan. Some critics of the tacit subsidy of medical education via reimbursement argue that there are too many doctors anyway, that teaching hospitals collect windfalls from Medicare and from insurance reimbursements, and that it's high time for a shakeout. But the market is too myopic to perform this task competently. It is far more efficient for a planning process to assess the demand for the next generation of doctors, and fine-tune how the subsidy is allocated.

A related form of damage is that, in this entrepreneurial environment, nonprofit institutions find themselves behaving more and more like for-profits—avoiding the burden of caring for expensive and hardship cases, limiting costly research and teaching, advertising for market share, conceiving of the healing enterprise as cost centers versus profit centers, and entering into dubious joint ventures that contradict the spirit of their original mission. To exquisitely complete the circle, the defensive imitation of for-profits by nonprofits then allows the big chains to argue that nonprofits are really not so different after all. Why, Columbia/HCA repeatedly asks in its public-relations materials, should nonprofits get special treatment?

These new market values seem to have been internalized even by those who stand for a different set of norms. One chief executive of a very distinguished teaching hospital sighed ruefully to a colleague, "The chairman of my board keeps reminding me that the market is always right"—as if he were belatedly learning an incontrovertible law of economics. But in necessarily mixed sectors such as health care, the market is often wrong.

FROM PREPAID GROUP HEALTH TO FOR-PROFIT HMO

As the entire medical marketplace has become more entrepreneurial, for-profit HMOs have been growing at the fastest rate. They overtook nonprofits for the first time in 1992, and now have about two-thirds of all HMO members.

In the new era of intensified marketization, HMOs have intensified their own cost-cutting. Especially in for-profit HMOs, doctors report increasing case-loads, less time to treat each patient, and pressure not to refer to specialists. As one HMO primary-care physician employed by Humana explained to me, the system of very short appointments functions effectively as a form of risk selection. Young and healthy patients who come in for the occasional sore throat like the system: their care is efficient and delivered with no out-of-pocket charge. Sicker patients, with complex symptoms and elaborate histories of multiple diseases, cannot possibly be treated in a fifteen-minute appointment. Those who have other options tend to leave. High turnover is inefficient for the system as a whole—new doctors need to take the time to learn about new patients; long-standing relations of trust get disrupted—but Humana likes it just fine, since the effect is to squeeze in young, healthy patients and squeeze out older, sicker ones. Of course, as the cost squeeze intensifies, nobody wants the older, sicker people, and illusory "savings" are achieved simply by denying them necessary care.

Older HMOs tend to follow the group-practice or "staff" model, whereby most participating physicians function in a cliniclike setting. Newer hybrids, such as the Independent Practice Association (IPA) or Preferred Provider Organization (PPO), are variants in which participating doctors are far-flung independent contractors who agree to take referrals at a discount and follow the plan's spartan approach to care. None of the teamwork benefits of a true group practice obtain; the purpose is simply to cut costs. The sponsoring organization regularly reviews its panel of physicians and, in the antiseptic jargon, "de-selects," i.e., fires, those "outliers" who consistently incur more expenses than average. Thanks to private managed care, the most conscientious physicians, who take adequate time to listen to patients and involve them in their treatment, and who use specialists as necessary, are under pressure to sacrifice their livelihood. One physician, Dr. David Himmelstein, an internist at Cambridge Hospital in Massachusetts, was conspicuously de-selected by U.S. Healthcare, after he wrote a guest editorial in *The New England Journal of Medicine* criticizing for-profit HMOs.

In the District of Columbia, the Blue Cross and Blue Shield system organized a Select Preferred Provider program that eventually included about half the doctors in the D.C. metro area. But unlike most such preferred provider networks, which accept any physician willing to accept discounted fees and to follow broad protocols, Blue Cross/Blue Shield created a data base and refused to enlist doctors who seemed to be ordering more tests, referring patients to specialists at above-average rates, and generating costly hospitalizations. Some states have laws requiring such plans to accept "any willing provider," but D.C. has no such law. At this writing, the Medical Society of the District of Columbia has filed suit to block the plan; similar suits have been filed in California, Florida, and Texas, over the way in which HMOs and other managed-care systems select and dismiss physicians.

A related problem in HMOs, especially for-profit ones, is the injection of conflicts of interest in the doctor-patient relationship. HMOs reimburse doctors in a variety of ways. Some pay flat salaries, or salaries based on the physician's caseload. But as the competitive market environment has intensified, more HMOs have been shifting to forms of payment that either share the HMO's annual profits with the doctor or, worse, place the doctor at financial risk for his medical decisions by giving her a flat fee per patient and then having the doctor bear the cost of treatment. A doctor who orders fewer tests, makes fewer referrals to specialists, and minimizes his patients' hospital stays reaps a financial bonus. One who behaves more conscientiously earns less, and is hectored, sanctioned, or fired.

Newspapers have reported innumerable scandals involving HMOs that skimped on necessary treatments, selectively marketed in crude ways, harassed participating physicians, and otherwise betrayed the promise of prepaid group health care. A number of HMOs put the physician and patient in an excruciating bind by refusing to compensate emergency-room care if the verdict turned out to be a false alarm. So, if a patient calls his primary doctor in the middle of the night reporting chest pains, and the doctor urges him to go to the emergency room, both can be penalized if the malady turns out to be digestive.

One HMO denied reimbursement when a biopsy revealed a breast lump to be benign. Of course, if the doctor, under the constraint of HMO guidelines, tells the patient to wait until morning and the heart attack turns out to be real, or the lump turns out to be malignant, the doctor rather than the HMO is likely to be sued.

When Tennessee became one of the few states to seek almost universal coverage, relying heavily on HMOs to cover the poor and near-poor, it set off a marketing stampede. OmniCare, the most aggressive of the companies, went so far as to enroll felons at the state penitentiary (who weren't eligible). OmniCare itself was only formed in 1993—its key organizer was a former state representative—to take advantage of the new TennCare legislation, which made some 1.2 million Tennesseans eligible for Medicaid-style HMOs. OmniCare is also under fire for aggressive risk selection. Its marketing strategy, according to *The New York Times*, explicitly includes avoidance of those likely to become sick. This is deplorable enough in ordinary insurance marketing, but even worse when most of the covered population were previously entitled to automatic coverage (under conventional Medicaid).

Perhaps the most notorious of the HMO scandals occurred in Florida, with its large retired population. Like Tennessee, Florida created financial incentives for Medicaid HMOs (but without seeking universal coverage for the near-poor). The result, as documented in an award-winning series by the *Sun-Sentinel* newspaper of Fort Lauderdale, was a gold-rush mentality coupled with shabby care. One large HMO, whose chief executive was making over a million dollars a year, was paying out only 50 percent of its receipts in patient care. Another actually kept all but twenty-three cents on the dollar. This compares with the 15- to 20-percent overhead ratio of non-Medicaid Florida HMOs. A number of patients had been de-selected (kicked out) after becoming ill. Following the *Sun-Sentinel*'s series, in December 1994, Douglas Cook, director of Florida's Agency for Health Care Administration, ordered a moratorium on the approval of new Medicaid HMOs.

There is also a plain contradiction between two of the key selling points of HMOs made by marketizers. In principle, HMOs save costs because they have a financial incentive to keep members healthy. But the other argument made by advocates of competition is that consumers discipline providers by shopping around among competing health "products." Obviously, an HMO with high turnover has no incentive to invest in the long-term health of its members. Paradoxically (and cynically), many HMOs showcase fitness centers, yoga classes, and the like, less as a public-health strategy than as a risk-stratification device. Healthier people are more likely to be attracted to a health plan that offers a free fitness center. Only in a universal system are such investments truly cost-effective, both for the society and the health-care system.

In a less ruthlessly competitive environment, there is much about the HMO model that is attractive. Traditional nonprofit prepaid group plans, with an ideology of service as well as consumer accountability, offer genuine opportunities to spend the same health dollars more efficiently and compassionately. By using public-health-style screenings, prepaid group plans can allocate expensive capital equipment more rationally. By emphasizing wellness, diet, exercise, regular checkups, and immunization, they can create a higher baseline level of good health among their members. By using nurse-practitioners, midwives, and outpatient procedures, and relying on second opinions, they can divert resources from overutilized venues to ones that have been starved for resources. By emphasizing team treatment and good communication within an on-site medical staff, they can realize genuine efficiencies. These trade-offs seem to work best, however, outside a context of competition for market share and profit maximization, where dollars saved are more likely to be diverted to shareholders or new acquisitions or lower charges for client corporations, rather than recycled within the HMO to more appropriate forms of treatment.

A good example of this kind of group health plan is the Group Health Cooperative of Puget Sound. That HMO, which operates in the spirit of the original prepaid group-health model, is owned by its consumer-members, not by an absentee corporation. It is not seeking to expand market share as an end in itself. By emphasizing wellness, and being parsimonious with the unnecessary use of testing and referral to specialists, GHCPS is able to redirect money to primary care. Patient satisfaction is consistently high. However, in the new environment of cost-cutting, good HMOs like Group Health of Puget Sound are under pressure to match the false economies of cheaper for-profit competitors, lest they be dropped by large employers as too expensive.

Some form of managed care is inevitable, whether in public systems or private ones. Unfortunately, in the hyper-entrepreneurial environment of the 1990s, where cost-cutting for its own sake is paramount, where the doctor is encouraged to think like an entrepreneur, where insurers are fiercely battling for market share, and where outright corruption is part of the landscape, a malign form of managed care may drive out the benign form.

If health care were an ordinary market, HMOs that treated patients shabbily would lose their customers. But at least three factors, characteristic of health-care markets, prevent this kind of discipline from operating.

First, consumers are imperfectly informed. HMOs spend billions of dollars on marketing campaigns, often misleading ones. But the customer is told little about the true financial incentives or hidden rules governing the HMO.

Second, the real consumer is the employer who typically pays the premium, not the patient. When for-profit HMOs market to employers, they tend to stress cost savings, not patient satisfaction.

The third problem is lock-in. Under present federal regulations, a Medicare HMO has to take any Medicare subscriber who subscribes, and the member is free to switch plans once a year. But there is no such rule for patients under age sixty-five. A patient with a pre-existing condition, or whose employer offers a single, take-it-or-leave-it plan, has no ability to switch HMOs, no matter how great his dissatisfaction.

Just as in the case of hospitals, as for-profit companies come to dominate the HMO sector, nonprofit HMOs defensively begin to imitate for-profit ones— risk selecting, limiting services, aggressively marketing, and building networks whose logic is more entrepreneurial than clinical.

MANAGED CARE AND MENTAL HEALTH

Mental health illustrates the clash of market and medicine at its extreme, since much diagnosis is subjective and much treatment can be dismissed as elective. Psychiatrists working for HMOs typically function more as gatekeepers than as therapists, encouraging troubled patients to use medication or short-term groups, instead of costlier psychotherapy or inpatient care. To a degree, this is legitimate. Society cannot afford to pay the cost of every ambulatory neurotic who might benefit from a long-term "talking cure." One patient with a moderately serious disorder who sought psychiatric treatment from the Harvard Community Health Plan reported to me, only half-jokingly, that the "gatekeeper" psychiatrist must have been chosen for the job because he was the sort of person in whom no one would want to confide. This patient fled. Eventually, she persisted and was assigned another therapist, who offered a total of three sessions. Unfortunately, such a deterrent strategy does not just discourage unnecessary psychotherapy. As a number of lawsuits have revealed, zealous HMOs also endeavor to bar people with major mental illnesses from necessary treatments, sometimes with tragic results.

In one case that I reported for *The New Republic*, a man named Lawrence Megge, a thirty-four-year-old machinist, killed himself and his wife after having repeatedly sought treatment for extreme depression, delusions, suicidal tendencies, and sexual abnormalities. Megge's health plan, SelectCare of Michigan, nominally had excellent mental-health benefits, but had contracted with a managed-care company called American Biodyne to take over its mental-health cases. As is typical with this kind of contract, known as a "carve-out," Biodyne took a few dollars per month per patient from SelectCare, and assumed the financial risk of their mental-health treatment. Biodyne boasts that it cuts the number of hospital admissions in half, and the average stay from fifteen to twenty days to less than a week. In the Megge case, Biodyne psychologists twice overruled emergency-room physicians who recommended that he be immediately hospitalized.

In most cases, managed-care entrepreneurs like Biodyne escape legal liability for this spartan gatekeeping via the disingenuous pretense that second-guessing doctors is something other than practicing medicine. Under civil commitment statutes, the doctor has a duty to hospitalize a patient who is "dangerous to self or others." Managed-care companies like Biodyne take the position that, if the doctor on the scene thinks the utilization reviewer at the end of the 800 number is really wrong, the doctor has a duty to hospitalize the patient and argue about who pays the bill later. This contention is doubly disingenuous, since the participating doctor's very livelihood often depends on not antagonizing the managed-care company.

In the Megge case, Biodyne and SelectCare settled a lawsuit filed by Megge's children for an undisclosed sum, reportedly in excess of a million dollars. But in most cases, plaintiffs' attorneys refuse to sue managed-care companies, because of the civil-commitment loophole. Instead, they sue the doctor first and the general health plan second. The American Psychiatric Association has sought state laws that would define the practice of managed care that second-guesses doctors as tantamount to the practice of medicine. This would appropriately expose companies such as Biodyne to the consequences of their actions. At this writing, no such laws have been enacted.

Two decades ago, the mental-health system was the extreme case of feast or famine. The typical health-insurance plan offered only minimal outpatient mental-health benefits, but if the subscriber was seriously ill, it would pay for sixty days of inpatient care, at several hundred dollars a day. This was a system crying out for rationalization. But despite the promise by managed-care companies to match condition with intervention through a seamless "continuum of care," ranging from medication to short-term therapy to day treatment and halfway houses to full hospitalization, this promise has not materialized—because, done properly, it is expensive. Risk selection is much cheaper. If patients with expensive conditions are driven away by the red tape and unfriendly personnel, this is of course just what the HMO wants. Great economies could certainly be realized by a system that offered a continuum of appropriate care—but a fragmented, profit-driven system does not get us there. A true continuum of mental-health care is more closely approximated in nations with universal health systems, in which there is far less financial incentive for profit maximizing or cost shifting.

THE ALLURE OF THE MARKET MODEL

For nearly two decades, market-oriented economists have sought marketlike remedies for the imperfections in health-care markets. The intellectual fathers of this movement include the aforementioned Alain Enthoven and Paul Ellwood. In the early 1960s, Enthoven was one of Robert McNamara's "whiz kids" at the Pentagon. In the 1970s, he was a supporter of universal, government-mandated health coverage. In the 1980s, he invented the "managed-competition" model that inspired the Clinton Health Security Plan; at this writing, he has given up on universal coverage entirely and jumped on the private-regulation bandwagon.

Enthoven, along with Paul Ellwood, the physician who conceived HMOs, is a leading member of the influential Jackson Hole Group, a network of market-oriented economists and health- and insurance-industry figures. The Jackson Hole Group is a cross-fertilization of several purposes—intellectual, entrepreneurial, political. For the insurance industry it has offered a model to stay in business, if and when the demand for universal health insurance becomes politically irresistible. For the economists, it offered a prestigious forum to try out a blend of market and extra-market concepts that changed the existing system only incrementally, and to earn lucrative consulting fees for certifying the soundness of pro-competitive reform.

Enthoven's big idea, widely embraced by other enthusiasts of pro-competitive regulation, is that solitary patients cannot serve the usual economic function of sovereign consumers, because of the well-known market failures described above. What Enthoven envisioned, therefore, was managed competition *among health plans*, with each offering a package of services and prices, and each having an incentive to control rather than inflate costs.

More recent writings on competitive reform have added the thought that, though individual patients are naïve and imperfectly informed health consumers, corporations are sophisticated consumers. The corporation, as a discerning buyer choosing among competing health plans, functions as a surrogate for the individual employee, carefully balancing cost and benefit. One enthusiast terms this "a shift from 'patient-driven' to 'payer-driven' competition between providers, with important resultant benefits in terms of prices and costs." Thus, market incentives, in service of more rational use of medical resources and cost containment, are at last brought to both sides of the health-care transaction.

Writing in 1980, Enthoven declared, "In an appropriately designed system of fair economic competition among various types of health plan, including traditional insurance and fee-for-service as one option, consumers who join health plans that do a good job of controlling costs would pay lower premiums or receive better benefits. Health plans that do a poor job of controlling costs would lose customers and risk being driven out of business. In the long run, the surviving health plans would be the ones that offer good value to their members. The health system would be transformed, gradually and voluntarily, from today's system with built-in cost-increasing incentives to a system with built-in incentives for consumer satisfaction and cost-control."

This one paragraph captures all the hopes, heroic assumptions, and, ultimately, fallacies of pro-market health-care reform. First, it assumes that competing health plans will take a high road of offering better service, rather than a low road of risk selection and secret financial incentives to participating doctors. Second, it assumes consumers will have a free choice among competing plans. Third, it assumes that good plans will drive out the bad ones, rather than vice versa. Fourth, it assumes that plans will not acquire a degree of monopoly power. And it presumes that consumers will be adequately informed about competing plans.

The use of the employer as proxy for the consumer entails another heroic assumption—that the corporation has the employee's best interests at heart. That may have described an earlier era, one already fading at the time Enthoven wrote, in which corporations and their employees had tolerably symmetrical bargaining power. Hard as it is to believe today, a generation ago corporations actually competed for employees by striving to offer very attractive health-benefit packages. Today, such corporations are the exception, and companies are increasingly giving employees stripped-down health plans, or only one choice of plan.

In effect, Enthoven relied on one extra-market norm and source of extra-market power—the custom of firms' providing good employee health coverage—to compensate for another aspect of market failure in health care—the imperfectly informed and disempowered health-care consumer. But as the labor market has become more of a spot market (see chapter 3), the company can no longer be relied upon to serve as surrogate health-care purchaser in the consumer's best interests.

At the core of pro-market reform is one more unreal premise—and a highly ironic one. The whole schema depends on a heroic degree of regulation, to prevent an opportunistic race to the bottom. One could fill an entire chapter discussing the kind and extent of regulations necessary to make such a system work. Enthoven himself, in the course of proposing a plan contrasting virtuous market incentives with dubious government regulation, calls for literally dozens of regulations necessary to make his system work.

In Enthoven's original (1978–80) managed-competition system, consumers would have a free choice once a year to switch plans; at least one traditional "indemnity" plan would have to be included among the options. Consumers would receive subsidies to buy their health-plan membership: "The subsidy might be greater for people with lower incomes than for people with higher incomes, more for the old than the young, larger for families than for individuals, more for people in one geographical area or bargaining unit than those in another. . . ." Further, each plan would have to use community rating (see page 143), cover a minimal package of "basic health services," and disclose extensive information. Enthoven has also proposed, in a plain contradiction, that higher premiums could be "charged to people in categories with higher average medical costs. Insurance is still made affordable for people in the higher cost categories by providing them with higher government subsidies." In his later, Jackson Hole plan (1988–91), Enthoven added the idea of risk adjustment, to compensate plans that attracted more costly populations—as well as dozens more regulations. But none of this spontaneously arises from private-market forces. It takes government to promulgate the regulations and pay the subsidies.

Though Enthoven inspired and lobbied heavily for Clinton's embrace of managed competition, in the end he deserted the Clinton plan. Clinton's advisers had added two key features that offended Enthoven's market sensibilities. They wanted, to the greatest extent possible within the managed-competition model, to break the link between employment and health insurance. Clinton envisioned that most employees would have a free choice of plan, purchased directly from a "health alliance" and subsidized by the employer. Only very large employers could sponsor their own plans. Second, Clinton added to the Enthoven plan a total national budgetary cap, in case managed competition by itself failed to restrain costs adequately. Ironically, Enthoven had written in his 1988 version of managed competition that "the presence of even several health plans in an area does not guarantee that competition will be lively. The market may be segmented, or a pattern of 'live and let live' may evolve." Yet Enthoven bitterly attacked Clinton's embellishment as "price control" and joined the opposition.

Clearly, pro-market reform turns out to require massive government regulation. And, contrary to the rest of free-market theory, it further presumes regulators with the wisdom, public-mindedness, and incorruptibility of philosopher-kings. Oddly, Enthoven and kindred spirits are almost oblivious to the regulatory platform on which their scheme depends. In a section of the very book that lays out his health plan, Enthoven includes a discussion headed "Regulation versus Competition." He declares: "Regulation often raises costs to consumers." And "Regulators are often 'captured' by the regulated." And "Regulation often retards beneficial innovation." And "Regulation often depends on coercion. . . . Coercion and uniform standards are wasteful." Yet every ground rule that Enthoven proposes to make his managed system work is, of course, a regulation, one that must be promulgated by none other than the government, warts and all.

In part, President Clinton was ridiculed because he took this problem seriously and attempted to stipulate—in a 1,364-page bill—just what an actual managed-competition regime would entail. For example, regulations would have to certify that plans met a certain basic standard. New government or quasi-government agencies would be necessary to manage and supervise the whole affair. Plan operators would be prohibited from resorting to most kinds of risk selection. Elaborate risk-weighting formulas would be necessary to compensate plans that ended up with sicker subscribers. Indeed, the very fact that consumers would be free to shop around once a year posed another practically insoluble problem. The rational consumer would tend to buy the lowest-cost insurance—until she got seriously ill. Then she would shift to the most expensive plan, with the best coverage. This dynamic tends to frustrate the whole logic of insurance—namely, risk pooling.

The unstated presumption is that all the players in the new market game play according to the rules of the Marquis of Queensberry. They compete, supposedly, by offering patients a wide choice among the most appropriate plans. Consumers then optimize their well-being by knowledgeably selecting the plan that best suits their needs, or by rationally calculating their health and taste for risk, and choosing to spend more or less on insurance premiums versus other outlays. As one scholarly paper put it, "Individuals can tailor their insurance plan to their own tastes—those who are willing to bear more risk can assume higher copayments, for example."

The academic innocence of this brand of theorizing is breathtaking. It presumes the survival of extra-market norms, of the very sort that are being relentlessly undermined by marketization itself. Compare this idealized picture of well-informed consumers and conscientious providers, dwelling happily in a self-correcting market, with the grubby world of kickbacks, lobbyists, risk selection, self-dealing, mergers and acquisitions, windfall profiteering, insurance-plan lock-ins, and really nasty strategizing to avoid subscribers likely to get sick. It ignores the prospect that a company such as National Medical Enterprises can get hit with a $379 million fine for multiple frauds, reorganize itself, change its name, merge, and re-emerge as a major player; that a company such as Golden Rule Insurance, which earns high profits by risk selection, does things like disallowing a $31,569 bill for heart-bypass surgery on the grounds that the subscriber "misrepresented" his health when he took out the policy—by failing to disclose high triglyceride levels.

The market enthusiasts leave out the ugly reality that profit-maximizing venues are rife with opportunism. To limit opportunism, consumers need roughly symmetrical market power with producers. The market may be tolerably self-correcting at dispatching opportunists when we are describing a market for, say, retail dry-cleaning—but not when the market is as imperfect as the one for health care. Here, far from being a rational and informed maximizer of consumer welfare, the patient is a sitting duck.

A further complication is that none of this stays put. Rationalization of a system of managed competition is a moving target. No sooner do regulators make moves than entrepreneurs make countermoves. The regulator is always playing catch-up. To get the flavor of just how potent are the incentives for aggressive risk selection, consider these statistics, derived by the health economist Karen Davis: In 1993, the most costly 10 percent of Medicare patients cost the Medicare program an average of $28,120 a year. The other 90 percent cost an average of just $1,340 a year. To the health-insurance entrepreneur, risk selection—avoiding the sickest—cuts far more costs than any conceivable administrative savings from better case management, bulk purchases, or second opinions. And though the disproportionate costs of treating the elderly in the final weeks of life get most of the publicity, the fact is that approximately the same percentages apply to the under-sixty-five population. Every age group is divided into the basically well and the seriously ill. For all age groups, on average, the sickest 1 percent of the population consume 28 percent of medical costs. So it takes astute regulation indeed to frustrate the incentive to risk-select. The more government cracks down, the greater the incentives—and rewards—to the entrepreneur who can concoct a device for risk stratification that the regulator hasn't yet thought of. The ideal of "managed competition," policed by competent regulators, is in short a kind of infinite regress. No sooner is the system tolerably stable than a new set of opportunisms intrudes, requiring a new set of regulatory responses.

Moreover, the entire regulatory process operates in a political cauldron, in which political investments pay handsome dividends. At this writing, the nursing-home industry is working with Republican allies to rescind federal regulations that mandate minimal standards of institutional nursing care, regulations that were enacted after countless scandals came to light involving aged, helpless patients—not a sovereign consumer among them—strapped to beds, lying in their own filth, because nursing-home operators maximized profits by minimizing staffing ratios. In several states, Blue Cross/Blue Shield is seeking legislative approval to convert to for-profit status, and in some places to get out of the indemnity market altogether, in favor of HMOs. Regulation is invariably a creature of the political process—and so is deregulation. The fact that pro-market reformers opt for regulation in service of a special hybrid called "managed competition" does not moot the political nature of the regulatory process.

A review of the recent economics literature on the use of competition to restrain costs and rationalize resources reveals a kind of intellectual tunnel vision. Enthusiasts imagine an idealized marketplace, where consumers are tolerably well informed and able to discipline providers, where providers are not opportunistic, where fragmentation is not itself a source of deadweight cost, where benign regulation precludes the game of pass-the-risk, and where the noninsurance of some forty million people is of no consequence.

HEALTH CARE AND INSURANCE PRINCIPLES

The insurance aspect of health care deserves special scrutiny. In general, insurance is a favorite device of market enthusiasts, because it is contractual, voluntary, private, and faithful to marketplace disciplines of price and risk. Insurance, therefore, is a fine example of improved efficiency via specialized knowledge and voluntary exchange. Life is full of risks, but risks can be insured, at an appropriate price, if they are spread among a broad enough population. An insurance entrepreneur who is astute at actuarial calculation and careful about where he markets his product can make a nice living.

In the case of casualty insurance, the insurer is indemnifying an individual or firm against possible losses that cannot be foreseen in the individual case but whose aggregate costs are broadly predictable based on past experience. By melding a large pool of those who will not suffer loss with those who will, the insurer is able to offer premiums at a rate low enough to attract customers and make a profit. This yields broadly efficient outcomes in the case of fire insurance, auto insurance, homeowner insurance, and even in seemingly hard cases such as life insurance and libel insurance. But, as we shall see, a fragmented and competitive system of private insurance does not yield efficient outcomes in health insurance.

The insurance business has its own set of special concepts. Three are worthy of special note here: moral hazard, adverse selection, and underwriting (in the special insurance sense of the word). Insurers worry, with justification, that the existence of insurance will influence behaviors in a way that makes payment of claims more likely. This is termed moral hazard. For example, fire insurance that exceeds the value of the property may be a temptation to arson. If a person prone to clinical depression can get large amounts of life insurance, he may contemplate suicide. A different kind of moral hazard operates when insurance coverage induces the insured person to be less safety-conscious. Insurers take special precautions not to create such perverse incentives.

A closely related concept is adverse selection. Insurers lose money not only when the existence of insurance yields behaviors that produce losses, but also when insurance attracts the people most likely to incur casualty. This was the worry back in the 1920s about health insurance: sick people would disproportionately buy it. Insurers deal with adverse-selection concerns by being very careful whom they insure, by fine-tuning the process of "underwriting"—

matching the risk of loss to the price of the premium—and by insuring very large pools.

Health insurance, however, does not cleanly fit these concepts. The whole logic of insurance is based on spreading risk. Some people are indeed more likely than others to get sick, mostly through no fault of their own. It may be reasonable for insurers to charge higher rates to smokers, whose behavior is voluntary and whose additional risk is calculable. But is it justifiable to deny coverage to someone who has had a past bout of cancer? Most people would say no, based on social values of comity and fair play, but a conscientious, profit-motivated insurer is constantly on alert to avoid high-risk cases (adverse selection). So private insurance companies routinely turn down cancer patients as "uninsurable."

To pursue the example, though smoking is partly implicated in some cancers, most victims of cancer contract the disease for reasons unrelated to their own behavior. Adverse selection misses the point, as does moral hazard. A smoker may be partly culpable if he winds up with lung cancer, but it is highly improbable that he smokes *because* he has health insurance. Indeed, smoking is more prevalent among lower-income individuals who are uninsured. People engage in self-destructive behaviors for largely nonrational reasons, not to collect insurance money. There are a wide variety of plausible strategies available to society to encourage healthful diet and exercise, to discourage domestic violence and harmful addictions—but denial of health-insurance coverage is not among them. On the contrary, a universal insurance system is among the most effective crusaders for healthful behaviors on the part of the entire population, because everyone is in the same risk pool, and the objectives are social rather than profit maximizing.

But private insurers, as market-motivated actors, are signaled by market mechanisms precisely to stratify risks, and not to insure people likely to get sick, or at least to insure them at a much higher premium. And this risk-selection behavior by insurance companies has intensified precisely as the health-insurance system has become more the creature of market forces. Risk selection is itself a source of cost, which does not arise in a universal system, where everyone is covered as a citizen. A Chicago School–oriented professor of law and economics solemnly explained to me that an insurance company sorting out prospective subscribers on the basis of who was likely to get sick was just as legitimate as a bank assessing the likelihood that an applicant for credit was likely to pay back the loan. This is a reasonable inference from market principles—and a telling indictment of them.

Prior to the 1970s, "community rating"—charging the same premium to everyone in a geographical area—was nearly universal, except in the insurance of small groups. "Medical underwriting"—screening out or charging higher rates to individuals or groups thought likelier to get sick—was considered unethical and contrary to the whole point of health insurance. But note that this was an extra-market value, and it lasted only as long as extra-market norms were dominant.

With the rise of for-profit commercial insurance, the temptation to introduce medical underwriting was irresistible. Commercial insurers begin with a large cost-disadvantage relative to Blue Cross/Blue Shield or nonprofit HMOs, because they need to earn a profit and because they must defray the cost of salesmen and other marketing expenses. Even the most administratively efficient commercial carriers start with a 15- to 20-percent cost disadvantage. As the commercials and the Blues began fighting it out for market share, the commercials began "risk selecting" and "experience rating" their health plans, in order to cream off healthier subpopulations. A large company with a relatively young work force was the ideal client. It would incur lower medical costs, and thus could be insured for a lower rate. Blue Cross, meanwhile, was continuing to charge a community rate, following the social-insurance principle of averaging low-risk and high-risk subscribers.

Once this practice began and was widely tolerated, it was inevitable that the commercial insurers would skim off the lower-risk populations, and that risk rating would drive out community rating. Today, less than 10 percent of private health insurance is community-rated. And this form of risk selection is only the camel's nose under the tent. Until fairly recently, the group insurers, like Prudential and John Hancock, that supplied health plans to big companies provided coverage to everyone who went to work for a given company—with no medical underwriting. Coverage was automatic. The risk pool was broad enough, the norms of comity were sufficiently well entrenched, and the insurance business was sufficiently lucrative, so that there was no need for this degree of risk stratification. Even if there was no longer risk pooling within the entire community, there was at least pooling within one large company plan.

No longer. As competition has become fiercer, it has become increasingly common for large insurers to demand medical examinations of new employees as a condition for including them in the group plan. Employees in high-risk groups or with "pre-existing conditions" are either denied insurance, charged a higher rate, subjected to a waiting period before insurance becomes effective, or even denied insurance for the specific condition that afflicts them. A report by the Office of Technology Assessment found that, by 1989, three insurance companies in four were screening individual applicants in order to risk-select in small group plans, and 58 percent in large group plans.

As testing and genetic screening have become more sophisticated, insurance companies have increasingly relied on tests to risk-select populations. Denial of health insurance to people who tested positive for the AIDS virus, and then to homosexuals and other groups deemed at risk, stirred enormous controversy. Initially, civil-rights advocates got some states to pass antidiscrimination laws, but by 1989 the insurance industry had fought back, and only California's law remained on the books. Neither the courts nor Congress has resolved whether the federal Americans with Disabilities Act of 1990 prohibits insurance companies from denying coverage to someone who tests positive for the AIDS virus. Traditionally, once somebody has insurance and becomes sick, the insurance plan is stuck with him. But a Texas company unilaterally canceled the health plan of an employee being treated for AIDS, and the courts held that, because the company was self-insured and hence not subject to ERISA, the employee had no rights to continuation of the health plan.

Risk selection is even more flagrant in the case of individual insurance. Self-employed people (a rising fraction of the work force) find insurance expensive, difficult to get, and universally subject to a medical examination. Insurers and HMOs that offer individual coverage routinely turn down 30 to 50 percent of applicants. In some states, laws require Blue Cross/Blue Shield to serve as insurer of last resort, and to offer coverage to individuals who are not eligible for group plans through their employer, though Blue Cross retains the right to defend itself against adverse selections by imposing long waiting periods before coverage becomes effective. HMOs that offer supplemental health insurance for people over age sixty-five are likewise prohibited from rejecting anyone, but have become astute at marketing their wares to relatively healthier people. One widely used trick is to offer meager pharmaceutical benefits, since the heavy use of prescription medicines is a very accurate proxy for general ill-health. Another is to advertise selectively to enlist healthier populations. In Florida, one HMO deliberately put its clinic up several flights of stairs to discourage frail elderly people from participating.

In a 1987 *Harvard Law Review* article, Karen Clifford and Russell Iuculano, who then represented the American Council of Life Insurance, contended that insurers have a fiduciary duty to differentiate people with identifiable health risks from healthier populations. "Failure to do so," they argued, "represents a forced subsidy from the healthy to the less healthy." Well, yes. This, after all, is the whole point. Deborah Stone, criticizing Clifford and Iuculano, writes: "The argument makes sense only if we understand the purpose of insurance as allocating costs to the people who generate them, rather than spreading the costs of misfortune and thereby making them more manageable. All insurance entails cross-subsidy. That is what makes it insurance instead of forced savings."

Social insurance, by its very nature, is different from commercial insurance. Let us recall that the entire issue of health insurance arises because society has made an *a priori* decision not to leave the public's health entirely to market forces and market-determined personal income. So measuring efficiency by conventional market concepts (in this case, avoiding the cost of treating the sick!) is the wrong criterion. To quote Stone again: "A system of competitive insurers based on medical underwriting guarantees that as insurers scramble for customers and seek to control their risks, society will be divided into more homogeneous risk classes, and more people will be left out of insurance pools altogether. From a commercial insurer's perspective, that may be good business practice. But from a social perspective, the splitting up of insurance pools means the erosion of mutual aid."

Of course, this does not mean that society can be oblivious to the problem of inexorably rising costs. But unless we choose to sacrifice the goal of promoting good health and treating illness roughly on the basis of need, the brand of efficiency promoted by market forces does not yield outcomes that are efficient by that test. On the contrary, market-led rationalization of the health-care system tends to increase deadweight costs and depress the ratio of costs paid to health benefits received.

MARKET INEFFICIENCIES

The most fundamental market inefficiency is the fact that some forty million uninsured Americans get their medical care, catch-as-catch-can, in the most inefficient manner possible. First, they tend not to get preventive care at all, because they cannot pay for it. Then, when they become acutely ill, they turn up at the most expensive venue in the whole system—the hospital emergency room. A frightened mother who shows up at an emergency room with a child having a 104-degree fever will cost the health-care system several hundred dollars. A similar visit to a clinic might cost fifty dollars. If she waits a day longer, until the child is sick enough to be admitted to the hospital, the cost will be in the thousands. Here again, there is no comparable inefficiency in a universal system; when people are sick, a lack of private resources is no constraint against seeing the doctor. Without a government mandate, the number of uninsured and underinsured people continues to grow. The free market cannot solve this.

The Paper Chase. The market aspects of the American health-care system impose immense, unnecessary administrative costs absent in a universal system. These include, first, a far greater degree of paperwork. The fastest-growing category of health-care job is claims clerk. Since there is no standard form or standard plan, each insurer has its own rules, reimbursement procedures, and formulas. These are a costly, time-consuming hassle for doctor and consumer alike. Forty-seven percent of the personnel employed in medical offices are clerical, and much of their time goes to dealing with insurance forms and patient

billing. Since 1970, the supply of physicians has grown by about 60 percent—
and the supply of medical administrators by 500 percent.

A patient conscientious about minimizing his own out-of-pocket payments
must often file (and refile) claims, and spend countless hours reaching busy signals or recorded messages, waiting on hold, repeating the same stories to different clerks. In the case of elderly people, many of whom have "Medigap" policies
to supplement what Medicare covers, claims must be submitted to Medicare,
then submitted all over again to the Medigap carrier. Pharmaceutical coverage,
which is not included in Medicare but is offered by Medigap plans, typically entails reimbursement one prescription at a time.

Insurance companies, of course, make mistakes. In this case, they have a financial incentive to make mistakes and to complicate the reimbursement procedures, since every dollar paid in ignorance or exasperation by the subscriber is
one less dollar paid out of insurance company funds. The more convoluted the
reimbursement procedure, the more the subscriber decides at some point that the
time fighting the insurance company yields diminishing returns, and just pays
the bill.

All of this wasted time represents a huge opportunity-cost seldom calculated
by market enthusiasts. Hospitals and doctors also waste an immense amount of
time processing claims and collecting bills. A consumer bold enough to challenge
the share of a bill paid by her insurance and to delay paying the bill until the matter is resolved, will be shocked to find that the hospital quickly sends the bill to a
collection agency. The collection agency's activity also represents a deadweight
loss to the whole system. Yet another source of unnecessary overhead is the
money spent on "benefits departments" in large corporations—another peculiarly
American device that does not exist in countries with universal health systems. In
effect, each part of our fragmented private system spawns a private bureaucracy
to deal with each other part. All of that time and money would be better spent on
health care. But the reimbursement maze is only the beginning.

For-profit health-care conglomerates and insurance companies also capture
large profits. These can be understood as more overhead costs. In the case of
Medicare, there is no residual profit, and administration consumes 2.4 percent of
total costs. In the best nonprofit group health plans, such as Kaiser-Permanente,
the plan pays out about ninety-five cents on every dollar of premium. The more
aggressive entrepreneurial health-care conglomerates pay out only about 70 percent—that is, HMO companies such as U.S. Healthcare keep thirty cents on the
dollar as profits. As Uwe Reinhardt, a health economist at Princeton, observed,
"Imagine if government burned 30 percent of the premium dollar."

Backseat Driving, Risk Selection, Marketing. A source of sheer waste
is the business of second-guessing doctors—one of the hottest growth industries

in the health-care sector. Utilization reviewers working either for insurance plans or for "fourth-party" specialized companies that contract with insurance companies themselves cost billions of dollars, and waste a good deal of the precious time of medical professionals. Some of this contributes to bad medical decisions—people ejected from hospitals prematurely, necessary treatments denied. This, in turn, leads to costly malpractice suits and more deadweight overhead.

A related deadweight economic loss is the administrative cost of risk selection and marketing. If the sickest 1 percent of the population consume 28 percent of total medical costs, no amount of managerial efficiency can compete with the sheer amount of money to be saved by astute risk selection. Far better to avoid covering the sick person in the first place. Medicare, as a universal system, has no such costs, since everyone over age sixty-five is covered. Hence, there is no need to bear the expense of processing applications, obtaining medical reports, or staffing underwriting departments in order to stratify risk, or to try to market the plan in competition with rival plans. Nor is there a need to recruit and monitor the financial cost-profile of doctors, since any qualified doctor may be a Medicare provider. So what is privately efficient is not socially efficient.

Private insurers spend billions of dollars on advertising. The premise is that this helps consumers choose the plan that best fits their needs. But the ads are bewildering, and often intended to risk-select rather than provide objective information. Ads typically tout benefits and prices, and make unflattering comparisons with competitors. But consider all the variables the hapless consumer must consider, not divulged in the ad: Which specialists are affiliated with the plan? How tough is the plan in restricting access to them? How likely am I to need expensive prescription drugs? How large a patient panel does my primary doctor have? What are the constraints on his freedom to practice that are not being divulged to me? Is my primary doctor likely to disaffiliate from the plan in disgust? How likely is the plan to go broke? Which hospitals will the plan let me use for what conditions, and how stable are those hospitals? The consumer is plainly unable to play the fabled role of wise discipliner of the market. Ironically, because of the success of marketing and the fears of unreliable coverage, many fearful and unwary consumers end up purchasing redundant policies. Again, none of these concerns or costs arise in a universal system.

In a weird reversal, the chief executive of Empire Blue Cross/Blue Shield of New York, a plan now recovering uneasily from a convoluted financial scandal, has called for tighter regulation of his own industry. In an op-ed piece in *The New York Times*, Michael A. Stocker called for legislation requiring full disclosure to subscribers of now secret treatment protocols and payment systems. Stocker also urged the state to require full emergency-room coverage. This plea is more than a little ironic, since it lays bare the market's failure to police itself.

A conscientious HMO would offer these rights-to-know and entitlements to treatment voluntarily—but it would be revealed as a high-cost provider, and it would be easy prey for less scrupulous competitors. Hence, legislation is necessary to limit opportunism. Marketization: meet regulation.

Note the irony: Under the present system, HMOs achieve some of their cost savings by misleading consumers. However, the regulatory remedy—disclosure to produce better-informed consumers—would require more costly policing and paperwork. This entire costly game of deception and regulation disappears in a universal system. Both the private market's inflation of costs and the government's imposition of countercosts are sheer waste compared with the available alternative.

Healing, Entrepreneurship, and Trust. The more "entrepreneurial" the system becomes, the more providers become pitchmen rather than healers. Doctors, of course, have always been part entrepreneur. They are a delicate blend of small businessmen, making sure they have enough customers and that their bills get paid, and healers with professional norms and a social mission. As both entrepreneurs and healers, doctors have been especially vigilant to make sure that third parties—especially government bureaucrats—stay out of the consulting room. But today the assault on both purse and profession is coming from private bureaucracies. As Theodore Marmor has observed, "[D]octors were guarding their left flank, but the attack came from the right." The rush to marketize is shifting the delicate balance in favor of crass entrepreneurship, but in a way that is efficient for neither physicians' clinical autonomy, resource allocation, nor patient care.

Traditionally in the United States, ethical norms have prevented doctors from taking a profit on drugs that they prescribed. En route to a recent medical convention, I was mistaken for an M.D. and given promotional material with the delightfully revealing slogan "Capitalizing on Capitation." The material promoted a line of dietary-supplement and weight-reduction products that the doctor could market right from his office. As the sales representative explained the concept, managed care was ratcheting down doctors' incomes, so here was a fine way to make up the loss by taking advantage of the captive customer. According to the taped pitch, "Interior Design Nutritionals has one of the only science-backed, self-directed wellness systems on the market. With this, you have the advantages of adding a very lucrative profit center to your practice, as well as extending a new and very valuable service to your patients." The marketing materials include three videos to play in the waiting area; a life-style questionnaire; a two-hundred-page handbook; and the "Healthy Alternative" products line, which includes antioxidants, minerals, botanical products, sports-nutritional products, and other dietary supplements that may or may not have any medical value. Patients who enlist are given a code number, so that the order can be credited to the referring physician. The doctor gets a 43-percent commission on all products sold; doctors who pitch the system to other doctors can get an additional commission of up to 24 percent on the sales of those doctors. The tape ends: "In a world where independent business people are losing control to run their own practices, there is a way to capitalize." Another piece of direct mail, encouraging physicians to bypass pharmacies and refer patients directly to wholesale drug repackagers, contains the headline "Why pass the buck? Every time you sign a prescription, it's like writing a check to a pharmacy."

Yale Professor Bradford Gray, in a study *The Profit Motive and Patient Care*, observes, "The devices of the salesman seem inconsistent with the [medical] fiduciary ethic. Seeking to create demand is quite different from seeking to evaluate need objectively." Unlike, say, a furniture salesman, a doctor is in a privileged position to sway a patient's decision. Gray adds: "Even though sales personnel are ethically and legally obligated to be truthful about certain matters, they have no ethical obligation to ascertain and act in their customers' best interests, and only the most naive consumers are unwary. The doctor-patient relationship, by contrast, is supposedly one of comparative trust."

A generation ago, a study of "physician-entrepreneurs" examined attitudes toward doctors who operated such sidelines as hemodialysis centers, ambulatory-surgery centers, pathology and radiology labs, sports-medicine centers, obesity clinics, and substance-abuse facilities. In 1972, such doctors themselves reported that their entrepreneurial ideology was "deviant and stigmatized among their colleagues." Today, as doctors are being trained to become more entrepreneurial, such conduct is increasingly normal. Professor Gray worries that conflicts of interest in such situations threaten the doctor's credibility and may "put patients in the position of having to follow the advice of someone they have reason to mistrust." Market incentives, contrary to their billing, also waste resources. A doctor with a financial stake is more likely to overtest and overprescribe. A 1988 study by the inspector general of the Department of Health and Human Services found that Medicare patients of doctors who had a financial stake in clinical labs received 45 percent more lab tests than Medicare patients in general.

Market Undervaluation: The Case of Vaccines. Some investments in public health are immensely cost-effective socially but not worth the candle to the entrepreneur. The epic example is childhood vaccines. As the proverbial ounce of prevention, vaccines save society untold suffering and medical expense. Dr. Anthony Robbins and his co-author, Phyllis Freeman, who directed a study of vaccines for the Rockefeller Foundation, calculated that childhood immunizations save at least ten dollars for every dollar expended. The trouble, however, is that the social return diverges sharply from the private return. Vaccines are immensely beneficial to society, but are not big money-makers for pharmaceutical companies. Whereas prescription drugs return profits to their manufacturer every time a prescription is refilled, vaccines are literally one-shot deals. Once a customer is immunized, he doesn't need to return.

As a result, private industry systematically underinvests in vaccine development. But even though vaccines are the ideal candidate for public development and distribution, the pharmaceutical industry strenuously resists efforts to turn vaccine production and distribution over to public agencies. Once even a low-profit area of drug development and production becomes socialized, the pressure is to reduce per-unit cost so that the maximum number of children benefit. Vaccines disseminated by the United Nations, or by public agencies in other nations, are typically sold for far less per dose than private pharmaceutical companies charge for comparable products. This shames the pharmaceutical houses, as well as cutting their profit margins. Social development, production, and distribution, even of a low-profit, low-volume product like vaccines, is a real threat. The private market cannot yield optimal outcomes, yet market actors don't want rivals to get a foot in the door.

In the United States, because of the fragmented nature of the health-care system, tens of millions of children go without available immunizations that are universal in other advanced countries. In the third world, where preventable conditions are epidemic, the failure of the global system to finance and distribute cheap vaccines causes billions of children to suffer needlessly. The market doesn't seem to mind.

Market Piggy-Backing: the Case of AA. Markets relentlessly seek to commodify things that are unsuited to market principles of impersonal exchange. Sometimes the market operates as a kind of parasite on extra-market values and institutions. An instructive case in point is Alcoholics Anonymous.

AA, despite some flaws, is a remarkable institution built almost entirely on volunteerism. People who can acknowledge they are alcoholics may attend AA meetings, at no charge. Giving something back is central to the AA ethic and part of the healing process. The entire institution lies beyond the process of market exchange. Except for the short-term process of clinical detoxification, AA seems superior to explicitly medical intervention.

Beginning in the 1960s, as health-insurance coverage became more generous and as many state legislatures began mandating that insurance plans cover treatment for substance abuse, many psychiatric hospitals and free-standing clinics began identifying substance-abuse treatment as a new profit center. A thirty-day course of inpatient treatment for alcoholism cost in the range of ten thousand dollars. But alcoholics often revert to drink. So nearly all the postdischarge plans have one prescription in common: Go to AA. The part of the system that finds alcoholism a source of profit is subsidized by the part of the system that depends on charity, spirituality, generosity, and empathy. If AA were turned into a fee-for-service business, its essence would be destroyed. Which approach is more "efficient"? Which pursues the logic of the market?

EFFICIENCY, HEALTH, AND CLASS

Healthfulness and long life are influenced by personal behaviors, which are themselves affected by social class. Self-destructive behavior patterns, such as smoking, unhealthy diet, lack of exercise, careless pregnancy, domestic and street violence, and myriad addictions, reduce longevity and health. The consequences of these behaviors impose costs on the explicitly medical part of the system, which then come at the expense of other potential outlays to benefit health. According to the *Journal of the American Medical Association* tabulation of the top ten causes of death, tobacco leads the list, accounting for 400,000 deaths a year; factors related to diet and exercise account for another 300,000; all infectious diseases rank fourth, causing 75,000.

Unhealthful individual behaviors and social pathologies are intimately connected with social class in three distinct and reinforcing ways. First, in an economy with gross income inequalities, poorer people are less likely to be effective members of the collectivity that benefits from the basic social measures such as nutrition, sanitation, and vaccination that broadly contour good health. Slum neighborhoods often have the public-health conditions of the third world, and morbidity and mortality statistics to match. Second, virtually every study on the subject shows that self-destructive behaviors are powerfully correlated with (lower) social class. Third, poor people tend to wait until they are sicker before they seek medical help, even in societies with universal health systems, and to use the health system less discerningly. So, to the extent that a market society exacerbates the extremes of class, it both depresses health for large numbers of people, and depresses the efficiency of society's health outlays.

Healthy families are a primary source of good health in children. The ways in which families influence the physical, psychological, and social health of their offspring are multiple, and closely correlated with class. Better-educated, better-off families are more likely to cultivate good habits of learning, communication, respectfulness, and hence self-esteem; good habits of diet, hygiene, bedtime, and hence wellness; regular preventive medical care, and hence resistance to disease; general parental supervision, and hence physical safety. Such families are less likely to be violent or otherwise dysfunctional. They are more likely to model caring and communicative behaviors, and hence a variety of life skills. All of these attributes are correlated with good health in children. Conversely, to be under great pressure to make ends meet is to bring home stress. To bring home stress is to place the family at risk, since parents stressed to the breaking point are less able to nurture healthy children. Hence, low economic status correlates with greater health risk, for oneself, one's spouse, and one's children.

Poor people, further, are more likely to lead unhealthy lives for occupational reasons; the poor are likely to be concentrated in more dangerous, more stressful, less secure, less rewarding occupations. Even when occupation is held constant, simply living in a poor neighborhood increases morbidity and mortality. Moreover, as the saint of the Catholic Worker movement, Dorothy Day, was wont to observe, the poor are not poor just in money, but in organization, knowledge, and self-respect. Income tends to correlate with education; education tends to correlate with healthful living habits.

Landmark research by the British epidemiologist Michael G. Marmot and his colleagues confirms that lower socioeconomic groups are more likely to smoke, less likely to take regular exercise, less likely to have hobbies, less likely to have healthy diets. These habits have a complex etiology, partly related to lack of information, partly to subculture, partly to low self-esteem and repressed frustration or rage that translates into self-destructive behavior. In their famous Whitehall Study, a longitudinal survey of the health of British civil servants, Marmot and colleagues found that the propensity to higher rates of sickness and death reflected relative as well as absolute socioeconomic status. Even though income, education, and nutritional standards were rising throughout the period of the Whitehall Study, the people in the upper-status jobs and upper income brackets continued to live longer and experience better health than those with jobs that offered less satisfaction, income, prestige, and control.

One of the best-established facts of mental-health research is that poorer people are at greater risk of mental illness and breakdown. The rich may spend more time in psychotherapy, but the poor are in greater need of help. To be in a life situation where one experiences relentless demands by others, over which one has relatively little control, is to be at risk of poor health, physically as well as mentally. As public-health scholars Jeffrey Johnson and Ellen Hall have observed, "The potential to control one's own environment is differentially distributed along class lines." Reviewing statistics on heart disease, they found that people at greatest risk tended to be in occupations with high demands, low control, and low social support. People in demanding positions but with greater autonomy were at lower risk. This is the case not only in societies like the United States, with very high inequality and incomplete health-care systems, but across the spectrum of industrial nations.

Public-health research indicates that active engagement in the healing process is itself conducive to healing. A "patient" literally means the opposite of an "agent"—one who is acted upon rather than one who acts. To be an agent of one's own health is itself restorative of health. Poor and working-class people are more likely to be disempowered; more likely to accept mistaken medical strategies passively; more likely to be intimidated by experts; less likely to take charge of their cases; more likely to be patients rather than agents. The *Journal of the National Cancer Institute* reports that men in the lowest social class have twice the cancer risk as those in the highest social class. That statistic expresses—and conceals—all the subtle and interconnected ways that lower socioeconomic status retards healing—greater environmental exposure, less access to care, less access to early and high-quality care, greater fatalism and pessimism, less willingness to become actively engaged in one's own healing.

With the weakening of unions and of the postwar welfare state, we can see a reversion to a two-class system in which a relatively small elite demands and gets empowerment, self-actualization, autonomy, and other work satisfactions that partially compensate for long work hours. Though the popular cliché imagines that it is the harried executive who drops dead on the golf course, epidemiological data confirm that lower-paid, lower-status workers are more likely to experience the most clinically damaging forms of stress, in part because they have less control over their work. They are less likely to be found on the golf course at all, or in other forms of healthful relaxation.

Of course, these subtleties all refer to extra-medical health differentials of social class. Uniquely in America, these interact with a grosser inequality—the fact that poor people are more likely to be uninsured and less likely to get routine medical care at all.

As all of the foregoing suggests, whether society embraces a broad strategy of primary prevention and broad healthfulness is a profoundly political question. The same social and economic forces that make America a highly stratified society, with gross imbalances of economic wealth and power, resist repairing those imbalances in a fashion that would improve our collective health. Inequality generated by market forces elsewhere breeds inequality in health. Changing unhealthy habits requires much more than exhortation to healthier personal behavior. Self-destructive behaviors—alcoholism, smoking, lack of exercise, exposure to toxic substances, unwanted early pregnancies, stressful ways of living generally—are themselves deeply embedded in the structure of social relations. To call for a broad strategy of wellness and public health is to call for a redistribution of economic and political power.

THE INFORMED CASE FOR UNIVERSAL COVERAGE

The American health-care system is a tangle of inequity and inefficiency—and getting worse as private-market forces seek to rationalize it. A shift to a universal system of health coverage would cut this Gordian knot at a stroke. It would not only deliver the explicitly medical aspects of health more efficiently and fairly, but, by socializing the costs of poor health, it would also create a powerful financial incentive for society as a whole to stress primary prevention. With everyone in the same system, universal health coverage would also enhance social empathy and cultivate a greater consciousness of the reality that health is a collective good, not just an individual one. In 1991, the General Accounting Office found that "if the United States were to shift to a system of universal coverage and a single payer, as in Canada, the savings in administrative costs would be more than enough to offset the expense of universal coverage."

The proof of this proposition is that every nation with a universal system spends less of its GDP on health care than the United States, yet has less intrusion into clinical decisions than in the U.S. system. And nearly every other nation with a universal system has longer life spans from birth (though roughly equivalent life spans from adulthood). Contrary to the propaganda of groups opposed to universal health insurance, most nations with universal systems also report greater patient satisfaction.

The reasons, by now, should be obvious. By their nature, universal systems spend less money on wasteful overhead, and more on primary prevention. Health-insurance overhead in the United States alone consumes about 1 percent of the GDP, compared with .1 percent in Canada. Though medical inflation is a problem everywhere, the universal systems have had far lower rates of cost inflation, and less convoluted strategies of cost containment. In the years between 1980 and 1987, total health costs in the United States increased at 2.4 times the rate of GDP growth. In nations with universal systems, they increased far more slowly. The figures for Sweden, France, West Germany, and Britain were 1.2, 1.6, 1.8, and 1.7 percent, respectively. In the United States, doctor bills increased at triple the general inflation rate, compared with less than double elsewhere.

The cost-containment mechanisms used overseas are complex and diverse, but most nations with universal systems use some form of overall ("global") limit on health-system outlays. This total national cap then translates into annual budgets for hospitals. The hospital, its health professionals and lay representatives, must set priorities and make difficult trade-offs within the context of that overall budget. This is not unlike what American HMOs do, with the crucial difference that there is no expenditure on risk selection or marketing, no diversion of profit to shareholders, and far less interference from outsiders.

With respect to doctor bills, there is typically annual negotiation between the health-care system and the medical societies. In universal systems that compensate doctors on a fee-for-service basis, such as Canada, the inexorable tendency to more costly treatment measures is offset by an annual ratcheting back of reimbursement rates, to keep the whole system within budget. In systems where doctors are salaried, such as Britain's, financial discipline is maintained by holding down salary schedules. In universal systems, governments tend to own most hospitals and control budgets for capital expansion, so the American habit of increased supply causing increased demand is less of a problem. Universal systems also bypass the perverse incentive of the search for the reimbursable procedure.

The absence of a universal system in the United States means there is no avenue for system-wide bargaining, and no overall cap on medical outlays. The private-market counterpart does ratchet down costs, but in a far less efficient manner. Cost containment, American-style, causes the shoe to pinch in the wrong places, while the forces of medical entrepreneurship are constantly looking to beat the system by looking for new profit opportunities.

Another ironic result of the American form of cost containment is that the United States now has the shortest average hospital stay of any advanced nation—not because this is medically efficient but because hospital stays are one of the easiest "cost centers" for insurance plans and HMOs to monitor. This is another aspect of the cops-and-robbers game of American-style managed care. U.S. hospitals tend to be very high-tech affairs—a legacy of the days when profit maximizing was based on maximizing reimbursement. But now that the game is minimizing costs, hospitals are literally too expensive to use. Remarkably enough, the United States spends the most money on health care, but has the fewest beds per thousand in population, the lowest admission rate, and the lowest occupancy rate—coupled with the highest daily cost, highest technology-intensiveness, and greatest number of employees per bed. European and Japanese hospitals tend to be lower-tech and less costly, and the system is far more willing to let the patient stay until she has recovered.

A related mismatch is the inefficient use of home care, nursing care, and psychiatric halfway houses in the United States relative to overseas. Because of the system's patchwork nature, many of the most efficient and humane modalities are not used in the American system, because insurance does not happen to pay for them. In the case of care for the infirm elderly, for example, nations with more social systems of health care typically offer a continuum, ranging from home-health-aide services, to individual apartments with nursing help on call close by, to assisted living and congregate housing, to U.S.-style medical-model nursing homes. In the United States, everything short of full nursing-home care is available only spottily, unless the individual can pay out of pocket. Short-term home health care is available under Medicare for patients recovering from acute conditions, but not as part of a long-term plan for keeping the frail elderly out of institutions.

As a result, many people who could benefit from home health aides or assisted-living apartments (for which Medicaid doesn't pay) are herded into nursing homes sooner than necessary; nursing homes are overutilized and underfunded; and a great deal of unnecessary hardship occurs, given that the same dollars could be spent far more rationally under a system of social provision. To the extent that Medicare pays for home care in some cases, this has attracted a new wave of for-profit companies seeking reimbursements, often shoving aside well-established community-based groups committed to an ethic of service.

One red herring in this whole debate is "rationing." Foreign universal systems are said to entail rationing, whereas the American system allegedly puts no constraints on available medical care. But, given the propensity of medical care to eat up most of the GDP, one form or another of rationing exists everywhere in the world. The real issue is whether it is rationing based on private purse or on medical need. A system that coddles wealthy patients with minor ailments but cannot find money for universal vaccinations is, of course, rationing. A system that spends millions keeping alive twenty-week premature babies, and subsidizing *in vitro* fertilizations, but has forty million people without basic health coverage, is also rationing.

Another red herring, one that surfaced in the debate over the Clinton bill, is the claim that a universal system would deprive individuals of the right to spend money out of pocket to supplement what was covered in any of the approved plans. This was based on a deliberate misreading of the bill. In reality, there is no system of socialized health care anywhere in the Western world that prohibits affluent people from buying additional treatment.

Even in the most socialized health-care systems, some services remain private and commodified. For example, long-term psychoanalysis and cosmetic surgery are unlikely to be covered by the universal system, and remain amenities for the well-off. However, the experience of most countries shows that, if the basic system provides a high quality of care, the vast majority of people will rely on it. The design of the system is crucial to that outcome. In Britain, the Thatcher government, which was hostile to the system, achieved an accelerating backdoor form of privatization by starving the National Health Service for resources, and driving those who could afford it to supplement the NHS with private health insurance. This logic tends to cumulate. As more doctors set up private practices and more middle-class people become dissatisfied with a starved public system, private medicine gains at the expense of social medicine. By the end of

Thatcher's reign, more than 15 percent of the British public had supplemental health coverage.

In Canada, by contrast, it is illegal for private vendors of insurance to compete directly with those offered by the public system, though they can offer supplements for services not covered. Though a small fraction of affluent Canadians go to the United States for elective surgery, the overwhelming majority stay within the universal system. If the level of the basic coverage is set high enough, it achieves a genuinely one-class system. If it is not, political support will erode as consumer desertion increases. In Canada, though health costs have inflated at a slower rate than in the United States, conservative provincial governments are pursuing a Thatcher-style campaign to erode the universal system by allowing private entrepreneurs to compete for the most remunerative customers.

Thus, the politics of a particular health regime is self-reinforcing. An egalitarian system of health care is solidarity-building. When everyone is in the same system, the more affluent and sophisticated demand high-quality care. And when solidarity values reign, there is also a logic to push outward and downward available services—more comprehensive immunizations, more wellness education, more preventive care. But when basic care is shabby, and it is attractive for the affluent to buy their way out, political support for the universal system dwindles and there is more pressure to divert resources to the individualistic, privatized alternative, diminishing social empathy or solidarity, and reducing support for the public-health approach.

A universal system, by its very nature, is more alert to all of the social ways to improve health—antismoking campaigns, universal screening and immunization efforts, wellness and exercise options, as well as better public education aimed at more healthful living. A purely privatized system is likely to be more fragmented, and less willing to pay for public health, or to grasp its logic.

In America, the overreliance on market logic and market institutions is ruining the health-care system. Market enthusiasts fail to tabulate all the costs of relying on market forces to allocate health care—the fragmentation, opportunism, asset rearranging, overhead, underinvestment in public health, and the assault on norms of service and altruism. They assume either a degree of self-regulation that the health markets cannot generate, or farsighted public supervision that contradicts the rest of their world view. Health care now consumes fully one-seventh of our entire national income. There is no realm of our mixed economy where markets yield more perverse results.

5 / MONEY MARKETS AND THE CORPORATION

THE PUREST MARKET

Financial markets are the very essence of capitalism. They are markets whose product is money itself. Financial markets serve the crucial function of joining investors with entrepreneurs. They allow corporations to obtain equity and debt capital from both large institutions and small savers. They signal informed (or speculative) judgments on the relative worth of myriad alternative investments. In that sense, money markets are among the purest of markets in their fidelity to the model of minute, continuous adjustment of price. A well-functioning stock or bond market displays supply and demand at its most elegant, as stock prices rise and fall in response to a blend of hard information, hunches, and investor expectations about the expectations of other investors.

Yet, ironically enough, this purest of all markets is unavoidably reliant on the state. For one thing, governments print money. Through fiscal policies and central banks, governments also influence its value. And though investors' supply and demand influence stock and bond prices and interest rates, they do so in a context substantially contoured by central-bank monetary policy. When interest rates briefly went to 21.5 percent in 1980, it had far less to do with inflationary expectations than with Paul Volcker's monetary policy. By the same token, the bull market of the 1990s had everything to do with gradually declining inflation and interest rates, which raised stock prices almost mechanically, and only a little to do with deregulation. A different set of central-bank policies would have produced a very different money market.

Commercial banks, a key part of the monetary system, are necessarily among the most heavily regulated of market institutions. The risk of ordinary market discipline, with severe punishment of innocent losers, is intolerable, and the temptations of opportunism are too great, for banks to be pure creatures of the market. Society has decided that unsophisticated people should not lose their life savings because of the misjudgment or corruption of a particular banker or the general consequences of a run on banks. And once government guarantees the deposits of small savers, government is at risk for their losses and needs to be a vigilant policeman. In addition, banking collapses pose grave systemic risk to the nonfinancial, "real" economy. The nineteenth-century era of relatively unregulated banking was replete with panics that had the effect of constricting the money supply and inducing depression in the rest of the economy.

Stock markets, though the exemplar of markets that clear with shifts in supply and demand, likewise operate within a substantially regulated system that defines property rights, mandates a variety of forms of disclosure, and prohibits a wide variety of transactions that consenting adults would otherwise pursue. As financial markets have undergone partial deregulation in recent years, a serious debate has ensued as to whether they and the economy would benefit from further deregulation. Is the present regime of regulation merely prudent, or does it interfere with efficiency gains that markets, in their genius, pursue when left alone? Or is there already too much marketization?

This question divides into two broad issues. The first has to do with systemic risk, safety, and soundness. As money markets become more speculative, are we playing roulette with the entire economy? The second issue involves the relationship between the financial economy and the real economy. Money markets are exquisitely capitalist in their unsentimentality. They are the antithesis of social compacts. An investor will sell out his position if he thinks the market has peaked, or tender his shares in a proxy battle if that seems to optimize his investment strategy—with nary a thought about how a merger, consolidation, or stock selloff will affect a community or work force that may have long years of affiliation with underlying assets about to be plundered.

Money markets epitomize both the market's genius and its myopia. The money market is concerned about today's price, and by definition today's price is the right price. Countless studies have shown that financial markets are very poor at predicting the profitability of an enterprise over the long term. Looked at retrospectively, stock prices are not good predictors of future performance. As the Yale economist Robert J. Shiller has observed, "Even if a market participant believes that information about a firm is of no fundamental value, he should trade on it if he believes others will use the information to make their trades. Paradoxically, traders may disregard information they think is meaningful for long-run profits and instead use information they think is spurious, because they believe that other market participants are using the spurious information. The goal for a portfolio manager is to be right in the short run if he wants to be around for the long run."

The efficiency of the daily trading market may not produce the optimal long-term result for the enterprise, and hence for the economy. Money markets, in short, are mostly spot markets, with prices that clear according to the laissez-faire model, based on educated guesses at best and reckless gambling at worst. The instruments of commerce, however, are not spot markets but complex institutions based on relationships. So the connection of the financial economy to the "real" economy of factories, farms, and firms is an imperfect fit.

Much of the recent debate about how much deregulation is optimal in money markets can be understood as a conversation about the relationship of the financial economy to the real economy. The partisans of ever-purer marketization argue that financial markets, by definition, are right in the way they value the assets of companies, and how they reorganize those assets. In this view, anything that gets in the way of the smooth functioning of money markets and their rearrangement of assets departs from the market's wisdom and incurs real economic costs.

This, once again, is the familiar appeal to *allocative* efficiency, juxtaposed against other forms of efficiency. But the freest possible money markets are often adept mainly at rearranging assets according to the strategy or fad of the day, displacing incumbents and enriching middlemen. That process may not optimize either high growth and full employment (the efficiency of Keynes), or technical advance over time (the efficiency of Schumpeter). Money markets often sacrifice long-term investment for short-term windfall.

"The market," after all, is a convenient abstraction. Adam Smith's unseen hand implies an impersonal and natural process. But in practice the role of the market is often played by individuals who are far more interested in quick returns than in maximizing the health of an enterprise for the long run. The latter sort of capitalists are also entrepreneurs, of course, but their own values are often not those of short-term profit maximization commended by the pure market ideal. They may be steelmakers who just love making steel, paternalistic heads of enterprises with deep roots in a community, or stubborn visionaries who keep plowing back profits into a company and letting the stock market be damned.

Enthusiasts of greater liberation of financial markets hold that such people are precisely the ones who need the unsentimental discipline of Wall Street. Critics of money-market capitalism reply that capitalists need nothing so much as respite from Wall Street. So relatively free financial markets are at once a useful and critical aspect of capitalism—and too important to be permitted to operate according to absolute laissez-faire. Nor does their partial encumbrance seem to harm their capacity to match individual investors efficiently with users of capital in industry and commerce.

These questions play out in several practical policy dilemmas. Should hostile takeovers and leveraged buyouts be encouraged as a strategy of holding managers accountable and "maximizing shareholder value"—or discouraged as speculative capitalism at its worst? To the extent that hostile takeovers are touted as forms of superior accountability, what other strategies of accountability might be more consistent with the long-term institutional health of the enterprise? Should "innovation" of financial instruments be encouraged, or limited as a source of speculative excess? Should banks and thrift institutions be further relieved of the remaining constraints on their ability to merge and to pursue non-banking lines of business?

In the 1980s, the issue was leveraged buyouts and hostile takeovers. The fad eventually fizzled when few junk bonds turned out to be reliable long-term investments. The market dried up, though it took more than a decade to correct its expensive failure. In the 1990s, the question is whether to rein in derivatives—hybrid investment instruments that add nothing of long-term value but merely facilitate new forms of speculation.

EFFICIENT FINANCIAL MARKETS

The debate is an old one. On one side are the institutionalists, beginning famously with Thorstein Veblen, who saw an economy of financial manipulators versus engineers. The financiers were useful to the extent that they supplied capital; they were parasites to the extent that they were mere speculators. Accordingly, proprietors of actual businesses were the ones who added real value to the economy, and they needed to be sheltered from purely financial pressures for quick returns. Keynes's version of the same point is articulated in an oft-quoted line from his *General Theory*: "Speculators may do no harm as a bubble on a steady stream of enterprise. But the position is serious when enterprise becomes the bubble on a whirlpool of speculation." As good a mainstream economist as Nobel laureate James Tobin could write that public policy needed to throw some "sand in the gears" of trading markets, a phrase that sounds heretical and almost Marxian. Why would a distinguished economist, one who presumably respects the pricing system and the allocative genius of markets, ever want to add friction to the smooth equilibration of supply and demand?

The reason is a variant on our theme. Taken to an extreme, the market's short-term pursuit of returns can be ruinous. Tobin's remedy for excessive financial churning was a tax on financial transactions—one intended to reward the long-term investor and damp down the impulse to short-run financial speculation. Other strategies for pursuing the same objective include tax favoritism for long-term capital gains (a policy that was on the books until 1981) and tax penalties for profits realized from quick speculative returns.

On the opposite side of the divide are those who insist that financial markets, like other markets, must be efficient—by definition. Throwing sand in their gears, in this view, is every bit as perverse as the metaphor implies. In financial markets as in others, interfering with the market's short-term impulse to clear—with the desire of traders to "truck and barter," in Adam Smith's phrase—brings terrible costs to allocative efficiency, since it prevents the full discipline of supply and demand. Favorable treatment of longer-term investments, likewise, is a distortion that impedes the normal shifting of capital among different assets as investors perceive opportunities for superior returns. By definition again, the investment that provides the higher return is the more deserving, and hence the more efficient use of capital.

In recent years, this set of claims has come to be known as the Efficient Market Hypothesis—whatever markets do is necessarily right. It is the financial-market counterpart of other claims about laissez-faire. This theorem has been used as an all-purpose defense of inherently speculative derivative financial instruments and the hostile-takeover movement, however dubious its outcomes, as well as a rationalization for a market that has become increasingly a trader's market rather than an investor's market, and as a rationale for bank deregulation.

In its "strong" form, first propounded by the economist Eugene Fama, the Efficient Market Hypothesis insists that the stock market knows everything about the value of a company that can be known; that all available information is rapidly diffused and embodied (capitalized) in the market's pricing of a stock. The hypothesis is a solemn version of the old economists' joke about the economics professor and his student walking across campus. "Look!" says the student. "There's a twenty-dollar bill on the sidewalk." But the professor knows better. "It can't be," he explains. "If it were a twenty-dollar bill, someone would have picked it up."

Like so much else in free-market economics, the hypothesis is a truism. If markets are rational, then the market is efficient by definition, and by definition its prices are accurate. All important information has already been processed by the market and capitalized in the value of the stock. If this is the case, then regulation is destructive, and new financial instruments that investment bankers dream up (no matter how speculative) are virtuous, and any transactions between consenting adults (which by definition are voluntary) enhance allocative efficiency.

There are several problems with this view of financial markets. As description, it is true only as tautology. When the stock market crashed, losing almost a third of its entire value, on October 19, 1987, there were scant changes in the prospects of the underlying assets represented by the stocks. The market was grossly mistaken either before, or after. Computerized program trading—the fruits of the financial "innovation" celebrated by marketizers—sent the ostensibly rational stock market into mindless free-fall. It took regulatory intervention to limit the destructive effects of this creature of the market, in the form of short-term liquidity advances by the Federal Reserve, and a bit later regulatory constraints on program trading by the SEC. Left alone, the "efficiency" of the financial market would only have produced more panic-selling and deeper damage.

A related problem is the tendency of trading markets to excess volatility. As recently as 1960, only 12 percent of the whole New York Stock Exchange turned over in a year. And there were virtually no derivative instruments other than old-fashioned futures markets, which played a legitimate hedging role for farmers and buyers of commodities, and a very small market in puts and calls. This, again, was the result of a combination of regulation and custom. The people who ran Wall Street three decades ago could still remember the consequences of excess volatility. Stability was fine by them. Today, financial markets turn over their entire value many times in a year. Who is to say that, on balance, this shift improves the ability of the real economy to get capital? What is clear, however, is that the volatility is itself a source of destabilization. Middlemen have an immense motivation to dream up more and more products—for volatility is their source of income, via commissions, reselling, and what amounts to insider trading. A trading market is a zero-sum game. It adds no real value to the economy. This draws off many billions of dollars that would otherwise be spent in the real economy. It diverts expert attention from the legitimate task of carefully analyzing and valuing the underlying assets, not to mention building real enterprises.

Most of the financial market in stocks and bonds is a secondary market. That is, most shares traded are previous issues, not new demands for investment capital. Day-to-day valuation is driven more by the (often irrational) perception of other investors' (often irrational) expectations than by discerning analysis of real companies. For more than half a century, critics have observed that market "prices have been based too much on current earning power, too little on long-run dividend-paying power." If that is true, then the market seriously misallocates capital. The Efficient Market Hypothesis compounds the sin by claiming to spare investors the need to give serious study to the actual companies represented by the securities traded in financial markets. Supposedly, investing can be reduced to a set of formulas.

A very fashionable variant of the Efficient Market Hypothesis is something called the Capital Asset Pricing Model (CAPM), which claims that the relationship between risk and reward can be reduced to a series of mechanical formulas. CAPM attempts to measure the risk of a particular investment relative to the stock market generally, and to calculate the trade-off between risk and antici-pated return. There is, to be sure, a broad correlation between risk and reward. That's why Treasury bills, which are virtually risk free, pay low returns. It's why bonds with longer maturities generally pay higher returns, since risk increases with time, even for relatively safe investments. But mechanical models such as CAPM generally measure risk and return in relation to broad averages, for ex-ample by comparing the volatility of a given stock with the volatility of the stock market as a whole. What they do not measure is unique risk, since unique risk is literally unknowable. We had no way of predicting, based on the recent past, that Microsoft would displace IBM or that Toyota would savage Chrysler. Some in-vestments are of course riskier than others, and mechanical formulas, while use-ful first approximations, are no substitute for hands-on knowledge. Taken to an extreme this leads to a system of capitalism without capitalists, in which the fel-low who devotes long years to building up an enterprise is a chump, while the clever fellow is the trader.

Efficient market theory manages to hold, simultaneously, that stock prices are both "rational" and substantially random. As if to mock the Efficient Market Hypothesis, a relative handful of astute long-term investors, the most celebrated of whom is Warren Buffett, have demonstrated that one can indeed beat the mar-ket, by careful study of the fundamental values of corporations, in the prudent manner commended by such old-fashioned scholars of securities analysis as Benjamin Graham and David Dodd. For thirty-five years, Buffett has averaged annual returns of 27 percent, by "steadily mining the imperfect prices that effi-cient market theory says do not exist," as Columbia Professor Louis Lowenstein puts it. There is a twenty-dollar bill on the sidewalk after all, but only the percep-tive notice it.

Defenders of free-market economics dismiss concerns about volatility and speculation by insisting that all investment is in a sense speculative. It is the tak-ing of a risk, a gamble against an unknown future. But that construction plays fast and loose with language and elides a key distinction. An investor in a real enterprise is taking a risk that the venture will pan out. If he is a hands-on owner, he is working to bring that result about. If he is a Buffett-style investor, he is looking very closely over the entrepreneur's shoulder, sometimes offering firm advice. This is a bet on a positive-sum game; there need be no loser. If the ven-ture thrives, real value will be added to the economy. Entrepreneur, investor, lender, worker, and consumer will all benefit. But a commodities play, an invest-ment in any other derivative instrument, or even a short-term trade in an old se-curity is a purely zero-sum transaction. Someone gains only to the extent that someone else loses.

Derivatives represent zero-sum financial markets at their most extreme. They are basically abstractions of certain features of underlying stocks and bonds that represent real assets. They include stock index futures, options, mortgage-backed instruments, bets on foreign-exchange markets, and a variety of other hybrids whose main benefits seem to be that they allow middlemen to make fortunes and speculators with a taste for high risk to evade old-fashioned margin restrictions.

Many derivative securities, such as those based on mortgages, involve disassembling individual income streams from the overall cash flow of an investment, and selling different pieces to investors who may have different needs or strategies. For example, a monthly mortgage payment can be divided into principal repayment and interest, or repayment over different time periods. Since a mortgage usually allows the borrower to pre-pay at his discretion, there is an element of unknowable risk for the creditor. The maker or buyer of a mortgage is nominally investing in a thirty-year note, but the mortgage may be pre-paid in a year. In principle, derivatives reduce risk, or at least allocate it more precisely, by taking moderately risky investments like mortgages and slicing them into less risky and more risky securities.

The problem, however, is that the riskier pieces are risky indeed, since they are somtimes highly customized and have no ready market if one needs to sell them. A derivative security may be based on a unique transaction, for which a bank writes a unique contract. The risk may be a complex blend of interest rates, currency prices, and other variables whose future is literally unknowable. A separate problem is that derivatives can be very highly leveraged—they sidestep the old regulatory effort to limit playing the market "on margin." So, in one sense, derivatives are designed to manage risk; in another sense, they invite highly speculative plays. If an investor bets wrong on which way interest rates are heading, he can be wiped out. In the bankruptcy of Orange County, California, blue-chip brokerage houses sold highly speculative derivative securities to the county treasurer, who should have known better, but didn't. For a while, he seemed to have the Midas touch. When the bottom fell out of the market for the securities he had purchased, county finances collapsed. Even large banks have taken large baths on derivatives. In 1994, clients of Banker's Trust New York, Inc., including Proctor & Gamble, took multimillion dollar losses on derivatives. Such seemingly sophisticated investors as Paine Webber lost $268 million; BankAmerica lost $68 million; investors in Piper Jaffray lost more than $700 million.

Thus the paradox of derivatives: a device invented to make risk more manageable leads to a market that is more speculative as a whole. Since the designers of derivatives make very lucrative commissions, they have a strong incentive to push the entire financial market in this general direction.

Michael Lewis's fine memoir, *Liar's Poker*, hilariously describes the rise and fall of Salomon Brothers and its mortgage-bond department, in which he worked. Salomon's chairman, John Gutfreund, and his chief mortgage-bond trader, Lewis Ranieri, transformed mortgage bonds from lackluster, low-risk instruments into highly speculative derivatives. Before the firm crashed, its mortgage department made multimillionaires out of many traders who hadn't yet reached their thirtieth birthday. In the Efficient Market Hypothesis, these instruments allow investors to make (or lose) money, and in the process to overcome some important market imperfections. But if one steps back, one must ask: What imperfection? The mortgage market has for fifty years been one of the economy's most efficient markets. Long before the invention of these risky hybrids, mortgage rates were only slightly over Treasury rates, and qualified homebuyers had no difficulty qualifying for credit. Derivative mortgage-backed securities have not increased the supply of mortgage credit, or lowered its cost relative to other benchmarks. Home mortgages still cost about one point more than comparable Treasury securities. Mainly, these securities have provided an outlet for one more form of gambling—and enriched the casino.

Scholarly critics of the Efficient Market Hypothesis point to a wide variety of empirical anomalies. The well-known "winner's curse" suggests that, in a pure auction market, the winner often overpays. Markets also betray odd, seemingly irrational "calendar effects." They crash in October, rebound in January, for no good fundamental reasons. One of the longest-running rebuttals to the Efficient Market Hypothesis is the fact that so-called closed-end mutual funds—which are mutual funds whose own shares are publicly traded—tend to diverge from the value of the underlying stocks that make up the fund. Smart investors ought to be able to make money by arbitraging that difference, and forcing the price back into alignment. Why they can't and don't has been the subject of much technical controversy. The funds often sell at discount, meaning that the market worth of the fund is less than that of its underlying assets. Nearly fifty years ago, Benjamin Graham called these discounts "an expensive monument erected to the inertia and stupidity of stockholders." Richard Thaler dryly comments: "It is important to remember that the statement 'price is equal to intrinsic value' is a testable proposition, not an axiom."

The Efficient Market Hypothesis has provided intellectual cover for the debt binge of the 1980s, the excesses of junk bonds and hostile corporate takeovers. It has counseled deregulation of financial markets generally, suggesting a world of undifferentiated financial institutions, with presumably well-informed investors and savers in the role of consenting adults. Since risk could be calibrated precisely against reward, the theory went, investors should be perfectly free to indulge their taste for risk. And purveyors should have the liberty to dream up whatever might attract the customers.

Since this conception of markets invokes only one brand of efficiency—the allocative sort—it ignores all the offsetting inefficiencies. Consider the real-world history of financial regulation, in banking and securities markets.

SECURITIES AND BANKING REGULATION

Even among advocates of deregulation, the Securities and Exchange Commission is generally held in high regard. The reason is that, for the most part, the SEC's brand of regulation is based on the principle of disclosure. The law requires that those who underwrite or make markets in securities disclose all material information that a prudent investor would want to know. Free-market economics, however grudgingly, admits that the correction of information failures is generally pro-efficiency, though it wonders why this task must fall to government.

Although business is generally averse to regulation, there is a broad constituency for an activist SEC on the part of investors. This tends to offset the pressure by investment bankers for less regulation. Corporations, likewise, are sometimes in the position of selling stock, sometimes in the position of investing in securities. As a result of these crosscutting pressures, there is more business support for an activist SEC than in the case of most regulatory agencies.

Note, first, that the SEC is needed to override the kind of market failure that existed in the 1920s when promoters could systematically mislead investors. Note, also, that the SEC in practice does a great deal more than mandate and police disclosure. The law prohibits insider trading and a variety of other abuses intended to manipulate stock prices or to deceive investors. The SEC is also responsible for policing accounting standards, which are the underlying basis for the required disclosures. This responsibility is currently delegated to the quasi-public Financial Standards Accounting Board, though there is an ongoing tug-of-war between the SEC segments of the financial community who desire more latitude for creative accounting.

The problem is that the new financial instruments and plays made possible by computerization, such as derivatives, interest-rate swaps, securitization of loans, and computerized program trades, regularly outrun the knowledge of investors and the capacity of the SEC to monitor and police the financial system. When derivatives became popular in the 1980s, the SEC and the Commodity Future Trading Commission struck an accord under which CFTC would regulate "futures" and the SEC would regulate "securities." As Thomas A. Russo, managing director of Lehman Brothers, observed in a recent speech, "The fallacy of this premise is highlighted best by foreign exchange options, which become securites when traded on a securities exchange, commodity options when traded on a futures exchange, and remain fundamentally unregulated when traded over-the-counter."

The purely financial part of the economy keeps moving further and further away from its ostensible role—the channeling of capital to the "real" part of the economy. It is only public regulation that keeps this tendency from turning self-cannibalizing. So even money markets, the most liquid and instantaneous markets of all, operate in a second-best world contoured by public regulation.

However, both the academic and the self-interested purveyors of laissez-faire resist extending regulatory oversight to new financial instruments that currently evade the SEC. For example, legislation proposed in 1994 by Senator Don Riegle and Congressman Henry Gonzalez, then the respective Senate and House Banking Committee chairmen, would have required sellers of derivatives to register with the SEC, and would have subjected them to the same disclosure and fair-marketing constraints as sellers of more conventional securities. Senator Byron Dorgan of North Dakota would go further and prohibit banks and other federally insured institutions from trading derivatives at all, except for legitimate hedging, where both sides of the transaction are covered. These reforms were sidetracked by the Republican 105th Congress and the general euphoria for laissez-faire.

The regulatory regime that governed banks and thrift institutions between the 1930s and the 1970s was emphatically a regime of the Second Best. It was a response to the destruction of the real economy that occurred when speculative financial markets went wild and then crashed. The Great Crash demonstrated the multiple failures of unregulated financial markets to self-correct—the manic delusion of investors, the deceptive pyramiding schemes offered by promoters, the excessive and self-intensifying market response to plunges in asset values.

Nearly a half-century later, just as the last bankers and brokers who personally experienced the Crash retired or died, financial markets and their scholarly paladins commenced a new romance with laissez-faire. The deregulation of banks and thrift institutions in the 1970s is an instructive story of second-best versus third- or fourth-best forms of accountability. As we briefly noted in chapter 1, the system of bank regulation devised in the 1930s limited exit, entry, and price. Yet banks could and did compete intensely for both depositors and borrowers, and served the goal of supplying capital to the economy with a minimum of speculative excess. This system of regulation, however, began unraveling in the 1970s. The broad causes for the shift were the new prestige of laissez-faire markets, the globalization of the financial economy, and the invention of institutions that circumvented the tight regulatory strictures on banks and thrift institutions. The immediate cause was inflation.

As long as inflation was low and stable, depositors could tolerate low, regulated passbook interest rates, and banks could finance long-term loans with relatively short-term deposits without fear of a dangerous mismatch. But as inflation in the 1970s crept upward, initially fueled by the stimulus of the Vietnam War, the collapse of the Bretton Woods system of global finance, and the first OPEC oil shock, depositors complained that their savings were earning less than the rate of inflation. In 1974, for example, the Federal Reserve's Regulation Q limited interest on deposits to 5 percent at banks and 5.25 percent at thrifts. In that year, the inflation rate was 11 percent.

Depositors, in effect, were subsidizing borrowers. Mortgage rates and rates on commercial loans were still relatively low, given rising inflation. A homeowner who took out a 7-percent mortgage in 1972 would enjoy a negative rate of interest for the next fifteen years of the loan. In addition, the interest would produce tax write-offs. As a bonus, the same inflation would eventually produce, on average, more than a trebling of the capital value of the house. The generation that bought homes before the late 1970s realized one of history's greatest (and broadest) financial windfalls.

Savers, by contrast, saw their financial wealth erode. By 1974, the low rate on passbook savings had become a populist consumer issue. Pressure to lift Regulation Q was felt across the political spectrum. Entrepreneurial bankers and state banking commissioners began finding ways around regulations prohibiting payment of interest on demand deposits (checking accounts). In Worcester, Massachusetts, an enterprising bank invented what it disingenuously called a Negotiable Order of Withdrawal, or NOW. When a depositor orders a withdrawal from his account and specifies that it be "negotiable," this is nothing but a check under another name. But regulators were willing to indulge the fiction. Checking accounts could not pay interest, but NOW accounts could. The Massachusetts banking commissioner went along. NOW accounts quickly spread to other states, and from savings banks to commercial banks. Congress was induced first to allow NOW accounts at federally chartered institutions, then to drop the fiction and to allow interest on checking accounts. The repeal of Regulation Q shortly followed.

Why did the banking industry join with consumer groups in pressing for the privilege of paying higher interest rates? In the same era, the pressure for market-rate earnings on savings deposits led to the invention of a new kind of financial institution, the money-market mutual fund, which became a major threat to banks. The Fidelity Corporation began selling shares in a mutual fund backed by investments in short-term money-market securities. The fund was not insured, but its investments were either guaranteed by government agencies, or were blue-chip. In addition, Fidelity arranged to connect a checking account to its mutual fund. You could place savings deposits in a money-market mutual fund, transfer them only as necessary to checking, and earn 7 percent when banks were paying only 5. The money was not insured by the FDIC, but millions of Americans saw it as safe enough.

When the Securities and Exchange Commission allowed Fidelity to sell shares in a money-market mutual fund that behaved much like a bank account, and when the banking authorities went along with the fiction that a NOW account was somehow different from a checking account, they began tugging on a thread that would eventually unravel the postwar regime of bank regulation. Marketization of the deposit side of the ledger quickly led to pressure to marketize the loan side as well, since banks needed to finance the higher interest payments with higher earnings.

By the mid-1970s, America's banks and thrift institutions were in the midst of a crisis of "disintermediation"—a fancy word for the fact that depositors were withdrawing funds from financial institutions in favor of other havens, which paid higher rates. Disintermediation was a massive crisis for the banking system, and not just because it meant a decline in banks' and thrifts' market share. Banks, and especially thrifts, often borrow short and lend long. When a financial institution makes a thirty-year mortgage loan at, say, 7 percent, that loan is backed by deposits of varying maturities, the longest of which will be perhaps four or five years. A typical bank has 30 to 40 percent of its deposits in demand deposits—money that can be withdrawn overnight. When money began pouring out of banks and thrifts into money funds, the banks suddenly found themselves without the deposits necessary to back their loans.

Traditionally, a "depository institution" is one that both takes in deposits and makes loans. As such, it is part of the nation's monetary system, since every time a bank makes a loan it creates credit and expands the economy's total supply of credit. Much of the nation's monetary policy is based on the system of "fractional reserve banking." This means that banks must keep a certain portion of their total assets in cash and other reserves, and lend only a specified multiple of those assets. In that fashion, the regulators can keep the total supply of credit on a manageable, noninflationary leash. But by the late 1970s, the banking system was under assault from hybrid creatures that took in deposits but did not make loans (money-market mutual funds), as well as ones that made loans but did not receive deposits (mortgage companies, the commercial-paper market, and the venture-capital market). Both depositors and borrowers could circumvent banks.

Thanks to a tolerant regulatory climate, some companies, like Sears, Roebuck, succeeded in breaching not only the wall between commercial banking and investment banking, but the more fundamental wall between finance and commerce, by having affiliated banks, stock brokerages, insurance companies, and real-estate subsidiaries, as well as department stores.

Though they did not make commercial loans and were not insured by the FDIC, as far as the consumer was concerned these hybrids looked liked banks and quacked like banks. Meanwhile, on the other side of the ledger, the host of nonbank banks began cutting into the very heart of the banking business—making commercial loans. It used to be that corporations relied on banks for their short-term credit. But increasingly, large corporations issue their own IOUs, sometimes underwritten by investment bankers, for direct sale to pension funds, insurance companies, and the general public. This market in commercial paper eliminates the bank's traditional role as judge of credit-worthiness and as middleman. It has removed a reliable and nearly risk-free source of the bank's business. By the same token, most consumers no longer use banks for auto loans, because the auto companies have their own financing operations, selling bonds in the money markets and using the proceeds to finance loans, sometimes at cut rates in order to promote sales. In some years, Ford Motor Company's profits from its financial business have exceeded its profits from making cars.

The paper that finances such nonbank lending is converted into securities, which are then sold by investment banks in the nation's money markets. Almost any such loan—an auto or mortgage loan, or for that matter a loan to Bolivia—can be "securitized." But of course, under the Glass-Steagall Act, commercial banks could not sell securities. So they were precluded from following the technological evolution of this new hybrid financial service into its logical end-markets. The banks did succeed in expanding into some other lines of business, by creative use of loopholes for bank holding companies. Some banks managed to use the holding company that nominally owns the bank to get into real estate, some kinds of insurance, and in a few cases stock brokerage. But, on balance, the gradual breach of Glass-Steagall has been a one-way street. Nonbanks—whose capital ratios are unregulated, who are not picked over by bank examiners, who lack deposit insurance—have swarmed into the quasi-banking business. And banks have not been able to swarm out. Note, however, that most of these shifts were not technologically inevitable, any more than the investment trusts of the 1920s were technologically driven. They required regulatory consent.

The final assault on the bank-regulatory regime came from globalization. Most foreign countries—the main exception being Japan—do not separate commercial banking from investment banking. So, whereas a U.S. bank is not permitted to underwrite a corporate bond in New York, its Zurich office is perfectly free to underwrite that bond in the Eurodollar market, nominally operating through a branch in the Netherlands Antilles. This means a market that could be operating at home is artificially driven offshore, where there is even less regulation.

All of these innovations had to be approved by the regulatory authorities. But since the mixed economy was under both ideological and practical assault, regulators and legislators saw little harm in letting innovation flower. To compete with money-market mutual funds for deposits and fend off the crisis of disintermediation, banks and thrifts won the right to pay higher rates of interest. But in order to do so, they had to earn higher interest on their investments.

Banks and thrifts could no longer remain the sleepy, by-the-numbers institutions of the 3-6-3 formula. The repeal of Regulation Q and the competition with money-market mutual funds produced a new set of pressures for entrepreneurial, go-go banking. The result was a series of highly speculative investments—in loans to third-world governments, in real-estate promotions, in equity positions in everything from oil wells to fast-food franchises—of the sort that an earlier generation of bankers and bank regulators shunned. And it led the financial industry to lobby Congress, successfully for the most part, for deregulation on a broad front, in order to permit the kind of high-yield investments that the banks needed.

Like the health-care industry, the banking industry does not exist in a political vacuum. Since the industry is heavily regulated, its ground rules are set by Congress. The American Bankers Association and the counterpart savings-and-loan leagues are among the capital's most aggressive lobbies. Throughout the 1970s, the banking lobbies successfully importuned Congress to repeal much of the post-Depression regulatory scheme. By 1981, this practical effort to keep banks competitive with new, less regulated competitors got a powerful ideological boost from the new Reagan administration, which esteemed deregulation as an end in itself.

In the case of thrift institutions, the pinnacle of this effort was the 1982 Garn–St. Germain Act, a bipartisan bill not unlike the 1981 tax act, which saw a bidding war between the two parties to give industry what it wanted. The act watered down regulation in several respects, and allowed thrift institutions to become far more speculative—with federally insured money. Violating the Theory of the Second Best, it removed an extra-market stick, but kept an extra-market carrot.

The result of this orgy of deregulation was the savings-and-loan collapse. The details were arcane, but at bottom the problem was very simple. Congress had substantially deregulated what thrift institutions could do, both in attracting and paying interest on deposits, and in making investments. A tiny savings-and-loan association with enough nerve could attract billions of dollars' worth of brokered money in national capital markets, by paying a quarter- or half-point over the going rate. To defray this above-market cost of capital, it then had to turn around and find above-market investments. Without quite appreciating what it was doing, Congress behaved as if banks were just another entrepreneur, without special fiduciary duties, without taxpayer-insured deposits. In a spectacular lapse, Congress and the Reagan administration deregulated nearly everything but deposit insurance, effectively inviting bankers to gamble with government-insured money.

Having set in motion a dangerously speculative form of deregulation, Congress, the bankers, and the newly politicized regulators also colluded to put off the day of reckoning. The whole game was predicated on the premise that thrift institutions could compete for deposits on the basis of price (interest) and earn enough money from loans and other investments to pay the inflated interest costs. As the investments became shakier and shakier, none of the players wanted to admit that the system had failed. Bankers used their influence with legislators and the administration to keep regulators from cracking down, in the hope that one more roll of the dice would make them whole. Many regulators, fearing a drain on the FDIC and FSLIC, conspired in the fiction that the investments would eventually pay off, and allowed banks and thrifts to lose still more money. When the reckoning finally came, this experiment in marketization cost the taxpayers $160 billion. In the aftermath, when regulators belatedly cracked down and nervous lenders became newly risk-averse, the economy then paid a second price in the form of loans called and credit denied.

According to the Congressional Budget Office, there is a further indirect cost, in that the estimated total borrowing for finance deposit-insurance losses will accrue interest costs of $15 billion a year. In addition to the direct costs of the bailout, CBO estimates indirect losses to the economy in the form of foregone output, totalling over $500 billion by the year 2000.

In the case of commercial banks, as opposed to thrifts, the counterpart debacle was the third-world loan calamity and the real-estate bust of the early 1980s. Like thrifts, banks found themselves under new pressure from close nonbank competitors that did not face the banks' regulatory constraints. Their traditional cash cow, blue-chip corporate lending, was undermined by the commercial-paper market and by new, esoteric forms of financing. So banks sought new, higher-risk customers.

Contrary to the Efficient Market Hypothesis, however, the banks had not anticipated the second OPEC oil shock and the interest-rate crunch of the late 1970s and early 1980s. Above-market third-world loans, which seemed great money-makers in the 1970s, turned sour in the 1980s, as high-interest rates turned into too much of a good thing and pushed Latin American economies into recession. Ordinarily prudent bankers failed to perceive that a real-estate bubble was only as durable as the business cycle. The money-center banks were allowed by an indulgent Federal Reserve Board to carry their underwater loans at book value rather than market value. Had the regulatory authorities followed their own usual rules, several of the largest money-center banks would have been ruled insolvent. Over more than a decade, the banks, encouraged by the regulators, kept lending new money to cover the interest payments due on old loans, while the Fed, the Treasury, and their foreign counterparts worked out elaborate schemes such as debt-equity swaps to clean up the banks' balance sheets gradually. The effect on Latin American economies was a decade of lost growth. Many observers contend that for most of the 1980s the Federal Reserve kept interest rates higher than necessary, guided by a desire to shore up the banks' earnings, to compensate for their earlier errors. Here was a case where the market (in the persona of the banks) failed disastrously, and was rescued only by central banks breaking the market's own usual accounting rules.

Nonetheless, the quest for further deregulation of the banking system continued—driven both by ideology and by the banks' need to find new sources of earnings. In the 1980s, brokerage houses, through junk-bond deals, derivative securities, and leveraged buyouts, were making the big profits, while banks struggled to shake off the effects of the third-world loan losses and the domestic real-estate bust. So banks were eager to break what remained of Depression-era regulatory shackles, and to gain the powers of their investment-banker rivals.

In the late 1980s, advocates of further deregulation focused on the one remaining pillar of the New Deal system of financial regulation—the Glass-Steagall Act. A brief flashback is in order.

Most of us dimly remember a famous photo of the financier J. P. Morgan, Jr., sitting incongruously with a circus dwarf on his lap. Morgan, at the time, was testifying under subpoena in an investigation by the U.S. Senate Banking Committee on the financial manipulations that helped trigger the great stock-market crash. (A PR agent had thrust the midget onto the portly Morgan as a sight gag.) Historians and economists generally conclude that the 1929 Crash had multiple causes, but in that winter of 1933 Congress was zeroing in on one particular villain—speculative investment schemes promoted by large banks with brazen conflicts of interest. In a typical scheme, the bank would underwrite a stock or bond, sell it to investors via a subsidiary "investment trust" (the forerunner of modern mutual funds), and even lend the investor the money to buy the bond. If a security underwritten by the bank turned sour, the bank redoubled its efforts to unload it on the public.

In the populist aftermath of the Crash, insider trading by bankers came in for particular and well-deserved indignation. In a five-part investigative series in *The New Republic* in the spring of 1930 sifting through the wreckage of Wall Street, John T. Flynn, then the magazine's financial editor, had unearthed scandalous details of how banks used investment trusts to peddle paper for corporate clients to unsuspecting investors who had trusted the bank to provide disinterested fiduciary advice. Investment trusts, Flynn concluded, were reasonable for investors with a taste for speculation—but bankers ought not be permitted to sponsor them.

When Congress moved to repair the financial system, it moved on multiple fronts. It converted the fledgling (and quasi-private) Federal Reserve System into a genuine central bank. It built a rigid wall between commercial banking and investment banking via Glass-Steagall. It created an entirely separate regulatory scheme for investment banking and stock brokerage, based primarily on the principles of disclosure and the prohibition of insider trading. Commercial banks got closer regulatory supervision, deposit insurance, and a prohibition against engaging in the riskier business of underwriting or marketing securities. Congress further acted to limit the interest that banks could pay depositors to help banks resist the temptation to indulge in more speculative ventures in pursuit of high returns.

The pieces of the scheme fit together logically. If banks were partially instruments of monetary policy, and if the government was ultimately backstopping them, then banks should not take excessive risks. An investor of more entrepreneurial bent was free to take his chances in the largely unregulated securities market, where he would be to an extent forewarned by the disclosure schema. But a depositor putting his money in the bank mainly for safekeeping and for modest interest could be sure it was safe. The Glass-Steagall schema also reflected the desire of competing financial magnates to euchre the House of Morgan, which was the one banker-broker that had managed to run both businesses competently.

Putting aside the conceits of the Efficient Market Hypothesis, the practical dissents against repeal of Glass-Steagall boil down to three: Letting banks become more speculative, with other people's insured savings, puts the whole system at greater risk. Combining banking, underwriting, and brokerage intensifies the conflicts of interest that already permeate the financial industry. And, as a practical matter, the idea of segregating a bank's insured activity from more speculative activity is an impossibility.

Remarkably enough, despite more than a decade of assault, Glass-Steagall still stands—but not because of the power of intellectual discourse or the appeal of regulation. Rather, the power of the several interest groups has been more than a match for the forces of deregulation. Big investment houses are not sure they want commercial banks invading their turf. Insurance companies, likewise, resist the threat to their industry. Most theorists of laissez-faire financial markets have argued that regulatory policy should recognize the inevitability of one big, undifferentiated "financial-services industry"; that the cleanest solution would be simply to acknowledge this and allow any financial company to compete in whatever lines of business it chose to pursue: commercial banking, investment banking, insurance, mutual funds, real estate—whatever.

The trouble with this solution, however, is that banks remain special creatures which enjoy a safety net of protections from the federal government. It is not practical for the government to permit a big bank to fail. But it is even less practical to extend the federal financial safety net to the entire economy. Yet, if a bank or its holding-company affiliates were permitted to take huge risks, and a mega–financial enterprise affiliated with a bank found itself on the brink of insolvency, the federal government would find itself holding the bag, lest the ailing affiliate drag down the ailing bank along with it. There has been more than one case, such as the previously bailed out Continental Illinois, where the bank improperly used its own assets to bail out a failing affiliate. Extending the federal safety net by proxy to the entire financial industry would intensify the moral hazard of excessive speculation by banks. But failing to do it would jeopardize the security of banks. The only solution is either to repair radically the existing breaches in the Glass-Steagall wall, or—paradoxically—to intensify supervision of newly deregulated bankers and brokers.

Sponsors of Glass-Steagall repeal have imagined a "firewall," separating the bank from its nonbank affiliates. In principle, a bank's investment-banking activities would be regulated by the SEC, in exactly the same fashion as a broker's. A bank could not bail out its nonbank businesses. But there are so many ways for a bank to use a brokerage to do favors for bank clients at the expense of the investing public that the firewall might not hold in a situation when a bank holding-company subsidiary such as a real-estate investment trust or a commodities firm got into serious trouble. As author and banking critic Martin Mayer testified to the U.S. Senate Banking Committee, "If you hadn't had Glass-Steagall, the entire third world debt situation would have developed differently, because they would have peddled this junk to the public as they did in the 1920s. . . . The temptation," Mayer warned, will be "to securitize the worst assets."

Congress can enact nominal strictures about how bank holding companies ought to behave, said Mayer, "But it isn't the bank holding company that makes this sort of decision, it is an executive whose world is about to come apart with the revelation of his lousy credit judgement in the XYZ matter. His wife's brother-in-law is on the board of the country club with the president of the underwriting subsidiary, and, what the hell, the loan will probably turn out to be all right."

Others, such as economist Robert Litan, have imagined a new creature, the "narrow bank." It would continue to have federal deposit insurance; in return, it would have very limited investment powers. The narrow bank would continue to be a safe harbor for small savers, and an instrument of government monetary policy. All other financial institutions would be free to pursue a more go-go approach—and let the investor beware. Still others, such as James Pierce, an economist at the University of California, would design the regulatory system around functions rather than nominal kinds of institutions. Regulatory safeguards would follow the type of financial services; for example, all institutions that offered checkinglike accounts would have banklike deposit insurance and banklike regulation. All companies in the securities business would be regulated like investment bankers.

Eventually, Congress will likely overhaul the financial-services industry. And there is a wide range of ways to mix and match. But as this brief history has suggested, it would be extremely unwise to deregulate it entirely. There are simply too many conflicts of interest, too many temptations to speculative excess, and too many systemic risks to leave the financial system entirely to the tender mercies of markets. Banking, like so many of the complex mixed sectors described herein, is a realm of the economy where greater competition paradoxically depends on greater regulation, if it is to fulfill its efficiency promise.

THE "MARKET FOR CORPORATE CONTROL"

For more than two decades, the exponents of the liberation of financial markets have argued that the right to manage a large corporation should be seen as a market just like any other. This became the theoretical rationalization for the hostile-takeover fad of the 1980s. The intellectual defenders of hostile takeovers contend that such takeovers serve the purpose of improving the efficiency of the market system by providing a more accurate price, and by allowing raiders to squeeze out inefficiencies tolerated by incumbent managers. Raiders were said to "maximize shareholder value"—and what could be a more desirable goal than that?

A hostile takeover occurs when a raider thinks that the stock market is undervaluing the shares of a particular company. The raider then makes an offer to buy a controlling interest, usually at a significant premium over the market price, and invariably with borrowed money. Once a company is "in play," the price is bid up and some kind of takeover usually occurs. Either the raider succeeds, or the target company finds some other, friendlier partner to take it over, sometimes called a "white knight."

After a buyout is consummated, the raider in effect has used the assets of the target company to collateralize the new debt he has incurred to finance the takeover. Now, in order to pay off the increased debt, the new owner must squeeze more revenue out of the assets he has acquired. This is sometimes done by closing less profitable facilities or achieving other consolidations, by laying off managers and workers, or by cutting the pay of those who remain. Sometimes a takeover is mounted only to sell off the assets afterward. In a "bust-up takeover," the raider is a pure middleman. He brokers or "arbitrages" between an old set of players—shareholders who in hindsight seriously undervalued their company, and managers who caused it to underperform—and new owners who pay a premium to buy it and who will necessarily squeeze out more return or lose their investment.

In principle, a raider (by definition) is better suited to run a target company than the incumbent managers. His willingness to pay a price in excess of the current market valuation signals that he must have a greater capacity to improve performance; otherwise he wouldn't pay the higher price. This is praised as a purer form of market discipline.

The opponents of hostile takeovers have often been cast as the mere defenders of incumbent management. Some doubtless are. But the real issue here is not whether a given set of managers gets to keep their jobs. It is whether this form of asset rearrangement is the best way of holding managers accountable and maximizing the performance of real companies. Often these were promoted mainly for their transactional value and the windfall returns they could provide to middlemen.

The problems with this form of market discipline are multiple. It would be one thing if the targets were badly managed companies that were running shareholder assets into the ground. But some of the targets have been America's best-managed corporations. Often the target company was attractive because it was so well run that it had squirreled away substantial cash, which was there to be looted. And some of the raiders knew nothing about the businesses they were acquiring. The proof of the pudding is that, as many studies showed, the stock price of the now bloated acquiring company often declined. Often, too, the new owners were not better managers; they were simply more ruthless about cutting the paychecks of longtime employees. The result was not a gain to "efficiency," but simply a transfer of income and wealth from worker to new owner. The more the new economy has been subject to this kind of rearranging, cost-cutting, and downsizing, the less are employees able to defend themselves.

There is also a paradox with respect to the theory that undergirds the takeover movement—the theory of efficient markets. Either the market price is efficient just before a raid is mounted, or it is efficient afterward. Given that the price dramatically rises once a takeover attempt is announced, it is hard to see how it could be efficient in both cases. A stock market that systematically undervalues many of its crown jewels is not an efficient market.

Raiders, of course, often guess wrong, too—the winner's curse again. For example, the Canadian Robert Campeau, who briefly won control of most of America's department-store chains, seriously overpaid. Many of them ended up in bankruptcy. In retrospect, the investment-banking concerns like First Boston, who staked Campeau (and reaped large transaction fees), guessed wrong about him, just as Campeau guessed wrong about how much he could wring out of his targets. But they had the motivation of enormous transaction fees virtually to throw money at Campeau. Louis Lowenstein, in a careful comparison of the balance sheets of three large retailers, compared two that had been the target of leveraged buyouts (Macy's and Federated) with one that had not (The May Co.). Between 1985 and 1989, debt payments overwhelmed the operating incomes of Federated and Macy's, both of which went bankrupt, while May continued to have manageable debt burdens and remained profitable.

Prior to the late 1970s, there were virtually no such hostile takeovers, because it was not considered fair play for an investment banker or a commercial bank to lend a corporation or an individual money with which to mount a raid on another company against the will of its incumbent board of directors. Such raids were not illegal; they were simply not done. If one wanted to acquire a controlling interest in a company, one either bought a large number of shares or negotiated a friendly merger. Institutional investors (pension funds, mutual funds, life-insurance companies) likewise followed the custom known as the Wall Street Rule. If they didn't like incumbent management, they did not actively use the power of their shares to displace the managers or even to modify their strategy; they simply sold the stock.

The recent history of the hostile-takeover movements begins with a tiny and quirky investment-banking firm, Kohlberg, Kravis, Roberts & Co. KKR had used borrowed money to finance several minor takeovers, but in 1978 it pulled off the leveraged buyout of a Fortune 500 firm, Houdaille Industries, a manufacturer of machine tools. KKR found its opening when Gerry Santarelli, the sixty-seven-year-old CEO, began contemplating retirement, and two younger executives were concerned about the succession. Houdaille, at the time, had almost no long-term debt. KKR sold Santarelli on a deal that became a model of the genre. They proposed to buy the company for $335 million—entirely with borrowed money. The interest on the debt would wipe out Houdaille's tax liability. They lured blue-chip lenders with 10- to 12-percent interest rates, then far above market. They lured investment bankers with about six million dollars in transaction fees. Santarelli would enjoy a windfall $3 million from the run-up of the stock. The two other executives were promised raises. And KKR would get to own the company. The deal succeeded. KKR was in business as a premier junk-bond impresario. Unfortunately, Houdaille, saddled with immense interest payments, failed.

Having been devised by a few Wall Street mavericks, hostile takeovers were supercharged by the regulatory and ideological climate of the 1980s. Junk-bond deals became the emblem of the decade. The interest on the new debt was tax-deductible, and under the Economic Recovery Tax Act (ERTA) of 1981, a raider paying a premium for a corporation in a tender offer could then take advantage of accelerated depreciation write-offs on an inflated asset base. Further, the middlemen making the immense profits on the transactions—lawyers, investment bankers, institutional investors—tended to be people of substantial political influence. They were a force for coherent ground rules, but above all they wanted the game to continue. To the extent that the Reagan SEC was involved at all, it acted to expedite the game, in line with the prevailing Chicago theory that shareholders benefit.

Once the first raiders demonstrated that hostile takeovers could be successfully mounted, they met with general approval from market-oriented financial economists. For raids seemed a marketlike solution to the problem in corporate governance posed in the 1932 classic work *The Modern Corporation and Private Property*, by A. A. Berle and Gardiner Means. As Berle and Means pointed out, the modern corporation bore little resemblance to its textbook picture, in which shareholders elect directors, and directors, as agents of owners, hire managers. By the 1920s, the corporation was already an entity run by a self-perpetuating board that was itself often the tame creation of the chief executive. The investor was passive. This was the famous "separation of ownership from control." Except for their nominal equity ownership and their fluctuating returns, the shareholders might as well have been bondholders—for they had no effective influence on management.

If shareholders have little influence over managers, then the efficiency of the corporate form as resource allocator is open to challenge. In the 1920s, the era when Berle and Means conducted their research, corporate assets were highly concentrated—the smoking gun was Means's calculation that the two hundred largest nonfinancial corporations controlled 49 percent of all corporate wealth. This, in turn, suggested a picture far from Adam Smith's. If the nominal owners did not control the managers, and if corporate wealth was highly concentrated, then competition was far from perfect, and the pricing of both products and stocks was wrong. Corporations enjoyed the power to rig markets, administer prices, and squirrel away excess profits on behalf of their managers.

"By surrendering control and responsibility," Berle and Means wrote, shareholders "have surrendered the right that the corporation should be operated in their sole interest." Their timing was superb. The research of Berle and Means helped strip the corporation of its presumed legitimacy, at a moment when history had provided the exclamation point. Their book fed into a broad stream of works that undergirded the economic interventionism of the Roosevelt era. Berle and Means both became New Dealers. Of the two, Means was more interested in corporate concentration, whereas Berle addressed the dwindling influence of shareholders.

In their view, economic concentration and financial manipulation were the twin villains of the piece. The remedy was a set of regulatory interventions to step up antitrust enforcement, to bring securities markets under much tighter regulation. Yet, in a sense, both men were reluctant New Dealers. The subtext of the book was the mourning of a presumed Eden when the real economy more closely resembled the atomized textbook economy, and markets were more nearly self-regulating.

Thus, the ideological import of their classic work was ambiguous. On the one hand, the actual shape of corporate capitalism seemed such a far cry from market discipline that it justified substantial intervention. The abuses of concentration and managerial capitalism were only compounded by the purely financial manipulation that they invited. On the other hand, there was the tacit message that, if the shareholder, the fallen hero of the piece, could just be restored to sovereignty, then much of the ongoing regulatory intervention might be superfluous.

Though the New Deal did significantly increase the oversight of financial markets, it did little to change the governance of corporations. The chartering of corporations remained a matter for state, rather than federal, law. The Wagner Act introduced a measure of what John Kenneth Galbraith later called "countervailing power"—but only in companies that were unionized. Nothing like the German or Scandinavian conception of state-mandated codetermination applied to U.S. corporations. Corporations remained purely accountable to their shareholders, not to a broader community of stakeholders. If the shareholder had ceased to be sovereign in practice, he remained the exiled sovereign in theory.

The postwar economy remained very much a managerial economy of the sort criticized by Means, but largely purged of the financial manipulation criticized by Berle. Financial capital, for the most part, was rendered usefully passive. New Deal regulation had separated investment banking from commercial banking. Securities regulation both required substantial disclosure, and prohibited most of the financial pyramiding that contributed to the speculative aspect of the Great Crash. Relatively high corporate taxation appropriated nearly half of the corporation's social product. But instead of rendering the corporation more accountable by dethroning the manager and empowering the shareholder, the interventionists of the postwar period constrained corporate excess via Galbraith's countervailing power of labor and of government. This was the era of stable, and arguably benign, oligopoly. Shareholders may have been dethroned, but the economy and the stock market both thrived.

After a decade or so of mediocre corporate performance, the hostile-takeover boom, ironically, harked back to Berle and Means. In the more than sixty years since Berle and Means wrote, the debate has come nearly full-circle. The prophets of the leveraged buyout claim to be restoring shareholder sovereignty, which should warm the hearts of Berle and Means. But they do so by way of financial speculation—Berle and Means's nemesis.

When corporate-takeover artists first burst on the scene, they claimed to be the invisible hand made flesh—a business-school version of populists. In theory, they embodied the democratic virtue of enhancing corporate accountability, the capitalist virtue of maximizing value for shareholders, and the social virtue of forcing the redeployment of underperforming assets on reluctant (and overpaid) corporate managers. In the mid-1980s, in the heyday of the takeover boom, *Time*'s cover feature on oilman Boone Pickens was sufficiently flattering for Pickens to distribute it in his publicity materials.

When the intellectual history of the Reagan era is written, one of the more revealing artifacts will be a chapter in the 1985 Economic Report of the President, titled "The Market for Corporate Control." The chapter is pure Chicago School theory, right down to its title, which is borrowed from a famous article of Professor Henry Manne, who argued three decades ago that corporate-takeover battles should be understood as markets no different from other markets. Manne and his disciples contend that whole corporations are simply commodities, "like apples," which exist in auction markets, and that takeover contests are simply rival teams of managers competing for the right to operate corporate assets. The management team that can command the highest price is, by definition, the highest-valued team.

Although the leveraged buyout (LBO) movement claims to be acting on behalf of the shareholder, the effect is almost the opposite of true shareholder empowerment. Though the raider is very much an engaged "shareholder," he often plays that role only on a transitional basis. The usual investors, often large institutions, are merely interested bystanders, enjoying windfall profits thanks to the accelerated trading and stock run-up wherever they can—but not increasing their supervision of managers. In the aftermath of a leveraged buyout, the corporation often has to divert money that would otherwise be invested in new plant and equipment, to pay off the higher debt. In contested takeovers during the 1980s, the premium paid by the raider averaged 80 percent. In some of the larger leveraged buyouts, such as RJR Nabisco and Kraft, it exceeded 100 percent.

Of course, the maximization of current shareholder value is hardly the only test of economic worth. Share prices were soaring in mid-1929, but this was a sign of fever, not health. One effect of takeovers is accelerating debt. The debt-equity ratio of U.S. corporations soared during the 1980s, before the LBO boom finally crashed into a sea of red ink and devalued junk bonds.

At the level of the firm, takeover fears only intensify the obsession with the quarterly bottom line, for when profits drop the stock may become undervalued, making it a target. Takeover worries also lead prudent managers to get rid of cash cushions, to raid pension funds, and to throw overboard anything that might make them a target. Often managers deliberately turn a swan back into an ugly duckling in order to make the firm less attractive to a potential raider. In cases like CBS's successful defense against Ted Turner, the target firm ends up uglifying itself by selling off some of its most profitable divisions, or taking on crippling debt, which depresses its own earnings for years to come.

Moreover, the claim that target firms are poorly managed underperformers is not borne out by the facts either. A study by Professor Lowenstein looked at all of the industrial firms that were targets of hostile takeovers during 1981. He found that they enjoyed a return on equity of 16 percent—well above average.

This finding only reflects common sense. Raiders are after good firms that happen to have depressed stock prices; they are not interested in paying premium prices for lemons.

Many of the takeovers, in hindsight, turned out to be bad deals. This is hardly surprising, since, as Michael Lewis put it in *Liar's Poker*, they were often the result of a twenty-six-year-old apprentice investment banker playing with his computer rather than a move by someone who knew something about the industry. There is a long catalogue of cases in which the acquiring firm, understandably, knew less about what it was buying than the established management, and proved to be an even worse manager. Several recent studies confirm that hostile takeovers indeed bid up the price of the target firm (as they would have to), but, interestingly, they tend to depress the performance of the raiding firm. Harvard economist Frederick Scherer found that companies that were acquired and then sold off had above-average profitability before they were acquired, but performed poorly afterward.

In the 1960s, it was very fashionable for financial economists to defend conglomerates on the theory that, with diverse lines of business, a corporation could operate like a miniature capital market, shifting capital into more profitable lines of business and out of lower-yield ones. Ironically enough, the same cheerleaders of the infallibility of the financial markets, who were praising conglomerate acquisitions in the 1970s, are now praising the efficiency of "bust-up acquisitions," in which a raider buys out a firm in order to sell off its pieces. Their rationale is that conglomerates were never very efficient in the first place.

Another intriguing phenomenon that gives the lie to the Chicago interpretation of the efficiency of hostile takeovers is the latest fad, the management buyout. Managers have found that two can play this game. The same device available to raiders—borrowing money and buying stock—is available to managers. Many have pre-emptively taken their companies private, using the same sort of junk-bond financing as raiders. Now, obviously, if the social justification for an unfriendly takeover is the claim that incumbent management was doing a poor job, the same claim cannot possibly apply when that same incumbent management buys out the shareholders. On the contrary, there is a pretty fair presumption that, if management is taking advantage of its privileged information and swooping in to buy out undervalued stock, then it is violating its fiduciary duty to its own shareholders. Almost by definition, if management can reap windfalls by buying assets at more than they are "worth," it should have paid the shareholders a higher price and let the shareholders get the windfall. And there is some evidence that a management preparing to go private can subtly act to drive down the stock price, in order to buy it back at a bargain later on, by investing in capital improvements, or overfunding pension plans and thereby depressing reported earnings. When management buys the company, there may be an invisible hand at work, but it is the invisible hand not of Adam Smith but of Alex Portnoy.

When one sets aside assumptions and gets down to cases, often the only factor that makes the deal pay at all is the tax angle. In his study of management buyouts, Professor Lowenstein found that, absent the tax subsidy, the return on equity in a sample of twenty-eight management buyouts would have been a paltry 6 percent. Hostile takeovers do produce gains for one class of shareholders—people who happen to hold shares in a target company on the eve of a bidding war—but, contrary to the Chicago view of financial markets, they don't automatically translate into gains to the national welfare. The reason lies in a double market failure.

The first is the failure of the stock market to reflect accurately the true "worth" of a given firm on a given day. Often the total value of a firm's shares is substantially less than its liquidation value, or the price it would fetch in a negotiated sale. But that is no proof that the present managers are inferior to the raiders. The shares may be depressed for any number of reasons, ranging from consumer confidence about the economy as a whole, to current high interest rates pulling money into the bond market, to industry-specific investor pessimism. In the late 1980s, with oil selling for about twenty-seven dollars a barrel, the shares of major oil companies were trading for an equivalent price of about three dollars a barrel for the oil they had in the ground.

A corporate raider is actually arbitraging between the market for the firm's shares, and the market for the entire firm. If the new rules of the marketplace provide that any company is up for grabs anytime a prospective raider can borrow enough money, then the entire real economy is turned into a speculative casino.

And this raises the second sort of market failure, the failure of an executive of an acquiring firm to represent the long-term interests of his own shareholders. Why, after all, would a raider pay a grossly inflated premium to acquire a firm in a hostile-tender offer, often far in excess of what the firm is worth, even to the extent of doing damage to the acquiring company? The answer is that the executive who plans the raid is typically feathering his own nest, not the firm's. A corporate executive's personal self-interest is not identical to the self-interest of the entire firm. Economists such as Herbert Simon (who received the Nobel Prize for the insight) have suggested that corporate executives often reap more personal gain by expanding the size of the firm than by maximizing its profitability; a mega-takeover is a quick way to maximize size.

Often, the stimulus to the takeover is less the real gain to be earned by shareholders or by a more efficient allocation of resources than the windfall, front-end fees to be reaped by insiders. These include payments to diverse promoters—accountants, lawyers, commercial bankers, investment bankers, and golden parachutes to executives. To these asset-rearrangers, the ultimate "efficiency" of the transaction is far less important than that the deal take place.

The irony of the hostile-takeover form of corporate accountability is that it (arguably) brings greater pressure to bear on managers—but by exposing them to the full force of financial markets at their most speculative. In that sense, it intensifies what is already a widely criticized flaw in American capitalism, its short-termism. What we really have here are two rival models of corporate accountability. At one extreme, the argument is that a speculative financial market serves shareholders, by displacing lazy managers and by fetching higher and presumably more accurate stock prices. But since a trading market is by definition a short-term market, this form of accountability intensifies a characteristic form of market failure—myopia.

An alternative regime would render corporate managers more accountable through a range of institutional reforms. A moderate version of this approach would discourage a purely trading market, and cultivate investors with longer-term horizons—an approach that some have called "relational" or "relationship" investing.

In the German and Japanese systems, this role is played principally by banks. Most Japanese stock shares are seldom traded. Either corporations hold each other's stocks, or stocks are held for the long term by banks, pension funds, and insurance companies. Raiding is unknown in Japan, since it is illegal for one corporation to acquire another against the wishes of the target company's board of directors. However, Japanese banks, precisely as long-term owners, are relentless in their supervision of corporations. German banks play more or less the same role. In both countries, corporations tend to have higher debt-equity ratios than in the United States. This is nonetheless prudent, because of the closer supervision by owners.

The rather shallower equities markets in Germany and Japan have also been criticized, with some justification. It is said that both Germany and Japan have an overly institutionalized form of capitalism, with too small a role for entrepreneurial, "risk-bearing" capital. This may have its problems, but one of the offsetting benefits is to give corporate managers some respite from the quarterly-performance mania necessary to satisfy a trader's stock market, yet without sacrificing necessary accountability. A German or Japanese chief executive who performs badly will be removed, not by a hostile takeover, but by the board, with the key bank often taking a lead role.

U.S. advocates of a more relational form of capitalism look to a variety of reforms, some in the structure of corporations, others in the structure of financial markets, tax laws, and the role of large institutional investors. Because of the Depression-era Glass-Steagall Act, prohibiting commercial banks from playing the role of investment bankers, and because of the broader tradition in the United

States separating finance from commerce, a German-style solution is improbable. So American advocates of long-termism tend to look to other institutional investors, such as pension funds, in the hope that they can play a more activist role in corporate governance.

The California Public Employees Retirement System (CALPERS), with its hundred-billion-dollar stock portfolio, is often cited as a model case of a large institutional investor taking a more activist role in corporate oversight. The former New York State comptroller, Edward V. Regan, has urged pension funds to become more engaged shareholders. In 1987, the California and New York public-employee pension systems teamed up to win a greater role from Texaco in nominating directors to that company's board. Since the mid-1980s, CALPERS and its allies in the shareholder-rights movement have thrown their weight around in proxy contexts and shareholder meetings, and have successfully challenged the management strategies of such giants as GM, IBM, Sears, and Time-Warner.

In 1989, CALPERS and the Pennsylvania Public School Employees Retirement System initiated—and won—a proxy fight against the management of Honeywell, Inc., of which they were major shareholders. But the reform, ironically, was intended to make Honeywell less able to defend itself against hostile takeovers. The big pension funds, unlike German banks, find themselves on both sides of the debate. In their quest for high returns, they sometimes insert themselves in the management of companies deemed to be underperforming. Yet some of their remedies, in this case weakening management's defense against hostile takeovers, only intensify the short-term nature of the trading market. Edward Regan, a strong advocate of a stronger role for institutional investors and a more relational brand of investment, also likes to boast that he saved the taxpayers of New York tens of millions of dollars in commissions by firing the fund managers and simply buying the stock index. This strategy, though cost-effective, also places large institutional investors on both sides of the question, since it is the antithesis of the Warren Buffett–style investor, who invests based on a careful study of fundamentals and plays a genuinely hands-on role.

For the most part, pension funds are there to maximize return, not to be hands-on managers. The typical pension fund owns hundreds of stocks, and it is simply not practical for it to play the role of engaged owner, except in a handful of cases. Its fiduciary obligation, moreover, is to its ultimate beneficiaries. The average institutional investor sells 40 percent of its portfolio within a year of purchase. During the LBO boom of the 1980s, pension funds were, in the main, part of the problem. They loved the stock run-ups created whenever a company was in play. They left the chore of restructuring, helter-skelter, to the takeover artists, rather than playing the role of patient capital. And this is not surprising, for an American pension fund is a far cry from a German bank, in its role, structure, and mission.

Still, if one embraces the view that the problem in corporate finance and governance is too much market, not too little, there is plenty that can be done. The Twentieth Century Fund's 1992 report on "Market Speculation and Corporate Governance" blamed the short-term horizons of corporate managers largely on the shift to more speculative, performance-oriented financial markets. The report made several recommendations. These included a change in capital-gains taxation to discourage short-term, speculative investing, as well as changes in the laws of corporate governance to allow shareholders and non-management directors to play a more activist role.

A more aggressive version of the same basic approach would tax stock transactions, as long proposed by James Tobin. This would create powerful incentives for investors, both institutional and individual, to look to the long-term, underlying value of corporations, and it would take much of the profit out of purely speculative trading. Senator Nancy Kassebaum and others proposed a bill, the aptly titled Excessive Churning and Anti-Speculation Act, which would impose a short-term capital-gains tax on pension funds—a 10-percent tax on the gains of securities held thirty days or less and a 5-percent tax on assets held 180 days or less. This is necessary because pension funds are tax-exempt, and their trading strategies would not be affected by changing the terms of the ordinary capital-gains tax. Kassebaum's intent was to discourage pension funds from trying to make short-term trading profits.

Pension funds and life-insurance companies, by their very nature, are seemingly the ideal long-term investor. They collect money that represents the deferred wages of employees or the premiums of people insuring their lives, and because early cashing in is either severely penalized or not possible at all, these investors (unlike banks) know that they will not be hit with sudden demands for cash. So the long-term-liability side of their balance sheets could usefully be matched with a long-term view of their assets (investments). However, because they are not banks, and because their investments are necessarily highly diversified, most pension funds and other institutional investors fall short of the long-sought hands-on owner. If they did take on a genuinely long-term outlook, it would likely stay relatively passive. Even at their best, such as the CALPERS brand of hands-on corporate monitoring, these measures retain a fairly traditional view of corporate governance, in which the corporation is responsible only to the owner—the shareholder. Such proposals, though usefully reducing the purely speculative aspect of financial markets, fall short of a "stakeholder" conception of the corporation.

TOWARD STAKEHOLDER CAPITALISM

Prior to the speculative era of the 1980s, the stakeholder aspect of the corporation was tacit. Often the management of large companies saw themselves as closely associated with the fate of a locality. Detroit was synonymous with automaking, Pittsburgh with steel, Seattle with Boeing. As corporations came to be seen as nothing but fungible sets of assets, this older conception was dismissed as sentimental and inefficient. However, if hyper-marketization itself brings new kinds of inefficiency, then it makes sense to reclaim and to formalize the stakeholder concept of the corporation.

Historically, corporations were granted special privileges and immunities from the crown, and later from the democratic state, for narrow privileges. The general-purpose joint stock company became widespread only in the nineteenth century. Some theorists of political democracy, such as David Ellerman, argue that the extension of political rights to citizens in the late eighteenth century was short-circuited, in that such rights were never extended to the workplace. One can imagine a wide range of remedies to the problem of managerial short-sightedness which entail Albert Hirschman's "voice" rather than enhanced Chicago-style discipline of the financial market.

German and Scandinavian codetermination is one such model. The employee does not quite have property rights in the enterprise, but is, via works councils, something close to coequal with the shareholder. There is a kind of dynamic tension between the equity that is purely bought and sold in financial markets, and the "sweat equity" that comes from having spent most of one's career working in an enterprise. In efficiency terms, there is a danger that a company purely accountable to its employees is at risk of paying excessive wages, and not investing enough. But one that is purely "accountable" to shareholders via the tender mercies of corporate raiders may well plunder its human and physical assets in a different way.

One useful home-grown model of stakeholder capitalism can be found in the blueprint prepared in early 1996 for a Senate Democratic task force on a high-wage economy, chaired by New Mexico Senator Jeff Bingaman (see "Responsible Corporations," page 108).

The Bingaman model is only one possible blueprint, but the general approach is worth contemplation, in the broader context of the debate about how to slow down financial speculation and still hold managers accountable. Basically, this approach concludes that financial markets, especially in their speculative incarnation, are an imperfect tool for corporate accountability. They only exacerbate the short-termism plaguing the economy, and exaggerate the gross inequalities by conferring windfalls on asset-rearranges. Even worse, they punish those with the longest-term loyalty to the enterprise—its workers. However, the alternative of passive shareholders and complacent managers is not any solution either.

Yet we need not choose between the destructive discipline of highly imperfect trading markets, and the imperfect passivity of the manager-dominated corporation. The stakeholder approach introduces two new players—regulatory policy and the work force. It does so by rewarding a high-road approach, and cultivating corporate institutions with a greater degree of accountability to the employees. In this way, stakeholder capitalism returns to an older, more corporatist conception of the joint stock company. It is not only the shareholders (who are here today, gone tomorrow) who have a legitimate stake in the enterprise, but also the employees, communities, and society as a whole.

If financial markets were an adequate, or an efficient, check on corporations, it would be harder to make the case that they should be supplanted or complemented with this "stakeholder" conception. One would have to argue for stakeholder rights on extra-market grounds, such as citizenship, or fairness, or workplace democracy as values worthwhile in their own right. And one would have to answer the usual rejoinder that this approach would be fraught with economic peril because it was pursuing political or social equity at the expense of economic efficiency. However, given what we have seen about speculative excess in banking and in the reliance on financial markets to restructure corporations, it is no longer a convincing premise that the financial-market form of discipline and accountability is the most efficient.

6 / MARKETS, INNOVATION, AND GROWTH

THE BLACK BOX

The purist view of efficient free markets offers little useful insight about the dynamics of innovation or its relationship to economic growth and material well-being. The market model holds that free competition, steering resources to their optimal uses based on supply and demand, will yield the best outcome available. To the extent that markets find it rational to invest in innovation, capital will be allocated accordingly. Growth will follow.

In this conception, the institutional details of technical progress are of scant interest. Market forces need only pursue allocative efficiency, and the technology available will naturally emerge. The nature of the technology, the institutional particulars of how and where it flourishes, the relationship between the structure of the firm, the society, and the culture of innovation—all of these were traditionally seen as a "black box," of interest perhaps to business historians but not of concern to economists. As the economist Joseph Stiglitz wrote in a scathing critique of the standard model, "there was no need to look into the black box called the firm: firms maximized profits [and] stock market value; if managers didn't, they would be replaced; and firms that didn't maximize value wouldn't survive. Accordingly, what went on inside the black box was mere detail."

This orthodox conception of growth, ironically, is static. Equilibrium occurs in the present tense. We need not worry about the institutional sources of technical learning, its relationship to growth over time, or the critical question of whether technical learning is truly optimized by perfect competition; like so much else in free-market economics, that question is solved more by assumption than by investigation.

The theory does acknowledge, somewhat grudgingly, departures from perfect competition that reflect the interplay of market forces, such as externalities and market power. But the orthodox view insists, first, that these don't matter enough to impeach the basic story. Second, the state should certainly not compound the imperfection. Third (and somewhat contradictorily), even where the private sector produces violations of free-market competition, such as monopoly, the market itself is the best source of remedy.

However, economic history since the industrial revolution strongly suggests that technical learning, not the process of perfect competition, drives growth over time. And as we shall see, innovation often flourishes in institutions that depart significantly from the idealized picture of economic equilibrium. That insight, in turn, opens the door to thorny practical questions. Which departures from perfect competition that occur spontaneously in the private sector should government policy tolerate? Which more explicit spurs to innovation should government actively organize or subsidize? And in an era of global competition, where state subsidies and research consortia can advantage particular national producers, what ground rules to harmonize or limit the total amount of subsidy are reasonable, feasible, symmetrical, and consistent with economic efficiency?

GROWTH IN ECONOMIC THOUGHT

Before turning to such policy questions, it is worth reviewing the debate of the theoreticians. In standard theory, economies are in or near equilibrium; growth results from the application of increasing amounts of capital and labor. The preferred form of growth is the substitution of labor-saving devices for human drudgery, not human beings working longer hours—so that each hour of human input yields more output. The economy accomplishes this with increments of physical capital.

However, the classical economists, particularly J. S. Mill, noticed that this conception led to one disconcerting inference: Over time, the law of diminishing returns holds that increasing application of capital relative to labor must bring smaller and smaller gains in total output. Hence, increasing capital intensity, paradoxically, must lead to declining rates of return to capital, and hence slower rates of growth. Mill reached this conclusion by neglecting the possibility of technological dynamism. It was Mill's prospect of diminishing growth—he predicted an eventual "steady state"—along with Malthus's belief that populations would expand faster than food supply, that led Thomas Carlyle in 1850 to brand economics "the dismal science." Late in the nineteenth century, Alfred Marshall sought to make a case that new technologies could yield increasing returns to scale, consistent with other assumptions of the classical school. But this conception was difficult to model and never quite became part of the basic paradigm. By the early twentieth century, the belief in diminishing returns to capital (and a general lack of interest in technology) was well entrenched in the classical canon.

In 1956, Robert Solow, who later won the Nobel Prize for his work on growth, examined U.S. data on the labor force, the capital stock, and the growth of total output. Solow found, somewhat to his surprise, that only about half of the actual growth in the U.S. economy between 1909 and 1949 could be accounted for by increasing inputs of labor or capital, and less than 20 percent of the increase in GDP per person employed could be explained by increases in the stock of capital. Something else was at work, because growth rates far exceeded what could be explained by the standard account. The growth attributable to some other inexplicable source Solow called the "Residual"—an algebraic term that economists use to mean some factor not explained by the equations. The consensus today is that Solow's famous Residual reflects the influence of technology and industrial organization, factors not studied systematically by conservative economics.

The reason is hardly mysterious: the same amount of physical and human capital can be combined in different ways. New technologies can squeeze more output out of the same dollar value of inputs. For example, investing a billion dollars in old, open-hearth steelmaking technology, as American steelmakers did in the 1960s, is obviously less conducive to productivity and growth than investing the same dollars in newer technologies such as oxygen furnaces and continuous casters. Technology affects how much output we get relative to a given dollar amount of capital input. Entrepreneurs make mistakes. They don't always use the best technology. Most economists now agree that technical learning is the paramount source of long-term economic growth. For economic theory and policy, the controversial question is whether technical learning is advanced or retarded by imperfect competition, and which departures from perfect competition might be conducive to increased technical innovation and growth.

What made Solow's paper so significant was that it represented a cautious invitation to heterodoxy, from a safely orthodox source. Solow has considered himself a neo-Keynesian, but emphatically within the mainstream. His more recent work has been devoted to reconciling a more complex historical and institutional story with the neoclassical view, not overthrowing it.

Earlier in the twentieth century, a number of more insurgent economic thinkers had offered frontal challenges to the idea that the economic problem was best understood as the allocation of scarce resources in equilibrium. Though they often argued with each other on the particulars, such theorists as Frank Knight, Edward Chamberlin, Nicholas Kaldor, Austin Robinson, and Joan

Robinson (a disciple of Keynes and a nemesis of Solow), among others, argued that market power, externalities, and information failures were so pervasive that nearly all actual competition was best understood as imperfect.

Rather than aggregating to a single, optimal, "general equilibrium," the real economy was constantly in disequilibrium. Each innovation produced new relationships between supply and demand, to the point where a general equilibrium was simply not a useful premise. Mini-monopolies were pervasive; therefore, within limits, firms had the power to set prices, not passively "take" prices, as the classical model held. So a great deal of actual competition therefore operated on a basis other than pure price. All of this occurred normally in the *private* economy, not as a result of government meddling. Thus, the idea of an optimal state, in which "no one can be made better off without someone else being made worse off," a condition known to generations of credulous graduate students as "Pareto Optimality," was simply a fiction. This was only one possible state, and a very improbable one, among an infinite variety of states; Pareto Optimality was neither the norm nor the optimum in a market economy.

ENTER SCHUMPETER

It was Joseph Schumpeter who argued most cogently that this brand of imperfect competition was not to be regretted as a departure from economic efficiency. On the contrary, if competition were truly perfect in textbook terms, and a producer had no influence over price but simply kept producing until his marginal price just equaled his marginal cost, profits would be competed away, and there would be nothing left over to invest in innovation.

Under conditions of imperfect competition, by contrast, a producer was not a passive "price-taker." Thanks to subtle differences in product and imperfect consumer-information, the producer enjoyed a degree of monopoly power. That allowed him to set prices that departed somewhat from the prices that would obtain under perfect competition. Schumpeter declared: "it is clear that every grocer, every filling station, every manufacturer of gloves or handsaws has a small and precarious market of his own which he tries—must try—to build up and to keep by price strategy, quality strategy—'product differentiation'—and advertising. Thus we get a completely different pattern [from] perfect competition. . . ." This departure permitted the producer to earn the slightly excess profits that economists call "rents." In the view of Schumpeter and his followers, rents were what induced innovation and financed technical advance and ultimately growth. Thus, departures from perfect competition were not to be regretted, but celebrated. They drove economic progress.

This came to be known as the "Schumpeterian Hypothesis": growth reflects innovation; innovation requires rents; and rents tend to be associated with large-scale and price-setting market power. "Perfect competition," wrote Schumpeter, "is not only impossible but inferior."

Because of its stylized and highly misleading picture of how market economies actually worked, said Schumpeter, the standard neoclassical description was simply a fiction. The theoretical structure of standard economics proposes a static equilibrium, but "capitalist reality is first and last a process of change," he wrote. "Equilibrium, even if eventually attained by an extremely costly method, no longer guarantees either full employment or maximum output. . . ." Hence, a measure of market power was virtuous. If economic concentration was not so extreme as to prevent competition and accountability altogether, bigness allowed the producer to earn the super-normal profits that financed the next round of technical innovation.

This revision sat very uneasily with neoclassical economists, since the entire paradigm had an immense investment, ideologically and methodologically, in the idea of the optimal, self-equilibrating market in which marginal price equaled marginal cost, and the whole process could be smoothly modeled. In sharp contrast to Adam Smith, many advanced students of economics in this century have been startlingly innocent of the actual institutions of commercial life; they were simply virtuosos at the math. A Schumpeterian economy, of imperfect competition, multiple disequilibria, price-setting power, and crucial institutional difference, was more indeterminate; much more difficult to model or reduce to equations; much less amenable to the deductive method of reasoning logically from axioms. Even worse, it allowed for the possibility that state intervention, and not just with respect to macroeconomics, could actually improve on market outcomes in some circumstances. As Robert Solow wrote acidly in 1994, commenting on a series of papers on growth and imperfect competition, "Schumpeter is a sort of patron saint in this field. I may be alone in thinking that he should be treated like a patron saint: paraded around one day each year and more or less ignored the rest of the time."

Schumpeter was a most unwelcome guest at the neoclassical table. Yet it was hard for the mainstream to reject him out of hand, since Schumpeter was such a celebrant of capitalism and of entrepreneurship. He thought it a superb, energetic, turbulent system, one that led to material betterment over time. He hoped it would triumph over socialism. He just didn't believe it functioned in anything close to the way the Marshallians did, and he was appalled that economists could apply an essentially static model to something as profoundly dynamic as capitalism. Schumpeter wrote presciently, "Whereas a stationary feudal economy would still be a feudal economy, and a stationary socialist economy would still be a socialist economy, stationary capitalism is a contradiction in terms." Its very essence, as the economic historian Nathan Rosenberg wrote, echoing Schumpeter, "lies not in equilibrating forces, but in the inevitable tendency to depart from equilibrium" every time an innovation occurs.

For the most part, orthodox economics never came to terms with Schumpeter. Instead, it simply cut him a very wide berth, and went on. Schumpeter died in 1950, during a period when standard economics was performing another delicate alchemy—the process of blending a few diluted drops of Keynes into the neoclassical formula, but not enough to curdle Smith, Ricardo, Mill, Marshall, Walras, and the rest. Schumpeter's views, though highly provocative and consistent with a capitalist sensibility, were never even accorded that dubious honor during his own lifetime.

The Schumpeterian view, nonetheless, had profound implications for economic theory, method, and policy. A generation after his death, Schumpeter was gradually rediscovered and partly rehabilitated, stimulating a new current of scholarly inquiry into the dynamics and history of technology. More recently, there have been heroic efforts to integrate economic history into the corpus of mainstream economic thought, revising the classical models to allow for price setting, imperfect competition, and technical learning.

The neo-Schumpeterian school includes prominent economic historians, including Nathan Rosenberg, Paul David, Richard Nelson, Sidney Winter, David Mowery, Zvi Griliches (the 1993 president of the American Economic Association), and Douglass North, the 1993 Nobelist in economics. The Schumpeterian approach likewise resonates with students of industrial organization and of technology—for example, F. M. Scherer, Giovanni Dosi, and Eric von Hippel—and such eclectic thinkers as the political economists Charles Sabel and Michael Piore. More broadly defined, it attracts students of business history, such as Alfred Chandler, Thomas McCraw, and Joseph Bower of the Harvard Business School, and David Teece of the University of California at Berkeley, who see virtue in oligopoly. Some self-consciously leftist economists—for example, Bennett Harrison, William Lazonick, and Sam Bowles— find this tradition's impeachment of the self-regulating market congenial, to the point of overcoming the intuitive leftist aversion to big business. And in the past decade, several entirely mainstream economists fluent in the mathematical idiom have offered Schumpeterian insights in a form that would pass muster with the model builders. These include Jean Tirole, the leader of what is sometimes called the "new," i.e., highly abstract and theoretical, industrial-organization economics; Joseph Stiglitz, the longtime editor of the *Journal of Economic Perspectives*, chair of President Clinton's Council of Economic Advisers, and a distinguished student of market imperfections; and Paul Romer, a Chicago-trained economist who has devised a new and prestigious theory of economic growth based on a more prominent role for innovation and a critique of how markets price it.

Romer's approach, now a major current in academic inquiry, goes under the name Endogenous Growth Theory. Romer's revisionism, first expressed in his 1983 doctoral dissertation, and published in the *Journal of Political Economy* in 1986, broadly holds that technological advance cannot be seen as something "out there," unrelated to supply and demand. Rather, innovation emerges from the internal dynamics of what business firms do. Romer tries to operate (barely) within the neoclassical school, prudently crediting the earlier work of Robert Solow. But whereas Solow's model treated technological advance as an external or "exogenous" force, resulting from idiosyncratic scientific progress and not easily explained in terms of measurable factors of production, Romer views innovation as "endogenous" to the process of (usually imperfect) competition.

THE REVISIONISTS

In short, there is now a major current in mainstream economic thinking that disputes the premise that the maximum rate of material progress requires the freest possible markets. "Neoclassical theory is simply an inappropriate tool to analyze and prescribe policies that will induce development," Douglass North observed in his 1993 Nobel Prize lecture. "It is concerned with the operation of markets, not with how markets develop." This roughly neo-Schumpeterian approach is less a school than a broad sensibility. To do justice to it would require a whole other book. But at the risk of oversimplifying, here are some essential points of broad agreement.

Technological advance, not allocative efficiency, is the main long-term source of economic growth. "The loss to society from the absence of perfect price competition is more than compensated by the gains in the long run, derived from innovation," Morton Kamien and Nancy Schwartz wrote in an early survey article summarizing the Schumpeterian view. Allocative efficiency, however, does not cease to matter. In a capitalist economy, innovation may reflect imperfect competition, but it must still be broadly subject to market discipline. As Schumpeter wrote presciently, "In capitalist reality, as distinguished from its textbook picture, it is not [price] competition that counts but the competition from the new commodity, the new technology, the new source of supply. . . . [C]ompetition of the kind we have in mind acts not only when in being but also when it is an ever-present threat. The business man feels himself to be in a competitive situation even when he is alone in his field." Indeed, the possibility of competition is precisely what differentiates market power in a capitalist setting from market power in a command economy.

At one extreme, state socialism and other forms of command economy can also assemble large quantities of capital and seemingly take advantage of innovation. But as the collapse of the Soviet Union demonstrated, Schumpeterian gain in a command economy has its limits. Absent some degree of price discipline, absurd misallocations of resources will eventually set in and overwhelm the technological benefits. At the other extreme, perfect market competition can also be ruinous, by competing away rents and leading to systematic underinvestment in innovation. In between, there is not one true equilibrium, but a variety of possible paths, with different technical trajectories, institutional particulars, and distributional consequences.

None of this can be usefully modeled as equilibrium in a social vacuum, because that model excludes economies of scale, market power, and rents. As Joseph Stiglitz explains, "Technological change (whether it occurs as a result of explicit expenditures on R&D or as a result of learning by doing) gives rise to economies of scale. R&D expenditures are fixed, *sunk* costs. Industries where R&D is important will naturally, then, be imperfectly competitive."

These dynamics, of course, vary widely with the structure of the industry. In some industries—such as pharmaceuticals, chemicals, and aircraft—there seems to be a virtuous circle of government influence, significant market power, and above-normal profits, leading to continual reinvestment in technical advance. In other industries—such as the U.S. auto and steel industries in the 1950s and 1960s—oligopoly led to technical stagnation and loss of market share to imports. In still others—such as software—there is a blend of market leadership (Microsoft) and fierce innovation by smaller players. But this is an industry in which the product is very close to pure knowledge, and the sunk capital costs are minimal. Innovation in computer hardware, such as microprocessors, seems closer to the Schumpeterian model of price power, imperfect competition, and rents financing further innovation, epic examples being Intel and Motorola. But it is precisely these institutional differences among industries that require a concrete analysis of the different forms of imperfect competition rather than an assumption of smooth equilibrations.

Yet another reason why technical advance cannot usefully be modeled as an equilibrium is that innovation is often "path-dependent." Once a technology follows a particular path, sunk investments in know-how and habit raise the costs of departing from that path. The most famous example is the QWERTY typewriter, a historical accident with prodigious staying power. Innumerable studies have shown that people could type faster and more accurately with a more logical configuration of characters. But alternatives to QWERTY have failed to win acceptance, because people have invested in learning QWERTY. "Technical progress," observes David Teece, "exhibits strong irreversibilities . . . because the evolution of technologies along certain trajectories eliminates the possibility of competition from older technologies, even if relative prices change."

For example, if we take into account hidden costs of congestion and pollution, rail travel may indeed be more efficient for distances of two hundred to five hundred miles. But once the United States stopped investing in the maintenance and upgrading of track, rolling stock, and rail technology, the cost of reversing history became prohibitive. Many computer enthusiasts swear that Apple has the more elegant and user-friendly technology, but the IBM system, backed by the marketing power of Microsoft Windows, has locked in hundreds of millions of users who find switching more trouble than it's worth.

Knowledge is not like other factors of production. Traditional economic theory presumes there is a general pool of available knowledge that can be purchased as needed—a metaphorical "book of blueprints." This view, however, is entirely misleading. Usable technical know-how is often local and cumulative, the product of concrete business or scientific subcultures. It cannot be modeled as simply one more fungible input of production. The process of incremental improvement in the art of production requires subtle, often local know-how—what Michael Polanyi called "tacit knowledge"; it entails localized learning by doing. Joseph Bower observes, "The difficulty experienced by General Motors in learning from the production practices of NUMMI, its own joint venture with Toyota, is dramatic evidence of how hard it may be to adapt readily available technology."

As Giovanni Dosi points out: "firms produce things in ways that are differentiated technically from the products and methods of other firms. . . . [T]he search process of industrial firms to improve their technology is *not* likely to be one where they survey the whole stock of national technical knowledge before making their technical choices. . . ." Technological pathways are "cumulative processes," says Dosi. What the firm can do in the future is constrained by what it has done in the past. Innovation "embodies complex and varying balances between public and proprietary forms of knowledge." Perfect competition would frustrate this process, not optimize it.

Paul Romer emphasizes the distinction between rival goods and nonrival ones and their relationship to technical advance. A rival good is a product that belongs either to you or to me—a car or a corned-beef sandwich. Only one of us can consume it. The market for rival consumer goods more or less follows the rules of supply and demand. A nonrival good, such as the invention of the blinking computer cursor, or the deliberate diffusion of sterile insects that retard reproduction of agricultural pests, or the dissemination of knowledge about how to prevent spread of epidemics, is available to all. Some rival goods are collective and generally available, such as fish in the sea. Other rival goods—even knowledge-based ones such as computer software—are proprietary. "Because it is so difficult to establish property rights over these kinds of goods, market outcomes are inefficient," Romer writes. "We over-fish, and under-provide sterile insects." That is, we overconsume "free" collective goods that are ultimately divisible, but underproduce ones whose rents are hard to capture but which add to the general welfare. "An approach to economic policymaking that neglects nonrival goods will miss most of the interesting issues," Romer concludes.

Economists have long accepted the proposition that "public goods," which are nonrival and nonexcludable, must be provided by government. But the recent swing to extreme conservativism, and the conviction that unleashed market forces can accomplish almost anything, has led to a trivialization of the significance of public goods.

Markets, left to their own devices, do not reliably price innovation. Before an innovation is devised, it is in society's interest to maximize the rewards to the innovator. That is why patents, trademarks, and copyrights are necessary to prevent innovations from being treated as free goods. Government creations of rights in "intellectual property" award rents, at least temporarily, to the innovator. But after the fact, it is in society's interest to maximize the diffusion of the new technique. Thus, as Romer notes, it is logically impossible for the same price to be "optimal" *ex ante* and *ex post*. Further, economic theory offers no intuitive answer to the issue of the "right" form or term of patent, trademark, and copyright protection. "We do not know whether a gene fragment or a programming concept such as overlapping windows should be protected by law," Romer writes. Institutions, both public and private, need to be invented to reconcile the somewhat contradictory goals of inducing—and diffusing—innovation.

Richard Nelson observes: "the portfolio of R&D investments generated by market competition can in no way be considered optimal. There is virtually certain to be a duplicative clustering of effort on alternatives widely regarded as promising, and neglect of certain long shots that, from society's point of view, ought to be explored as a hedge. Thus market failure is rampant in this system."

Research and development—knowledge itself—is the economy's most famous positive externality. In a perfect market economy, a firm that develops a new process, a company that invests heroically in workers' skills, will not capture the full social return on the investment, since some of the new knowledge will be imitated by competitors and broadly diffused. Hence, private businesses notoriously underinvest in both human capital and research. Studies have shown that the social return from research-and-development investments exceeds the private return by 35 to 60 percent.

Economist Edwin Mansfield and colleagues, in one of the classic studies of the subject, put the median social return on R&D investment at 56 percent, whereas the median private return was only 25 percent. Mansfield also found that, in 30 percent of the cases he studied, the private return was so low that no private firm, in hindsight, would have made the investment. Yet every single investment in this sample yielded high social returns and worthwhile innovations. Another careful recent study, comparing private and social rates of return by industry, found disparities as high as a private return on investments in scientific instruments of 16.1 percent, versus a total social return of 128.9 percent on the same investment. Though even conventional economists agree that private firms systematically underinvest in research and innovation, because they will not capture the full return, orthodox economics pays this dilemma scant attention, because it is almost impossible to model, and because the implications impeach the standard paradigm.

The closer a good comes to "pure knowledge," the less do its production and sale resemble the textbook picture of competition. Marginal price is supposed to equal marginal cost, but the marginal cost of producing another copy of a software program is a minuscule fraction of its price, since most of what is being sold is embedded knowledge, not plastic and packaging. Contrary to the textbook conception of production costs, the cost of producing an additional unit of a software package is close to zero. (With the ability to send and receive software via the Internet, it is sometimes literally zero.) The standard description of "perfect, price-taking competition," Romer writes, "is logically inconsistent with the private production of non-rival goods" such as knowledge-based products.

Information failures and externalities, both positive and negative, are far more pervasive and important than laissez-faire economics presumes. In 1991, prior to her appointment as President Clinton's chief economist, Professor Laura Tyson was completing a book on managed trade, to be published under the aegis of the influential and very mainstream Institute for International Economics (IIE). Tyson was an advocate of some forms of managed trade, partly on the ground that the United States needed to retain and increase its capacity to produce and innovate in technically dynamic industries; and partly to create a roughly equitable second best in a trading system far from an Adam Smith world. If other nations were more interventionist and protectionist than the United States, managed-trade remedies might be necessary to level the playing field, even though the resulting field would not be one of perfect competition. This, of course, violated the conventional view of the allocative benefit of buying from the current low-cost producer even if that producer's home markets were closed to U.S. exports.

IIE, eager to publish a presentable managed-trade advocate but anxious about the product, put Tyson through a series of review panels, where mostly orthodox trade economists challenged her draft manuscript. At one point in a lively debate, it became clear to all that much of Tyson's argument hinged on the fact that subsidy of innovation generates broad positive externalities. This was widely conceded, until one notable simply declaimed, "But you can't measure externalities." That ended the discussion. In fact, as the research noted herein suggests, economists have managed to measure externalities. However, in standard economics measuring is far less prestigious and persuasive than modeling. And innovation, by its nature, cannot be modeled. "[T]he outcome of inventive activity is not really predictable," Zvi Griliches recently wrote in his American Economics Association presidential address. "True 'innovation' is an innovation. If it were knowable in advance, it would not be one and the innovators would not be able to collect any rents."

This more structural view of the logic of imperfect markets also changes the way one thinks about remedies. In the traditional view, the cure for a negative externality is simple: use taxes or charges to force a polluter to internalize the full social cost, and leave the market's allocative preferences essentially undisturbed. But this approach doesn't necessarily produce the technical advances that may be the more efficient remedy to pollution; it may merely raise costs. By setting explicit standards, direct regulation can induce the invention of new technologies. Contrary to the conservative view that such regulation is mostly cost and scant benefit, cost-benefit analysis typically fails to include the full benefit of raising the entire trajectory of technical advance (see chapter 8, below). Without regulation, entire categories of technical innovation, such as pollution control, are far less dynamic, since there is little private-market demand and hence little R&D.

The large company, with significant economies of "scale," "scope," and "speed" as well as steep "learning curves," is often the natural habitat of both technological and organizational innovations. Because of these superior contributions, we can forgive the large company a degree of market power and divergence from the "price-taking" behavior of the virtuous hypothetical firm described by Alfred Marshall. The dean of American business historians, Alfred Chandler, in his two master works, *The Visible Hand* and *Scale and Scope*, described the new type of business enterprise that emerged in the late nineteenth century. It was large, integrated, hierarchical, and made possible a hitherto unprecedented scale and volume of production, as well as market power. "The new potential for greatly increased speed and volume of production generated a wave of technological innovations that swept through Western Europe and the United States creating what historians have properly termed the Second Industrial Revolution." These superior efficiencies, based on scale and on technical and organizational innovation, finally refuted Mill's dismal conclusion that increasing quantities of capital would eventually be futile because of diminishing returns.

The firms that maximized these new economies of "scale" (high volume and decreasing unit costs), "scope" (different products using the same expertise and the same managerial and distributive network), systematic innovation, and speed of production were a far cry from the atomized, price-taking firms of classical theory. Their efficiency was strategic, not allocative. And their structure was often oligopolistic. "Such oligopolistic competition in these capital-intensive industries sharpened the product-specific capabilities of workers and managers. These capabilities plus retained earnings from profits of the new technologies became the basis for the continuing growth of these manufacturing enterprises," Chandler writes. "Firms did grow by combining with competitors (horizontal integration) or by moving backward to control materials and forward to control outlets (vertical integration). . . ."

An oligopoly structure of industry, rather than either monopoly or perfect competition—at least in many industries—seems most compatible with high rates of investment in innovation. Economists Kamien and Schwartz, summarizing empirical evidence for the Schumpeterian view, noted that research-and-development outlay tended to occur disproportionately in large firms, but within limits. The evidence on balance suggests that "a market structure intermediate between monopoly and perfect competition would promote the highest rate of inventive activity." Moderately high concentration—30- to 50-percent market share by the four largest firms—seems to be consistent with both competitive discipline and high levels of R&D outlay, but monopoly power beyond that degree apparently retards it.

Large, integrated firms, as David Teece observes, are able to realize more of the return from innovation than are small, fragmented ones. "Integrated firms need not sell their innovations in order to capture value from them." Richard Nelson has also pointed out that large, integrated firms facilitate the flow of new technology from the laboratory to the production floor, with less worry of cross-firm leaks of proprietary information.

The economic history of the last century demonstrates that well-entrenched companies, including both oligopolies and regulated monopolies, can use market power to capture rents, invest in R&D, and cheapen the cost of the product over time. A good illustration of Schumpeterian efficiency versus allocative efficiency may be seen in the airline industry, before and after deregulation. The era of airline regulation guaranteed airlines stable profits, and hence assured airline manufacturers customers for new generations of planes. The new planes, rather than the process of allocative efficiency, drove down the real cost of flying. A jumbo jet can fly a passenger from point to point at approximately one-eighth the cost of a DC-3. The increased price-competition and presumed allocative efficiency after deregulation competed away rents, and retarded the rate of technical innovation.

The Internet is a splendid illustration of the power of nonmarket institutions and motivations in creating key innovations. Its enabling technology and antecedents were created by the Pentagon, for military purposes, via ARPA-net. Subsequently, a consortium of universities piggy-backed on ARPA-net, for research purposes. The Internet is governed by a nonprofit consortium. Interestingly, too, as the Internet broke out and became a technology used by millions of ordinary consumers via the World Wide Web, hundreds of thousands of institutions and individuals began offering information at no charge, via "web sites" and "home pages" that they sponsored for the intellectual satisfaction, ego gratification, or publicity value. It was only in 1995 that market-motivated purveyors of goods and services began horning in, in a very uneasy symbiosis with the original users, who were highly individualist, as per the market model, but who resented the commercialism.

The following chart is dramatic proof of the power of innovation under a regulated regime versus the rather feeble gains to allocative efficiency under a more laissez-faire approach. It compares the drop in the inflation-adjusted price of airline travel and transatlantic telephone service; all prices are in inflation-adjusted 1990 dollars.

	Air travel per passenger mile	A three-minute New York–London phone call
1930	.68	244.00
40	.46	188.00
50	.30	53.20
60	.24	45.86
70	.18	31.58
80	.10	4.80
90	.11	3.32

Note that the real cost of air travel dropped steadily and dramatically during the regulated era—most dramatically during the 1970s, even though the price of fuel quadrupled between 1973 and 1979. During the first decade of deregulation, airline costs actually rose. The price of telephone calls during the era of the Bell-regulated monopoly fell even faster than air travel. Competition came to long-distance service in the early 1980s; the decline in the price of an average call continued after 1980, but at a much slower rate than during the previous decades. Long-distance telephone service actually increased in cost in the early 1990s, reversing a century-long trend. Excess competition may be frustrating scale economies.

Perfect competition, in a great many industries, turns out to be practically unbearable. If customs, norms, or regulations do not provide some respite from pure price competition, private firms will find ways to regulate privately or cartelize themselves partly. "In many major markets of major importance," Joseph Bower writes, "few if any of the conditions necessary for a free market are satisfied. In particular, numbers [of producers] are small, barriers to entry and exit exist, competition is on the basis of corporate strategy rather than price, and government intervention is widespread."

Bower's decade-long research examines what firms actually do in industries that either are structural oligopolies (a few firms dominating commerce) or have significant characteristics of imperfect markets, or have commodity characteristics that would lead to ruinous price-competition. Such industries typically have high sunk costs, insufficient product differentiation, and the risk that full price-competition would drive down the price to the level of the variable cost— with the risk of mutual ruin. Bower argues, persuasively, that it is better to have firms stay in business, where they can keep innovating, rather than have perfect, and mutually ruinous, price competition. He poses the question: What sorts of norms or benign forms of collusion prevent this mutual ruin? He formulates this intriguing question in game-theory terms, as a collective-action problem. Unlike most neoclassical economists, he views a positive-sum solution as beneficial not just to the "collusive" firms, but to broad economic welfare.

Bower takes the example of hotels, a business where only a few landmark hostelries are distinctive enough to enjoy real market power, and one in which total price-competition would be truly ruinous. Why don't hotels engage in cut-throat pricing, Bower wonders? "Downtown hotels are large capital investments, often $100 million." The "product," lodging for a night, has low marginal cost and disappears each morning. Even labor is a relatively fixed cost. In order to keep service at a high level, hotels prefer to maintain steady employment. At the same time, though there is overcapacity in many cities, room prices retain a degree of relative stability that seems inexplicable. Just as interesting, hotels do not steal large blocks of business from each other, although it would be a simple matter to call a corporate or trade-association event planner and offer a better deal. What are called "definite bookings" are sacrosanct, whether or not there is any enforceable contract. "There is no badmouthing of competitors."

Bower finds that potent norms such as these mitigate mutually ruinous competition, and hold prices at a level consistent with reasonable profits. He concludes: "Recognition by owners and top management of the importance to business of the overall reputation of the city, the habit of dealing cooperatively with large groups or individual overflow situations, and the long life of the sunk cost represented by a hotel seems to provide the basis for a friendly balance of competition and price cooperation." Bower found similar patterns in industries as diverse as commodity chemicals, reinsurance, even the wholesaling of used cars. In each case, customary norms mitigated pure price-competition, and informal sanctions punished opportunists. Market leaders, the villains of traditional antitrust theory, are actually virtuous, because they set patterns that prevent mutually destructive price-wars.

In Germany, Japan, and Korea, there is a far more tolerant view of cartels than in Britain and the United States. The national innovation system in these countries allows for fierce strategic competition between competing industrial groups, but the competition is typically on the basis of quality and technical excellence rather than price. The Japanese system also affords a complex skein of tacit contracts and reciprocal loyalties between supplier and primary producer, between wholesaler and retailer, between firm and bank, and between worker and firm. Foreign trade worked superbly for Japan, as long as it was one-way. When American firms, more accustomed to price competition, sought to crack Japan's home market, resistance was fierce, because the American companies were not party to Japan's tacit norms. Western economists studying Japan have had to deny what they see, since Japan plainly violates the price system, yet has grown at quadruple the rate of the United States.

Market activity does not operate in isolation but needs to be understood in the context of a "national innovation system." A national innovation system is the implicit and explicit set of institutions, public and private, that influence a nation's propensity to innovate. It includes a variety of structural factors beyond the allocative efficiency of markets. Some of these elements violate perfect competition but add to the economy's innovative efficiency. They include the quality of public bureaucracies; the ability of business and government to work collaboratively rather than as adversaries; the extent and nature of government expenditures on R&D; the governing structure of business firms; the effect of financial markets on the time horizons of firms; the technical and scientific culture of universities and their linkage to industry; tax incentives to savings and investment versus consumption; and the culture of labor-management relations.

All of these structural factors affect the ability of firms and nations to innovate and to compete globally. Large multinational firms do not operate in a sociopolitical vacuum, but are beneficiaries or victims of the national innovation system of their home country. When a German or a Japanese multinational competes in the U.S. domestic market, or head to head against U.S.-based firms in third-world markets, each firm brings with it the scientific, financial, governmental, and labor-relations legacies of the domestic soil in which it is rooted. Pure laissez-faire, therefore, is not an option, since we cannot erase history. And, in line with the General Theory of the Second Best, it is not at all clear that relative movements in the direction of laissez-faire necessarily leave us better off.

VIRTUES OF IMPERFECT COMPETITION

This broadly Schumpeterian line of inquiry and analysis removes the presumption that measures that throw the economy off its equilibrium course distort economic efficiency and hence retard growth. That, in turn, opens the door to both a different view of how private markets actually work—whether scale and price power can be virtuous—and also to the issue of whether state intervention can sometimes induce innovation that the market misses. As economists Elhanan Helpman and Gene Grossman observed in a summary of the recent contributions to growth theory, the new view of growth and innovation casts doubt on the premise of a market-determined optimum, in two distinct respects: "First, [allocative] efficiency dictates marginal cost pricing, but innovation requires the existence of monopoly profits. Second, [allocative] efficiency demands that investment returns be fully appropriable, but the characteristics of knowledge suggest that spillovers will be prevalent."

Although the new view of growth has a great deal of empirical evidence to back it up, and has made substantial inroads into the reigning neoclassical paradigm, it is as if editorial writers, popular commentators, and politicians had never encountered this vein of economic thought. For the most part, press commentary consciously or unconsciously presumes a largely outmoded view of the price system based entirely on allocative efficiency, in which perfect markets maximize the efficient allocation of investment, and optimize growth and well-being. Thus, press accounts of economic issues repeat, mindlessly, truisms about the superiority of laissez-faire that reflect exclusively allocative conceptions of efficiency.

In fairness to my colleagues in the press, much of the responsibility rests with the economics profession. Even among the most heterodox economists, especially those wishing to retain their good standing in the neoclassical church, there remains an almost intuitive reverence for markets and a skepticism of state intervention. This hesitancy reflects the potent bias of what it means to be a mainstream economist. Even in the thick of a demolition of classical economics, critics feel constrained to issue disclaimers that they, too, are skeptical of the competence of governments. Economic historians Richard Nelson and Sidney Winter, at the close of a landmark book demolishing the neoclassical view of growth, conclude nonetheless with the obligatory disclaimer that "governments are quite limited in the things they can do well." And further, "The attempt to optimize and accordingly to control technological advance will . . . lead not to efficiency but to inefficiency."

Indeed, with the exception of self-defined heretics, who don't mind the professional ostracism, one can discern a pattern: the more that an insight or finding departs from the received neoclassical wisdom, the more the economist bends over backward to deny its implications for theory and policy—especially the conclusion that state intervention, done carefully, might improve outcomes.

MIT economist Paul Krugman, for example, did pioneering work challenging the truism that the freest trade led to the optimal outcome. That premise, one of the most universally held within orthodox economics, is based entirely on the allocative conception of efficiency. But Krugman noticed that, in a world of technological dynamism and economies of scale, temporary restraints on free trade could create opportunities for capture of rents and technical learning—a good description of postwar Japan and South Korea, not to mention pre–World War I America. Krugman, stumbling on the implications of Schumpeter for the standard view of trade, immediately took great pains to distance himself from the policy implications of his theoretical work, both to maintain his standing as a mainstream economist and to avoid giving aid and comfort to interventionists.

For the most part, the mainstream critics are very cautious about jumping from fairly dramatic revisions in the premise that perfect competition is the optimum—to interventionist-policy recommendations. Paul Romer, a sometime co-author of Krugman, has observed that economists tend "to duck the complicated political and institutional issues . . . and instead to work backwards from a desired policy conclusion to a simple economic model that supports it. According to this approach, if we want to discourage counterproductive restrictions on trade and foreign investment in most countries of the world, then the right model is one with perfect competition so that intervention can be shown to be always and everywhere a mistake."

Thus, though the modern analysis of innovation and growth removes the presumption that the freest possible market and most perfect form of competition leads to the maximum material well-being, it does not lead most economists to commend state intervention. Yet it does permit a more open-minded exploration of several policy dilemmas. And it allows us to recognize that, in areas where markets are far from optimal, no policy is also a policy.

If free markets in fact do not optimize outcomes, one must still weigh necessarily imperfect policymaking against imperfect markets. That question, of "market failure" versus "polity failure," is a whole other discussion, to be treated at length in chapter 9.

ECONOMIC DEVELOPMENT AND THE STATE

Armed with this Schumpeterian view of innovation and growth, we now turn from economic theory to economic history, much of it rife with violations of the textbook model of perfect competition. Feudal, premodern restraints on markets were properly criticized by Adam Smith. Their removal permitted a more competitive and dynamic modern economy to emerge. Still, the history of the actual economic development of most nations is a far cry from the model of perfect competition. State subsidies for education, research, infrastructure, state incubation of infant industries, protection of sheltered home markets, have been part of the development strategies of nearly all capitalist nations, including the United States. For the most part, these departures from perfect competition did not grow out of dissident economic theories. They were intuitive responses by national leaders to practical policy dilemmas, often reflecting the fact that foreign-policy goals and economic ones are inextricably linked in practice.

The first industrial nation was of course Great Britain. Not surprisingly, British economists such as David Ricardo found a scientific basis for instructing other nations to import British industrial goods rather than incubating their own industries. Subsequent industrializing countries faced the practical dilemma of whether simply to buy British, or to attempt to develop manufacturing competence domestically. This question involved considerations of sovereignty and military security as well as economics. It also posed balance-of-payment concerns, since the terms of trade tended to favor manufactured goods heavily.

Looking at efficiency in static, allocative terms, as a snapshot at a moment in time, it was plainly more "efficient" simply to import British goods, which were momentarily better and cheaper, just as classical economists commended. However, taking a long-run perspective, the leaders of most emerging nations grasped the fact that their future well-being depended on learning how to manufacture products at home, even if this meant temporarily subsidizing, protecting, and forgoing purchase of the cheaper British good. This describes nineteenth-century Germany's efforts to industrialize, inspired by the economist Friedrich List. It describes French state-led development from Colbert to Mitterrand, as well as the economic nationalism of Japan, Korea, Brazil, and almost every emergent industrial nation, including those reputed to embrace free markets, such as Taiwan, Singapore, and Hong Kong.

This approach also describes the nation most deeply skeptical of state power at its founding, and the one most fervently committed to laissez-faire economics today—the United States. It is too easy to believe that the United States was born as a laissez-faire nation, and embraced the mixed economy only in the extraordinary circumstances of the Great Depression. In reality, right from the era of the Articles of Confederation, federal and state governments have intervened in a variety of ways to promote economic innovation and development.

The new nation suffered acutely from a lack of financial capital. Most of the economy's capital value was in the form of the millions of acres of public lands owned by the government, which nearly doubled after the Louisiana Purchase of 1803. Despite the new nation's belief in limited government, the development of these lands (agriculture then dominating economic output) was anything but laissez-faire. As historian Frank Bourgin has observed: "It is apparent that the value of the public lands must have greatly exceeded that of the entire private sector, and the government acted in the capacity of private landlord in making disposition of them. Nor should it be forgotten that it was the government that set the terms: the free market did not set the price; the public acres could not be sold without first being surveyed and then sold by platted location and at prices specified by law."

Federal policy, for more than a century, encouraged small freeholding, through homesteading, agricultural extension, and the building of roads, canals, and rails, because of a conviction that this form of land tenure was consistent both with a republican form of government and with development of the virgin economy. Beginning with the Land Ordinance of 1785 and the Northwest Ordinance of 1787, policy explicitly rejected the more marketlike approach of selling off land in large private tracts to the highest bidder—though this was a sore temptation, given the nation's war debt.

A market approach, leading to a large concentration of landholding, was no mere theoretical dilemma. The Founders were acutely aware of the incompatibility of republican government and the feudal landholding that characterized most of Europe. Prior to the American Revolution, speculative land companies had already secured significant land grants. They enjoyed very significant influence both in the courts of the English kings and in the territorial legislatures, and their influence delayed ratification of the Articles of Confederation. The early policy of the Republic deliberately favored what economists would call "use values" as opposed to "exchange values"—an explicit repudiation of the idea that market price should determine ownership and disposition of land.

Government also aided development of canals and railroads, both through credits and through land subsidy, which raised the value of contiguous lands owned by freeholders. George Washington's first annual message recommended a national policy of advancing "agriculture, commerce, and manufactures by all proper means." Treasury Secretary Alexander Hamilton's 1791 Report on Manufactures argued explicitly that the young country needed to promote the industrial arts as well as agriculture. This first statement of the case for an industrial policy, like so many others after it, was occasioned partly by a concern for military security. In commissioning the report, the House of Representatives had requested Hamilton to prepare a plan to enable the United States to become "independent of other nations for essential, particularly for military, supplies." However, Hamilton took this as license to make the case for a more general promotion of manufactures, calling for a government "board" to promote manufactures, arts, agriculture, and commerce, with a subsidy fund to be run by the board. Though the board was never enacted, the Hamiltonian view had broad influence.

Even Thomas Jefferson, usually characterized as laissez-faire and agrarian in contrast to the interventionist and pro-industry Hamilton, was deeply opposed to the more marketlike approach of land speculation. As a framer of the Declaration of Independence in the 1770s, a member of Congress in the 1790s, and as the president who negotiated the Louisiana Purchase, Jefferson championed government planning and subdivision of the new lands, and small freeholding by yeomen who would actually work the land. Jefferson also actively sponsored public improvements, in education, science, and transportation. Albert Gallatin, Jefferson's Secretary of the Treasury, drew up a ten-year plan for the construction of national roads and waterways. In 1802, the federal government began a policy of granting public lands to local public schools. In his second inaugural address, Jefferson proposed a broad program of building schools, roads, river and harbor improvements, and canals. The War of 1812 further stimulated federal support for a national transportation system.

In 1816, President James Madison signed a law imposing a high protective tariff, and creating a Bank of the United States. Canal building was greatly enhanced by the creation of the Army Corps of Engineers in 1824. As Arthur M. Schlesinger, Jr., has noted, "The project of national economic expansion, based on internal improvements, tariff protection, the Bank and land legislation, soon acquired a name—the American System."

State governments were even more activist in support of economic development. The economist Carter Goodrich estimates that government supplied approximately 70 percent of the capital for the construction of canals and 30 percent for railroads, in contrast to Britain, where railroads were built entirely by private capital. The armories of nineteenth-century America were also the sources of both the invention and diffusion of much industrial innovation.

Despite the popularity of Adam Smith, David Ricardo, and the free-trade doctrines in nineteenth-century Whig Britain, these views had little appeal either on this side of the Atlantic or on the European continent. France, whether nominally monarchist or republican, maintained a statist view of development. In the German-speaking lands, the economic prophet was the Swabian economist Friedrich List, an advocate of state-led development, yet a staunch political liberal. And in the United States, as Schlesinger writes, "As striking as the extension of government intervention was the absence of opposition on grounds of economic theory. When interventionist policies were attacked, they were opposed as inexpedient or impractical, not as violations of immutable economic law. Businessmen welcomed government favor. . . . The radical democrats were hostile to government favoritism, not to government intervention per se." Jacksonian radicalism, Carter Goodrich wrote, "was based on a desire to keep business out of government . . . rather than a desire to keep government out of business."

Later in the nineteenth century, government pursued a highly successful "industrial policy" for the main industry of the day, agriculture. Through the Morrill Act of 1862, the federal government used land subsidies to sponsor a uniquely successful system of agricultural and mechanical colleges. Government sponsored agricultural research as well as the diffusion of scientific knowledge through an agricultural extension system.

The United States was also especially successful in both incubating pure science, and developing institutions for its application and diffusion. Many of these were public, either government-aided industrial labs, or government-sponsored state universities. Historians David Mowery and Nathan Rosenberg observe that land-grant colleges were crucial in giving the United States technological leads in such fields as metallurgy and mechanical and electrical engineering. MIT, originally a public institution, pioneered chemical engineering. Comparing Britain with the United States and Germany, Mowery and Rosenberg observe: "A tradition of minimal public support for [technical] education in Britain did nothing to improve the number or the professional training of British engineers, who are still much scarcer than in Germany or the United States. In addition, Britain did not develop the informal links between higher and technical education that were important in the industrial research systems of the United States and Germany."

It was only in the late nineteenth century, with the increased power of large business combines, the rupture of the reform coalition of small freeholders by the Civil War, and the spread of the doctrine of Social Darwinism, that intellectuals and conservative politicians began arguing that government should stay out of the private economy. Laissez-faire was advanced as a national creed, despite the anomalous fact that business continued to enjoy subsidies and high protective tariffs. "The peculiarly American version of laissez-faire," Schlesinger dryly observed, meant "aid from the state without interference from the state."

Politically, however, this first romance with laissez-faire was relatively short-lived. The administrations of Theodore Roosevelt and then Woodrow Wilson produced a burst of progressive regulation, as well as redoubled government efforts to promote science, technology, and industry. The First World War and its aftermath dramatically increased government collaboration with industry and stimulated technical advance. Even during the heavily Republican 1920s, Herbert Hoover's brand of conservatism was more corporatist than laissez-faire, and government-business collaboration during that conservative decade was extensive.

Two new industries were emblematic: aviation and radio. Although aviation was invented in the United States, our government gave the fledgling technology little support during its first decade, while Germany and France both heavily subsidized their emerging industries. After the outbreak of war in Europe and the early German use of planes both for reconnaissance and combat, Congress in 1915 established a National Advisory Committee for Aeronautics (NACA) to promote U.S. scientific advances in aviation.

NACA quickly intervened to settle a patent dispute between Glenn Curtiss and the Wright-Martin Company, which was threatening to retard large-scale aircraft production. This resulted in a cross-licensing agreement, and freed rival producers to make use of leading-edge technologies. NACA, collaborating with the U.S. Army, also developed the Langley Memorial Aeronautical Laboratory at Langley Field, which soon (in 1920) built a wind tunnel and dynamometer lab. NACA pioneered testing techniques, produced more advanced airfoil designs and better wind tunnels, helped perfect retractable landing gear, and pioneered the "NACA Cowl" for air-cooled engines, reducing wind resistance and cutting airframe drag by nearly 75 percent, according to historians Mowery and Rosenberg. All of this took place more than a decade prior to the era of mass passenger service. This was a classic case of the circular failure of private-market forces to commit sufficient capital to yield necessary innovations, because a mass market had not yet emerged and there was no assurance the investment would be recouped. Public support of technology, through NACA, helped bridge over that market failure.

Meanwhile, the government created mass aircraft demand through the U.S. Post Office. With the collapse of military demand for aircraft after World War I, total U.S. production dropped from a peak of fourteen thousand planes in 1918 to just 263 planes in 1922. However, the Kelly Air Mail Act of 1925, giving private contractors the right to transport airmail, created a new government market ahead of the yet unborn passenger market, spurring private research and production.

The government also virtually organized the structure of the aircraft industry, by encouraging the creation of "trunk carriers" to provide passenger as well as mail service. This was done first under the postmaster general, through the 1930 McNary-Watres Act, which provided extra payments for carriers using large, multi-engine planes, and even empowered the postmaster general to orchestrate mergers. By the early 1930s, most mail carriage was in the hands of three large carriers, which became Eastern, American, and United. In 1938,

Congress consolidated airline regulation under the Civil Aeronautics Board, removing authority from the Post Office but deliberately maintaining the structure of large trunk airlines, which were treated as a regulated cartel.

Thus, the combination of wartime aircraft orders, NACA, postal subsidies, and rate and route regulation stimulated development of this key industry in several complementary respects. NACA created a supply-side technology subsidy, and a publicly funded locus of research and expertise. War and postal contracts produced a demand-side stimulus. Rate and route regulation guaranteed a stream of earnings. Taken together, these policies dramatically accelerated technical innovation both in the public and private sectors, and brought the era of mass commercial service into being far more rapidly than private-market forces could have done. World War II, of which more later, further accelerated all these dynamics.

The commercialization and technical development of radio were likewise a direct outgrowth of government actions. In Europe, where telecommunications was a government function, radio technology was already more advanced than in the United States. On the eve of World War I, the two dominant companies in radio transmission were British Marconi and the German firm Telefunken. During the war, the U.S. Navy took control of domestic and transatlantic radio communications, using high-frequency alternators, which permitted long-distance ship-to-shore communication. AT&T secretly pursued vacuum-tube technology, working with the U.S. military. But after the war, British Marconi, which already held most of the key patents, was on the verge of buying the alternator patent and other crucial technologies from GE and AT&T. This led to a flurry of concern in President Wilson's Cabinet, and in 1919 the navy organized a "Radio Corporation of America"—RCA—as a consortium to retain and develop crucial radio technology.

The firm that soon became America's leading consumer-electronics company was launched by government, and with an injection of public capital. GE, AT&T, Westinghouse, and the U.S. Navy were the prime stockholders. The secretary of the navy had a seat on the board. RCA was envisioned in 1919 as holder of key radio patents and as a common carrier for marine telecommunications. But RCA rapidly expanded into production of commercial and consumer radio receivers and transmitters. The government quickly became concerned that it had created a monopoly in the unanticipated field of commercial radio. In 1926, the Justice Department negotiated a comprehensive antitrust settlement confining RCA to the manufacture of home receivers; AT&T had to sell its RCA stock but was awarded a monopoly in the production of transmitters; GE was forced to spin off RCA as a separate company, and to license patents to competing radio-set manufacturers.

Here is a telling example of the Theory of the Second Best. Although private firms were involved, the emergent radio industry had little to do with free markets. The jockeying for national control of radio transmission was mainly the work of governments motivated by military objectives. When RCA emerged as a consumer-electronics firm, as an indirect result of U.S. government actions, this "second-best" creation then produced a third-best—a radio monopoly. Once again government had to move, this time to restore competition. But here, too, the remedy was not entirely marketlike; rather, it was a blend of antitrust enforcement, competition, and cartelization. No "first-best" solution (pure marketization) was institutionally possible, because radio technology dwelt in a realm affected by multiple government actions.

With World War II, followed almost immediately by the Cold War, government's involvement in the national system of technical innovation took a quantum jump. Prior to World War II, government had often helped organize new industries, and had subsidized applied research, most notably in agriculture. However, government's support for basic science had been minimal. With the war's onset, government became both a major purchaser of technically advanced products, and a subsidizer of basic and applied research.

Many, if not most, of today's key industries received immense benefits from the military. The earliest computers were largely a response to the military's need for cryptography. Jet aircraft were the direct result of wartime contracts and research spending. World War II was an immense demand-side boost to the production of everything from aircraft to machine tools, computers, aluminum, synthetic rubber, etc., etc, as well as a human-capital program and a boon to scientific research.

In 1945, Vannevar Bush, the wartime director of the Office of Scientific Research and Development, published a celebrated report, "Science: The Endless Frontier." Bush, responding to a request from President Roosevelt on the postwar organization of government aid to science, proposed what ultimately became the National Science Foundation. NSF, though motivated mainly by defense concerns, subsidized mostly basic science. During the half-century after World War II, the U.S. commercial economy enjoyed immense research and technology subsidies, most of them contradicting our professed faith in laissez-faire, thanks to the Cold War. U.S. R&D spending for most of the Cold War period exceeded the combined spending by other advanced industrial nations.

Today government supports innovation in multiple ways. Direct federal R&D money accounts for about eighty billion dollars, or about 40 percent of all the R&D spending in the economy. Government procurement, much of it for products that embody advanced technologies, creates a market worth more than $200 billion. The federal government runs some 745 federal laboratories. It directly sponsors some forty-nine thousand fellowships, traineeships, and research assistantships in graduate-level science and engineering.

The commercial spinoffs from Cold War–sponsored military research include supercomputers, advanced microprocessors, computer networking and computer-controlled machine tools, advances in metallurgy and materials sciences, optical-fiber cable, and much more. Ostensibly civilian industrial laboratories, notably Bell Labs and RCA's Sarnoff Labs, received extensive research subsidies and procurement contracts from the Pentagon. Though the semiconductor was invented at Bell Labs, that worthy private institution owed its existence partly to the regulated, rent-capturing monopoly that was AT&T, and partly to the loving support of the military. Refinement of future generations of semiconductors and microprocessors benefited immensely from the military's insatiable appetite for smaller and faster computers.

The fact that this was a surrogate industrial policy rather than an explicit one had both benefits and costs. Among the costs were the ideological cost of having to insist that America really didn't believe in such things. The deliberate incubation of certain advanced technologies for national-defense purposes was an unfortunate exception to the prevailing free-market dogma. Any spillovers were incidental, and (as we told our incredulous trading partners) even regrettable. Another cost was that two industrial cultures grew up, one accustomed to military patronage, cost-plus contracts, and very long planning horizons, the other accustomed to competing for commercial markets and satisfying Wall Street's shorter-term imperatives. When defense contracts dwindled, many technically elegant companies could not make the transition. Research collaboration between competing firms that did not involve national-security goals was long disallowed as violating antitrust doctrines. Cultivation of export markets for many high-tech products was discouraged or prohibited, lest they fall into the wrong hands.

But the benefits were also significant. In a society loath to sanction direct government involvement in the economy, World War II and the Cold War allowed hundreds of billions to flow to research and development. The Pentagon also functioned as an agency of technical diffusion. The system of having a few prime contractors and two tiers of subcontractors required big companies to share advanced process-technology with small ones. Quite unintentionally, this worked as a kind of technological extension system. The Defense/technology system also functioned as a kind of investment bank for ultra-high-tech projects; the Defense Advanced Research Projects Agency (DARPA) almost single-handedly spawned the supercomputer industry, which was needed to design missiles, model the effects of nuclear weapons, and crack codes. Indeed, during the postwar boom the two main institutions counteracting the short-term horizons dictated by the structure of American financial markets were the Pentagon, with its very long planning horizons and deep pockets, and the several technically dynamic industries that were regulated cartels.

Policies to promote technologies or industries are widely considered vulnerable to pork-barrel pressures. However, during the Cold War the necessary secrecy of the Defense connection substantially insulated federal technology policy from the need to pander to powerful legislators. If the United States was secretly developing highly sensitive technologies in specialized machine tools needed to build aircraft and submarines, or supercomputers to break codes, this was too important and too secret for pork-barrel politics. To a remarkable degree, Congress trusted Defense scientists to seek out the experts, without regard to region or congressional district. The Defense science establishment was sometimes quietly (and impotently) criticized in Congress for concentrating federal resources in a few elite research universities—MIT, Berkeley, Stanford, Cal Tech—but to little effect. Pork-barrel politics operated at the level of procurement politics with epic battles over whether General Dynamics or Boeing would get major aircraft contracts. But this didn't interfere with the basic science.

Federally funded science was also politically insulated by a new institution: peer review. Prior to the era of mass federal funding of science, large private foundations such as Rockefeller and Carnegie had devised informal peer review of grant proposals, in order to get expert advice and prevent favoritism. This system was explicitly written into the statutes setting up the National Science Foundation and the National Institutes of Health, to keep the allocation of research dollars from being politicized. It is a fine example of how the political process can devise innovations to save itself from its coarser tendencies. Peer review, though used by government agencies, can be located culturally in a "third sector" that is neither market nor state. Research grants are allocated neither bureaucratically nor politically, nor via market forces, but on the basis of blind evaluations by the expert scientific community. The system seems to work better than either political or market allocation.

During the same postwar era, the U.S. government poured hundreds of billions of dollars into biomedical research, in this case not mainly for defense purposes but as an outgrowth of the same national consensus that government should support basic research. The National Institutes of Health, created in 1944, spend about eight billion dollars yearly, roughly matching the research dollars contributed by the private pharmaceutical and medical-device industry. Throughout the postwar era, pharmaceuticals have consistently been among the most profitable major industries and were among the most reliable export leaders. The newer biotech industry has also benefited substantially from government support of the health sciences, most recently through the multibillion-dollar project to map the human genetic system. Even the Gingrich Republicans, contrary to their professed ideology of laissez-faire and budget-cutting, have increased funding for NIH because of the plain benefits to industry.

Note here a three-way nexus of government support of innovation that promotes a leading-edge industry. NIH grants to the graduate training of scientists, to the funding of research labs, and to more applied investigations serve to advance the scientific knowledge that is the basis for "downstream" commercialization of products. Government patent protection of pharmaceutical products and government toleration of monopoly prices both err on the side of generosity, allowing companies to reap large rents that are then invested in further innovations. Finally, the Food and Drug Administration—the dreaded regulatory presence—functions as a blue-chip certification agency widely respected worldwide. FDA approval gives export products of American drugmakers global credibility. Thus, a three-way violation of allocative laissez-faire—research subsidy, pricing protection, and regulatory intrusion—together have helped incubate one of America's crown-jewel industries.

INTERVENTION AND INNOVATION

This brief history is worth recalling, on several counts.

First, it gives the lie to the idea that the United States has historically been a laissez-faire nation. Despite the constitutional restraints on state power and the generally libertarian national creed, government action for economic and industrial development is deeply ingrained in our heritage. As an emerging nation seeking to develop, industrialize, and maintain its sovereignty, the early American Republic looked warily on foreign financial and commercial influences. For most of its history prior to World War I, the United States had a high external tariff. It also engaged in significant and highly interventionist industrial policies, both directly and as a byproduct of the military. The claim that pure laissez-faire is optimal policy turns out to be quite recent, and out of character with most of American history.

Second, there is now a sharp disjuncture between the policy the United States pursued for most of its first two hundred years, and the advice it now proffers to today's developing economies. Most emergent nations have in fact followed the developmental path of the early United States, using state power to blend technical learning and economic development with a tolerable measure of sovereignty. But in recent years, the U.S. government and American private investors have used America's significant global diplomatic leverage to move emergent economies onto a path very different from our own: to promote entree for foreign private capital, ban discrimination in favor of domestic production, and turn away from public investment, public regulation, public subsidy, and public ownership.

The IMF and the World Bank, which are substantially American proxies, have also used their significant influence to warn developing nations first and foremost to "get prices right" and trust market mechanisms in economic-stabilization policies, rather than using government credits or industrial policies for economic development. So confident is contemporary opinion of this approach that American free-market economists and diplomats typically read laissez-faire policies into their views of successful late-industrializing nations such as Japan and South Korea, whose actual policies have been the opposite.

Finally, our history vividly demonstrates the power of innovative, as opposed to allocative, efficiency. One cannot experimentally rerun history. However, it is very hard to believe that the United States in the year 2000 would be a more prosperous nation if the nineteenth-century federal and state governments had never promoted the development of railroads and canals, if we had never set up state universities, agricultural and mechanical colleges, and agricultural extension, if there had been no government program to accelerate development of radio, civil aviation, semiconductors, pharmaceuticals, and basic research in the sciences, and had the immense technical stimulus of World War II and the Cold War never happened. It is even more improbable to believe that Japan or South Korea would be more prosperous today had they just waited for private-market forces to follow the dictates of allocative efficiency and failed to take heroic steps to industrialize.

At this point in the argument, the good free-marketeer will object that it is too easy to emphasize only the successes. It is true that many canal and rail enterprises in nineteenth-century America went bust; that public-investment schemes in Mexico, Brazil, India, and even France have often failed to pay off. Economists Linda Cohen and Roger Noll, in an emblematic book, *The Technology Pork Barrel*, emphasize such failures as the Jimmy Carter–era Synfuels Corporation, the Clinch River Breeder Reactor, and the proposed SuperSonic Transport (SST)—which Congress in the end failed to approve in 1971. Of their six case studies, only one, the government-financed communications satellite, later spun off into the private Comsat corporation, was deemed an unambiguous success. Cohen and Noll conclude from this relatively small and rather biased sample that, though government subsidy of pure science can be cautiously defended, government attempts to sponsor the "commercialization" of technologies usually backfire. They declare, "The overriding lesson of the case studies is that the goal of economic efficiency—to cure market failures in privately sponsored commercial innovation—is so severely constrained by political forces that an effective, coherent national commercial R&D program has never been put in place."

Note, however, two oddities in this rather convoluted wording. First, the subject of the inquiry—a "coherent national commercial R&D program"—is something of a straw man. It is specified in such a way that most of the successes are excluded by definition. The development of radio, microelectronics, supercomputers, jet aviation, numerically controlled machine tools (all generated via Pentagon funding), and biotech breakthroughs built on NIH support—not to mention our longest-lived and highly successful "industrial policy" of increasing agricultural productivity—was not precisely the fruit of deliberate, narrow-focus efforts to "commercialize R&D," though that was very much the effect and the broader intent. Second, Cohen and Noll take a jaundiced, "public-choice" view of the hopelessness of the political process. Yet one wonders how the same flawed political process was able to legislate such gems as DARPA, NIH, NSF, and the national laboratories, all of which incubated technologies that led to commercial innovations.

Alas, economic theory doesn't definitively settle this question. We do know, from the notional dialogue between Schumpeter and Smith, that the contest between allocative efficiency and dynamic technical gain is broadly indeterminate. Industrial history strongly suggests that violations of pure allocative efficiency often pay off. But we also know that gross and prolonged transgressions against the price system can also bring grief. And, contrary to economists such as Cohen and Noll, we know that polities as well as markets are capable of cumulative learning and invention. The SST was closed down (by liberals), just as the Synfuels project was defunded (by conservatives). Peer-reviewed science was invented by the public sector, as were agricultural extension, the self-amortizing mortgage, and precompetitive research consortia.

This review of economic history and theory should at least impeach the presumption that free markets optimize technical learning. But which policy interventions are most likely to play to the strong suit of market discipline, while simultaneously compensating for the failure of pure markets to maximize innovation and minimizing risks of bureaucratic or political myopia? For most classical economists, the choice is fairly easy: if you must depart from the price system, do it in the most marketlike manner.

There is a new urgency to this debate, because America's technology and industrial policies can no longer hide behind the Cold War. Either there is a legitimate and widely accepted rationale for violations of laissez-faire to promote innovation, or the twin hammers of budget-cutting and ideological attack will gradually deplete the public subsidy of technical innovation. How much R&D spending government continues to provide will reflect competing budgetary priorities. These will be fought out in a new climate of fiscal scarcity which itself reflects the broad assault on government's ability to do anything competently. In the fiscal year 1996 budget, government support for research and development declined in real terms. Major research universities, such as MIT, Berkeley, Cal Tech, and Carnegie-Mellon, faced hidden cuts in federal R&D support through changes in the overhead formula.

Much of government's funding even for basic research has in effect been concealed in the Pentagon budget, which has fluctuated between one-half and two-thirds of all federal spending for R&D. Nondefense R&D in recent years has hovered around 1.8 percent of GDP, or about 50 percent less than in Germany or Japan. Directly or indirectly, the Pentagon provides nearly half of all federal support for university math and science, and over 40 percent of federal support for engineering.

Just as defense funding disguised general support for science, the recent defense cuts have been disguised reductions in science spending generally. Until the early 1990s, large research universities such as MIT were allowed extremely generous overhead payments in connection with military contracts for both basic and applied research. Large overhead payments assume the delicate fiction that the contract covers part of the university's fixed costs, as well as costs directly attributable to the contract. (In reality, the university would incur the same basic costs for its physical plant and its administrators' salaries, even if it lost the contract.) These somewhat inflated overhead payments were permitted because of the military's long-term alliance with research universities. The Pentagon knew, intuitively, that having such institutions flourish was in the broad national interest; this was a disguised form of general subsidy. With the new budgetary climate, the fiscal relationship has become more adversarial, and overhead formulas have been cut.

FROM INDUSTRIAL POLICY TO RESEARCH PARTNERSHIP

Prior to the ideological swing to the right in 1994–95, a new consensus was emerging to finally settle the sterile industrial-policy debates of the late 1970s. In this new consensus, most mainstream economists have accepted that government has a legitimate, if modest, role to play in promoting "precompetitive" research and development—outlays that private-market forces would not optimally finance and whose fruits would be broadly diffused. This was nothing more than an acknowledgment of a positive externality that had long been disguised in defense spending.

The earlier debates over whether the United States should have an "industrial policy" were misleading, because the goals were ambiguous, even to supporters, and because each side tended to exaggerate the other's position. To some, industrial policy was the latest euphemism for the long-standing left-liberal interest in national economic planning. More narrowly cast, industrial policy was a response to the deindustrialization suddenly occurring in basic industries such as autos and steel.

Some early advocates, such as Robert Reich, viewed industrial policy as a strategy for easing transitions out of failing industries into dynamic ones where

America's superiority was also suddenly under assault. For others, such as Bennett Harrison and Barry Bluestone, industrial policy was a government commitment to help revive industries mistakenly dismissed as defunct, industries whose real problem was a combination of bad managerial decisions and adversarial labor relations domestically, and subsidies and aggressive trade practices overseas.

Market-oriented economists, regardless of party, saw mischief in the entire approach. Charles Schultze was fond of remarking that *ad hoc* bailouts at least did less damage than grand industrial-policy schemes. Debate degenerated into a tussle over whether government was more competent than markets to "pick winners." Industrial policy was attacked for presuming to rescue industries that the invisible hand was properly consigning to the scrap heap. The debate was conducted in an odd idiom of "sunrise" versus "sunset" industries, quite ignoring the fact that some of the most advanced technologies operated, potentially or actually, in such supposedly rust-belt industries as steel and autos. Industrial policy was also seen as archaically nationalist, at a time when the national identity of multinational firms was blurring.

The Carter administration, cautioned by its own economists, sponsored a few *ad hoc* industrial policies—an embryonic "tripartite" (industry-labor-government) program for modernization of the steel industry, small technology subsidies to raise productivity in shoe and apparel manufacturing, and also, rather guiltily, supporting the Chrysler loan guarantee. With the election of the Reagan administration in 1980, the idea of government policy's deciding which domestic industries should be explicitly supported dropped from public debate.

Yet the question of how public policy should promote innovation did not go away. Rather, with the imminent end of the Cold War, the issue was reframed as technology policy. Even in two conservative Republican administrations, defense planners were concerned that technologies vital to the national defense might be lost, either because of dwindling military appropriations or because of superior foreign producers, or both. Under the Reagan and Bush administrations, a fierce ideological battle continued between technological nationalists and economic libertarians. Richard Darman, head of the Office of Management and Budget, declared at a Cabinet-level meeting, "Why do we need a semiconductor industry at all? If our guys can't hack it, let it go." Michael Boskin was quoted as declaring—he later denied the quote—"Computer chips, wood chips, potato chips, what's the difference, they're all chips." This was the standard wisdom regarding allocative efficiency: one dollar of GDP is as good as another, and the market is the best determinant of what is produced. If Japan pushes American producers out of the semiconductor industry—even by being protectionist, this must somehow be the market speaking.

Meanwhile, Democrats (who still controlled Congress) mounted a rearguard action using the defense interest in key technologies to fashion a more explicit national technology policy. Prodded by legislation fashioned by New Mexico Democratic Senator Jeff Bingaman, the Pentagon in 1989 identified twenty-two technologies deemed crucial to the national defense. These turned out to run the entire high-tech gamut. In effect, this effort flushed out the fact that military concerns functioned as a surrogate industrial policy; it also looked ahead to the end of the Cold War, when that surrogacy would no longer be sufficient. In addition, the Reagan administration continued an intermittently hard-line trade policy, especially vis-à-vis Japan, which forced the government, however uncomfortably, to define which technologies and industries mattered to America and which ones did not.

During the 1980s, several laws written by a coalition of defense Democrats, industrial-policy Democrats, and "fair-trade" Republicans were signed into law by Presidents Reagan and Bush. Legislation passed in 1983 and expanded in 1988 allows private corporations to develop collaborative research projects with the national laboratories. A small-business R&D fund was established in 1982 to aid in commercialization of new process technologies. In 1984, waivers were written into the antitrust laws, allowing industry research consortia. These were liberalized in 1993. Essentially the same coalition supported the establishment of SEMATECH, with the frankly interventionist purpose of maintaining and advancing American leadership in production of semiconductors. SEMATECH was funded on a fifty-fifty basis by participating private firms and the Pentagon. The 1988 trade act enlarged the old National Bureau of Standards into a new National Institute of Standards and Technology, and created a civilian Advanced Technology Program to help firms develop "precompetitive" technologies. In 1989, DARPA was given explicit authority to serve as a venture-capital bank for defense and dual-use technologies, such as advanced semiconductors, X-ray lithography used in the fabrication of semiconductors, and flat-panel display screens. The national laboratories, artifacts of the warfare state, shifted their emphasis to collaborations on civilian technologies.

With President Clinton's election in 1992, this approach gained new allies in the White House. Vice President Gore was an enthusiastic backer of a more assertive federal R&D presence. The 1994 Economic Report of the President, in marked contrast to such reports during the Republican 1980s, enthusiastically supported "technology initiatives" to "correct market failures," both in basic research and precommercial technology, and even in commercial applications.

Despite net cuts in the overall federal budget, the Clinton administration significantly increased funding for technology subsidies. The Advanced Technology Program, for example, was increased from $36 million in its first year, 1991, to $431 million in 1995. The Commerce Department also launched an industrial extension service, the Manufacturing Extension Partnership, modeled on agricultural extension. Under Clinton, the federal government also pursued more explicit industrial policies to develop more fuel-efficient and low-pollution cars, as well as an Environmental Technologies Initiative housed at EPA, and a five-year, \$22-billion defense-conversion project to help military contractors shift production facilities to commercial applications.

Laissez-faire critics of technology policy and industrial policy usually paint a caricature of a bureaucratic czar or a corrupted Congress arbitrarily picking winners—arrogantly presuming to outguess the market. The actual process by which government supports technologies, for example via SEMATECH or the national labs, is far more consultative, consensual, and iterative. Despite the earlier polarization of views on industrial policy, by the early 1990s there was something of an intellectually defensible middle ground: government would increase efforts both for basic science and for applied research in technologically dynamic industries, both to maintain American competence in emerging technologies and to compensate for the dwindling defense role. This was not exactly industrial policy, in the sense ridiculed by economists such as Cohen and Noll, but it was certainly a big departure from trusting the free market. There was widespread recognition in both parties that, with the decline in defense spending, explicit civilian technology policy had to make up the gap.

Even so, with the Cold War's end and the decline of military outlays for R&D, the expansion of civilian subsidies to basic science and applied technologies has not made up for the military cuts. And the sweeping budget cuts of 1995–96, stimulated by the Republican embrace of a more fundamentalist laissez-faire, utterly gutted the Clinton innovations.

Thus, the threat to the new middle ground on government support of innovation is both ideological and budgetary. And there is a real irony in this aspect of the latest right-wing lurch of American politics. For, although there is now a respectable consensus among economists that government can add to national well-being by supporting technical advance, that constructive role is being undermined by the broader ideological attack on government per se. Much the same process is occurring in the area of pro-competitive regulation—to which we now turn.

7 / REGULATED COMPETITION

THE INEVITABILITY OF REGULATION

In the celebration of markets, regulation is an unnecessary and counterproductive drag on efficiency. The hero of the story, as usual, is the price system. Regulation alters the prices that would obtain in a laissez-faire market, thus changing the allocation of resources and supposedly depressing total output.

As we have seen, however, regulation often facilitates commerce in second-best realms where perfect competition is structurally unattainable. If we look back on health care and on financial markets, it is evident that regulated competition is necessary to compensate not just for isolated "market failure," but for huge discrepancies between the theory and the practice. In necessarily imperfect markets even the deliberate construction of "marketlike" incentives is itself another form of regulation.

In reviewing the economic history of the past century, it may be startling to realize that until quite recently something like two-thirds of this highly capitalist, privately owned economy was very substantially regulated. Indeed, the most dynamic industries of this century—electric power, telecommunications, aviation, radio and television, and information technology, among others—have been subject to regulatory constraints on entry, exit, price, demand, supply, profit, and terms of competition.

Likewise, in the financial sector, banking, underwriting, stock brokerage, and insurance have been heavily regulated. As we saw in chapter 6, many advanced industries were influenced—and incubated—by Pentagon decisions to buy and subsidize technologies. Other major industries affected or operated by government, such as education, scientific research, transportation, and basic infrastructure, were far from free markets. This regime was not laissez-faire, but evidently it was broadly efficient in the aggregate: the zenith of the era of regulation—the postwar boom—was the most successful period of American capitalism.

Regulation, emphatically, did not supplant market forces. On the contrary, privately owned firms continued to be subject to pressures from consumer markets and capital markets as well as from regulators. But they maximized their profits within a context structured by regulatory constraints. And this altered outcomes, often for the better. Looked at dynamically over time, these regulatory influences may well have produced more innovation, more diffusion to a broader public, a faster decline in price, and more effective consumer choice than their absence would have achieved.

Thus, it is a serious mistake in industries with scale economies or partial monopolies to view regulation as a simple alternative to the market mechanism. Rather, as Richard Vietor points out in a brilliant and somewhat neglected book, *Contrived Competition*, government regulation "shapes the structural characteristics of the market in which the firm does business." Within that "contrived" structure, which may well be a significant improvement on a laissez-faire Hobbesian war of each against all, *entrepreneurs continue to behave as profit maximizers*. They innovate. They cut costs. They cultivate customers.

For example, electric utilities in this century have been subject to regulation of their rate of return. That meant they could maximize company earnings only by maximizing diffusion of service. They necessarily took advantage of scale economies, operating according to the core economic principle that increasing demand is associated with declining cost, whatever the source and direction of causality. This made cheaper electric power more widely available, and raised company earnings. In this context, for half a century the electric power industry's productivity grew at an average annual rate of 5.5 percent, at a time when overall productivity growth was 1.7 percent a year. It is very hard to believe that unregulated competition, with the severe risk of excess capacity, would have improved upon that remarkable record.

In diverse industries, entrepreneurs constrained by the rules of monopoly franchise and rate regulation internalized norms consistent with their necessary strategy of profit maximization. Electric-company executives, AT&T officials, and airline magnates all became virtual missionaries for the ideal of universal service. Schumpeter trumped Smith.

Of course, some industries, as they mature, are natural candidates for greater marketization. For example, the postal monopoly may have been necessary to promote commerce and communication in a young, developing nation most of whose capital was in the form of land and labor rather than financial wealth. The vigorous competition of UPS and FedEx suggests that postal service—at least major parts of it—is amenable to private competition. The telephone monopoly may have been more efficient for getting the entire country wired, whereas new technologies may well facilitate more innovation and consumer choice in a regime of greater competition.

Yet it is a mistake to conclude that government intervention was appropriate only in an earlier state of development, or that globalization and recent technological changes moot the need for regulation entirely. In highly imperfect markets such as health care, telecommunications, electric-power generation, or airlines, opportunism, oligopoly, and asymmetric bargaining power do not disappear. With new technology, they simply take different forms. If left to private forces, the result typically frustrates both allocative efficiency and consumer sovereignty. Despite the persistent quest for the grail of a perfect, self-regulating market, the need for ground rules never disappears.

Since the 1970s, a near consensus has emerged that the regulation that characterized that earlier era is now unnecessary and unwise. The burden of proof has shifted to those who would supplement competition with regulation. Enthusiasts of deregulation contend either that regulation, with the wisdom of hindsight, was always excessive; or that recent changes in technology, industrial structure, and global competition have overwhelmed whatever case for regulation applied in an earlier time.

With Newt Gingrich's 1994 Contract with America, the hostility to regulation intensified. The marketizers attacked not only the remnants of economic regulation, which had been under assault from most free-market economists since the 1970s, but even health, safety, and environmental regulation, an area where most economists have accepted that externalities exist.

As I will suggest in this chapter, a market economy still needs a substantial dose of regulation to perform as well as it is able. The instruments of regulation can often use the incentives and disciplines of markets. In many industries, regulated competition can be superior to older forms of direct regulation—of prices or rates of return. But regulated competition still requires intelligent, public-minded regulators.

WHY REGULATE?

Conventionally, regulation is classified as either economic or social.

Economic regulation—of price, entry, profit, and terms of competition—is justified when particular markets, for structural reasons involving economies of scale and market power, fail to be effectively self-correcting. The classic case is a regulated public utility.

Social regulation is generally used to overcome negative spillovers ("externalities"), as in the case of antipollution regulation, or failures of information and bargaining power, as in health and safety regulation. This chapter deals with economic regulation in three key industries. Chapter 8 will address social regulation. Here is a brief taxonomy of why market economies can benefit from regulation.

Natural Monopolies. We regulate some industries because they work more efficiently as monopolies. It would be wasteful and duplicative to have two parallel gas pipelines, two sets of telephone poles, two parallel rail lines, or two electric grids. Neither supplier could cover his costs by running at half-capacity, and both would soon have to raise prices or go out of business. Left alone, one would likely absorb the other. A natural monopoly is typically efficient when it has overwhelming economies of scale (one firm can produce at lower total cost and higher volume than several). For the logic of a regulated monopoly to work, government policy also regulates exit and entry, to protect the producer's monopoly franchise from opportunistic competitors.

Once we tolerate a monopoly, the producer is no longer subject to the discipline of competition. A monopolist left to its own devices would likely raise prices, leaving consumers to pay more money for less product. Of course, in principle the consumer is free not to buy the product. But in many natural monopolies, such as electricity, water, and transit, the product is a virtual necessity, and consumer demand is fairly inelastic; hence the consumer cannot discipline the monopolist.

A variation on this theme is regulation intended to prevent "ruinous" competition. Although the very idea of ruinous competition is out of fashion today, in the 1930s the economy was afflicted with massive overcapacity. Desperate businesses kept cutting prices, which only added to the glut and drove prices (and purchasing power) down further. This dynamic compounded the general deflationary spiral of the Great Depression. Eventually, market forces might have squeezed out all this capacity and rationalized what remained—but at an even lower level of output, employment, and income.

Artificial Monopoly and Antitrust. Government also regulates to save the market from its own antimarket excesses. Though some monopolies are arguably natural, many reflect abuses of market power in industries that could be efficiently competitive. Scale can be virtuous, but when one or a few firms dominate a potentially competitive market, they may collude at the expense of potential entrants, and of consumers. Overt price-fixing is only the most extreme monopoly practice. Firms that enjoy market power also retard competition with coercive or anticompetitive mergers, discriminatory or predatory pricing, cross-subsidies, retail-price maintenance, tying or bundling arrangements to force buyers of one product to buy another, and so on. Antitrust laws make these practices illegal. The paradox here is that a degree of regulation is necessary in order to safeguard competition and allow markets to work more nearly in the textbook fashion.

Scarcity and the Public Interest. Other industries are regulated because of real or perceived scarcity. Once, the electromagnetic spectrum seemed finite. The FCC stepped in both to allocate the spectrum according to use, and to award licenses. This in turn required public-interest criteria and administrative proceedings to award and then renew licenses. In this case, entry and exit were regulated, but not price. Not surprisingly, broadcasting earned super-normal profits, until close substitutes such as cable channels and home video appeared. Lately, thanks to microwave, cable, cellular, satellite, and other new technologies, there may well be an infinite number of communications channels. There is still a residue of public-interest concern affecting broadcasting, but scarcity is no longer the governing factor. Change, however, sometimes cuts the other way and enhances monopoly power. For example, at busy airports, takeoff and landing rights are also scarce public resources. These used to be regulated, but are now subject to private monopolies. The unregulated scarcity confers market power— and price-gouging.

Safety and Soundness. Other economic activities are regulated to assure safety and soundness. This is especially true of financial industries, such as banking, stock brokerage, and insurance. Here the rationale is a blend of concerns about "information failure" (the consumer is not sophisticated enough to tell which bank or brokerage is sound), fiduciary obligations (the banker or broker is holding other people's money), and systemic risk. Banking, as we have seen, is simply too important to leave to the tender mercies of market discipline. In the nineteenth-century era of "free banking," financial panics regularly spread to the real economy, wiped out the savings of innocent consumers and businesses, and deepened depressions. The state regulates financial industries, because the state would have to bail them out in the event of catastrophe.

Health, Safety, Environment. We also regulate to protect ourselves from market assaults against the human and natural environment. The common rationale is that market pricing fails to discern serious negative externalities. This will be treated in chapter 8.

These are the economist's stylized rationales for regulation. Today, as intellectual fashions have changed and political-power balances have shifted, there is a widespread belief that most of these rationales no longer apply. In evaluating whether this claim is true, we should remember as a matter of economic and political history that none of these regulatory systems resulted from bloodless expert analysis of externalities, information failures, natural monopolies, bargaining asymmetries, and the like. For the most part, they resulted from gross abuses of private economic power—followed by exposé, indignation, social conflict, struggle, and ultimately political remediation.

In the event, the market failures that inspired regulation were far from subtle. Congress created the Interstate Commerce Commission in 1887 because railroad magnates were consolidating, colluding, and using monopoly power to charge farmers extortionate rates. From the company's economic point of view, and as a matter of economic theory, small shippers had less market power and often no effective alternatives. They had to pay whatever the railroad charged. Big customers might have shipping alternatives so they would have more bargaining power to demand lower rates. The railroad, needing to cover its enormous fixed costs, charged whatever the market would bear. But society (reasonably) determined that these disparities were fundamentally unfair, and had deleterious economic consequences to small producers, hence to society. The pricing structure wrought by "market" forces—in this case, the railroads— was neither natural nor optimal. During the same era, the first John D. Rockefeller was using his market power to extract secret rebates from shippers, which allowed his Standard Oil Trust to underprice competitors that he was seeking to squash or gobble up. In 1890, Congress passed the Sherman Act to deal with monopolization, coercion, and price fixing, which were then rampant in diverse emerging industries. It enacted the Pure Food and Drug Act in 1906 after exposés of disgusting working and sanitary conditions in slaughterhouses. During the same era, states began creating public-utilities commissions (beginning in 1907) to avoid the Hobson's choice of either inefficient fragmentation of gas, electric, and phone systems, or unregulated monopoly price-gouging under the aegis of a single dominant firm. The states also stepped in to limit the power of employers to take advantage of vulnerable children and adult workers. These measures were all enacted to deal with flagrant abuses, either of the ideal of free competition, or of vulnerable people. Often the formal economic rationales came only after the fact.

In a stylized taxonomy of why and when to regulate, it is all too easy to ignore that the generally more mannered competition of our own era is itself the legacy of a century of regulation; too easy to overlook that much regulation reflected changing values and balances of political power, and that failure to regulate would not have yielded efficient laissez-faire markets but would merely have entrenched a different set of inequities and inefficiencies. By agreeing to a sterilized idiom of market failures, externalities, and the like, one can back into an acceptance of an overly mechanical view of economic man, in which narrow conclusions necessarily follow from narrow premises, realities of political and market power are excluded, and entire debates about the nature of the good society are foreclosed by tacit definition.

THE RISE AND DECLINE OF REGULATION

From the late nineteenth century through the 1970s, regulation came in three broad waves. The economic regulation that began in 1887 and extended through the progressive era of Theodore Roosevelt and Woodrow Wilson was intended to remedy the abuses of economic concentration. New Deal regulation, though it had diverse strands, largely pursued economic stabilization, to remedy deflation and overcapacity by regulating entry, exit, price, and rate of return. A third wave of regulation, lasting from roughly 1965 to 1977, addressed health, safety, and the environment. This was a whole new impeachment of markets, with a new arsenal of regulatory remedies.

By the end of the New Deal, independent regulatory commissions were effectively a fourth branch of federal government. Radio and telecommunications were regulated by the FCC; rail, trucking, and barge traffic was regulated by the ICC; civil aviation by the CAB (routes and fares) and the FAA (safety and technical standards); gas and oil by the FPC; nuclear energy by the AEC; securities and stock exchanges by the SEC; and banking by four different federal agencies and the forty-eight states.

Other regulation, notably of public utilities, was also shared with the states. The federal courts made clear, beginning in 1877, that states did have the power to regulate prices and conditions of service for local gas and electric companies, street railways, telephones, and the like. As it evolved, state public-utility regulation computed the utility's cost structure, which became the "rate base" upon which was calculated a reasonable rate of return. Utility companies made regular requests for rate changes, which were subjected to exhaustive evidentiary hearings. Over the long haul, state PUCs did a commendable job of simulating markets, and stimulating innovation and diffusion. Public utilities were able to earn a broadly competitive rate of return, given their relatively low risk. The gains of ever-increasing productivity were broadly shared with ratepayers and shareholders. And regulated utilities had little difficulty securing capital. The politics were also complex. In the absence of state or federal regulation, municipal franchises for gas and electricity service were often products of corrupt local politics. Gas and power interests, in the late nineteenth century, fought among themselves, and ended up largely embracing state regulation as a strategy of more coherent consolidation. Like so much else in the Progressive era, the regulatory regime that emerged was a complex blend of civic reformism and self-interested industry lobbying. What was not possible, however, was a pure market solution. Abuses, opportunism, and monopoly were too pervasive; in a democratic society, one way or another politics had to intrude.

If we look at the actual economic history of these industries in the late nineteenth and early twentieth centuries, it is evident that the absence of regulation would not have produced stable, benign competition of the textbook sort. More likely, we would have seen fragmentation, as was the case with the early gas, electric, and telephone industries, followed by consolidation and private monopoly or cartel, as occurred with oil, telephones, steel a century ago, and airlines after 1978. In industries with even some characteristics of natural monopolies, nature seems to abhor atomized competition. If government doesn't act, private regulation ensues.

Public regulation reached its apex in the late 1960s. A burgeoning consumer movement spearheaded by Ralph Nader, with allies in the press and champions in Congress, could call attention to corporate abuses, and legislators would respond with new regulatory initiatives. Between 1965 and 1977, Congress enacted some twenty new major regulatory laws, governing clean air, clean water, toxic waste, occupational safety and health, highway safety, consumer-product safety, and truth in lending and credit reporting, and creating an elaborate new regime for assessing environmental impacts, as well as expanded financial regulation through measures such as the Community Reinvestment Act. But within a decade, the era of regulation was suddenly spent. The reversal came with stunning speed. The word "deregulation," which only entered popular discourse in 1976, had become a widely shared policy objective by 1978. What changed?

Regulatory Capture. Disillusion came from right, center, and left. Interestingly enough, the counteroffensive did not begin with business. Though organized business emphatically resented the new wave of Nader-style social regulation, for the most part big regulated companies like AT&T, the airlines, electric utilities, broadcast networks, and so on had made their peace with a regulated regime, and used their political influence within it rather than against it.

In the political center, there was disillusion with both the machinery and the politics of regulation. A generation after Roosevelt, too many regulatory agencies had become overly cozy with the industries they ostensibly regulated. An influential 1955 book by Marver Bernstein proposed the theory of "regulatory capture," which quickly became a social-science staple. There was, critics held, a life cycle of regulatory agencies. After a few decades of vitality, they tended to ossify or become clients. The regulators of the Roosevelt generation, who grew up as idealists working in FDR's alphabet soup of commissions, found during the postwar boom that they had highly marketable skills. All they had to do was to switch sides, and counsel or lobby for the regulated industry. They could even remain good nominal Democrats—this, too, was a marketable affiliation that kept alive useful contacts with key Democratic legislators. Even if public-interest regulation was possible in theory, it was evidently difficult in practice. A report to incoming president John Kennedy by James Landis, former head of the SEC and CAB, called for a basic shake-up of the system.

Further left, Ralph Nader was a blistering critic of bureaucracy and regula-tory capture. A series of muckraking reports by the first Nader's Raiders, with arch titles like *The Interstate Commerce Omission*, presented a highly unflatter-ing picture of these agencies. Many of the newer consumer agencies, such as the National Highway Traffic Safety Administration and the Occupational Safety and Health Administration, owed their existence to the legislative efforts of Nader and his allies. Yet Nader was quite willing to abolish agencies such as the Civil Aeronautics Board, which he considered beyond redemption. Though Alfred Kahn and his staff were cautiously advancing the idea of "regulatory re-form" of the CAB in 1977, Nader had already called for the agency's outright abolition—in 1975.

Curiously, the left-wing critique of regulatory capture tended to meld with a conservative critique of the very idea of regulation. The consumer movement's love-hate relationship with regulatory agencies reflects an ideological ambiva-lence among American reformers, which dates at least back to Louis Brandeis. Some, like Brandeis, wanted to extirpate bigness and restore a world more like that of Jefferson and Adam Smith. Other reformers, such as Herbert Croly and later J. K. Galbraith, saw large scale as a necessary feature of modern industrial life, something to be wrested from purely private purposes and domesticated for a broader public interest, through regulation or what Galbraith termed "counter-vailing power."

For those in the Brandeis tradition, who included one strand of New Dealers and later Ralph Nader, consumer sovereignty remained an intact ideal. The challenge was to make sure markets did not become rigged by monopolists or used deceptively against consumers. For these reformers, the favorite reme-dies were antitrust, disclosure, labeling, and only occasionally the deliberate countermanding of the price mechanism. Brandeis was sometimes on both sides of this question; he supported the right of manufacturers to dictate retail prices, because he thought it defended small business against large, monopolistic retail chains. Although Nader named his organization Public Citizen, the rhetoric and imagery were substantially those of the marketplace. For all of Nader's tactical radicalism, the ideal was an informed, vigilant, and sovereign *consumer*.

Thus, when the full-blown attack on regulation matured in the late 1970s, its natural defenders were hobbled by a somewhat equivocal set of first principles. Rather than a coherent theory of what Charles Lindblom astutely called the limited competence of markets and a commitment to a social-market brand of capitalism, most liberal reformers harbored the earlier liberal ideal of a perfected market system. American reformers also tended to be energized by an exaggerated hostility to big business, rather than a more measured conception of a mixed economy in which business was promoted but domesticated as a responsible social partner. It was easier to demonize business than broker a European-style contract with it. Thus, if a regulatory agency had been "captured" by business, and seemed to be serving the purposes of business, this was a capital crime, and the remedy was execution of the agency. The extended hearings on regulatory reform of the mid-1970s, sponsored by the Senate's most effective liberal, Edward Kennedy, quickly became a contest between the two parties to see which could be the better champion of complete economic deregulation.

Economists as Ideologues. On the right, the main ideological influence in favor of deregulation was less the militance of the business community than the broad shift in the economics profession, partly described in chapter 1. When business did become more militantly anti-regulation in the 1980s, it consummated a three-way rendezvous—with an energized conservative movement and a newly fundamentalist economics profession.

Laissez-faire economists found the entire regulatory system an affront to the discipline of markets and a source of bureaucratic waste. Professor Murray Weidenbaum, later President Reagan's chief economist, widely publicized his calculation that regulation was costing American business $102 billion a year. Weidenbaum made no serious effort to place this cost estimate in context by calculating offsetting benefits, but his statistic gained wide currency.

The conservative Law and Economics movement enjoyed growing influence. Robert Bork, in a series of scathing articles culminating in a 1978 book, *The Antitrust Paradox*, argued that prosecutors and courts were ignorant of the basic laws of economics, and that nearly all antitrust interventions had an effect opposite to the one intended—they suppressed self-renewing competition. The market anomalies and abuses that spawned regulation in the first place were suddenly of scant interest. (As a paid consultant to AT&T in the mid-1990s, Bork oddly reversed field and warned that the rival Baby Bell companies had to be regulated.)

As regulatory agencies and their missions proliferated, liberal as well as conservative economists grew disillusioned. "The central policy prescription of microeconomics," wrote Alfred E. Kahn in his two-volume master work, *The Economics of Regulation*, "is the equation of price and marginal cost." Otherwise, consumers buy more, or less, than the optimal quantity, and producers misallocate resources. But in regulated industries, Kahn observed ruefully, price seldom equaled marginal cost.

For Kahn and a chorus of other critics, regulation of rates and of entry and exit distorted economic activity. Regulated utilities were rife with cross-subsidies. Potential innovators were denied the opportunity to compete. Consumers were denied innovation and choice. Regulated industries, moreover, tended to overinvest in physical capital, since their permissible return was computed as a fraction of their capital costs. Even with the best will in the world, regulators could not price services properly, since hearings took time, and the resulting rate schedules suffered from "regulatory lag."

Some regulated industries enjoyed windfall profits (as in the broadcasting industry's exorbitant return on investment), whereas others had chronic losses (as in passenger rail service). The problem was partly structural. It was difficult if not impossible to allocate precisely how much of, say, the AT&T cost base should be charged to local, versus long-distance, service. But regulatory inefficiency was also the result of the failure of regulators and judges to appreciate basic principles of economics. These were the themes of a library full of books and scholarly articles published during the 1960s and 1970s. Economist F. M. Scherer, a relative liberal, wrote in his 1970 text on industrial organization, "The Supreme Power who conceived gravity, supply and demand, and the double helix, must have been absorbed elsewhere when public utility regulation was invented."

Also writing in 1970, Alfred Kahn was promoting more marketlike regulation, acknowledging that some industries needed to be regulated but pushing regulated prices more closely in line with marginal costs. As chairman of the New York State Public Service Commission from 1974 to 1977, Kahn used marginal-cost principles to raise peak prices for electricity from three and a half cents per kilowatt hour to thirty cents a kilowatt hour on hot summer nights. This discouraged casual use, limited peak demand, and thus minimized the need for costly new construction that would have raised everyone's rates.

By the time Kahn took over as President Carter's chairman of the CAB in 1977, the movement for regulatory reform was quickly becoming a movement for deregulation. Initially, Kahn moved to allow airlines much greater latitude in offering discount fares, and granted applications for new routes, something the CAB had long discouraged on the grounds that it would result in "ruinous competition." By 1978, Kahn was presiding over complete deregulation of airline fares and routes, and the abolition of the CAB.

The Airline Deregulation Act of 1978, as another early advocate, Yale management-school dean Michael Levine, later wrote, "to an unusual degree was the legislative embodiment of an academic consensus." It was, Levine observed, "a relatively rare 'natural experiment' with which to evaluate the predictions of academics." Kahn, who long prided himself on being an institutionalist, a student of concrete industrial detail, told an airline executive that he really didn't need to know much about planes. They were all, he declared famously, "marginal costs with wings." Newly enamored of complete deregulation, Kahn set out to make sure that regulation could not return.

Though Democrats retook the White House in November 1976, the economists' support for deregulation only intensified. Charles Schultze, Jimmy Carter's chief economist, created an office of regulatory review in the Office of Management and Budget, to rein in wayward regulators in ostensibly independent commissions. This leash was tightened under Republican Presidents Reagan and Bush, and loosened only slightly under Clinton.

For the generation of economists that came of age in the 1970s and afterward, the older concern with market imperfections seemed archaic. Industries that appeared to be natural monopolies might be competitive after all, if government would just stop restraining competition. Entrepreneurship was so potent that antitrust, except in the most extreme cases, only interfered with the market's own self-cleansing tendencies. Except in very special circumstances, "ruinous competition" was a contradiction in terms; the more competitors, the merrier.

As far as consumer protection was concerned, the first generation of Law and Economics scholars proved to their own satisfaction that the common law was a far more reliable and efficient source of remedy than legislation by the too easily corrupted political system. Later, when judges tightened liability standards and juries began rendering more generous damage awards, many Law and Economics partisans reversed field and called for legislation to rein in courts—ignoring the plain inconsistency of their arguments.

Even in the rare areas where an economist might make an uneasy case for regulation, the debate shifted to arguable "market failure" versus almost certain "polity failure." The theory of public choice, the gift of economics to political science, made it all too clear that regulators were unlikely to regulate in a true public interest, whatever that was. Hence, almost all of the economics profession—the "expert" witnesses most likely to be called—weighed in on the deregulatory side.

Inflation. Classic regulation was also a victim of the inflation of the 1970s. In some industries, such as electric utilities, inflation played havoc with pricing assumptions. Until the quadrupling of oil prices, utilities lived in a stable world whose entire logic was based on scale economies and long-term reductions of costs. Regulated utilities could price "ahead of markets," confident that scale economies, technical breakthroughs, and therefore steadily declining prices would attract sufficient additional customers to justify the artificially low initial price. This was precisely what occurred during much of the twentieth century in core regulated consumer industries such as telephones, electricity, and air travel. The fact that prices might diverge from marginal costs at any given time was less important than that regulation guaranteed the producer a reasonable return, and enabled a system in which prices were declining steeply and usage expanding steeply over time.

The inflation of the 1970s turned this settled world upside down. Rate structures presumed rising use and declining costs. When fuel prices quadrupled, the reality was suddenly one of escalating costs. The more power the utilities sold, the more money they lost. But reversing the usual strategy and discouraging usage was hardly painless either, for it moved in the wrong direction on the cost curve, and led to scale diseconomies. The more electricity the ratepayers conserved, the less income the utilities had to amortize a very costly installed generating base, which had been constructed based on projections of ever-increasing use.

By an unfortunate coincidence, OPEC's hike in oil prices followed almost immediately on the first wave of environmental regulation. In addition to paying higher fuel costs, utilities were having to spend money installing the first generation of costly antipollution technologies. Self-taught energy economists such as Amory Lovins began arguing, plausibly, that conservation was a superior substitute to new generating capacity, and that electric power should be priced accordingly. All of this was perfectly logical as part of the new conservation ethic, but it threw nearly a century of regulated utility economics into reverse and destabilized the entire regime. These dynamics generated financial pressures both for rate hikes to cover costs, and for new rate structures to discourage usage. But these remedies only intensified the squeeze on utilities and the cost to consumers—generating more political pressure to end the monopoly and allow in competitors, further undermining the old system.

Though regulation was a useful scapegoat for the inflation of the 1970s, in retrospect nearly all of the inflation was initially macroeconomic—the excessive stimulus of the Vietnam War. This was intensified by an external sectoral shock—the oil-price increases, whose effects became embedded in the economy. Regulation was a trivial factor. But if regulation did not cause inflation, inflation undermined regulation, both mechanically and ideologically. Concern that regulation was frustrating competition and hence raising prices became a key part of the deregulatory mantra of the 1970s.

Technology. Economic regulation can be credited with providing stable long-term profits which finance technical innovation, but in the end innovation can undermine regulatory regimes. The emblematic example is telecommunications. As long as phone service required wires, it made sense to treat AT&T as a single regulated monopoly with scale economies. With microwave long-distance service, however, and with cellular phones increasingly a local wireless option, the purely technical rationale for phone service as a natural monopoly weakens.

By the same token, the new generating technologies also undermined traditional assumptions in the generation of electric power. In the 1960s and 1970s, huge thousand-megawatt generators were seen as the threshold of scale efficiency. With that degree of sunk cost, departing from the traditional monopoly franchise was unthinkable. But in the 1970s and '80s, new gas-fired turbines, small cogenerating technologies, and nontraditional, decentralized sources of renewable wind, solar, and geothermal power made possible a wholly different configuration of the industry.

Ostensibly, technical changes, as well as inflation, undermined the regulated banking system. With instantaneous computerized transfer of funds anywhere in the world, technology seemed to link global markets and undermine national regulation. But in many respects, the global system of finance was more laissez-faire from the nineteenth century through the 1920s. Even though the technology was rudimentary, money could still be exchanged and transferred globally via telegraph rather than fax and modem, but almost instantaneously. It was policy choices, not technology, that caused the shift to a more regulated regime in the 1930s. Similarly, the shift back to banking deregulation (and airline deregulation) in the 1970s and 1980s had less to do with technology than with ideology.

Look again at the telephone business. Technologically, competitors could have entered the consumer phone-equipment business anytime in the last century. It was the Bells' monopoly, formalized in FCC policy, that prevented them from doing so; technology was a minor factor. Independent telephone companies were plentiful a century ago. They were weakened by AT&T's predatory tactics, until the existing telephone oligopoly was stabilized and regulated by federal policy beginning in 1913. Again, technology had little to do with it. So, although technical change often stimulates pressure for deregulation, technology does not dictate it.

The fact remains that, in industries where there is even partial monopoly power, economies of scale, and structural limits on consumer sovereignty, a pure free market does not yield optimal outcomes. New technology may expand the realm of possible competition in such industries, but regulatory regimes and policies are necessary to establish common ground rules, fair access, universal service, and consumer protection. The particulars of private regulation will vary according to the structural characteristics of the industry. But its complete absence is likely to lead to a regime of private regulation, which often ends in consolidation and abuse of monopoly power.

Let us look more closely at three key industries that epitomize the logic of regulated competition: telecommunications, airlines, and electric power. All three were traditionally regulated either as natural monopolies or oligopolies, on the premise that they had overwhelming economies of scale. Thus, entry, exit, price, and terms of service were subject to regulation. A producer got a monopoly franchise and a guaranteed rate of return, and had to provide universal service with limited price-discrimination.

One of these industries, airlines, has been entirely deregulated with respect to entry, product, and pricing—everything except safety. In the United States today, anybody can start an airline, fly anywhere, charge any price, as long as the craft are certified airworthy and the pilots certified competent.

The other two industries are today a complex blend of regulation and competition. To the extent that regulation continues, it is intended to supervise terms of access and maintain fair ground rules for emerging competition.

I will argue that the shift to complete deregulation in airlines was a self-defeating mistake, which holds important lessons for other policy realms such as telecommunications. It would have been far more efficient and more conducive to true competition if the CAB had stayed in business, promoted greater competition, monitored the experiment, and selectively regulated the airlines. Likewise, greater competition in telecommunications and electric power paradoxically requires a regulatory presence.

TELECOMMUNICATIONS AS REGULATED COMPETITION

Until the AT&T breakup, the telephone company was regulated as a public utility, though aspects of the industry were potentially competitive. In the old system, subscribers not only got a dial tone; even the phone was owned by Bell. But AT&T did not pay much attention to the instrument at the end of the telephone line. AT&T made its money by extending service to new customers, expanding its rate base while it developed new technology to lower costs of wiring and switching. The telephone receiver was not a profit center, and the technology of the black rotary dial phone barely changed in two generations. Here was a case where monopoly really did suppress innovation. Entrepreneurs hungered to invent and market devices that could be hooked up to AT&T's phone lines. But these were fiercely resisted by AT&T, disingenuously, as "foreign" equipment that might damage its system, and—more to the point—that impinged on its monopoly franchise.

In a series of cases that came to a head in the 1968 Carterfone decision, the FCC and the courts gradually permitted non-Bell producers to sell devices for home use that competed directly with AT&T's manufacturing subsidiary, Western Electric. Almost simultaneously, AT&T faced a similar and more serious challenge to its long-distance monopoly, again thanks to technological advances. With microwave technology, long-distance competition became technically feasible. In 1969, the FCC, by a four-to-three vote, allowed MCI, the first microwave competitor, to enter the relatively narrow business of selling "private-line" connections to business users, presumably insulated from AT&T's mass consumer market.

MCI, however, got cute. After filing tariffs with the FCC to authorize interconnections between AT&T's switchboards and its own dedicated private lines, MCI abruptly targeted the entire consumer market. Through "Execunet," unveiled in 1975, MCI offered ordinary consumers the ability to use an AT&T touch-tone phone, punch up MCI's dial tone, and connect to any AT&T subscriber in the country via MCI's competing long-distance microwave service. AT&T, outraged, accused MCI of filing misleading tariffs, and the FCC withdrew its approval. MCI then took AT&T to court—and won. This opened the floodgates to competing long-distance service. Charles Brown, chairman of AT&T, complained that he faced a "fence with a one-way hole": competitors were allowed in to poach on his customers, but, as a regulated monopoly, AT&T could not venture out.

In the 1970s, Congress, the FCC, and the courts wrestled with the dilemma of how simultaneously to safeguard the magnificent system of cheap, universal telephone service, yet to allow the competition that the new technology was making possible. AT&T fought "creeping deregulation" on two fronts. In the political arena, AT&T pressed (unsuccessfully) for legislation to limit competition. In the marketplace, AT&T stepped up its battle against competing suppliers of equipment and purveyors of long-distance service—often fighting dirty. AT&T imposed spurious technical barriers, charged exorbitant rates for interconnections, made customers of long-distance competitors dial as many as twenty-two digits, and sought to degrade the quality of competitors' signals.

As a result of these tactics, AT&T, for the third time in its century-long existence, fell afoul of the antitrust authorities. The first antitrust challenge to AT&T's ruthless tactics against surviving independent phone companies had resulted in a 1913 agreement with the Justice Department, known as the Kingsbury Commitment. AT&T promised to cease buying up independent phone companies, to allow the remaining independents interconnections with the Bell System, and to sell Western Union, which AT&T had acquired in 1909. This deal ushered in the era of AT&T as a stable, regulated monopoly.

In a second major antitrust suit, initiated in 1949, the Justice Department had alleged that AT&T's exclusive buying arrangements with its subsidiary, Western Electric, were harming independent manufacturing companies and retarding development of better, cheaper phone equipment. The antitrust suit initially sought divestiture of Western Electric. However, in 1956 the government settled for a consent decree, requiring AT&T to license technology freely to competitors, restricting its operations to common-carrier communications, and specifically keeping AT&T out of the emerging data-processing business.

In 1974, stimulated by AT&T's tactics against its new rivals, the Justice Department sued again. It was this suit that led to the breakup of the Bell System in 1982–84. The settlement, approved by Federal District Judge Harold Greene, created seven highly regulated operating telephone companies, and a partly deregulated AT&T able to offer almost everything but local phone service.

At the same time, the FCC and the courts determined that AT&T was still a "dominant carrier" in the long-distance business, and subjected AT&T to a series of pricing, reporting, and regulatory requirements designed to make sure that AT&T would stop using its market power to strangle its fledgling rivals. On an interim basis, these included outright subsidies of competitors. AT&T's market share in long distance has gradually fallen to under 60 percent.

But as technology has continued to unfold, Judge Greene, appeals courts, Congress, and the FCC have continued to modify the terms of engagement. As countless analysts keep pointing out, information technology is creating the eventual convergence of three hitherto distinct industries—telephone, cable, and broadcasting—with the new world of networked personal computing. In addition, electric-power companies may well get into the telecommunications business, along with other nontraditional providers of wireless and satellite services. One can imagine a single industry with multiple competitors, all in the business of bringing a wire or wireless connection to the home or office, offering a gateway to an infinite offering of voice, information, data-processing, entertainment, educational, and financial services.

The Internet suggests an even more pluralist model, in which myriad providers offer diverse gateways between the home and a global information web, and the web itself is a largely unregulated set of autonomous overlapping pathways. One very laissez-faire analyst, Peter Huber, terms this model "geodesic," and sees no reason for it to be regulated at all. Monopoly bottlenecks are no problem, Huber likes to say, because there are "many bottles and many necks."

That view, however, is far too sanguine. Even in a world of multiple providers and convergence of cable, telephone, and broadcasting, a regulatory role will be needed indefinitely. Why? Because this emerging superindustry is highly segmented, and major sectors are still either natural monopolies with substantial economies of scale and scope, or unnatural monopolies with lingering market power to fend off competitors.

In theory, the emerging telecommunications market is wide open to free competition. But in practice, competition requires countless regulatory determinations of what is fair play. Competitors often necessarily operate on each other's right of way. Upstart long-distance carriers usually lease phone lines from the very company they are trying to displace. Local start-up phone companies need to piggy-back on the Baby Bells. Cable companies must often rent space on electric-utility towers or telephone poles. Competitors offering plain or enhanced phone services need access to the local phone-company grid.

Contrary to Huber, many of these industries do enjoy control over some key bottleneck, and each views the others as actual or potential rivals. Absent regulation of ground rules, no rational competitor will allow its rivals into a sheltered market on equal terms. The stakes are too high, the opportunities for anticompetitive behavior too tempting.

Regulators are needed to determine what is truly competitive and what is still a natural or contrived monopoly, and to establish fair rules of competition accordingly. This is, of course, a very different mission from the traditional one of setting fair rates of return and ruling on prices and services proposed in AT&T tariff filings. But it is still regulation, since in its absence companies would price their services differently and resort to different competitive (or anticompetitive) tactics. There is no space in a nontechnical book to address every regulatory issue in the new, convergent telecommunications industry. But here are some lingering issues unlikely to be resolved efficiently by market forces:

Spectrums and Standards. The national telecommunications system is a blend of wired connections and wireless use of the broadcast spectrum. Even though technology has enlarged the capacity of the electromagnetic spectrum and complemented it with cable, copper, and fiber-optic connections, the government must still determine which portions of the spectrum will be reserved for what broad uses, revising them periodically as technology evolves, and awarding licenses to users.

In 1994, the FCC began auctioning licenses on one small portion of the spectrum newly reserved for personal wireless communication devices. This was hailed as a more marketlike improvement over earlier procedures, in which the FCC had awarded licenses either administratively or by lottery. The advantage of an auction is that it allows private-market players to make informed judgments about the economic worth of limited-spectrum rights, to make investments, and to work to make the investment pay off. The auction also produces revenue in exchange for the sale of rights to airwaves that are in some sense "public." The auctioning of the spectrum is a fine example of more marketlike regulation—*and* of the lingering need for regulators.

Before auctions could proceed, the FCC had to determine which parts of the spectrum should be redirected to what new uses, whether the rights were being sold for a finite period or in perpetuity, how the auction would be conducted, whether royalties would be paid after the license was obtained at auction, how many competitors were considered sustainable in each market area, whether licenses could be freely traded in a secondary market, whether competing bidders could communicate their intentions with one another, and a host of other ground rules. The answers were not intuitively self-evident from pure-market principles, since this policy was being superimposed on institutional and historical facts that themselves reflected a second-best world. Though this used a marketlike mechanism, it was emphatically a contrived market.

Moreover, though advocates of laissez-faire view the regulatory role as merely transitional, none of these policy dilemmas is a one-time occurrence. As the FCC monitors the results and as technology keeps changing, the FCC (and/or Congress) will doubtless modify the terms of future auctions. In the closely related issue of technical standards and incumbent windfalls, Congress and the FCC face another unavoidable set of policy decisions that markets cannot make for them. Should the government allow existing broadcast licensees to offer advanced digital television (ATV)? Should there be a separate allocation of new ATV channels? Should government require that ATV signals be received by conventional TV sets, or only by new equipment? And since new technology allows five or six channels in the spectrum bandwidth of one old channel, should incumbent license-holders get this windfall to do with as they see fit? Should they be allowed to divide and sell off excess bandwidth? Should they split their windfalls with the public? Or should the FCC take back the entire excess spectrum from incumbent licensees and reallocate it? As technology keeps evolving, variations on these issues will keep emerging. Public regulation as traffic cop, even as it uses more marketlike principles, remains a public good.

The development of the explosively successful market in cellular phones depended on regulatory policy. The FCC, after extensive hearings, decided in 1984 to award franchises for two competing cell-phone providers in each local market area. One of these could be the local Baby Bell; the other could be AT&T, or anybody else. The FCC initially determined that allowing more than two competitors would be inefficient, since the establishment of a cell-phone network requires very costly construction of transmitters (Schumpeter trumps Smith again). By 1996, cell-phone service has become available to about 90 percent of Americans, and nearly every franchise is a monopoly or duopoly. As the technology evolves, and the next generation of portable communications devices relies on other wireless technologies, more fragmented competition is being authorized. But this will also require a new set of regulatory determinations.

Given that other portions of the spectrum continue to be reserved for a wide variety of uses, ranging from military purposes to conventional radio and television, specialized commercial uses, and the like, it is fantasy to think that market forces alone could allocate the entire spectrum with no regulatory guidance. For that to occur, government would first have to abandon the multiple social purposes that underlie the current spectrum allocation, and lock in place windfall "possessions" of public spectrum. Even if government did so, a free-for-all would likely prove institutionally inefficient and unstable. In the "gold-rush" auction of the entire spectrum, many investors would guess wrong and overpay. The morning after, there could well be a new round of fire sales, followed by extreme institutional disruption, then consolidation and cartelization, very likely leading to cries for a new round of regulation.

"Asymmetric Regulation." Partial deregulation of the telephone industry has not solved the problem of Charley Brown's "fence with a one-way hole." It has only intensified it. Asymmetric regulation occurs when a local phone company or electric company subject to rate-of-return regulation is forced to be provider of last resort, but also to compete with others subject to no such mandate. It also occurs when what we might call a recovering monopoly, such as AT&T, is being weaned by regulators from its former monopoly status but still enjoys substantial market power that it could abuse.

When unregulated competitors are permitted to enter a regulated local-telephone market, they can skim the cream, by offering more attractive rates to more profitable customers—typically the high-volume business customers that had been subsidizing residential ones. In addition, many large businesses are now partly bypassing the local phone company by leasing lines and operating their own systems.

The logical conclusion of this asymmetry is not hard to discern. The most profitable lines of business of regulated operating phone companies will be peeled off, leaving fewer ratepayers to pay for the installed base, and the remaining residential customers with ever-higher rates. This could lead to a kind of death spiral, in which the regulated phone company loses its best customers and becomes marooned in a money-losing submarket as high-cost provider. This dilemma has caused local phone companies both to resist the new competition and to seek the right to diversify defensively.

But consider the opposite problem. Local phone companies have a huge amount of market power, since they control more than 99 percent of local phone loops. Except in a few pilot areas, anybody who wants to sell long-distance, data-processing, or other services to a telephone customer must pay to tap into the grid of the local phone company. As long as this monopoly remains, there is the risk that the local phone company, usually a Baby Bell, will charge an exorbitant rate for access. These excess profits, in turn, can allow the local phone company to selectively lower its own rates for basic local service, and underprice competing local phone providers seeking to break in.

If the system "tips" in the direction of competitors skimming all the cream, the cost of basic local service could skyrocket, and the universal system would be compromised. Universal service, let's recall, is not a natural goal of markets, but a social goal with spillovers that pay economic dividends. If the system tips the other way, and local phone companies successfully fend off competitors, a regulated monopoly will simply turn into an unregulated one. By paying attention to which way the system is tipping, regulators can achieve a reasonable balance.

A good illustration is the delicate question of volume discounts. Many local and long-distance competitors lease wires from AT&T or from one of the Baby Bells. They then resell the service, often with technical enhancements, to the public or to specialized business niches such as local area computer networks. Discounts to resellers are partly set by supply and demand and partly by regulators. If the discount is too steep—say, 50 percent—the incumbent carrier in effect subsidizes its competitors' prices, and its own demise. If the discount is too shallow—say, 5 percent—few competitors will crack the market.

As competition increases in telecommunications, there is a related risk of excess capacity. In the 1990s, there has been a competitive race to lay optical fiber. Unlike copper wire, a single optical fiber can carry hundreds of thousands of calls. The marginal cost of adding an additional call is practically zero, so each competing firm has an incentive to build volume. By 1995, it was estimated that the nation had enough copper and optical fiber already installed to supply our long-distance needs four times over, and the race was continuing.

In the short run, overcapacity lowers prices, as companies race to sign up customers. But somebody has to pay for all that new infrastructure. It is not at all clear that wiring the country four times over is an efficient use of resources. At some point, regulators may need to discourage further excess. A historic parallel is the railroad boom of the nineteenth century. Rival rail companies, in an industry that was a natural monopoly, raced to build lines, often duplicative ones. In the short term, there were price wars—usually followed by consolidation and price gouging. By the midtwentieth century, the Interstate Commerce Commission was the target of well-deserved criticism. Rail regulation (and passenger rail service) eventually failed, for reasons having partly to do with the nation's preference for subsidizing highways. But in the heyday of rail traffic the failure to have any regulation would likely have led to far worse distortions.

As technology has evolved and deregulation has proceeded, the Baby Bells have gradually diversified into a far-flung set of information, video, cable, and long-distance businesses. But the Baby Bell is also still the local phone company. If a local phone company bets wrong on an extraneous investment, its ratepayers will likely absorb a substantial part of the cost, through either higher rates or degraded service. Remember that, in most parts of the country, full competition to provide basic phone service is a long way off and may never be cost-effective.

For example, there has recently been a thicket of consumer and regulatory complaints against U.S. West, the former Bell company that serves the fourteen-state Rocky Mountain region. U.S. West has aggressively moved into overseas ventures, as well as acquiring cable franchises in states outside its primary operating region. But that has left it with less money for the humdrum business of installing telephone lines.

In the mid-1990s, U.S. West invested $2.5 billion to acquire a share of Time-Warner, $1.8 billion to buy a cable company in Atlanta, and billions more on overseas ventures. During the same period, hundreds of installers and customer-service representatives serving U.S. West phone customers were laid off, and tens of thousands of customers for basic telephone service were made to wait weeks or even months for installation. It costs U.S. West about two thousand dollars to install a new line once capacity has been exhausted, and as much as four thousand per new line in remote rural areas. U.S. West, however, has reduced its outlays for new lines in several states of this fast-growing region, claiming (implausibly) that it underestimated demand. Several state public-utilities commissions are investigating whether U.S. West has unreasonably diverted revenues from regulated phone service to other ventures. Though they don't have authority to prohibit U.S. West's outside investments, they do have the power to condition rate increases on specific reinvestments of ratepayer funds. And a few states with assertive regulators, including Tennessee and Vermont, have ordered regulated Bell companies to spend more money on their networks.

During this era of partial deregulation, the net outflow of capital from regulated Bell operations to nonregulated activities has significantly increased. In the 1987–89 period, the first two years when Baby Bells were freed to pursue outside ventures, $1.733 billion flowed out from rate-base operations to nonregulated activities. In 1990–92, that doubled to $3.579 billion—money that was diverted from maintaining, expanding, and upgrading the phone grid. Complete deregulation would likely intensify the race by regulated utilities to abandon basic service and pursue more profitable lines of business, leaving many phone customers either without basic service, or with service only at prohibitive rates.

The policy dilemma is whether competition between unregulated and partially regulated carriers can be rendered more symmetrical and sustainable. Professor Eli Noam, who directs the Institute for Tele-information at Columbia University, seeks to reconcile competition with universal service. He proposes mandating a complex system of transfer payments. The basic idea is that all companies offering telecommunications services would pay a prorated fee, to help defray the costs of maintaining the basic grid and financing cheap, universal basic service.

Professor Noam advocates this approach as a more "transparent" and "marketlike" substitute for the older forms of cross-subsidy, and more efficient than other mechanisms, such as access charges or taxation. His approach is certainly ingenious. But it is nothing if not . . . regulation. In the old days, cross-subsidy of basic service was internal to AT&T. Under Noam's plan, public policy sets a goal—cheap, basic, universal phone service—that markets would not otherwise achieve. In order to reconcile this outcome with the competition that the new technology allows, government has to design and administer, or at least supervise, a more subtle system of cross-subsidy. Moreover, as companies and their accountants learn how to "game the system," and as new technologies come on line, the terms of transfer require periodic review and refinement—by government regulators concerned about the broad public interest. Noam's work, emblematic of a whole genre that celebrates competition and deregulation, is not quite as free of regulation as it supposes.

Another prominent enthusiast of deregulation, Professor William Baumol, the father of the theory of contestable markets, argues that local telephone companies, cable companies, long-distance carriers, and new players should all be allowed into each other's markets. But, unlike many of his economist colleagues, Baumol recognizes that in key submarkets major players will retain substantial market power; thus, he endorses the continuing need for regulation—not traditional rate-of-return regulation, but regulation nonetheless.

Among other mechanisms, Baumol proposes ceilings and floors on prices. Floors are necessary to prevent powerful former monopolies like the Baby Bells from using predatory pricing to keep out new competitors. Ceilings are necessary to keep producers with monopoly power from selectively gouging consumers. Seemingly, a monopolist might be either improperly underpricing or improperly overpricing—but it is hard to appreciate that in segmented markets both abuses can occur simultaneously. In fact, this is exactly what occurs in segmented, monopolistic industries like telecommunications and airlines. As Professor Baumol writes (with J. Gregory Sidak), "A regulated firm wishing to keep out or destroy competitors can, if permitted, set uncompensatory prices for services in which it faces rivals, making up the shortfall from its high profits on those of its services in which it enjoys a monopoly."

As noted, the Baby Bells enjoy monopoly control of the local "loop" connecting the customer with the central switching station. In addition to fending off local competitors, the Bells have used this monopoly to extract exorbitant access charges from long-distance companies needing to connect with customers. These charges have been estimated by independent economists at seven to eight times costs, and account for just under half of the Baby Bells' total profits. Regulation of one sort or another is necessary to determine fair access charges to the local grid. When there is only one seller, the "free market," by definition, does not set a fair price.

Competition Between Regulated Industries. In the coming information era, one can imagine head-to-head competition between three different kinds of partially regulated companies—local and long-distance phone companies, electric-power companies, and cable companies—as well as brand-new entrants such as purveyors of wireless communication. Champions of marketization imagine the brokering of a giant deal and an ensuing competitive free-for-all, where any entrepreneur can offer any service. But since the basic line of business of each of these industries is a partly regulated monopoly, none of them is a pure exemplar of a free market. And since there is also a policy goal of universal phone and electric service, as well as nondiscriminatory and cheap basic cable service, totally unregulated competition runs the risk that money will be diverted to targets of opportunity and universal service will unravel. At the very least, the new world of competition requires sophisticated regulators to set ground rules to assure that none of the industries competing from behind semiprotected fortresses gains an unfair advantage against either consumers or the other industries, or abandons its core service.

In effect, the information highway is being constructed from the excess profits earned from ratepayers in three monopolistic, semiregulated industries. As a matter of economic theory, this process worked well enough when there was a closed system and a single company (AT&T). But it is by no means clear that the benefits of competition among two or three competitors will compensate for the inefficiency of redundant construction. Remarkably, long-distance rates actually began rising in 1992, and they rose at a steeper rate in 1993 and 1994. For the previous decade, they had declined every year. Nor is it clear that resources collected from ratepayers will not be diverted, as they have been especially by cable companies and Baby Bells, to extraneous and speculative uses. At the very least, regulators need to stand by to make adjustments, both in the terms of competitive engagement and in the entire premise of competitive regulation.

One can imagine several possible regimes to facilitate the seeming oxymoron of "regulated competition." One element, achievable through a variety of means, is relatively free competition with shared responsibility for universal service. Eli Noam's transfer-payment system is one of many possible approaches to that end. Another principle, already being used by the FCC and several state regulatory commissions, is "price-cap regulation." Rather than explicitly setting prices the way they used to, regulators mandate permissible price ceilings. The company is free to charge less, but not more. If the phone company, or electric company, can lower its costs and achieve additional savings, it can reap higher profits. But in most cases, the regulator mandates both a declining price-cap, to induce improvements over time, and a formula that requires the sharing of gains between the company's stockholders and its ratepayers.

Supporters of price-cap regulation emphasize that it is more marketlike than setting prices service by service, or targeting a fair rate of return. Price caps do rely more on economic incentives, but they are really a kind of rate-of-return regulation measured retroactively. If the regulator has underestimated gains from productivity or from monopoly power, and profits seem excessive, the regulator will lower the price cap after the fact. In order to make this judgment, the company needs an accounting system that segregates costs and revenues by line of business, and the regulator needs access to it. This is, of course, still regulation.

The FCC has used price-cap regulation on both AT&T and interstate operations of the Baby Bells. This has been hailed as marketlike, but the actual price-cap regulation of the Baby Bells has been widely criticized as overly generous. Since the AT&T breakup, the profits of the Baby Bells have regularly exceeded those of other regulated utilities and of American industry generally. Between 1988 and 1992, the Bells averaged 14.5-percent return on equity, compared with 11.5 percent by industry as a whole. In the decade prior to deregulation, the totally regulated Bell System earned profits only a point or two above the ten-year Treasury-bond rate. This more modest return was entirely appropriate, since Bell rates of return were virtually guaranteed, and investors enjoyed one of the private sector's most risk-free investments. But in the years since the breakup, the Baby Bells have earned over seven points above the ten-year Treasury-bond rate. So there is a good case that the actual price-cap is being set too generously, and is allowing the Baby Bells excess profits that in turn give them bottleneck market power to fend off competitors.

The FCC has used a "productivity factor," set at 2.4 percent per year in 1991, to estimate a reasonable rate of productivity increase, and ratchet back the price cap by that amount each year. But at a 1995 review, the FCC concluded that this factor understated the actual rate of productivity growth. The FCC raised the factor, lowered the price cap, and forced the Baby Bells to share more of the productivity gains with consumers. Without this kind of discerning oversight, consumers would suffer, and real competition would erode.

Though it is possible, in very high-density areas like Manhattan, to imagine the early arrival of multiple vendors of local phone services, it will be a long while before this becomes a reality in most of America. In 1996, less than 1 percent of local telephone customers had a choice of more than one supplier. In pilot areas of direct competition such as Manhattan and Rochester, New York, competition for local phone service has posed more regulatory questions, not fewer. For example, on what terms can competitors "piggy-back" on the phone lines of established companies? Can telephone service be offered by cable operators, and electric-power companies, and other businesses that happen to have wires and to own rights-of-way? And on what terms, with what protections against cream-skimming, and what interconnection requirements and residual obligations to the overall grid?

In most regions, scale economies make it difficult for new entrants to compete with established local phone companies. As competitors enter these markets, regulatory policy needs to pursue at least rough justice between new entrants and old, regulated phone monopolies. In one harbinger of regulated competition, the New York Public Service Commission took nearly two years to negotiate an elaborate set of ground rules that allow the local phone company, Rochester Telephone (a non-Bell independent), to pursue other lines of business. In return, Rochester Telephone accepted head-to-head competition by Time-Warner, which operates the local cable franchise. The commission's order ingeniously combines two elements. Both companies are subject to price-cap regulation; rates are frozen for seven years, and the two phone companies can keep whatever they save. The commission also devised an elaborate "settlements" formula for interconnection fees. The company whose subscriber initiates a call pays a fee to the company serving the subscriber to whom the call is placed. Again, this sort of competition is anything but a free market, since it is subject to carefully specified ground rules, and it is competition between two companies that are in part sheltered monopolies. This is more aptly described as a regulated cartel, with a degree of price and quality competition. If nothing else, regulators will still be necessary to make sure that neither phone company is abusing its market power to harm the other or to keep out additional entrants. At this writing, Rochester Telephone's competitors have barely made a dent on the incumbent's monopoly.

At minimum, as competition for local phone service emerges, regulators will need to make sure several preconditions apply: full access to Bell's right-of-way with fair access charges; "portability" of local phone numbers when subscribers shift to a competing phone company; no extra digits required for non-Bell customers; a balanced "settlements" scheme to give competing phone companies fair compensation for connecting subscribers to each other's customers; full cross-listing for all customers in the telephone directory; and equal access to the customer base for billing and marketing purposes. The FCC has identified no fewer than 266 elements of fair access.

A concrete discussion of these practical dilemmas in a historically regulated industry makes a laughingstock of the Coase Theorem. If the regulators simply went away and left private businesses with monopoly powers to negotiate fair, symmetrical outcomes, the result would be either chaos or cartel. To the extent that producers reached accommodation with each other, the loser would be the consumer. And lawyers would be litigating the details indefinitely.

Monopoly and Kindred Assaults. In an industry with lingering scale economies and monopoly elements, an efficient shift to partial competition requires vigilant policing by regulators. A good case in point is the cable industry. In 1984, the Reagan administration sponsored legislation to deregulate the cable industry, pre-empting local regulation. The award and pricing of cable franchises by local government has been rife with corruption and price-gouging. Typically, a cable company came into a city promising low rates; after it won the franchise, rates went up dramatically. The 1984 Cable Television Act basically freed local cable monopolies to charge whatever they liked. The theory was that the consumer was free to do without, and to rely on over-the-air reception, home video, movies, and other close substitutes for cable.

However, to many households cable had become a necessity or at least a habit. Absent price competition, cable companies could earn extraordinary rents. These windfall profits, reaped from an unregulated but captive rate base, were used not just to expand cable services but to build conglomerate empires. Companies like Viacom and TCI expanded into ownership of other entertainment, TV networks, book publishing, and so on. Armed with huge cash hoards, they became some of the biggest players in the hostile-takeover game. In 1992, Congress repealed the 1984 act, and reimposed price regulation of basic cable service. This was the only bill passed over President Bush's veto. Cable companies remained free to charge what the market would bear for popular extra channels, on the theory that the customer was free to refuse to buy, but the FCC regulated profits on basic service. In 1994, to howls of rage from the industry and from enthusiasts of "free markets," the FCC ordered a three-billion-dollar rollback of basic cable rates. In fact, the cable industry was a classic natural monopoly. In another age, it would have been regulated as one. And, unlike the regulated AT&T monopoly of yore, which was prohibited from diversifying, the cable monopolists were using their rents less to build the information highway than to finance an acquisition binge. Cable was in fact a splendid candidate for reregulation. Because of the cable industry's concentrated political power in local politics, where franchises were awarded (often corruptly), it was also a candidate for Federal regulation.

As public policy tries to nurture greater competition in realms that are not pure natural monopolies, such as long-distance service and perhaps local phone service in dense urban areas, there is a delicate middle ground between allowing cream-skimmers to wreck the economic logic of universal service, and allowing the market power of the incumbent phone monopoly to fend off competitors. Though the right to offer phone service and to set prices is increasingly deregulated, the access charges that local phone monopolies charge to long-distance carriers and local competitors cannot be entirely deregulated. Nor can the other terms on which competitors can access each other's customers.

In principle, it is easy to stipulate that everyone can compete in anyone else's formerly proprietary industry. In practice, there remain very thorny and complex issues of symmetrical access. In the real world, legislation doesn't begin with a clean slate, but with the historical fact of incumbent industries with substantial market power resulting from a legacy of past regulation.

Consumer Abuses. The new world of semiregulated competition also invites a new cornucopia of consumer abuses, which themselves require new regulatory decisions. Here are just a few:

Caller-ID.   New technology has made it possible to identify the source of an incoming call. Local phone companies saw caller-ID as a new profit opportunity, and began offering the option to subscribers. Though many customers would like to know who is calling them, they may not wish their identities to be known to callers. This offered yet another profit opportunity. The phone company would not only offer caller-ID; it would offer caller-ID *blocking*. One can easily imagine an infinite regress, in the fashion of *Mad* magazine's "Spy Vs. Spy." Regulators soon stepped in to fashion rules. In most states, if the phone company offers caller-ID, it must also offer caller-ID blockage.

"Slamming."   With deregulation of long-distance service, anybody can go into the business. But how to invade the customer base of AT&T, MCI, and the other large incumbent players? Current FCC regulation provides that, before a long-distance carrier can claim a customer, the customer must give written approval. In 1993 and 1994, upstart long-distance entrepreneurs began sending misleading direct-mail solicitations, advising that the recipient had won a contest. To collect the prize, you had only to sign and return the form. In tiny and hard-to-notice print, the form also authorized a change in your long-distance carrier. AT&T and MCI, a bit less crudely, resort to premium awards ("$20 of free calls") that also lure the unwary consumer into switching carriers. Not only does regulation need to differentiate permissible from deceptive forms of bait, it also needs to stipulate acceptable technical standards, interconnection requirements, provision for operator services, and so on.

In 1995, after receiving more than four thousand consumer complaints, the FCC proposed antislamming regulations, requiring that authorizations to change long-distance carrier be clearly identified as such, and separated from all promotions. This also came in the wake of lawsuits by long-distance carriers, charging each other with improperly purloining customers. Note again the mockery of the Coase Theorem. In theory, consumers and competing providers will settle all of this by negotiation. In practice, such negotiation is inconceivable. Regulation involves a modest one-time cost and sets clear ground rules for seller and consumer alike. Its absence would invite endless deception, counterdeception, hassle—and litigation.

COCOTs. A "COCOT" is not a small furry animal but an acronym for a Customer-Owned, Coin-Operated Telephone. In most states, there has been a proliferation of "public pay phones" not owned by the local phone company, charging double or triple the permissible regulated rate. Though the state public-service commission usually regulates rates that the local phone monopoly may charge, the owner of an independent pay phone may charge anything at all. Independent phone companies, charging fifty cents or more for a local call, market such pay phones to owners of bars, restaurants, gas stations, shopping malls, parking lots, airports, and other quasi-public spaces. The independent phone company pays a fee, or splits the profits with the business that has bought or leased the pay phone. The fiction is that this high-priced pay phone "belongs" to the restaurant or bar, which is merely "reselling" the service to the unsuspecting customer, just as I might charge you for making a call on my private phone.

This device, however, frustrates the policy goal of keeping public coin-phone service cheap and plentiful. In a kind of Gresham's law, expensive public phones drive out cheap ones. You don't see very many ten-cent pay phones side by side with fifty-cent phones, because the high-priced pay phone yields the bar a higher income than the low-priced one. Why doesn't the local incumbent phone company complain? The local phone company is likely to be barely breaking even or losing money on its pay phones, which are mandated by regulators and are a nuisance to service. It is just as glad to see somebody else take over the responsibility. And by getting users accustomed to paying fifty cents for a coin call, the COCOT softens the public up for the next rate increase that the local phone company wants, and also trains the caller to stop fumbling for coins and to reach instead for a credit card—a service that the local phone company just happens to offer, at a higher per-call cost. If "markets" are left to decide in a monopoly context such as this one, windfall profits are reaped from captive customers, and a traditional public convenience—the cheap public coin phone—is left to wither.

What are the proper terms of engagement here? Should the local phone company still be required to provide and service so many coin phones? Should there be a limit on what the COCOT can charge? Should the COCOT phone be required to provide operator, 911, and directory-assistance service? Should it provide free interconnection to the long-distance company of your choice? Should we just give up on the public-policy good of cheap coin-phones as a public convenience? Alas, only regulatory policy can decide.

Gouging Galore. What is true of COCOTs, caller-ID, and phony long-distance carrier "contests" is also true of junk faxes, automated telemarketing machines, the issue of who pays for charges on a stolen credit card, 900-number abuses, extra charges by hotels for connection to a long-distance carrier, and a host of other consumer issues not resolved by greater competition. On the contrary, intensified price-competition only drives suppliers to look harder for these disguised forms of price-gouging. Like it or not, these issues and opportunities for abuse will only proliferate. And enlightened regulation continues to be indicated.

Enduring Competition Policy. Some enthusiasts see these systems of marketized regulation merely as way stations en route to pure competition. That, however, is extremely unlikely. Ten or twenty years hence, if we do reach a world where companies that began as phone companies, cable companies, power companies, and others are all competing to bring information services to homes and businesses, there will still be a welter of issues, ranging from universal service, cross-subsidy, interconnectivity, access charges, sharing of right-of-way, market dominance, and consumer abuses, that cannot be solved autonomously or efficiently by private-market forces. The more complex the issues, the more sophisticated the regulators will have to be. Moreover, none of this operates in a political vacuum. If we do follow the laissez-faire advice and simply deregulate, the ensuing chaos and erosion of cheap, universal service would likely lead to a clamor for some form of reregulation.

In short, competition in industries that are partial monopolies requires a competition policy—a regulatory platform that channels, configures, and governs the process of competition. This is not identical to the older form of public-utility regulation, nor is it simply antitrust.

Some readers may wonder why antitrust is not sufficient. As the foregoing discussion suggests, achieving competition in telecommunications is extremely complex and iterative; it requires careful monitoring, the mandating of fair play, and periodic revision of rules. In the case of the AT&T breakup, some of this process was carried out pursuant to an antitrust settlement. But Judge Greene's ongoing supervisory role in the AT&T case was virtually unprecedented, and it is far from ideal. Normally, antitrust remedies are imposed long after damage is done. In extreme cases such as the AT&T divestiture, the remedies take on the characteristics of entire regulatory regimes. But the courts are not designed to play this role, and it is far better for regulatory regimes to be conceived and applied as creatures of explicit policy and ongoing agency supervision.

The emerging regulatory regime in telecommunications will structure competition that otherwise would be a blend of monopolistic and ruinous. By definition, regulation (even of the pro-competitive sort) requires regulators. In

1995, some of the more extreme Republicans in Congress sought to demonstrate their deregulatory fervor by dramatically cutting the FCC budget, as if this would somehow lead to less regulation and presumably more competition. A large faction of congressional Republicans also balked at the 1996 telecommunications bill, which was emphatically pro-competitive, on the ground that it wasn't sufficiently laissez-faire. But by now it should be clear that, in industries such as this, regulation and competition are not antithetical; they are complementary.

AIRLINE DEREGULATION

Based on our discussion of telecommunications, airline deregulation can be understood as an epic case of how not to proceed. Regulatory reform gradually led to complete deregulation. The regulatory agency, the CAB, was put out of business. When the results confounded the predictions of its sponsors, there was no agency to make a course correction—to return to regulated competition in order to mandate fair play. And most of the professional economists whose predictions had been confounded by the actual course of the experiment remain highly defensive about the results and reluctant to open the door to reregulation.

As a matter of theory, airline deregulation was premised on several interconnected assumptions. First, airlines were not a natural monopoly after all. Skyways were not like rail lines or pipelines; any number of planes could fly any number of routes. Airlines, properly understood, did not really have large sunk capital costs, since planes could easily be rented, bought, and sold. Because of the relative ease of going into the airline business, there were no serious barriers to entry other than those posed by regulators. And although there was a good deal of apparent monopoly power at many airports—with only two or three carriers accounting for most of the traffic—this, too, was an artifact of regulation. The theory of contestability held that actual competition was not necessary to discipline dominant incumbent firms. The mere threat of competition—"contestability"—would discipline providers. The reasoning was pure Chicago School economics, though its most effective proponents in the academy were relative liberals such as Professor Baumol: Logically, whenever super-normal profits appeared, a competitor would jump into the market to take advantage of them. Armed with that knowledge, existing airlines would price their services as if there were actual competition. "It is the threat of entry," Alfred Kahn testified to a House subcommittee in 1977, "that will hold excessive price increases in check." This dogma as applied to airlines was based more on logical inference than the study of actual markets.

The existing regulated regime was criticized by economists on several grounds. Regulated prices were widely thought to be too high. After extensive hearings in 1974–75, the Kennedy subcommittee concluded that prices were 40 to 100 percent higher than they should be. As evidence, a number of observers cited the fares on unregulated intrastate service, most notably in California and Texas. In 1974, a passenger flying the 338 miles between San Francisco and Los Angeles on Pacific Southwest Airlines paid $18.75, whereas a traveler on the only slightly longer Boston–Washington route of 399 miles was charged $41.67 on any of the carriers regulated by the CAB. Critics also noted that unregulated airlines in Texas and California tended to fly fuller than their regulated counter-parts—strongly suggesting that the regulated carriers were overpriced and thus deterring usage. Southwest Airlines, competing within Texas against CAB-certified incumbents, also introduced simple peak and off-peak fares. Advocates of deregulation anticipated that such fares would become the norm in a deregu-lated airline system. The Kennedy hearings also produced evidence that regula-tion had failed to keep fares closely aligned with costs. Some routes were subsidizing others, which was inefficient. Deregulation, Kahn and other experts predicted, would bring prices and costs efficiently into closer alignment.

Another vivid piece of evidence for the belief that fares were too high was the observation that airlines, barred from competing on price, were wastefully competing on frills, such as luxury meals and free champagne. This not only gave travelers more services than they would have freely bought in an unregu-lated market; it led to often ridiculous and costly regulatory proceedings. For ex-ample, on the lucrative New York–Florida run, Delta actually filed a laborious complaint before the CAB against rival Northeast's promotion offering steaks "cooked to order." Delta solemnly alleged that the offending steaks were mostly cooked in advance, and merely *reheated* to order. This dispute consumed months of deliberation, until it was abruptly and mercifully mooted when Delta acquired Northeast.

Regulation, as both liberal and conservative critics noted, was overly solic-itous of existing carriers, whose profits it guaranteed against ruinous competi-tion. Between 1950 and 1974, the CAB had received seventy-nine new carrier applications, and rejected every one. The deregulators believed not only that free competition would lower prices, but that it would bring them more closely into line with costs, just as theory predicted.

In 1977 and 1978, Kahn and the CAB moved toward deregulation by au-thorizing increased competition on routes. The CAB began to issue operating authority to all qualified applicants, dismissing the worry of overcapacity or ru-inous competition. If a route did turn out to be overserved, said the board, "one (or more) carriers will find it unprofitable to continue operating in this market and will withdraw. Should that occur, we would interpret it as a sign that the type of service provided by it is not desired by the public. The choice is more effi-

ciently made by the marketplace than by the Board." The board, in another ruling liberalizing competition, opined that "market forces would more likely result
in optimum service at optimum fares, for the market selection process operates
continuously and efficiently." Note the splendid indifference to whether this describes an idealized market or an actual one. Armed with these convictions,
Kahn, the Congress, and the Carter administration fully deregulated the airlines,
with a five-year phase-in. When Reagan appointees took over in 1981, they
phased out interim regulation even faster than planned. In 1985, the CAB went
out of business.

A Failed Experiment. What followed defied nearly all of the predictions.
Concentration increased. New competitors went bankrupt. Fares became a crazy
quilt, diverging wildly from costs. Market power and predatory pricing intensified. The major airlines became a private cartel—yet a strange blend of monopoly in some segments and ruinous competition in others. Despite selective
gouging, airline earnings plummeted. Between 1990 and 1994, the airlines had
five straight money-losing years, collectively losing thirteen billion dollars.

For a few years, new entrants like People Express and New York Air attempted to compete on the basis of price, with no-frills fares and novel forms of
management, marketing, and ownership. But the major carriers were able to use
their market power to underprice the upstarts selectively, and drive all but one
(Southwest) out of business. To wreck the business strategy of a People Express
or a New York Air, you didn't need to match all of their fares—just enough to
lure away sufficient customers to drive their load factors below break-even.
Armed with computers and sophisticated techniques of targeting, the majors
price-discriminated with a vengeance. *The Wall Street Journal* reported that
some of the selective deep-discount fares were coded "FU," just to make sure the
cut-rate carriers got the message. By the mid-1980s, all but one of the post-1978
upstarts were either in bankruptcy or acquired by one of the major carriers. The
industry was becoming steadily more concentrated.

Here, seemingly, was a flagrant case of predatory pricing. But the Reagan
antitrust division, steeped in Chicago economics, insisted that predatory pricing
was logically improbable. The Justice Department did not intervene. Nor did
the government do anything to block the wave of mergers and acquisitions.
All twenty-one of the proposed mergers brought before the Department of
Transportation in the 1980s were approved. The four largest airlines increased
their market share from 42 percent in 1985 to 75 percent by 1989. But the deeper
mischief is not in the concentration of the industry on average, but at particular
hubs. At Baltimore, USAir's market share went from 24.5 percent in 1977 to
60 percent in 1987, and over 80 percent at this writing. Concentration ratios
of above 80 percent now apply at Atlanta, Cincinnati, Detroit, Memphis,

Minneapolis, Pittsburgh, St. Louis, Salt Lake City, etc., and duopoly domination exists at Chicago, Denver, and Dallas–Fort Worth. Though there is token competition at some of these cities, a passenger desiring nonstop service to more than a fortuitous handful of destinations is virtually forced to deal with the dominant carrier.

As new competitors were driven out, concentration increased. Instead of providing more consumer choice, deregulation led to dominance of major routes by one or two carriers. Interestingly, too, most of the increased concentration resulted not from major carriers' crushing and then absorbing failing upstarts but, rather, from established airlines' combining with each other and tolerating each other's hub domination. By 1988, 85 percent of all airline markets were monopolies or duopolies.

The proponents of deregulation assumed that it would yield a simplified fare structure, with standard fares and deep discounts for those willing to stand by or to book far in advance. But computerization allowed the deregulated airlines both to match each other's fares and defeat price competition, and to use price discrimination to squeeze out the maximum sum that a customer could be made to pay. Instead of a simplified fare structure, airline pricing became so complicated that passengers on the same flight might be paying literally dozens of different fares. This system, known as "yield management," charges the passenger who cannot book in advance and stay over a Saturday night three or four times as much as the promotional fare. As the date of the flight approaches and the plane gets fuller, the fare keeps going up and the discounts disappear. Mysteriously, on the few remaining routes with head-to-head competition, the fares are usually identical between nominally competing airlines. The marginal cost of servicing an empty seat is about six dollars. By charging a stand-by passenger seven dollars, the airline would make a dollar profit. But the airlines would rather fly half-empty than offer last-minute bargains that might bust their entire pricing strategy. So much for marginal price equaling marginal cost.

One of the most contentious issues is whether prices have fallen thanks to deregulation. Ticket prices, on average, have indeed fallen—but they fell faster before deregulation. Revenue per passenger mile, adjusted for changes in fuel prices, fell at an annual rate of 2.7 percent in 1967–77 and 2.0 percent in 1978–88. And most of the postderegulation price decline occurred in its first two years, when competition truly was vigorous. Inflation-adjusted prices have been essentially level since the early 1980s. Stated another way, airline prices per mile ("yields") adjusted for inflation declined by an average of 2.5 percent annually between 1950 and 1978, but only by 1.7 percent between 1978 and 1994. Between 1980 and 1994, labor costs and fuel declined as a fraction of total operating expenses, but leasing expenses increased significantly. Airlines, with shaky earnings and little capital reserves, borrowed to the hilt and had to lease planes (which is more costly) rather than purchase them. In a climate of intensified competition, airlines also paid higher commissions to travel agents than before deregulation, as each airline vied for business with the other in a kind of reverse price war. Supporters of deregulation emphasize that the vast majority of today's tickets carry some kind of discount, but these are discounts from astronomical full-fare rates. The Bureau of Labor Statistics calculates that inflation-adjusted average fares were basically flat between 1967 and 1979—despite sharply rising fuel prices—but rose some 50 percent in the subsequent decade. One widely cited technical study by Brookings economists Clifford Winston and Steven Morrison claims that travelers have saved six billion dollars thanks to deregulation. But two-thirds of these savings are attributed to the "greater convenience" of more flights, by calculating the estimated value of a business traveler's time. This is nonsensical. In the real world, business travelers adjust schedules to fit flight times. If you plan in advance to depart at four rather than ten, you don't twiddle your thumbs waiting to take off; you use the time in your office to get work done or you squeeze in another client.

It is also misleading to compare today's discounted fares with the coach fares prevailing before 1978, since most off-price fares are encumbered with restrictions that represent a serious cost unacknowledged by the deregulators. The traveler who thinks she might need to revise plans is forced either to forgo that right or to pay an astronomical full coach or first-class fare. Occasionally changing plans is a natural and normal part of life. Restricting that freedom or charging disproportionately for the privilege represents a real loss to consumer welfare. It is reasonable compensation for the inconvenience to the airline to charge a small penalty—say, fifty dollars—for changing flights. But under the present system, a passenger who has to change an advance-purchase Saturday-night ticket often faces an effective penalty of many hundreds of dollars. The public has been trained to accept this as normal. Free-market economists defending deregulation neglect to count this very real cost, which aggregates to far more than the savings imputed to more frequent flights.

Proponents claimed that deregulation benefited the average person, since it forced business travelers to pay higher fares while the "discretionary" traveler enjoyed steep discounts. It is true that the deep discounts on selective seats have increased discretionary flying. But in fact large businesses—typically those with more than about half a million dollars' worth of air travel annually—are able to negotiate significant bulk discounts for their travelers. The price is essentially the restricted fare, but without the restrictions. So discretionary passengers able to book far in advance save money, as do large corporations, but the casual traveler in between gets a gouging.

The biggest airline customer of all is the U.S. government. Washington uses its market power to negotiate very steep discounts for government travel. On the

Boston–Washington run, where the basic coach fare has lately been as high as $596 round-trip, a government employee pays as little as $125—and doesn't need to stay over a Saturday night—thanks to a deal the government has negotiated with USAir. In effect, the general traveling public subsidizes the government. In many industries and transactions, bulk purchases make economic sense, since they are cheaper for the seller to service. But air travel is not one of these, since air tickets still have to be assigned one at a time, whether or not they are nominally purchased in bulk. The government is able to negotiate these cut-rate fares only because it enjoys market power not available to the ordinary citizen. It would be far better for government not to think of itself as proprietary consumer, but to use its regulatory power to benefit the entire citizenry, by mandating simpler and cheaper universal fares.

The deregulators, it turned out, fundamentally misconceived the dynamics of the airline business. As an industry with little product-differentiation—one airline seat is quite like another—and strong scale economies, the industry could not stand open price-competition. Faced with deregulation, the major airlines have resorted to a variety of devices to segment markets, use discriminatory pricing, and otherwise defend themselves against ruinous competition. (Alfred Kahn blames many of the unexpected outcomes on the failure of the Reagan administration to fight predatory pricing and its toleration of mergers. But if the antitrust enforcers ever got really serious and forced true head-to-head price-competition and regulated nothing else, the airlines would likely go broke.) The anticompetitive devices of the deregulation era include the following:

Airline Ownership of Reservation Systems. The major computer reservations systems owned by American (SABRE) and United (APOLLO) are relied on by about 70 percent of travel agents and account for 71 percent of seat bookings. These give the airlines instant feedback on how full flights are, and facilitate price discrimination. They also make it harder for upstart airlines to break in. A challenger's flights are not likely to be in your travel agent's master computer; or if they are, they will typically be hard to find. The traveler has to be aware that smaller airlines like America West and Kiwi exist, and be willing to press the travel agent to offer their flights. Airline control of reservation systems also enables the majors to give travel agents extra commissions to steer passengers to favored flights, known in the business as "override commissions." These legal bribes are not generally known to the customer. In 1983–84, Reagan-administration antitrust officials considered whether to force the airlines to divest computer reservation systems. Instead, the government settled for inadequate regulations against only the most extreme anticompetitive tactics.

Michael Levine, one of the early advocates of deregulation, served for a time as an airline chief executive. He has observed:

An airline whose CRS [computer reservation system] is used by travel agents has access to a very accurate picture of both its own and its rivals' business patterns. Through the CRS an airline can track the effect of price changes, see roughly how much of a rival's seat inventory is assigned to a given discount fare classification, measure how much full-fare business it attracts compared to rivals, and track changes in city-pair flows. . . . It can even see how loyal its own frequent flyers are. A CRS owner can then use this information to distort market signals to its rivals, leading them to make incorrect decisions. When a CRS owner sees travel agents making bookings on a rival airline's flights, it can intervene through targeted incentive programs in an attempt to switch business. By responding selectively, it can temporarily distort signals the market sends to competitors, in order to persuade the rivals to abandon fares, schedules, or even routes where, absent these secret interventions, its offerings would be preferred by customers.

Frequent-Flyer Programs. These are a splendid device intended to frustrate shopping around, an activity essential if a competitive system is to work. Rather than seeking the lowest possible fare, travelers are induced to stick with a favored carrier in order to earn mileage credits. This masquerades as something for nothing, but of course somebody has to bear the costs of "free" tickets. The airlines must charge more for paying seats than they otherwise would, to finance all those nonrevenue seats. Corporate treasurers are generally too intimidated to insist that frequent-flyer credits for company travel be returned to the firm—a measure that would restore a lot of shopping around. Even the IRS has been stymied by the issue of whether to tax frequent-flyer tickets. And the public has been so conditioned—mistakenly—to view frequent-traveler plans as a bargain that prohibiting them would be politically unthinkable.

Incumbent Power at Airports. The airline business was thought to be "contestable," but new competition has been frustrated both by the market power of incumbent airlines and by the shortage of takeoff and landing rights (known in the trade as "slots"). Slots are often limited because of airport congestion. At the nation's busiest airports—Washington National, Chicago O'Hare, New York's La Guardia and JFK—nobody can break in, because all the slots are taken. In principle, these slots are for sale. But they are owned by incumbent airlines who would rather keep them idle than see them go to a new competitor. So they are priced so high that they render competition uneconomical. Current FAA rules allow a carrier to use only 55 percent of its slots. A competitor needs not only to land, but to get the passenger through the jetway to the terminal. At many airports, there is also a limited number of gates; many hundreds of unused gates, as well as slots, are tied up by dominant carriers. At some airports, incumbent monopoly airlines have "majority-in-interest" clauses, giving them a veto power over the airports' ability to construct additional gates and thus let in competitors. In a reasonable regime, this would be prohibited.

Even at airports that are in principle "contestable," the municipal or private owner of the airport is often forced into a fortress partnership with the dominant carrier, heavily subsidizing its facilities and agreeing to contractual terms that make it prohibitive for new competitors to enter the market. Moving a big hub means the loss of thousands of jobs, and local mayors tend to be very compliant partners. In effect, local taxpayers subsidize the dominant airline's monopoly. This system makes local public officials complicit in a system of monopoly pricing that soaks local residents twice—once as taxpayers, and a second time as airline passengers.

Fortress Hubs.   The most novel innovation of deregulation has been the hub-and-spoke system. Instead of flying nonstop, point to point, as under CAB regulation, airlines increasingly organize flights around a hub. Over time, a single airline has come to dominate most of the fifty major hubs, such as Pittsburgh, Charlotte, and Baltimore (USAir), Atlanta (Delta), Nashville (American), St. Louis (TWA), and Minneapolis (Northwest). Defenders of deregulation argue that the hub-and-spoke system allows airlines greater flexibility, enabling them to serve more pairs of cities with relatively fewer planes. That may be so, but the darker side to the hub-and-spoke system is that it has allowed the airlines to carve up the skies into a system of shared monopoly. If a carrier dominates a hub, it can charge exorbitant fares. Hubs also allow dominant airlines to work out joint marketing agreements with "commuter" carriers by simulating common ownership and locking in the traveler. Most "United Express" and "American Eagle" flights, for example, are owned by a company other than United or American, though they carry United and American flight numbers. The common reservation and ticketing ("code-sharing") makes it almost impossible for the traveler to choose different airlines for different segments of the flight. In principle, airlines could challenge each other's hubs. This of course would benefit the consumer, but not the airline. The tacit understanding in the industry is: You stay out of my hub, I'll stay out of yours, and we'll all make a living.

Ironically, however, the airlines are not making a reliable living. In the nearly two decades since deregulation, the airline industry's annual net profit margin has averaged less than 1 percent. "There is no denying that the profit record of the industry since 1978 has been dismal, that deregulation bears substantial responsibility, and that the proponents of deregulation did not anticipate such financial distress—either so intense or so long continued," Alfred Kahn has conceded.

The system of cartelized deregulation has produced the worst of both worlds. There is fierce competition on contested routes, such as New York–Los Angeles, and price-gouging on the uncontested ones. The monopoly rents subsidize the competitive routes. Over time, the airlines have learned that everyone (except the public) benefits when there are as few contested routes as possible. Travelers have grown accustomed to a familiar pattern: gradually, one airline comes to provide all of the convenient, nonstop flights between more and more city pairs. Such large cities as Baltimore (USAir) and Cleveland (Continental) and Minneapolis (Northwest) have joined the growing list of near-monopoly hubs. The popular Boston–Washington run used to be serviced by Delta, Northwest, and USAir. At this writing, only USAir provides jet nonstops, and the fare is over $500. Between St. Louis and Kansas City, the fare is over a dollar per seat mile, compared with a cost of about thirteen cents. Critic Paul Dempsey calculates that it is literally cheaper to cover the two hundred miles by taxi! In theory, some of the competitors should quit the prestige routes where price wars periodically break out—but they don't. This is one more behavior in which the practice defies the theory.

Airlines take advantage of selective market power and short-term urgencies. In the short run, the demand for business travel is relatively "price-inelastic": a business traveler who has to make a meeting will pay almost anything the airline charges. But the airlines' gouging is penny-wise and pound-foolish, for it gradually creates price resistance. Over the long term, customer demand is more price-elastic than it seems. Businesses noticing rising air-travel bills shift to fax, telephone, and teleconferencing—and discourage air travel except when indispensable. The current pricing system depresses air travel by people who would fly if prices were more reasonable and predictable.

Instead of more consumer choice, lower fares, and greater reliability, deregulation has degraded service in multiple ways.

Fewer Nonstops.   A fuel-efficient, wide-body 767 can deliver a passenger from New York to Los Angeles for about 40 percent less than it costs to fly two 737s with a change of flights in Denver or Dallas. The stopover consumes more fuel, more ground time, more crew-servicing, and uses a plane that is less fuel-efficient to fly. But nonstops increase head-to-head competition, whereas the hub-and-spoke system increases market power and the ability to price-discriminate. Since deregulation, nonstops have become increasingly scarce. And the airlines have been using relatively more recycled 737s, and fewer modern, fuel-efficient wide-bodies. This not only subjects passengers to less comfortable flights, but also denies the aircraft industry the orders with which to generate cash flow for the next generation of even more efficient planes (Smith plus a dose of anticompetitive behavior stymies Schumpeter). These extra costs and inconveniences are left out of the laborious calculations of Messrs. Winston and Morrison. If one credits greater frequency of flights to deregulation, shouldn't one debit the extra time en route spent on a cramped 737 too small for the executive even to unfurl his laptop?

"Circuity." A related efficiency loss is that people are having to travel more miles (and be charged for the inconvenience). For example, Boston–San Francisco direct is a distance of 2,429 miles. Boston–San Francisco via Dallas is 3,024 miles, takes about four hours longer, and increases the risk of a missed connection. Circuity adds millions of passenger hours per year. The statistics showing how prices have dropped since deregulation are based on actual miles flown, which are more than they should be. What is the benefit of having more flights from which to choose if the paradoxical result is more time spent in the air? Circuity and the hub-and-spoke system have also added needlessly to the nation's construction bill. Denver had to build a new airport, at astronomical cost, not because increasing numbers of people suddenly desired to visit Colorado, but because United and Continental were using Denver so intensely as a hub. Most cross-country travelers would have preferred to see Denver from the air, as they continued on their way via a nonstop flight.

Loss of Service. In 1978, 515 nonhub airports had regularly scheduled service. By 1995, 167 had service terminated, while only 26 gained new service. Since deregulation, many cities that once had jet service have been forced to settle for smaller, more cramped, unpressurized, and more hazardous commuter flights. It is not that the jets are less efficient to operate in the strict economic sense of costing more per passenger mile. It is, rather, that small commuter planes fit better into the airline's hub-and-spoke marketing-and-pricing strategy. The argument that some communities have received more flights per day and that frequency trumps other aspects of convenience defies common sense. People are able to plan for air travel if there is a reasonable degree of frequency. Surely many residents of small cities would prefer two 737s a day to six twenty-eight-seaters.

Airline Safety. Although overall airline safety statistics have improved since 1978, continuing a long upward trend that predates deregulation, the intense competition spawned by deregulation has caused some airlines to skimp on safety. The ValuJet crash in June 1996 called attention to the fact that new, cut-rate airlines were more inclined to contract out vital maintenance to companies over which they have less direct control. Deregulation was supposed to leave airline fares and routes to market forces but maintain strict government control over airline safety. However the general antiregulation climate not only abolished the CAB, but abolished entire categories of reports that used to be filed with either the CAB or the FAA, which influence government's capacity to monitor safety violations. In addition, fiscal pressures have left the FAA with fewer inspectors per aircraft, and have led to more indirect monitoring, in which government supervises the airline's systems and records, rather than direct monitoring of repairs and inspections of airworthiness.

An Aging Fleet.   Over time, the source of increasing productivity in airlines is not harder-working pilots and flight attendants, but new generations of planes. Before deregulation, the public was guaranteed predictable fares and the airlines were guaranteed a reasonable return. This gave them the cash flow to invest in ever more efficient planes. Since deregulation, the purchase of new equipment has dwindled, and the U.S. commercial fleet has become one of the world's oldest. At this writing, one-third of the planes in our skies are over twenty years old, and exceed the life span projected by the planes' designers. The GAO estimated in 1989 that the percentage of superannuated planes would double by the year 2000. There are currently several hundred jetliners mothballed in the Arizona desert, the casualties of the more than 150 airline bankruptcies since deregulation. With all these extra planes glutting the market, the airlines keep deferring purchases of new aircraft.

Astronomical and Capricious Fares.   Reasonably predictable fares are a public convenience. There is literally no other service industry where two people buying the identical product are charged prices that vary by a factor of three or four to one. Nor is it reasonable for travelers to pay exorbitant penalties because their plans change. Though prices per mile can reasonably vary modestly because of different population densities and other legitimate cost-differentials, there is no economic reason to tolerate fares of more than a dollar per passenger mile on some routes and less than eight cents on others. The economists who brought us deregulation implicitly recognized this when they confidently (and mistakenly) forecast that free markets would bring prices more closely into line with marginal costs. When the opposite occurred, this anomaly was justified on the ground that "the market did it." But these are not competitive markets. Because of the nearly unanimous chorus of economists endorsing airline deregulation, the public has been brainwashed into believing that the current fare structure, with its convoluted rules and encumbrances, is reasonable and even convenient. Deregulation is so in vogue as an abstract principle that few politicians dare to say anything against it.

In the late 1980s, a small San Francisco company called Marketel tried to take the logic of airline deregulation to its ultimate conclusion. Why have only ten or twenty different fares on the same plane, when you could have an infinite number? Marketel's idea was to use computers to set up a bid-and-asked market in airline tickets. That way, the demand-elasticity of each prospective customer could translate into a perfectly correct fare. Planes could fly full, since the last customer would pay just the right fare to buy the last available seat. There could even be a secondary, trading market in air tickets. The idea flopped. Armed with equal market power, too many passengers would likely wait until the last minute and hammer down prices to marginal costs. Alternatively, speculators might try to corner the market in a particular flight and extract the rents currently being extracted by airlines. Either way, a true auction market in airline seats would deprive the airlines of their remaining power to set prices—and bankruptcy would ensue. Marketel's idea was an epic illustration of the limits of free-market theory as applied to a structurally monopolistic industry. The airlines needed this invention like they needed leprosy. No airline agreed to cooperate with Marketel.

A Conspiracy of Silence. In the past few years, some of the braver sponsors of deregulation have sheepishly acknowledged that it didn't work out as planned. Mark S. Kahan, who served at the CAB under Alfred Kahn, wrote:

> Of the six intellectual assumptions behind airline deregulation, four have been proven completely false. Deregulators believed that airline size was not critical to efficient operations. The marketplace, to the contrary, has ruled that bigger is better. Deregulators believed that barriers to entry are low in the airline business. Experience has demonstrated that they are very high. Deregulators believed that increased competition would produce low unrestricted fares. In fact, it has produced a bewildering array of discriminatory prices. Deregulators believed that travel agencies were obsolete as well as potentially misleading channels of information and distribution. But travel agencies became more powerful than ever. A fifth assumption, that the antitrust laws would restrain competitive abuses, has been negated by the policy default of two administrations. . . .

Michael Levine, in his influential 1987 review article, commented on the importance of market power. It was widely thought that the big airlines "should have been at a *disadvantage* in comparison to the new entrants," Levine noted. The "holdover firms were overweight, possibly arthritic, dinosaurs, threatened by nimble, lean, and aggressive new entrant carriers." But, funny thing; only the big players survived, using their market power to crush much more efficient competitors. To a great extent, Levine notes, they did it by trading more fuel-efficient planes (747s, 767s) for less efficient ones (737s and DC-9s).

Even Alfred Kahn, in writings and speeches over the past decade, has allowed himself some guarded second thoughts. "I doubt most of us were prepared for . . . the generally dismal profit record of the past ten years," he wrote in 1988. "We advocates of deregulation were misled by the apparent lack of evidence of economies of scale." And: "the persistence—indeed—intensification of price discrimination has been a surprise." And: "Most of us probably did not foresee the deterioration in the average quality of the flying experience. . . ." And: "I should have recognized that the naturally monopolistic or oligopolistic character of most airline markets . . . would continue—indeed expand—under deregulation." Kahn even adds, belatedly and rather Delphicly, that perhaps some residual price regulation should have been maintained: "I hope I do not shock anybody by observing that I probably would have been very reluctant to abandon price ceilings entirely had I had the choice."

Yet Levine and Kahn insist that the experiment, however flawed, should not be abandoned. Kahn has averred that the best remedy would be tougher antitrust enforcement, expansion of airport capacity, and entry of foreign competitors. He did concede, in painfully qualified language, that "it is not possible in principle to reject the reimposition of price ceilings to protect travelers subject to monopolistic exploitation, where restoration of more effective competition proves to be infeasible." But this is hardly a ringing endorsement of reregulation. Indeed, his article ends with a reiteration of the wisdom of "seeking consistently to move in the direction of the first-best functioning of a market economy, rather than the second- or third-best world of command and control."

Levine, concluding a book-length article on how deregulation misfired, ends with a rather feeble call for only two major reforms: divestiture of airlines' computer reservation systems, and partial taxation of frequent-flyer benefits. His final words: "Just as it would be folly to forgo feasible, demonstrable improvements because they represent 'government intervention,' it would be folly to let recitals of inevitable imperfections create a mandate to return to a world of regulation and intervention that we know will be far more imperfect and rigid than the one we have now."

But we know no such thing. These contradictory and defensive second thoughts by some of the fathers of deregulation attest to the power of the paradigm and the continuing victory of assumption over contradictory evidence.

The airline industry, like telecommunications and electric power, cries out for regulated competition. Though few admit it, the biggest mistake of the deregulators was abolishing the CAB. Had the CAB stayed in business and approached airline competition the way the FCC dealt with telephone competition, the public might have truly benefited. For one thing, regulators could have continued to monitor the experiment. They could have prohibited the anticompetitive practices noted herein. They could have been a major analyst of industry trends and a regular intervenor in antitrust proceedings against predatory pricing. Armed with a clear competition-policy rather than a cruder mandate to deregulate, they never would have allowed the anticompetitive mergers of the early 1980s. The effectiveness of Judge Greene in the telephone-divestiture case owed a great deal to the continuing presence of the FCC. But with no CAB, the Transportation Department does not keep adequate statistics on concentration, pricing, loss of service, circuity, and other indicators that would suggest how the experiment is working.

In fairness, the actual CAB (as opposed to an ideal one) may have been corrupted beyond remediation. Unlike the FCC or the SEC, which are well run, have an institutional commitment to a public interest, and are responsive to multiple constituencies, the CAB by the 1970s was something close to a captive of its client industry. However, given the rising consumer consciousness about abuses in the airline industry, it is possible to envision giving the FAA new authority to supervise a system of regulated competition that would be a significant improvement over what now exists.

Regulated Airline Competition. How would regulated competition work in the airline industry? Regulators could set a zone of tolerable prices, to reflect actual costs more nearly. The same computers that make it possible for unregulated airlines to price-discriminate could enable regulators to calculate appropriate pricing zones, just as public-utility regulators do in other industries. Floors on prices would prevent cross-subsidy and ruinous competition. Ceilings would prevent opportunistic price-gouging. In between, there could be a range of price and quality competition. Something like this was actually under consideration in the mid-1970s, until the fever for full deregulation struck, and this regime is precisely what is evolving in the marketlike regulation of other semimonopoly industries.

There are miscellaneous consumer abuses that could be prohibited by pro-competitive regulation. Airlines regularly use bait-and-switch techniques, advertising deep-discount fares that turn out to be available only on a few seats. They cancel or consolidate scheduled flights with no warning when they fail to attract enough passengers. They keep squeezing more and more passengers into narrower spaces—an abuse that cries out for regulation. They have even cut costs by reducing the amount of fresh air in cabins.

A new regime of regulated competition would bar plainly anticompetitive assaults, prohibiting a race to the bottom. Dominant airlines would no longer be permitted to tie up unused gates and slots. The proprietary computer reservation systems would be divested, to be succeeded by an industry-wide cooperative reservation system regulated by government, or even one operated by government. This new system, unlike the existing ones, would allow equal access.

There would also be a limit on "yield management." An airline would be allowed a small number of different fares on the same route, to reward the passenger willing to book far in advance or to stand by at the last minute. But there could not be ten or twenty different fares, or continual fare manipulation, or ratios of four to one between the cheapest and most expensive fares. Nor could there be unreasonable bulk discounts, otherwise known as discriminatory rates. If this sounds vaguely familiar, it is almost precisely the set of abuses and remedies that prompted Congress to create the Interstate Commerce Commission more than a century ago. Despite new technologies, some things don't change.

Another good idea to discourage discriminatory or predatory pricing would be to require that, whenever a major carrier announced a price cut to match or beat a competitor's lower fare, it should be required to keep that published fare in effect for a stipulated period of time. One expert suggested three to five years. The author of that idea was Alfred Kahn—in 1978, before deregulation.

A regulator would likely look askance on the kind of monopoly hubs that have become normal in the airlines. Professor Paul Dempsey, one of the rare academic experts critical of airline deregulation, suggests a regulatory schema whereby an airline would be permitted to be dominant at just one hub. Beyond that, Dempsey proposes that airlines be prohibited from controlling more than 60 percent of the traffic at a given major airport. Either the regulators could broker an agreement under which competitors would trade slots, yielding multiple competition at large airports, or large carriers could simply be broken up. In smaller airports, where scale economies create true natural-monopoly conditions on many routes, there could be more direct price-regulation, again using floors and ceilings, and with periodic review of pricing patterns by the regulator.

It would also serve economic efficiency and the public interest for regulators to encourage more nonstop flights on long-distance routes. The regulatory agency might grant an operating certificate for five or ten years on major long-distance routes. Airlines might bid competitively for such certificates, stipulating a fare structure or fare zones, to be reviewed every few years. "A monopoly," Robert Bork writes, "is not worth much if you have to bid competitively for the right to own it."

Note that this proposed schema for airlines is very much like the regime of regulated competition in telecommunications. In industries with monopoly elements, it takes regulation for the public to realize the benefits of competition. The FCC doesn't permit broadcasters to tie up unused channels, because the airwaves are a scarce public resource that should not be appropriated by monopolists. Why should government allow an airline to tie up scarce gates and slots? We have elaborate rules to make sure that competing phone companies can use each other's rights-of-way. Why doesn't public policy follow a similar approach in the case of airlines? The answer is that the 1978 Airline Deregulation Act has become a sacred cow. Economists with private misgivings have too much invested in the success of the experiment to admit that it failed. Because of the intellectual and political hegemony of the marketizers, there is almost no acknowledgment that in airlines, as in telecommunications and electricity, a dose of regulation would enhance both competition and efficient use of scarce resources. Alas, the ideology of laissez-faire is the enemy of efficient markets.

ELECTRIC POWER

For the first three-quarters of the twentieth century, electric companies dwelt in a stable and predictable realm where steadily declining costs of production and steadily increasing consumption were natural complements. In the 1930s, electric utilities began offering aggressive volume discounts: the more you consumed, the less you were charged per kilowatt hour. The Tennessee Valley Authority (TVA), whose explicit mission was to electrify the Tennessee Valley and bring power to more homes, businesses, and factories, pioneered a radically promotional "declining-block" rate structure: the first 50 kilowatt hours per month were billed at 3 cents per kilowatt hour, the next 150 kilowatt hours at 2 cents, the next 200 at 1 cent, and the remainder at 0.4 cent. This system yielded an average rate paid by TVA customers of just 0.7 cent per kilowatt hour for the average fully electrified home, at a time when the national average was about 5.5 cents.

The gamble paid off, much as Henry Ford had demonstrated during the same era that lower prices would increase sales of his cars. Within three years, the price of electricity in the TVA region was far below the national average, whereas usage was 60 percent higher. There was a close relationship between TVA's ability to build new, efficient generating capacity (through hydropower) and its success in making sure that its power would be sold. TVA's astute marketing soon produced a "load factor" of 70 percent—meaning that 70 percent of generating capacity was actually demanded, a very high rate among utilities.

Other privately owned power companies followed suit. The basic dynamic here was steadily increasing productivity, built upon three factors: *scale economies,* which came with increasing usage; *continuing technological advances,* amortized with the profits of these ever-widening sales; and *declining real prices of inputs* (coal, oil, and hydropower). Paradoxically, the regulated environment encouraged risk. Utilities could take daring risks, pricing ahead of markets, partly because they knew their profits were guaranteed even if they momentarily guessed wrong. Dynamic efficiency was superior to allocative efficiency. In the literature on deregulation, especially works written during the past twenty years, this history tends to be ignored or forgotten.

Contrived Competition. Electric power has substantial monopoly aspects, but it is also an example, *par excellence,* of regulated competition. Early in this century, electric utilities were regulated in most states by public-utility commissions. But by the 1920s, private utilities had combined in large, multistate holding companies intended to circumvent state regulation. Conservative state and federal administrations acquiesced. For a decade, the steady decline in consumer prices halted. A series of investigative hearings in the 1920s and 1930s revealed widespread abuses, such as padding of expenses, deceptive transfer pricing, and overvaluation of assets, which artificially took advantage of monopoly power and raised rates.

In the 1930s, President Roosevelt, who had been a critic of the private-utility industry while governor of New York, aggressively promoted a three-part policy which today would be called regulated competition. First, he sponsored federal regulation of utility holding companies, via the 1935 Public Utility Holding Company Act. Second, Roosevelt promoted public power. TVA, the Bonneville Power Authority, and other examples of "yardstick competition," as the contemporary phrase went, not only diffused electric power to a broader consuming public, but also demonstrated a reasonable set of baseline prices—public power consistently underpriced private power by 15 to 21 percent. Third, FDR encouraged municipalities with private power systems to view the threat of public power as a way of disciplining incumbent utilities. The New Deal offered communities low-interest federal loans for municipal power systems. Roosevelt compared this threat to "a birch rod in the cupboard to be taken out only when the child gets beyond the point where a mere scolding does no good." Interestingly, the idea of competition for the right to provide a monopoly franchise was revived half a century later by conservatives, as part of the argument against regulation. But, of course, that discipline operates only in the context of regulation.

As the economist and economic historian William Emmons has observed, the regulatory regime of the 1930s used "direct and indirect competition in reducing electricity prices without threatening the financial viability of the utility operating companies. . . ." It did this by allowing most utilities to remain monopolies, thus maximizing scale economies, but maintaining the threat of competition and providing the alternative of public power, as well as tightening regulation.

Interestingly, too, the regime introduced in the 1930s effectively dealt with the problems of monopoly pricing and overcapacity. Between 1890 and 1920, the price of electricity had dropped dramatically. But in the 1920s, privately owned industries, imperfectly regulated and wielding monopoly power, stopped passing along price cuts to consumers. Real prices were actually a bit higher in 1930 than in 1920. As the Depression deepened, and fewer people could afford electric power, real prices rose dramatically between 1930 and 1933, frustrating scale economies. With the introduction of public power and federal regulation in the mid-1930s, the virtuous pattern of declining prices, technical advances, and increasing usage resumed. This reminds us not to assume that technology alone will produce a straight line of declining real costs, or that competition is maximized by the absence of regulation. The interwar period demonstrated quite the opposite. As Emmons concluded, "Roosevelt perceived a dual nature in the power of competition: in certain instances, an indispensable tool for industry reform and renewal, but in others, a destructive impediment to economic stabilization."

Competition and Crisis. In the 1970s, the combination of a perceived energy crisis, inflation, and the availability of new technologies produced a very different challenge to the electric-power industry and its regulation. As I have suggested above, rising prices and the conservation ethic generated a new wave of support for strategies both to discourage usage and to allow consumers and businesses to find competing suppliers. However, because of the problem of huge sunk costs and scale economies, ruinous competition remained a genuine problem in the electric-power industry. In the 1978 Public Utilities Regulatory Power Act (PURPA), Congress required utilities to let independent producers onto their grid, and encourage alternative forms of "renewable energy." The Energy Policy Act of 1992 further stimulated independent generation, by authorizing a new category of essentially unregulated wholesale generating companies. The act also promoted the wholesale purchase of electricity among utilities (known as "wheeling"), in the belief that this form of increased competition would lower prices.

Several states now permit large industrial customers to buy electric power from sources other than the local power company, and some large companies generate their own electricity. Many states require utilities to procure new generating capacity by independent bid rather than direct construction. If the power company wants to build new capacity, it must tender a bid against competing bidders. At this writing, nonutility producers account for about 7 percent of total electric power. In the next decade, that will rise to about one-third. Electric utilities have partly shifted to a strategy of "demand management"—finding ways to earn money by helping their customers conserve—rather than the old strategy of supply management, which usually meant increasing generating capacity.

The old system was based on monopoly franchise and vertical integration. For the most part, the regulated monopoly was responsible for the production, distribution, and final sale of electric power. In the emerging regime, these elements are being "unbundled," as the phrase has it. This shift to greater competition and demand management is seemingly good both for consumers and for conservation. But because of the continuing elements of natural monopoly, scale economies, and dilemmas of overcapacity, there remain unavoidable regulatory issues that pure markets could not resolve efficiently. It is still a goal of public policy that electric power be universally available on demand. The incumbent power company, which used to enjoy a monopoly franchise, now faces a problem known in the business as "stranded assets." It owns hugely expensive generating stations built in another era, which were expected to be amortized by steadily expanding usage. But if industrial users can generate their own electricity, and utilities themselves can buy from cheaper sources, the provider of last resort is stuck with expensive assets and declining sales—which portend higher prices. In a competitive climate, large utilities with excess capacity in effect dump cheap power on each other's markets. This lowers prices in the short run but leads to ruinous competition and higher costs in the long term.

There is a distributional question here, for which free-market theory cannot provide a theoretically "correct" answer: who shall bear how much of the cost of this transition. The big utilities stuck with expensive generating capacity ("stranded assets") were behaving rationally at the time they made the investments. Moreover, under the previous regulatory regime, government guaranteed them a fair rate of return on the investments. But if regulators, under a new, partly marketized system, stick utilities and their shareholders with the full cost of the shift, utilities may have trouble finding investors in the future. Conversely, it isn't entirely fair for small users to get stuck with the full bill, since society (reasonably) has decided that electric power be broadly available and cheap. Clearly these costs will have to be shared. There is no intuitively right answer to the question of who bears precisely how much of the cost—and no substitute for discerning, public-minded regulation. In Britain, where the Thatcher administration privatized the system of electric utilities, the government found that it was losing the benefits of an integrated system. With competition and fragmentation, industry's costs declined, but the prices charged to consumers rose. The Thatcher government found that to make privatization work, it needed a whole new overlay of regulation in order to encourage long-term investment, prevent gouging of consumers, and achieve the necessary economies of an integrated electric power system.

There is an emerging consensus that generation and aspects of distribution of electric power can be partly deregulated, but the final sale remains a true natural monopoly. It would make no economic sense to have two parallel sets of power lines to the home, and, unlike in telecommunications, there is no wireless technology to transport electric power. There are also economies associated with vertical integration. It is efficient for the retail utility to meter the user, to keep track of peak power needs, and to determine the wholesale sources of power feeding the grid. Fragmentation of this industry would defeat economies of coordination as well as of scale. Three of the most enthusiastic and prestigious advocates of marketization, William Baumol, Paul Joskow, and Alfred Kahn, caution in a recent paper against complete deregulation: "the efficiency benefits flowing from competitive generation could be entirely dissipated or even more than offset by the deteriorated coordination. . . ."

What are some solutions? Several state regulators have encouraged competition in wholesale power generation, but with mandated transmission fees or access charges, so that all providers share the cost of maintaining the grid and the cost of paying off sunk investments from an earlier era. Some regulators require big industrial users that generate their own power or buy it from "off-system" independents to pay a charge to reflect the "option value" of being able to buy supplemental or emergency power from the local regulated utility. The premise here is that it costs the utility and its other ratepayers money to maintain the standby capacity that the industrial customer is not currently using. Many states have shifted from traditional rate-of-return regulation to "incentive regulation," keeping a ceiling on permissible retail prices, but allowing utilities to keep part of savings that they can reap from productivity improvements.

Another approach is to charge "entrance fees" to new suppliers of power, or "exit fees" to customers that leave the overall grid. All of these measures reflect regulators' efforts to grapple with the overcapacity dilemma. In the absence of such regulatory moves, the undercutting of scale economies would massively shift costs onto residential consumers, and leave the local utility as high-cost provider in a dwindling market—a slower-fused version of the 1930s dilemma.

A related policy conundrum is whether to permit regulated power companies to diversify, and how much. The 1992 act allowed utilities to invest in unregulated, independent generating companies, and in overseas electric-power ventures. For a utility executive facing a dwindling core business and declining rates of return, diversification is a natural impulse. But it poses inescapable regulatory issues, such as the need to segregate ratepayer income from other sources of capital, and the question of how ratepayers are affected when an enterprising utility executive guesses wrong. In the mid-1980s, Arizona Public Service, the state's regulated power company, took a flyer in real estate and insurance. It lost a bundle. Many states now limit extraneous investments by regulated utilities to 10 percent of sales. Most utilities are limiting their diversification to closely related businesses, such as unregulated power sale or investment in power generation and supply abroad.

Some extreme enthusiasts of marketization urge full free-market competition for the final sale of power to the home. But unregulated retail competition would be an inappropriate and inefficient reliance on markets. It would exacerbate the stranded-asset problem, lead to rampant overcapacity, undercut scale economies, and put the supplier-of-last-resort out of business. If this approach is to work at all, it requires regulators to allow the incumbent utility to charge the independent an additional transmission fee, to reflect the cost of maintaining the system as a whole. Without regulation, a fee that was too high would deny the independent's access to the customers. One that was too low would fatally disadvantage the incumbent.

Most observers see the business of electric power evolving into one where generation, distribution, and final sale of power are increasingly de-linked. The wholesale purchase of power is becoming a blend of long-term contracts and spot markets. Integrated power companies manage their risks by continuously monitoring trends and adjusting their mix of contracts and spot purchases. Big industrial customers of electricity, which used to subsidize residential customers, are now able to negotiate lower prices in exchange for long-term contractual commitments. If retail consumers are eventually able to choose from among competing power suppliers, it will only be under a carefully specified set of rules.

All of this is more "marketlike" than the traditional monopoly-franchise system—but hardly unregulated. Some of these issues are merely transitional. In another generation, many of the "stranded assets" of an earlier era will be fully amortized, and the overhang will cease to be a special dilemma. But the overcapacity problem will not go away, nor will the fact that the final linkage of the home to the grid remains a natural monopoly. At the end of the day, this industry remains a classic candidate for regulated competition. Competition has its benefits in some sectors, but only if carefully managed by regulators.

THE REAL ANTITRUST PARADOX

A final word is in order about antitrust. Antitrust has long been accepted, even by relative enthusiasts of markets, as the exception to the claim that markets do things better than regulators. If private-market actors drive out competitors, or use monopoly power, the usual market forms of discipline cease to operate. Private-market actors, paradoxically, frustrate the market mechanism. Antitrust enforcement is perhaps the oldest form of pro-competitive regulation. However, as the foregoing discussion has suggested, antitrust enforcement is too slender a reed on which to construct an entire competition policy. A regulatory regime is more effective than sporadic antitrust interventions when the object is the structuring or restructuring of an industry that is inherently monopolistic. Antitrust does have an important place in industries that are naturally competitive and otherwise mostly unregulated.

In the past twenty years, the exponents of a purer laissez-faire have increasingly argued that markets are so self-cleansing that in most cases antitrust interventions are superfluous and harmful. By definition, nearly anything that private economic agents do is given a presumptive safe-conduct pass; it is "market-like"—by definition—and hence virtuous. Although the very purpose of the antitrust laws is to prevent the undermining of markets, the enforcement agent is often the state; hence antitrust is suspect.

This view is well represented in the work of Robert Bork, law professor, former federal appellate judge, and rejected Supreme Court nominee. Bork's critique is worth very careful review, for his argumentation is an exceptionally good illustration of the deductive sophistry which insists that the results of private activity must be optimal.

In his 1978 book, *The Antitrust Paradox*, Bork mounted a broadside attack on prevailing antitrust doctrines, Justice Department and Federal Trade Commission enforcement activities, and recent Supreme Court decisions, for allegedly ignoring basic economics. The paradox to which Bork referred was his view that antitrust laws, intended to enhance competition, actually interfered with optimal competitive outcomes by frustrating the profit-maximizing activities of private-market actors. Note again the familiar logical sleight of hand: whatever the private sector does *must be* marketlike, hence efficient, hence optimal. By definition, markets are the essence of competition. Thus, private markets cannot not yield anticompetitive results, even when they appear to strangle competition—rather in the same way that pre-1989 "people's republics" could not be antidemocratic since they were governed in the name of the people.

A good case in point is predatory pricing. Bork dispatches even the possibility of predatory pricing, with this stunning bit of deductive logic: "The predator would already be maximizing profits in all markets and so would have no way of increasing profits elsewhere to finance predation." Bork efficiently dispenses with the need for empirical inquiry by defining the problem out of existence. But note the assumptions loaded on that one glib sentence. First, it is assumed that the market leader is pricing his product in an exactly efficient way. This is improbable, because firms make price changes all the time; and they would have to be out of an optimal equilibrium for some period, observing the possibility for improvement, before making the price adjustment. So nobody is in precise equilibrium all the time. Second, even if the firm in question were maximizing profits, that is not necessarily consistent with maximized consumer welfare. Even Chicago School economists—George Stigler and Arnold Harberger, among others—have long acknowledged that a monopolist can raise price, cut output, and thereby maximize his own well-being but not that of the public. Before the radical and tautologically laissez-faire position of the Law and Economics movement, the scholarly and regulatory arguments revolved around the question of what market share presumptively implied excessive market power. But Bork and company blithely assume that even old-fashioned monopolies are optimal, else they wouldn't exist. Since laissez-faire theory dictates that companies must be pricing efficiently, both for their own benefit and for that of consumers, it must be so.

The airline story demolishes Bork's view of predatory pricing, because the pricing strategy of the major carriers worked so well. The price cutters were either driven out or forced to merge. To turn Bork's logic around on him, this predatory-pricing strategy "must have" served the profit-maximizing welfare of the major airlines, else they wouldn't have pursued it. But of course that doesn't mean it maximized consumer welfare. Even granting his other premises, Bork's most palpably absurd claim is that the monopolist could not *finance* the cost of the price cut. Here, empirical evidence overwhelms Bork's deductivism. The essence of market leadership is deep pockets. Temporarily diverting profits in order to warn or discipline a price cutter is hardly a practical impossibility, or even theoretically inconsistent with the claim that the monopolist is profit-maximizing. The pages of antitrust litigation are replete with evidence of deliberate, temporary, and sometimes savage price cuts, in industries as diverse as airlines, steel, beer, tobacco, cable TV, and trash hauling.

It is instructive to contrast Robert Bork with Alfred Chandler, previously cited as an apostle of the Schumpeterian virtues of scale and scope. Both come to similar conclusions regarding the benefits of bigness—but from entirely opposite conceptions of how the economy operates. For Chandler, the classical picture is misleading, because price power is pervasive, and beneficial, at least up to a point. For Bork, market power is also extensive—but somehow Bork finds significant market power fully consistent with a model of perfect competition. He does this, again, by deduction and tautology. By definition, the market must be producing outcomes that are perfectly efficient; otherwise it wouldn't be a perfect market. In Bork's view, mergers, with rare exception, are deemed efficient, because they "must be" virtuous attempts to capture superior economies of scale, rather than vicious efforts to diminish competition. Even apparent monopolies are creatures of the discipline of the marketplace. In the contrast between Chandler's picture of the economy and Bork's, Chandler comes off as the more convincing, because his work is rooted in the history of the actual economy rather than in deductive reasoning from a premise of perfect competition. Chandler finds evidence for substantial price-power, and finds it virtuous precisely because it departs from the premises of perfect-market theory. Bork looks at the same price-power and pronounces it a perfect market. Remarkably, too, nowhere does Bork cite Chandler (or demonstrate anything like Chandler's grasp of actual industries).

To the uninitiated observer, these Chicago propositions about the impossibility of monopoly are childishly circular. Yet, because of their logical elegance and their congeniality to America's biggest businesses, they have had enormous intellectual influence, in the law schools, in the academic study of economics, and of course in practical politics. Not long after *The Antitrust Paradox* was published in 1978, Ronald Reagan was elected president, and conservative economic theorists took over key policy positions. Stanford University law professor William Baxter became head of the Justice Department's Antitrust Division. The department virtually ceased blocking mergers or bringing predation cases. The Federal Trade Commission, responsible for enforcing the Clayton Act, also went into a deep coma.

Bork and the Chicago critics are more convincing when they argue that the more extreme antitrust policies of the 1960s and early 1970s overreached, to the point of harming concentrations of market power that may well have been beneficial to innovation and hence welfare. The government spent hundreds of millions of dollars trying to break up IBM. By the time the case came to a head, IBM had misjudged the market and was the victim of new competitive pressures. Personal computers and, later, local-area computer networks were displacing mainframes. Personal computers, though introduced by IBM, quickly became commodity products, and IBM was the high-cost provider. IBM made a disastrous misjudgment in allowing little Microsoft control of operating software on which IBM depended, and soon software rather than hardware was the most dynamic part of the industry. But the fact that competitive forces dislodged a dominant incumbent in the computer industry hardly demonstrates that the market is always self-correcting in more monopolistic industries.

With the election of Bill Clinton in 1992, and the appointment of Assistant Attorney General Anne Bingaman, antitrust policy returned to something of a happy medium—not resisting size or market power per se, but keeping a weather eye on its anticompetitive abuses. Interestingly, when the Clinton administration revived antitrust enforcement after a twelve-year hiatus, one of the first targets was the airline industry. In 1993, Northwest attempted to pursue the familiar predatory selective price-cutting strategy against little Reno Air. The Antitrust Division, with strong support from the Department of Transportation, put Northwest on notice that, if they selectively undercut Reno's fares, they were risking prosecution. Northwest backed off. The resulting increase in price competition and consumer choice must, even in Bork's terms, increase total welfare, since it slides down the demand curve and generates more product and lower cost—even though Northwest evidently would not have preferred this outcome.

The Justice Department also got into an instructive tiff with U.S. District Judge Stanley Sporkin, over whether the Antitrust Division let Microsoft off too lightly in agreeing to a settlement rather than proceeding to trial on charges that Microsoft resorted to illegal anticompetitive practices. Microsoft's competitors accused it, among other allegedly predatory actions, of publicizing nonexistent products to be unveiled at some unspecified date, as a way of dissuading customers from buying new products from Microsoft's competitors. These imaginary software products are known in the trade, delightfully, as "vaporware." There is also much anecdotal evidence that Microsoft improperly uses information received from competing software companies developing applications software for use with Microsoft's Windows operating system. Microsoft is said to pass this information along to its own developers of applications software, thus using its market power in operating software to undercut competing applications products. Microsoft has also used tying requirements with hardware manufacturers to head off competing operating systems.

All of this recalls kindred dilemmas in the market power of banks and brokerage houses—which were resolved by Congress in the Glass-Steagall Act, separating commercial banking and investment banking—and in the telephone industry, where the FCC and the courts have laboriously taken steps to prevent incumbent phone companies from using their market power to strangle infant competitors.

At a hearing on whether to approve the consent agreement, internal Microsoft documents were introduced by three of Microsoft's smaller rivals, purportedly showing that company policy approved and rewarded the practice of "pre-announcing" nonexistent vaporware.

"These documents are conspiratorial documents," declared Judge Sporkin.

"Your honor, it's called competition," shot back the lawyer for Microsoft, in a beautiful exposition of Chicago theory. "It's the very heart of a free market economy." In other words, whatever private competitors do must *ipso facto* represent free-market competition—even when the practices are evidently anticompetitive.

Yet Justice Department documents and interviews regarding the Microsoft case suggest that the relation of market power to innovation was very much on the department's mind as it moved to settle rather than litigate the case. Here was the government, taking on one of the crown jewels of American high-tech industry. Though Microsoft may have begun as the brainchild of Bill Gates and a few of his hacker friends, it was now a $50-billion giant. Its capacity to keep innovating was not unrelated to its position of preponderant market leadership. Remembering the lengthy and enervating antitrust case against IBM, on the eve of IBM's own fall from grace, Anne Bingaman walked a careful tightrope between discouraging Microsoft from using its market power to savage smaller rivals—and resisting moves that might undercut Microsoft's own earned market leadership. Though respect for the innovative power of a market leader is nowhere in the antitrust laws, it was very much on the minds of the Justice Department—and rightly so. In the settlement, Microsoft agreed to cease several practices that its competitors deemed anticompetitive under the continuing supervision of the Justice Department. Eventually an appeals court upheld the Justice Department's consent agreement with Microsoft.

In the Schumpeterian dilemma of allocative versus innovative efficiency, the proper role of antitrust policy remains tantalizingly inconclusive. It appears that industries with fairly standardized products, such as airline tickets, hotel rooms, and commodity chemicals, must be allowed a degree of collaboration and norms that resist pure price-competition, as Joseph Bower recounts, or competition will turn ruinous. When ruinous competition looms, the private-industry response is characteristically to create a cartel or a wave of mergers and consolidations, as in the oil industry or the airline industry. This form of private price-regulation solves the industry's problem of excessive price-competition, but not necessarily in a way that maximizes consumer welfare. It simply shifts a great deal of surplus from consumers to producers. Whether this surplus is necessarily plowed back into innovation is also something of an open question, not mechanically settled by economic theory. At the point where market power in potentially competitive industries simply extracts the surplus from consumers, there is a role for antitrust. In industries characterized by scale economies and natural monopoly, the remedy involves regulation. Bracketing both antitrust policy and economic regulation is the idea of competition policy. It is hard to conceive of efficient commerce without it.

So: regulation is dead—long live regulation. In spite of itself, economic theory has contributed to a new hybrid: pro-competitive regulation. By so doing, economic theory has demonstrated, despite its prejudices against the polity, that social learning is possible after all. And pro-competitive regulation requires nothing so much as subtle, competent, public-minded regulators.

8 / REGULATING THE HUMAN ENVIRONMENT

THE MARKET'S ASSAULTS

In a mixed economy, the state intervenes to protect citizens from a variety of assaults that laissez-faire forces would otherwise produce. These include the spewing of pollutants into the air and water, the manufacture of dangerous products, the coercive power of private business to condition employment on unsafe working conditions, and other "contracts of desperation" that do not reflect truly voluntary transactions.

Many such abuses are the consequence not just of price inaccuracies but of imbalances in private knowledge and bargaining power. The consumer can't be expected to know with precision if her hamburger is poisoned, if the lawnmower will cut his foot off, if the water is safe to drink. The factory worker can't know whether an industrial compound risks producing cancer ten years into the future. The individual citizen doesn't have the basis to insist that the local public utility burn cleaner fuel or develop lower-polluting technology—except via government regulation.

To conceive of these assaults as "externalities" is helpful in understanding the dynamics of how markets fail to price accurately, but often conveys too narrow a conception of what is at work. For these issues often involve public values that are impossible to reduce to a simple economic calculus. They also raise distributional questions that cannot be reduced to efficiency terms.

Deciding that nobody shall be subjected to workplace chemicals that are clearly toxic yields very different distributive outcomes than allowing individuals of different economic circumstances to bid for the right to avoid exposure. Neither approach is *a priori* more "efficient." If producers are no longer permitted to dump waste products at their pleasure, or to shift hazards onto workers and consumers, the remedy necessarily entails a broad shift in the regime of property rights, not merely a fine-tuning of prices. To use contrived markets and narrowly economic incentives to reach social goals is one possible remedy, but not necessarily the best one. And, of course, it is also a form of regulation.

In the pricing of pollutants and employee or consumer injuries, the market's inability to price accurately is the norm. The remedy for these and kindred abuses entails broad public-policy goals, not mere corrections of narrow, isolated "market failure." Policy goals here flow from a recognition that society as a whole may choose to award itself certain common minima—clean drinking water, wholesome working environments, presumptively safe prescription drugs and foodstuffs—that market forces neglect or even deliberately frustrate to save short-run costs. A still broader goal is to vouchsafe the environment to future generations, or to achieve high living standards at lower overall environmental cost. These are civic goals that myopic markets cannot identify. So the purpose of public policy in this realm is not just to compensate passively for market imperfections, but to ratify public values and stimulate social learning.

Moreover, common objectives that involve environment and health are often poor candidates for the staple of economic analysis—the premise that economic transactions can usefully be understood as analogous to a physical equilibrium. In physics, if you exert force on a moving object, you will deflect it from its equilibrium path. Remove the perturbation and the object normally will return to equilibrium. In our humble supermarket example, the same is roughly true of, say, the price of orange juice. If an early frost depresses the supply of orange juice and raises the price, consumers will turn to substitutes. When the price returns to normal, a few buyers may have acquired a taste for cranberry juice, but most of the previous buyers will return.

The environment, however, exhibits *irreversibilities*—something that does not occur in equilibrium analysis. The depletion of the ozone layer and the process of global warming are results of accumulated biochemical changes that may not be easily reversed even after pollution levels are reduced. If reversal is possible at all, it may come at disproportionate, even prohibitive cost. A worker who contracts lethal cancer because of repeated exposure to benzene stays dead. Likewise an entire species that becomes extinct. The price system is of only limited use here, because all attempts to price a life, let alone a species, are at best partial. There are values at stake here that cannot be reduced to price. So standard economic analysis is not a good fit with environmental dilemmas.

Nonetheless, efforts to regulate environmental assaults are not free. So policymakers have to use available tools and devise new ones, to weigh environmental goals against other economic goals, to find "least-cost" solutions, and to look for approaches that yield net economic benefits—sometimes by stimulating whole new ways of doing things at lower net cost to the environment. Here, markets and marketlike incentives can be useful policy tools. But "incentive regulation" operates via a regulatory platform that itself overrides laissez-faire pricing; and direct regulation not only has different distributional consequences but is sometimes more efficient economically.

The wave of social regulation that began in the late 1960s resulted from a new public consciousness about the deteriorating natural environment. The consensus was remarkably broad. Most of the landmark environmental bills were signed by a Republican president, Richard Nixon, with bipartisan support. There seemed no other area where it was so widely agreed that market forces, left to themselves, yielded intolerable and unsustainable outcomes. This shift resulted from a change in social values rather than private "tastes"—a broad acceptance that environmental degradation was cumulative, that the air and water could no longer be treated as a free sink, and that employees need not bear a disproportionate share of industry's hazards. By the time the wave crested, in the mid-1970s, Congress had added new systems for regulating clean air and water, toxic substances, food and drugs, the workplace, and consumer products generally.

Twenty years later, there is a broad counterreformation against health, safety, and environmental regulation. In this insurgent view, most of these matters can efficiently be left to market forces after all, if government will just get out of the way. The fact that some concerns about resource shortages were overstated has been used to impeach the need for environmental regulation generally.

As with so much else that we are addressing herein, the backlash against social regulation extends from far right to center and even center-left—and includes much of the mainstream economics profession. As usual, the vehemence of economists' opposition reflects indignation that government is violating the price system. The critics' complaints boil down to these:

Social Regulation Is Expensive. By costing industry on the order of 2 percent of GNP, regulation allegedly depresses growth and adds to inflation. Investments mandated by bureaucrats cause industry to divert funds to uses that add nothing to productivity. This complaint was trotted out by affected industrial groups in the case of virtually every antipollution law proposed during the 1970s. Some critics went even further. The late Professor Aaron Wildavsky, in an article titled "Richer Is Safer," went so far as to claim that health-and-safety regulation actually depressed health and safety. Wildavsky's reasoning was impeccable. Richer societies tend to have longer life expectancies. Economic growth requires investment. Health-and-safety regulation diverts investment, hence depresses growth, hence detracts from health and safety. Conclusion: if you want a healthy society, don't invest in health. It did not occur to Wildavsky that a society might choose a development path that maximized both growth and health.

As the discussion in chapter 6 suggested, this view excludes the possibility that investment in advanced processes that are lower-polluting and safer for workers often pushes industry to a higher trajectory of productivity. Yes, richer is safer; but safer is also richer. A society in which people can confidently drink tap water is richer than one where the affluent buy bottled water and the poor get dysentery, but it is rich in a different and more egalitarian way. A cleaner industrial process is often a more efficient one. The record is full of cases where industry at first insisted that it could not possibly meet an emissions standard, or find a substitute for a hazardous chemical, but it quickly turned out that the mandate could be met—and with technical breakthroughs that had spillover benefits.

Social Regulation Is Self-Defeating. As Albert Hirschman observed in his classic work, *The Rhetoric of Reaction*, a staple argument of opponents of reform dating back at least to Edmund Burke is the claim that social intervention invariably backfires. Hirschman labels this the Perversity Thesis. For Burke and the conservative opponents of the French and other revolutions, social reform backfired because it undermined settled institutions and loosed forces that ultimately ruined liberty, prosperity, and civil order—the very goals of the reformers. For modern conservative economists, regulation backfires because it violates a market equilibrium. Society, by definition, is already getting exactly what it wants, and the market is doing the best it can. The do-gooder arrogantly disturbs that equilibrium, but people will get what they desire one way or another. At the end of the day, the main result of the regulation will be cost.

There are several recent classics of this genre. Professor W. Kip Viscusi claimed that medicine containers with government-mandated safety caps increased accidental poisonings because parents, frustrated by the hard-to-open lids, either deliberately bought drugs in conventional packaging or left caps open. In a similar vein, Chicago School economist Sam Peltzman argued that auto seat-belts and other safety features actually increased auto fatalities, since they gave drivers a false sense of security and induced them to drive more recklessly. Some natural equilibrating mechanism must dwell deep in the driver's soul: make the car 10 percent safer, people will drive 10 percent faster. Brookings economist Robert Crandall has contended, in the same spirit, that fuel-efficiency standards increase accidents, because they lead automakers to make smaller, more hazardous cars. All of these studies fail to consider the possibility that such regulation stimulates social learning, and is efficient after all. I will return to this shortly.

Social Regulation Is Mostly Unnecessary. Until the counterrevolution of the 1980s, it was generally accepted by economists that negative externalities were widespread. The classic case is an upstream factory that costlessly dumps its waste into the river, polluting the water of people downstream. For modern economists dating back almost a century to Arthur Pigou, the preferred solution in a second-best (imperfect-market) world was to levy a tax on the pollution. This would force the polluter to internalize the cost of the externality, give the polluter a more accurate price signal of what his pollution cost society, use a market-price mechanism to induce a desirable behavior change, and leave the pricing system otherwise undisturbed. A third-best, more bureaucratic solution was direct regulation.

But in "The Problem of Social Cost," Ronald Coase proposed that it didn't really matter whether the government regulated or not, as long as private transaction costs and information costs were low. Private parties, either directly or through the courts, had the capacity to bargain out an equitable settlement. Coase's article used several homey examples from actual court cases—a train's sparks risk igniting a nearby farmer's crops; a doctor shares a building with a small factory, whose machinery disturbs the doctor's practice. Coase showed easily how voluntary negotiation could yield an optimal solution and satisfy both parties. This comported beautifully with the Chicago notion that all transactions are essentially voluntary, and it usefully removed the need for government. Coase, very belatedly, explained that he was taking the case of "zero transaction costs" as a hypothetical, not as reality. In 1988, he wrote: "It would not seem worthwhile to spend much time investigating the properties of such a [zero-transaction-costs] world. What my argument does suggest is the need to introduce positive transaction costs explicitly into economic analysis so that we can study the world that exists. This has not been the effect of my article." In the real world, alas, bargaining by private parties does not reliably solve externality problems. There is too much asymmetry of knowledge and power. One can, of course, level that playing field and allow fair bargaining to commence—but this also entails . . . regulation.

Social Regulation Is Arbitrary. Economics is often described as the study of how society allocates scarce resources. As health, safety, and environmental regulation proliferated in the 1970s, it infuriated many economists that policymakers seemed to presume society had an infinite supply of time and money with which to meet health and environmental goals. Charles Schultze wrote, in 1977, that "efforts to improve the environment, while far from a failure, are unnecessarily expensive and bogged down in Rube Goldberg regulations, legal snarls, and games between regulators and industry as enforcement deadlines draw near. . . . [E]ven the sympathetic observer finds it hard to recognize many of the regulations as anything but absurdities." Schultze, in a book with Allen Kneese, lamented the sheer technical complexity of the task. "There are up to 55,000 major sources of industrial water pollution alone. A regulatory agency cannot know the costs, the technological opportunities, the alternative raw materials, and the kinds of products available for every firm in every industry." For Schultze, Kneese, and kindred critics, the remedy was to use economic incentives to meet social goals.

Judge Stephen Breyer, before his elevation to the U.S. Supreme Court, began his 1992 Oliver Wendell Holmes lectures with these words: "We regulate only some, but not all, of the risk that fills the world." Breyer decried the sheer arbitrariness of what society chose to regulate and how inconsistently it determined what was worth the cost. Government often went to heroic lengths trying to reduce the last 10 percent of risks, Breyer noted, while it virtually ignored other, more significant risks. He invoked federal circuit-court rulings, themselves influenced by the Law and Economics movement, ridiculing public policy for spending $250 million to ban asbestos, saving perhaps five statistical lives over the next thirteen years, or half the expected death toll from ingested toothpicks. The problem, Breyer concluded, was a combination of "tunnel vision," the random selection of agendas, and inconsistency in public-policy priorities. He called "not necessarily for deregulation but for a serious effort to prioritize, and perhaps to reallocate, our regulatory resources."

Regulators Can't Get It Right. For some political moderates such as Breyer, the solution is not complete deregulation but a better system for setting regulatory priorities. Breyer ended his Holmes lectures in good progressive-era fashion, by calling for a body of super civil servants, who would be "above politics," and who would be responsible for sorting out contending conceptions of the public good. Breyer actually invoked the French bureaucracy, the object of scorn on the *Wall Street Journal* editorial page, as a positive role model. Given that not everything can or should be regulated, it is sensible to have an overarching process to set priorities. In fact, this is just what OMB currently does. But for more conservative critics, the remedy is not a better system of setting regulatory priorities or a better class of bureaucrat. The whole enterprise of government intervention is doomed, either because of "regulatory capture" by affected interest groups, or "rent seeking" by bureaucrats, or because bureaucrats can't possibly know as much as markets.

Consumers Get Exactly What They Deserve. The most fundamental premise of the Law and Economics critique is that all transactions are voluntary. If this is the case, then consumers who wanted safer products or less risky occupations would buy something else, choose a different line of work, or purchase insurance against risks. The fact that they don't is proof that they are getting just what they want, and have no need for pesky lawyers or regulators. This view is used to attack both regulation and tort remedy. That consumers, in their role as citizens, often choose to modify market outcomes by supporting health, safety, and environmental regulation is attributed not to civic values but to the influence of rent-seeking politicians.

All of these criticisms are based on heroic and improbable views of the efficiency of markets. Despite very real flaws in government regulation, the fact remains that the laissez-faire market does pollute, does produce avoidable injuries, does distribute hazardous products. A market transaction also exists in historic time, influenced by prior asymmetries of circumstance, custom, and economic power. In practice, the Coasean world, where all externalities are happily negotiated away by voluntary private action, or where market processes dictate the precisely right payment of premiums for extra risks, seldom seems to materialize.

The market's more subtle defenders acknowledge these limitations, and fall back to a second line of defense. If we must regulate, they say, let us at least use the insights, tools, and disciplines of the market. These forays are worth careful attention, and need to be disentangled. Some of the approaches, like Public Choice theory, inappropriately and disingenuously impose market concepts upon a realm that is properly civic, and define public purpose out of existence. Other initiatives, such as the provisions of the 1994 Republican Contract with America, are mainly tactical assaults aimed at rolling back the reach of government. Still other measures, such as tradable emission rights, invoke market principles ingeniously to facilitate efficient regulation.

REGULATING CONDITIONS OF WORK

The issue of employee health and safety nicely illustrates the limits of markets and even of "marketlike" regulation. One doesn't have to be Marxist to notice a pervasive imbalance of bargaining power between a wage or salary worker and the owner of an enterprise. Commentators since Adam Smith have observed that most ordinary employees have little savings to fall back on. A worker out of a job for a more than a few weeks will starve. "Many workmen could not subsist a week, few could subsist a month, and scarce any a year without employment," Smith wrote. "In the long run the workman may be as necessary to his master as his master is to him, but the necessity is not so immediate." In 1995, economist

Edward Wolff confirmed that little had changed in more than two centuries. The median member of the work force, Wolff calculated, was about three months away from destitution if he lost his job.

The higher the unemployment rate at any given time, the less bargaining power the worker has relative to the boss. Since the broadening of political democracy to wage workers, the political process has used policy and law to level this playing field in a variety of ways, ranging from unemployment compensation, the right to collective bargaining, pension laws, health and safety laws, efforts to avert depressions, workers' compensation, modifications of the traditional employment-at-will doctrine, and so on. As political consciousness has shifted and democracy has broadened, common-law limitations on the liability of employers for worker injuries have also shifted somewhat in favor of workers. Note again that, despite the economist's idealized conception of "efficiency," there is no single, optimal, and enduring set of prior ground rules. The relative rights and bargaining capacities of employees and owners are embedded in history, custom, law, and politics.

A century ago, wage workers had almost no ability to collect damages for injuries or illnesses incurred on the job. A few industrial states, beginning with Massachusetts in 1877, did provide for factory inspection, but these protections were rudimentary. Prevailing legal doctrines were severely stacked in favor of the employer. A trinity of almost insurmountable common-law defenses dating to 1841 included: (1) the doctrine of contributory negligence, which immunized the employer from damages if an industrial accident resulted even partly from the worker's own carelessness, no matter how hazardous the working conditions; (2) the "fellow-servant" doctrine, which got the employer off the hook if negligence by a fellow employee contributed to the accident; and, most broadly, (3) the theory of "assumption of risk," which deemed that an employee who took a job freely and voluntarily assumed all risks associated with it. This stacking of the legal deck was of course highly political. It advantaged employers and disadvantaged employees. It is intriguing how closely the assumption-of-risk doctrine parallels modern theories of law and economics.

In the Progressive era, reformist exposés documented appalling rates of industrial accident and disease. One study in 1908 estimated that 35,000 workers were killed and 536,000 injured every year, out of a work force of about 30 million. Between 1907 and 1912, industrial accidents caused nearly 10 percent of all deaths of male Americans, 23 percent of deaths among miners, and 49 percent of deaths among electrical linemen. Upton Sinclair's famous exposé of conditions in the packinghouse industry, later woven into his novel *The Jungle*, was remembered for its exposure of filthy meat. But Sinclair's main intent was to rally the national conscience against the dangerous working conditions, not the food. "I aimed at the public's heart," he famously wrote, "and by accident I hit it in the stomach."

In the Progressive era, public opinion and courts became more sympathetic to workers. A detailed study of industrial conditions in Pittsburgh, underwritten by the Russell Sage Foundation, reported that Pittsburgh workers won eighty-eight of 304 industrial-injury lawsuits heard in 1907 and 1908. In the more Progressive states, according to one study, between 60 and 80 percent of plaintiffs had their awards upheld on appeal in the years between 1905 and 1910. These increasing damage awards led to a perceived crisis of employers' liability, prefiguring the tort-reform "crisis" of the 1990s. Between 1900 and 1911, employer-liability premiums more than doubled. Progressive agitation also led thirty-two state governors or legislatures to appoint commissions to investigate worker injuries in the years 1903–19.

Like so much in the Progressive era, the public-policy response reflected an ambiguous blend of civic and labor pressure for reform, coupled with business's desire to limit the financial damage. By 1910, the National Civic Association and the National Association of Manufacturers were lobbying actively in favor of workmen's-compensation statutes. Workmen's compensation had begun in Germany under Bismarck in 1894, and soon spread to much of Europe. Beginning in 1902, several American states formed commissions to study the problem of work accidents. The report of the Russell Sage Pittsburgh Survey, influential in Progressive circles, called for economic incentives to encourage accident prevention. In 1908, Congress passed a bill endorsed by President Theodore Roosevelt creating a limited workers'-compensation scheme for federal employees. Montana passed the first state workers'-compensation law the following year, though it was ruled unconstitutional by the courts. By 1912, ten states had passed similar laws, and by 1920 forty states had some form of workers' compensation. However, prior to the New Deal, a majority of states had optional rather than mandatory workers'-compensation systems. Employers in those states were free to remain uninsured and take their chances with the common law of liability. Though states themselves served as insurance carriers in several of the more Progressive states, the private-insurance industry successfully lobbied for the business, and the entire system was gradually privatized by the 1950s.

Limits of Workers' Compensation. Though not understood quite in the current terms of the Law and Economics movement, workmen's compensation was one of the earliest forms of incentive regulation. The system guaranteed workers a modest measure of compensation for accidents on the job. In return, workers were generally denied access to the courts, and payments were capped at actual economic loss—or less. Increasingly, employer premiums were "risk-rated"—companies with the most costly accidents paid the highest premiums.

Had this system been a faithful reflection of the true social cost of worker injuries and occupational illnesses, workers' compensation would have more fully internalized the costs of those accidents to firms, and firms would have responded with much greater health-and-safety consciousness. But evidently it was not. As I will suggest below, even an "optimal" workers'-compensation scheme can be only a partial remedy to occupational hazards. On the eve of the New Deal, the typical weekly compensation payment was capped at 50 percent of wages, or a maximum of ten dollars a week. The purchasing power of the average workmen's-compensation benefit was actually lower in 1929 than in 1915. Though less egregiously than the earlier common-law doctrines, the workers'-compensation system still stacked the deck in favor of employers. Half a century later, when Congress geared up to supplement workers' compensation with more direct "command-and-control" regulation via OSHA, worker injuries were still epidemic.

Why was workers' compensation only a partial remedy? For one thing, its terms were set politically. Employer groups effectively resisted more expansive compensation schemes. Workers' compensation in most states excluded occupational illness. Indeed, it was publicity about illnesses such as black-lung disease, asbestosis, and byssinosis (from cotton dust) as much as rising concern about accidents that swung public opinion to first to MSHA, regulating mine safety, then to OSHA.

State compensation laws remained a patchwork. A 1968, pre-OSHA report by the Labor Department found that the state-to-state death rate from workplace accidents varied from a low of nineteen deaths per hundred thousand workers to a high of 110 deaths. Fourteen thousand workers were still being killed every year on the job, and two million were suffering disabilities, resulting in a yearly loss of 250 million man-days of work. Four hundred thousand people suffered from occupational diseases.

Most studies found that prevailing compensation levels significantly undercompensated workers even for their narrow wage loss. In the 1960s, the average state still paid a worker less than half of the worker's former wage; payments were not adjusted for inflation, and there was no compensation for pain and suffering. In a minimalist compensation regime, insurance premiums, averaging about 1 percent of payroll, accounted for only a fraction of the actual costs borne by employees. Even the system of experience rating, intended to target the most dangerous employers, was capped and was only partly based on actual accident records. So it was far cheaper for industry to pay the premiums than to invest in serious re-engineering measures to reduce accident and disease.

Why not raise workers'-compensation payments to reflect economic losses fully, and thereby use market incentives to induce more realistic investments in safety? One line of the 1972 Commission Report on State Workmen's Compensation offers a revealing clue: "As the proportion of wages replaced is increased, the worker will . . . have less incentive to return to work." Workers' compensation is necessarily partial. The very concept of disability is anything but precise. Overly generous disability schemes in the United States and abroad have been criticized as promoting freeloading. Conversely, a meager compensation standard uses economic necessity to compel workers to return to the job, even amid real pain and suffering. The point is that a "correct" compensation standard, striking a balance between defraying economic loss and discouraging freeloading, is not "correct" for purposes of inducing the optimal level of investment in safety at the work site. There is not one correct price; the market, by itself, cannot get there from here. Some conservative scholars have proposed "decoupling" the portion of compensation payments that are intended to compensate from those intended to deter. But this, of course, would require still more regulation.

More broadly, as we saw in chapter 3, the market model poorly describes labor markets. In theory, workers freely shop for jobs, and are accurately informed about the relative risk of different jobs. As good, rational maximizers of their utility, workers weigh risks and gains. Hazardous occupations should command wage premiums in order to induce workers with a "taste" for challenge to bear the additional risk. This, however, is a fable. In practice, there are multiple constraints on worker mobility and bargaining power; a variety of factors influence wages; workers often are poorly informed about job risk and even less well informed about risk of occupational disease. Some workers may irrationally accept exposure to extreme risk because they have been acculturated to believe that this is a manly thing to do. In a climate of less than full employment, less than perfectly symmetrical information, and relatively weak trade unions, workers can be made to bear a disproportionate cost.

In the debates leading up to OSHA, industry representatives and their academic allies repeatedly made the argument that, if actual workers wanted higher levels of health and safety, their representatives would have made safety a higher priority in collective bargaining. But, said industry, unions tended to emphasize wages and fringe benefits rather than safety. In economic jargon, this was the workers' own "revealed preference." Therefore, it was professional do-gooders and not workers themselves who were agitating for unrealistically risk-free workplaces. This argument, however, is misleading. Surveys have repeatedly shown that low-paid workers tend to internalize society's low valuation of their worth, and place a low economic value on their health. Low-paid workers also characteristically have less bargaining power. The remedy for this is not to force safety into a contest with living standards, but to change the terms of bargaining so workers are not constrained economically to bargain away their own health. When health-and-safety regimes do come into being, they are highly popular with workers. Once again, "revealed preference" turns out to be nothing but denied options.

Further, company doctors, nurses, and industrial hygienists, presumably the first line of defense against worker illness and injury, are also beholden to the same employer and subject to the same asymmetries of power. Doctors who worked for Johns Manville, the largest maker of asbestos, knew for decades that workers were being exposed to a highly toxic substance. Their qualms came to light only after a massive class-action suit and political struggle for legislative reform. Company doctors were also of little use in the efforts to reform black-lung disease and byssinosis. The rare doctor who made a fuss was often black-balled in mill towns where the owner was like a private potentate. To conceive of this coerced silence as mere market failure misses the point utterly.

Enter OSHA. As enacted in 1970, OSHA required employers generally to furnish employment "free from recognized hazards so as to provide safe and healthful working conditions." It authorized a rule-making process, empowering OSHA to set standards, on both a routine and an emergency basis. It established a process for workplace inspections, with fines for noncompliance, and allowed the secretary of labor to shut down plants in cases of imminent hazard. It created a number of new employee rights, including the right to participate in inspec-tions, the monitoring of hazards, and access to information about inspectors' findings. The law also set up a National Institute of Occupational Safety and Health, and a national commission on the reform of workers'-compensation laws. One of its most far-reaching provisions, criticized by many economists as ignoring cost, required OSHA to set standards that assure "to the extent feasible, on the basis of the best available evidence, that no employee will suffer material impairment of health or functional capacity even if such employee has regular exposure to the hazard . . . for the period of his working life." In writing this lan-guage, Congress explicitly rejected efforts by the steel and chemical industries to water down the language to refer to "economic" feasibility. In upholding OSHA's cotton-dust standard, the Supreme Court later found that Congress had not intended to set up a narrow cost-benefit test, but to mandate a threshold level of safety.

What happened after OSHA became law is a good illustration of how an administration hostile to regulation can subvert its intent. The Nixon Labor Department did not address the more glaring hazards to workplace health. Rather, it moved quickly and indiscriminately to set more than four thousand *pro forma* standards, by writing into federal regulation existing private trade-association codes of conduct. It was this process that led to the widely ridiculed

OSHA standards for the size and shape of toilet seats, the color of life vests (orange), solemn instructions on how workers should climb ladders, and so on. The political right and its allies in the economics profession then attacked these standards as the product of "bureaucrats" rather than of a conservative administration pursuing the course of least resistance. By the time Nixon left office in August 1974, only two major standards for genuine hazards had been issued—on asbestos and on fourteen high-risk industrial carcinogens. In 1978, the Carter administration, far more friendly to health and safety, discarded over nine hundred OSHA standards as silly or unnecessary, and began targeting serious rather than nominal violations.

Left and right have both criticized OSHA. The left has criticized it mainly on three grounds—for being bureaucratic rather than participatory in its design, for failing to target major hazards in setting its inspection priorities, and for letting off offenders too lightly (the average penalty is a fine of a few hundred dollars). The two post-OSHA Democratic administrations have sought to respond to all of these criticisms. The Carter administration, working with unions, agreed to promote and help fund workplace Committees on Occupational Safety and Health (COSH). These so-called COSH groups offered an embryonic alternative to bureaucratic enforcement. An informed and educated work force was a far better source of health and safety than an occasional inspection. But from industry's viewpoint, COSH groups had the unfortunate side effect of increasing the activism and efficacy of unions, and the program was killed early in the Reagan administration.

Critics in the economics profession have used OSHA as a classic case of wrongheaded command-and-control regulation. Moderate conservatives, such as Professor Viscusi, contend that even imperfect workers' compensation, by relying on market principles, is a far more cost-effective way of reducing worker injuries than a regime of standard-setting and inspections. In a 1983 book pointedly titled *Risk by Choice*, Viscusi wrote, "By coupling stringent regulations with an ineffective mechanism for enforcement, OSHA has done little more than serve as a form of systematic harassment of the private sector." Viscusi finds the entire approach wrongheaded, since it overrides marketplace verdicts. His presumption is that the preregulation pattern of workplace hazards is the result of free worker choices: "Uniform standards do not enlarge worker choices; they deprive workers of the opportunity to select the job most appropriate to their own risk preferences. The actual 'rights' issue involved is whether those in upper income groups have a right to impose their job risk preferences on the poor."

This is an astonishingly credulous view of the labor market. The reasoning is reminiscent of the U.S. Supreme Court's notorious 1905 *Lochner* v. *New York* decision, in which the court struck down a law limiting bakers to a ten-hour day on the grounds that this interfered with freedom to contract. Viscusi, presuming that OSHA was imposed by upper-class reformers, is evidently unfamiliar with OSHA's actual political history. The two groups most responsible for OSHA were the Black Lung Association, a group of forty-three thousand rank-and-file coal miners, and the Oil, Chemical and Atomic Workers Union.

The claim that more hazardous jobs pay appropriately compensatory high wages is not borne out by the evidence. Coal mining, for example, pays relatively high wages not because it is hazardous—it paid low wages before the 1940s, when it was even more hazardous—but because of the strength of the United Mine Workers. Textile mills, prior to OSHA, exposed workers to significant risks of byssinosis, yet were consistently one of the lowest-paid industries. Work in assembly-line poultry factories in Arkansas and the Carolinas is dirty and grueling, and has accident records and repetitive motion injuries far above average, but pays slightly above minimum wage. Why did workers take these jobs? They perceived that they had few practical alternatives.

Contrary to the claims by Viscusi and others that OSHA is nothing but ineffective harassment, there is solid evidence that OSHA, even with its enforcement gaps, has reduced worker injury and illness. Workplace death rates have steadily declined from about seventeen per hundred thousand workers at the time of OSHA's enactment to fewer than eight per hundred thousand workers today. For private-sector workers, the death rate declined by 43 percent. Occupational injuries have also dropped, though at a lower rate, from about eleven per hundred thousand workers to about eight and a half.

In the present ideological climate, Professor Viscusi is a relative moderate. He argues that requiring industry to buy risk-adjusted workers'-compensation insurance is a more marketlike and hence a more cost-effective strategy for reducing worker injuries than an OSHA-style regime of standards and inspections. Mandated workers' compensation, of course, is itself a form of regulation. More extreme conservatives, such as Richard Epstein, insist that even workers' compensation is a self-defeating transgression of the market. Epstein writes, "If the compensation system were such a good idea, employers and employees would have adopted some version of it voluntarily." Presumably, workers know perfectly well what they are doing. Those who pursue hazardous occupations are voluntarily exercising their risk-selection preferences, for which they are fairly compensated. If the compensation were not fair, industry would not attract enough workers and would have either to raise the wage or to reduce the risk. This reasoning is almost pathetically tautological, yet these men have significant influence. A decade ago, the Law and Economics fraternity touted the common law as superior to regulation. Now many in this group worry that the common law itself is too generous to victims, and propose statutory limits.

Regulation as Mother of Invention. Opponents of investments in health and safety tend to overstate the cost of compliance with OSHA standards, and understate the benefits. For example, the textile industry bitterly opposed OSHA's imposition of tough standards on cotton dust, which had caused acute byssinosis ("brown-lung disease") in eighty-four thousand active workers at the time the standard was adopted in 1978, as well as disability in another thirty-five thousand former textile workers no longer employed. Before the final cotton-dust standard was issued, industry estimates of the compliance costs ranged from $875 million to nearly $2 billion. Five years later, OSHA concluded that the actual capital costs will total about $245 million.

Textile workers are exposed to cotton dust in the early, more labor-intensive stages of textile production—opening, cleaning, and carding the raw cotton and then drawing out the fibers—prior to the more mechanized process of spinning the cleaned and blended cotton into yarn, spooling the yarn, and finally weaving it into cloth. Automation was already under way at the more modern plants, but it was accelerated by the OSHA cotton-dust standard. Whereas the caricature of health-and-safety compliance portrays it as a purely extraneous function and cost, tacked on to a production process that is already—by definition—as efficient as it can be, in practice greater health and safety measures are typically "designed in" to new generations of production technology. According to a study for the Office of Technology Assessment, the textile industry came into compliance with OSHA's cotton-dust standard by modernizing and automating the dirtiest phases of the manufacturing process:

> The necessity for making changes in plant machinery for OSHA compliance created an opportunity for engineers to make other equipment improvements simultaneously. Similarly the process of changing plant machinery to improve profitability made it easier to make changes that would improve dust control. In many cases, the timing of modernization and of compliance efforts fit hand-in-glove.
>
> In other cases, the process of modernization has brought plants into compliance almost automatically. . . . [N]ew sophisticated machinery has lower dust tolerance and, therefore, requires a cleaner work environment. Downtime on new faster machines is more expensive, so automatic, traveling cleaners have become important for the healthy maintenance of capital as well as labor. The chute-fed card system is more productive when enclosed. That enclosure also eliminates employee exposure to cotton dust.

Technology-forcing regulation also rewards the more modern and productive segments of the industry, by raising the costs of the dirtiest and least modern firms. If industry really could profit by installing cleaner machinery, why did the textile industry not seize that opportunity prior to OSHA? Because, as long as manufacturers were able to externalize costs of dirty and inefficient manufacturing onto their workers, one logical spur to innovation was absent. In the history of the market economy, capital improvement has typically occurred in nations, regions, and industries where human labor is scarce and costly, not where workers are cheap and expendable.

The same story of industry resistance and overstatement of compliance costs occurred with the OSHA standards for vinyl chloride, and for grain dust. Vinyl chloride, a chemical gas, is the key ingredient in polyvinyl-chloride plastic, America's second most widely used plastic. In the early 1970s, epidemiological studies demonstrated that low concentrations of vinyl chloride could cause otherwise rare liver cancer as well as lung and brain tumors. When OSHA, in 1974, after lengthy technical study, proposed a regulation limiting worker exposure to one part per million, chemical companies warned that the standard could lead to the demise of the entire polyvinyl-chloride industry. In fact, within eighteen months of the regulation, over 90 percent of the industry was in compliance at far less cost than originally projected. The actual costs were about 7 percent of the projected costs. In the course of meeting the standard, the industry developed or accelerated installation of new technologies, including computer-controlled manufacturing systems that significantly raised productivity as well as reducing exposure. Polyvinyl chloride output more than doubled during the 1970s.

Regulation and "Voice." The stylized economists' debate about "command-and-control" regulation versus marketlike regulation and reliance on the common law is instructively misleading in three respects.

First, it overlooks the fact that direct regulation and incentive regulation can be complements rather than opposite alternatives. A more robust form of workers' compensation would doubtless induce industry to invest more money in safer workplaces. But it is unlikely that this brand of incentive regulation could be perfectly tuned. Occupational diseases take many years to incur costs, and are highly concentrated in particular industries. Risk rating, the targeting mechanism of workers' compensation, is backward-looking; it reflects historic experience with claims; it doesn't fully charge the most hazardous industries the full cost. As the accounts of OSHA's cotton-dust and vinyl-chloride standards suggest, it was more efficient for government to set standards than to rely on the slow pressure of compensation costs to spur innovation.

Second, this polarized debate overlooks the fact that direct ("command-and-control") regulation and incentive regulation both offer a broad continuum of possible approaches and efficiencies. The Nixon administration's brand of direct OSHA regulation was cynical and inept, and gave the whole approach a bad name. The traditional workers'-compensation regime was more marketlike, but the incentives it imposed on industry were too weak to internalize costs fully. An ideal regime would combine better-adjusted workers' compensation *and* a better targeted regulatory system of standards, inspections, and mandated employee involvement. Incentive regulation and direct regulation both involve the interaction of public policy and technical change, which are necessarily iterative processes. Direct regulation, much more dramatically than incentive regulation, can accelerate technical breakthroughs.

Third and perhaps most important, the usual economists' characterization of "command" regulation completely ignores the fact that regulation not only changes industry's cost curves; it can also increase workers' voice and thus alter the industrial culture of decision-making. This, in turn, opens the door to more collaborative and hence less bureaucratic solutions. Safety-and-health enforcement in Canada, Sweden, Germany, and Austria relies much more heavily on front-line workers and on worker-manager problem-solving than on periodic inspections by government officials. This alternative approach has the virtue of raising worker consciousness about health and safety and empowering employees to participate in discussions about technical solutions and investment decisions; it also creates another venue for worker-manager collaboration, and saves scarce bureaucratic resources for emergencies, chronic offenders, technical assistance, and long-term research. In the static economic calculus of costs and benefits, this kind of benefit is overlooked, because it is not on the free-market economists' methodological radar screen. It is a kind of social invention beyond the ken of the market, and beyond the lens of the market celebrant.

In Sweden, a 1974 law requires every workplace with five or more employees to have an elected safety steward, and workplaces with fifty or more employees must have a labor-management health-and-safety committee. These committees decide how to spend the company's health-and-safety budget; they approve the selection and monitor the work of the company doctor, nurse, safety engineer, and industrial hygienist. In one sense, this regime is more highly regulatory than the U.S. approach—but it "regulates" by changing the power relationships and the subculture of the work site, not by increasing government supervision. The result is far more joint problem-solving at the workplace level, and far less intrusion by state inspectors. Remarkably enough, since the system was established, it has required far fewer inspections relative to workplaces than have taken place in the United States. One statistic speaks volumes. The ratio of officials in Sweden's technical standards office to its legal office is twenty-five to one. The same ratio at OSHA is one to one. Appeals to the Swedish government tend to involve requests for technical assistance rather than help in resolving disputes. Inspections in the Swedish system aim at improving safety and devising remedies for problems, rather than imposing punishments. Though statistics are not perfectly comparable, Swedish occupational injuries and deaths are about one-third lower than U.S. levels.

The American approach is more adversarial, in three distinct and paradoxical respects. There is a more antagonistic and litigious culture of labor-management relations—but employees end up with less real power. The function of government inspections in the U.S. system is more punitive—but the fines are usually so low as to be mere slaps on the wrist. Because the American system is more bureaucratic, the process tends to emphasize formal compliance—inspections completed, standards met or flouted, fines meted out, reports written—rather than real problem-solving. Court challenges are far more frequent, and inspectors are under pressure from superiors to document their findings to provide evidence for possible legal cases. This, of course, raises suspicions on all sides, deters free sharing of information, and leaves little time for cooperative remedy.

All of the foregoing is grist for the antiregulators. But it seems beyond the imagination of the critics of regulation to imagine that government intervention could alter the local terms of engagement and thus lead to lower levels of conflict and more win/win solutions at the work site. The most basic paradox of the limits of the characteristically American brand of regulation is this: As an individualistic society, we tend to be more litigious and adversarial. More highly regulated, corporatist, and group-oriented nations seem better able to use collectivities to assure standing in society, and prevent weaker members of society from being trampled, and to do so in a less bureaucratic fashion. The emphasis is less on "rights"—a characteristically individualistic and Anglo-Saxon concept—than on membership, solidarity, and mutual responsibility within the group, in this case the workplace. An atomistic view of society as nothing more than a set of markets misses these possibilities altogether.

Steven Kelman contrasts adversarial and "accommodationist" ways of social bargaining and problem-solving. He observes: "Accommodationist institutions encourage achieving agreement by establishing a forum for negotiations. Furthermore, to the extent that participants become part of an ongoing small group, agreements are encouraged because of psychological processes that tend to occur in such groups and provide normative inducements toward agreements in general. . . . Negotiations among small ongoing groups also frequently act psychologically to promote the development of agreement-encouraging preferences and perceptions that would not have existed without the ongoing relationship." Note how diametrically opposed this is to the market model of man, in which relationships are arm's-length, contingent, and transitory, and motivations are purely instrumental and self-interested rather than collective and empathic.

The Clinton administration, to its credit, sought to move OSHA enforcement toward a more consensual and less bureaucratic approach. On the eve of the 1994 election, the House Education and Labor Committee reported an OSHA-reform bill, requiring among other things joint labor-management health-and-safety committees, and targeting by OSHA of high-risk industries and work sites. The bill never became law; however, the Clinton Labor Department has used its administrative discretion to shift to performance standards rather than measuring its success by the number of inspections or fines. OSHA has also increased its targeting of the most hazardous employers. Under a pilot project in Maine, the 203 employers with the worst records were given the choice of developing their own comprehensive safety-and-health programs or, as OSHA put it bluntly, "being put on a priority list for a wall-to-wall inspection." All but two companies complied. During the first eighteen months of the program, participants identified and abated hazards at a rate fourteen times higher than OSHA's own rate of hazards identified via inspections. OSHA, of course, has a limited number of inspectors. Had OSHA inspected Maine work sites at random, only about twenty of the companies with the worst records would have been inspected in any given year.

It is foolish and misleading to tar all social regulation with the same brush. Just as markets can yield efficient or inefficient outcomes, so can regulation. Just as markets evolve, so do regulatory regimes. As long as they operate in a climate that is not antiregulation per se, astute regulators learn by doing and wherever possible empower private actors to meet public standards rather than pursuing the ultimately futile course of direct policing. The stereotype of "command and control" misses the rich range of possibilities on the ground.

In practice, if we take a close look at, say, the FCC effort to devise an auction system for spectrum allocation, or the OSHA pilot project in Maine, or the New York State Public Utilities Commission's experiment in telephone competition in Rochester, or the EPA's accomplishment in tradable pollution rights (discussed below), one comes away with great respect for the integrity and discernment of the regulatory process. These cases conform neither to the stereotype of the imperious bureaucratic czar, nor to the Public Choice picture of a regulator who is nothing but the passive product of vectors of special-interest influence. Regulatory proceedings, at their best, can be an example of what the political scientist Jane Mansbridge has called "deliberative democracy." They can be iterative and educative, and can pursue an authentic public purpose. This is, of course, not costless—but it yields benefits. And it is hard to wax indignant over the cost of this public business in a nation where private-market forces choose to spend six billion dollars a year on cat food. The alternative to good regulation is not no regulation; it is bad regulation.

MEASURING COSTS AND BENEFITS

The recent attack on social regulation relies on a variety of market concepts. These include cost-benefit analysis, which usually finds that the cost of regulation outweighs the benefit; the assumption of a behavioral equilibrium, upon which regulation cannot improve; and the application of free-market analysis to judges and courts, lately attacking even the common law as a violation of efficient markets. Though it is always fair to ask whether particular regulations are efficient ways of addressing failures of markets, this line of attack tends to build in a bias against regulation per se.

Cost-benefit analysis illustrates the severe limits of the market model as an analytic tool kit. Seemingly, it makes perfect sense to measure benefits against costs. The logic appears unimpeachable: A society has limited economic resources. All regulatory constraints consume resources that the economy might better invest elsewhere. Before imposing such expenses, we should be sure that the benefit outweighs the cost. So far, so good. Every president since Jimmy Carter has ordered regulators to use some version of cost-benefit analysis, and the 1994 Republican Contract with America sought to write a very stringent version of this doctrine into law.

However, the practical problems with cost-benefit analysis are multiple. For one thing, cost-benefit analysis applied to worker health and safety uses a narrowly financial valuation of human life based on earning power. Cost-benefit analysis therefore creates a profound methodological bias against the idea of a social floor on standards—an idea that flows from extra-market values. Cost-benefit analysis also ignores distributive implications. Social cost is treated as if it were indivisible, rather than a cost disproportionately borne by front-line workers and other vulnerable people. (Chicago economics would say this apparent vulnerability is an illusion. Workers in hazardous occupations have freely chosen their lot in life, which is a precise blend of their marginal productivity and their taste for risk.)

More broadly, cost-benefit analysis attempts to bring into the price-auction system things that most people think should not be for sale. The Emancipation Proclamation, as Steven Kelman has observed, was not subject to an inflation-impact analysis. As Kelman aptly points out, it is a fallacy to extrapolate from how people value things in purely private transactions to collective values and public goods. Placing a "priceless" commodity—such as Central Park, or a clear view of the Grand Canyon—into a realm that deliberately precludes its sale is itself a collective decision that denies that commodity valuation according to market principles. Looking for a shadow market price or a cost-benefit test for such public goods alters their fundamental character, "reducing it to a mechanistic, mimicking recalculation based on private behavior," Kelman observes.

For society, the cost of injury or disease is average and abstract. For the individual, it is personal and profound. This is why Congress wrote OSHA to mandate a safe workplace broadly, and not a safe workplace subject to cost-benefit tests. This regulatory approach levels the playing field: society as a whole becomes the guarantor, and the worker on the front line is no longer presumed expendable subject to narrow financial criteria. When there are flat prohibitions against externalizing costs onto employees, the ingenuity of industry is boundless.

There is, in the cost-benefit exercise, a not very subtle class bias. The people who suffer the injuries and deaths from occupational hazards and diseases are almost never corporate executives, accountants, or economists. It is all too easy to reduce the suffering of front-line workers to so many "statistical lives," and to conclude airily that it isn't worth half a million dollars to save one statistical life—that the money would be better invested elsewhere.

Methodologically, the attempts to weigh costs against benefits are revealingly ghoulish. The two most widely used methods of valuing a life are the Discounted Future Earnings (DFE) approach and the Willingness to Pay (WTP) method. The former values a person's life by projecting the value of lifetime earnings lost because of premature death or disabling injury, and then discounts them into present dollars to adjust for future inflation and implied lost interest income. The latter method literally takes surveys or looks at other contexts to determine what people think their life and health are worth. This logic not only reflects and reinforces the class bias of the whole approach—the life of an executive is worth more than that of a minimum-wage worker—but, taken literally, it also produces some bizarre conclusions.

For example, the future earnings stream of an unemployed or retired person, or a homemaker outside the wage economy, is zero. And the earnings stream of a severely handicapped person is negative, since she is a net cost to society. So, in cost-benefit terms, their premature death would yield a net benefit. Of course, even the free-market economist resists that conclusion. But why? The answer is that society places a value on human life beyond narrow market criteria. We don't allow people to sell themselves into slavery or to sell off their body parts or their right to vote. The criminal law treats the murder of a homeless person as a matter just as serious as the murder of a corporate executive. Punishments may be moderated according to extenuating circumstances or motivations, but not according to the victim's economic worth. Historically, this was not always the case. The social consensus on the equal value of a human life for civic and criminal purposes is relatively recent. At this writing, even Messrs. Posner and Epstein have not proposed graduating penalties for capital crimes according to market criteria, but one awaits further developments.

Do I exaggerate? In the area of civil law, the cost-benefit philosophy of human life has already made significant inroads. The successful effort to cap damage awards for pain and suffering reverses the more social conception that your pain and my pain have the same worth, even if I earn more than you do. The 1995 "tort-reform" legislation caps pain-and-suffering awards at $250,000, and limits further awards to actual economic damage. This means that a homemaker or a retired or handicapped person collects little, no matter how extreme the negligence or how grotesque the suffering, because such people can demonstrate scant economic loss. As former Yale Law School dean, now judge, Guido Calabresi has observed, "The willingness of a poor man, confronting a tragic situation, to choose money rather than the tragically scarce resource [his health or safety], always represents an unquiet indictment of society's distribution of wealth."

Cost-benefit analysis also has a static view of benefit. As we saw in the case of OSHA standards on cotton dust and vinyl chloride, when the law denies industry the option of taking a "low road" of externalizing costs onto workers, it often propels technology onto a higher trajectory, with cumulative benefits to productivity as well as health over time. Since innovation feeds on itself and the future is not perfectly knowable, it is impossible to calculate accurately the total future benefit of mandating cleaner technology now.

Work by Nicholas Ashford and colleagues at MIT demonstrates repeated cases where environmental regulation similarly promoted new, more efficient technologies. For example, EPA's regulation prohibiting manufacture of polychlorinated biphenyls (PCBs) used in insulation beginning in 1980 led Dow Corning, Westinghouse, and GE to introduce new capacitor designs. OSHA's limits on industrial lead stimulated the battery industry to accelerate development of new technologies. The day the EPA ban on ozone-depleting fluorocarbons went into effect, American Cyanamid introduced a new pump spray cheaper to produce and more efficient than aerosol cans. The cost of attaining standards to control emission of nitrous oxides turned out to be overstated by a factor of at least two, and as much as five.

In health-and-safety regulation, the undercounting of benefits relative to costs is also reflected in the usual methodology of weighing costs against discounted future earnings. By deflating future earnings into current dollars, cost-benefit analysis devalues the benefit of saving workers from injury and disease over an entire lifetime. During the 1980s, OMB used a relatively high discount rate of 10 percent. This means that a regulation that would produce a million dollars' worth of benefits in fifty years is discounted to a value of less than ten thousand dollars today. Costs, however, are incurred in current dollars. So benefits are systematically discounted against costs.

The attempt to assess cost-benefit ratios by divining willingness to pay is

not much better, since countless game theory studies and psychological experiments have demonstrated that willingness to risk life and limb varies widely according to context, and, as Richard Thaler observes, valuations "are commonly
constructed in the process of elicitation." This is not the result of "mispercep-
tions" that could be corrected by training people to be better rational economic
actors.

It is impossible to divorce valuation preferences from values. In the context
of hiring a hit man to carry out a contract killing, the market value of a life is
under ten thousand dollars. In the context of the gray market in private adoptions
of healthy white infants, it is above twenty-five thousand. Ask people what they
would pay to avoid losing their own lives and the amount varies immensely.
Government agencies, going through cost-benefit exercises, have placed the
value of saving a life via regulation at anything from about a hundred thousand
to over ten million dollars. As Professor Thomas McGarrity has observed, economic theorists impute rationality and adequate information to ordinary individuals, but when presented with evidence that ordinary people are neither
consistent nor technically precise in their actual assessment of risks, the same
experts then shift ground and disparage the perceptions of ordinary people as uninformed. Kenneth Arrow once wrote, "We have the curious situation that scientific analysis imputes scientific behavior to its subjects. This need not be a
contradiction, but it does seem to lead to an infinite regress."

The point is not that government agencies should ignore cost when assessing the economic feasibility of compliance with a standard. Obviously, they
should take cost into account. The point, rather, is that the usual methodology of
cost-benefit analysis is flawed. It should be used as one tool among many, not the
definitive criterion. It makes sense to ban some health and safety hazards outright. By succumbing to cost-benefit analysis, we can easily forget that one legitimate business of public policy is to set collective goals. Some goals properly set
thresholds of acceptable safety; below the threshold, there are no permissible
economic trade-offs. Once a goal is set—no cancer-causing chemicals in human
food, cars that can withstand crashes of thirty miles an hour, no further environmental degradation of clean air, etc.—then it makes sense to pursue the most
cost-effective way of achieving the goal. But cost-effectiveness—the cheapest
way to a specified goal—is a very different concept from allowing cost-benefit
criteria to dictate the goals in the first place. Used as the definitive test, cost-
benefit analysis takes values that ethical norms or legal mandates have placed
beyond economic calculus and puts them back on the auction block.

DOES REGULATION ALWAYS BACKFIRE?

In theory, if markets are already optimizing outcomes, regulation can only make things worse. Conversely, if regulation can sometimes make things better, then markets must not always be optimizing—and the entire laissez-faire paradigm (not to mention the life's work of Chicago-style economists) is called into question. Grasp this logic and you will understand why this brand of economist invariably "proves" that regulation always backfires, and so fiercely resists contradictory evidence. Note also the asymmetry in the debate and the extremism of the Chicagoans. Advocates of a mixed economy do not insist that regulation always improves on markets—only that it sometimes improves on some markets, and that one must get down to cases. But the Chicago view holds that regulation is never warranted. Even the "mainstream" neoclassical school often takes the Chicago view as a presumption and suspects that imperfect regulation will prove even more distorting than imperfect markets.

Auto Safety. Professor Sam Peltzman's work on auto safety is a wonderful illustration. The Motor Vehicle Safety Act of 1966 required all new cars to be equipped with certain safety features, such as lap belts, padded dashboards, energy-absorbing steering columns, whiplash-resistant headrests, and antipenetration windshields. Safety engineers calculated that these requirements reduced the likelihood of death or serious injury by 15 to 35 percent. The actual trajectory of auto injuries and deaths since 1966 seems to have borne this out. But Peltzman wrote an influential article in 1975 contending that the act, remarkably, had actually caused more traffic deaths.

According to Peltzman, deaths of pedestrians, motorcyclists, and bicyclists increased, presumably because drivers aware of lower risks to themselves were driving faster and less carefully. Peltzman defended this conclusion with an elaborate set of regression equations relating auto death rates to such variables as alcohol consumption, per-capita income, driving by youths, etc. Based on these variables, he projected an anticipated fatality rate, which he compared with the actual rate. Of course, if Peltzman had found that regulation actually improved outcomes, that would really have been news. But these Chicago models almost never do. One can be forgiven for suspecting that the modeler keeps tinkering until they yield the desired result.

Other analysts, who varied Peltzman's specifications only slightly, came up with opposite results. Peltzman doesn't deny that the actual rate of highway fatality has declined, and declined more rapidly than it did prior to enactment of safety regulation. He merely speculates that it would have declined even more without safety regulation. Much of Peltzman's rationale is based on the dubious claim that rising living standards—in good Chicago fashion, he dubs this a "secular increase in the value of human capital"—should have led people to value their lives more and hence to drive more safely. Of course, nobody who drives carelessly expects to be killed; and the loss of economic utility from death is infinite and thus unquantifiable. Moreover, in the years after 1973, living standards for most Americans declined. By Peltzman's logic, this should have led them to drive more recklessly (*ceteris paribus*, of course). But, oddly enough, the downward trend in auto fatalities continued.

As a good Chicagoan, Peltzman rules out the possibility of social learning. However, one of the byproducts of health-and-safety regulation is a great deal more awareness by manufacturers and consumers of safety issues. The very act of fastening a seat belt subtly reminds the driver of the possibility of an accident. Over time, seat-belt use has steadily increased, from next to nothing a generation ago, to 65 percent in 1994. Manufacturers have heavily featured safety in their ads, which also reinforces consumer consciousness of the issue. In fact, traffic accidents and fatalities have continued to decline dramatically in the past twenty years, from 3.5 fatalities per hundred million vehicle miles in 1974, to 2.1 in 1990.

Fuel Efficiency. Another staple in the attack on auto regulation is the claim that pollution-control requirements have increased auto injuries and deaths. Robert Crandall and John Graham argue that government-mandated fuel economy has increased highway deaths "by several thousand additional fatalities over the life of each model-year's cars." The villain of the piece, for Crandall and Graham, is the 1975 Energy Policy Conservation Act, which mandated fuel-efficiency requirements known as Corporate Average Fuel Economy (CAFE) standards. By the 1985 model year, all auto producers had to have a fleet average of at least 27.5 miles per gallon (implementation was delayed until 1988). This was command regulation, *par excellence*. Crandall and Graham argue that CAFE caused automakers to reduce vehicle weight and therefore vehicle safety. Using a very sophisticated model, they calculated that CAFE has caused an 18-percent reduction in predicted weight, which in turn was responsible for a 27-percent increase in occupant fatality risk. Like Peltzman, they admit, rather sheepishly, that the actual number of auto deaths has continued to decline, but speculate that "the decline in car occupant fatalities from 1980 to 1985 might have been more dramatic had CAFE not been in effect."

Though their regression equations are highly complex, their method is crude and misleading in one telling respect. They use weight as a proxy for safety, relying on a 1984 study by Leonard Evans of General Motors, which statistically correlates "car mass" with the likelihood of occupant fatality. What

Crandall and Graham fail to consider, however, is the possibility that the safety regulation so despised by Peltzman might have combined with the CAFE regulations that they abhor to produce cars that were *both more fuel-efficient and safer.* (This would require conceding benefits from two separate kinds of regulation working in tandem.) In fact, as data from the National Highway Traffic Safety Administration (NHTSA) suggest, automakers have learned how to produce lighter, safer cars. Contrary to Crandall and Graham, the plain fact is that since 1974 fuel economy has increased by 100 percent, and fatalities have declined by 40 percent.

By manipulating equations and focusing on aggregates rather than studying the actual industry, Crandall and Graham simply miss the real story. As technology evolved, prodded by regulation, less efficient and less safe cars were replaced by safer, more efficient ones. Fuel efficiency no longer correlates neatly with fragile construction. In the 1980s, many flimsy cars were replaced by more solid cars that were also more efficient to run. For example, the VW Rabbit replaced the extremely dangerous VW Beetle. The Rabbit was the lighter vehicle, but it combined a 25-percent improvement in gas mileage with a 44-percent drop in fatality rate. The lighter, more efficient, and safer Escort replaced the heavier, more dangerous Pinto. The safer, more efficient General Motors J-cars replaced the tinny Chevette. The original, tiny Honda Civics introduced in the mid-1970s were replaced by larger, lighter, safer, and more fuel-efficient Civics in the 1980s. In every case, fatality rates went down.

The simplistic equation of weight with safety, followed by algebraic manipulation of statistics, is a characteristic economic method that misses the rich institutional detail of what has actually occurred. In several books and articles by Crandall, there is a total of one page that goes into (superficial) detail about the actual evolution of auto technology. There is little discussion of the trajectory of technical innovation in the industry. Had Crandall and Graham pursued that approach, they would have found that the first generation of subcompacts was indeed light, fuel-efficient, and hazardous. But over time, both imports and domestic cars have become roomier yet lighter, less dense yet more crash-resistant, and more economical to run yet safer. The CAFE requirements coupled with safety standards induced automakers to design in both safety and fuel efficiency, as they spent eighty billion dollars engineering a whole generation of more advanced cars.

In 1974, the average new-car weight was 3,938 pounds, the average fuel efficiency was fourteen miles per gallon, pollution was almost unlimited, and fatality rates were double their present rate. In 1990, fuel efficiency had exactly doubled, hydrocarbon emissions had been reduced by over 90 percent, fatalities were halved—and the average car weight was down to 3,178 pounds.

The Crandall-Graham approach illustrates still another instructive fallacy in the usual econometric technique. It assumes that the economic method can reliably isolate variables, holding other things equal. That makes formal algebraic sense, but not historical or dynamic sense. The use of regression equations can disentangle separate variables only to a degree, because we can't rerun history. The conclusions are therefore misleading. Federal standards requiring cars that were both safer and more fuel-efficient stimulated a cumulative process of social and technical learning. It may seem possible algebraically to simulate what "would have" occurred if one of these requirements—fuel efficiency—had not been in effect. But this exercise is illusory, since the regulation itself stimulated technical breakthroughs that allowed automakers to devise materials and designs that combined lighter weight and greater safety. And, absent CAFE standards, we don't know if those breakthroughs would have occurred. Cars might well have remained heavier and more dangerous.

Crandall, to his credit, rejects Peltzman's analysis of auto safety. Reworking Peltzman's equations, Crandall and three co-authors calculated in their 1986 book, *Regulating the Automobile*, that safety regulation had reduced auto deaths by about 30 percent. Conducting a conventional cost-benefit analysis, they pronounced auto-safety regulation cost-effective. This conclusion seemed to unnerve the authors, who speculated that other factors might be at work, such as rising damage awards by juries.

In 1995, Crandall published a new book, with Pietro Nivola, titled *The Extra Mile: Rethinking Energy Policy for Automotive Transportation*. The book repeats the canard about fuel efficiency's leading to more dangerous cars, but adds a new argument that higher gasoline taxes—a more marketlike brand of regulation—would be a far more efficient route to reduced fuel consumption and pollution than direct regulation. The advocacy of higher fuel taxes is sensible—other advanced nations have taxes averaging over two dollars a gallon—but Crandall and Nivola needlessly set up an either/or choice. Contrary to their claims, direct regulation of pollution, safety, and fuel efficiency have combined to produce cleaner, safer, and more efficient cars. If we want to deter unnecessary driving even more, and to create additional economic incentives for producers to make and consumers to buy even more efficient cars, that's fine, too.

Note once again the distributional bias in the more marketlike approach. With direct regulation of safety and fuel efficiency, everyone benefits from enhanced safety and cheaper operating costs, regardless of his or her economic means. Wealthy people remain free to buy gas-guzzlers, and to pay for the privilege. Poor people can economize by buying the cheapest, most fuel-efficient cars, but are precluded from choosing to save a few dollars by purchasing cars without seat belts, head restraints, or shatterproof glass. There is a good "marketlike" argument that, by denying the poor this spurious liberty, society saves money, since society as a whole would have to absorb the increased medical costs of increased injuries.

As I conclude this discussion, the morning paper brings news that Honda Motor Company has developed a gasoline engine that meets California's tough emission standards scheduled to take effect in 1997. The standards, which will reduce hydrocarbon and particulate emissions by over 90 percent, were bitterly criticized, by the big three U.S. automakers and by economists, as costly and unrealistic. But they are apparently feasible after all. Higher energy taxes would raise the cost of driving, and induce more fuel-efficient engines only indirectly if at all. Direct regulation evidently gets us more fuel-efficient cars and cleaner air much more expeditiously.

Poisonous Bottle Caps. One final illustration of dubious analysis of regulation is the controversy about "childproof" medicine bottle caps. In a classic article in the *American Economic Review*, "The Lulling Effect," Professor Viscusi speculated that these caps actually increased childhood poisonings by lulling parents into careless behavior. He does not demonstrate this directly but infers it statistically, citing Peltzman's earlier work suggesting a backfiring effect to seatbelt regulation. The bottle-cap regulation was issued by the FDA in 1972. Viscusi admits that the rate of childhood aspirin poisonings dropped from 2.6 per million children in 1971 to 0.6 per million by 1980, a dramatic improvement in the previous trend—but insists that this cannot be credited to the safety caps. He blandly asserts in a companion paper that "almost all accident trends have declined throughout this century as society has become richer." But it was after 1973 that this trend reversed, so one cannot credit diminished aspirin poisonings beginning in 1973 to general average wealth effects.

More ominously, Viscusi notes that the percentage of aspirin poisonings associated with safety caps rose after 1972. This, of course, is unremarkable, since the fraction of aspirin sold with safety caps rose, too. He also states that almost half of aspirin poisonings are associated with bottles that had been left open, concluding that parents must have decided it wasn't worth the trouble to close the bottle. He concludes that thirty-five hundred additional children have been poisoned annually because of the safety caps, and that "consumers have been lulled into a less safety-conscious mode of behavior by the existence of safety caps." But the plain fact remains that childhood poisonings have dramatically declined since the caps were mandated, and Viscusi offers no study of actual consumer behavior and no direct evidence for his assertions. These are rather statistical inferences from an implausible and unverified view of human behavior.

Recently, the *Journal of the American Medical Association* published a comprehensive statistical study on child-resistant packaging of prescription drugs. The study found that child-resistant packaging was associated with an annual reduction of 1.4 percent in childhood deaths from accidental ingestion of prescription drugs, or the prevention of 460 childhood deaths over two decades.

REGULATORS AND COURTS

At the heart of laissez-faire theory is the idea of rational economic actors' maximizing their utility by freely choosing among alternatives. From this core premise, theorists posit that all private choices are free of coercion, since the actor is always free to choose another course. In the purest Chicago version of the theory, the only force that interferes with this magnificent, optimizing process is the state; hence state regulation is to be resisted. The state is always coercive; the market, never.

It logically follows from this view that courts are generally preferable to regulators, since civil courts are venues of private bargaining whereas legislation and regulation are corrupted by the usual process of "rent-seeking." Left-wing legal scholars have long argued that the rules and resources of the legal system tend to reflect the inequities of capitalist society. Conservative legal theorists, in a neat inversion, respond that the common law is an efficient counterpart to the market and that its rules should emulate markets. Twenty years ago, Law and Economics theory generally held that, if regulators just left well enough alone, the body of common law would gradually evolve and become more efficient. This would occur in almost Darwinian fashion, because inefficient rules were more likely to be litigated. Over time, good, efficient decisions would naturally drive out bad, inefficient ones. Hence, the common law was superior to any system of regulatory law.

Taking no chances, the founding fathers of the Law and Economics School also set up a series of all-expenses-paid institutes and seminars for judges, to expose them to the evolving body of scholarship. These seminars, sponsored by the ultra-conservative Law and Economics program at George Mason University, were underwritten by the Olin, Scaife, Smith Richardson, Bradley, and other conservative foundations, as well as large corporations. At this writing, some six hundred judges—about half the nation's federal judges—have been through the program, which George Mason's Law School Dean Henry Manne affectionately calls "Pareto in the Pines." A 1993 report by the Alliance for Justice noted that these all-expenses-paid two-week events in resorts appeared to violate the canon of the Judicial Code of Conduct prohibiting judges from accepting gifts. Several leading Law and Economics scholars were appointed to the federal appellate courts by Presidents Reagan and Bush.

But despite the increasing influence of Law and Economics theory, courts did not respond the way theory predicted. And lately, Law and Economics theorists have directed their bitterest criticism not at regulators but at courts.

The Attack on Product Liability. A delicious case in point is the supposed crisis of product liability. During the past several decades, the courts have gradually made it easier for consumers to win damage awards, overturning the old standard of *caveat emptor*. Juries, freed from archaic doctrines that had stacked the deck in favor of corporations, began awarding generous damages to victims of corporate negligence. This trend seemed to reflect shifting public consciousness about the victims of industrial society, just as a similar wave of social conscience had appeared in the first decade of the twentieth century.

Law and Economics scholars, however, view the system of laws and courts as just another market and just another candidate for cost-benefit analysis. The tort system, they argue, should be understood not as an instrument for the exercise of rights of membership in civil society but as a system of deterring accidents and providing insurance against unforeseen hazard. Looking at the rising costs of damage awards, they observed that lawsuits were a highly inefficient way of holding manufacturers accountable for products that killed or maimed consumers, since about 50 percent of the total cost of liability to American industry goes to pay "transaction costs"—the expenses of operating the court system, and the fees captured by lawyers. Only half the cost to industry, in other words, trickles down to benefit the victims.

Defying the theory, the common law was not evolving in the direction of Chicago-style efficiency. Rather, it was shifting the costs of hazards from consumers to capitalists. So, in the 1980s, leading Law and Economics scholars rather awkwardly reversed position on the evolutionary theory of the common law, viewing courts as well as regulations as encroachments on the market, and calling for federal legislation to limit jury awards. This became the intellectual basis for the tort-reform movement that bore legislative fruit in the 1990s as state after state rolled back tort awards and standards of liability. Law and Economics scholars maintained a discreet silence on the delicate question of whether the giant corporations lobbying Congress for regulatory limits on damage awards were mere rent-seekers. A cynic might notice more than a little opportunism in this intellectual reversal.

Traditionally, American courts recognized a "privity rule," which originated in a famous 1840 English case in which the court held that a negligent supplier of a defective product was liable only to those with whom he had dealt directly. Only plaintiffs with a direct contractual relationship—"in privity"— could sue. Producers also escaped liability by writing all-purpose disclaimers, which courts permitted to serve as contracts disavowing responsibility in the event of injury or death. By buying the product, the consumer was the unknowing party to a contract denying him recourse. These doctrines began eroding as early as 1916, in a New York State Court of Appeals decision written by Judge (later U.S. Supreme Court Justice) Benjamin Cardozo allowing recovery of damages against manufacturers who were plainly negligent. But it was not until 1960 that the Supreme Court of New Jersey set a new standard of "strict liability" that was soon applied widely by other courts. In *Henningsen* v. *Bloomfield Motors*, the New Jersey court held that a woman injured by a car with a defective steering mechanism could recover damages from both dealer and manufacturer. In the years that followed, courts increasingly imposed strict liability standards on manufacturers, and juries obliged with more liberal damage awards.

In principle, when an avoidable accident implicates a faulty product, tort law tries to sort out how much of the risk the manufacturer knew or should have known, how much was unknowable, and how much was the fault of the consumer. Whether the common law errs on the side of the consumer or the manufacturer at any given time, under a given legal standard, must be an empirical question. Scholars in the Law and Economics tradition have objected that recent standards and jury awards impose excessive costs on manufacturers; and that the large cut taken by lawyers renders the tort system an inefficient mechanism of both deterrence and compensation. Defenders of a strict liability standard respond that the recent rise in liability costs is merely the correcting of a historic imbalance. Couched in these terms, the debate is pragmatic and reasonable. America is indeed a highly litigious society; generous damage awards do invite more litigation. At some point, obviously, such awards would be excessive.

Where Law and Economics scholarship borders on self-parody, however, is in its claim that product markets are so perfect that consumers ordinarily deserve little if any relief. Some of its most influential leaders, such as Yale law professor George Priest, argue that tort remedy is mostly unnecessary, since it is more "efficient" for consumers to "self-insure"—i.e., bear most of the risk of manufacturer negligence. Here is the logic: When the consumer buys a product, he is or he should be aware of possible risks. Purchasing the product at the posted price is a voluntary assumption of risk. If the consumer cared more about those risks, he would demand indemnification, or would spend more money to buy a less risky product, or seek to insure himself against the risk before he made the purchase. Priest and kindred scholars argue that there are two types of loss involved in accidents caused by hazardous products—losses to health, life, and working time (which are already covered by insurance) and intangible losses. The fact that consumers don't insure against intangible losses is taken as proof that they are assuming risks voluntarily. The fact that no such insurance exists is proof that consumers really do not care about the risks of hazardous products and that the prevailing market price is a fair one which has built in all such contingencies. Consumers evidently have a "taste" for saving money in the purchase price rather than protecting themselves from hazards. They "self-insure." This is our old friend "revealed preference."

Hence, judicial standards imposing liability on manufacturers and large damage awards by juries—not to mention consumer-product safety regulation, which is even worse—amount to gratuitous economic waste and interference with free choice. Even all-purpose manufacturers' disclaimers (of the sort deemed unenforceable today) are perfectly legitimate, since these can be understood as freely negotiated contracts between producers and consumers. Misguided judges, as Priest puts it, "have forced upon consumers an unwanted and inefficient form of insurance contract" (meaning the right to collect damages!). Though it may look to the naked eye as if producers prior to the era of strict liability merely took advantage of consumers, the reality is that consumers were getting exactly what they wanted (by definition) until meddlesome courts intervened.

The logic is so preposterous on its face that the reader who is innocent of this vein of scholarship may think I am describing only the most extreme proponents. Would that this were so. This school of legal theory has become depressingly mainstream. Its adherents include some of the most prestigious jurists at Yale, Berkeley, Harvard, UCLA, and Stanford, as well as Chicago, and are well represented among Reagan-Bush appointees to the federal appellate bench. Conservative foundations have spent millions of dollars to endow chairs to propagate this view, and law schools, bending the usual rules that appointment decisions are not influenced by benefactors, have gratefully accepted the money. Republican Senator Spencer Abraham of Michigan is a leading graduate of this school of theory, and the political crusade for "tort reform" is based on these doctrines. Even relative moderates at the law schools have felt compelled to conduct discourse in this oddly deductive idiom.

The theory, among its other flaws, misdescribes how consumers actually behave. It describes, rather, how they "should" behave were they socialized to live according to the precepts of a Chicago economics textbook. When a consumer buys anything from a lawnmower to a food processor to a can of tuna, the risk of injury or death is ordinarily far from her mind. Yet all of these products have caused injury and death because of manufacturer negligence. In the language of less extreme economic theory, the consumer is "imperfectly informed," and faces high "opportunity costs" should she choose to spend precious time becoming fully knowledgeable. In more common parlance, life is too short. No consumer could take the time to inform herself perfectly about the relative risks of everyday products, much less calculate precisely risks measured against the products' features and prices. Some of these risks are literally unknowable.

Rather, the consumer relies on the presumption that the product will perform as advertised. In economic terms, the manufacturer enjoys a degree of market power, and has passed along the risk to the consumer.

Also, the consumer may be vaguely aware that, if the lawnmower cuts her foot off or if the tuna contains botulism toxins, she can sue. This awareness, in turn, may suggest on further thought that the manufacturer likely has taken care to avoid such suits. As long as this is the case, it isn't surprising that insurance markets have not spontaneously arisen to insure consumers against unknown hazards. Indeed, if such markets were to arise at all, they should logically have come into being in the days before 1960—when legal doctrines were stacked in favor of producers, and consumers were at far greater risk. But at that time, there was neither liability insurance nor a more costly class of products for which manufacturers had agreed to indemnify consumers against injury. The absence of such insurance hardly proves that consumers knowingly incurred a risk and that manufacturers should therefore be held harmless against the results of their own negligence.

Law and Economics theorists point out that insurance markets against such risks do exist, but it is the manufacturer rather than the consumer who buys the insurance—to insure against the cost of lawsuits. (It is the rising cost of such insurance that has led to the trumpeted crisis in product liability.) Many Law and Economics scholars argue that it would be more "efficient" if consumers rather than producers bought insurance, since that would eliminate most lawsuits and the attendant waste of transaction costs (lawyers and courts). They are confident that, if regulatory distortions were removed and courts went back to the ancient standard of *caveat emptor*, the market would do the rest. But this remedy runs into a second rejoinder. If consumers rather than manufacturers were stuck with insurance costs, then the entire deterrent effect of possible litigation would be removed from the manufacturer, increasing incentives to disregard safety. The ordinary economist's term for this problem is "moral hazard."

The premise at the heart of this odd body of theory is that markets work with perfect efficiency. The true preferences of consumers can be inferred from the price they are willing to pay. Any anomalies can be solved in marketlike fashion by insurance and by the freedom to contract. But a much more plausible analysis is simply that a market system, precisely because of imperfect information, asymmetries of power, and lags in deterrent mechanisms, provides ample latitude for opportunism.

Logically, Ford might have been deterred from manufacturing a car with an exploding gas tank (the Pinto) for fear of its reputation. It was not. With some diligent investment in public relations, its reputation quickly recovered. The executives at Johns Manville who knowingly exposed workers to premature death from asbestos production were long gone by the time the company was bankrupted by damage claims. Manufacturers shifted burdens of unsafe products to consumers as long as the courts let them get away with doing so. That is hardly proof that consumers desired this outcome.

As one scholarly paper by critics Steven P. Croley and Jon D. Hanson aptly titled "What Liability Crisis?" has observed, there are really two externalities at work when consumers are maimed or killed by unsafe products. First, the manufacturer, with superior market power and information (and, prior to 1960, biases in legal doctrine), externalizes the risk onto consumers generally. Second, since actual injuries are highly personalized rather than borne by consumers as a whole, consumers who don't experience injuries displace the entire economic cost onto those who do. Thus, society as a whole underinvests in safe products—another case of market failure. Consumer insurance would only spread these risks, not ameliorate them, because it would misallocate costs.

On reflection, the Law and Economics attack on the "product-liability crisis" is wonderfully ironic. In principle, the interplay of insurance and private litigation creates market-style incentives for manufacturers to invest appropriate sums in the prevention of hazards to consumers. It combines compensation for victims with deterrence aimed at manufacturers, all without the interference of rent-seeking regulators. The rational, profit-maximizing corporation invests in safety to the point where the cost of further investment would exceed the benefit derived from averting lawsuits and insurance costs. But evidently this market is not working: industry is not investing the right amount in safety, and consumers are not collecting the correct compensation. Contrary to the earlier claim that the common law was more marketlike than regulatory law, Law and Economics theorists now generally argue that the fear of lawsuits does not make corporations pay appropriate attention to safety. Corporations are paying too much in liability insurance. Middlemen are taking too much compensation. Some injured consumers are getting windfalls; others get nothing. The problem, by definition, cannot be the market, so it must be the structure of the law. Hence the crusade to rein in damage awards.

Given these startling inefficiencies of the tort system, a less extreme enthusiast of laissez-faire could reasonably conclude that regulation is a superior alternative to litigation. Although consumer-safety regulation is not free of costs, it does have the virtue of mandating standards that prevent a great deal of consumer injury and death before the fact, rather than seeking damages afterward. It also has the virtue of clarity. The authors of a prestigious volume on the product-liability crisis wrote that "the uncertainty of the tort system is its greatest vice, magnifying risks of liability while disconnecting them from unduly risky conduct." But to embrace regulatory remedies as an alternative to inefficient litigation would tear out the very heart of Law and Economics theory.

Looking at the rising costs of jury awards for unsafe products, Law and

Economics theory has run into a logical wall. The heart of the theory is the claim that markets work. But if all markets worked, consumers would be aware of knowable product risks and would buy insurance against unknowable risks rather than taking their chances with litigation. To deal with the fact that markets evidently don't work this way, Law and Economics scholars have proposed a variety of marketlike substitutes for tort remedy. Some of the most vehement critics, such as Peter Huber, have proposed mandating more disclosure of product risks. Others would create a market in "immature tort claims"—insurance companies would buy rights to collect negligence judgments, pay off consumers, and then settle with producers. This would reduce legal fees and trim exorbitant damage awards (some might say it would add even more middlemen). Still others have proposed bringing into being consumer-liability insurance. The alert reader will notice how each of these proposals immolates the theory. If markets worked, none of these interventions would be necessary. So we are no longer in the virginal world of laissez-faire; we are only debating the details of regulation.

Lately, Law and Economics theory has managed to come down on all sides of the question of whether regulation could ever be superior to the common law. Some theoreticians who are normally antistate got so incensed at the perceived excesses of common law that they became improbable converts to the cause of regulation. Professor Viscusi allows himself some guardedly kind words for regulators, and Professor Stephen Sugarman calls for abolition of the tort system and increased regulatory powers. The purest Chicago theorists, such as Richard Epstein, end up attacking both regulation and common law, as improper interferences with markets—somehow not noticing that property rights themselves are creatures of law, that law is the product of legislation, and that legislation reflects politics. Neither courts nor regulators exist in a sacred, purely market realm.

Law and Economics theory keeps bumping up against the fact that some market or other isn't working, and keeps proposing ingenious regulatory mandates that would compel the market to behave the way the theory says it should behave spontaneously. But if the market were truly self-correcting, none of these crutches would be required. The issue ceases to be whether all markets are self-regulating—they are evidently not—but only which brand of regulation is desirable. In this fashion, the logical core of Law and Economics theory implodes.

In this debate, the choice is posed as the inefficiency of bureaucratic regulation versus the inefficiency of tort remedy. Most Law and Economics theorists seek to achieve efficiency by doing away with regulation and making courts work more like markets, via disclosure, contract, and insurance schemes. There are, however, alternatives to both the utopia of perfect markets and the caricature of leaden bureaucracies. One attractive alternative is better peer-regulation, backed by greater consumer and worker "voice," with the tort system and regulatory remedy on standby in the background.

Medical Malpractice. A good case in point is medical malpractice. Malpractice damage awards have been criticized, as adding to health-care inflation, leading to costly "defensive medicine," and even driving doctors out of the profession. Of course, if malpractice suits were made more difficult, that would not make medical care a more efficient market; it would just shift risk and cost from doctor to patient. This crisis is also exaggerated—the actual costs are about three billion dollars annually, three-tenths of one percent of the national health bill. Even so, three billion dollars is not a trivial sum, and the money would be better spent on patient care.

Malpractice suits exist because there is a great deal of medical negligence. The most careful study to date, in *The New England Journal of Medicine*, found an avoidable-injury rate in 3.7 percent of hospitalizations, and an "iatrogenic" (doctor-caused) death rate of half of one percent. That means about eighty thousand patients die in hospitals because of preventable mishaps. This occurs in part because doctors are notoriously lax about reporting each other's mistakes, and hospitals are reluctant to discipline doctors. A 1986 law, the National Health Care Quality Improvement Act, protects medical staff against retaliation if they report cases of medical incompetence, and sets up a national data bank on doctors who have been disciplined. But in 1994 only one hospital in four reported even a single case of disciplinary action against doctors. The pattern of disciplinary actions by state medical-licensing boards also varies widely, from a high of about 1 percent of doctors disciplined in states with tough medical boards, to less than one-tenth of that rate in lax states. In 1994, there were just 2,675 such disciplinary actions nationally, measured against an estimated eighty thousand wrongful deaths. So, despite escalating malpractice awards, tighter self-regulation is coming only slowly.

Tougher peer-supervision is one intelligent remedy. The more consumer-oriented health-maintenance organizations do an excellent job of monitoring doctors' prescription practices and use a team approach to risk prevention. In the Boston area, the rising cost of malpractice insurance led the teaching hospitals associated with Harvard University to create a nonprofit Harvard Risk Management Foundation. The corporation provides malpractice insurance at lower cost than commercial insurers, but, more important, it explores patterns of sloppy clinical practice and seeks to educate practitioners in risk prevention. For example, anesthesiologists had faced escalating lawsuits for wrongful patient death. The job of the anesthesiologist is not just to anesthetize the surgical patient, but to make sure all the patient's vital signs are in good order. While the surgeon performs the operation, the anesthesiologist keeps the patient alive. If a patient dies on the operating table, the anesthesiologist is usually sued. With the cooperation of the anesthesiologists' professional society, the teaching hospitals instituted a concerted program mandating operating-room procedures and standards for anesthesiologists. After the program was adopted, losses from wrong-ful injury or deaths declined by more than 50 percent. If malpractice awards had been capped, the economic signal would have been weaker. Absent the new clinical discipline, patients would have continued to suffer injury and death.

Here is a case where the combination of a consumer law encouraging tougher disciplinary action coupled with a tort system instilling a fear of lawsuits led to appropriate remedial action, based on an appeal to professionalism—three different extra-market incentives working in tandem! The hospitals were re-sponding to an economic signal—rising malpractice-insurance costs—but their response cannot be understood as a "market" without denuding that term of use-ful meaning. Would that more doctors and medical societies poured resources and creative effort into this sort of preventive remedy rather than spending their effort lobbying Congress to water down tort law.

One scathing critique of American medical-malpractice costs laboriously compared U.S. statistics with the far lower rate of lawsuits, malpractice awards, and insurance costs in Europe, lamenting America's costly litigiousness. At the very end of the article, the author noted as an afterthought that "England, France, Germany, and Japan all operate under systems of socialized medicine. . . ." Law and Economics theorists seem oblivious to the possibility that social standards offer a whole systemic alternative to litigation, perhaps a more efficient as well as more equitable one. Reining in litigation is one "solution" to the inefficiency of tort claims, but a solution that imposes disproportionate social cost on con-sumers rather than producers.

Litigation and Innovation. Another staple in the Law and Economics attack on product liability suits is the claim that escalating liability costs discour-age innovation. Here, the theory is that manufacturers, fearful of lawsuits against unknowable hazards, become increasingly reluctant to put new products and processes on the market. The high theorists reach this conclusion via the usual deductive method, just as they once deduced that the common law had to be-come more efficient over time. But empirical research based on surveys and capital-investment data suggests that fear of lawsuits has two opposite incentive effects. Some manufacturers in some industries redouble innovative efforts, to replace more dangerous products with less dangerous ones. Others narrow their innovative efforts to products with lower risks. Discouragement of innovation seems to be concentrated to a relatively few industries.

Advocates of tort reform are particularly indignant that an industry subject to consumer regulation can be subject to litigation as well, if the regulator failed to detect a hazardous product. This is seemingly a kind of double jeopardy. In the crusade for tort reform, industry fought hard to change federal law so that certifi-cation of products by regulators would amount to a kind of all-purpose Good

Housekeeping Seal. This view overlooks the fact that the regulatory process, unfortunately, is itself politicized. Enforcement standards vary according to the political sympathies and ideologies of administrations, and even the most intrusive regulatory regime is not capable of policing every possible hazard.

Some of the most devastating safety and health hazards were not caught by regulators, in part because manufacturers covered up what they knew. The exploding Ford Pinto gas tank and the Dalkon Shield intrauterine device, which rendered many of its users permanently infertile, slipped through the regulatory net, because conservative administrations had weakened enforcement. It turned out, in both cases, that manufacturers had known of the risks but had marketed these products anyway. These facts came to light only through litigation.

At the same time, it is certainly fair to argue that some limit on damage awards is reasonable. Having the world's most litigious society serves the goals of neither efficiency nor justice. But one reaches this conclusion not by a simple invocation of laissez-faire. On the contrary, a great deal of death and injury can be prevented by regulation and by social invention—both of which are often better correctives to market failure than recourse by victims to the courts—or simple *caveat emptor*.

One must conclude, finally, that systems of regulation, litigation, changing public values, professional self-policing, and social bargaining interact with each other in indeterminate ways. All influence the complex relationship between consumer safety and economic efficiency. As abstractions, many policy questions in this realm have no neat theoretical answers. One must get down to cases. There are good and bad systems of regulation, as well as good and bad standards of litigation. Some forms of regulation and of litigation evidently induce constructive innovation, reducing hazards and increasing economic efficiency. Other forms incur excess costs, and deter innovative remedy. The best blend of litigation, regulation, and social bargaining will vary according to the particulars of diverse industries. And regulation, like rules of common law, is subject to evolution, social learning—and politics. Though the *a priori* Law and Economics theories offer a satisfying certitude, they are no substitute for the grubby business of exploring the real world.

If we review this debate, it is clear that the search by Law and Economics theorists for the laissez-faire grail of a market unpolluted by politics is a doomed quest. In a democracy, the chain of causality leads inexorably back from law to politics to public opinion. In a democracy voters often choose to complement their consumer roles with a civic role. The common law is anchored in a set of ground rules just as surely as is statute law; each is the creature of prior legislation, which itself reflects norms, values, and political choices. The effort to differentiate regulatory law (inefficient rent-seeking) from the common law (efficient evolution) proved sterile, and ludicrously so. If I may indulge one gloat, there is sublime justice in the fact that the celebration of the efficient and marketlike common law backfired in a litigation explosion.

INCENTIVE REGULATION: THE CASE OF CLEAN AIR

The foregoing discussion impeaches the credibility of the market utopians. It is not meant to suggest there is no place for market incentives in regulatory policy. We saw in chapter 7 that pro-competitive regulation can serve some economic goals. Such regulation can also serve social goals, though it is not invariably superior, or always appropriate. A nice case in point is clean-air regulation.

In the past quarter-century, environmentalists lost one major argument with free-market economists, and won another. The argument they lost had to do with the alleged scarcity of raw materials. Many environmentalists made the error of projecting forward the rising cost of energy, in a straight line. If oil had quadrupled from three dollars a barrel to twelve in 1973, and then trebled again to thirty-six dollars in 1979, it would surely be a hundred dollars a barrel by century's end. At this writing, oil fluctuates narrowly between seventeen and twenty-two dollars a barrel. Natural gas is so cheap that some utilities are paying producers of alternative energy sources, such as wind power, *not* to supply them with electricity contracted for a decade ago. Many latter-day Malthusians forecast sharply rising prices of basic raw materials. In a famous wager, economist Julian Simon offered environmentalist Paul Ehrlich a bet in 1980 that the price of a basket of raw materials would be lower in 1990. Simon won.

The environmentalists had overlooked the law of substitution. Most commodities and products have close substitutes. When a given product becomes ridiculously expensive, the market tends to purchase substitutes, or invent them. With the rise of the information economy, one of the most important products combines silicon—sand—which is almost free, with knowledge, which is infinite.

This is not to say, of course, that society is using all of the earth's resources wisely, or pricing them appropriately. Some of the planet's most plentiful resources, such as water, are suddenly in scarce supply in major regions of the globe, because of overirrigation, overcultivation, and pollution. The price of oil may not be too cheap relative to the world's total energy reserves, but it may be far too cheap in terms of the hidden damage wrought by burning hydrocarbons. Here again, a price that is correct for one purpose may be wrong when measured by other criteria—another profound limitation of the market mechanism.

The debate that the environmentalists won unambiguously had to do with the waste products of an industrial society. Even if the resource scare was at best premature, the pollution scare was all too real. Without the new wave of regulation that began in the 1970s, the air and water would have gotten progressively dirtier, toxic waste would have flowed with impunity, and worker injuries and damage to the public health would have continued to escalate. Some of the planetary effects, such as global warming, acid rain, and progressive deforestation, bordered on the irreversible. These were problems that market forces simply couldn't solve. Government, with all of its own imperfections, had to intervene.

Around the time of the twenty-fifth anniversary of the first Earth Day, in April 1995, there was a wave of books and articles celebrating good environmental news—the air and water were cleaner, technologies were more energy-efficient, resources were plentiful, forests were coming back, endangered species were recovering. These happy outcomes, newly fragile thanks to a resurgent conservative Congress, were hardly the work of an invisible hand; they were triumphs of political mobilization, changed public consciousness—and regulation.

The first wave of regulation, in the 1970s, started with health criteria and attempted to reduce pollution at its source, by requiring industry to use the "best available technology" to achieve compliance with standards for air quality, water quality, control of toxic substances, and so on. There was a deliberate strategy of "technology forcing." For example, the 1970 Clean Air Act mandated a 90-percent reduction in hydrocarbon and carbon-dioxide pollutants from automobiles by the 1975 model year, even though the technology to meet those standards did not yet exist. (The standards had to be postponed, but in the 1980s cars met and exceeded them, thanks to the technology that had been induced by the regulation. Today, auto-emission control is a seven-billion-dollar industry.)

This approach was relentlessly criticized by opponents of regulation, and by free-market economists, for mandating standards with insufficient regard to cost, and for using systems of "command and control" rather than incentives to induce compliance. The term is loaded, and misleading; its origin is military, and it suggests rigid hierarchy. The fact is that any system of laws relies on commands. Thou shalt not run a red light, or cheat the IRS, or rob a bank. Thou shalt honor property rights in a variety of highly specified ways. The issue is not whether these are "commands," but whether the goals of public policies are sensible and attainable, and whether their means are appropriate to the specified goals.

The economists contrasted bad "command-and-control" regulation with good "incentive" regulation. After several false starts and very limited uses of marketlike regulation, the approach got a full field test with the enactment of the acid-rain program, part of the 1990 amendments to the Clean Air Act. These amendments included the first large-scale program to carry out tradable emission rights, in this case to reduce emissions that cause acid rain. At this writing, the approach seems a genuine success: the use of marketlike incentives to carry out a regulatory goal.

The original Clean Air Act of 1970 required the new Environmental Protection Agency to reduce pollution in two basic ways. EPA sets "ambient" standards, for maximum allowable concentrations of selected pollutants in the air. These include sulfur dioxide, carbon monoxide, nitrogen dioxides, lead, hydrocarbons, and so on. EPA also regulates emissions of pollutants at their source. The country is divided into 247 air-quality regions, and the states, through State Implementation Plans, seek to meet EPA's standards through permits which limit allowable emissions. The air-quality regions are considered "attainment areas" or "nonattainment areas," depending on whether they are in compliance with ambient standards. Nonattainment areas are typically subject to more stringent regulation at the pollution source. All of this is the sort of thing that free-market economists deride as command and control. It requires bureaucrats to make judgments about tolerable pollution levels, chemical by chemical. It mandates limits, and plans for reductions. It deliberately embraces standards aimed at "technology forcing," and is seemingly oblivious, or at least insensitive, to cost.

The principal sources of air pollution are autos, electric utilities, and, to a lesser extent, factories and incinerators. In the early years of air-quality regulation, several problems became apparent. States had neither the information nor the resources to collect data on all sources of pollution. Some emission standards specified in EPA's initial goals turned out to be technically infeasible or prohibitively expensive. Over time, most states came into compliance on most standards, but other problems emerged. At the outset, the designers of the 1970 Clean Air Act made a decision to require higher standards for new generations of production technology. This seemingly made sense. Cleaning the air at acceptable cost was a long-term endeavor. Eventually, old sources of pollution would be phased out. It seemed far more cost-effective to require that new factories and power plants design in cleaner technologies than to expensively "retrofit" old plants. Thus, the most stringent emission requirements were applied to new pollution sources.

This approach, however, partly backfired. It turned out that many power plants and other factories had much longer lives than projected, especially with repair and renovation. In 1990, over two-thirds of the power-plant emissions responsible for acid rain were coming from plants at least twenty years old. The imposition of more stringent pollution-control requirements on new facilities increased the marginal cost of building a new plant. So the more costly emissions standards required of new sources perversely discouraged adoption of newer technology. A second problem was that the cheapest approach to meeting standards for ambient air quality—tall smokestacks—merely exported the problem. In the first generation of air-quality regulation, tall stacks seemed the ideal solution. Spewing pollutants high into the atmosphere resulted in a cleaner local environment and allowed states to comply with ambient standards sooner.

Unfortunately, what went up came down elsewhere. The sulfur dioxide and nitrous oxides from factories and public utilities in the Midwest, many of which burned cheap, dirty, high-sulfur coal, fell to earth in the form of acid rain hundreds of miles away in New England and Canada. Acid rain killed fish, denuded forests, ruined crops.

The acid-rain problem had been well documented since the 1960s, but Congress remained deadlocked for nearly two decades on how to control it. The dilemma was how to share costs. The biggest culprit was dirty coal, plentiful in Appalachia and widely used by electric companies in the American heartland. The Midwest was responsible for a disproportionate share of acid-rain deposits, but controlling those emissions directly would not only raise local electricity costs; it would also shut down many of the high-sulfur coal mines of West Virginia, Pennsylvania, and Kentucky, costing tens of thousands of jobs. The Southern and Western states, the latter having much cleaner coal available for export, were unwilling to bear the cost of the Midwest's cleanup. The Midwest was unwilling to incur higher costs for electricity, which would produce regional competitive disadvantage. So deadlock continued.

In the meantime, the economists continued to refine their case for incentive regulation—in this case, emissions trading. Though allowing sales of the "right to pollute" at first struck many environmentalists as a way to sanction pollution and degrade parts of the country that were still clean, the economists aptly pointed out that a perfectly pristine environment was beyond the realm of possibility. That being so, the public-policy challenge was how to achieve the most pollution control for the least cost—whatever public policy deemed that pollution control to be. A system that created and then allowed trading in permits to pollute, though odious at first blush, had several virtues.

Before the creation of marketable emission rights, a utility that emitted sulfur dioxide beyond the permissible limit had four basic options. It could shift to lower-polluting fuel; it could add antipollution technology, usually flue-gas desulfurization devices known as "scrubbers"; it could construct a new, more modern facility; or it could rely on conservation to reduce output and hence pollution. A more efficient utility, whose total emissions were already below the allowable cap, had no particular reason to lower them still further, even though this might be technically feasible and cheap.

With the addition of tradable emission rights, the dirty utility had a fifth option. It could buy the right to pollute, on the open market. Meanwhile, the clean utility had a new opportunity to profit. It could reduce its emissions even further—and have more permits to sell. The virtue of this approach was that it allowed decentralized market forces to seek out the "least-cost" way of reducing pollution in the system as a whole. If it turned out to be cheaper for an electric power company in Ohio to shift from coal to natural gas in order to come into compliance with emission limits, the executives of that utility would pursue that course. But if it turned out that the same amount of pollution could be reduced even more cheaply by a more modern utility in, say, Colorado, then it would be more cost-effective for the Ohio utility to buy surplus emission rights from the Colorado utility. The same amount of acid-rain pollution would be reduced, but at less cost.

Mandating a Market. The emissions-trading approach offered an elegant improvement over conventional regulation. As Nancy Kete, an EPA official, has observed, "Under an emissions trading scheme, sources get credit for going beyond the minimal control that would otherwise be specified. While conventional regulation is designed to force a firm to internalize its social *costs* [italics added] . . . emissions trading schemes are designed to internalize social *goals* in firms' production decisions."

In the fifteen years prior to enactment of the 1990 amendments, EPA had experimented with marketlike regulation in several realms. Beginning in 1974, EPA allowed firms to treat their total emissions as a "bubble." Reductions of pollution within one facility below the level required by law could be credited to other company facilities. In addition, firms that wanted to build new facilities in regions out of compliance with air-quality goals could offset new emissions by reducing old pollution sources. Within limits, firms could also trade these credits to other firms. Industry made only very limited use of this approach. The market for emission rights was fairly shallow and informal, and few companies used it. Moreover, there was no national market, because different states had different standards.

Critics aptly pointed out that many states began with unrealistically high baseline calculations of emissions of pollution. For many utilities, allowable rates exceeded actual rates. Thus, a utility might receive tradable credits for purely paper "reductions." This in turn undermined the trading market, since the apparent property right in a marketable credit was only as reliable as this year's allowable emission levels. As regulators became more sophisticated about measurement, and baseline levels of acceptable emission were lowered, the tradable credit would evaporate. Economists, however, continued to tout this approach. Marketable pollution rights were also used, in a limited way, in clean-water regulation, and in the phaseout of leaded gasoline and of chlorofluorocarbons (CFCs), which cause depletion of the ozone layer.

With the acid-rain amendments of 1990, the application of market principles to environmental protection got its first full-scale adoption. To review how this came about is to appreciate how essential the policymaking process is to the development of such regulatory hybrids. Before the acid-rain policy could be implemented, a great deal of political jockeying was necessary, since divergent interests needed to be accommodated. There was no intuitive right answer to the question of how much of the burden each region should bear, since their pre-existing cost structures were the result of historic accidents (plentiful, clean coal deposits in the West, dirty coal in the East and Midwest) coupled with the prior willingness of public policy to let pollution costs be treated as free to the polluter. Policy was suddenly changing the rules, and there was no "one-best" way to allocate the costs, save through political bargaining.

Fortuitously, political forces happened to be in a propitious alignment. By 1990, environmentalists and economists, who had been wary adversaries a decade before, had managed to find some common ground. Most mainstream environmental groups, initially put off by sales of the right to pollute, had warmed to the idea of marketable permits—if they were locked into a stable regulatory structure guaranteed to reduce overall emissions over time. All but the most doctrinaire of economists recognized that such a market required significant prior regulation. Canada was usefully applying diplomatic pressure. Scientific evidence of the cost of doing nothing was mounting. EPA staff had done a good deal of the preliminary technical work. And in the White House George Bush, a moderate conservative who had run on a pro-environment platform, had appointed as EPA administrator a relative liberal in William Reilly. The more conservative Reagan administration had sought simply to weaken the Clean Air Act. But the philosophy of marketlike regulation suited the Bush administration nicely—it was both pro-environment and pro-market—and the Bush White House became its champion.

Beyond the political challenge was a policy challenge. Pre-1990 experiments with tradable pollution credits had shown that a robust market would not emerge spontaneously, because of uncertainties and transaction costs. Before a large-scale market in tradable permits could be constructed, policymakers had to answer several complex technical questions. What was an achievable national goal for the reduction of acid-rain deposits? Should there be limitations on emission rates relative to output, or a total limit on allowable tons of pollutant? What timetable? How should the market in permits be structured? How would the initial stock of permits be distributed? Who would monitor plants to make sure they were not exceeding allowable emissions? Which pollutants would be covered? And so on.

Though marketlike, the resulting system was no free market. Indeed, conservative critics objected precisely on these grounds. "[T]radable permits do not represent a truly free market approach to reducing acid rain," lamented Terry Anderson and Donald Leal in a Coasean critique titled *Free Market Environmentalism*. "A government agency still must determine the level of permits, and the permits do not force polluters to compensate those harmed by pollution. In this system, the political process determines the initial or optimal pollution levels, not the polluters bargaining with those who bear the cost of the pollution." Exactly.

But imagine what it would take, à la Coase, for polluters to compensate those harmed by acid rain. How is a camper in Acadia National Park encountering a denuded campsite, or a logger in Canada, or a fisherman in upstate New York, to know which of the many thousand polluters should be asked to pay what share of the damage? How should they seek redress? How is the damage to be priced? What institutional bargaining process could conceivably produce equitable results at reasonable costs? The entire premise is preposterous on its face. Imagine, too, the conservative outcry if millions of people harmed by acid rain tried to mount a massive class-action suit against thousands of diverse polluters. We would hear the usual gripe about litigious excess. The collective-action problem facing the approach of Coasean case-by-case redress is insurmountable. The likely result would be continued polluting. Even from a market perspective, regulation is the far more efficient approach.

In reviewing the legislative history of the 1990 amendments, one must be impressed by the technical, political, and legislative work that went into the final design of the strategy. Eventually, after thousands of pages of testimony, the administration and Congress set a goal of a ten-million-ton reduction in the chemicals that cause acid rain, which translated into an allowable emission level of 8.9 million tons of sulfur dioxide by utilities by the year 2000. To placate Midwestern congressmen and senators, dirty plants were given extra emission allowances as incentives for early compliance.

The public-utility industry vehemently opposed the acid-rain amendments, as did most state regulators. They fought the entire approach of tradable permits. With the approach gaining support, they sought to weaken both the timetable and the allowable cap. As Nancy Kete, a careful student of the legislation, observes, "For all the public complaints about 'command and control' regulation, complying with the pre-amended Clean Air Act was essentially risk-free for electric utilities. As regulated monopolies, utilities don't face much competition, and they pay lower capital costs than other companies, and are allowed to charge their customers for necessary expenditures, prudently made." But the Bush administration's plan finally offered a viable compromise between Northeastern and Western legislators who wanted acid-rain regulation and Midwesterners who opposed it, and in the end regional politics trumped special-interest politics.

The 1990 law creates a market in emissions "allowances." Each allowance is the right to emit one ton of sulfur dioxide. The allowances were allocated to existing utilities according to a complex formula, whose result is a gradual ratcheting down of the total national amount of sulfur-dioxide emissions. Allowances are freely tradable. Under an agreement with EPA, the Chicago Board of Trade has offered an options market in them. Emissions allowances trade at about $80, and have declined with falling compliance costs.

Unlike broadcast frequencies, this market was not intended to be a money-maker for the government, and is deliberately revenue-neutral. The money paid from one utility to another stays within the utility industry. Every plant must have monitoring instruments, and report emission levels to EPA. No utility may emit pollutants in excess of the allowances that it holds. The EPA's computerized system keeps track both of emission levels, plant by plant, and of holdings of allowances. A small number of allowances were held in reserve for new plants and for independent power producers. For the first time, this system allowed the Clean Air Act to yield significant reductions in old as well as new sources of sulfur dioxide.*

What we have here is the use of market incentives, but within a highly contrived and regulated context. While tradable permits allow greater flexibility in one sense, they depend on command and control in other respects. The national ceiling is of course the creature of regulatory policy, not the market. The monitoring of emissions requires an extensive regulatory presence. Utilities are fined two thousand dollars for each ton they emit in excess of their allowances. Deliberate violations are subject to criminal penalties. The program imposes a net cost on the industry of three to four billion dollars a year, which goes for a gradual upgrading of power-generation facilities to yield cleaner power—and cleaner air. The benefit in health, and in reduction of acid-rain losses to crops and fisheries, is far greater. EPA estimates that the tradable-permit approach is about a billion dollars a year cheaper than conventional regulation. There was no pure-market solution to this problem.

To establish this entirely artificial market, government had to invent and then guarantee a new kind of property right. The very limited success of tradable pollution rights prior to the 1990 amendments suggests a period of trial and error before public policy came up with a kind of property right that private-market actors would trust. This is not unlike the gradual evolution of other artificial property rights created by the state, such as patents, trademarks, and copyrights, which are also subject to periodic refinement as technology changes.

Note also that this approach was only one possible "marketlike" approach. One popular alternative, a pollution tax, would seemingly be simpler, but in practice would be less flexible and would not have the same benefits in inducing

---

* A separate national cap was applied to non-utility polluters, who account for only about 10 percent of acid rain–causing emissions. The 1990 act ratchets down the other principal source of acid rain, nitrogen oxides, but does so by imposing direct limits rather than tradable allowances.

relatively clean utilities to operate even cleaner, for it would offer them no reward. Nor is the tradable-permit approach a once-and-for-all government intervention that can leave the rest to the market. Government will have to decide whether the 8.9-million-ton limit can be left alone after 2000, or be ratcheted down further. Public policy will also need to decide whether reduction of nitrogen-oxide emissions, still subject to conventional regulation, should join the tradable-permit system. And there will be other course corrections. The market in sulfur-dioxide allowances is working reasonably well at this writing, but it is not without some glitches. For example, some utilities that are well within compliance limits are hoarding allowances rather than trading them. They are doing this, prudently, in case they need them in future years, when the price might be higher. This frustrates the design of a smooth trading market, reduces the current supply, and raises the price for utilities that need allowances now. The regulators may need to up the ante to discourage hoarding.

Finally, the success of incentive regulation in the case of acid rain does not mean that it is a suitable approach for every kind of environmental regulation. This works for acid rain because the problem is national, the sources of pollution are disparate and essentially fungible, and the technology for measuring emissions is relatively precise. The tradable-permits regime can involve a blend of command-and-control and incentive regulations. Other kinds of regulation necessarily require commands directly. A great many chemicals, for example, are so toxic that it makes policy sense simply to ban them rather than to rig up some kind of market in the right to use them at a very high price.

In sum, there is plenty of room for the market and marketlike regulation in achieving social goals—just as there is room for the market in a mixed economy. But incentive regulation and the price mechanism do not offer a superior approach at all times, in all cases. And incentive regulation is still regulation. Only people with a utopian view of markets should find these conclusions surprising.

In early 1996, EPA, responding to a Congressional mandate, dutifully prepared a 392-page cost benefit analysis of the 1970 Clean Air Act. The costs of compliance, EPA found, were approximately $436 billion over 20 years. The benefits, to improved health, reductions in lost work days, agricultural productivity, and reduced clean-up benefits, were between $2.3 trillion and $14 trillion. The pricing of pollution by free markets simply was not capable of this calculus.

The system in which the private market operates is inevitably structured by law and by democratic choices. Those choices can contrive a relatively efficient, or inefficient, brand of mixed economy. But the quest for a perfectly pure free market, or an economy free of political influences, is an illusion.

9 / MARKETS AND POLITICS

THE INEVITABILITY OF POLITICS

Our tour of the virtues and limits of markets necessarily takes us back to politics. Even a fervently capitalist society, it turns out, requires prior rules. Rules govern everything from basic property rights to the fair terms of engagement in complex mixed markets such as health care and telecommunications. Even the proponents of marketlike incentives—managed competition in health care, tradable emissions permits for clean air, supervised deregulation of telecommunications, compensation mandates to deter unsafe workplace practices—depend, paradoxically, on discerning, public-minded regulation to make their incentive schemes work. As new, unimagined dilemmas arise, there is no fixed constitution that governs all future cases. As new products and business strategies appear and markets evolve, so necessarily does the regime of rules.

The patterns of market failure, our tour reveals, are more pervasive than most market enthusiasts acknowledge. Generally, they are the result of the immutable structural characteristics of certain markets and the ubiquity of both positive and negative spillovers. Unfettered opportunism is more widespread in economic life than free-market theory admits. In much of the economy, sellers are not reliably held accountable by buyers. In markets where the consumer is not effectively sovereign (telecommunications, public utilities, banking, airlines, pure food and drugs), or where the reliance on market verdicts would lead to socially intolerable outcomes (health care, pollution, education, gross inequality of income, the buying of office or purchase of professions), a recourse purely to ineffectual market discipline would leave both consumer and society worse off than the alternative of a mix of market forces and regulatory interventions.

Another paradox: markets are rather stronger and more resourceful than their champions admit. The basic competitive discipline of a capitalist economy can coexist nicely with diverse extra-market forces; the market can even be rendered more efficient by them. These include both explicit regulatory interventions and the cultivation of extra-market norms, most notably trust, civility, and long-term reciprocity. As we have seen in markets as varied as banking, public utilities, and health care, entrepreneurs do not sicken and expire when faced with "contoured competition"; they simply revise their competitive strategy and go right on competing. Norms that commit society to resist short-term opportunism can make both the market and the society a healthier place. Pure markets, in contrast, commend and invite opportunism, and depress trust.

We have also seen, contrary to the theory of perfect markets, that much of economic life is not the mechanical satisfaction of exogenous preferences or the pursuit of a first-best equilibrium. On the contrary, many paths are possible—many blends of different values, many mixes of market and social, many possible distributions of income and wealth—all compatible with tolerably efficient getting and spending. The grail of a perfect market, purged of illegitimate and inefficient distortions, is a fantasy—and a dangerous one.

The marketizers make one powerful point: everything cannot be regulated. But neither can everything be deregulated. So the practical task is to determine when regulation improves efficiency, what sort of regulatory strategies to pursue, which regulations take precedence over others, and where is the point of diminishing returns. The real world displays a very broad spectrum of actual markets with diverse structural characteristics, and different degrees of separation from the textbook, libertarian ideal. Some need little regulation, some a great deal—either to make the market mechanism work efficiently or to solve problems that the market cannot fix. Someone has to make such determinations, or we end up in a world very far from even the available set of second bests.

Rules require rule-setters. In a democracy, that enterprise entails democratic politics, competent public administration, and reliable courts. The only alternative is *non*-democratic politics, whose public administration and courts are likely less competent, and certainly less accountable and legitimate.

The market solution does not moot politics. It only alters the dynamics of influence and the mix of winners and losers. By the same token, the attempt to relegate economic issues to "nonpolitical" bodies, such as the Federal Reserve, does not rise above politics either. It only removes key financial decisions from popular debate to financial elites, and lets others take the political blame. A decision to allow markets, flaws and all, free rein is just one political choice among many. *There is no escape from politics.*

QUIS CUSTODET?

The issue of how precisely to govern markets arises in libertarian, democratic nations like the United States, and deferential, authoritarian ones like Singapore. It arises whether the welfare state is large or small, and whether the polity is expansive or restrained in its aspirations. Rule-setting and the correction of market excess are necessarily public issues in social-democratic Sweden, in Christian Democratic Germany, in feudal-capitalist Japan, and in Tory Britain. The highly charged question of the proper rules undergirding a capitalist society pervaded political discourse and conflict throughout nineteenth-century America, even though the public sector then consumed less than 5 percent of the GDP.

The political process, of course, can produce good sets of rules for the market or bad ones. Thus, the quality of political life is itself a public good—perhaps the most fundamental public good. A public good, please recall, is something that markets are not capable of valuing correctly. Trust, civility, long-term commitment, and the art of consensual deliberation are the antithesis of pure markets, and the essence of effective politics.

As the economic historian Douglass North, the 1993 Nobel laureate in economics, has observed, competent public administration and governance are a source of competitive advantage for nation-states. Third-world nations and post-communist regimes are notably disadvantaged not just by the absence of functioning markets but by the weakness of legitimate states. A vacuum of legitimate state authority does not yield efficient laissez-faire; it yields mafias and militias, with whose arbitrary power would-be entrepreneurs must reckon. The marketizers advising post-Soviet Russia imagined that their challenge was to dismantle a state in order to create a market. In fact, the more difficult challenge was to constitute a state to create a market.

Norms that encourage informed civic engagement increase the likelihood of competent, responsive politics and public administration, which in turn yields a more efficient mixed economy. North writes: "The evolution of government from its medieval, Mafia-like character to that embodying modern legal institutions and instruments is a major part of the history of freedom. It is a part that tends to be obscured or ignored because of the myopic vision of many economists, who persist in modeling government as nothing more than a gigantic form of theft and income redistribution." Here, North is echoing Jefferson, who pointed out that property and liberty, as we know and value them, are not intrinsic to the state of nature but are fruits of effective government: "stable ownership is the gift of social law, and is given late in the progress of society."

The more that complex mixed markets require a blend of evolving rules, the more competent and responsive a public administration the enterprise requires. It would be nice to be able to argue that an expansive and competent state logically requires a vibrant democracy. Alas, a look around the world suggests that this is more a value preference than a logical imperative. As the social philosopher Ralf Dahrendorf has observed, it is unfortunately possible to have a strong, competent state and a relatively weak democracy. This is precisely the East Asian model of capitalism. However, it is also possible to have a relatively strong state and a strong democracy. The nations of the European Union, especially in Northern Europe, rely more heavily on the state, and also have higher levels of political participation via voting, partisan activism, and work-site representation. Strong civic institutions help constitute the state, and also serve as counterweights against excesses of both state and market.

AMBIVALENT AMERICA

The United States, historically, combined a strong democracy with a relatively weak and fragmented state. This blend is embedded into the structure of our constitution. It seemingly reflects our liberty-loving national character. The relationship between a strong democracy and a strong state is a conundrum at the absolute core of our constitutional founding. At first, libertarian Americans adopted a weak state, in the Articles of Confederation. But as Madison, Hamilton, and Jefferson successfully argued, a stronger state was necessary precisely to secure and guarantee the rights of a free people.

Nineteenth-century America was justly celebrated for its honeycombed voluntary associations, which observers like Tocqueville saw as the social basis of civic republicanism. If the common man was to be self-governing, he needed to hone those civic skills and habits in myriad "small republics"—and to beware of distant central government.

For a century, the American champions of popular sovereignty associated it with limited government. Conversely, the partisans of a stronger state were generally more skeptical of the democratic role of the common man, seeing democracy as potentially the instrument of majoritarian tyranny, and looking instead to the "best men" to lead a Republic that would combine adequate, if limited, state power with checks and balances on majoritarian impulses. Hamilton wrote in *Federalist* 70 that "energy in the [federal] executive is the leading character in the definition of good government." Strong state equaled weak democracy, and vice versa. This axis defined the Federalist/anti-Federalist debate. Both sides eventually converged on the point that an effective state was necessary to guarantee individual political rights, but continued to dispute the state's proper role in the economy.

That conventional polarity, however, began breaking down late in the nineteenth century, when progressive critics began associating the weak state of the Federalist founders with a blockage of desirable public purposes. The first fully fleshed version of this critique was Professor Woodrow Wilson's *Constitutional Government*, published in 1885.

A century after the founding of the first modern democracy, there were now emergent examples of nations whose constitutional systems combined a measure of popular rule with stronger public administration and more effective parliamentary government. The British model of the king-in-Parliament, now embodied in a Cabinet selected by a (qualified) mass electorate; the Prussian blend of a very strong state with a limited parliamentary democracy; and the French Third Republic, democratically elected but drawing on an older tradition of *étatisme*, all suggested that more than one structural model of democracy was possible. The young Wilson, then a political-science professor, was writing at a time when the American Republic was hamstrung by narrow and seesawing partisan alignments, substantial corruption, undistinguished chief executives, and frequently divided party control of Congress and the presidency. Wilson, an internationalist influenced by European commentary and envious of European institutions, argued that the U.S. Constitution should be amended to shift the American Republic in a more parliamentary direction.

This, of course, did not occur. But in Wilson's own presidency a quarter-century later, and *a fortiori*, in Franklin Roosevelt's New Deal, a stronger executive, a more professionalized public administration, and even a more "developmental" conception of the state did emerge. The constitutional obstacles to strong government, however, remained. Only at rare moments, such as the New Deal and the 89th Congress of Lyndon Johnson's Great Society, were partisan majorities in Congress large enough to constitute *de facto* parliamentary majorities and to bridge over the structural weakness of the American state.

Despite the enlargement of the administrative state in the twentieth century, Americans have continued to debate whether a strong state is the ally or enemy of a strong democracy. Most Americans, like the Founders, have remained resolute civic republicans. As James Morone has written, "At the heart of republican politics lay the subordination of individual interests to the common good, the *res publica*. The ideal was not simply the sum of individual private interests, but a distinct public interest with an objective interest of its own."

In the past quarter-century, however, free-market economists have taken this debate in a wholly new and disturbing direction. Extrapolating from the economic model of man, this new current of thought impeaches politics as well as government, because of their common, allegedly negative, effects on the efficiency of the market. The counsel of this radical view is to limit the scope of polity and state alike. So, whereas the need to govern markets seemingly leads back to politics, the fundamentalist market model offers a blanket rejoinder: politics is a hopelessly self-defeating endeavor. This view converts the case for the market into a frontal challenge to the most basic aspirations of political democracy.

THE MARKET AS ANTIDEMOCRATIC THEORY

This current of thought goes under the name of Public Choice or Rational Choice theory. These are very similar in their essential claims, and I am here terming both Public Choice. This influential vein of social science offers an astonishingly cynical view of political democracy. Public Choice functions as the stand-in for the free-market economist in debates about what can reasonably be entrusted to politics and government. In Public Choice theory, the demonized state makes an almost perfectly Manichaean mirror image of the idealized market. The sacred economy is at constant risk of being violated by a profane polity. The core claim is that systematic error and opportunism are as endemic and logically inevitable in the political enterprise as self-purification is in the marketplace. That premise then gives the Public Choice theorist an all-purpose trump to any demonstration of market failure: *Yes, the market perhaps does fail from time to time, but political interference will only make things worse.* Public Choice theorists, in their zeal to impeach economic intervention, go further and impeach democracy itself.

This set of conclusions is less demonstrated from the observation of actual political life or the concrete study of comparative political norms and institutions than it is deduced from axiom, logical inference, and the extrapolation of the market model. Logically, if economic man maximizes self-seeking behavior in the economic realm, he also pursues selfish gain in social and political life. But where markets are self-correcting, politics is self-infecting. This presumption then leads to a series of syllogisms that "prove" that politics must lead to chaotic, rapacious, or perverse outcomes. The conclusion then inevitably follows that the most prudent course is to make the political and governmental realm as narrow as possible. The next ten pages may seem somewhat arcane, but the reader should persist. For the influence of this body of work has been immense in providing self-confident theoretical underpinnings for the appalling claim that intervention in the economy is perverse because democratic life is doomed.

Modern Public Choice theory has several strands, but all are projections of the behavioral assumptions of free-market economics. The classics include Anthony Downs's 1957 book, *An Economic Theory of Democracy*, James Buchanan and Gordon Tullock's *The Calculus of Consent* (1962), and Mancur Olson's *The Logic of Collective Action* (1965). These works closely parallel the model of human motivation depicted by Friedman, Stigler, Becker, and the Chicago School of economics. A work that predates this tradition, but which is often invoked as a pillar of Public Choice theory, is Kenneth Arrow's *Social Choice and Individual Values* (1951). The Law and Economics tradition, discussed in chapter 8, closely parallels this brand of theorizing.

Whereas earlier democratic theory viewed the process of group formation and expression as a healthy and necessary avenue of representative democracy ("pluralism"), Public Choice theory sees interest groups as the collective expression of individual selfishness, invariably at the expense of the collectivity. Both economic and political life, of course, are filled with uncertainty, imperfect foresight, opportunism, and frustrated expectations. But Public Choice theory awards all the self-correcting mechanisms to the market realm, and all the self-destructive ones to the polity.

The competition of the marketplace, though less than perfect, is seen as a tolerable approximation. In contrast, the ostensible competition of the democratic polity is mostly sham, because of the power of incumbents, agenda-setters, single-purpose groups, and the ignorance of voters. In the market, consumers are imperfectly informed but it doesn't much matter, because purveyors of bad products at high prices will eventually be punished. The imperfect knowledge of voters, on the other hand, leads to interest-group domination of politics and disastrous results. The same consumer who somehow has all the information he needs to buy a car or invest in a stock is a hopeless patsy in the voting booth. The businessman whose opportunistic impulses are held in tolerable check by the threat of competition in the marketplace becomes an unleashed tyrant when he enters democratic politics, notwithstanding electoral competition.

In his *Economic Theory of Democracy*, Anthony Downs argued that the usual conception of political democracy was illusory. Citizens seldom made informed choices, because information had costs that outweighed expected benefits ("the information-seeker continues to invest resources in procuring data until the marginal return from information equals the marginal cost"). The absence of adequate information led "rational men to make systematic errors in politics." Citizens did not pursue a common good. As in economic life, they pursued self-interest. Political parties and their standard-bearers, rather than being understood as coalitions devoted to a shared public philosophy, should be seen as individuals whose principal motivation is to be elected (and re-elected) in order to extract unearned windfalls from the collectivity. It logically followed from these premises that leaders pander to the "median voter" in order to attain, and cling to, public office. But since the median voter is uninformed, and since organized groups dominate politics, the democratic ideal is substantially a sham. Downs's book was in the realm of pure theory and logical manipulation, in narrative form supplemented by algebra. It contained no empirical or historical description of the actual political process.

Complementing Downs, Buchanan and Tullock pushed further on the idea of the individual in the political arena seeking to maximize his individual benefits and shift costs to others, confronting a "calculus not unlike that which he must face in everyday economic choices." A central premise of their emerging theory was the ubiquity of "rent-seeking" in politics, whether by organized interest groups, politicians, or bureaucrats. A "rent," as noted above, is an excess profit—a presumptively illicit return that would be competed away in a perfect market. By analogy, a political "rent" is a benefit that a rational voter would not willingly confer but that a wily interest group or bureaucrat is able to extract from a naïve or disorganized electorate. (The phrase "rent-seeking," as applied to politics, was originally Professor Anne Krueger's.) Elected officials, in this view, are seen primarily as the agents of organized narrow interests. In the work of more extreme theorists such as Richard Posner, government taxation, public outlay, or income transfers are understood as nothing more than theft.

Here is an emblematic passage from James Buchanan:

> The basic notion is a very simple one and once again it represents the transference of standard price theory to politics. From price theory, we learn that profits tend to be equalized by the flow of investments among prospects. The existence or emergence of an opportunity for differentially high profits will attract investment until returns are equalized with those generally available in the economy. What should we predict, therefore, when politics creates profit opportunities or rents? Investment will be attracted towards the prospects . . . [and] that investment will take the form of attempts to secure access to the scarcity rents. When the state licenses an occupation, when it assigns import or export quotas, when it allocates TV spectra, when it adopts land-use planning, we can expect resource waste in investments to secure the favored plum. . . . As the expansion of modern governments offers more opportunities for rents, we must expect the utility-maximizing behavior of individuals will lead them to waste more resources in trying to secure "rents" or "profits" promised by government.

Consider the breathtaking assumptions in this mild-mannered prose. Buchanan, first, assumes that the perfect market of idealized price theory is a reasonable proxy for economic reality. The distortions in ordinary commerce are simply assumed away, as is the reality of more than one kind of efficiency. Buchanan's is the Smithian efficiency of the price system, under presumed conditions of perfect competition. The preregulation prices derived by markets are presumed optimal. Buchanan assumes that the state licensing of, say, doctors and engineers, or the state allocation of scarce broadcast spectra, is pure cost. He says nothing about the cost of *not* regulating necessarily imperfect markets. Note also the mechanical application to the political realm of concepts that are dubious even as economic theory. Note the imputation of pure opportunism to the civic and political enterprise. The idea that some public administrators or citizen activists might actually be pursuing a broad public good is also assumed away.

This largely mechanistic, noninstitutional and ahistoric mode of analysis is characteristic of the first generation of Public Choice theory. Kenneth Arrow's "Impossibility Theorem," from his 1951 book, is widely cited as a kind of Rosetta stone of Public Choice theory that translates politics into economics and demonstrates once and for all the futility of political efforts at social betterment. Arrow basically rendered the schoolyard game of rock-paper-scissors into complex algebra to demonstrate that group-choice outcomes are logically indeterminate. If rock crushes scissors, and scissors cuts paper, but paper covers rock, then we have no way of knowing who wins.

This commonsensical insight gave rise to a whole genre of political-science theorizing, known as "cycling," which holds that voters are logically incapable of getting what they want. By analogy, if groups in politics have multiple preferences on diverse issues, it can be demonstrated algebraically and logically that outcomes cannot be predicted in advance, and that multiple possible coalitions and outcomes are logically consistent with the same hierarchy of individual preferences. Public Choice theorists extrapolate from this unimpeachable formal syllogism to conclude that voters cannot logically get what they want out of politics, and that political outcomes are largely the result of who happens to get control of agendas and how choices are structured.

This conclusion, of course, is an empty truism unless one gets down to cases. Political history is replete with examples of voter preferences being frustrated—and other examples of majorities' getting approximately what they wanted—and still other cases of evolving public debate and education changing public opinion. The real story is in the rich historical and political detail that Public Choice theory usually leaves out.

Likewise, Mancur Olson's influential work, *The Logic of Collective Action*, is widely invoked to prove the ubiquity of "free-riding" in political life. Through the same sort of logical chain of reasoning, Olson argues that a rational individual will choose not to expend effort on legislative or civic life, since the "cost" (in information gathered and time expended) will invariably outweigh the scant individual benefit. This logically leads to an electoral politics dominated by progressively smaller, more highly focused, and more selfish groups, and to a legislative politics dominated by logrolling at the expense of the general good. It also logically dictates that most people will not get what they want out of politics: "unless the number of individuals in a group is quite small, or unless there is coercion or some other special device to make individuals act in their common interest, rational self-interested individuals will not act to achieve their common or group interests." This must come as a surprise to the myriad trade associations and other interest groups whose members collectively spend billions of dollars to influence legislation.

Law and Economics scholars use this same deduction to urge a new, radical form of judicial activism on courts: if the legislative process is not genuinely expressing the majority will, then it lacks legitimacy and courts should freely ignore ostensible legislative intent in deferring to the older common law. This logic has been repeatedly invoked by Justice Antonin Scalia, relying on Public Choice theory. The traditional rationale for judicial activism was to protect minority rights from being trampled by legislative majorities. Public Choice turns this on its head, using economic theory to license courts to overrule legislators in the name of higher economic rationality—often protecting a status quo of economic elites.

In this way, the celebration of the market has become an insidious form of contempt for political democracy. Excluded by definition are the possibility of deliberation leading to social learning, institutional refinement, and an evolving conception of the common good. Indeed, the essence of the theory is to deny that such a thing as the common good exists, except as the sum of selfish individual goods. Those who posit a collective good, or an ethic of public-mindedness, are mere "sentimentalists" pursuing an unscientific mirage.

This body of thought seemingly provides expert witness for the claim that we should minimize political intervention in the economy. Concluding a long and balanced discussion of Public Choice theory that pointed out many of its empirical weaknesses, Dennis C. Mueller wrote that "the best and simplest way to avoid the rent seeking problem is to avoid establishing the institutions that can create rents, that is the regulations and regulatory agencies that lead to rent seeking." In other words, even if the claim that politics is mainly the art of rent-seeking is tautological and unproved, better to take no chances. This is the normative conclusion (and premise) of most Public Choice pieces.

Once again, the uninitiated reader may find these descriptions of politics so extreme and tautological as to wonder why I am spending several pages describing this peculiar body of theory. Well, James Buchanan and Kenneth Arrow are both winners of the Nobel Prize in economics. Anne Krueger is president of the American Economic Association. At last count, roughly half the articles in the flagship *American Political Science Review* proceeded from a Public Choice orientation.

The proof of the banality of Public Choice is in its empirical application. When the second generation of Public Choice scholars sought to apply their theory to the actual world of politics, it fell embarrassingly flat. Their attempts at empirical application characteristically fail in two ways. Either the theory turns out to be painfully wide of the mark, or it reduces to a body of truisms that either are trivial or necessarily depart from its theoretical footings.

For example, one of the most fundamental embarrassments to Public Choice theory is the "paradox of voting." Public Choice theory logically predicts that people won't vote. By the lights of the theory, voting is plainly irrational, since the costs exceed the benefits, and the odds of your vote's actually affecting the outcome are infinitesimal. (The odds of a single voter's ballot's being decisive are roughly equivalent to the odds of being run over by a car en route to the polling place.) Unfortunately, people do vote. They brave bad weather to vote. They vote when they are certain the other guy will win. In third-world countries, they brave the risk of retaliation and assassination. What an odd way to maximize one's utility.

If people do vote because of extra-rational values, Public Choice theory still might be able to explain variations in turnout based on rational utility-maximization. But no. Affluent people, for example, value their time more highly than poor people, but typically have much higher rates of voting. Public Choice twists itself into ingenious knots to explain the paradox of voting while preserving the theory. In general, Public Choice theory preserves its explanatory power precisely to the extent that it relaxes its core assumptions.

The most parsimonious explanation for the voting paradox, of course, is that Public Choice theory misdescribes political man. Citizens don't always free-ride. They bring goals and values to politics that sometimes transcend self-seeking. They vote to express ideological preferences, beliefs about what is good for the collectivity, or to signal solidarity with democracy itself. Remarkably enough, the same is true of some elected officials, who are often larger and more public-spirited than the sum of their constituents.

In an important empirical rebuttal, the political scientists Donald Sears and colleagues at UCLA correlated individual voting behavior with a voter's own perceived economic condition and his perception of the overall economic condition of the nation. Contrary to the radical individualism that Public Choice theory projects, voters tended to reward or punish incumbent legislators based on how they perceived the *collectivity* to be doing, not how well the voter was doing personally.

In Public Choice theory, deliberation is taken to be mere logrolling, never legitimate consensus-building or problem-solving, let alone a quest for the public good. There is little respect for the dynamics of minds changed by expert testimony, argumentation, or the pleas of ordinary people. Anyone who has observed legislative hearings close up knows that some legislation is pure logrolling, and other cases reflect an iterative process of social learning and a search for common ground. One gets the sense that Public Choice scholars neither like nor appreciate politics.

It is in the area of empirical application and concrete prediction that the theory has suffered its greatest setbacks. In the 1970s and 1980s, many Public Choice theorists began describing the seemingly irresistible growth of public spending and inflation as beautiful illustrations of the sublime explanatory power of their theory. As individuals, voters might want stable prices and balanced budgets, but because of the failure of politics to translate their true individual preferences accurately into policy (Arrow's Impossibility Theorem), the ubiquity of Olson's free-riders, and the universal rent-seeking by Buchanan's selfish interest groups, voters were denied what they really desired. Thus, a welter of Public Choice works "proved" how the ineluctable growth of the welfare state, the inflation of the late 1970s, and the budget crisis of the 1980s all resulted from Public Choice dynamics in politics, and all harmed the economy.

Unfortunately for the theory, each of these supposedly chronic maladies has reversed itself, despite politics—or, more accurately, through politics. In virtually every advanced industrial country, the public sector has stopped growing. In the Maastricht Treaty, members of the European Union have now committed themselves to limit the public debt to 60 percent of GDP, and one year's public deficit to 3 percent. In the United States, both parties are now committed to the even more austere course of budget balance. The inflation crisis of the 1970s also subsided, thanks to policy interventions.

Even more interesting (and more damaging to the theory) is *how* these changes came about. Supposedly, the pressure of free-riding and of interest-group domination leads to insurmountable obstacles to sensible fiscal policies. Supposedly, too, politicians are mainly interested in being re-elected. But in the past decade, each of these factors was somehow suspended.

To review recent events is to notice the large role of ideology and of "conviction politicians." Even the most cursory reading of political history will demonstrate that political life has both pragmatists and ideologues. Presidents Eisenhower, Nixon, Ford, Kennedy, Bush, Carter, and Clinton ran and governed as pragmatists. They sought the political center, roughly as Public Choice theory presumes—but also out of their own conviction that the center offered the most appropriate policies. At times, each also spent substantial political capital and took real political risks to advance policies he believed good for the country, sometimes winning and sometimes suffering humiliating defeat.

In contrast, Franklin Roosevelt, Harry Truman, Barry Goldwater, George McGovern, Walter Mondale, and Ronald Reagan were conviction politicians. Goldwater and McGovern ran principled campaigns and lost badly. Roosevelt and Reagan took positions far from the prevailing political center, and succeeded in moving public opinion in their direction. The same is true of many legislators.

American political history is replete with "profiles in courage"—legislative bravery on behalf of a perceived public good that often cost the legislator his seat. Several Democratic congressmen walked the plank for Bill Clinton and fiscal discipline in 1994, voting for a deficit-reduction package that included tax increases which would likely be unpopular with their constituents. Many Republican freshmen who ousted the Democratic incumbents in the November 1994 midterm election have taken positions far to the right of their constituents, costing some their seats.

Ironically enough, the entire conservative counterrevolution that began in 1981 embarrasses its intellectual allies in the Public Choice fraternity. Though allied with business-interest groups that want deregulation and tax reduction on opportunistic grounds, the Reaganites were driven mainly by ideological zeal— a principled conviction that big government was bad for American society. Initially Reagan and his allies, deliberately or inadvertently, behaved the way Public Choice theory suggests—they cut taxes but did not significantly reduce spending. Historians will long debate whether this was a purposive tactical ploy to create a permanent deficit with which to hammer public outlay—or an accidental miscalculation that later proved to be a tactical master stroke. However, since the late 1980s, deficit reduction has been the paramount fiscal goal, and the budget-balance coalition has offered the electorate mainly pain—significant reductions in public spending coupled with little tax relief. Yet deficits are coming steadily down. This crusade, now a bipartisan article of faith among political elites, totally defies the Public Choice conception of legislative behavior.

It is not surprising that Public Choice would be an empirical failure, for it misdescribes political motivation. Some politicians are pure pragmatists and even mere errand boys for interest groups; others are driven by ideology. Some are self-seeking; others altruistically pursue a collective good. What is true of politicians is also true of voters and activists. Environmentalists and antiabortion activists cannot pass a conventional cost-benefit test, unless we twist language and logic to define preference for a pristine environment or the rights of the unborn as a purely private "taste." Likewise, the white politicians and voters who supported civil rights for blacks felt they were righting a long-delayed historic wrong, even though they were doing so at cost to their own racial privilege. Lyndon Johnson's famous aside as he signed the 1964 Civil Rights Act, "There goes the South," was all too prophetic as an epitaph for the Dixiecrat party, and hardly reflective of a Public Choice politician. The first generation of black voters who braved economic and physical retaliation to cast ballots did so in the belief that they were building a better society for their children.

Why would such a banal and tautological body of theory win such wide respect and influence in the academy? One can identify three broad reasons.

The first is the influence of free-market economics. Public Choice, as both its adherents and detractors declare, is the application of the economic model to political life. The economic model has never had more prestige than in this era, both in academia and in political life. Public Choice theory represents both the incursion of free-market economics into other disciplines, and the hapless efforts of other social sciences (whose domains are inherently less mechanical) to emulate formalistic economics. Relatedly, Public Choice commands academic respect because of its scientific pretensions. Building models, rendering theories in algebra, and manipulating what is quantifiable carry more prestige than historical, institutional, or qualitative research. Even if the results are trivial, formalistic, and tautological, and even when they are empirically falsified, the proponents can argue (as Public Choice scholars often do), "At least we try to be scientific."

A second reason is that skepticism about politics resonates with the American character, history, and institutions. As James Morone explains in *The Democratic Wish*, Americans simultaneously expect a great deal from their politics, yet profoundly mistrust it. They want benefits from government, yet hobble it constitutionally, administratively, and fiscally. They invoke the democratic ideal, but limit it. This core contradiction yields voter frustrations that periodically erupt in self-defeating remedies. Sometimes the result is a quixotic effort to take the politics out of politics. Examples are the elite crusade in the Progressive era to denature political issues into questions of purely technical expertise. The current counterpart is the movement for mechanical strictures such as constitutional limitations on taxing and spending, balanced-budget mandates, and term limits. The opposite impulse seeks to take politics away from the illegitimate politicians and restore it directly to the people through popular referenda. Both of these approaches turn out to be dysfunctional. Complex issues remain unresolved, voters remain frustrated, and democratic politics never quite returns to the mythic "people." Public Choice theory, viewed in this light, is the formalistic expression of the popular belief that voters never get what they really want and that you can't trust politicians. Of course, with all its blemishes, politics is the necessary regime of democracy. The more that "politics" is decoupled from "democracy," the more the Democratic Wish is frustrated.

Third and perhaps most important, Public Choice theory and its close cousin, Law and Economics, are very reinforcing of the laissez-faire ideal and thus very congenial to society's most powerful. Who, after all, loses when society pursues political mobilization of propertyless voters, a broad welfare state, substantial economic regulation, and redistributive taxation? When nonwealthy voters, who are most vulnerable to the vicissitudes of markets, organize themselves into a political force, leaders and policies ensue that change society's distribution of power and wealth. If that enterprise, however, can be discredited and dismissed as either economically perverse or politically futile, elites have less to fear from countervailing political action. (Just to help the free market of ideas along, conservative foundations have spent tens of millions of dollars subsidizing research by sympathetic academicians with the premise that their work will help propagate this faith.)

Looking back on different conceptions of the relationship of a strong state to strong democracy, we see that the application of the economic model offers something radically new. In the era of the constitutional founding, there were fierce debates about the power and construction of central government and the nature of democratic representation. But all sides to the debate invoked the virtues of democratic self-governance. In the Progressive era, clean-government reformers tried to depoliticize many public questions. But they championed more professionalized public administration and stronger regulation. Public Choice theory, uniquely, damns democratic politics and government alike.

REVIVING THE POLITY

The alternative to leaving everything to markets on the ground that government is chronically incompetent, of course, is the revival of politics and public administration. Public Choice theory—the trespass of free-market economics into democratic politics—dooms this as a hopeless enterprise. However, if I have persuaded the reader that markets do not always optimize, and that politics does not inevitably make outcomes worse, then at least we can open a discussion about how to energize the polity, both as an end in itself and in order to place correction of market failure in competent and accountable hands.

It should go without saying that in a political democracy we need robust forms of popular participation and the cultivation of norms of public-spiritedness. It seems appalling, at this late date, to have to restate the case for democracy. Why, after all, do we want a political democracy in the first place? Why not let public office be sold, and put democratic rights up for bid? A reconsideration of the case for democracy helps put into perspective the new utopian conception of markets.

First, we need democracy as a bulwark against tyranny. Lord Acton is still apposite: "Power tends to corrupt, and absolute power corrupts absolutely." The American Revolution and the other democratic revolutions that followed took political power out of the hands of arbitrary monarchs and gave it to the people. The need to carefully balance the democratic wish against the threat of tyrannical majorities is a more subtle endeavor, one that also pervades our constitutional founding. The virtues and complexities of democracy are deeply ingrained in our collective consciousness as Americans, perhaps our most precious heritage as a nation. To argue that this entire quest is illusory is to forget what happens to nations when democracy fails.

Second, we need democracy for the development and expression of our selfhood. To be a free man or woman is to express opinions, participate in deliberations, have some influence over the shape of the collectivity. One achieves self-expression as a consumer, but also as a citizen—the latter often in richer ways. If the realm of the polity is shrunken and the political enterprise is straitened, then the individual is stunted. As the political philosopher Hanna Pitkin wrote, invoking sages as diverse as Aristotle and Hannah Arendt, "What distinguishes politics [is] the possibility of a shared, collective, deliberate, active intervention in our fate, in what would otherwise be the byproduct of private decisions. . . . [T]he distinctive promise of political freedom remains the possibility of genuine collective action, an entire community consciously and jointly shaping its policy, its way of life." These concerns have preoccupied free men and women ever since the first democracy of the Greeks, and these timeless issues are not mooted by the momentary ascendance of laissez-faire economics.

Third, we need to cultivate civic skills and norms if democracy is to be more than the formalistic ritual or interest-group charade that Public Choice theory cynically projects. Obviously, there are limits to the time the average citizen has to exercise the arts of self-government, just as there are limits to the time she has to comparison-shop. However, a society in which citizens allocate time to vote, participate in voluntary associations and political parties, attend local school-board and PTA meetings, and even have some democratic expression at the workplace is likely to be a healthier, more trusting, and more resilient society than one in which democratic forms are passive and formal. Rather than trying to expand the market to the polity, it would be salutary to extend democratic rights and deliberative principles to areas of the marketplace where they are weak or absent, such as the workplace.

Fourth, if the limits of markets require us to entrust government with functions beyond the minimal one of keeping public order and enforcing basic property rights, then we need an even stronger politics and democracy. Some societies are evidently able to combine expansive and efficient public administration with relatively weak or formalistic democracy, because of predemocratic traditions of strong government and authoritarian cultural predispositions. Many of the democratic nations with the most competent states inherited effective bureaucracies from their own predemocratic eras. Nations as diverse as Japan and Sweden had traditions of deference to legitimate authority that conferred great power on royal bureaucracies, which were then retained and rendered accountable to parliamentary institutions.

By contrast, Americans are not noted for their deference to authority. Almost everywhere else, authority came first; liberty was extracted afterward. In America, as Madison observed, liberty came first; consensual authority had to be constructed later. To have an effective state, we need a strong, vital democratic and civic life in order to render it legitimate and accountable. Contrary to Public Choice theory, the cultivation of public-spiritedness and robust participation in all levels of politics and government are worthwhile for their own sake.

These four rationales for political democracy ought to be familiar. Here is a fifth one that is more novel, and more immediately relevant to our discussion of market and polity: we need the habits and institutions of a strong democracy *precisely to keep markets in their place* and to provide resilience during those historical periods when the market goes haywire and makes ordinary people vulnerable to the appeals of tyrants. Looking back on our turbulent century, one appreciates Karl Polanyi's account of marketization uprooting premodern forms of security and stability, and leading to modern forms of despotism. Reading history, one grasps that it was the nations with strong democratic traditions that escaped dictatorial remedies to economic disorder. At points during the Great Depression, that outcome did not seem so inevitable. But our long-standing habits as a free people with vigorous civic institutions ultimately stood us in good stead.

The United States came through the economic turbulence of this century with democratic institutions intact. More than a century of experience with civic republicanism, the long tradition of voluntary association, and the deep national conception of democracy as a public good gave most Americans an intuitive resistance to the appeal of fascism or communism. The democratic habit served us well as an economic shock-absorber. Germany, Italy, Japan, much of Latin America were not so fortunate. Bolshevik Russia, with just a few short months of parliamentary democracy, chose bread over liberty, and ended up losing both.

Despite their recourse to highly stylized models, champions of the pure-market model cannot reasonably place it outside history. If we are to keep the market from overrunning everything else we hold dear, we need competent states. And if we don't want the state to be its own source of tyranny, we need strong democracy.

Even though the ideological theme of our era is that politics hobbles the efficiency and dynamism of markets, it is worth paying attention to the opposite malady. In many ways, markets are today assaulting and undermining democratic politics—ideologically and institutionally. As Arthur Okun, contradicting the Public Choice fraternity, aptly observed, politics necessarily exists in an entirely separate realm from markets. Because its first principles of membership are so different, politics cannot be understood as merely an extrapolation of economics. Yet, lately, the market has been inexorably encroaching on the polity, in both practice and theory.

In addressing the revival of political life, we need to be clear that we are discussing three distinct, though interrelated institutions—the polity, the state, and the community. Earlier conservative liberals associated a strong community and a vital polity with a weak state. Today's conservatives make a particular villain of the state, contribute to the cynicism about the possibilities of politics, and associate the private institutions of community with markets. However, there is ample evidence that the market, taken to an extreme, can weaken state, polity, and community alike.

MONEY AND POLITICS

A capitalist democracy exists in necessary tension between the contradictory principles of one-citizen/one-vote and one-dollar/one-vote. Money buys nearly everything else, and keeps trying to buy what should not be for sale in politics. Lately, money has become newly influential in political life. As campaigns become more expensive, money tends to drive out more civic forms of political participation. Politics is increasingly becoming an enterprise built on polling, mass mailing, and paid TV commercials, all of which cost lots of money and involve few citizens. Politicians spend a great deal of their time raising money and cultivating wealthy donors. Several of our most public-minded legislators have recently quit public life because they found the fund-raising imperative so demeaning and corrupting.

Sometimes this dynamic frustrates democracy by leading to the literal buying and selling of votes. But the corrosive effect on democracy operates in several more insidious ways. It creates a climate in which large donors and fund-raisers have privileged access to elected officials. This is a form of "special-interest" politics rather different from that posited by Public Choice theory. It is not a case of individuals organizing themselves into groups or coalitions to maximize their legitimate influence as voters. It is, rather, the use of money to directly purchase illegitimate influence in defiance of the core democratic principle of one-person/one-vote. This brand of politics has the effect of allowing the large donor to go to the head of the queue. Rare is the politician who will not take a phone call from a large donor or fund-raiser.

Money-driven elections feed into a brand of politics that leaves out ordinary voters, except as objects to be manipulated by polling, focus groups, mass mailings, and paid TV spots. Politics becomes an exercise in raising funds to pay for the expert polling, the production of commercials, and the purchase of TV time. The genre places a premium on negative campaigning, for which TV is particularly well suited. Over time, the result is an escalating cynicism on the part of ordinary voters. What sticks in the voters' minds is less any one argument or commercial than the general negativism, a sense that the whole show is manipulative, and that all politicians are scoundrels. Real issues, and the possibility of real constructive change, are excluded. People stop participating in more authentic, civic ways. Voting seems futile, and turnout declines.

Money also skews group participation. In money-dominated politics, money-driven lobbying tends to drive out authentic grass-roots activism based on popular mobilization of citizen-activists. A new, charming term has crept into politics—"Astroturf lobbying." This is a pun on the older concept of "grass-roots lobbying," in which coalitions of voters did not rely primarily on Washington-based lobbyists but put pressure on their elected representatives from the heartland. By contrast, Astroturf lobbying, like Astroturf, simulates the real thing. Large amounts of money can almost instantly create an approximation of a true grass-roots campaign. Underwritten by well-heeled special interests, money can create letterhead organizations, enlist local citizens in front groups, and create the impression of a true grass-roots rebellion.

For example, in the battle over communications deregulation in 1995–96, the Baby Bells and the cable industry organized broad coalitions with letter-writing campaigns and full-page ads, purporting to represent consumers as well as narrow interests. The legislative battle boiled down to AT&T versus the Baby Bells. True consumer groups, concerned about everything from monopoly cable power, to the maintenance of cheap basic telephone service, to ground rules for the Internet, were hopelessly outspent and outshouted. Another fine example is the "Wise Use Movement," a pseudo–mass movement ostensibly committed to the peaceful coexistence of economic development and the environment. Though the movement cultivated the image of a broad coalition of ordinary people, it was in fact dominated by commercial mining and logging interests. The more that ordinary people come to believe that politics is dominated by moneyed interests, the less politics seems worth participating in.

Note the difference between this analysis of civic and political degradation and that offered by market-influenced theories of politics. According to Public Choice theory, the threat to meaningful democracy is the influence of selfish interest groups generally. Because critics attracted to this brand of theorizing tend to be pro-market and anti-redistribution, their examples of "rent-seeking" are often those of the state aiding the poor. James Buchanan illustrates the perverse outcomes from democratic incursions into the marketplace: "If mothers with dependent children are granted payments for being mothers, we can predict that we shall soon have more such mothers. If the unemployed are offered higher payments, we predict that the number of unemployed will increase." Buchanan has little to say about disparities of private economic power and their effect on political influence. In the world of Public Choice, all interest groups are created equal, and equally pernicious.

By contrast, the special-interest abuses I have in mind involve the superior and disproportionate access purchased by money. In a market society, as Charles Lindblom presciently wrote two decades ago, business enjoys a "privileged position." Democratic politics is the realm in which ordinary people make up for the disproportionate power exercised by organized money. If senior citizens, by dint of their numbers, can convince sympathetic legislators that it makes sense for the government to redress a serious market failure by providing universal medical insurance for the elderly, that action has to enjoy a greater presumptive legitimacy than the case of nursing-home operators persuading legislators via campaign contributions to water down regulations specifying minimal standards of care. The one initiative comports with the basic principle of democratic politics—voting. The other violates it by substituting the political currency of cash.

Public Choice theory is almost entirely silent on the disproportionate purchase of influence by big money. There is a presumed symmetry of welfare mothers and bankers, and an equivalence of corruption. It is, however, possible to rotate Public Choice theory slightly on its axis and come up with an analysis that sounds almost Marxian. The political scientist Thomas Ferguson offers what he calls an "investment theory of politics." Conventional Public Choice theory, Ferguson writes, "privileges voters [in general], who are said to exercise control over at least the broad shape of public policy." By contrast, Ferguson's "investment theory holds that voters hardly count unless they become substantial investors. When the ranks of significant investors are limited to relatively small numbers of elite actors commanding disproportionate shares of politically mobilized resources, mass voting loses most of its significance." Except when ordinary, nonrich voters are in a state of high mobilization via parties, unions, or other instruments of representation, there is a fundamental asymmetry between the interest-group influence of rich and poor.

Contrary to Public Choice theory, one needn't conclude that the corruption and degradation of politics are intrinsic or inevitable. The relative influence of money in politics, and, conversely, the relative health of more authentic participation, have ebbed and flowed in our political history.

Whether money is kept in its place has profound implications for how the polity operates. When money dominates politics, entire questions are kept off the agenda. The dependence of politicians on money brokers changes the perceived spectrum of legitimate public issues. It rules out issues that may have broad popular support but little appeal for economic elites. In chapter 4, I discussed the problem of slow growth, rising inequality, and stagnant living standards for most working Americans. There are remedies for each of these problems. Strikingly, each of them is currently off the policy agenda, because of an elite, bipartisan consensus that it is bad to criticize the Federal Reserve, that full employment is necessarily inflationary, that deficit reduction takes precedence over public remedy, that global competition precludes durable workplace compacts, and that the labor movement is an archaism. There is thus no political remedy for the pocket-book frustrations of most voters. No wonder people stop voting.

Unless we want our republic to degenerate into a new plutocracy—an oligarchy of the wealthy and fortunate—we face a twin challenge: to keep the market from ruining the polity and to renew the institutions of healthy civic and political life.

The first task entails strengthening the barriers that constrain the influence of money in politics. Full public financing of elections would be a good start. The Supreme Court's 1976 *Buckley* v. *Valeo* decision allowed wealthy people to spend unlimited sums financing their own candidacies. It also permitted unlimited private outlays on causes or candidacies as long as they were "unaffiliated" with a candidate's official campaign. This ruling has blocked a regime of pure public financing of elections. Absent an improbable constitutional amendment, a second-best remedy would be to construct a system of public financing for which candidates could qualify only if they refused private money. It would be wise to broaden the emerging practice of having broadcasters give candidates free TV and radio time, with the proviso that the candidate himself must appear and that produced spot-ads with "production values" be prohibited. Candidates for public office should not be treated like commodities. Not surprisingly, the democratic countries that provide public financing and public air time generally have shorter, cleaner, more substantive campaigns and higher voter turnouts.

Much of the degradation of political democracy is the result precisely of market forms and norms taking over the political process. A prime culprit is television, a medium first of marketing, and second of purveying entertainment useful for delivering a mass audience to a sponsor. Education and deliberation, much less civic uplift, are not part of this equation. "Entertainment," as critic Neil Postman writes, "is the supra-ideology of all discourse on television. No matter what is depicted or from what point of view, the overarching presumption is that it is there for our amusement and pleasure. . . . A news show, to put it plainly, is a format for entertainment, not for education, reflection, or catharsis." As television becomes the pre-eminent avenue of politics, market principles and entertainment values begin crowding out civic ones. Candidates are attractive or not, as products. "The problem is not that television presents us with entertaining subject matter," writes Postman, "but that all subject matter is presented as entertaining."

RENEWING POLITICAL LIFE

Democratic theorists have long debated whether democracy is essentially representational or necessarily participatory. When Joseph Schumpeter argued that democracy could be understood mainly as a contest of competitive leadership, he was only echoing the more conservative and patrician of America's Founders. Direct democracy was held to be impractical, even in the much smaller American Republic of the 1780s. The Federalists imagined that the duty of a representative was to act in the stead of the common man, to do what he would do if it were practical to put the entire community in one location. The legislature, as John Adams put it, "should be an exact portrait, in miniature, of the people at large. . . . [I]t should think, feel, reason, and act like them." For Jefferson, legislatures were a necessary inconvenience to be tolerated only because it was not possible for the people to act "directly and personally."

Conservative liberalism, dating back to John Locke, has a privileged place in the American political creed. In Locke's conception, the most serious enemy of liberty was the state. Lockean liberals hold that we need republican instruments of government to establish individual rights, not to pursue collective purposes. We need self-governance to protect ourselves from each other, and from the Leviathan state. Free-market economists are Lockean liberals. The market is the realm of private choice and accomplishment, which flourishes when the polity is wise enough to leave well enough alone. Markets, by definition, are never instruments of private tyranny.

The political scientist Benjamin Barber, in his classic work, *Strong Democracy*, argues that the "thin democracy" of radically individualist liberalism is too weak a reed to defend against either tyranny, passivity, or the predations of markets. "Strong democracy," in contrast, envisions citizens "made capable of common purpose and mutual action by virtue of their civic attitudes and participatory institutions rather than their altruism or their good nature." Barber contrasts this with formal Lockean democracy, which is merely representational and minimalist. In the same spirit, Jane Mansbridge, a political scientist at Harvard, challenges the concept of democracy that is merely an "adversarial" clash of interests, and puts forth instead a democracy that is consensual and deliberative. From her study of politics in a small town, Mansbridge finds that, at least some of the time, deliberation and persuasion can break down barriers of presumed opposite interests, while cultivating civic and empathic skills.

For libertarian conservatives, this vision of participatory democracy is a mirage. Where legislative consensus appears, it is likely to be mere logrolling. Where "strong democracy" takes charge, it does so by trampling minority rights or expropriating private property. In the libertarian view, the more of society and economy that the state attempts to influence, the further it wanders from the participatory ideal, and the more it risks rendering the collectivity ungovernable. If we want strong democracy (itself a questionable goal to Public Choice theorists), we had better have a weak state.

Yet this is far too straitened a conception of the possibilities of politics and governance. In this century, the expansion of state constraints on the market and the expansion of the province of personal liberties have gone hand in hand. Plentiful employment, respite from arbitrary private power via social insurance and trade unions, expanded civil rights, and protections from environmental calamities wrought by markets all *increased* personal security and liberty for ordinary people—no loss of liberty resulted. Despite the libertarian triumphalism of our own age, there is in fact no historical instance of F. A. Hayek's famous Road to Serfdom beginning with an established democracy that attempted an excess of public planning and ended in tyranny. The totalitarian states—the Soviet Union, Nazi Germany, Fascist Italy, imperial Japan—were in no case the results of previously democratic states biting off more of the economy than they could chew. All were societies where democracy itself was too weak.

Is it realistic, in the late twentieth century, to imagine a revived realm of democratic participation? To begin with, we need to reclaim the idea that there is a legitimate public space that is more than the sum of individual private interests. And we need to revive avenues of civic engagement.

The most basic act of civic participation is voting. The United States has consistently the lowest rate of voting among all the major democracies. In 1992, just 38 percent of eligible citizens cast ballots for president. In 1994, the Gingrich revolution was wrought by a bare 51 percent of the 39 percent of eligible citizens who bothered to vote. The steady decline in voting turnout is also skewed by class. Poorer people are generally more pessimistic and cynical about the possibility of political efficacy; in moments when democracy is in disrepair, they tend to defect first. Currently, the professional and entrepreneurial class votes at rates approximating those of Western Europe. The voting rate of poor and working-class voters is below 20 percent. That gives the affluent approximately three effective votes for every one of the poor's.

Low voting turnout results from the decay of political institutions, the rising cynicism about the possibility of political action leading to constructive change, and the obstacles to participation, which are higher in the United States than in other democracies. The United States, almost uniquely, requires a two-step process of advance registration as a precondition to actual voting. This was introduced late in the last century, ostensibly to combat fraud but also to depress increased participation by working-class voters. The United States also votes on a Tuesday, which is not a mandatory work holiday. One constructive step was taken in 1994, when Congress, over the strenuous objection of most Republicans, enacted the "Motor Voter" bill. This automatically registers citizens when they apply for drivers' licenses, public-assistance benefits, and other transactions that require proof of identity and citizenship. A further constructive step would be to shift Election Day to a Saturday or Sunday.

Voting, however, is only the most elemental act of citizenship. It is also necessary to renew and enlarge those spheres of community life where people are in the role of citizens rather than consumers. In the current era, the trend is largely in the opposite direction, as public institutions are privatized and the shopping mall becomes the new public square.

One useful approach is to expand realms where people play a civic rather than a market role. President Clinton's national volunteer program, AmeriCorps, spends relatively modest sums, but Republican conservatives understandably oppose it. Such endeavors incubate civic, as opposed to marketplace, values. A young person who has spent a year tutoring in a slum, or working with a multiracial group on a recreation or housing program, is a bit less likely to grow up to be a pure libertarian defining satisfaction as entrepreneurship and viewing the poor as deserving losers. Other such realms are the Public Health Service, the Urban Teacher Corps, and the Peace Corps.

Another promising initiative is the idea of the "policy jury," in which ordinary citizens are brought together and invited to resolve a difficult public-policy issue. I participated in one of these affairs, whose subject was the budget deficit. I was the expert liberal witness, opposed by former Republican Representative Vin Weber in the role of expert conservative witness. Each of us was backed up by a team of specialists on specific topics. Twelve ordinary people, compensated with a trip to Washington and a modest honorarium, spent the better part of a week boning up on fiscal issues. At the end of the week, they voted to cut defense spending, increase outlays for health and education, raise taxes on the wealthy, and reduce but not eliminate the deficit. The Jefferson Institute, and University of Texas political scientist James Fishkin, among others, have all sponsored variants of this model of civic education and participation.

One of the enemies of civic engagement is time pressure. As the society has become more marketized, and as income distribution becomes more polarized, most ordinary people face a terrible time squeeze. There is barely enough time to juggle work and family, let alone participation in civic and political activities. In order to reclaim civic space from market space, we need to take some of that time back. Shorter working hours, mandatory parental leave, paid child-care benefits would all leave more time for civic activity. A more egalitarian distribution of income would also give more people the effective choice of giving up some of their workday to participate in community events.

RECLAIMING CIVIL SOCIETY

There is, at this writing, an instructive debate between right and left over ideological ownership of the voluntary sector, which is neither state nor market. In the 1960s, community participation was very much a cause of the New Left. In the 1970s, through the writings of Richard John Neuhaus, Peter Berger, Michael Novak, and Robert Woodson, among others, a new generation of conservatives appropriated Tocqueville, and began praising the benefits of voluntary associations and "mediating institutions"—church, family, Little League, PTA, even trade-union local—as private alternatives to the welfare state.

Were state and market, respectively, the friend or the enemy of these beneficial communitarian institutions? The right painted a picture of the welfare state crowding out voluntary and charitable associations. The New Left had its own qualms about the bureaucratic welfare state, but prized the new wave of community institutions—antipoverty organizations, community-development corporations, self-governing tenant councils—many of which were in fact launched and subsidized by government.

The debate cannot be settled in the abstract. One must get down to cases. Some instruments of the bureaucratic welfare state may well operate at the expense of voluntarism. On the other hand, that is not entirely bad. A retired person, fortified by a Social Security check and a Medicare card, has less need to patronize the local soup kitchen, as well as more time and self-confidence to become engaged in the community's civic life. Some of the most dynamic private civic institutions are allies of public ones. PTAs are adjuncts of the quintessential local public institution, the public school. Trade unions, the premier institution of working-class representation and direct participation, exist in the shelter of the Wagner Act, which (in principle) protects unions from employer retaliation. For the past thirty years, publicly funded social services have increasingly worked through nonprofit community agencies, and the majority of such agencies rely on a blend of local voluntary energy and public funds.

Conversely, a great deal of local voluntarism is harmed by the excesses of the market. For every corporation that "adopts a school," sponsors a Boy Scout troop, or organizes an employees' service club to clean up a local mile of interstate highway, there are others that are reducing their commitment to community charities and services because of the relentless pressure of the bottom line. An employee fearful of his job security has less time or inclination to volunteer for the Little League. The old days of the paternalistic corporation, anchored in the locality and committed to the community, have given way to a new wave of absentee- and shareholder-owned corporations driven by quarterly stock performance and viewing the locality as little more than a flag of convenience. This trend is emblematic of an age in which corporations are freed of regulatory and customary constraints and behave precisely like the profit maximizers commended by pure free-market theory.

As they have cut back the social-service state for more than fifteen years, conservatives have waited in vain for private charity to take up the slack. On the contrary, corporate substitutes for social provision are evaporating. Private pension plans are covering a dwindling fraction of employees. Employer-provided child care remains a lofty goal and an elusive reality. Collectively, corporate profits are at an all-time high, but in a deregulated and marketized environment the individual corporation experiences itself as under relentless competitive pressure—and such fringe benefits seem unaffordable frills. This is why such benefits need to be provided socially, if they are to be reliably provided at all. The very corporation liberated by deregulation is also freed from premarket commitments to community and charity.

The free-market right today has its own agenda of civic renewal, stressing local government and voluntary mediating institutions—George Bush's Thousand Points of Light. In late 1995, Indiana Republican Senator Dan Coats introduced a nineteen-point "Project for American Renewal," proposing to use public resources and policy to energize civil society. The plan includes a five-hundred-dollar tax credit for donations to charitable organizations—in effect, the government would reimburse everyone's first five hundred dollars of charitable giving; an equal tax credit for those who provide home care to the needy; vouchers for women choosing to deliver unwanted babies in religious or charitable maternity homes; yet another tax credit to subsidize adoptions; and federal demonstration programs on mentoring, "Role-Model Academies for At-risk Youth," and a "Kinship Care Act" to place troubled children with extended-family members rather than in foster homes. Yet another bill would mandate and subsidize counseling and a compulsory waiting period for couples with children seeking divorce.

Though a resolute conservative, Senator Coats inadvertently found himself on both sides of the state-versus-civil-society debate. For he plainly proposed to use government to shore up (a conservative version of) civil society. This was too much for the libertarians to the right of Coats. In a special issue of the Heritage Foundation's magazine, *Policy Review*, several conservative intellectuals pounced on Coats's plan. David Boaz, executive vice president of the libertarian Cato Institute, minced no words:

> The nature of government doesn't change when it is charged with conservative social engineering rather than liberal social engineering. . . . [N]early every one of the bills would further entangle the federal government in the institutions of civil society. . . . Despite all that we've learned about the failure of government, Coats just doesn't seem to get it. His proposals reflect the Washington that Roosevelt built, the Washington where, if you think of a good idea, you create a government program. But ultimately, you either believe in individual liberty, limited government, and free markets, or you end up inviting the coercive state into every nook and cranny of civil society.

This is the ascendant public philosophy: markets are self-perfecting, "civil society" somehow exists in a state of nature independent of civil government, and even public efforts to shore up families and voluntary associations are, by definition, illegitimate. But there is good evidence that an excess of market, not state, is killing civil society.

The political scientist Robert Putnam has investigated the across-the-board decline of civic involvement in America, which he broadly terms "social capital." Putnam finds a steady decline in social connectedness and trust, which pervades all social classes. He dismisses such popular explanations as rising public cynicism in the aftermath of such national civic traumas as the Kennedy assassination, the Vietnam War, and Watergate. Rather, he finds that the "long civic generation," which came of age in the Great Depression and World War II, an era when government and politics enjoyed greater legitimacy and prestige, has not passed its stock of social capital and civic engagement to its children. Interestingly enough, private civic engagement was at its peak during the zenith of the welfare state and the mixed economy—perhaps because more nonaffluent people were able to participate in civic life, and because politics itself enjoyed more legitimacy.

A particular villain, for Putnam, is television. Civic engagement, he finds, began declining just as TV viewing began increasing. The average American now watches four hours of television per day. High-volume TV viewing, Putnam reports, correlates with low civic engagement and diminished trust: "Controlling for education, income, age, race, place of residence, work status, and gender, TV viewing is strongly and negatively related to social trust and group membership, whereas the same correlations with newspaper reading are positive. Within every educational category, heavy readers are avid joiners, whereas heavy viewers are likely to be loners. . . . In other words, each hour spent watching television is associated with less social trust and less group membership. . . ."

TV is both the emblem and the reality of a heavily marketized society. Audiences are assembled in order to sell products. Satisfaction of hedonic impulse, in perfect keeping with the market imperative to maximize utility, is promised by commercials; but the satisfaction is often fleeting. The result is a generation of channel-surfers with little loyalty to show, to product, or to political label. A pitchman may produce a momentary impulse to purchase a product, but the cumulative result is cynicism. As a form of acculturation, much less of civic education, commercial TV produces empty calories.

Neil Postman's fine book, *Amusing Ourselves to Death*, poses a notional debate between the century's two great dystopian novelists, Huxley and Orwell. Orwell imagined that the television screen was an instrument of direct totalitarian surveillance and subjugation; it both monitored ordinary citizens and conveyed messages from Big Brother. Huxley's brand of tyranny was more insidious. By taking "Soma," the populace amused itself to death; it lost ancient liberties without being aware of the loss. Our Soma is television.

As a number of analysts have observed, television itself purveys a particularly passive and sterile form of politics, while it epitomizes the market experience. Putnam suggests several distinct ways in which television depletes social capital, including direct time displacement, inducement of passivity and cynicism, and the crowding out of more engaging leisure pursuits that require more effort, more individual development, and more cultivation of social skills.

If Putnam and Postman are right, the satisfactions of the market, taken to an extreme, crowd out the satisfactions of the engaged life of a free, discerning people. If anything, Putnam's critique is too easy on the market and too single-minded in blaming television, because he largely leaves out social class. In a sense, Putnam's message is that, if we are a producing a generation of couch potatoes, it's our own fault. But that lets the dominant economic forces in society off the hook too easily. The collapse of civic institutions has a disproportionate negative effect on poor and working-class Americans, since the polity is the one avenue of voice and redress for citizens with scant material possessions. When the social fabric thins, more affluent people can buy their way out with private schools, guarded or gated communities, private social clubs, and individual psychotherapy (about which one scholarly critic subtitled a book *The Purchase of Friendship*). People with less purchasing power obtain these needs socially, or go without.

It has long been a staple of political science that the poor depend more than the rich on institutions of political and civic representation. For example, the decline of trade unionism has a particularly negative impact on the social capital and political influence of working-class citizens. Most surveys show that poorer people are less socially engaged to begin with, because of time pressures and higher passivity and cynicism. In many working-class communities, the prime institutions of social connectedness and democratic voice are church and union. Both are on the decline. It is all too fitting that the decay of working-class political and civic institutions occurs in an era when the market is hegemonic.

Another distinguished student of civic life, Sidney Verba, reports in his most recent book with colleagues Kay Lehman Scholzman and Henry E. Brady that "participatory inequality" is accelerating and is highly skewed by social class. Concluding an encyclopedic empirical investigation of civic participation, they report:

> Over and over, our data showed that participatory input is tilted in the direction of the more advantaged groups in society. . . . The voices of the well educated and the well heeled—and, therefore, of those with other politically relevant characteristics that are associated with economic and educational privilege—sound more loudly. . . .

Inequalities in activity seem to be more pronounced in the United States than in other democracies. Moreover, they seem to be more pronounced with respect to political rather than non-political activity. . . . [S]o long as inequalities in education and income persist—and income inequality in America has become more pronounced of late—so long as jobs continue to distribute opportunities to practice civic skills in a stratified manner, then individuals will continue to command stockpiles of participatory factors at very different rates.

Since the early 1970s, widening inequality has been associated with greater commodification. In plain English, this means that many things that were once basic social amenities now depend on private purchasing power, which is increasingly unequal. The recent increase in working time, coupled with the greater stress of juggling paid work and parenting, likewise seems at first glance characteristic of the "fast-track" affluent, professional class. However, the upper class can afford private, in-home nannies, which may leave children with scant "quality time" with their natural parents, but at least creates reliable and secure care the rest of the time. Less affluent people find themselves reliant on helter-skelter child-care arrangements, risking child abuse and neglect, and extreme parental stress. This increased time pressure also squeezes out what a European friend calls "the third life"—the aspect of life built around neither work nor family, but around life-affirming sociability.

When two candidates for President Clinton's attorney general had to withdraw because they had failed to pay Social Security taxes for paid nannies, the Reverend Jesse Jackson quipped that in the black community folks didn't need nannies—they had grannies. This is a good illustration of how lower-income groups rely on informal networks of mutual help, whereas the upper class buys a commodity. But as the rich get richer and the poor get poorer and once stable working-class communities turn into slums, those networks of extended families weaken. In short, the civic deterioration and the increased stresses associated with social and economic changes of the past twenty years are not uniformly distributed, but are heavily skewed according to social class.

REINVENTING GOVERNMENT

Besides reviving the vitality of politics and the fabric of civil society, those who believe in a mixed economy necessarily rely on government. So strong is the market vogue, however, that many relative liberals as well as conservatives take pains to disparage government. The first recent president to win an election warning about the excesses of the federal government was not Ronald Reagan but Jimmy Carter. President Clinton, likewise, won his election advertising himself as a different kind of Democrat—different, presumably, from his predecessors who saw government as a counterweight to the market and as an instrument of collective betterment. And in his 1996 State of the Union Address, Clinton emphatically declared that "the age of big government is over."

In late 1995, I was on a panel with Massachusetts Senator John Kerry, who was heading into a close re-election campaign. The audience was three township Democratic committees—mostly liberal activists. In 1994, the state's other Democratic senator, Edward Kennedy, had won re-election by seventeen points, in a campaign that deliberately embraced liberal themes of the defense of entitlement spending and the incomes of working families. Kerry, in contrast, seemed to be defining himself as a different Democrat. At one point, he asked rhetorically, "Who in America is in favor of more regulation?"

This happened to be the same week that the papers were filled with reports of for-profit Health Maintenance Organizations giving participating doctors secret rebates for not referring patients to specialists, of insurance companies selling confidential information, and of pharmaceutical companies marketing unsafe or unproven drugs. As it happens, millions of Americans look to regulation to protect them from the opportunistic assaults of the pure market. It is not helpful when the ostensible advocates of the mixed economy sound an uncertain trumpet.

Clinton's embrace of the "Reinventing Government" theme initially seemed a welcome alternative to the right-wing view that government could do nothing right. The idea borrowed heavily from the 1992 surprise best-seller of the same name, by David Osborne and Ted Gaebler. Osborne became an adviser to the Clinton White House, and Reinventing Government was institutionalized under Vice President Gore as the "National Performance Review"—a top-to-bottom campaign to bring greater efficiency to government.

The Osborne-Gaebler book was emblematic of the neoliberal impulse. It was partly a defense of the idea that government had a major role to play in stabilizing a necessarily mixed economy, and partly an embrace of the fashionable idea that government itself had to become more entrepreneurial, flexible, and (inevitably) marketlike. The authors began by declaring (in bold type) "**First, we believe deeply in government.**" But then they called on government to become less rule-bound and bureaucratic, and more entrepreneurial. Much of the book was a plea to liberate the creativity of public servants, and to hold them accountable for results rather than formal compliance with regulations. Countless examples were offered of model agencies that had done just that.

The Gore National Performance Review began quite in that spirit. But much of it rather carelessly became part of the general current of government-bashing, boasting of how much paperwork had been cut, by how much budgets had been reduced, rather than contributing to the philosophical defense of a mixed economy, a more dynamic and creative public sector, and enhancing the morale of public servants. Oddly, Gore's interim report of the National Performance Review, *Common Sense Government*, released in September 1995, was published commercially in an edition by Random House with an introduction by Philip K. Howard, author of *The Death of Common Sense*, a crude broadside against government regulation. Gore's report ends by calling for more privatization and competition, citing as an example the partly privatized U.S. Postal Service. "Is the U.S. Postal Service improving, in part, because it must now compete with UPS and FedEx? Certainly. Can such competition improve the performance of other service-oriented government operations? Of course."

As is often the case, such simple sloganeering leaves out much of the story. The Postal Service, necessarily, still has a monopoly on first-class mail. It has a mandate to bring universal postal service to every address in America, to meet a public-policy purpose, not a market one. This necessarily entails cross-subsidy, which violates market pricing principles. The Postal Service does compete with FedEx and UPS on courier service, but not fairly. Thanks to lobbying by FedEx and UPS, the Postal Service is prohibited from offering bulk rates, which means that FedEx and UPS can skim off nearly all of the lucrative business market. Even the federal government uses FedEx rather than the Postal Service for overnight courier service, because regulations successfully imposed by its competitors prohibit it from contracting with the government at a competitive rate. The market may deliver the goods cheaply, but it often fights dirty.

The effort to modernize and streamline government, without pandering to the attack on government, is necessarily a delicate balancing act. The idea of introducing competition to the public sector is generally salutary, but competition can have one ideological meaning if the intent is to bring greater efficiency, and quite a different one if the purpose is to strip government of necessary resources. Government has increasingly relied on private contractors to carry out public programs, in realms as diverse as trash collection, social services, and prisons. Several critiques of privatization initiatives have made clear that the vaunted efficiencies are squandered when government itself loses the core competence to supervise the contractor, and a public monopoly simply gives way to a *de facto* private one. In many localities, one dominant private curbside recycling company or school-bus company or prison contractor simply drives out competitors.

Often, the ostensible cost-savings achieved by privatization turn out to be merely cost-shifting. I investigated the privatization of ambulance service in the suburbs around Boston. The actual cost of operating an ambulance is roughly comparable, whether the operator is a public agency or a private ambulance company. The main difference is that the private contractors are more aggressive at billing health insurance companies. The private companies, however, avoid the city of Boston, with its high concentrations of uninsured people. Suburban taxpayers save money, because their towns no longer have tax-supported ambulances. But there is no net gain to "efficiency" or to society.

Other candidates for privatization, such as prisons, pose public issues beyond economic efficiency. State monopoly on criminal justice has been the hallmark of a modern, democratic society. The evidence on whether private corrections actually saves money is mixed. But even if it does, do we really want to contract out elements of the criminal justice system? Although, in principle, proprietors of private jails are acting as agents of the state, there is no way to avoid the privatization of some discretionary acts that influence the liberty (or denial of liberty) of citizens. John Donahue, in a critique of prison privatization, quotes the chief of one private detention center, who was trying to offer reassurance that his guards were not abusing their authority: "I review every disciplinary action: I'm the Supreme Court."

The Ford Foundation and the John F. Kennedy School of Government give a series of annual awards for enterprise and innovation in government. The subtext of this effort is rather different from that of Newt Gingrich's Contract with America, or even Vice President Gore's National Performance Review. It is that government is necessary, and with a little encouragement and adequate resources it can be rendered a lot more accountable and satisfying, both for its public consumers and for the people who work in it. One of the 1995 award-winners was the OSHA project cited in chapter 3. OSHA demonstrated that a great deal of enforcement could be done via self-certification, as long as effective plans were in place and employees were involved in the policing. The scarce resource—government inspectors—was reserved for the dirtiest, most hazardous plants with the worst safety records. With this innovation, everyone won. Companies with good records got out from under bureaucratic regulations. Those with poor records were given closer scrutiny, and incentives to improve. Employees were empowered. And OSHA officials were retargeted to useful work rather than paper-shuffling.

Another double-edged example is the public-school-choice movement. Libertarian opponents of direct government services want to supplant publicly administered public schools with private institutions supported by vouchers. For-profit corporations such as Chris Whittle's Edison Project become lobbyists for this innovation. A pure voucher system, however, has distributive consequences. An affluent parent can take the value of the voucher and supplement it privately, whereas a working-class parent has only the value of the voucher. Such a system allows private schools to be parasites on the public system, and leaves the most costly students with dwindling resources. A defensible middle ground is a measure of school choice within the public system, which introduces constructive competition and innovation without diverting public resources outside the public system. However, depending on how school-choice experiments are structured, the result can be to promote new energy and innovation, or to set up a rival private bureaucracy.

The Swedish Social Democratic government has launched several experiments allowing private contractors to submit competitive bids against projects of certain public-sector agencies. This encourages the public agencies to become more innovative, and in fact the public agency often wins the contract. The Social Democrats, however, as unabashed advocates of a mixed economy and strong public administration, take great care to make clear that the intent is more effective public services, not government-bashing.

Yet another very double-edged issue is "devolution"—the idea of returning government to a level closer to the people. In principle, this makes great sense. Its most fervent recent advocates were the New Left communitarians of the 1960s. The current, conservative version of devolution, which replaces federal entitlements with block grants, mainly passes along liabilities for social problems to the states and cities, stripped of adequate fiscal resources.

Since the New Deal, many social and economic interventions have been assumed by the national government, either because states and localities lacked the fiscal resources or the administrative competence to deal with them, or because reform was blocked by the power of entrenched local economic elites. To "return" these problems to levels of government ill equipped to cope with them—at the same moment that lower levels of government are denied adequate funding—is to set in train a self-fulfilling prophecy in which government is stripped of resources and then adjudged terminally incompetent. The sometime defenders of government should think twice before embracing this formula. Devolution of some public functions makes great sense, when combined with national resources and adequate financing.

Government as a share of total GDP now averages over 40 percent in the advanced industrial democracies. It is just over 30 percent in the United States and as high as 60 percent in Scandinavia. This range is evidently a tolerable ceiling. Most people want a balance of private income and services that are provided collectively. There is little popular support today for massive increases in government outlay, but even less support for repealing major government programs. However, as public spending is stabilized, and even reduced, the broad need for government remains, as a forum for deliberation as well as a source of economic stabilization, regulation, and collective provision. To hobble government, or to contract out most of its functions, is not to render it more efficient. It is clear that government cannot do everything, but neither can private markets. As we have seen, while various forms of fiscal discipline can enhance the efficiency of government, much of what government does is necessarily outside the market's logic of private purchasing power and private profit-maximization.

CONCLUSION

We have now experienced more than two decades of the celebration of markets and denigration of government. This represents an alliance of free-market economists, their allies in other social sciences and in the press, ideological conservatives, and business lobbies that want liberation from public regulation. It is a very potent alliance, even if its story of how society works is fantastic.

As this book has sought to illustrate, the case for the market is much more of a mixed case than its champions insist. Some domains are inherently beyond the reach of the market. They belong to the province of rights, which by definition cannot be alienated or sold. These include the sanctity of one's person (human beings may not be sold, no matter how great their desperation); the prohibition or commercial exchange of one's vote or of public office; of free speech, of professions, of honors and awards, of military service, or of products such as illegal drugs and weapons that society has deemed too dangerous for private exchange. We can all think of common violations of these principles, even as we can agree, with minor differences, that they should be upheld.

Such proscriptions have little to do with "efficiency," but everything to do with the good society. Breaching them would hardly bring greater prosperity or increased liberty. That the market keeps seeking ways to bring such exchanges into ordinary commerce suggests just how potent is the market impulse, and why it requires necessary constraints.

Other incursions are more insidious. Conflicts of interest, in scientific research, in medicine, finance, law, journalism, in public office and other positions of trust, invariably stem from individuals compromising legal or customary extra-market standards in exchange for monetary rewards. A society that believes that the market is always the most efficient arbiter and the source of the maximum efficiency and liberty will be dangerously blind to such trespasses. It will seek to resolve these conflicts by finding ways to marketize nearly everything.

Even in more narrowly economic realms, markets do a great deal well, but they fall far short of being perfectly self-regulating. They often lead to deprivations of personal liberty and economic security that are no less painful for representing authority that is private rather than public. They spill over into realms where they don't belong. One observes this by looking at actual markets, not at models.

If markets are not perfectly self-correcting, then the only check on their excesses must be extra-market institutions. These reside in values other than market values, and in affiliations that transcend mere hedonism and profit maximization. To temper the market, one must reclaim civil society and government, and make clear that government and civic vitality are allies, not adversaries. That enterprise, in turn, requires a more effective politics, both as the emblem of a free democratic people and as the necessary counterweight to the inflated claims about markets. If we are to balance markets with other social goals, that requires an engaged and informed electorate, as well as healthy, legitimate political institutions.

No real-world society has attained the ideal the libertarians commend. The closer ours gets to that vision, the more resistance is likely to set in. A society that was a grand auction block would not be a political democracy worth having. And it would be far less attractive economically than its enthusiasts imagine. We must beware this utopia, as we have been properly wary of others. Everything must not be for sale.

Notes

1 / THE RESURGENT MARKET

13 **diamond cartel:** see Edward Jay Epstein, *The Death of the Diamond* (London: Hutchinson, 1982).

16 **externalities:** see A. C. Pigou, *The Economics of Welfare* (London: Macmillan, 1920).

19 **Second Best:** K. Lancaster and R. G. Lipsey, "The General Theory of the Second Best," *Review of Economic Studies* 24, no. 1 (October 1956): 11–32.

21 **bank failures:** Federal Deposit Insurance Corporation, Annual Report (Washington, D.C., 1992), 127.

22 **a pure free market:** In the nineteenth century, banks issued their own notes, which could be cashed at a discount, depending on the bank's reputation and (often) on the geographic distance from the issuing bank. Lately, extreme monetary conservatives have reopened the case for free banking. For a modern libertarian argument in favor of free banking, see Lawrence H. White, *Competition and Currency* (Washington, D.C.: Cato Institute; and New York: New York University Press, 1989). See also R. G. King, "On the Economics of Private Money," *Journal of Monetary Economics* 12 (1983): 127–58.

25 **Tobin:** This is a famous quip, confirmed to the author.

Harberger: Arnold C. Harberger, "Monopoly and Resource Allocation" *American Economic Review, Papers and Proceedings* 44 (May 1994): 77–87.

Okun: Arthur M. Okun, "Potential GNP: Its Measurement and Significance," Proceedings of the Business and Economic Statistics Section, American Statistical Association, Washington, D.C., 1962, 98–103; reprinted in Arthur Okun, *Economics for Policymaking: Selected Essays of Arthur M. Okun*, ed. J. A. Pechman (Cambridge, Mass.: MIT Press, 1983), 145–58; see also Arthur Okun, *The Political Economy of Prosperity* (Washington, D.C.: The Brookings Institution, 1970).

25 **Schumpeter:** Joseph A. Schumpeter, *Capitalism, Socialism and Democracy* (New York: Harper & Brothers, 1943).

26 **South Korea:** see Alice H. Amsden, *Asia's Next Giant* (Oxford: Oxford University Press, 1989).

Kurth: interview with the author and in various lectures.

27 **Kelley:** Maryellen Kelley and Todd A. Watkins, "The Defense Industrial Network: A Legacy of the Cold War" (Carnegie-Mellon University, Pittsburgh, Pa., 1992, photocopy).

Schumpeter/Smith disjuncture: In technical terms, economists speak of a production-possibility frontier, which describes the maximum combination of goods that can be produced at a given level of inputs and technology. "Static efficiency," based on supply and demand, is said to optimize that output of goods. However, changes in technology can "push the production frontier outwards"—increase the goods that can be produced with the same amount of labor and capital. Orthodox economists assume that free competition maximizes the process of technical invention. However, static efficiency does not maximize the process of innovation and push that frontier outwards.

North: Douglass North, "Economic Performance Through Time," *American Economic Review* 84 (June 1994): 359–68, quote at page 367; this is North's Nobel Lecture, delivered on December 9, 1993, in Stockholm.

Tawney: R. H. Tawney, *The Acquisitive Society* (New York: Harcourt, Brace and Co., 1929), 29.

28 **Friedman:** Milton Friedman, *Capitalism and Freedom* (Chicago: University of Chicago Press, 1962); Milton Friedman and Rose Friedman, *Free to Choose* (New York: Harcourt Brace & Co., 1980).

31 **Friedman:** Milton Friedman, *Essays in Positive Economics* (Chicago: University of Chicago Press, 1953); and *A Program for Monetary Stability* (New York: Fordham University Press, 1959).

Drucker: Peter Drucker, "Toward the Next Economics," in Daniel Bell and Irving Kristol, eds., *The Crisis in Economic Theory* (New York: Basic Books, 1981), 4.

32 **"strict monetary rule":** Friedman, *Program for Monetary Stability*.

Natural Rate of Unemployment: Milton Friedman, "The Role of Monetary Policy," *American Economic Review* 58 (March 1968): 1–17.

33 **Friedman:** Friedman, *Capitalism and Freedom*, 13.

Law and Economics: see Richard Posner, *Economic Analysis of Law* (Boston: Little, Brown, 1986).

Coase: Ronald H. Coase, "The Problem of Social Cost," *Journal of Law and Economics* 3 (October 1960): 1–44.

34 **Public Choice:** see Anthony Downs, *An Economic Analysis of Democracy* (New York: Harper & Row, 1957); Anthony Down, *Inside Bureaucracy* (Boston: Little, Brown, 1967); Gordon Tullock, *The Politics of Bureaucracy* (Washington, D.C.: Public Affairs Press, 1965); and Gordon Tullock, *Toward a Mathematics of Politics* (Ann Arbor: University of Michigan Press, 1967).

35 **Okun:** Arthur Okun, *Equality and Efficiency: The Big Tradeoff* (Washington, D.C.: The Brookings Institution, 1975).

Schultze: Charles L. Schultze, *The Public Use of Private Interest* (Washington, D.C.: The Brookings Institution, 1977).

"trade-off": Okun, *Equality and Efficiency*, 38.

Economic Illusion: Robert Kuttner, *The Economic Illusion: False Choices Between Prosperity and Social Justice* (Boston: Houghton Mifflin, 1984).

Okun on rich and poor: Okun, *Equality and Efficiency*, 30.

Schultze quotes: Schultze, *Public Use*, 6, 18.

36 **Kneese and Schultze:** Allen Kneese and Charles Schultze, *Pollution, Prices, and Public Policy* (Washington, D.C.: The Brookings Institution, 1975).

37 **Enthoven:** Alain Enthoven, *Health Plan* (Reading, Mass.: Addison-Wesley, 1980), 113.

Kelman: Steven Kelman, *What Price Incentives?* (Boston: Auburn House Publishing, 1981), 7

2 / THE IMPERIAL MARKET

39 **"The market needs a place":** Arthur Okun, *Equality and Efficiency: The Big Tradeoff* (Washington, D.C.: The Brookings Institution, 1975), 119.

40 **Fundamental Theorems:** A. C. Pigou, *The Economics of Welfare* (London: Macmillan, 1920).

behavioral assumptions: For example, Gary Becker has written, in *The Economic Approach to Human Behavior* (Chicago: University of Chicago Press, 1976), 5, "The combined assumption of maximizing behavior, market equilibrium, and stable preferences, used relentlessly and unflinchingly, form the heart of the economic approach" and can be applied to human behavior in all fields. I heard George Stigler, speaking at an AEA event, declare that there was no Nobel Prize in any of the other social sciences because "they already have a prize in literature."

general equilibrium: see Kenneth Arrow and Gerard Debreu, "Existence of an Equilibrium for a Competitive Economy," *Econometrica* 22 (1954): 265–90.

41 **Schultze:** interview with the author.

42 **The "marginalist revolution":** of the late-nineteenth century is the work of A. Stanley Jevons, Leon Walras, and later, Alfred Marshall. A good discussion for the lay reader is Robert Lekachman, *A History of Economic Ideas* (New York: McGraw Hill, 1959), 229–97.

de Jouvenel quote: quoted in Brandon Robinson, "Psychological Assumptions, Conceptions of Value, and Economic Theory" (unpublished paper, 1972), 3; citing Bertrand de Jouvenel, "Efficiency and Amenity," in Kenneth Arrow and Tibor Scitovsky, eds., *Readings in Welfare Economics* (Nobleton, Ontario: Richard D. Irwin, Inc., for the American Economic Association, 1969), 109.

43 **on smoking:** see Robert Rabin and Stephen D. Sugarman, *Smoking Policy: Law, Politics and Culture* (New York: Oxford University Press, 1993).

44 **suicide:** Daniel S. Hammermesh and Neil M. Soss, "An Economic Theory of Suicide," *Journal of Political Economy* 82 (January/February 1974).

"De Gustibus": George J. Stigler and Gary S. Becker, "De Gustibus Non Est Disputandum," *American Economic Review* 67 (March 1977), 76–90.

Becker-Stigler quote on "music capital": Ibid., 80.

"we would welcome": Ibid., 89.

Hirschman: Albert O. Hirschman, *Rival Views of Market Society and Other Recent Essays* (New York: Viking, 1986), 147.

45 **Veblen:** Thorstein Veblen, *The Place of Science in Modern Civilization and Other Essays* (New York: B. W. Huebsch, 1919).

Simon quote: Herbert Simon, *Models of Man* (New York: John Wiley & Sons, 1957), 198.

Thaler quote: Richard H. Thaler, *The Winner's Curse: Paradoxes and Anomalies in Economic Life* (New York: Free Press, 1992), 121.

Daniel Kahneman and Amos Tversky: See Daniel Kahneman and Amos Tversky, "Prospect Theory: An Analysis of Decision Under Risk," *Econometrica* 47, no. 2 (1979): 363–91. See also Daniel Kahneman, Jack L. Knetsch, and Richard Thaler, "Experimental Tests of the Endowment Effect and the Coase Theorem," *Journal of Political Economy*, 98 (December 1990): 1325–48.

46 **theatre tickets:** Amos Tversky and Daniel Kahneman, "The Framing of Decisions and the Psychology of Choice," *Science* 211 (January 30, 1981): 453–8.

Cornell experiment: Thaler, *Winner's Curse*, 65.

Thaler's preferences vs. meta-preferences: Ibid., 99.

47 **Frankfurt:** Harry G. Frankfurt, "Freedom of the Will and the Concept of a Person," *Journal of Philosophy* 68 (1977): 5–20.

Whitman: Walt Whitman, "Song of Myself," in *Leaves of Grass* (New York: The Lowell Press, 1953 [1855]).

Sen: Amartya Sen, "Rational Fools: A Critique of the Behavioral Foundations of Economic Theory," *Philosophy and Public Affairs* 6 (1977): 317–44.

Lutz and Lux: Mark A. Lutz and Kenneth Lux, *Humanistic Economics: The New Challenge* (New York: Bootstrap Press, 1988), 110–11.

Hirschman quote: Hirschman, *Rival Views of Market Society*, 148.

Radin quote: Margaret Jane Radin, *Contested Commodities* (Cambridge, Mass.: Harvard University Press, 1996), 21.

Sagoff on public values: Mark Sagoff, *The Economy of the Earth: Philosophy, Law and the Environment* (New York: Oxford University Press, 1988), 25.

48 **Sagoff on consumer versus citizen:** Ibid., 8, 53.

Waldman, "Spend the optimal amount": Steven Waldman, "The Tyranny of Choice," *The New Republic*, January 27, 1992, 23.

48 **Waldman: "The more choice available":** Ibid., 24.

Lane: Robert E. Lane, *The Market Experience* (Cambridge: Cambridge University Press, 1991), 25.

49 **Sagoff quote:** Sagoff, *Economy of the Earth*, 45.

50 **Sagoff on anti-social preferences:** Ibid., 102.

Calabresi and Melamed quote: Guido Calabresi and A. Douglas Melamed, "Property Rules, Liability Rules, and Inalienability: One View of the Cathedral," *Harvard Law Review* 85 (1992): 1089–128.

Heilbroner quotes: Robert L. Heilbroner, *The Nature and Logic of Capitalism* (New York: W. W. Norton, 1985), 115, 140.

51 **Dole quote:** *Newsweek*, July 1, 1996, 31.

Lieberman speech: September 29, 1995, Washington, D.C.

Wall Street Journal: quoted in *Business Week*, October 2, 1995, 26.

Gingrich speech: to Republican fund-raising dinner, September 13, 1992.

52 **Streeck:** Wolfgang Streeck, "Beneficial Constraints: On the Economic Limits of Rational Voluntarism" (paper presented to the Society for the Advancement of Socio-Economics, New York, 1993), 12.

Esping-Andersen: Gøsta Esping-Andersen, *Politics Against Markets: The Social Democratic Road to Power* (Princeton: Princeton University Press, 1985).

53 **Okun quote:** Okun, *Equality and Efficiency*, 13.

Tobin: James Tobin, "On Limiting the Domain of Inequality," *Journal of Law and Economics* 13 (October 1970): 269.

Walzer's blocked exchanges: Michael Walzer, *Spheres of Justice* (New York: Basic Books, 1983).

54 **Heinrich Pesch:** See *New Catholic Encyclopedia*, vol. 11 (New York: McGraw Hill, 1967), 195. See also entry "solidarism," in vol. 13, 419–20.

Isaiah Berlin on negative freedom: Sir Isaiah Berlin, *Four Essays on Liberty* (London: Oxford University Press, 1969), 124.

Berlin on Robinson Crusoe: Ibid., 135, 156.

Berlin, "The liberty of the strong": Ibid., 170.

55 **Zelizer:** Viviana Zelizer, *Pricing the Priceless Child: The Changing Social Value of Children* (New York: Basic Books, 1985).

57 **Schor:** Juliet B. Schor, *The Overworked American* (New York: Basic Books, 1991).

Schor, shopping: Ibid., 108.

58 **Schor, leisure skills:** Ibid., 162.

59 **Magic Penny:** Malvina Reynolds, "Magic Penny," copyright, 1955, 1958, Northern Music Co. and MCA Music Publishing Co.

Robertson: Sir Dennis Robertson, "What Does the Economist Economize," in *Economic Commentaries* (London: Staples Press, 1956), 147–55.

Schultze: Schultze, *The Public Use*, 18.

60 **Monty Python:** quoted in Thaler, *Winner's Curse*, 6.

afterlife consumption: Corry Azzi and Ronald Ehrenberg, "Household Allocation of Time and Church Attendance," *Journal of Political Economy* 38, no. 1 (1975): 27–56; cited in Amitai Etzioni, *The Moral Dimension: Toward a New Economics* (New York: Free Press, 1988), 26.

61 **experiments on perceptions of fairness:** See Daniel Kahneman, Jack L. Knetsch, and Richard H. Thaler, "Fairness as a Constraint on Profit-Seeking: Entitlements in the Market," *American Economic Review* 76 (1986): 728–41; reprinted in Richard H. Thaler, *Quasi Rational Economics* (New York: Russell Sage Foundation, 1991), 199–219.

tipping: Thaler, *Winner's Curse,* 212.

62 **economists free ride:** Gerald Marwell and Ruth Ames, "Economists Free Ride, Does Anyone Else?" *Journal of Public Economics* 15 (1981): 295–310.

64 **efficient breach:** See Deborah A. DeMott, "Beyond Metaphor: An Analysis of Fiduciary Obligation," *Duke Law Journal* 1988, no. 5: 879–94; see also Frank H. Easterbrook and Daniel R. Fischel, "Contract and Fiduciary Duty," *Journal of Law and Economics* 36 (1993): 425–7.

65 **DeMott quote—can "witlessly provide":** Deborah A. DeMott, "Contesting the Fiducial Line: Legal Theory and the Duty to Be Loyal" (paper presented at the 1994 Society for the Advancement of Socio-Economics sessions, Paris), 1.

DeMott on fiduciary obligation: Ibid., 10.

Titmuss: Richard Titmuss, *The Gift Relationship* (London: George Allen & Unwin, 1970).

blood donation as "free gift": Ibid., 95.

blood donation statistics: Ibid., 32.

free-market economists on efficiency in the blood market: M. H. Cooper and A. J. Culyuer, *The Price of Blood* (London: Institute for Economic Affairs, 1968), 157.

66 **antitrust case:** cited in Titmuss, *The Gift Relationship*, 161.

Titmuss's three conclusions: Ibid., 157.

commercialization of blood donation and GNP: Ibid., 205–6.

survey revealing altruism and gratitude: Ibid., 227.

survey revealing reciprocity and duty: Ibid., 234.

Rhoads on positive externality: Steven E. Rhoads, *The Economist's View of the World* (Cambridge: Cambridge University Press, 1985), 188

3 / THE MARKET FOR LABOR

69 **Michael Polanyi on tacit knowledge:** Michael Polanyi, *Personal Knowledge: Towards a Post-Critical Philosophy* (New York: Harper & Row, 1962).

70 **voice:** Albert O. Hirschman, *Exit, Voice, and Loyalty* (Cambridge, Mass.: Harvard University Press, 1970).

70 **Efficiency Wage Theory:** see Andrew Weiss, *Efficiency Wages: Models of Unemployment, Layoffs, and Wage Dispersion* (Princeton: Princeton University Press, 1990), and J. E. Stiglitz, "Theories of Wage Rigidity," working paper, National Bureau of Economic Research, Cambridge, Mass. (Working Paper no. 1441.)

71 **Granovetter:** Mark S. Granovetter, "The Strength of Weak Ties," *American Journal of Sociology* 78 (1973): 1360–80; and Granovetter, "The Sociological and Economic Approaches to Labor Markets," in George Farkas and Paula England, eds., *Industries, Firms, and Jobs: Sociological and Economic Approaches* (New York: Plenum Press, 1988).

72 **Stiglitz:** Joseph E. Stiglitz, "The Invisible Hand and Modern Welfare Economics," working paper, National Bureau of Economic Research, Cambridge, Mass., 1992 (Working Paper no. 3641), 12.

73 **secondary labor markets:** Peter Doeringer and Michael Piore, *Internal Labor Markets and Manpower Analysis* (Lexington, Mass.: D.C. Heath, 1971).

74 **Okun quote:** Arthur Okun, *Prices and Quantities: A Macroeconomic Analysis* (Washington, D.C.: The Brookings Institution, 1980), 59.

Weiss, "the lower the wage": Weiss, *Efficiency Wages*, 5.

Weiss, "If all workers were identical": Ibid., 42.

75 **workers bidding to keep their jobs:** Paul Starr, "Bidding For Your Job," *The American Prospect*, fall 1995, 95–6.

contingent work force: "Managing a Contingency Work Force to Promote Flexibility and Increase Profitability," conference of the Institute for International Research, Chicago, Ill., July 1994.

76 **virtual corporation:** William Davidow and Michael S. Malone, *The Virtual Corporation* (New York: Harper Business, 1992).

human capital: For a nuanced discussion of labor relations in the new, contingent corporation, see The Aspen Institute, "Tomorrow's Corporation," conference report, July 1993.

77 **writings that congratulate corporations:** see, for example, Thomas A. Kochan and Paul Osterman, *The Mutual Gains Enterprise* (Boston: Harvard Business School Press, 1994); see also Rosabeth Moss Kanter, *World Class* (New York: Simon and Schuster, 1995).

spared the ax: The ordeal of downsizing, Heckscher writes, tends to produce "more patience and loyalty than one might expect." Charles Heckscher, *White Collar Blues* (New York: Free Press, 1995), 57.

78 **Piore and Sabel:** Michael Piore and Charles Sabel, *The Second Industrial Divide* (New York: Basic Books, 1984).

quintessence of laissez-faire: George Gilder, *Microcosm: The Quantum Revolution in Economics and Technology* (New York: Simon and Schuster, 1989); Peter W. Huber, et al., *The Legal Assault on the Economy*, 3 vols. (Washington, D.C.: National Legal Center for the Public Interest, 1986); John Naisbitt and Patricia Aburdene, *Reinventing the Corporation* (New York: Warner Books, 1985); and *Megatrends 2000: The New Directions for the 1990's* (New York: Avon Books, 1990).

79 **For descriptions of "high-road" companies:** see Barry Bluestone and Irving Bluestone, *Negotiating the Future* (New York: Basic Books, 1992); and Thomas A. Kochan and Paul Osterman, *The Mutual Gains Enterprise* (Boston: Harvard Business School Press, 1994).

Sidney Harman: interview with author.

Powersoft: Rosabeth Moss Kanter, "Nice Work If You Can Get It," *The American Prospect*, fall 1995, 55.

82 **generation of Keynesian strategies:** These included, at one extreme, the grand strategy of the Swedish Keynesians to use macroeconomic measures to get the economy close to full employment, supplemented by "active labor-market policies"—training, public employment, job-matching—coupled with centralized wage bargaining to get to virtual full employment with low inflation. In the United States more moderate neo-Keynesians proposed using tax incentives to keep wage demands from outstripping productivity growth. These policies are described in the author's *The Economic Illusion* (Boston: Houghton Mifflin, 1984). For a theoretical discussion see Arthur Okun, *Prices and Quantities: A Macroeconomic Analysis* (Washington: The Brookings Institution, 1980).

Ross et al.: see, for example, William Lazonick's *Comparative Advantage on the Shop Floor* (Cambridge, Mass.: Harvard University Press, 1990).

83 **Charlotte:** E. B. White, *Charlotte's Web* (1952; reprint, New York: HarperCollins, 1980), 39.

Becker: Gary Becker, *The Economics of Discrimination* (Chicago: University of Chicago Press, 1971).

84 **Marshall:** Alfred Marshall, *Principles of Economics*, 8th ed. (London: Macmillan, 1938), 15.

Sigmund Freud: Erik Erikson, *Identity and the Life Cycle* (Psychological Issues monograph, vol. 1, no. 1; New York: International Universities Press, 1959).

Lane: Robert E. Lane, *The Market Experience* (Cambridge: Cambridge University Press, 1991), 235–8.

85 **"principals" and "agents":** John W. Pratt and Richard J. Zeckhauser, *Principals and Agents: The Structure of Business* (Boston: Harvard Business School Press, 1985).

"shirking": William Lazonick, *Competitive Advantage on the Shop Floor* (Cambridge, Mass.: Harvard University Press, 1990).

86 **widening of inequality:** Barry Bluestone, "The Inequality Express," *The American Prospect*, winter 1995, 82–3; see also Lawrence Mishel and Jared Bernstein, *The State of Working America* (Washington, D.C.: Economic Policy Institute, 1994).

Thurow: Lester C. Thurow, *Generating Inequality* (New York: Basic Books, 1975). Quote is from an adaptation: Thurow, "The Redistribution of Wealth," *Working Papers for a New Society*, winter 1996, 23.

87 **Frank and Cook:** Robert Frank and Philip Cook, *The Winner-Take-All Society* (New York: Free Press, 1995).

executive compensation: Graef Crystal, *In Search of Excess* (New York: W. W. Norton, 1991), 27; see also "Executive Pay," *Business Week*, April 26, 1993, 56–79. *Business*

Week reports that in 1992, the total compensation of the average CEO was 157 times that of an average factory worker, up from 42 times in 1980, compared to a ratio of 32 to 1 in Japan (see page 59).

88 **on whether earnings inequality was mainly due to the baby boomers:** see Frank Levy and Richard Michael, "An Economic Bust for the Baby Boom?" *Challenge*, March-April 1986, 33–9; and Frank Levy, *Dollars and Dreams* (New York: Russell Sage Foundation, 1987); see also Frank Levy and Richard Murname, "U.S. Earnings Levels and Earnings Inequality: A Review of Recent Trends and Proposed Explanations," *Journal of Economic Literature* (September 1992).

89 **on transitional benefits and subsidy of retraining:** see Robert B. Reich, *The Work of Nations* (New York: Vintage Books, 1992).

For a general defense of the Reagan economic program: see Robert L. Bartley, *The Seven Fat Years* (New York: Free Press, 1992).

90 **Kaus:** Mickey Kaus, *The End of Equality* (New York: New Republic Books/Basic Books, 1992).

Murray and Herrnstein: Charles Murray and Richard Herrnstein, *The Bell Curve* (New York: Free Press, 1994).

D'Souza: Dinesh D'Souza, *The End of Racism* (New York: Free Press, 1995).

91 **on Mexican wages:** see Harley Shaiken, "Going South: Mexican Wages and U.S. Jobs after NAFTA," *The American Prospect*, fall 1993, 58–64.

92 **on imbalance of purchasing power in the third world:** see Walter Russell Meade, *Mortal Splendor* (Boston: Houghton Mifflin, 1987); see also Meade's "American Policy in the Antemillennial Era," *World Policy Journal* (Summer 1989), especially 403–11.

Robert Reich: see Reich, *Work of Nations*.

93 **End of Laissez-Faire:** Robert Kuttner, *The End of Laissez-Faire: National Purpose and the Global Economy after the Cold War* (New York: Alfred A. Knopf, 1991).

94 **Eisner quote:** Robert Eisner, "Opening Up the Growth Debate," *Wall Street Journal*, September 25, 1995, 14; see also Eisner's "Our NAIRU Limits: The Governing Myth of Economic Policy," *The American Prospect*, spring 1995, 58–64.

Joan Robinson: see Milo Keynes, ed., *Essays on John Maynard Keynes* (London: Cambridge University Press, 1975), Robinson's quote on social bargaining at page 129; see also Robinson, *What Are the Questions and Other Essays* (Armonk, N.Y.: M. E. Sharpe, 1980).

inflation and wage restraint in United States: see Leon Lindberg and Charles S. Maier, *The Politics of Inflation and Economic Stagnation* (Washington: The Brookings Institution, 1985), especially Colin Crouch, "Conditions for Trade Union Wage Restraint," 105–39.

Weitzman: Martin Weitzman, *The Share Economy* (Cambridge, Mass.: Harvard University Press, 1985).

on inflation/unemployment and the alleged trade-off: see Michael Bruno and Jeffrey Sachs, *The Economics of Worldwide Stagflation* (Cambridge, Mass.: Harvard University Press, 1985), especially chapter 11, 217–42.

95 **long-term interest rates:** see Economic Report of the President 1994 (Washington, D.C.: Government Printing Office, 1994).

96 **Bluestone:** Barry Bluestone, "The Polarization of American Society: Victims, Suspects, and Mysteries to Unravel" (report to the Twentieth Century Fund, March 1995), 21.

97 **decline in pension coverage:** Pension Rights Center, Washington, D.C.

98 **"President Roosevelt wants you":** Saul D. Alinsky, *John L. Lewis: An Unauthorized Biography* (New York: Vintage Books, 1970 [1949]), 71.

99 **Weiler:** Paul C. Weiler, *Governing the Workplace: The Future of Labor and Employment Law* (Cambridge, Mass.: Harvard University Press, 1990).

100 **Freeman and Medoff:** Richard B. Freeman and James L. Medoff, *What Do Unions Do?* (New York: Basic Books, 1984).

workers unlikely to reveal true preferences: Ibid., 9.

unionism can be a plus: Ibid., 12.

unions reducing inequality: Richard B. Freeman, *Labor Markets in Action* (Cambridge, Mass.: Harvard University Press, 1989), 203.

101 **Freeman on union effect on profits:** Ibid., 212–14.

Reich's influential book: Robert B. Reich, *The Work of Nations* (New York: Vintage Books, 1991).

102 **"High Skills or Low Wages":** "America's Choice: High Skills or Low Wages" (Rochester, N.Y.: National Center for Education and the Economy, 1990).

Rothschild: Michael Rothschild, "The End of Scarcity and the Politics of Plenty," *The New Democrat*, summer 1995, 8–12.

103 **Newman:** Katherine Newman and Chauncey Lenon, "The Job Ghetto," *The American Prospect*, summer 1995, 64–5.

productivity and employee compensation: Lawrence Mishel, "Rising Tides, Shrinking Wages," *The American Prospect*, fall 1995, 60–5.

wages of dropouts and graduates: Bluestone, "Polarization of American Society," 10.

104 **Howell:** David Howell, "The Skills Myth," *The American Prospect*, summer 1994, 81–90; see also Howell, "The Collapse of Low-Skill Wages: Technological Shift or Institutional Failure?" (Annandale-on-Hudson, N.Y.: The Jerome Levy Economics Institute of Bard College, 1996).

105 **costs of restoring 1979 income distribution through education:** Bluestone, "Polarization of American Society," citing calculation by James Heckman, "Assessing Clinton's Program on Job Training, Workfare, and Education in the Workplace," working paper, National Bureau of Economic Research, Cambridge, Mass., 1993 (Working Paper no. 4428).

earnings rise in Europe: Richard B. Freeman, ed., *Working Under Different Rules* (New York: Russell Sage Foundation, 1994), 12–13.

productivity growth in United States and Europe: World Bank, World Development Report (Oxford: Oxford University Press for the World Bank, January 1995).

106 **inequality and growth:** see Andrew Glyn and David Miliband, eds., *Paying for Inequality* (London: Institute for Public Policy Research and Rivers Oram Press, 1994); see especially Chapter 9, Adn Corry and Andrew Glyn, "The Macroeconomics of Inequality," 205–16.

Card: see Andrew Card and Richard Freeman, "Small Differences That Matter: Canada Vs. the United States," in Freeman, *Working Under Different Rules*, 189–222.

Blank: Rebecca Blank, "Does a Larger Social Safety Net Mean Less Economic Efficiency?" in Freeman, *Working Under Different Rules*, 161.

107 **skills of the American work force:** "America's Choice: High Skills or Low Wages!" (report of the Commission on the Skills of the American Workforce, National Center on Education and the Economy, Rochester, 1990), 4.

108 **gain-sharing strategy yields:** see Bluestone, "Polarization of American Society"; Osterman and Kochan, *Mutual Gains*, and Kanter, *World Class*.

4 / MARKETS AND MEDICINE

111 **Evans and Stoddart quote:** R. G. Evans and G. L. Stoddart, "Producing Health, Consuming Health Care," in Evans et al., eds., *Why Are Some People Healthy and Others Not?* (New York: Aldine De Gruyter, 1994), 55.

112 **Japanese life expectancy:** Michael G. Marmot, Martin Bobak, and George Davey Smith, "The Influence of Social Inequality on Health" (paper presented at Authors' Working Conference on Society and Health, Boston, Mass., October 1992), 20 and appendix table 4.

Enthoven's "paradox of excess and deprivation": Alain Enthoven and Richard Kronick, "A Consumer-Choice Health Plan for the 1990s," *New England Journal of Medicine* 320 (1989): 29.

113 **White:** quoted in Lawrence D. Brown, "Competition and the New Accountability," in Richard J. Arnould et al., eds, *Competitive Approaches to Health Care Reform* (Washington, D.C.: Urban Institute Press, 1993), 223.

116 **government licensing of professionals:** see Walter Gelhorn, "The Abuse of Occupational Licensing," *University of Chicago Law Review* 44 (fall 1976): 6–27.

Harris statistic on best possible health care: Louis Harris and Associates, *Making Difficult Health Care Decisions* (Cambridge, Mass.: The Loran Commission, June 1987), 5.

117 **William Baumol:** William J. Baumol, "Containing Medical Costs: Why Price Controls Won't Work," *The Public Interest* (fall 1988): 37–53.

doctors' income and inflation: Senator Daniel Patrick Moynihan, a colleague and friend of Professor Baumol's, contributed a singular disservice to the health policy debate by repeatedly insisting that "Baumol's Law" was a primary source of inflation of health costs, and that therefore other strategies of cost containment were barely worth the trouble.

doctors' incomes: in 1929, 53 percent of doctors had annual incomes below $4,000, according to the 1933 President's research committee, cited in David J. Rothman, "A Century of Failure," in James A. Morone and Gary S. Belkin, eds., *The Politics of Health Care Reform* (Durham: Duke University Press, 1994), 18.

117 **professionalization of physicians:** see Paul Starr, *The Social Transformation of American Medicine* (New York: Basic Books, 1982), especially pages 102–27.

118 **sickness funds:** Ibid., 241.

evolution of Blue Cross: Ibid., 295–7.

119 **employer-provided insurance:** Karen Davis, Gerard F. Anderson, Diane Rowland, and Earl P. Steinberg, *Health Care Cost Containment* (Baltimore: Johns Hopkins University Press, 1990), 105.

health-care cost ratio: "National Health Expenditures, 1986–2000," *Health Care Financing Review* 8, no. 4 (1987): 1–36.

120 **passive intervention:** Paul Starr and Gøsta Esping-Andersen, "Passive Intervention," *Working Papers for a New Society*, July-August 1979, 14–26.

121 **Medicare cost containment:** Karen Davis et al., *Health Care Cost Containment*, 17–18.

hospitals' increasing capital intensity: D. Salkever and T. Bice, "The Impact of Certificate of Needs Controls on Hospital Investment," *Milbank Memorial Fund Quarterly* 54, no. 2, 185–214, quoted in Davis, *Health Care Cost Containment*, 23.

122 **history of Ellwood and HMOs:** Davis, *Health Care Cost Containment*, 134.

HMO costs: Sidney Wolfe et al., "Mangled Competition," *The American Prospect* (spring 1994), 118, citing Health Insurance Association of America and Group Health Association of America data.

125 **lawsuits against "double bookkeeping":** see Bureau of National Affairs, *Managed Care Reporter*, July 19, 1995, 70.

126 **Medicare as scapegoat:** see Mathew Miller, "The Medicare Boom," *The New Republic*, December 11, 1996, 20–3.

127 **Columbia/HCA:** see "Balance Sheets That Get Well Soon," *Business Week*, September 4, 1995, 80–4.

Goodlark Hospital and Nashville Memorial Hospital: Robert Kuttner, "Columbia/HCA and the Resurgence of the For-Profit Hospital Business," *New England Journal of Medicine* 335, no. 6 (1996): 446–51.

128 **Curley:** remarks by John E. Curley, Jr., at the Catholic Health Assembly, Minneapolis, Minn., June 5, 1995.

uncompensated care at Kendall Regional Hospital: see "Balance Sheets," *Business Week*, 84.

129 **legal rules regarding conversion of charity and nonprofit hospitals:** see Linda B. Miller, Robert A. Bestiary, and Thomas M. Barr, "State Attorneys Generals' Authority to Police the Sale and Conversion of Not-For-Profit Hospitals and HMOs" (Washington, D.C.: Volunteer Trustees Foundation for Research and Education, 1995).

131 **distinguished teaching hospital CEO quote:** confirmed to me by CEO's colleague.

131 **Humana material:** author's interview with Humana physician who requested anonymity.

132 **Himmelstein:** David Himmelstein, "Extreme Risk: The New Corporate Proposition for Physicians," *New England Journal of Medicine* 333, no. 5 (December 21, 1995): 1706–80.

HMO abuses: John K. Iglehart, "Health Policy Report: Physicians and the Growth of Managed Care," *New England Journal of Medicine* (October 27, 1994): 1167–71.

133 **doctor's liability for following HMO guidelines:** see Public Citizen Health Research Group, *Health Letter*, February 1995, 1.

Tennessee's OmniCare: see "A Free-for-all in Swapping Medicaid for Managed Care," *New York Times*, October 2, 1995.

Sun-Sentinel series: "Profits from Pain," Ft. Lauderdale *Sun-Sentinel*, December 11–20, 1994.

135 **Megge case:** see Robert Kuttner, "False Profit," *The New Republic*, February 6, 1989, 21–3.

137 **quote on alleged benefits of payer-driven competition:** David Dranove, "The Case for Competitive Reform in Health Care," in Richard J. Arnould et al., *Competitive Approaches to Health Care Reform* (Washington, D.C.: Urban Institute Press, 1993), 69.

Enthoven quote: Alain C. Enthoven, *Health Plan: The Only Practical Solution to the Soaring Cost of Medical Care* (Reading, Mass.: Addison-Wesley Publishing Company, 1980), xxii.

139 **First Enthoven quote on subsidies:** Ibid., 71.

Enthoven on variable subsidies: Ibid., 81.

Enthoven's Jackson Hole plan: Alain C. Enthoven, "Managed Competition of Alternative Delivery Systems," *Journal of Health Politics, Policy and Law* (summer 1988): 316.

Enthoven on market segmentation: Alain C. Enthoven, *Theory and Practice of Managed Competition in Health Care Finance* (New York: North Holland, 1988), 97.

Enthoven on regulation and coercion: Ibid., 111–13.

140 **"Individuals can tailor insurance plans to their own tastes":** Dranove, "The Case for Competitive Reform," 76.

National Medical Enterprises: "Analysts Cheer NME Fraud Settlement," *Modern Healthcare*, April 18, 1994, 2.

Golden Rule: "Health Insurer Profits by Being Very Choosy in Selling Its Policies," *Wall Street Journal*, September 20, 1994.

141 **Medicare data:** analysis by Karen Davis, Commonwealth Fund, New York.

expenses of sickest 1 percent: computations by Marilyn Moon, Urban Institute, Washington, D.C.

143 **Chicago School economist:** interview with author.

144 **on erosion of community rating:** see Rashi Fein, *Medical Care, Medical Costs* (Cambridge, Mass.: Harvard University Press, 1986), 29–31.

144 **Office of Technology Assessment report:** U.S. Congress, Office of Technology Assessment, "Medical Testing and Health Insurance," OTA-H-384, 69.

145 **anti-discrimination laws:** Deborah A. Stone, "AIDS and the Moral Economy of Insurance," *The American Prospect*, spring 1990, 62–74.

Clifford and Iuculano: quoted in Stone, "AIDS and the Moral Economy," 65.

Stone quotes: Ibid., 65, 68.

146 **medical clerical personnel:** John Canham-Clyne, Steffie Woolhandler, and David Himmelstein, *The Rational Option for a National Health Program* (Stony Creek, Conn.: Pamphleteer's Press, 1994), 45.

growth of physicians and administrators: Ibid., 81.

147 **Reinhardt:** quoted in John K. Iglehart, "The Struggle Between Managed Care and Fee for Service Medicine," *New England Journal of Medicine* 331, no. 1 (July 7, 1994): 67.

148 **op-ed piece:** Michael A. Stocker, "The Ticket to Better Managed Care," *New York Times*, October 28, 1995.

149 **Theodore Marmor:** interview with author.

"Capitalizing on Capitation": from a marketing audiotape distributed at a medical meeting in Boston, September 1995.

150 **Bradford Gray quotes:** Bradford H. Gray, *The Profit Motive and Patient Care* (Cambridge, Mass.: Harvard University Press, 1991), 183–4.

1972 study on physician attitudes: Michael S. Goldstein, "Abortion as a Medical Career Choice: Entrepreneurs, Community Physicians, and Others," *Journal of Health and Social Behavior* 25 (June 1984): 211–29, quote at 225; quoted in Gray, *Profit Motive*, 185.

Gray on conflicts of interest: Gray, *Profit Motive*, 186.

underproduction of vaccines: Phyllis Freeman and Anthony Robbins, "The Elusive Promise of Vaccines," *The American Prospect*, winter 1991, 80–90.

152 **ranking of causes of death:** *Journal of the American Medical Association* 207, no. 18 (November 10, 1973): 2207–12.

153 **poor neighborhoods and health:** see Donald L. Patrick and Thomas M. Wetzler, "Community and Health," in Benjamin C. Amick et al., eds., *Society and Health* (Oxford: Oxford University Press, 1995), 46–92.

lower socio-economic groups and health: Michael G. Marmot, Martin Bobak, and George Davey Smith, "Explanations for Social Inequalities in Health," in Amick et al., *Society and Health*, 172–210.

Whitehall study: Michael Marmot et al., "Health Inequalities among British Civil Servants: The Whitehall II Study," *The Lancet* 337 (1991): 1387–93.

mental health and socio-economic status: see August B. Hollingshead and Fredrick C. Redlich, *Social Class and Mental Illness* (New York: John Wiley & Sons, 1958); see also M. Harvey Brenner, *Mental Illness and the Economy* (Cambridge, Mass.: Harvard University Press, 1973).

153 **Johnson and Hall quote:** (from paper presented at Authors Working Conference on Society and Health, Boston, Mass., October 16, 1992); see Jeffrey V. Johnson and Ellen M. Hall, "Class, Work, and Health," in Amick et al., *Society and Health*, 247–71.

heart disease and control over one's environment: see Johnson and Hall, "Class, Work, and Health," 257–8; see also Marmot et al., "Health Inequalities," 187–91.

active engagement in the healing process: see Robert Karasec, *Stress and Health* (New York: Basic Books, 1989).

154 **poverty and cancer:** P. Eastman, "Cancer Cases Rise as Social Class Declines," *Journal of the National Cancer Institute* 88 (1996): 490–2.

155 **GAO report:** U.S. General Accounting Office, *Canadian Health Insurance: Lessons for the United States* (Washington, D.C., 1991), 6.

overhead costs in the United States and Canada: Canham-Clyne, Woolhandler, and Himmelstein, *The Rational Option*, 43.

statistics on health-insurance costs: William A. Glaser, *Health Insurance in Practice* (San Francisco: Jossey-Bass, 1991), 432.

comparative statistics: "DataWatch," *Health Affairs* 13, no. 4 (fall 1994): 100–12.

156 **average length of patient stays:** *OECD Health Facts and Trends* (Paris: OECD, 1993); see also John K. Iglehart, "The American Health Care System: Community Hospitals," *New England Journal of Medicine* 329, no. 5 (July 29, 1993), chart at page 373.

157 **Clinton bill:** Elizabeth McCaughey, "No Exit," *The New Republic*, February 7, 1994, 21–5.

5 / MONEY MARKETS AND THE CORPORATION

160 **stock markets and financial performance:** see Louis Lowenstein, *What's Wrong with Wall Street? Short-Term Gain and the Absentee Shareholder* (Reading, Mass.: Addison-Wesley, 1988); and Thomas Lee Hazen, "Rational Investments, Speculation, or Gambling," *Northwestern Law Review* 86, no. 4 (summer 1992).

Shiller quote: Robert J. Shiller, "Who's Minding the Store?" in Robert J. Shiller, ed., *Report of the Twentieth Century Fund Task Force on Corporate Governance* (New York: Twentieth Century Fund Press, 1992), 13–14.

162 **Veblen:** Thorstein Veblen, *The Theory of Business Enterprise* (New York: Charles Scribner's Sons, 1904).

Keynes quote: John Maynard Keynes, *The General Theory of Employment, Interest, and Money* (1936; reprint, New York: Harcourt Brace Jovanovich, 1964), 159.

Tobin's "sand in the gears": James Tobin, *The New Economics One Decade Older* (Princeton: Princeton University Press, 1974).

on removing incentives for short-term speculation: see James Tobin, "On Limiting the Domain of Inequality," *Journal of Law and Economics* 13 (October 1970); and "On the Efficiency of the Financial System," *Lloyds Bank Review* (July 1984).

163 **Fama and the Efficient Market Hypothesis:** Eugene Fama, "The Behavior of Stock Market Prices," *Journal of Business* 38, no. 1, 34–105.

164 **stock turnover:** Lowenstein, *What's Wrong with Wall Street?*

Capital Asset Pricing Model: H. Markowitz, "Portfolio Selection," *Journal of Finance* 7 (March 1952): 77–91; and J. Tobin, "Liquidity Preference as Behavior towards Risk," *Review of Economic Studies* 25 (February 1958): 65–86.

165 **Graham and Dodd:** see Benjamin Graham and David L. Dodd, *Security Analysis* (New York: McGraw Hill, 1934).

Lowenstein quote: Louis Lowenstein, "The Predator's Accomplice," *The American Prospect*, spring 1994, 72.

166 **losses on derivatives:** House Committee on Banking, Finance, and Urban Affairs, *Recent Derivatives Losses*, serial no. 103-169 (Washington, D.C., October 5, 1994), 59.

Salomon Brothers and mortgage bonds: Michael Lewis, *Liar's Poker* (London: Hoder and Stoughton, 1989).

167 **critics of Efficient Market Hypothesis:** see Richard H. Thaler, *The Winner's Curse: Paradoxes and Anomalies in Economic Life* (New York: Free Press, 1992).

Graham: quoted in ibid., 181.

Thaler: Ibid.

168 **Russo quote:** Thomas A. Russo, "Derivatives Regulation" (talk given at a meeting of the Futures Industry Association, Washington, D.C., March 4, 1994).

170 **inflation rate:** see 1994 Economic Report of the President (Washington, D.C.: Government Printing Office), 363, table C-61.

history of NOW accounts: T. F. Cargill and G. G. Garcia, *Financial Deregulation and Monetary Control: Historical Perspective and the Impact of the 1980 Act* (Stanford: Hoover Institution Press, 1982).

Fidelity: for a history, see Joseph Nocera, *A Piece of the Action; How the Middle Class Joined the Money Class* (New York: Simon and Schuster, 1994), especially 231–49.

174 **CBO estimates:** Congressional Budget Office, *The Economic Effects of the Savings and Loan Crisis* (Washington, D.C.: Congressional Budget Office, 1992), 50.

Federal Reserve and bank solvency: see William Greider, *Secrets of the Temple* (New York: Simon and Schuster, 1987).

175 **Flynn:** John T. Flynn, "Investment Trusts Gone Wrong," *The New Republic*, April 2, 1930, 181–4; April 9, 1930, 212–16; April 16, 1930, 240–2; April 23, 1930, 267–9; April 30, 1930, 294–6.

177 **Mayer quotes:** Robert Kuttner, "The Fire Wall," *The New Republic*, June 20, 1988, 13–15.

"narrow banks": Robert E. Litan, *What Should Banks Do?* (Washington, D.C.: The Brookings Institution, 1987).

177 **Pierce:** James L. Pierce, *The Future of Banking* (New Haven: Yale University Press, 1991).

179 **studies on fate of target company after takeover:** For a good summary, see John C. Coffee at al., eds., *Knights, Raiders, and Targets: The Impact of the Hostile Takeover* (New York: Oxford University Press, 1988).

Campeau: See Louis Lowenstein, *Sense and Nonsense in Corporate Finance* (Reading, Mass.: Addison-Wesley, 1991).

comparison of Federated and Macy's: Ibid., 30–51.

180 **on the Houdaille buyout:** see George Anders, *Merchants of Debt* (New York: Basic Books, 1992).

on Houdaille's demise: see Max Holland, *When the Machine Stopped* (Boston: Harvard Business School Press, 1989).

181 **1932 classic work:** Adolf A. Berle and Gardiner C. Means, *The Modern Corporation and Private Property*, rev. ed. (New York: Harcourt, Brace and World, 1967).

Berle and Means 1920s calculation: Ibid., 33.

Berle and Means quote: Ibid., 312.

183 **"Market for Corporate Control":** Henry G. Manne, "Mergers and the Market for Corporate Control," *Journal of Political Economy* 73 (1965): 110–12.

premiums paid by raiders: see Lowenstein, *Sense and Nonsense*, 76.

186 **"relationship" investing:** see Shiller, "Who's Minding the Store," 6–8.

187 **CALPERS:** Ibid., 76.

On CALPERS's role in the shareholder rights movement: see "Big Companies, Big Problems," *New York Times,* February 6, 1996, sec. B.

CALPERS vs. Honeywell: see Shiller, ed., *Report of Twentieth Century Fund*, 77.

40 percent annual turnover: Ibid., p. 76.

Twentieth Century Fund report recommendations: Ibid., 105–110.

189 **Ellerman:** see David Ellerman, *The Democratic Worker-Owned Firm* (Boston: Unwin Hyman, 1990).

6 / MARKETS, INNOVATION, AND GROWTH

191 **Stiglitz quote:** Joseph Stiglitz, "Symposium on Organizations and Economics, *Journal of Economic Perspectives* 5, no. 2 (1989): 15.

192 **Marshall:** see Alfred Marshall, *Principles of Economics*, 8th ed. (London: Macmillan, 1938).

193 **Solow:** Robert M. Solow, "A Contribution to the Theory of Economic Growth," *Quarterly Journal of Economics* 70 (1956): 65–94.

194 **imperfect competition:** For a summary, see Louis Makowski, "Imperfect Competition," in John Eatwell et al., eds., *The New Palgrave*, vol. 2 (New York: Macmillan, 1987), 723–6.

194 **Pareto Optimality:** Vildredo Pareto, *Manual of Political Economy* (1927; reprinted London: Macmillan, 1971).

Schumpeter quote: Joseph A. Schumpeter, *Capitalism, Socialism and Democracy* (1943; reprinted London: George Allen & Unwin, 1961), 77, 80.

195 **Schumpeter on perfect competition:** Ibid., 106.

Schumpeter on capitalism and change: Ibid., 77.

Schumpeter on equilibrium: Ibid., 80.

Solow on Schumpeter: Robert M. Solow, "Perspectives on Growth Theory," *Journal of Economic Perspectives* 8, no. 1 (1994): 45–54, quote at page 52.

Schumpeter on "stationary capitalism": quoted in "Capitalism in the Postwar World," in R. Clemence, ed., *Essays of Joseph Schumpeter* (Cambridge, Mass.: Addison-Wesley, 1951), 174.

196 **Rosenberg quote:** Nathan Rosenberg, "Joseph Schumpeter: Radical Economist," working paper, Canadian Institute for Advanced Research Program in Economic Growth and Policy, Toronto, May 1993 (Working Paper no. 10), 2; see also Nathan Rosenberg, *Inside the Black Box* (Cambridge: Cambridge University Press, 1982); and Nathan Rosenberg, *Exploring the Black Box* (Cambridge: Cambridge University Press, 1994).

neo-Schumpeterians: see Richard R. Nelson, ed., *National Innovations Systems* (Oxford: Oxford University Press, 1993); Douglass C. North, *The Economic Growth of the United States 1790–1860* (New York: W. W. Norton, 1966); Douglass C. North, *Structure and Change in Economic History* (New York: W. W. Norton, 1981).

Scherer: see Frederic M. Scherer and Mark Perlman, *Entrepreneurship, Technological Innovation, and Economic Growth: Studies in the Schumpeterian Tradition* (Ann Arbor: University of Michigan Press, 1992).

Piore and Sabel: Michael Piore and Charles Sabel, *The Second Industrial Divide* (New York: Basic Books, 1984).

Chandler and McCraw: see Alfred D. Chandler, Jr., *Scale and Scope: The Dynamics of Industrial Capitalism* (Cambridge, Mass.: Harvard University Press, 1990); and Thomas K. McCraw, *Prophets of Regulation* (Cambridge, Mass.: Harvard University Press, 1984).

Lazonick: see William Lazonick, *Competitive Advantage on the Shop Floor* (Cambridge, Mass.: Harvard University Press, 1990).

Harrison: Bennett Harrison, *Lean and Mean* (New York: Basic Books, 1995).

Stiglitz: see Joseph E. Stiglitz, *Economics of the Public Sector* (New York: W. W. Norton, 1986).

197 **Romer's Endogenous Growth Theory:** Paul Romer, "Increasing Returns and Long Run Growth," *Journal of Political Economy* 94, no. 5 (1986): 1002–35.

North's Nobel Lecture: Douglass C. North, "Economic Performance Through Time," *American Economic Association* 84, no. 3 (June 1994): 359.

Kamien and Schwartz: see Morton Kamien and Nancy Schwartz, "Market Structure and Innovation: A Survey," *Journal of Economic Literature* 13, no 1 (March 1975): 1–37, quote at page 15.

197 **Schumpeter quote:** Schumpeter, *Capitalism, Socialism, and Democracy*, 84–5.

198 **Stiglitz quote:** Joseph E. Stiglitz, "The Invisible Hand and Modern Welfare Economics," working paper, National Bureau of Economic Research, Cambridge, Mass. (Working Paper no. 3641), 24.

on QWERTY: see Paul David, *Technological Choice, Innovation, and Economic Growth* (Cambridge: Cambridge University Press, 1975), 1–15; see also Paul David, "Understanding the Economics of QWERTY," in William N. Parker, ed., *Economic History and the Modern Economist* (Oxford: Basil Blackwell, 1986), 30–49.

Teece quote: David Teece, "Design Issues for Innovative Firms: Bureaucracy, Incentives, and Industrial Structure" (Stockholm: The Prince Bertil Symposium, June 1994), 4–5.

199 **on "tacit knowledge":** Michael Polanyi, *Personal Knowledge: Towards a Post-Critical Philosophy* (New York: Harper & Row, 1962); see also William Lazonick, *Competitive Advantage on the Shop Floor* (Cambridge, Mass.: Harvard University Press, 1990).

Bower quote: Joseph Bower, "The Organization of Markets," working paper, Harvard Business School Division of Research, Cambridge, Mass. (Working Paper no. 92-093), 20.

Dosi quote: Giovanni Dosi, "Sources, Procedures, and Microeconomic Effects of Innovation," *Journal of Economic Literature* 26 (September 1988): 1120–71, quote at page 1130.

Dosi on "cumulative processes": Ibid., 1147.

Romer on rival and nonrival goods: Paul Romer, "Two Strategies for Economic Development: Using Ideas and Producing Ideas," working paper, Canadian Institute for Advanced Research, Program in Economic Growth and Policy, Toronto, May 1992 (Working Paper no. 4), 18–19.

200 **Romer on patents for gene fragments:** Ibid., 20.

Nelson quote: Richard R. Nelson, "Roles of Government in a Mixed Economy," *Journal of Public Policy and Management* 6, no. 4 (1987): 541–57, quote at page 549.

on social returns of research exceeding private returns: see 1994 Economic Report of the President (Washington, D.C.: Government Printing Office), 190; see also Zvi Griliches, "Research Cost and Social Returns: Hybrid Corn and Related Innovations," *Journal of Political Economy* 66 (1958): 419–31.

Mansfield: Edward Mansfield et al., "Social and Private Rates of Return from Industrial Innovations," *Quarterly Journal of Economics* 41 (May 1967): 221–40.

201 **another study of private and social return:** Jeffrey I. Bernstein and M. Ishaq Nadiri, "Interindustry R&D Spillovers, Rates of Return, and Production in High-Tech Industries," *American Economic Review Papers and Proceedings* 78, no. 2 (May 1988): 429–34.

Romer quote: see Romer, "Two Strategies," 21.

202 **Griliches quote:** Zvi Griliches, "Productivity, R&D, and the Data Constraint," *American Economic Review* 84, no. 1 (March 1994): 18.

Chandler quote: Alfred Chandler, "What Is a Firm?" unpublished paper, Harvard Business School Business History Seminar, Cambridge, Mass., September 17, 1991, 3.

203 **Chandler on oligopolistic competition:** Chandler, "What Is a Firm?" 6.

Kamien and Schwartz on inventive activity: Kamien and Schwartz, "Market Structure," 32.

benefits of "moderately high concentration": Ibid., 23.

Teece quote: David Teece, "Design Issues," 51.

204 **costs of air transport and international phone calls:** Gary Hufbauer, "World Economic Integration: The Long View," *International Economic Insights* 11 (May-June 1991), cited in Richard J. Herring and Robert E. Litan, *Financial Regulation in the Global Economy* (Washington, D.C.: The Brookings Institution, 1995), 14.

205 **rising long-distance rates:** Gantam Naik, "Costs of Control," *Wall Street Journal*, March 20, 1995, R10.

Bower quote: Joseph Bower, "The Organization of Markets," working paper, Harvard Business School, Cambridge, Mass. (Working Paper 92-093), 1–2.

Bower on hotels: Ibid., 13–14.

Bower on norms in the hotel industry: Ibid., 14–15.

207 **Helpman and Grossman:** Elhanan Helpman and Gene H. Grossman, "Endogenous Innovation in the Theory of Growth," working paper, Canadian Institute for Advanced Research, Toronto, 1994 (Working Paper no. 20), 21.

Nelson and Winter: Richard R. Nelson and Sidney G. Winter, *An Evolutionary Theory of Economic Change* (Cambridge, Mass.: The Belknap Press of Harvard University Press, 1982), 394–5.

208 **Krugman:** see Paul R. Krugman, ed., *Strategic Trade and the New International Economics* (Cambridge, Mass.: MIT Press, 1986), 18–19. Krugman wrote, cautioning against activist industrial policies, "New thinking about trade does not yet provide simple guidelines for policy . . . [T]here is a risk that interest groups that have a stake in trade policies will simply find in the new ideas an excuse to advocate policies that are not likely to benefit the nation as a whole."

Romer on trade and perfect competition: Romer, "Two Strategies," 5.

209 **dissident economic theories:** Practically the sole exception early in the nineteenth century was the Swabian economist Friedrich List, whose two major books, *The Natural System of Political Economy* (1837) and *The National System of Political Economy* (1841), proposed both a political philosophy of liberalism and an economics of state-assisted development; see W. O. Henderson, *Friedrich List: Economist and Visionary* (Totowa, N.J.: Frank Cass and Company, 1983).

210 **Bourgin quote:** Frank Bourgin, *The Great Challenge: The Myth of Laissez-Faire in the Early Republic* (New York: George Braziller, 1989), 24.

Washington quote: Arthur M. Schlesinger, Jr., *The Cycles of American History* (Boston: Houghton Mifflin, 1986), 220.

211 **Hamilton:** quoted in Bourgin, *The Great Challenge*, 90.

Schlesinger on the "American System": Schlesinger, *Cycles of American History*, 223.

211 **Carter Goodrich:** quoted in Ibid., 224.

armories: See David A. Hounshell, *From the American System to Mass Production: 1800–1932* (Baltimore: Johns Hopkins University Press, 1984).

Schlesinger quote: Schlesinger, *Cycles of American History*, 226.

212 **Goodrich:** quoted in Ibid., 228.

Mowery and Rosenberg: David Mowery and Nathan Rosenberg, *Technology and the Pursuit of Economic Growth* (Cambridge: Cambridge University Press, 1989), 100.

Schlesinger on the "peculiarly American version of laissez-faire": Schlesinger, *Cycles of American History*, 234.

213 **NACA Cowl:** Mowery and Rosenberg, *Technology and Pursuit*, 182.

215 **Bush report:** Vannevar Bush, "Science: The Endless Frontier" (Washington, D.C.: Government Printing Office, 1945).

216 **technological extension system:** see Maryellen R. Kelley and Todd A. Watkins, "The Defense Industrial Network: A Legacy of the Cold War," monograph (Pittsburgh: Carnegie-Mellon University, 1992).

219 **imputation of free market policies to state-led Asian economies:** For a critique see Alice H. Amsden, *Asia's Next Giant: South Korea and Late Industrialization* (Oxford: Oxford University Press, 1989).

Cohen and Noll: Linda R. Cohen and Roger G. Noll, *The Technology Pork Barrel* (Washington, D.C.: The Brookings Institution, 1991).

Cohen and Noll quote: Ibid., 378.

220 **Pentagon support for research:** Michael Davey, "DOD Support for University-Based Research," CRS 94-1001 (Washington, D.C.: Congressional Research Service), cited in Science and Government Report, Washington, D.C., February 1, 1995, 2.

222 **Darman and Boskin quotes:** source: Clyde R. Prestowitz.

223 **Bingaman's twenty-two critical technologies:** Department of Defense Authorization, Fiscal Year 1990–91, Hearings before the U.S. Senate Committee on Armed Services: part 7, Defense Industry and Technology, March-April 1990 (Senate Hearing 101-251), 14–15.

1994 Economic Report of the President: "Through collective action we can sometimes correct such 'market failures,' and thereby improve the ability of private markets to serve social goals." *Economic Report of the President* (Washington, D.C: Government Printing Office, 1994), 169.

7 / REGULATED COMPETITION

226 **Vietor:** Richard H. K. Vietor, *Contrived Competition: Regulation and Deregulation in America* (Cambridge, Mass.: Harvard University Press, 1994), 21.

230 **history of regulation:** see Thomas K. McCraw, *Prophets of Regulation* (Cambridge, Mass.: Harvard University Press, 1984).

231 **history of state regulation of public utilities:** see Paul Stephen Dempsey, *The Social and Economic Consequences of Deregulation* (New York: Quorum Books, 1989).

232 **Bernstein:** Marver Bernstein, *Regulating Business by Independent Commission* (Princeton: Princeton University Press, 1955).

233 **Landis report:** James M. Landis, *Report on Regulatory Agencies to the President-Elect*, printed for use of the Senate Committee on the Judiciary, 86th Cong., 2nd sess., 1960.

Interstate Commerce Omission: Robert Fellmeth, *The Interstate Commerce Omission: Report of Ralph Nader's Study Group on the Interstate Commerce Commission and Transportation* (New York: Grossman Publishers, 1971).

Nader's call for abolition of the CAB: Martha Derthick and Paul Quirk, *The Politics of Deregulation* (Washington, D.C.: The Brookings Institution, 1985), 162.

"countervailing power": John Kenneth Galbraith, *American Capitalism: The Concept of Countervailing Power* (Boston: Houghton Mifflin, 1952).

Brandeis on bigness: see Louis D. Brandeis, *The Curse of Bigness* (New York: Viking, 1934); see also Philippa Sturm, *Brandeis: Beyond Progressivism* (Lawrence, Kans.: University of Kansas Press, 1993), especially chapter 4.

234 **Lindblom:** Charles E. Lindblom, *Politics and Markets* (New York: Basic Books, 1977).

Kennedy hearings: U.S. Senate Committee on the Judiciary, Subcommittee on Administrative Practice and Procedure, *Civil Aeronautics Board Practices and Procedures*, 94th Cong., 1st sess., 1975; see also Steven Breyer, *Regulation and Its Reform* (Cambridge, Mass.: Harvard University Press, 1982), especially 317–40.

Weidenbaum on the costs of regulation: Murray L. Weidenbaum, *Government-Mandated Price Increases* (Washington, D.C.: American Enterprise Institute, 1975).

Bork: Robert H. Bork, *The Antitrust Paradox* (New York: Basic Books, 1978).

Kahn quote: Kahn, *Economics of Regulation*, vol. 1, 65.

235 **overinvestment in physical capital:** The classic work demonstrating the tendency of firms subject to rate-of-return regulation to overinvest is H. Averch and L. Johnson, "Behavior of the Firm under Regulatory Constraint," *American Economic Review* 52 (1962): 1052–69.

Scherer quote: F. M. Scherer, *Industrial Market Structure and Economic Performance* (Chicago: Rand McNally, 1970), 537, quoted in Derthirk and Quirk, *Politics of Deregulation*, 162.

Levine: Michael Levine, "Airline Competition in Deregulated Markets: Theory, Firm Strategy and Public Policy," *Yale Journal on Regulation* 4 (1987): 393–495.

236 **Kahn on marginal costs with wings:** cited in Paul Stephen Dempsey and Andrew R. Goetz, *Airline Deregulation and Laissez-Faire Mythology* (Westport, Conn.: Quorum Books, 1991), 335.

237 **the effect of conservation on traditional utility pricing:** see George Sterzinger, "Why Utilities Can't Be Conservationists," *Working Papers for a New Society* (September-October 1981): 17–19.

Amory Lovins: Amory Lovins, *Soft Energy Path* (San Francisco: Friends of the Earth, 1977).

239 **Carterfone decision:** FCC Docket 16942, "Carterfone," adopted June 26, 1968; see Peter Temin with Louis Galambos, *The Fall of the Bell System* (Cambridge: Cambridge University Press, 1987).

240 **Charles Brown quote:** see Robert Kuttner, "Ma Bell's Orphans," *The New Republic*, March 17, 1982, 17–23.

241 **Huber:** see Peter Huber et al., "The Geodesic Network II: 1993 Report on Competition in the Telephone Industry" (Washington, D.C.: The Geodesic Company, 1993).

242 **on spectrum auctions:** see Evan Kwerel and Alex D. Felker, "Using Auctions to Select FCC Licensees," working paper, Federal Communications Commission, Office of Policy and Plans, Washington, D.C., May 1985 (Working Paper no. 16).

246 **Bell operating companies' spending on local networks:** see William Page Montgomery, "Promises versus Reality: Telecommunications Infrastructure, LEC Investment and Regulatory Reforms," paper presented to Institute of Public Utilities, Williamsburg, Va., December 12, 1994.

  outflow of money from rate base: calculations by Marc Cooper, research director, Consumer Federation of America.

  Eli Noam: see Eli M. Noam, "Beyond Liberalization III," *Telecommunications Policy* 18, no. 9 (1994): 687–704.

247 **Baumol:** William J. Baumol and J. Gregory Sidak, *Toward Competition in Local Telephones* (Cambridge, Mass.: MIT Press, 1984).

  Baumol: Ibid., 85.

248 **rising long-distance rates:** Gautam Naik, "Costs of Control," *Wall Street Journal*, March 20, 1995, sec. R, citing Labor Department data.

249 **Baby Bells' excess profits:** testimony of Marc Cooper of the Consumer Federation of America on S. 1822, The Communications Act of 1994, before the Senate Committee on Commerce, Science, and Transportation, February 23 and May 18, 1994, 71–3, and 549–51.

250 **Rochester agreement:** State of New York, Public Service Commission, "Opinion and Order Approving Joint Stipulation and Agreement," Opinion no. 94-15, November 10, 1994.

  FCC and fair access: see Federal Communications Commission, "Draft Implementation Schedule for S. 652, The Telecommunications Act of 1996," revised March 25, 1996.

255 **theory of contestability:** The idea, in technical terms, was that even natural monopolies could reach efficient equilibria without regulation, as long as their markets were contestable—able to be challenged by prospective competitors. The notion was first put forth in 1968 by Harold Demsetz, a Chicago School economist, in his article "Why Regulate Utilities," *Journal of Law and Economics* 11 (1968): 55–65. In the 1970s it was carried forward, interestingly enough, under the sponsorship of AT&T. The most complete statement came in 1982, in W. Baumol, J. C. Panzar and R. D. Willig, *Contestable Markets and the Theory of Industry Structure* (New York: Harcourt Brace Jovanovich, 1982).

255 **Kahn testimony:** quoted in Dempsey, *Consequences of Deregulation*, 224.

256 **excess airline fares on regulated routes:** see Breyer, *Regulation and Its Reform*, 300.

steaks reheated to order: Robert Kuttner, "Plane Truth," *The New Republic*, July 17 and July 24, 1989, 21–23.

quotes from CAB rulings: cited in Dempsey, *Consequences of Deregulation*, 182.

257 **code "FU":** *Wall Street Journal*, "Airlines May Be Using a Price-Data Network to Lessen Competition," June 28, 1990, sec. A.

258 **revenue per passenger mile:** Dempsey, *Consequences of Deregulation*, 245, 255; Paul Dempsey, *Airline Management: Strategies for the Twenty-First Century* (Phoenix: Coast Aire, forthcoming 1997).

259 **Winston and Morrison:** Steven Winston and Clifford Morrison, *The Economic Effects of Airline Deregulation* (Washington, D.C.: The Brookings Institution, 1986), 15–18.

261 **Levine quote:** Michael E. Levine, "Airline Competition in Deregulated Markets: Theory, Firm Strategy and Public Policy," *Yale Journal on Regulation* 4 (1987): 393–492, quote at pages 461–2.

262 **quote on dismal profit record:** Alfred Kahn, "Airline Deregulation: A Mixed Bag but a Clear Success Nonetheless," *Transportation Law Journal* 16 (1988): 229–48; see also Kevin C. Murdock, "The Effects of the Development of Hub-and-Spoke Route Structures on Pricing in the Deregulated Airline Industry," Ph.D. diss., Woodrow Wilson School, Princeton University, 1989).

263 **Dempsey quote:** interview with the author.

264 **loss of service:** Andrew Goetz and Christopher S. Sutton, "The Geography of Deregulation in the U.S. Airline Industry," *Annals of the Association of American Geographers* (forthcoming 1997).

265 **airliners stored in the desert:** Fedex Aviation Services, "Total Stored Aircraft," January 1995. Worldwide, over a thousand modern jet and turbojet aircraft were mothballed in 1993, according to Walsh Aviation Research of Annapolis, Maryland. The number has dropped to about nine hundred in 1995.

266 **Kahan quote:** Mark S. Kahan, "Confessions of an Airline Deregulator," *The American Prospect* (winter 1992): 39.

Levine on market power: Levine, "Airline Deregulation," 406.

267 **Kahn quote:** Alfred Kahn, "Surprises of Airline Deregulation," *American Economics Association Proceedings* 78, no. 2: 316–18, 320.

Kahn conclusion: Alfred Kahn, "Deregulation: Looking Backward and Looking Forward," *Yale Journal on Regulation* 7 (1990): 325–54, quote at page 349.

Levine quote: Levine, "Airline Deregulation," 494.

269 **published fare:** cited in Appeals Judge D. Cudahy, "The Coming Demise of Airline Deregulation," *Yale Journal on Regulation* 10, no. 1 (1993): 1–15, reference to Kahn memo at page 7.

Bork quote: Bork, *The Antitrust Paradox*, 234.

270 **TVA history:**   McCraw, *Prophets of Regulation.*

TVA's load factors: McCraw, *Prophets of Regulation*, 240–1.

271 **Roosevelt and yardstick competition:**   see William M. Emmons, "Franklin Roosevelt, Electric Utilities, and the Power of Competition," *Journal of Economic History* 54, no. 4 (December 1993): 880–907, statistic at page 896.

Roosevelt quote: Ibid., 884.

Emmons's "direct and indirect competition":   Ibid., 887.

272 **Emmons on Roosevelt's dual nature of competition:**   Ibid., 902.

274 **against complete deregulation:**   William J. Baumol, Paul L. Joskow, Alfred A. Kahn, "The Challenge for Federal and State Regulators: Transition from Regulation to Efficient Competition in Electric Power," monograph, December 9, 1994, quote at page 29.

276 **Bork quote:**   Bork, *The Antitrust Paradox*, 145.

279 **Microsoft and rivals:**   see "Judge and Attorneys Duel over Microsoft," *Wall Street Journal*, January 23, 1995, sec. B.

8 / REGULATING THE HUMAN ENVIRONMENT

283 **2 percent of GNP:**   Robert W. Hahn and Robert N. Stavins, "Incentive-Based Environmental Regulation: A New Era from an Old Idea?" *Ecology Law Quarterly* 18, no. 1 (1991): statistic at page 27.

"Richer Is Safer":   see Aaron Wildavsky, "Richer Is Safer," *The Public Interest*, summer 1980.

284 **regulation inducing technical breakthroughs:**   see Nicholas Ashford, Christine Ayers, Robert F. Stone: "Using Regulation to Change the Market for Innovation," *Harvard Environmental Law Review* 9 (1985): 419.

Rhetoric of Reaction: Albert O. Hirschmann, *The Rhetoric of Reaction* (Cambridge, Mass.: Belknap Press of Harvard University Press, 1991).

Viscusi: see W. Kip Viscusi, *Risk By Choice* (Cambridge, Mass.: Harvard University Press, 1983).

Peltzman: see Sam Peltzman, "The Effects of Auto Safety Risk Regulation," *Journal of Political Economy* 83 (1975): 677–725.

Crandall: see Robert W. Crandall and John D. Graham, "The Effect of Fuel Economy Standards on Automobile Safety," *Journal of Law and Economics* 32 (April 1989): 97–118.

285 **Pigou:**   Arthur Cecil Pigou, *The Economics of Welfare* (London: Macmillan, 1920).

Coase: Ronald H. Coase, "The Problem of Social Cost," *Journal of Law and Economics* 3 (October 1960): 1–44.

Coase quote: Ronald Coase, *The Firm, the Market, and the Law* (Chicago: University of Chicago Press, 1988), 15. For a devastating discussion of the uses and misuses of Coase, see Steven G. Medema (University of Colorado, Denver) and Warren J. Samuels (Michigan State University), "Ronald Coase and Coasean Economics: Some Questions,

Conjectures, and Implications," paper presented to the meeting of the American Economic Association, December 1994.

285 **Schultze:** Charles Schultze and Allen V. Kneese, *Pollution, Prices and Public Policy* (Washington, D.C.: The Brookings Institution, 1975), 4.

286 **technical complexity:** Ibid., 88.

Breyer: Stephen Breyer, *Breaking the Vicious Circle: Toward Effective Risk Regulation* (Cambridge, Mass.: Harvard University Press, 1993), 3.

ingested toothpicks: Ibid., 14.

Breyer quote: Ibid., 19.

287 **Adam Smith on workers:** Adam Smith, *The Wealth of Nations* (1776; reprint New York: Modern Library, 1937), 84.

288 **Wolff:** Edward Wolff, *Top Heavy* (New York: Twentieth Century Fund, 1995).

on history of common law doctrine on worker risk: see Nicholas A. Ashford, *Crisis in the Workplace: Occupational Disease and Injury* (Cambridge, Mass.: MIT Press, 1976), 48.

1908 study: cited in Nicholas A. Ashford and Charles C. Caldart, *Technology, Law, and the Working Environment* (New York: Van Nostrand Reinhold, 1991), 8.

deaths caused by industrial accidents: Anthony Bale, "America's First Compensation Crisis: Conflict over the Value and Meaning of Workplace Injuries under the Employers' Liability System," in David Rosner and Gerald Markowitz, eds., *Dying for Work: Workers' Safety and Health in Twentieth Century America* (Bloomington: Indiana University Press, 1987), 34–52.

Upton Sinclair: quoted in Gabriel Kolko, *The Triumph of Conservatism* (Chicago: Quadrangle, 1963), 103.

289 **Russell Sage study:** Crystal Eastman, "Work Accidents and the Law," The Pittsburgh Survey, Russell Sage Foundation, New York, 1910.

state reform commissions: Harry Weiss, "Employers' Liability and Working Conditions," in Don D. Lescohier, ed., *Working Conditions*, vol. 3 of John R. Commons, ed., *History of Labor in the United States* (New York: Macmillan, 1935), statistic at page 572.

prior to the New Deal: Weiss, "Employers' Liability," 579.

290 **risk-rated premiums:** John Commons, as a leading crusader for workers' compensation, urged that premiums be related to accident experience, making in effect an argument that worker injury should be recognized as an externality.

shrinking purchasing power of workmen's compensation: Weiss, "Employers' Liability," 605.

variation in worker injuries and deaths: testimony by Secretary of Labor Willard Wirtz on S. 2864, Occupational Safety and Health Act, before the Subcommittee on Labor of the Senate Committee on Labor and Public Welfare, 90th Cong., 2nd sess., 1968, 69–72.

average state programs: Sar Levitan, Peter E. Carlson, and Isaac Shapiro, *Protecting American Workers: An Assessment of Government Programs* (Washington, D.C.:

Bureau of National Affairs, Inc., 1986), 103; see also the report of the National Commission on State Workmen's Compensation Laws (Washington, D.C.: Government Printing Office, 1966), doc. no. 496-632.

290 **premiums averaging 1 percent of payroll:** Benjamin W. Mintz, "OSHA: History, Law, and Policy" (Washington, D.C.: The Bureau of National Affairs, Inc., 1984), 9.

291 **1972 Commission Report:** quoted in Ashbrook, *Crisis in the Workplace*, 393.

292 **OSHA provision:** Public Law 91-596, sec. 6(b)5 (1970).

293 **Viscusi on systematic harassment:** W. Kip Viscusi, *Risk by Choice* (Cambridge, Mass.: Harvard University Press, 1983), 10.

Viscusi on uniform standards: Viscusi, *Risk by Choice*, 80.

294 **statistics on declining worker injuries and deaths:** National Safety Council, "Accident Facts" (1994).

more extreme conservatives: Richard A. Epstein, *Takings: Private Property and the Power of Eminent Domain* (Cambridge, Mass.: Harvard University Press, 1985), 250.

295 **cotton dust deaths, disease, and costs of compliance:** Ruth Ruttenberg, "Compliance with the OSHA Cotton Dust Rule: The Role of Productivity Improving Technology" contract no. 233-7050 (Washington, D.C.: Office of Technology Assessment, 1983), 32–37.

quote from OTA report: Ruttenberg, "Compliance with OSHA," iii.

296 **polyvinyl chloride:** Thomas O. McGarrity, chapter 9 of *Reinventing Rationality: The Role of Regulatory Analysis in the Federal Bureaucracy* (New York: Cambridge University Press, 1991).

industry's response to polyvinyl-chloride regulation: see Ruth Ruttenberg, "Regulation Is the Mother of Invention," *Working Papers* (May-June 1981): 45–9; see also Marianne P. Brown and John Froines, "Technological Change at the Workplace" (Los Angeles: UCLA Institute of Industrial Relations, 1979), 24; and Steven Kelman, *Regulating America, Regulating Sweden: A Comparative Study of Occupational Safety and Health Policy* (Cambridge, Mass.: MIT Press, 1981).

297 **ratio of inspectors in the U.S. and Sweden:** Kelman, *Regulating America, Regulating Sweden*, 147.

298 **Swedish occupational injuries and deaths:** see Steven Early and Matt Witt, "The Worker as Safety Inspector," *Working Papers* (September-October 1980): 21–9; see also Kelman, *Regulating America, Regulating Sweden*.

Kelman quote: Kelman, *Regulating America, Regulating Sweden*, 142–4.

299 **Maine program:** OSHA internal documents provided to the author.

300 **Emancipation Proclamation:** Steven Kelman, "Cost-Benefit Analysis: An Ethical Critique," *Regulation Magazine* (January-February 1981): 33–8, quote at page 36.

Grand Canyon: Ibid., 38.

302 **Calabresi:** quoted in Thomas O. McGarrity, *Reinventing Rationality*, 70.

Ashford and colleagues: Nicholas Ashford, Christine Ayers, Robert F. Stone, "Using Regulation to Change the Market for Innovation," *Harvard Environmental Law Review* 9 (1985): 419.

302 **PCBs and industrial lead:** Ibid., 419–65.

American Cynamid pump spray: Ruttenberg, "Regulation Is the Mother of Invention," 46.

cost of attaining nitrous oxide standards: U.S. Environmental Protection Agency, Office of Air and Radiation, *Clean Air Marketplace* (June 1993): 3; see also Gregg Easterbrook, *A Moment on the Earth* (New York: Viking Penguin, 1995).

303 **Thaler quote:** Richard H. Thaler, *The Winner's Curse: Paradoxes and Anomalies in Economic Life* (New York: Free Press, 1992), quote at page 91.

McGarrity quote: McGarrity, *Reinventing Rationality*.

Arrow: Kenneth Arrow, "Rationality of Self and Others in an Economic System," *Journal of Business* 59 (October 1986): 391; quoted in Thaler, *The Winner's Curse*, 61.

304 **Peltzman:** Sam Peltzman, "The Effects of Automobile Safety Regulation," *Journal of Political Economy* 83 (August 1975): 677–725.

305 **decline in fatalities:** see Leon J. Robertson, "A Reply," in "Notes and Communications," *Journal of Economic Issues* 11, no. 4 (December 1977): 672.

auto fatality statistics: National Highway Traffic Safety Administration data.

Crandall and Graham: Crandall and Graham, "Effect of Fuel Economy Standards," 98.

drop in vehicle weight, increase in fatalities: Ibid., 111.

Crandall and Graham quote on declining fatalities: Ibid., 112.

Crandall and Graham's reliance on car mass: Ibid., 110.

306 **Rabbit, Pinto, and Chevette:** *The Safe Road to Fuel Economy* (Washington, D.C.: Center for Auto Safety, 1992), i.

auto weight, fuel efficiency, and fatalities: Ibid., 2.

307 **Crandall and Nivola:** Robert Crandall and Pietro Nivola, *The Extra Mile: Rethinking Energy Policy for Automotive Transportation* (Washington, D.C.: The Brookings Institution, 1995).

308 **Honda:** Frank Swoboda, "Honda Announces Gas Engine Meets Anti-Pollution Goals," *Washington Post*, January 7, 1995.

The Lulling Effect: W. Kip Viscusi, "The Lulling Effect: The Impact of Child-Resistant Packaging on Aspirin and Analgesic Ingestions," *American Economic Review* 74, no. 2 (1984): 324–7.

Viscusi quote: W. Kip Viscusi, "Consumer Behavior and the Safety Effects of Product Safety Regulation," *Journal of Law and Economics* 28 (October 1985): 527–53, quote at page 540.

quote on consumers being lulled: Viscusi, "The Lulling Effect," 327.

309 **study on child-resistant packaging:** Gregory B. Rodgers, "The Safety Effects of Child-Resistant Packaging for Oral Prescription Drugs," *Journal of the American Medical Association* 275, no. 21 (June 5, 1996), 1661–5.

"Pareto in the Pines" and foundation support for Law and Economics semi-

nars for judges: see Henry G. Manne, "An Intellectual History of the School of Law, George Mason University" (Arlington, Va.: Law and Economics Center, George Mason University, 1993), Pareto quote at page 10; see also "Justice for Sale," report by the Alliance for Justice (Washington, D.C., 1993). Appendix A lists sitting judges who have had tuition scholarships to attend Law and Economics seminars.

310 **"in privity":** The rule in modern form dates from the case *Winterbottom* v. *Wright*, in which a Royal Coachman named Winterbottom was injured when the coach he was driving collapsed. However, the judge held that since the Royal Mail, and not coachman Winterbottom, had a contract with the coachmaker, the unfortunate Winterbottom could not sue.

311 **Cardozo and Henningsen:** In *MacPherson* v. *Buick Motor Company*, Judge Cardozo, on the New York State Court of Appeals, wrote a majority opinion holding the Buick Motor Company liable in a case where a car's wheels had collapsed, injuring the plaintiff, even though MacPherson had bought the car from a dealer and not from the Buick Motor Company. In *Henningsen*, the New Jersey Supreme Court allowed the plaintiffs to sue both dealer and manufacturer, effectively ending the privity rule. The Court also held that any express (limited) warranty narrowing the implied warranty that the car was fit to drive was unenforceable. This discussion draws on Steven P. Croley and Jon D. Hanson, "Rescuing the Revolution: The Revived Case for Enterprise Liability," *Michigan Law Review* 91, no. 4 (February 1993): 683–797.

Priest: George L. Priest, "The Current Insurance Crisis and Modern Tort Law," *Yale Law Journal* 96 (1987): 1544–6.

312 **consumers getting what they wanted:** "A [manufacturer's] disclaimer . . . is the functional equivalent of provisions, common in other contracts, that explicitly require one of the parties to take certain actions to prevent breaches or to insure for losses from uncertain events. The theory predicts that disclaimers of liability and exclusions of coverage will be observed in consumer warranties for those specific allocative or insurance investments that the consumer can provide more cheaply than the manufacturer. In this view, disclaimers and exclusions can be said to be demanded by consumers because of the relative cheapness of consumer allocative investments of self-insurance." George L. Priest, "A Theory of the Consumer Product Warranty," *Yale Law Journal* 90 (1987): quote at page 1313.

314 **"What Liability Crisis?":** Steven P. Croley and Jon D. Hanson, "What Liability Crisis?: An Alternative Explanation for Recent Events in Products Liability," *Yale Journal on Regulation* 8, no. 1 (1990): 1–111, especially pages 9–10.

prestigious volume: Peter W. Huber and Robert E. Litan, eds., *The Liability Maze* (Washington, D.C.: The Brookings Institution, 1991), 20.

315 **details of regulation:** As Croley and Hanson acidly observe, the Law and Economics group attacking product-liability law "share the implicit but inexplicable premise that all markets work except one: the market for liability insurance." Croley and Hanson, "What Liability Crisis?" 727, *n* 185.

Epstein: see Richard A. Epstein, "The Unintended Revolution in Products Liability Law," *Cardozo Law Review* 10 (1988): 2193; see also Epstein, *Bargaining with the State* (Princeton: Princeton University Press, 1993).

316 **rate of malpractice:** Troyen Brennan et al., "Incidence of Adverse Events and Negligence in Hospitalized Patients: Results of the Harvard Medical Practice Study," *New England Journal of Medicine* (February 7, 1991): 370–84.

disciplinary actions: Public Citizen Health Research Group, "Ranking of Serious Doctor Disciplinary Actions," *Health Letter* (May 1995), 8.

anesthesiologists: James F. Holzer, "The Advent of Professional Standards for Professional Liability," *Quality Review Bulletin* 16, no. 2 (February 1990).

317 **England, France, Germany quote:** Gary T. Schwartz, "Product Liability and Medical Malpractice," in Huber and Litan, *The Liability Maze*, 75.

effects of product liability on innovation: W. Kip Viscusi and Michael J. Moore, in an article generally critical of product-liability litigation, report that an extensive survey by the Conference Board found 36 percent of respondents reported that liability costs led them to discontinue products, and 30 percent said that liability concerns led to decisions against introducing proposed new products. However, 35 percent credited product-liability pressures in a favorable way for improving product quality, and 33 percent said such concerns led to improved safety of the entire product line. Viscusi and Moore, "An Industrial Profile of the Links between Product Liability and Innovation," in Litan and Huber, *The Liability Maze*, 81.

319 **Simon-Ehrlich debate:** Norman Myers and Julian L. Simon, *Scarcity or Abundance* (New York: W. W. Norton, 1993), especially pages 205–6.

320 **anniversary of Earth Day:** Easterbrook, *A Moment on the Earth.*

321 **emissions coming from old power plants:** Nancy Kete, "The Politics of Markets: The Acid Rain Control Policy in the 1990 Clean Air Act Amendments (Ph.D. diss., Johns Hopkins University, 1993), 118. My discussion of the history of acid rain legislation follows Kete.

322 **deadlock:** Ibid., 220, reports that nine midwestern and border states accounted for 65 percent of the SO_2 pollution by the nation's utilities.

323 **Kete quote:** Ibid., 290.

problems with "bubble" regulation: Robert W. Hahn and Robert N. Stavins, "Incentive-Based Environmental Regulation: A New Era From an Old Idea?" *Ecology Law Quarterly* 18, no. 1: 1–42.

324 **Anderson and Leal quote:** Terry L. Anderson and Donald R. Leal, *Free Market Environmentalism* (Boulder, Colo.: Westview Press, 1991), 154, quoted in Kete, *Politics of Markets*, 2.

325 **Kete quote:** Ibid., 170.

9 / MARKETS AND POLITICS

330 **North quote:** Douglass C. North, "Institutions and Economic Growth: An Historical Introduction," *World Development* 17, no. 9 (1989): 1319–32, quote at page 1323.

Jefferson quote: Benjamin Barber, *Strong Democracy* (Berkeley: University of California Press, 1984), xv.

331   **Ralf Dahrendorf:**   Ralf Dahrendorf, "A Precarious Balance: Economic Opportunity, Civil Society, and Political Liberty," *The Responsive Community* (summer 1995): 13–39.

   Federalist quote: Alexander Hamilton, John Jay, and James Madison, *The Federalist* (1788; reprint New York: The Modern Library, 1962), 454.

332   **Wilson:**   Woodrow Wilson, *Constitutional Government* (Boston: Houghton Mifflin, 1885).

   Morone: James A. Morone, "Hidden Complications," *The American Prospect*, summer 1992, 40–9, quote at page 47.

333   **Downs:**   Anthony Downs, *An Economic Theory of Democracy* (New York: Harper & Brothers, 1957).

   Buchanan and Tullock: James M. Buchanan and Gordon Tullock, *The Calculus of Consent* (Ann Arbor: University of Michigan Press, 1962).

   Olson: Mancur Olson, *The Logic of Collective Action* (Cambridge, Mass.: Harvard University Press, 1965).

334   **Arrow:**   Kenneth Arrow, *Social Choice and Individual Values* (New York: John Wiley & Sons, 1951; 2nd rev. ed. New Haven: Yale University Press, 1963).

   pluralism: see V. O. Key, Jr., *Politics, Parties, and Pressure Groups* (1942; reprint New York: Thomas Y. Crowell Co., 1963).

   Downs on cost-benefit calculus: Downs, *Economic Theory of Democracy*, 215.

   Downs on systematic error: Ibid., 10.

335   **Buchanan and Tullock quote:**   Buchanan and Tullock, *Calculus of Consent*, 73.

   Buchanan quote: James Buchanan, "The Economic Theory of Politics Reborn," *Challenge* 31, no. 2 (1988): 4–10, quote at page 8.

336   **Arrow quote:**   Arrow, *Social Choice*.

337   **Olson quote:**   Olson, *Logic of Collective Action*, 2.

   Law and Economics rationale for overturning statutes: see William N. Eskridge, "Politics without Romance: Implications of Public Choice Theory for Statutory Interpretation," *Virginia Law Review* 74, no. 2 (March 1988): 275–98; see also Frank Easterbrook, "Statutes' Domains," *University of Chicago Law Review* 50 (1983): 533, 544–47.

   "sentimentalists":   see discussion in Steven Kelman, "Public Choice, Public Spirit," *Public Interest* 87 (spring 1987): 80–94.

   Mueller quote: Dennis C. Mueller, *Public Choice II* (Cambridge: Cambridge University Press, 1989), 245, quoted in Green and Shapiro, *Pathologies of Rational Choice*, 11.

   roughly half of recent political science articles: Donald P. Green and Ian Shapiro, *Pathologies of Rational Choice Theory* (New Haven: Yale University Press, 1994), 3.

338   **odds of one's vote counting:**   Daniel A. Farber and Philip P. Frickey, *Law and Public Choice* (Chicago: University of Chicago Press, 1991).

   Donald Sears and colleagues: cited in Kelman, "Public Choice, Public Spirit."

338 **Public Choice:** The reader interested in a more systematic deconstruction of Public Choice theory should consult two fine recent critiques, Green and Shapiro, *Pathologies of Rational Choice*; and Farber and Frickey, *Law and Public Choice*.

341 **Morone:** James A. Morone, *The Democratic Wish* (New York: Basic Books, 1990).

342 **Public Choice damns both democratic politics and government:** Here is a schematic chart that shows different theoretical stances towards a strong democratic polity and a strong state. I place the Progressive era in the Strong State–Weak Polity quadrant because of the Progressive impulse to depoliticize many issues in favor of technocratic experts. Oddly, many leading Progressives of that era also sought to expand direct democracy, without sensing the contradiction.

POLITY

	Strong	*Weak*
Strong	New Deal Great Society European Social Democrats	Hamilton Progressive era East Asian authoritarians
STATE		
Weak	Lockeans anti-Federalists Jacksonians	Public Choice theorists

343 **Pitkin quote:** Hanna Pitkin, "Justice: Relating Public and Private," *Political Theory* 9: 327, 344–45, quoted in Frank Michelman, "Law's Republic," *Yale Law Journal* 97, no. 8 (July 1988): 1503–4.

346 **Buchanan quote:** Buchanan, "Economic Theory of Politics."

347 **Lindblom:** Charles E. Lindblom, *Politics and Markets* (New York: Basic Books, 1977).

Ferguson: Thomas Ferguson, *Golden Rule, The Investment Theory of Party Competition and the Logic of Money-Driven Political Systems* (Chicago: University of Chicago Press, 1995), 28.

348 **Postman:** Neil Postman, *Amusing Ourselves to Death: Public Discourse in the Age of Show Business* (New York: Viking Penguin, 1984), 87–8.

Schumpeter: Joseph A. Schumpeter, *Capitalism, Socialism and Democracy* (1943; reprint, London: George Allen & Unwin, 1961).

349 **Adams:** quoted in Morone, *Democratic Wish*, 40.

Lockean liberals: see discussion in Barber, *Strong Democracy*, p. 15.

Barber quote: Barber, *Strong Democracy*, 117.

350 **Hayek:** F. A. Hayek, *The Road to Serfdom* (Chicago: University of Chicago Press, 1944).

352 **conservative ethic of communitarianism:** see Peter Berger and Richard John Neuhaus, *To Empower People: The Role of Mediating Structures in Public Policy* (Washington, D.C.: American Enterprise Institute, 1977).

353 **Coats program and Boaz quote:** Senator Dan Coats, David Boaz, et al., "Can Congress Revive Civil Society?" *Policy Review* 24 (January-February 1996): 25–33, quote at pages 32–3.

354 **Putnam:** Robert D. Putnam, "The Strange Disappearance of Civic America," *The American Prospect* 24 (winter 1996): 34–49.

Putnam quote: Ibid., 47–8.

Postman: Postman, *Amusing Ourselves*.

355 **Verba et al.:** Sidney Verba, Kay Lehman Schlozman, and Henry E. Brady, *Voice and Equality* (Cambridge, Mass.: Harvard University Press, 1995).

Verba et al. quote: Ibid., 512–13 and 533.

356 **increase in working time:** see Juliet L. Schor, *The Overworked American: The Unexpected Decline of Leisure* (New York: Basic Books, 1992).

357 **we believe deeply in government:** David Osborne and Ted Gaebler, *Reinventing Government* (Reading, Mass.: Addison-Wesley, 1992), xii.

358 **Gore:** Al Gore, *Common Sense Government: Works Better and Costs Less* (New York: Random House, 1995).

Howard: Philip K. Howard, *The Death of Common Sense* (New York: Random House, 1994).

National Performance Review quote on Postal Service: Gore, *Common Sense Government*, 139.

359 **detention-center chief quote:** John D. Donahue, "Prisons for Profit: Public Justice, Private Interests" (Washington, D.C.: Economic Policy Institute, 1988), 23.

Index

PERMISSIONS ACKNOWLEDGMENTS

Grateful acknowledgment is made to the following for permission to reprint previously published material:

MCA Music Publishing: Excerpt from "Magic Penny," words and music by Malvina Reynolds, copyright © 1955, 1959 by Northern Music Company, copyright renewed. Northern Music Company is an MCA Company. International copyright secured. All rights reserved. Reprinted by permission of MCA Music Publishing.

Python Productions Ltd.: Excerpt from "Banker Sketch" from *The Complete Monty Python's Flying Circus, All the Words, Vol. 2* (Pantheon Books, 1989). Reprinted by permission of Python Productions Ltd., London.

The University of Arkansas Press: "Purity" by Reed Whittemore from *The Past, The Future, The Present: Poems Selected & New* by Reed Whittemore (1990). Reprinted by permission of The University of Arkansas Press.

A NOTE ABOUT THE AUTHOR

Robert Kuttner is founding coeditor of the liberal bimonthly *The American Prospect* and a contributing columnist for *Business Week*. His weekly editorial column, originating in the Boston *Globe*, is syndicated by the Washington *Post*. He was the longtime economics correspondent of *The New Republic*. His articles have also appeared in *The Atlantic Monthly*, *The New Yorker*, *Harvard Business Review*, *Dissent*, *New England Journal of Medicine*, and other leading journals. He is author of four previous books on economics and politics. Mr. Kuttner has taught at Harvard's Institute of Politics, at Boston University, at Brandeis University, and at the University of Massachusetts. Previously, he served as chief investigator for the U.S. Senate Committee on Banking, Housing and Urban Affairs and as a national staff writer on the Washington *Post*. He lives in Brookline, Massachusetts, with his wife and their two children.